rome

FODOR'S TRAVEL PUBLICATIONS

NEW YORK • TORONTO • LONDON • SYDNEY • AUCKLAND

WWW.FODORS.COM

Contents

KEY TO SYMBOLS

- Map reference
- Telephone number
- Opening times
- Admission prices
- Underground station
- Bus or tram number
- Train station
- Tours
- Guidebook
- Restaurant
- Café
- Shop
- Toilets
- Number of rooms
- Parking
- No smoking
- Air conditioning
- Swimming pool
- Gym

UNDERSTANDING ROME

Rome is the world's greatest historical city, its staggering monuments, museums, galleries and architectural treasures spanning almost 3,000 years. Nowhere else will you find such a surfeit of artistic riches, from the grandiose ruins of imperial Rome to the glories of the Vatican, and from sculptural masterpieces of the baroque to the golden age of the Renaissance. But although history has left a considerable legacy, it is not the legacy of a modern capital city and Rome sometimes strains to live up to its contemporary role. Traffic and pollution can be a problem, as can the pressure imposed by many millions of visitors on an already overburdened infrastructure. But Rome has survived three millennia, and today, as monuments are restored and problems confronted, its timeworn face is slowly adapting to the needs of one more in a long line of new centuries.

LAYOUT OF THE CITY

Rome belongs to no single historical period, but is a patchwork of ancient, medieval and modern sights. At the same time, it is small enough to explore by foot, all but a handful of its main sights being in, or close to, the place where it all started—the Foro Romano. To the north of the Forum lies Piazza Venezia, heart of the more modern city, linked by roads that strike off to the four points of the compass: Via dei Fori Imperiali leads south, back past the Forum to the Colosseo; Via IV Novembre heads east towards a mostly newer 19th-century quarter; Via del Corso strikes north to Piazza del Popolo, passing close to Piazza di Spagna and the shopping streets around Via Condotti; and Via Corso Vittorio Emanuele II runs west towards St. Peter's and Vatican City. This last street also bisects the *centro storico*, or historic centre, the area where most of the sights are, and which includes two of the city's most captivating squares: Campo dei Fiori and Piazza Navona. This area is bounded to the west by the curve of the River Tiber, across which lies St. Peter's and, to the south, the more traditional Trastevere area, known today for its restaurants and nightlife. Farther south still is the nightlife district of Testaccio.

CLIMATE

Rome has a marked Mediterranean climate, characterized by summers that are hot and dry, with possible thunderstorms (especially in July and August) and temperatures up to 38°C (100°F). Winters are short and mild, with temperatures that average 14°C (58°F) and rarely fall below freezing. Spring (late March–May) is usually brief and autumn (September–November) long: Both can be prone to spells of heavy rain or humid weather. October and November are the wettest months.

THE ECONOMY

Rome may be the Italian capital, but it is far from being its economic fulcrum. It lacks the financial clout of Milan, the heavy manufacturing base of Turin or the international maritime reach of Genoa. Most jobs are in the service sector, in particular those parts of it that provide for the city's millions of visitors. The state is also a big employer, with many jobs in local and national government. Office workers outnumber industrial workers by about six to one. Manufacturing firms are mainly small-scale family concerns, economic mainstays that help counter what might otherwise be a debilitating unemployment problem.

THE SEVEN HILLS OF ROME

According to tradition, Rome was built on seven hills, but 3,000 years of occupation and urban planning means that it is difficult to see the contours of the ancient city. Look closely, however, and the hills are still there, playing host to all manner of historically important sites.

Legend has it that the **Palatine Hill** was the site of Romulus's ancient city. In the middle of the group, it became the seat of power and the residential district of choice, and give us the word 'palace' after the elegant houses of the patrician classes who built on its summit. Today, you can see the remains of temples and palaces on the hill, as well as the Orti Farnesiani—the 16th-century gardens of the Farnese family. To the northwest is the **Capitoline Hill,** once a fortified stronghold and later, following the building of the Temple of Jupiter, a religious hub. The Capitoline has two summits: the Arx, where a temple to Juno was built, and where the church of Santa Maria in Aracoeli stands today; and the Asylum, where Romulus allowed refugees from other towns to stay, and which is now Piazza del

Ancient ruins on the Palatine Hill (left and middle), and the medieval piazza on the Capitoline (right)

Campidoglio. North of the Capitoline is the **Quirinal Hill,** which, during the imperial age, was the largest residential area. Here is the Palazzo del Quirinale, home of the popes from 1573, then the official residence of the king until Italy's unification in 1870. It is now the seat of the president of the republic. Just to the south lies the **Viminal Hill,** the smallest of the seven, running towards Termini station. Farther south again is the largest of all the hills, the **Esquiline Hill,** where Nero built his Domus Aurea, the Golden House. Below this and to the east of the Palatine is the **Caelian Hill,** stretching across the city from the Colosseo to San Giovanni in Laterano. The **Aventine Hill,** the most southerly of all the seven hills, is divided from the Palatine by the Circo Massimo. It was tradtionally the home of the working classes.

POLITICS

Italy's politics are largely Rome's politics, the city having been a political hub for millennia: head of an empire that once covered much of the known world, the headquarters of the Roman Catholic Church for almost 2,000 years, and—more recently—the seat of Italy's national government. It has been capital of a united Italy since 1870 and of the present Italian republic since 1946, when the monarchy was abolished by popular referendum. The two houses of the Italian parliament are here, the Senate (in the Palazzo Madama) and Chamber of Deputies (in the Palazzo di Montecitorio); members of both houses are elected for five years. The city's Palazzo del Quirinale is home to the Italian president, elected by both houses and regional representatives for seven years. Most power, however, is wielded by the prime minister, who is usually the leader of the party with a majority of seats in the Chamber of Deputies. The present prime minister is controversial media-magnate Silvio Berlusconi. Much day-to-day administrative business in the city is carried out by the Comune di Rome, or city council, which has its headquarters in the Palazzo Senatorio in Piazza del Campidoglio on the Capitoline Hill.

SOCIETY

Rome sits on a social and economic faultline, with the more prosperous and more dynamic Italy to the north and the more traditional and generally less wealthy Italy to the south. As such, its inhabitants exhibit a variety of traits, from the lingering Mediterranean habits of the siesta and a generally laid-back attitude to life, to a more northern European sensibility that finds expression in obvious displays of material wellbeing and the increased all-day opening of shops and offices. Rome's inhabitants also share the largely liberal values of Italians as a whole, values that can come as surprise to those who still see Italy as a country hidebound by religion and history. Divorce and abortion, for example, have been legal for decades, while one of Europe's lowest birth rates belies the notion of Italians in thrall to the Church. Indeed, while most Romans are Catholics, less than 10 per cent regularly attend church services. To speak of Romans these days, however, is not only to speak of the familiar Fellini-esque stereotypes, as the last decade has seen the arrival of many thousands of immigrants, notably from the Philippines and eastern Europe, an influx that is slowly changing the city's face.

Toll motorway (Turnpike)
Motorway (Expressway)
Major road
Atlas section

Labaro

La Giustiniana

VIA CASSIA

SR2

SR2bis

GRANDE RACCORDO ANULARE (GRA)

VIA CASSIA

Tomba
di Nerone

VIA FLAMINIA

Selva
Candida

Ottavia

Sant'
Onofrio

VIA TRIONFALE

Tor di
Quinto

VIA   DEL   FORO

Palmarola
Nuova

Torrevecchia

Villa
Glori

Parid

Casale
Selce

Casalotti

Primavalle

VIA DI

BOCCEA

Pinciano

CITTA DEL
VATICANO

Villa
Borghese

VIA DEL CORSO

Monte-
spaccato

SS1

VIA AURELIA

Villini

Villa Doria
Pamphilj

Giancolo

Tevere

Trastevere

Palatino

Massimina

VIA DELLA PISANA

VIA OSTIENSE

SS

Pisana

Corivale

VIA

Portuense

Garbatella

Ostiense

La
Pisana

PORTUENSE

Magliana

VIA C. COLOMBO

EUR

VIA LAURENTINA

AUTOSTRADA ROMA-FIUMICINO

Magliana

VIA DEL MARE

VIA C COLOMBO

E80

Tevere

SS8

Acilia

Vitinia

SR 148

GRANDE

THE BEST OF ROME

BEST ROMAN MONUMENTS

Castel Sant'Angelo (see page 73): This imperial mausoleum sits grandly by the banks of the Tiber.

Colonna di Marco Aurelio (see page 78): Magnificent third-century AD bas-reliefs cover this massive column.

Colosseo (see pages 74–77): Its partially ruined state hardly dents the impact of this vast amphitheatre.

Foro Romano (see pages 84–89): The focal point of the Roman Empire for almost a thousand years.

Pantheon (see pages 120–121): Hadrian's temple is Rome's best-preserved ancient monument.

Detail of Ponte Sant'Angelo, leading to Castel Sant'Angelo (above)
The Tempio di Saturno in the Foro Romano (left)

BEST PAINTINGS AND SCULPTURES

Bernini's *St. Teresa* (see page 137): This statue, in Santa Maria della Vittoria, has been called one of the most erotic in Italy.

Gaul Committing Suicide (see pages 112–113): One of the most dramatic statues of the Classical age, at Palazzo Altemps.

Laocoön (see page 109): A virtuoso Classical sculpture and the highlight of the Musei Vaticani's extensive sculpture collection.

Marcus Aurelius (see pages 100 and 118): Either the original in Musei Capitolini or the copy in Piazza del Campidoglio.

Michelangelo's *Pietà* (see page 68): Now behind glass in St. Peter's following a vandal's attack.

Paolina Borghese (see page 93): Canova's statue in the Museo e Galleria Borghese leaves little to the imagination.

Raphael's *Transfiguration* (see page 109): In the Vatican's Pinacoteca, long considered the city's most sublime painting.

San Luigi dei Francesi (see page 133): An otherwise modest church, made exceptional by a trio of paintings by Caravaggio.

Stanze di Raffaello (see page 106): Four rooms in the Musei Vaticani with stunning allegorical frescoes by Raphael.

Villa Farnesina (see page 146): Surprisingly few people visit this Trastevere villa, which has an exceptional series of frescoes by Raphael and Baldassare Peruzzi.

Michelangelo's Pietà in the Basilica di San Pietro (above)

BEST SHOPS

Castroni (see page 164): Stands out even in Rome, which has more than its share of good delicatessens.

La Città del Sole (see page 163): A long-established store crammed with educational and high-quality toys.

Coin (see page 171): A popular department store and Rome's best bet for one-stop shopping.

Frette (see page 170): Internationally recognized for fine Italian linens and sleepwear.

Giorgio Sermoneta (see page 168): Gloves, gloves and more gloves.

Spazio Sette (see page 170): A vast and tempting range of furnishings, gadgets and other items for the home.

Volpetti (see page 165): Rome's best deli is worth a trip if you want to buy food to take home.

There is no shortage of shopping opportunities in Rome (above)
If you like your nightlife late and loud, head for Testaccio (below)

BEST BARS AND CLUBS

Alibi (see page 186): One of the longest-established of the Testaccio clubs, with a delightful summer terrace.

Gilda (see page 189): If you must see and be seen, this has for many years been the place to come in central Rome.

THE BEST OF ROME

Jonathan's Angels (see pages 187–188): Quirky to a fault, this eccentrically decorated bar is popular with locals and visitors.
Piper Club (see page 190): Piper was trendy before the word was coined, and decades later it's still popular.

Pizza al fresco (above)

BEST PLACES TO EAT

Alberto Ciarla (see page 232): The best place to eat fish and seafood in Rome—but at a price.
Il Convivio (see page 238): Creative regional cuisine served in spacious modern surroundings.
Da Agusto (see page 239): Trastevere used to be the home of the simple trattoria; this is best of the handful that survive.
Dai Tre Amici (see page 240): All the bustle and old-fashioned fittings you could want from a traditional Roman restaurant.
Der Pallaro (see page 241): This trattoria seems to have been there for ever, and offers a reliable Roman home cooking.
Pizzeria La Montecarlo (see page 248): Simple, inexpensive food with good service.
Pizzeria Popi Popi (see page 248): A long-established pizzeria in Trastevere, with outside tables in summer.
Roof Garden 'Les Etoiles' (see page 250): fine food, with a sensational view of St. Peter's.

BEST CAFÉS

Antico Caffè della Pace (above)

Antico Caffè della Pace (see page 233): One of Rome's prettiest bars, and a lovely place to sit, indoors or out.
Bar Capitolina (see page 234): This bar has few rivals when it comes to views of ancient Rome.
Café di Marzio (see page 237): One of two good cafés in Piazza Santa Maria in Trastevere (the other is Café dell'Arancia—see page 237).
Sant'Eustacchio (see page 251): Rivals the nearby Tazzo d'Oro (see below) for the quality of its coffee, but has the bonus of somewhere to sit.
Tazzo d'Oro (see page 252): Join the queues at this café for what many Romans consider the city's best cup of coffee.

BEST LUXURY HOTELS

Grand Hotel de la Minerve (see page 266): An excellent position overlooking the Pantheon.
Hassler (see page 266): The traditional luxury hotel of choice for visiting film stars and other VIPs.
Hotel de Russie (see page 267): This is by the far the best of Rome's modern hotels, a blend of the classic and the contemporary.

Lord Byron Hotel (see page 268): An art deco villa in leafy, out-of-town Parioli, away from the bustle of the city.
Raphael (see page 270): More intimate than many of the city's luxury hotels, with romantic rooms behind an ivy-covered façade.

The roof terrace of the Raphael hotel (right)

BEST EXPERIENCES

Don't miss the Palatine Hill when you visit the Foro Romano. It's a leafy retreat with pretty gardens and sweeping views of the ancient city (see page 110–111).

Walk up the Gianicolo Hill, and stroll along the ridge (Passeggiata del Gianicolo) that overlooks Rome. (see page 90)

Visit Campo dei Fiori in the morning, partly to take in one of the city's quainter squares, but also to enjoy the sights, smells and sounds of the its best market (see pages 122–123).

When it starts to rain, don't dive for just any available cover, but head for the Pantheon, where the water pouring through the deliberately left hole in dome is one of the city's most evocative sights (see pages 120–121).

Join the Romans walking along the Via Appia Antica (see page 146)—the road is traffic-free on Sundays and public holidays.

It's not just the traffic that causes problems for scooter riders (above)

Drink coffee in the Piazza Navona. Although you pay a premium to sit at a café table in the square (left), it's worth it to watch the constant parade of people, and to admire Bernini's famous central fountain (see pages 124–125).

Climb to the top of the dome at Basilica di San Pietro (see page 71). The views from the top, over the Vatican gardens and back into the city, are stunning.

Eat an ice-cream in Piazza Navona (see pages 124–125): Tre Scalini makes the best *tartufi* in the city, or try a poison apple—ice-cream, coated in chocoate, with an alcoholic filling.

Enjoying an ice-cream (above) Making a wish at the Trevi Fountain (left)

Throw a coin into the Fontana di Trevi (see pages 80–81): Throw the first coin backwards, over your shoulder, into the fountain and make a wish to come back to Rome; a second coin makes the wish come true.

The Villa Borghese (see page 146) is popular at weekends with picnicking families. If you want to do more than relax, take a walk through the park (see pages 208–209) or visit the Museo Nazionale Etrusco at Villa Giulia (see page 147).

Window shopping in the Via dei Condotti (left) The floodlit Colosseo (below)

Mingle with the *bel mondo* on the world-famous shopping avenue, Via dei Condotti (see page 157), where you'll find all the top fashion names: Armani, Fendi, Gucci, Max Mara, Valentino, Versace and (on Via Bocca di Leone, cutting across Via Condotti) Yves Sant Laurent.

Visit the Colosseo and Foro Romano on a summer evening, when they're floodlit (see pages 74–77 and 84–89).

Living Rome

Life goes on for modern Romans in the shadow of their ancestors (above)

Keeping the city clean (top left) and policed (left) is a full-time job, but older romani take time to relax in the sun (above)

Life in
Ruins

It's not always easy living with 3,000 years of history. Monuments tend to get in the way, and the Forum occupies a prime piece of centro storico (historic centre) real estate. But Romans have grown used to the challenge. Writer and historian Georgina Masson summed up the way Rome lives with its past when she called the city a palimpsest: a sheet of parchment used over and over again, with the new text written over the faded original or squeezed in between the lines. Rome is just such a sheet of parchment, except that it has many more overwritings than other cities, and far fewer rubbings-out. This reuse is seen in single buildings—as in the Teatro di Marcello, a Renaissance palace grafted onto a first-century bc theatre— but it is also seen in the ground plan of the city: Piazza Navona curves to follow an ancient racetrack and public parks mark out the boundaries of former private estates.

Rome's Archaeology

A celebrated scene from Fellini's Roma shows workers who are drilling a new metro line suddenly breaking through into a room decorated with spectacular classical frescoes, which begin to fade as soon as they come into contact with the atmosphere. The wealth of archaeological remains is one of the main reasons why Rome has only two metro lines, neither of which goes through the heart of the centro storico. The new C line, which has been on the drawing board for decades, will bridge the gap, and planners intend to make the most of this underground wealth, rather than hiding it. Stations will allow access to previously hidden archaeological sites, like the Teatro di Pompeo, and some tunnels may be lined with clear acrylic sheet to allow glimpses of illuminated ruins.

Rome's abundance of public drinking fountains fascinates visitors (right)

As the city's streets are so crowded, it makes sense to drive a small car, like the Fiat 500 (below)

The ancient aqueducts, like this one along Via Appia Antica (below), brought water into Rome

Look for the city's motto, *senatus populusque romanus,* on statues, but also on rubbish bins and drain covers (below left)

A detail from the fountain in Piazza della Rotonda (left)

Romans En Masse

Romans are good at high-density living. It breeds habits that may appear rude or discourteous to those from more sedate cultures, but that are often determined by sheer force of numbers. Queuing three or four abreast is often the only way not to spill out of the door and down the street: but you can be sure that everyone in the queue knows exactly who came in after them (in doctors' waiting rooms, new arrivals will always ask, 'Chi è l'ultimo?'—'Who's last?'). The same goes for parking, which is all to do with making the most of the available space—even if this means parking facing into the edge of the road (a feat that the archetypal Roman car, the Fiat 500, is uniquely designed to perform).

Acqua Potabile

Between 312BC and AD206, 11 aqueducts were built to provide classical Rome with fresh water. These feats of engineering passed both overland (well-preserved sections of the Acquedotto Claudio can still be seen on the road to Ciampino airport) and underground, bringing more than a million cubic metres (35 million cubic feet) of water a day into the capital. Despite the fact that most of Rome's modern water supply is guaranteed by a huge underground reservoir called the Peschiera, inaugurated in 1949, three of the old aqueducts (the Acqua Marcia, the Appio–Alessandrino and the Vergine) are still in use, though the routes they follow are slightly different now. Many older Romans can still be seen filling up bottles from certain single-aqueduct fountains: They swear it tastes better than the water that comes out of the taps.

Living Latin

There have been a number of attempts by Roman politicians and power brokers down through the ages to co-opt the Glory That Was Rome. In 1347, rabble-rouser Cola da Rienzo persuaded the citizens to revolt against their aristocratic bosses and establish the Senate once more on the Capitoline (this new Republic lasted precisely six months). Even the popes got in on the act, giving themselves the high-sounding Latin title Pontifex Maximus (chief bridge-builder). And Mussolini pushed the Roman parallels for all he was worth, adopting the Roman *fascio littorio* (a ceremonial bundle of sticks) as his party symbol. Today, Rome's city council continues the tradition, inscribing its motto SPQR (*senatus populusque romanus*— the Senate and the Roman people) on everything from trams to drain covers.

Auditiorium Moved

Inaugurated in December 2002, the Auditorium is the biggest new building project to have been unveiled in Rome for a number of years. Designed by Italian architectural superstar Renzo Piano— whose career was launched as Richard Rogers' partner on the Centre Georges Pompidou in Paris—this three-hall city of music is the new home of Rome's premier Santa Cecilia classical music academy and orchestra. But the €140-million complex risked not being built at all when remains of a huge Roman villa were discovered on the site. In the end, the whole project was simply shifted around on its axis to create room for the archaeological area, which has now become an added visitor attraction, complete with small museum.

Mother Teresa is one of many modern day candidates for canonization (below left)
The Vatican is still a place for pilgrimage, and the Pope says weekly public Masses (left and below)

Vatican
Secrets

The dialect expression '*Quanno more er papa, ne fanno n'artro*' (When the Pope dies, they just make another one) expresses the fatalistic, cynical approach of the average *romano* towards the religious mini-state in his or her midst. The indifference has been mutual: It was only in 1929, with the signing of the Lateran Pact, that the pope recognized the existence of a unified Italy, and today there is still a reserve in the Vatican's dealings with the city outside its walls that has sometimes been interpreted as wilful secrecy. But reticence is in the nature of the Holy See, which is not only the arbiter and preserver of the Catholic faith. It is also, in more worldly terms, a well-oiled para-governmental organization, whose 4,000 employees service 950 million Catholics worldwide. Like any such concern, it has public areas—such as Basilica di San Pietro and the Musei Vaticani—and strictly private sections, hidden behind the imposing Leonine Walls. This is where the various ministries of the Vatican State are housed; but there are also more mundane necessities, like the tax-free Vatican supermarket and filling station.

The Conclave

The conclave, or the election of a new pope, is one of the world's most mysterious ballots. It's strictly one cardinal one vote, though the Holy Spirit is allowed (indeed expected) to influence the outcome. Eighteen days after the pontiff's death, the cardinals are locked into the conclave area, which comprises the Sistine Chapel and some adjoining rooms. Voting takes place twice a day until a successful candidate emerges. At the end of each session, the voting slips are burned. In the event of a deadlock, the slips are mixed with wet straw to produce a plume of black smoke. When a pope is finally chosen—usually after several days—a plume of white smoke (*la fumata bianca*) rises from the chapel.

Religious articles (left, below and on opposite page), both tacky and tasteful, are on sale throughout the city
The Swiss Guard (far left) still wear uniforms designed by Michelangelo

Despite ill health, the Pope (above) makes frequent public appearances

The Man Behind the Uniform

The Swiss Guards are the subject of countless tourist photos. But evidence of strong passions stirring behind their picturesque 16th-century uniforms came on the evening of 4 May 1998, when young vice-corporal Cecil Tornay killed himself after shooting dead his commanding officer, Colonel Alois Estermann, and Estermann's wife, Gladys Meza Romero. In a recent book, *City of Secrets,* journalist John Follain claims that the murders were not, as the Vatican claimed, the result of a fit of madness, but a premeditated act by a man frustrated by his lack of promotion, by the end of a homosexual affair he had been having with Estermann, and by the scorn heaped on his proposals for improving the efficiency of the 500-year-old papal guard.

The Vatican Online

The Vatican may be a male-dominated organization, but one branch at least is in female hands. Sister Judith Zoebelein, an American Franciscan nun, is the mind behind the Holy See's website. Brought over in 1991 to expand the Vatican's rudimentary computer network, she soon became involved in setting up the website (www. vatican.va), which was launched in earnest over Easter 1997. The three computers that initially handled the Internet traffic were called Michael, Gabriel and Raphael, after the three archangels. After a million hits in the first three days, contacts settled to their present average of 50,000 per day. Available in six languages, the Vatican website gives access to over 25,000 Holy See documents, including some in the Vatican Secret Archives.

Working for God

The Holy See's 600 clerical staff and 3,300 lay workers may not be paid global corporate rates, but staff loyalty is boosted by a range of tax breaks and other perks, which include free health care and subsidized rents. Vatican workers pay around a third less for fuel than they would across the border in overpriced Italy—which explains the popularity of Vatican City's two fuel pumps. The employees-only Vatican supermarket also offers substantial savings, though the patchy selection of items on offer can recall Eastern Europe before the fall of the Wall. The only part of the complex that is open to outsiders is the Vatican pharmacy, which stocks certain medicines that are unavailable in Italy (a doctor's prescription is required).

John Paul II—the Saintmaker

Pope John Paul II has created more saints than any other pope in history, and more than all the popes of the previous four centuries. As of March 2003, the tally stood at 465. The Polish Pope has also smoothed the road to sainthood, reducing the interval between the death of the candidate and the initiation of the lengthy process from 30 years to just five. The first step, beatification, is a courtroom-style 'cause' in which the prosecuting attorney—the original 'devil's advocate'—argues against the person's holiness. Full canonization requires two proven miracles to take place after beatification. Even for those on the 'fast track' to sainthood, like Mother Teresa of Calcutta, the full process will take a minimum of 15 years.

Art isn't confined to Rome's museums (above)
Taking your pizza away can save on cost (far left),
as can drinking your coffee at the bar (below)

Insider's **Rome**

Sometimes it's not the obvious things that strike you about a city. It might be a detail, like the scent of cherry blossom in spring, the leisurely walking pace, or the way Italian banks seem geared towards keeping people out. In Rome, for example, the Colosseo is a top tourist priority—but so is crossing the road in one piece. At first this might seem a vain hope, as cars and Vespas are often reluctant to stop even for those waiting at crossings. But it becomes a lot easier if you observe the local technique, which seems to be stride out purposefully, all the while staring the oncoming driver or motorcyclist firmly in the eye. Roman drivers, after all, have no desire to mow down pedestrians: It messes up their car and makes them late (or, rather, later) for appointments. A little inside knowledge also helps make sense of other local stimuli, from soccer graffiti to stray cats; and mastering Roman habits such as not drinking cappuccino after lunch and not leaving tips of more than five per cent will do wonders for your self-esteem, though hard-up waiters may be less impressed.

Caffè Culture

Coffee is a serious business in Rome and has little to do with the Americanized genre peddled in London or Seattle by lookalike chains. To do *caffè* as the Romans do, a few rules are in order. First, opt for tradition over variety: Mochacchino is unheard of, as is any form of flavoured coffee. Second, respect the time of day: Cappuccino is a breakfast drink, and no Roman would dream of ordering it after lunch or dinner. Third, learn the terminology: If you want an espresso, just ask for *un caffè*; if you want a little more water, it's *un caffè lungo*; if you just want a coffee stain in the bottom of the cup, ask for *un caffè ristretto*.

Locals find the best way to get around the city is by scooter or on foot, while the feline population finds another use for cars (bottom)

The Cat Ladies

Visitors to Rome are often surprised, and sometimes shocked, by the number of stray cats that roam ownerless around the city's archaeological sites. There are large communities in the Forum, in the sunken Area Sacra in the middle of busy Largo Argentina, around Caius Cestius's Pyramid and in the adjacent Cimiterio Protestante, where Keats and Shelley are buried. But although they are not as well groomed as pampered single-owner apartment cats, these strays are in fact well looked after. An army of voluntary *gattare* (cat ladies) feed the cats, report illnesses or deaths to the city council vet, and provide extra comforts such as wooden cat houses.

Giallorossi or Biancocelesti?

Rome has two Serie A (premier league) soccer teams: Roma and Lazio. They share the 85,000-capacity Stadio Olimpico, scheduling home matches on alternate Sundays (stadium time-shares are common in Italian soccer: AC Milan and Inter have the same arrangement in Milan, Juventus and Torino in Turin). The teams also recently alternated the league title, which was won by Lazio in 2000 and Roma in 2001. Both teams are often referred to by the colours they wear: Roma are the *giallorossi* (yellow-and-reds), while Lazio are the *biancocelesti* (white-and-light-blues). Roma supporters are concentrated in the city itself, and tend to be more Leftist (soccer, like everything else in Italy, is politicized), while Lazio supporters hail more from the hinterland, and mostly veer to the Right.

The *Motorini* Invasion

As anyone who has tried to cross Piazza Venezia during the rush hour can testify, Rome has been invaded by motorcycles and *motorini* (light, 50cc mopeds and scooters) in the last 15 years. It now has a staggering 600,000 motorized two-wheelers: that's one for every five inhabitants, more than any other city in the world. Rome's balmy climate is one reason for the boom, but it's also connected to the fact that going by scooter can more than halve journey times across the city, and it makes it a lot easier to find a parking space. All two-wheelers are now supposed to have catalytic exhausts, though there are still plenty of unmodified Vespas buzzing around.

Faith in the Future

It was not only in ancient times that Romans put their faith in soothsayers and augurs. Around 100,000 Romans visit one of the capital's estimated 1,700 *maghi*, or magicians, every year. Some come for help with unrequited love affairs, others because they believe that enemies have put the *malocchio* (evil eye) on them. With names like Zorzi and Osiris, these modern soothsayers have websites and advertise on buses. Their customers range from professional types to housewives, and even Fellini used to consult a Turinese *mago* called Rol. In the Lazio region as a whole, the annual turnover of these tarot-readers, palm-readers and crystal-ball-gazers is estimated at over 75 million euros.

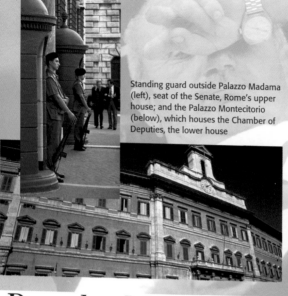

Standing guard outside Palazzo Madama (left), seat of the Senate, Rome's upper house; and the Palazzo Montecitorio (below), which houses the Chamber of Deputies, the lower house

Controversial prime minister, Silvio Berlusconi

People, Money and Power

Romans are quick to complain whenever the city's place as the nation's capital—and as the spiritual home of one of the world's largest religions—causes them any grief. Hold-ups resulting from anti-government demonstrations or motorcades ferrying heads of state to and from the airport are frequent, and are part of any self-respecting romano's repertoire of excuses for being late. But the city benefits from its special status, too; major events like the 1990 World Cup and the Jubilee Year in 2000 saw a huge influx of funds to the capital, which is looking better now than it has for a number of years.

The Eternal City has a diversified economy, based on small-scale trade and service concerns; tourism and, more recently, IT are two important sectors. As a consequence, Rome has been largely immune to the post-industrial shake-ups affecting northern cities such as Milan and Turin, where heavy industry accounts for a larger slice of the cake. On the political front, Rome is currently split—acrimoniously at times—between the centre-left loyalties of the city and provincial councils, and the centre-right orientation of both the Lazio region (of which Rome is the capital) and the national government, to which the city plays host.

Silvio Berlusconi

A man who owns three of Italy's seven national TV channels is allowed to make legislative decisions that affect his rivals; the same man, who is under investigation on bribery charges, uses his parliamentary powers to curb the power of the magistracy. But Italians have been living with such paradoxes for some time. For Silvio Berlusconi, media magnate turned centre-right political crusader, whose moneymaking career began when he charged his schoolmates for help with their homework, is currently in his second term as prime minister. The first, in 1994, lasted only seven months; the second, which began in June 2001, looks set to run a little longer if Berlusconi can dodge the judges and rein in his talent for gaffes.

Whether at work or play, Romans like to dress well (left, far left and bottom), but immigration (below left) has changed the face of the city

Small families are now more common in modern-day Rome (right)

A Modern-Day Melting Pot

It was only in 1976 that Italy became a net importer of people: For over a century, Italians were more used to being immigrants than receiving them. Romans have had plenty of experience of outsiders: In the 25 years following the unification of Italy in 1870, the city's population doubled. Today's immigrants, though, come not from Abruzzo or Campania but from the Philippines, Romania and Poland (in that order), plus a host of other developing and developed countries. The African and Asian communities congregate around Piazza Vittorio, near the station, where it is not unusual to see impromptu cricket matches in the park in summer. Integration has been slow; most Romans still use *la filippina* as a synonym for the cleaning lady.

The Roman Art of Getting By

The *arte di arrangiarsi*— the old Roman knack of muddling through and of turning even the least promising situation to some advantage— extends to matters of finance and employment. The classic example is the *portiere condominiale*, the porter who, in the more well-heeled areas of the city, sits in a tiny booth at the entrance to an apartment block, screening visitors and taking messages. The *portiere*, who generally lives with his family in the basement apartment, earns a subsistence wage, collected via a tax levied on the apartments' owners. But this is supplemented by a whole range of other activities: procuring documents, doing the shopping, watering plants, taking calls from lovers—all of which carry extra fees.

Mamma's Children

These days, the image of a prosperous, pasta-serving *mamma* surrounded by dozens of kids is way off the mark. Italy has one of the world's lowest birth rates, at 9.1 per 1,000 inhabitants, and one of the lowest fertility rates, with 1.2 children born per adult woman (compared with 1.7 for the UK and 2.0 for the US). But *mamma* still exercises a strong influence on the few kids she does have: At the last count, 56 per cent of 25- to 29-year-olds still lived at home, and the number is increasing. According to Italian statistical institute Eurispes, the two figures are connected: 'Young people are getting married less, and until they do marry they prefer to live at home.'

Rome's mayor, Walter Veltroni

Walter Veltroni

Roman mayor Walter Veltroni took over city hall in May 2001, inheriting the job from fellow left-wing politician Francesco Rutelli. If Rutelli is being groomed as a challenger to Silvio Berlusconi's centre-right government, Veltroni seems content for the moment to be top Rome dog. His main achievement so far has been to persuade the national government to channel 300 million euros into city funds. But he's a smart cookie and should make his mark by pushing through the long-awaited new *piano regolatore*, the first Rome town-planning blueprint for 40 years, which aims to put an end to the unregulated building that plagues the capital.

19

Raphael's frescoes in the Musei Vaticani dwarf visitors (above), while a statue from the Palazzo dello Sport at the EUR watches over a runner (left)

Wealthy families sponsored much of the building work, and their emblems, like the Barberini bees (right), can often be picked out

Art and

Architecture

Rome is too full of life and noise and theatre to lie down quietly and agree to be a museum. But this is all to the benefit of the tuned-in visitor. Caravaggio's striking *chiaroscuro* canvases in the churches of San Luigi dei Francesi or Santa Maria del Popolo are likely to seem forced and artificial until, emerging into a Roman summer evening, you see how the golden light really does slant in sideways, leaving dark pools of shadow. Bernini's baroque creations, like the Four Rivers fountain in Piazza Navona, translate the city's love of theatre and spectacle into a concerto of stone and water. To uncover Rome's artistic jewels, a little patience is needed. Alongside top tourist attractions like the Sistine Chapel are lesser known treats such as the church of Santi Quattro Coronati, with its medieval cloister, and that of Santa Prassede, with its Byzantine mosaics. There are quirky architectural one-offs, such as Bramante's miniature *tempietto* in the church of San Pietro in Monitorio, and one or two unexpected modern classics, including Mazzoni's Termini station and Libera's Marmorata post office.

Pietro Cavallini

Few tourists realize that one of Italy's great medieval frescoes is not in Tuscany but in Rome. In its nascent realism, Pietro Cavallini's late 13th-century *Last Judgement* in the church of Santa Cecilia is a clear anticipation of the Renaissance. Late, great Italian art critic Federico Zeri went so far as to suggest that Cavallini, rather than Giotto, may have been responsible for the St. Francis cycle in the Upper Basilica at Assisi; and a recent book by Zeri disciple Bruno Zanardi lends support to the claim by demonstrating the clear stylistic analogies between the Santa Cecilia frescoes and the Upper Basilica cycle. The jury is still out—so catch Cavallini before he becomes a household name.

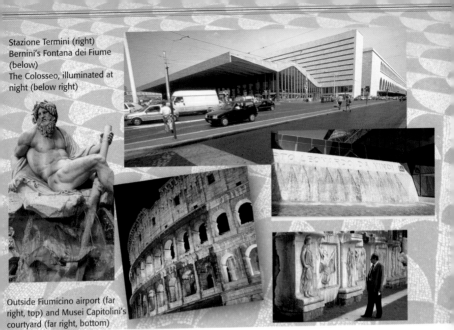

Stazione Termini (right)
Bernini's Fontana dei Fiume (below)
The Colosseo, illuminated at night (below right)

Outside Fiumicino airport (far right, top) and Musei Capitolini's courtyard (far right, bottom)

The Perfect Blue

Renaissance painters, and their patrons, observed a rigid hierarchy of hues. It is easy for us today to appreciate the value of the silver and gold pigments that enriched the altarpieces of the Middle Ages, and that derived directly from the precious metals themselves. But few modern observers realize that ultramarine blue was just as valuable: Extracted from lapis lazuli, it was a costly Arabian import. Contracts would stipulate the grade to be used, in order to prevent its replacement with the inferior German blue (a copper carbonate). Without lapis lazuli, the deep blue firmament that provides the luminous backdrop of Michelangelo's *Last Judgement*, on the altar wall of the Sistine Chapel, would by now have faded to grey.

Fascist Architecture

Mussolini may have made those trains run on time, but it was architecture, rather than punctuality, that he bequeathed to the Romans. Fascism is kept alive today only by a fringe of far-right nostalgics, but the clean, sharp, marble-faced buildings that encapsulated the regime's dreams of a Brave New World are still standing, in silent reproach to the lack of identity and vision of their postwar counterparts. Leading examples are the Foro Italico, built between 1928 and 1935 to host the Olympic games; the model suburb of EUR to the south of the city, which includes Adalberto Libera's groundbreaking Palazzo dei Congressi; and Termini station, with its soaring cantilever roof, completed after the war to a 1930s design by Angiolo Mazzoni.

Private Wealth Makes Public Art

In terms of masterpieces per square metre, Rome does not have a gallery to compare with the Ufizzi in Florence or the Accademia in Venice. But what it does have is a wealth of private collections that have remained substantially intact. The Museo Galleria Borghese, the Palazzo-Galleria Doria Pamphilj and the Ludovisi collection in Palazzo Altemps are fascinating because of the personalities that lie behind them and the way they illuminate the history of taste. The Ludovisis, for instance, thought nothing of asking baroque sculptors such as Alessandro Algardi to 'improve' the classical statues they owned. Meanwhile, Scipione Borghese's mixture of hedonism and seriousness comes through in his eclectic collection, which veers from the religious piety of Raphael's *Deposition* to the worldly eroticism of Correggio's *Danaë*.

The Rarity of New Buildings

Compared to London, Paris or Berlin, Rome has little contemporary architecture of any breadth or vision. Red tape is one problem; so is the sheer lack of sites in a city where nothing is ever knocked down. Well, almost nothing. Of the handful of new projects that represent Rome's long-awaited architectural reawakening, the most controversial is the new casing for the Ara Pacis monument, designed by American architect Richard Meier. Until recently this graceful classical altar, brought to light in the 1930s, was housed in a fascist-era pavilion, which was demolished to prepare the ground for Meier's boxy white Ara Pacis Museum. The ensuing political row blocked work on the project and is likely to keep this masterpiece of Roman art out of bounds to visitors for quite some time.

Gregory Peck recognized Audrey Hepburn's star quality when they starred together in *Roman Holiday* (left): He insisted her name was put above the film title
Federico Fellini (bottom left)

Marcello Mastroianni and Sophia Loren (above), two of Italy's greatest exports, starred together in over a dozen films

Hollywood on the
Tiber

Rome has always seen itself as one big movie set. Much of the city's theatre is spontaneous: rows erupt, jokes are cracked—Romans love playing to the gallery. It's no surprise, then, if this talent for spectacle should take more organized forms, and the natural medium for the city's show-off instinct is cinema. The golden age of the Roman film set was in the 1950s and 1960s, when low-budget swords-and-sandals movies, many shot in the city's historic Cinecittà studios, alternated with intense neorealist classics such as De Sica's *Umberto D* or Pasolini's *Accattone*, shot on location in the city's depressed inner suburbs. And then there were the Americans, attracted to 'Hollywood on the Tiber' by low labour costs.

Today, you can hire a Vespa to re-enact *Roman Holiday* (though helmets are now compulsory) or mime the chariot race from *Ben Hur* in the Circo Massimo. But don't attempt a *Dolce Vita*-style dip in the Trevi Fountain: The resident policeman's main job these days is to foil any would-be Anitas and Marcellos.

Albertone

When actor Alberto Sordi died in February 2003, a quarter of a million Romans turned out for his funeral. In almost 200 films, 'Albertone' (Big Alberto) had become a screen icon.

But Sordi (above) was no action hero. With his *faccia da mammone* (mummy's-boy face), he embodied a new type of Italian of the postwar generation: Outwardly modern and besotted with American values (as in *Un Americano a Roma*, 1954) but in reality profoundly Italian; outwardly the Don Giovanni (as in Fellini's *I Vitelloni*, 1953) but in reality ill at ease with women. Later in life, Sordi became an unofficial Roman elder statesman; he was even made mayor for a day on his 80th birthday.

Anthony Minghella (top right) filmed parts of *The Talented Mr. Ripley* (1999) on location in Rome

Cameron Diaz (far right) with Martin Scorsese on the set of *Gangs of New York* (2002). The actress was nominated for a Golden Globe for the role of Jenny Everdeane

Anita Ekberg (right) in *La Dolce Vita* (1960), the film that introduced the word *paparazzi* into general use

STUDIOS

Cinecittà

It was not until the 1930s that Rome emerged as the capital of Italian cinema ahead of two early contenders, Turin and Florence. Inaugurated by Mussolini in 1937, the Cinecittà studios covered what had been until then a huge area of farmland on the Via Tuscolana. The studios worked flat out until the wartime lull, then returned to health in the 1950s on the back of a string of American productions, from *Roman Holiday* (1952) to *Cleopatra* (1963). Meanwhile, Federico Fellini (far left), who claimed that the real world never matched the heightened reality of a studio set, was weaving his cine-matic fantasies in Studio 5. The 1970s and 1980s saw a drastic decline in Cinecittà's fortunes, with TV pro-ductions outnumbering feature films.

The Not So Sweet Life

Perhaps the most iconic Italian film of all time, Federico Fellini's *La Dolce Vita* was shot in Rome between March and September 1959. It was not an easy birth: The film's original producer, Dino De Laurentiis, pulled out at the last moment, alarmed by the 'chaotic' script and Fellini's refusal to replace Marcello Mastroianni with Paul Newman. Shooting was equally eventful. The famous Trevi Fountain sequence was shot on a freezing night in March, with Anita Ekberg shiver-ing in her backless ball dress. Ever the enter-tainer, Fellini turned his megaphone to the crowd and said:

'Where would you find another like her? I've made her do things a circus horse wouldn't do. And now I'm throwing her into the water.'

The Return of the Americans

The Americans are back. Although the days when Rome was known as 'Hollywood on the Tiber' are long gone, when stars such as Cary Grant, Ava Gardner, Charlton Heston and Elizabeth Taylor kept the paparazzi of the Via Veneto snap-happy, the 1990s saw a significant return of big-budget international productions to the com-petitively priced Cinecittà studios. First came two Stallone action vehicles, *Cliffhanger* and *Daylight*; interior scenes of *The Portrait of a Lady* and *The Talented Mr Ripley* were also shot here. Then, in the autumn of 2000, the heavy artillery moved in, when Martin Scorsese built a replica of 1860s New York on the studio backlot for *Gangs of New York*. With DiCaprio and Diaz in town, it was paparazzi paradise once again.

Italian Cinema

It's not quite true that nothing has happened in Italian cinema since those glorious art house days of Fellini, Pasolini, Antonioni and Bertolucci. But it's an understand-able assumption, as few contemporary Italian films are distributed abroad, and those that are tend to languish in cineclub ghettos. The exception to the rule is Roberto Benigni, whose Oscar-winning *La Vita è Bella* (Life Is Beautiful) was a huge international hit. But Benigni is not really representative of the new Italian cinema, which is at its most incisive in the films of Roman auteur Nanni Moretti (*The Son's Room*, 2001), veteran political filmmaker Marco Bellocchio (*The Divinity Lesson*, 2002), and the emotional tangles of Young Turk (literally, as he was born in Istanbul) Ferzan Ozpetek (*Ignorant Fairies*, 2002).

From head to toe, and everywhere in between, if it's stylish, you can buy it in Rome

La Bella Figura

Roman Style

Understand *bella figura* and you're halfway to understanding the Romans. *Bella figura* is a little bit presence, a little bit self-respect and a little bit being careful not to let the side down. It's what *carabinieri* motorcycle cops are communicating when they lean against their Moto Guzzis in jodhpurs and wraparound shades; it's what makes kids from the depressed outer suburbs dress up on Saturday night as if they were in Beverly Hills. The opposite is *brutta figura*, to show oneself up. In Rome, it's not so much what you've got, it's what you project.

If style is all about care for one's appearance, an instinct for what looks good and the abilty to project self-confidence, most Romans have it in bagfuls. All three qualities can be observed during the evening *passeggiata*. Though not as strong a tradition as it is in other towns farther south, the custom of walking up and down observing others who are also walking up and down reaches critical mass along Via del Corso on Fridays and Saturdays between 5 and 8pm. But if style is interpreted in the more North European sense of originality and standing out from the crowd, many Romans would fail to qualify. Roman style tends to be fairly conformist, opting for the prevailing designer uniform rather than going out on a customized limb. In fashion terms, Rome is more provincial, but also more relaxed, than Milan, Italy's *capitale della moda*. The only big designer to have made his power base in the city is Valentino, though the Fendi siblings and a few mavericks such as Roberto Cappucci are a strong supporting act.

Valentino

Though he hails from Voghera in the north of Italy, Valentino (below) long ago adopted the Eternal City as the hub of his fashion empire. Valentino Garavani, as he was christened in 1932, moved down to Rome in 1959 after a stint as an apprentice in the couture houses of Paris. It was the White Collection in 1967 that really made his name; before long he was dressing such divas as Jackie Kennedy and Elizabeth Taylor. The designer's Roman headquarters is at Rampa Mignanelli, just behind the Spanish Steps, where the *alta moda* (haute couture) collections are presented in January and July.

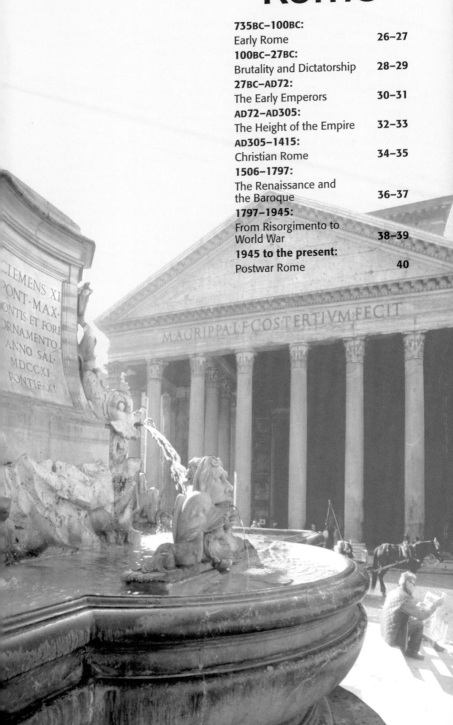

The Story of Rome

Early Rome

The legend goes that Romulus and Remus were the twin sons of Mars and a vestal virgin. Left to die on the banks of the Tiber, they were cared for by a she-wolf and fed by a wood-pecker. The brothers grew up to be robbers and wandered with a band of men. Romulus took possession of the Palatine Hill and founded Rome, very precisely, at eight o'clock in the morning on 21 April 753BC. Remus set up his rival kingdom on the Aventino. Eventually, Romulus killed Remus and his power grew. The legend rings true in one respect: the gaining of imperial power through violence and murder within the family, which was to become a familiar pattern in Roman history.

All civilizations have their creation myths, like the tale of Romulus and Remus. We know for certain that tribes had colonized the Seven Hills of Rome by 1000BC, between the Etruscans to the north and the Greeks to the south. The Etruscans soon dominated the city and brought with them much of what we regard as typically Roman: irrigation, temple-building, gladiatorial displays and togas. Their aristocratic rule was oppressive, and the last of the kings was driven out in 509BC. The following republic was a system of power-sharing among noble families, but rights for commoners were gradually won, set out in the Twelve Tables in 450BC and displayed in the Forum.

Over the next two centuries the Romans conquered Italy and moved inexorably beyond. They defeated the Carthaginians so, by the end of the Third Punic War in 146BC, the Roman Empire comprised Italy, the western Mediterranean and Asia Minor. Strict warrior values had created it, but the aristocracy appropriated land and wealth, leaving soldiers and peasants almost nothing. Attempts at reform from the top, led by the Gracchi brothers, and from the bottom in the form of slave revolts, achieved nothing. By 100BC the rulers of Rome had become violent, selfish and dictatorial.

735 BC

Via Appia Antica was built in 312BC and is still paved with its original basalt cobbles (above left)

The she-wolf is the symbol of Rome. This statue is from the Musei Capitolini (above right)

By the second century BC, the Roman Empire was expanding (right)

The Rape of the Sabine Women

Romulus's fledgling state needed women, so he decided to steal some. In 750BC, he invited the nearby Sabine tribe to attend a ceremony in honour of a newly discovered holy altar to the god Concus. The Sabines came peacefully, and Romulus and his armed men simply ran away with their women, 683 of them if legend is true. Strangely enough, after a few skirmishes both sides agreed to avoid a ruinous war and co-operate. Romulus, with typical Roman pragmatism, then ruled over the Seven Hills jointly with the Sabine chief, Titus Tatius. This joint-rule system entered Roman government: Consuls often worked in pairs, as did many of the other officers of state.

The Rape of Lucretia

According to tradition, in 509BC Sextus Tarquinius, the son of the Etruscan king, went to visit Lucretia and her husband, Collatinus, one night, and they fell to discussing virtuous wives. Lucretia, a true Roman matron, was strict and irreproachable, and Tarquinius, aroused by this, determined to seduce her. He came back when she was alone, threatened her and then raped her. With her honour gone, Lucretia committed suicide after telling her husband what had happened. This act represented everything that was wrong with a corrupt and selfish Etruscan monarchy, which was plundering the country and trampling on Roman virtues, so Collatinus and his powerful friends rose up in revolt. The people of Rome supported them, the King was forced into exile and the republic was established.

The Capitoline Geese

In 390BC, an army of Gauls surrounded Rome. The smaller Roman army withdrew and evacuated the city except for the Capitoline Hill, where the soldiers were besieged. One night a former consul, Marcus Manlius, woke to hear the honking of a gaggle of geese, which the starving soldiers had not eaten because they were sacred to Juno. Manlius looked over the wall in time to see the shield of a Gaulish soldier about to climb over. He knocked him back, and a volley of stones and javelins from the other soldiers sent the Gauls crashing down the hill to their deaths. The Capitoline Hill never was taken, but the Gauls stayed in Rome for seven more months, and left only when they got a hefty ransom.

The Gracchi Brothers

The tribune Tiberius Gracchus attempted to break up the great estates of the rich and distribute the land to the poor, especially former soldiers, who were wandering the country. The Senate, composed of the owners of great estates, was horrified to see public support for Tiberius and hired a band of thugs to kill him. He was beaten to death with a chair leg outside the Capitoline temple, and 300 supporters were thrown into the Tiber. In 120BC his brother Sempronius met the same fate over the same issue, and 3,000 followers were murdered. These acts of shocking violence by the very men supposed to uphold the law set the scene for the fall of the republic 60 years later.

Romulus populated his new city with women abducted from a nearby tribe (left)

1OOBC

Most of what is known about the Etruscans comes from their pottery and artwork (left)

The Palatine Hill is rich with archaeological remains (above)

Honking geese warned of a surprise attack by the Gauls (left)

Brutality and Dictatorship

Riot, unrest and civil war in the first century BC led to the emergence of the army and ruthless dictators as the guarantors of public order, gladly supported by the Senate. The brutal rule of Sulla was followed by the first triumvirate in 70BC, composed of Pompey, Crassus and Julius Caesar. They resisted all attempts by the Senate, somewhat belatedly, to regain democratic power. The triumvirs eventually turned on each other. In 49BC Julius Caesar crossed the Rubicon from his territories of Gaul and took control of Rome; by the following year he was sole ruler of the empire. Caesar was an autocrat who demanded total obedience: the republic was finally at an end. The Senate nevertheless rallied its forces, albeit for the last time, and a group of conspirators murdered the dictator in 44BC. What followed was a contest for power between the impulsive, emotional Mark Antony and the icy, calculating Octavian. Antony was absent from Rome for long periods during his spectacular love affair with the queen of Egypt, Cleopatra, while Octavian built up his military base in the western part of the empire. After moving against Antony and defeating him at the Battle of Actium in 31BC, Octavian secured the empire for himself to become the first emperor, Augustus.

100BC

Marius and Sulla

Gaius Marius (pictured below, top left), the son of a farmer, and Lucius Cornelius Sulla (pictured below, middle left), an aristocrat, played out the murderous rivalry that Romulus and Remus had set as the Roman pattern. The men had once been comrades, but, as the republic was about to collapse, Marius, seven times consul, wanted to break the power of the Senate; Sulla was determined to oppose him. Marius massacred the Senate and thousands of aristocrats in 87BC. After Marius' death, Sulla murdered his foe's army. He formed a dictatorship and paraded through the streets protected by a vicious force of 10,000 slaves, the Cornelii. When Sulla abruptly stepped down and retired to the country, he left Rome brutalized and the Senate ripe for overthrow.

Julius Caesar ignored warnings to 'beware the ides of March' (below)

Spartacus

There were three slave revolts between 140 and 70BC. Life depended on the caprice of the master: 'Lighten a ship by throwing out the slaves, not the horses,' Cicero said, while the philosopher Seneca thought slavery the worst shame of the empire. Spartacus, possibly a deserter, was a slave in the gladiator barracks in Capua in 73BC, when he escaped with 70 other gladiators and weapons from the kitchens. They hid on the slopes of Vesuvius and were soon joined by other escaped slaves and gladiators. Spartacus wanted to lead his men to freedom across the Alps, but his followers sought to plunder the surrounding countryside, attracting punitive action from Rome. For two years Spartacus' army (120,000 strong at its peak) managed to defeat all the forces the Roman senate sent to deal with it. Eventually, in 71BC, his forces were defeated at Brindisi, and 6,000 slaves were crucified along the Appian Way. Spartacus himself died in battle and his body was never found.

Cicero

Cicero was Rome's best lawyer, a respected author with political skills that made him consul in 63BC, a position usually reserved for the aristocracy. These were violent times—killing was state policy—and he spent much time on murder trials. In 80BC the young Cicero made his reputation defending Sextius Roscius for the murder of his father. In a barnstorming speech he described the horrible punishment for this: being tied up in a sack and thrown into the sea. Then Cicero dared to suggest that a servant of Sulla, the dictator of Rome, was the real murderer, since he wanted the Roscius estates. Sensationally, the jury believed him, Roscius was acquitted and the young lawyer was on his way.

The Assassination of Julius Caesar

Julius Caesar was dictator of Rome. 'Regard what I say as law,' he declared. When the Senate, gritting its teeth, knelt before him, Caesar stayed seated. In the atmosphere of brutality and murder that he had used himself, the arrogant dictator's fate was sealed. A group of conspirators planned his murder for 15 March 44BC in the Senate. Caesar seemed not to fear assassination, taking no great precautions, and the night before he died said he wanted a quick and unexpected death. He ignored all warnings. The conspirators stabbed him 23 times, and a strange detail is recorded: He put his toga around his head, then drew the bottom around his thighs to preserve his modesty. He knew he was going to fall.

Antony and Cleopatra

In 41BC Mark Antony, joint ruler of the empire, became captivated by Cleopatra during her spectacular entrance to Tarsus, on a bejewelled ship with silver oars, dressed in cloth of gold. Antony left his wife, and he and Cleopatra were crowned as semi-divine rulers of Egypt. Rome was outraged: Antony had abandoned his country and ideals. His co-ruler, Octavian, declared war and met Antony's navy at Actium in 31BC. The battle went to Octavian, and Cleopatra sailed away. Antony had to choose. He still had his armies and his wealth: Rome might still be his. He sailed after Cleopatra and lost everything. They committed suicide together the next year.

Cicero was a great lawyer and statesman, but later fell from grace (right)

Mark Antony's obsession with Cleopatra lost him the city of Rome. The pair later died in a joint suicide pact (left)

The Ponte Fabricio, built in 62BC, is the oldest bridge in Rome (below)

$27BC$

The Early Emperors

The 41 years of Emperor Augustus' rule (27BC–AD14) were looked back on as the Golden Age by the Romans. He halted expansionist wars, set up a government bureaucracy and transformed the face of Rome itself. Too shrewd to accept the title of emperor—he was called 'First Citizen'—Augustus held all major posts in government, the army and religion for life, while leaving the forms of the republic intact. The glory of his reign notwithstanding, it set the scene for the breath-taking excesses that followed: Tiberius, Caligula and Nero were known for lust, perversion and cruelty. A well-ordered bureaucracy ensured the empire almost ran itself: Germanicus easily suppressed revolts in Germany (AD14–16), and great public buildings rose throughout Italy. However, Tiberius (AD14–37), fearing conspiracy, invoked laws to suppress any opposition; Caligula (AD37–41) despised the Senate so much that he planned to turn the empire into an autocracy. Fear and oppression seeped into government, and the emperors depended on the Praetorian Guard to terrorize opponents. Claudius (AD41–54) bribed the Praetorians well, but the reckless actions of his successor, Nero (AD54–68), antagonized the Senate and lost him the army's support. Nero fled the city and committed suicide in AD68.

Augustus

The first emperor, Augustus (previously know as Octavian; ruled 27BC–AD14), lived in a modest villa by the Palatine, but he made the city splendid, saying, 'I found Rome built of brick; I leave it clothed in marble.' This was not personal vanity; Rome had to be grand in the eyes of the world and orderly for its citizens. A hundred public buildings were raised; *insulae*, tenements for the poor, were limited in height to 25m (80ft). The city was divided into 250 precincts, each with its own police force and fire brigade—the poor made do with wood, not marble, and Rome was forever in flames. To deal with this, Augustus' architect, Agrippa, created a remarkable system of six aqueducts, which brought in over a billion litres (220 million gallons) of water a day.

27BC

Augustus, whose Golden Age saw the arts flourish (left)

The great fire of Rome in AD64 was reputed to have been started by Nero (below)

The original Pantheon was built in 27BC, but the inscription on the front is all that remains of that building (above)

Caligula

The notorious Caligula (ruled AD37–41) suffered a traumatic childhood and probably had some kind of mental illness. His appearance—tall, thin, bald and hollow-eyed—was truly frightening. Stories about his private life are outdone only by his amazing extravagance. He sailed along the coast in jewel-studded galleys fitted with baths and dining rooms. He offered dinner guests tit-bits made of gold. Mountains were levelled and plains raised for his public buildings, all at high speed since everything was done under threat of death. He showered people in the streets with gold and liked rolling around on heaps of it. The coffers were soon empty. In one year, it is estimated, he spent 3 billion sesterces, the entire revenue of Tiberius' 23-year reign.

Claudius

It was easy to make fun of Claudius (ruled AD 41–54) in his lifetime. He stammered and trembled, gave way to screaming anger, and stuffed himself with so much food and drink he often fell asleep in the middle of a banquet. His mother called him a monster whom Nature had begun but failed to complete, and he was regularly the focus of practical jokes. As often happens, the embittered, humiliated man retreated to the world of books and learning. He made himself a formidable scholar. Pliny regarded Claudius as one of the greatest minds in the empire. Claudius wrote a treatise on dicing, a study of the Roman alphabet and a 20-volume Etruscan history whose loss is a tragedy for historians.

Nero

Nero (ruled AD54–68) wanted to be a great actor and athlete. Progressing from private theatricals, he made his debut in Naples during an earthquake, warbling to his lyre and dressed in garish wig and robes. He entered competitions and, naturally, won. During a tour of Greece, he won 1,808 prizes, including one for a race when he'd fallen out of his chariot and been knocked senseless. Contemporaries giggled over his awful acting, but he was probably just mediocre. The doors were locked when he performed and the audience, bored to tears, endured endless applause and encores. More seriously, the Senate abhorred Nero's neglect of government business and rose against him. Deluded to the end, he fled Rome crying, 'What a loss I shall be to the arts!'

St. Peter in Rome

Peter probably visited Rome in the AD50s and it's almost certain that he died there during the persecution of the Christians begun by Nero around AD64. Some of those martyrs were torn to pieces by animals, others smeared with pitch and burned as human torches in the Circus of Nero to illuminate night-time races. According to early Church tradition, Peter was crucified upside-down at his own request, feeling unworthy to be killed in the same way as Christ. In AD324, Constantine built a church on the site of the Circus of Nero, which was subsequently replaced by Julius II's basilica that we see today. In the crypt of the great basilica is a place that tradition glorifies as St. Peter's grave.

Nero is best remembered for his debauchery and extravagance (right)

$AD72$

The gladiatorial games were noted for their brutality, with the emperor deciding if the fallen gladiator should live or die (far left)

This obelisk, now in Piazza del Popolo, was brought from ancient Egypt by Augustus (left)

The Height of the Empire

For nearly two centuries, the citizens of Rome enjoyed peace and wealth. The five 'good emperors' of the Antonine dynasty—Nerva, Trajan, Hadrian, Antoninus and Marcus Aurelius (ruled AD81–180)—worked with the Senate, and the empire expanded to its greatest limits. Soon, though, its very size proved its undoing. A huge army of approximately half a million men, composed of many different nationalities, could not easily be controlled. The army started to dictate policy, and local commanders were often made emperor without ever seeing Rome. In AD193 the Praetorian Guard put the empire up for sale—the winner lasted 66 days in power. In all, some 50 emperors came and went in the period up to the rule of Diocletian in AD286.

The enormous territories in the east meant Rome no longer occupied its central role. Recognizing that the empire was ready to collapse under its own weight, Diocletian divided it into the Western and Eastern empires, under two rulers, which brought some respite from political tension. Diocletian then tackled a much greater force for change, the Christians. He persecuted them ruthlessly, but the conversions went on and the Church continued to grow and develop, with converts increasingly coming from all ranks of society.

The Colosseum

The ruins of the Colosseo, built AD79–96, dominate the city today, as the games once held in it dominated so much of Roman life. Their equivalent today is the hugely expensive blockbuster movie with its pampered stars, but there the similarity ends. A successful gladiator might be adored by the whole city, but, as Seneca said, 'this was a serious business—pure murder.' The games themselves probably evolved from Etruscan funeral games, and this echo of the underworld never left them. At the games of Trajan in AD107, for example, 80,000 people watched 10,000 men fight to the death over a period of four months. As they became an instrument of social control, more frequent games with greater cruelty kept the populace quiet.

The Colosseo (left)
Porta Pia, built in AD 271–75, was one of the main gates in the Aurelian Walls (below)

AD 72

Triumphal arches, like this one dedicated to Titus, were built to celebrate military victories (below)

PIVS·IIII·PONT·M
·SVBLATA·NOMENTANA·EX
·VIA·M·PIAN

Trajan

During Trajan's reign (ruled AD98–117) the *Pax Romana* (Roman Peace) extended over a huge empire, from Scotland to Portugal, over the Sahara to the borders of Persia, and into Germany. Trajan expanded the empire to its limits, his armies following the routes of Alexander the Great. Trajan was a typical mixture of Roman brutality and magnanimity. The Dacians (modern-day Transylvanians) were completely subdued by him. Their gold was taken to Rome and thousands of men and women brought there as slaves and gladiators. Yet Trajan forbade the persecution of Christians, causing the governor of Bithynia, worried about that troublesome group, to write that 'they create the worst kind of precedent and are out of keeping with the spirit of the age.'

Hadrian

Hadrian (ruled AD117–138) spent most of his time journeying through the empire and usually left a building or two behind him. In Britain, he constructed a wall across the north to keep out marauding tribes. In Egypt, an entire city, Antinopolis, was raised in memory of his friend, Antinous. Two buildings in Rome express the opposites in his personality, the cool-headed administrator and the imperial master. The Pantheon is a masterpiece of design—classical, deceptively simple, perfectly symmetrical, the work of the man who revised the codes of tax and the law. His tomb, on the other hand, turned out to be an immense piece of unsubtle grandeur, so vast that medieval Romans used it as a fortress. It's now within Castel Sant'Angelo.

The Feasts of Elegabalus

Even by Roman standards, Elegabalus (ruled AD218–221) is astonishing. He was a teenage Syrian covered in make-up, jewels and silk, and the tales of his luxury are astounding. He liked to swim in pools stained yellow with saffron, and walk on roses and lilies. At his feasts guests lay on couches of solid silver; one evening the food was blue, the next it was green. He liked to eat peacocks' tongues, then suddenly would demand nightingales' tongues instead. Once, 600 ostrich heads were served and guests ate their brains. Not surprisingly, the guests often fell asleep in a stupor. Elegabalus' idea of fun was then to lock them in the hall, and send in tame bears and lions to wake them up.

Rome Without an Emperor

In AD300, over a thousand years after Romulus occupied the Palatine Hill, the emperors left Rome. The vast city was a rich brew of contrasting nationalities, from Arabians to Britons and Turks. The emperor himself might be African or Spanish, but he had always respected Rome as the focal point of the world: Diocletian had no such scruples. He came from Dalamatia, toured the empire as all the emperors had done, and it's likely that he did not even see Rome until he was almost 60. He didn't like the excess and corruption, and found Milan to the north and Nicomedia to the east far more practical as capitals. They were built up swiftly and soon became as grand as the Eternal City itself.

Trajan was a popular emperor, despite spending most of his reign abroad (below left)

Hadrian (left) built his mausoleum north of the Tiber. Today, it is in the Castel Sant'Angelo (right)

305

Piazza Navona's racetrack shape follows the lines of Domitian's AD86 Stadium (left)

Emperor Aurelius built the city's fortification walls in AD271 (above)

SPQR

IMP·CAESARI·NERVAE·F
TRAIANO
OPTIMO·PRINCIPI

ANNO·XI
A·FASCIBVS·RENOVATI

Christian Rome

Christianity became the state religion under Diocletian's successor, Constantine (AD306–37). Although he moved the capital to Byzantium, Rome became the empire's spiritual hub. Increasingly, the western borders were under threat from Goths and Vandals. The city was sacked several times and in AD476 the last Roman emperor, Romulus Augustulus, was deposed. During centuries of war between the Byzantine Empire and the Goths, the popes acquired territory known as the Papal States and the authority to crown the Holy Roman Emperor. The emperor of Germany claimed rights over the election of the pope, and only under Innocent III (1198–1216) did papal power finally become independent.

Throughout this turmoil Rome shrank to a provincial town. In AD546, reduced to rubble by the Goths, it was deserted for weeks. The papacy alone ensured Rome's survival, but its very wealth and power sparked such feuding that the popes fled to France from 1307 to 1377. The demagogue Cola di Rienzo set up a republic based on ancient principles during this period, but it soon collapsed. The return of the papacy was marred by the Great Schism of the West, when popes and antipopes fought for control of the Church, each backed by half of Europe. Only in 1417 did the Vatican gain its position as the residence of the true pope.

The Conversion of Constantine

No one is sure when Constantine converted to Christianity. Was it at the vision of a flaming cross in the sky in AD312, or at his deathbed baptism in AD337? Despite being the son of St. Helena, who found the True Cross, did he genuinely convert at all? What mattered was that a spirit of Christianity began to pervade the empire. A master who mistreated his slaves was punished, children were protected from abusive parents, prisoners no longer fought in gladiatorial displays, which were denounced by Constantine as 'bloody spectacles'. Much money was spent on erecting churches, many at sites linked with events of the New Testament. Constantine himself gave up imperial power, and the honour of being high priest of the state religion now went to the Bishop of Rome.

$AD305$

Constantine (right)
This 12th-century mosaic, from the church of San Clemente, is a wonderful example of Byzantine art (below right)

Pope Gregory the Great was a particularly pious man, who founded several monasteries (left)

The Arch of Constantine, from which this detail comes, was built to commemorate his defeat of the last pagan emperor, Maxentius, in 312 (above)

The Sack of Rome

The Goths, being driven out of their own lands by invading Huns in AD370, moved south into Greece and then, in AD400, under their leader Alaric, attacked Italy. The Italians begged Alaric to stop, but he told them of a voice urging him on: 'It says to me, "Go to Rome and make that city desolate."' The day came when he besieged the city itself. Alaric told ambassadors from the city to give him all their gold, silver and slaves. Horrified, they asked what he would leave them. 'Your lives,' he replied. The Goths stripped Rome of everything in four days and left behind a traumatized city, which had been inviolate for 800 years.

Visigoth leader Alaric (below)

Pope Gregory the Great

Gregory I combined the grandeur of his position with the simplicity of a true Christian, eating sparingly and giving money to the poor. His revision of the Mass introduced Gregorian chant. He sent St. Augustine to England to convert the Anglo-Saxons ('not Angles but angels'). Gregory became pope in AD590, a testing time: Rome was gripped by plague (the previous pope had died of it). He arranged penitential processions in Rome to ask for God's mercy. On his procession near the Tiber, he had a vision of an angel in the sky sheathing a bloody sword; from that moment the plague ended. The building beneath the vision, Hadrian's Tomb, was renamed Castel Sant'Angelo. On his death, Gregory was made a saint by popular acclamation.

The mosaic of Mary Enthroned, in the church of Santa Maria in Trastevere (right)

Charlemagne, Holy Roman Emperor

Pope Leo III was attacked by jealous rivals who wanted the wealth of the papacy for themselves; he also needed to separate the Church from the influence of the Byzantine Empire. He was fortunate to find his saviour in Charlemagne, king of the Franks, a truly great leader, enlightened and energetic. Charlemagne arrived in Rome and Leo was reconciled with his enemies. They then played out a little charade: Charlemagne, who happened to be wearing splendid robes, went to St. Peter's on Christmas Day AD800 to attend Mass. Suddenly, the Pope drew out a crown, put it on the amazed King's head and declared him Holy Roman Emperor. Rome now had a worthy successor to the likes of Trajan and Hadrian.

Charlemagne's coronation as Holy Roman Emperor marked the revival of the Western Empire (below right)

The Popes Leave Rome

The medieval Church was cursed by its wealth and power. Everyday corruption was so great, and papal elections themselves so violent, that the popes were driven out. For almost 70 years from the beginning of the 14th century, the papacy resided in Avignon, in the south of France. For a while the popes were safe, but the greed of King Philip of France (which lay behind his original invitation) soon infected the Court of Avignon, giving robbers much to plunder. The poet Petrarch, a man of immense public influence, pleaded with the popes to come back to their traditional home. Finally, it was a young mystic, Catherine of Siena, who succeeded in convincing Gregory XI to return to Rome in 1377.

The Renaissance and the
Baroque

The papacy dominated Rome completely. Clement VII, trying to lessen the power of the Habsburg emperor by a treaty with France, drew down on himself the terrifying Sack of Rome in 1527. After this, the energy of the papacy was taken up with the Counter-Reformation. Paul III (1534–39) approved a new order, the Jesuits, whose members pledged their services to the pope and tackled heresy. Papal wealth continued to attract the Roman nobility. Some were monsters, like Roderigo Borgia (Pope Alexander VI, 1492–1503); others were great patrons of the arts, such as Urban VIII (Maffeo Barberini, 1623–44), who issued a directive for public building.

Rome's glory was the baroque. Still, Julius II (1503–13) brought the Renaissance masters to the city and commissioned Rome's great Renaissance artist, Bramante, to rebuild St. Peter's in 1506. In the 17th century the flamboyant baroque architecture of Bernini and Borromini filled the city, and much of the Gothic and Romanesque disappeared. Sometimes, building materials from ancient monuments were used. The papal coffers were emptying fast, and Rome's influence and importance all but vanished in the 18th century. As the century ended, Napoleon annexed the Papal States into the French Empire and forced Pope Pius VII to come to France as a virtual prisoner.

The Sistine Chapel

Julius II and Michelangelo were both strong-willed men who secretly enjoyed their tempestuous relationship. When Julius sent envoys to arrest the artist, who had left Rome in a huff, Michelangelo returned with a rope around his neck, a childish symbol of imprisonment. In 1508 Julius commissioned Michelangelo to decorate the ceiling of the Sistine Chapel. He wanted a pattern of circles and squares bordered by the Twelve Apostles. Michelangelo retorted he would paint anything he liked. Wisely, Julius let him alone, fully understanding the nature of his genius. However, after four years of painting, it was only when Julius threatened to hurl the man off his scaffold that Michelangelo showed off his masterpiece, one of the greatest frescoes in the world.

1506

Despite protesting that he was a scuptor and not a painter, Michelangelo (above) designed and painted the ceiling of the Sistine Chapel (left)

Crowning of the Virgin by Filippo Lippi and assistants used the newly discovered principles of perspective (right)

Charles V and the Sack of Rome

The armies of the Habsburg emperor Charles V, in his war against the French, fought on Italian soil and entered Rome in May 1527. It was the last of the barbarian sackings of the city and in some ways the worst: 20,000 German, Spanish and Italian soldiers occupied Rome and stayed for nearly a year. Their leader died in the assault, and the troops ran out of control, raping, murdering and burning every day. The Pope escaped into the Castel Sant'Angelo. Many of the Germans were Protestants and delighted in smashing all evidence of Catholicism, including countless artworks. Rome was left in ruins and the population fell to 30,000. This catastrophe could well have brought about the end of the Renaissance.

The Trial of Galileo

In 1633 Galileo was charged with 'grave suspicion of heresy' and summoned to Rome for trial by the Inquisition. His bold advocacy of Copernican theory—that the earth revolved around the sun—provoked Church authorities, who interpreted Scripture as saying the opposite. As the 69-year-old Galileo was ill, his patrons, the Medicis, attempted to have the trial held in Florence, but the Pope insisted on Rome. Galileo was interrogated four times, finally under threat of torture, and recanted. He was found guilty and sentenced to unlimited imprisonment. However, the Church was not harsh. The Pope, once Galileo's patron, let him leave Rome for house arrest, and many of the prelates secretly supported him. He was allowed to work and write until his death in 1642.

Roman Baroque: Borromini and Bernini

If the Renaissance belonged to Florence, then the baroque belonged to Rome. Its two greatest practitioners, Gian Lorenzo Bernini (1598–1680) and Francesco Borromini (1599–1667), loathed each other with that ancient Roman fratricidal passion. Bernini, aristocratic and urbane, produced sophisticated work; Borromini, plebeian and hot-tempered, was wild and untamed. Borromini's genius led him to create beautiful churches in the cramped spaces of Rome. Bernini, never a trained architect, produced flamboyant sculptures of angels, tritons and saints. It all ended tragically. Old and frustrated, Borromini committed suicide; Bernini went smoothly on, blackening his rival's name.

The Grand Tour

Wealthy young Englishmen of the 18th century were expected to travel to France and Italy as clumsy youths and come back polished gentlemen. The tours could last four years, and Rome was the high spot, for various reasons: 'Look, listen, learn—and buy' was one of them. Young lords with money to burn returned with paintings, sculptures, coins and anything else the dealers could sell. More tellingly, Britain was conscious of her growing empire, and where better to educate her young men in ruling it than Rome, the blueprint of all empires? The young John Northall, an 18th-century traveller, wrote in 1752, 'One is confronted by emperors, consuls, generals…a cast of almost 2,000 years backwards, and the past becomes present.'

1797

Bernini's fountains and statues, like the Fontana dei Fiumi in Piazza Navona (left) and Borromini's churches, including Sant'Ivo alla Sapienza (right) characterize baroque Rome

The colonnade and piazza of St. Peter's (above) were designed in 1656 by Bernini, as was most of the interior (left). The floor plan, however, remains Michelangelo's

THE RENAISSANCE AND THE BAROQUE 37

From Risorgimento to World War

For centuries, Italy had been a collection of states under the control of foreign nations. The shock of Napoleon's occupations was felt across Europe, not only by the Papal States, annexed by the French between 1797 and 1814. A wave of nationalism swept the Continent; Germany was unified, as was Italy eventually. Rome kept out of the great movement of this Risorgimento (resurgence). The papacy was unwilling to give up its political power. Even when Garibaldi and Cavour united the country in 1860, the Pope held off until he was forced to join in 1870. Rome became the capital and administrative hub of the new country. Immense government buildings went up and boulevards cut through the city. Papal political power vanished completely and the popes withdrew until the onset of fascism in the 1920s, when Mussolini finally recognized the Vatican State. The fascists had great dreams for Rome as the capital of a new empire, but many of these had to be postponed with the onset of the war. Mussolini was overthrown in 1943 and Rome was ruled directly by the Germans. As the war ended, Rome was threatened with massive destruction during the Allies' battle for control. Then the Germans sud-denly left—Hitler had declared Rome an 'open city'.

1797

Napoleon and Pius VII

'Being master of Italy, I considered myself master of Rome,' Napoleon announced in his memoirs. He didn't like opposition and decided that the Pope should cease to have any political power. Moreover, since France ruled most of Europe, it made sense to the Emperor for the Pope to establish himself in Paris. Pius VII was told to come to Paris for Napoleon's coronation in 1804. He was treated rudely by the Emperor, and the Romans, outraged, felt a new affection for a pope they previously hadn't much liked. Napoleon consolidated his power ruthlessly, Rome was declared second capital of the empire and his son was made king of Rome in 1811.

The Lateran Pact (below), signed in 1929, on behalf of the King and the Pope, recognized the Vatican as an independent state

Revolution in Rome

The year of revolution in Europe came in 1848 as people called for more freedoms. For a few months Rome experienced a social experiment, a kind of welfare state that anticipated modern systems by a hundred years. Republicans drove Pope Pius IX out in the autumn. Pius allowed a free press and granted amnesty to all political opponents, but would not support a war for the unification of Italy. The romantic revolutionary Giuseppe Mazzini became part of the triumvirate of Rome and for three months ruled as an idealist socialist. He pardoned his enemies, introduced progressive taxation and rehoused the poor. It was not to last. The French restored the Pope in 1849, and Mazzini fled the country.

The Capital of Italy

After 1860, when Italy was united, it lacked its true capital. The new king of Italy, Vittorio Emanuele II, had been king of Piedmont and lived in Turin. The Pope refused to recognize unification and was protected by French troops. In 1870, when Garibaldi finally occupied Rome, the Pope, like the emperors of the collapsing empire, fled from his territories into St. Peter's, declaring himself 'the prisoner of the Vatican'. Garibaldi passed the Law of Guarantees, promising to defend the Pope and granting him a pension. The Pope retaliated with *Non Expedit,* forbidding Italians from participating in the new state. This had little effect, and the king occupied the Pope's residence, the Quirinale Palace, when Rome was declared the official capital in 1871.

The March on Rome

Italy could not be ruled without Rome, and in his bid for power, Mussolini's dramatic march on the city in 1922 was more a piece of theatre than political warfare. Although Mussolini controlled large forces throughout Italy and reviewed 40,000 soldiers in Naples on 24 October, he could not have fought a civil war. Four days later a fascist army of 16,000 surrounded Rome. Since most of them had arrived by train and were poorly organized, they presented no great threat to the city. The royal army was well run and equipped, and up until the evening of the 27th the King seemed determined to resist Mussolini. Fearing civil war, the King relented and the fascists entered Rome. Mussolini was soon declared prime minister.

The Lateran Pact

Almost 60 years had passed since Garibaldi had occupied the papal territories. The Lateran Pact of 1929, which became part of the constitution of the republic, settled the differences between the Vatican and the kingdom of Italy. The Pope became head of an independent state measuring 43ha (106 acres) and received 2 billion lire compensation for the loss of all lands in 1870. The pact established Catholicism as the state religion of Italy and made it a required subject in all schools. In return, the papacy recognized the unification of the country. At the time, public imagery showed the pope, the monarch and the dictator as the three pillars of the state. Today, only the papacy survives.

Giuseppe Garibaldi meets King Vittorio Emanuele II (far left) Pope Pius VII (middle) Early nationalist Giuseppe Mazzini (left)

When Mussolini's Blackshirts marched on Rome in October 1922 (left), they met little opposition from the King

1945

Garibaldi was a popular leader, and there are many monuments dedicated to him (left)

Dominating Piazza Venezia is the monument to Vittorio Emanuele II, the first king of unified Italy (below)

Postwar Rome

The new republic of Italy enjoyed a postwar boom. For a few years in the 1950s Rome became the hub of fashion and hedonism, summed up in Fellini's film *La Dolce Vita,* made in 1960, the same year Rome hosted the Olympics. The 1970s were marred by terrorism from both extreme Right and Left. One of the worst acts, the kidnap and murder of Prime Minister Aldo Moro, took place in Rome in 1978. Protests and demonstrations eventually led to the election of a communist city government in 1976, which did much to improve housing and a chronic transportation problem. Further to this, plans for the new millennium, *Roma Capitale,* extended the metro and improved the bus system.

The Treaty of Rome

The Treaty of Rome was signed on 25 March 1957 by six European nations, thereby creating what would become the European Union. Echoes down the centuries are strong: Much of the EU today comprises the vassal states of the former Roman Empire, and the inclusion of Turkey would see the ancient territories reunited after a split of 1,700 years.

A New Constitution

A referendum in 1946 voted against the monarchy. The King's ties with Mussolini and his flight from Rome when German troops attacked after the fall of the fascists made him unpopular, and the new constitution aimed to prevent a return of either the monarchy or fascism. Parliament elects a president, who then nominates a prime

minister for parliament's approval. In 1946, Luigi Einaudi was elected as the first president. He took up residence in the Quirinale Palace, home of popes and then the king, almost 2,000 years after Julius Caesar destroyed the Republic of Rome.

Jubilee Year 2000

The first papal Jubilee was held in 1300, but the truly ancient is always present in Rome, and the idea actually goes back to Old Testament times when, every 50 years, a jubilee cancelled all debts and required the redistribution of land. John Paul II (below right), in the same spirit, urged the cancellation of Third World debt—a suggestion greeted with varying degrees of enthusiasm by the lenders in question. Throughout Jubilee Year 2000, Rome welcomed more than 30 million people; every day pilgrims waited from dawn to pass through St. Peter's special Holy Door, gaining a rare indulgence. Many free events and concerts were held, the largest of which was World Youth Day, when 2 million young people gathered for an open-air Mass celebrated by the Pope.

Murdered prime minister Aldo Moro (far left)
Pope John Paul II (left)

1945 to the present

The Treaty of Rome, signed on 25 March 1957, was the first step towards creating the European Union (below)

Italian President Giovanni Gronchi (front row, second from left) opened the 1960 Olympic games (right)

On the Move

ARRIVING

By Air

Rome has two airports: Fiumicino (officially Aeroporto Leonardo da Vinci) and Ciampino (Aeroporto G. B. Pastine).

Fiumicino, 36km (22 miles) southwest of the city, has been Rome's main gateway since 1961, and over the past 40 years it has been refurbished and extended into the Mediterranean's largest airport. On average, its four runways handle more than 30 flights an hour. It is the destination of most scheduled international and domestic flights, including Air Canada, Alitalia, British Airways, Cathay Pacific, Continental Airlines, Delta, Japan Airlines, Lufthansa and Qantas. The airport has three terminals, plus a satellite, which is linked by an automated shuttle, the Sky Bridge. Terminal A handles domestic flights, Terminal B handles international and some

domestic flights and Terminal C (including the satellite) handles international flights only. The airport is open 24 hours.

In the arrivals areas *(arrivi)* of terminals B and C there are cash dispensers *(bancomats)*, foreign exchange facilities *(cambio)*, lavatories and public phones. Coffee and light refreshments are available, as is limited shopping (newspapers, magazines and sweets). Not all of these facilities are open 24 hours.

The best way to get to the city centre from Fiumicino is by fast train. The Leonardo Express runs from just outside the airport to Termini station. The service runs every 30 minutes between 6.37am and 11.37pm, takes around half an hour and costs €8.80 one way. There are other,

more frequent trains that stop at Tiburtina, Tuscolana, Ostiense and Trastevere (but not Termini). These smaller stations are usually not as convenient for visitors as Termini. These services operate from 5.57am to 11.27pm. Outside of these times a night bus runs between the airport, Termini station and Tiburtina station. There are four buses through the night (1.15, 2.15, 3.30 and 5am), which leave from near the international arrivals area. The journey costs €5 one way, and you can buy your ticket on the bus.

Rome's congested streets mean that travelling by taxi into the city can take longer than by train. The 36km (22-mile) journey takes anything from 30 minutes to 2 hours, so prices

GETTING TO CENTRAL ROME FROM THE AIRPORT		
AIRPORT	**FIUMICINO (FCO)**	**CIAMPINO (CIA)**
	Aeroporto Leonardo da Vinci (Fiumicino) Via dell'Aeroporto di Fiumicino, 320 00050 Fiumicino (Roma) Tel 06 65951 (switchboard)	Aeroporto G.B. Pastine (Ciampino) Via Appia Nuova Tel 06 794941
TAXI	€40 plus	€35 plus
TRAINS	Fast train, around 30 minutes—€8.80 Stopping train, 50 minutes—€4.70	
BUS/METRO		25-minute bus journey to Anagnina metro station (line A)—€1.03, plus standard BIT metro ticket—77c

Both of Rome's airports have wheelchair access to all facilities. See page 54 for more details.

RETURNING HOME
Fiumicino

The Leonardo Express takes about 30 minutes to reach the airport. The ticket costs €8.80, and the service runs from 5.52am to 11.52pm. If you are using the stopping train from Tiburtina, Tuscolana, Ostiense or Trastevere, the journey time is approximately 50 minutes, and trains run from 5.36am until 11.36pm. A one-way ticket costs €4.70. When arriving by train, allow at least an extra quarter of an hour to get from the station to the check-in desk.

If you need to travel outside these times, the night bus runs from Tiburtina to the airport, also calling at Termini. The service runs at 12.30, 1.15, 2.30 and 3.45am, and costs €3.62. You can buy your ticket on the train.

Ciampino

The airport bus from Anagnina metro station operates between 6.10am and 11pm, and costs €1.03. Remember to allow extra time to get to the check-in desk. If you travel outside these times, you will need to get a taxi.

> For information on getting around Rome, see pages 45–52. For information on driving in Rome, see page 52.

TIPS

● Avoid taxi and hotel touts who will approach you at the airport. Use only licensed (yellow or white) taxis.

● Buy your return train ticket when you arrive at Fiumicino. The queues are much longer at Termini, and the ticket will not become valid until you stamp it on your return journey.

● You will find suitcases with wheels a godsend at Fiumicino. It is quite some distance between baggage reclaim and the exit, and for some stretches you cannot use a baggage trolley, particularly on the homeward journey.

than Fiumicino, which means it has fewer facilities. However, there are cash machines, a foreign currency exchange, public phones and lavatories.

A bus service connects the airport to the Anagnina metro station (line A), running between 6.50am and 11.40pm. There is a machine just outside the arrivals terminal for tickets, which cost €1.03 one way. The metro runs every 5 to 10 minutes, and takes 25 minutes. You will need a standard BIT ticket, costing 77c. For other ticket options, see page 46.

Once the trains stop running, a taxi is your only option. The fare will be from €35, but there are surcharges for journeys between 10pm and 7am, on Sundays and public holidays, and for each item of luggage.

At both airports, smoking is permitted only outside the airport buildings.

vary, but will cost upwards of €40. If you have small children or heavy luggage, it might be worth using a taxi, but there are surcharges for journeys to and from the airport, for each item of luggage, on Sundays and public holidays, and between 10pm and 7am.

Ciampino is Rome's second airport and, at 16km (10 miles) to the southeast, it is closer to the city. It is primarily a military airport, but also handles chartered flights and some budget airlines, such as easyJet and Ryanair. It is much smaller

USEFUL TELEPHONE NUMBERS AND WEBSITES

AIRPORTS

FIUMICINO
● ☎ 06 6595 3640/6595 4001 (flight information)
● ☎ 06 6595 4252/6595 6777 (lost and found)
● ☎ 06 892021 (railways information)
● ☎ 06 6595 3794 (taxis)
● Fax 06 6595 3000
● www.adr.it
● Tourist office at International Arrivals, Terminal B. Open daily 8am–7pm (www.romaturismo.it)

CIAMPINO
● ☎ 06 794941 (flight information)
● ☎ 06 7949 4728 (lost and found)
● ☎ 06 7949 4225 (lost property)
● www.adr.it

By Car

In the days of the empire, all roads led to Rome, but in these modern times, all roads lead to the Gran Raccordo Anulare, known as the GRA. This 70km (43-mile) road completely encircles the city, and is always busy. Its 30 exits can make the GRA seem confusing, but there are only a few junctions that you need to worry about.

From Fiumicino airport, take the Autostrada Roma Fiumicino, which leads to the GRA. If you are coming from Ciampino you will need to follow the Via Appia Nuova. From Florence or Pisa, take the A1, also known as the Autostrada del Sole. Visitors arriving from Naples should also use the A1, while those coming from Abruzzo or the Adriatic coast should follow the A24.

Wherever you join the GRA, make sure you know which exit you need; your hotel can tell you which one is best. You should make sure staff at your hotel

know that you will be arriving by car, and that you have somewhere to park. (See also Driving, pages 52–53.)

If you are arriving by car, but don't want to use your car in Rome, you can leave it in long-term car parking (*lungo sosta parcheggio*) at Fiumicino Airport and take the train into the city. Parking costs €18.50 for 24 hours (tel 06 6595 5175).

By Train

There are rail connections between Rome and many other European cities, most of which

end at Termini station and are operated by FS (Ferrovie dello Stato), the state-run railway. Contact RailEurope for more information (tel 1-877 257 2887 or www.raileurope.com in the US or Canada; tel 08705 848 848 or www.raileurope.co.uk in the UK).

For journeys to or from smaller stations, you will need to use a *locale* train, which is a stopping service, but if you are coming from another major Italian city, your best option is a faster Intercity train. There is also a Eurostar service, which runs from Milan, Turin, Genoa, Bari, Naples, Florence and Venice. This service is faster than the Intercity, but you need to reserve your ticket in advance.

Termini is Rome's main station. It is a large, busy station on the edge of the *centro storico*, with a tourist office, banks and cash machines, shops, bars, a post office, telephones, newsagents, a

pharmacy, foreign exchange and left luggage. The area is popular with pickpockets.

By Bus

Most long-distance buses terminate at Tiburtina, to the northeast of the city. Although the station is some way out of the city, it is well served by the metro (Line B) and by a bus service (No. 492).

Eurolines runs buses from more than 100 European cities. For details of routes and tickets, see the company's website (www.eurolines.com).

TIP

- If you are arriving by car and staying in the heart of Rome, you will need a permit to drive in the city. If you are staying in a hotel, the staff can arrange this, otherwise you will need to contact STA on 06 5711 8333.

CAR RENTAL

All major rental firms, and some local ones, have desks at both airports and also in town. However, car rental is expensive in Italy and you can often get a better deal if you arrange it before you leave home. The minimum age for renting a car is between 21 and 25 (depending on which company you use), and you will need to have held a driving licence for at least a year. Most firms require a credit card as a deposit. Accident rates are high in Rome, so check that you have adequate insurance cover. Most car rental contracts include breakdown cover: make sure you know who to call.

Rental company	At Fiumicino	At Ciampino
Auto Europa	06 6501 7450	
Avis	199 100133	06 7934 4195
Europcar	06 6501 0879	06 7934 0378
Hertz	06 6595 4701	06 7934 0095
Italy by Car	06 6529133	
Maggiore	06 6501 0678	06 7934 0368
Sixt	06 6595 3547	(at Maggiore desk)

GETTING AROUND

Once in the city, you will find that Rome is quite compact—it is only 4km (2.5 miles) from Basilica di San Pietro to Termini station as the crow flies. Exploring the city on foot gives you the opportunity to cut through side streets, stop for coffee in one of the many bars and generally slow the pace. If walking is not your thing, or if the distance is too great, your best option is to make use of the city's efficient public transportation service.

LA METROPOLITANA

The metro system (la metropolitana) has been designed primarily to bring commuters into the city, and is not as comprehensive as similar systems in other countries. However, its two lines can be useful for getting across town, and avoiding Rome's congested streets.

BUSES

Rome's bus service is more useful for visitors, as it can often get you closer to the sights. By using a combination of bendy buses and electric minibuses, you can get within striking distance of most of the sights in this book. Remember, you can change buses as often as you need, within the time constraints of your ticket.

TRAMS

The tram system is less comprehensive, usually operating on the outskirts of the city.

For metro, bus and tram information, call ATAC on 800 431784 (toll-free). Lines are open Mon–Sat 8–8. Alternatively, visit the organization's website on www.atac.roma.it.

TAXIS

Taxis are useful for late-night travel, but will not necessarily save you much time. And remember, while you are stuck in Rome's busy streets, the meter is still running, making this an expensive way to travel.

ON TWO WHEELS

Scooters can be a good way of seeing the city, but only if you are already used to handling two-wheeled vehicles. Bicycles are ideal for getting around traffic-free areas, such as Villa Borghese, but traffic fumes and Rome's hilly terrain make cycling on the city's streets a less attractive prospect.

TIPS

- Peak times for public transport are roughly 7.30–9, 12.30–1.45 and 7.30–8.30.

- Beware of pickpockets on busy buses, trams and metro services, especially on the lines popular with visitors.

- Buses, trams and the metro can be uncomfortably hot during the summer.

BY CAR

The advice to anyone wishing to drive in Rome is—don't! Restricted access, busy, narrow streets, bad driving and inadequate parking can mean this is a stressful way to spend your holiday. If you really must drive, stay alert and remember that pedestrians have right of way. See pages 52–53 for more information on driving in Rome.

DISCOUNTS

Children under 10 travel free on public transportation if they are accompanied by an adult; discounts are also available to students. Other discounted fares are available only to residents.

Traffic around Piazza Venezia needs a helping hand from the vigile urbano (traffic police)

Metro, Bus and Tram

Rome's public transportation service, run by ATAC, is cheap, frequent and reliable. There are around 282 bus routes, six tram routes and two *metropolitana* (metro) lines, but don't be daunted: you will find you only need a select few to get to where you want to go. Your first stop should be ATAC's information office, where you can pick up a transport map—*Mappa dei Trasporti Pubblici*. This is free, and gives details of buses, trams, the metro and the night buses, with transport and ticket information in English and Italian. The office is just outside Termini, in Piazza dei Cinquecento (open daily 7.30am–7pm; tel 800 431784; most staff speak English).

TICKETS

Apart from the night bus (see page 50), you must have a ticket before boarding your chosen method of transportation. There are ticket machines in the metro stations, and tickets are also sold in most tobacconists (*tabacchi*) and in some bars—look for the ATAC sticker in the window. An increasing number of bus stops now have automated ticket machines.

The cheapest ticket is the *biglietto integrato a tempo* (BIT), usually just referred to as *un biglietto* (a ticket). They cost 77c, and can be used 75 minutes from validation for any

number of bus or tram trips, plus one metro journey. They can also be bought as a block of 10 tickets. Although you won't make a cash saving by buying them this way, you will save time by having a ticket available when you want it, without having to search for a *tabacchi*.

One-day passes (*biglietto integrato giornaliera*—BIG) are also available. They are valid for unlimited use on buses, trams and the metro, and on trains operated by both CO.TRA.L—who run services to other major cities— and FS—the state-run railway—until midnight on the day they are first used, and cost €3.10. They are not valid on the tourist lines (see page 220) or on the non-stop service to Fiumicino airport.

The only other type of ticket that might be useful for visitors is the seven-day pass (*carta integrata settimanale*—CIS), which costs €12.40 and is valid on the same modes of transportation as the BIG. You must write your name and the dates it is valid for on the front of the ticket.

VALIDATING YOUR TICKET

Whichever type of ticket you choose, it must be validated the first time you use it. At metro stations the validation machines are located just before the escalators, where you descend to the trains. Buses and trams have machines on board. If you are using a BIT ticket, you must stamp it when you use it on the metro, too. Other than this one exception, you do not need to stamp your ticket every time you change vehicles.

It is illegal to travel without a validated ticket. Ticket inspectors make regular checks, and if your ticket doesn't have a valid stamp, you will be fined. The fixed-rate fine is €51 plus the price of your ticket, and ignorance is no excuse.

BUSES

Rome has two types of bus: standard, single-decker buses and small electric minibuses. Most routes are covered by the

Standard buses (far left) and electric minibus (left)

standard buses, but minibuses operate on routes 116, 117 and 119. They are not very comfortable, even if you manage to get one of the eight hard plastic seats, but they are the only buses small enough to cope with Rome's narrow streets.

Bus Stops

At every bus stop there is a board showing the route number, the headstop (or *capitolinea*—where the route starts) and a list of the main intermediate stops for each bus that uses this stop. Your stop will be circled. The last journey of the day will usually start from the headstop at around midnight, after which it will be replaced by a night bus (see page 50).

Boarding the Bus

You should usually board the bus through the rear doors *(salita)*, making sure you validate your ticket on the way in. If you have already validated your ticket you may enter by the front or back doors *(entrata)*. You should use the middle doors, marked *uscita*, to leave the bus. Always try to use the correct doors, as the Romans do, but if the bus is busy you can leave by the front or rear doors. This door etiquette doesn't apply to minibuses, which have only one door.

METRO (METROPOLITANA)

Rome's metro system has two lines (A and B), which make roughly a cross shape, intersecting only at Termini. A promised third line, running north-west to southeast, has been on the drawing board for years. Its construction has been hampered by the discovery of archaeological remains, which have to be assessed before work can proceed (see page 12).

Entrances to metro stations are marked with signs showing a large white 'M' on a red

background, and there is usually more than one entrance—for example, on either side of a busy street. Just below street level are the ticket machines—remember to buy and stamp your ticket before you go down to the trains. Handy boards at the bottom of the escalator show you the route direction to help you identify your platform.

Although predominantly a commuter service, the metro provides a good cross-city service, and is always very busy—there is usually standing room only. This makes it very hot, particularly in summer, and the crowds are also a good cover for the pickpockets who operate on these trains. Look out for the route map inside the metro

Bus showing entrance and exit doors (top) Modern tram (above)

ROMAN BUS STOPS
Line numbers
Each bus number that runs from this stop is shown, together with selected points on the whole route. This stop will be circled.

Bus times
The first and last bus times are shown at the bottom of the column. This is the time they leave the headstop (at the top of the list), not when they leave this stop.

MAIN TOURIST BUS ROUTES

Certain bus routes are useful, as they link a number of places of interest. Below are four routes of particular interest to visitors.

64

Palazzo Massimo alle Terme, Terme di Diocleziano
Mercati Traianei
Piazza Campo dei Fiori
Castel Sant'Angelo
Basilica di San Pietro

Termini · Piazza della Repubblica · Via Nazionale · Piazza Venezia · Largo di Torre Argentina · Piazza Sant'Andrea della Valle · Corso Vittorio Emanuele II · Lungotevere Porta · Cavalleggeri · Stazione di San Pietro

• *denotes nearest stop to place of interest*

116

Museo Keats-Shelley
Villa Borghese
Palazzo Altemps
Piazza Navona, Sant'Ivo alla Sapienza

Via di Porta Pinciana · Piazza Barberini · Via del Tritone · Piazza di Spagna · Piazza San Silvestro · Piazza Ponte Umberto I · Corso del Rinascimento · Piazza Campo dei Fiori · Piazza Farnese · Lungotevere Sangallo · Ponte Vittorio Emanuele II · Terminal Gianicolo

Because of Rome's one-way system, some buses, like route 116, follow different roads on their outward and return journeys

116

Piazza Navona, Palazzo Altemps, Sant'Ivo alla Sapienza
Museo e Galleria Borghese, Villa Borghese
Pantheon, Santa Maria sopra Minerva

Terminal Gianicolo · Lungotevere Gianicolense · Via Giulia · Piazza Farnese · Piazza Campo dei Fiori · Corso del Rinascimento · Piazza Rotonda · Piazza Colonna · Via del Tritone · Piazza Barberini · Via Vittorio Veneto · Viale San Paolo del Brasile · Piazzale Canestre · Viale del Cavalli Marini · Via di Porta Pinciana

87

Piazza Navona, Palazzo Altemps, Sant'Ivo alla Sapienza
Fori Imperiali
Foro Romano
San Clemente

Piazza Cavour · Corso del Rinascimento · Piazza Sant'Andrea della Valle · Largo di Torre Argentina · Piazza Venezia · Piazza Colosseo · Via Labicana · Piazza San Giovanni in Laterano · Piazza Tuscolo · Via C. Baronio · Largo Colli Albani carriage—it shows you on which side of the carriage the doors will open at each stop, giving you a fighting chance of getting there before the train pulls away from the station. Services run between 5.30am and 11.30pm (12.30am on Saturdays), after which you will have to use the night bus service (see page 50).

TRAMS

Rome's six tram routes operate mostly on the outskirts of the city

Buses can be held up by cars, pedestrians and even horses

and are not as useful to visitors as the buses or the metro. However, route 19 will take you to Piazza del Risorgimento, the closest public transportation

point to the Basilica di San Pietro and the Musei Vaticani. From here, it runs around the northern edge of Villa Borghese, close to Villa Giulia and the Museo

ON THE MOVE

BUS BUSTER CHART

Use this chart to find out which buses or trams you'll need to catch to travel from one destination to another. Follow the rows of squares horizontally and vertically from the name of the destinations until they meet. This square contains the route number. Only the most frequent services have been included. Numbers on white squares are direct. Numbers in shaded squares show that you have to change. Start out on the first route listed, then change to the second. Look at the key to find out where you must change. The W symbol indicates a walk of usually less than 1km (about half a mile).

Routes change regularly, so check an up-to-date timetable or bus map before setting out.

CHANGE AT:
- Torre Argentino
- Lungotevere Marzio
- Vittoria Colonna
- Diocleziano (to Repubblica)
- Manzioni (to Tritone)
- Termini
- San Silvestro
- Orazio (to Piazza Cavour)
- Piazza Venezia
- Fori Imperiali
- Santa Maria Maggiore
- Palazzo Esposizione
- Piazza Cavour
- Fiume
- Risorgimento
- Ferrari (to Lepanto)
- Nazionale

Destinations (diagonal): BASILICA DI SAN PIETRO · CASTEL SANT'ANGELO · COLOSSEO · FONTANA DI TREVI · FORI IMPERIALI · MUSEO BORGHESE · MUSEI CAPITOLINI · MUSEI VATICANI · PALAZZO ALTEMPS · PALAZZO BARBERINI · PALAZZO DORIA PAMPHILJ · PALAZZO MASSIMO · PANTHEON · PIAZZA CAMPO DEI FIORI · PIAZZA NAVONA · PIAZZA DI SPAGNA · S. CLEMENTE · S. GIOVANNI IN LATERANO · S. MARIA MAGGIORE · S. MARIA IN TRASTEVERE · VILLA GIULIA

W																			
40/87	87																		
62	64	85, 850																	
40	46, 62, 63, 916	85, 87, 850, W	W																
116	116	3, 360	52, 53	175/52															
64	46, 62, 85, 87, 63, 916 850	81, 95, 628	W	95															
W	23	87/492	492	492	490	23													
492	W	87	W	87	116	81, 628	492												
62	62	175	W	175	52, 53	95	492	116											
40	46, 62, 63, 916	175	W	W	95	W	492	W	62, 63, 95, 492										
64	64	75	175	64, 170	910	64	492/64	70	175	64, 170									
116	W	87	W	87	910/64	W	492	116	W	64, 70									
40	46, 62, 63, 916	87	62	64	116	46, 916	492	W	116	62, 64	64	W							
40	W	87	W	87	116	81, 628	492	W	116	W	70	W	W						
40/87	913, W	117	W	175	119	H, 64, 70, 117	913	W	11	W	64/117	W	116	W					
40/87	87	W	85, 850	85, 850	52/85	87	49/87	87	175/85	85, 850	84/117	85, 850	87	87	117				
40/70	87	85, 850	85, 850	85, 850	910/714	87	49/87	87	70/714	85, 850	714	85, 850	87	87	117	117			
64	70	75	71	84	360	70	70	70	W	70	W	70	70	70	71	W	714		
280	280	3	H	H	910/H	780	23	116	116	H	H	8	W	W	116	3	87/8	71/H	
19	926	87/962	52	628	52	628	19	628	52	628	70/19	628	628	628	87/628	87/628	360/495	23/19	

GETTING AROUND 49

Nazionale Etrusco, the Galleria Nazionale d'Arte Moderne and Bioparco, as does route 3. Route 3 also runs through the south of the city, ending up in Trastevere. Route 8 goes to Trastevere (and beyond), starting at Via Torre Argentina, not far from Piazza Venezia.

NIGHT BUSES

From around midnight, Rome's public transportation system is replaced with night buses. The only exception to this is tram line 8, which runs until 2am. On the bus stops, the night bus routes are easily recognizable by the dark blue owl logo and on the bus, the letter 'N' will follow the route number. A night bus also follows as close as possible to each of the metro lines: Bus 55N follows line A, and bus 40N follows line B.

Night buses have conductors, and you can buy a BIT ticket on board for €1. Don't forget that if you have a BIG (one-day) ticket it will run out at midnight, so will no longer be valid.

DISCOUNTS

Children under 10 travel free if accompanied by an adult. There are no discounts for seniors (unless resident).

To qualify for discounts, students should contact their students' union to get an ISIC (International Student Identification Card) before leaving home. Cards can also be issued by CTS (Centro Turisimo Studentesco), as can Euro<26 cards for non-students aged under 26 (contact www.cts.it in Italy, www.ctstravel.co.uk in the UK or www.ctstravelusa.com in the US).

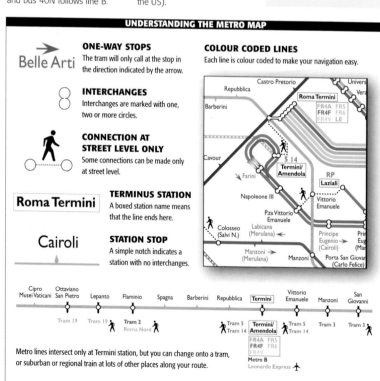

UNDERSTANDING THE METRO MAP

ONE-WAY STOPS
The tram will only call at the stop in the direction indicated by the arrow.

INTERCHANGES
Interchanges are marked with one, two or more circles.

CONNECTION AT STREET LEVEL ONLY
Some connections can be made only at street level.

TERMINUS STATION
A boxed station name means that the line ends here.

STATION STOP
A simple notch indicates a station with no interchanges.

COLOUR CODED LINES
Each line is colour coded to make your navigation easy.

Metro lines intersect only at Termini station, but you can change onto a tram, or suburban or regional train at lots of other places along your route.

Bicycles and Scooters

Seeing the city on two wheels has its advantages: Traffic jams and parking restrictions are not the problem they are for visitors in cars. However, Rome's busy streets are not for the uninitiated, and if you've never ridden a scooter or bicycle in a busy city, Rome is not the place to start. Bicycles are best reserved for exploring the quieter parts of the city, but don't forget—Rome is built on seven hills.

To rent a scooter you must be over 21 and hold a full driving licence. You will usually need to leave your passport and/or a credit card as a deposit. Crash helmets are compulsory, and you should also wear gloves, shoes that enclose your feet, trousers and long sleeves.

If you are exploring the city by bicycle, helmets are not compulsory, but they are recommended. As with scooters, you will be asked to leave your passport or similar ID as a deposit. There are bicycle stands at Piazza del Popolo, Villa Borghese and Piazza Navona.

WHERE TO RENT A BICYCLE OR SCOOTER IN ROME

NEW SCOOTER FOR RENT
(scooters only)
Via Quattro Novembre 96a/b
☎ 06 679 0300
🕒 Daily 8.30–8

SCOOT-A-LONG
Via Cavour 302
☎ 06 678 0206
🕒 Daily 9.30–7.30

BIKE E SCOOTER RENTAL
Via Cavour 80/a
☎ 06 481 5669
🕒 Daily 9–7

ROMA RENT
Vicolo de' Bovari 7/a
☎ 06 689 6555
🕒 Daily 8.30–7

RONCONI
Via San Leo 22
☎ 06 881 0219
🕒 Daily 9–1, 4–8

TRENTO E SCOOTER
Termini station
Multiservice, platform 1 - Via Marsala
☎ 06 4890 5823
🕒 Daily 9–6.30

ROMA IN SCOOTER
Corso Vittorio Emanuele II 204
☎ 06 687 6922
🕒 Daily 9.30–6.30

● Vespa means 'wasp'—named after the buzzing sound made by their engines.

BICI E BACI
Via del Viminale 5
☎ 06 482 8443
🕒 Daily 8–7

SCOOTER RENT JOY RIDE
Via Cavour 199
☎ 06 481 5926
🕒 Daily 9–7

TREVI TOURIST SERVICE
(scooters only)
Via dei Lucchesi 31/32
☎ 06 6920 0799
🕒 Daily 10–10

HAPPY RENT
(scooters only)
Via Farini 3
☎ 06 481 8185
🕒 Daily 9–7

SCOOTER FOR RENT
Via della Purificazione 84
☎ 06 488 5485 (also fax)

SAFE CYCLING TIPS

● Wear bright clothing in the day, and fluorescent clothing and lights at night.

● Make other road-users aware of your movements. Indicate clearly and in advance.

● Watch out for people opening doors of stopped or parked cars.

● Don't cycle down the inside of traffic when there is a right turning ahead.

● Helmets are not compulsory, but are advisable.

● Wear gloves, and cover your knees and elbows.

● Always lock your bicycle to a fixed object.

Taxis

Rome's busy streets and one-way systems mean that taxis are not the most economical way of getting from A to B, but there may be times when they are your best bet.

Always use official, licensed taxis, which are either yellow or white, and have an illuminated 'taxi' sign on the roof. You should avoid the many unlicensed taxis operating in Rome, as you have no way of knowing if they are adequately insured.

Taxis can be hailed on the street, but it is easier to get one from the *fermata dei taxi* at Termini, Piazza Venezia, Largo di Torre Argentina, Piazza San Silvestro, Piazza di Spagna or Piazza Sonnino (in Trastevere).

If you want to be sure of a taxi, or you need to be collected from your hotel, it is best to telephone for a radio taxi. You cannot book a radio taxi in advance, so allow enough time to get to your destination. The company gives you a reference, plus the timescale within which the taxi is expected to arrive. Radio taxis start charging from the time they leave to pick you up, so the meter will not be at zero.

TIPS

- Use only licensed cabs.

- Except in radio taxis, make sure the meter is set to zero at the start of your journey.

- The meter still runs when the taxi is stationary (eg in traffic jams).

TAXI FARES

All taxi fares are controlled by the meter, and a list of charges, in several languages, should be displayed inside the taxi.

For journeys within the city, the charges are as follows:

Fixed charge: €2.33
(€3.36 on Sundays and holidays, €4.91 between 10pm and 7am)

Increments: 11c every 141m (154yd). Stationary/slow-moving traffic: 11c every 19.2 seconds.

Surcharges for: each item of luggage; journeys to and from Fiumicino.

RADIO TAXIS

La Capitale	☎ 06 4984
Cosmos Radio Taxis	☎ 06 88177
Radio Taxi	☎ 06 3570
Radio Taxi Nuova Eurocosmos	☎ 06 880 5461
Radio Taxi Tevere	☎ 06 41571

Driving

What with restricted access, busy, narrow streets, bad road skills and poor parking, driving in Rome can be a stressful experience. However, if you decide you can't do without your car, here are some points to bear in mind:

Do carry your registration and insurance documents and driver's licence. You will need to produce them if you are stopped.

Don't dazzle oncoming traffic. Cars manufactured to drive on the left should adjust their headlights—kits are widely available.

Don't drive too fast. The speed limit in built-up areas is 50kph/ 31mph; outside built-up areas, 110kph/68mph; motorways (autostrada), 130kph/81mph (if your car is over 1100cc).

Do carry a warning triangle and display a nationality sticker (unless you have Euro-plates).

Do carry a first-aid kit, fire extinguisher and spare bulbs.

Don't use undipped headlights in towns or cities.

Do use dipped headlights when driving in tunnels, even if they are well lit, and when driving outside built-up areas.

Don't drink and drive—penalties are severe. The legal level is below 0.05 per cent of alcohol in the bloodstream.

Don't allow children under four years old to travel without a suitable restraint system. Children under 12 years old cannot travel in the front of the car without an adapted restraint system.

Do wear a seatbelt. They are compulsory in the front and rear of the vehicle (where fitted).

Don't use a mobile phone when driving.

Don't drive in shoes that do not fully enclose the foot.

DRIVER'S LICENCES

Both UK and US driver's licences are valid in Italy, but it is recommended that you also carry a translation. In the UK, the new licences with photographs and the pink, EU-style ones include a translation, but if you hold an older, green licence, you should either update the licence or apply for an International Driving Permit. Holders of US driver's licences should also apply for an International Driving Permit. These permits are not compulsory, but are easier to understand. They also act as another form of identification. Permits can be obtained from the Italian state tourist offices or many national motoring organizations (including the AA and AAA).

Drivers must be at least 18 years of age and hold a full driver's licence.

ACCIDENTS

If necessary, call the police (tel 112) and ask any witness to stay and make a statement. Do not admit liability. Exchange details (name, address, car details, insurance company's name and address) with other drivers.

BREAKDOWNS

If you break down, turn on your hazard warning lights and place the warning triangle 50m (164ft) behind the vehicle.

The Automobile Club d'Italia (ACI) provides a free service to foreign-registered cars. If they cannot repair your car at the roadside, they will tow you to a garage. You can contact ACI 24 hours a day by calling 116. They will need to know where you are,

your vehicle registration (license plate) number and the make of the vehicle.

FUEL

Filling stations in Rome are small, and generally keep shop hours, closing all day Sunday. Lead-free fuel is called *benzina senza piombo* or *benzina verde*; leaded fuel is still available in some places. Some filling stations, particularly those on the GRA, are open 24 hours.

TRAFFIC RESTRICTIONS

Most of the *centro storico* is covered by the Limited Traffic Zone, which restricts access to permit holders from 6.30am to 6pm Monday to Friday, and 2pm to 6om on Saturdays. Electronic systems are in place to record the number of unregistered vehicles and to issue fines. If you need to drive in the restricted area, fax details of your registration number and length of stay to STA on 06 5711 8259. If you are staying in a hotel, the staff will usually do this for you.

PARKING

Parking in the *centro storico* is limited and expensive. Street parking is indicated by blue lines and costs €1 per hour—buy your ticket from the nearby vending machines (which only take coins) or at tobacconists or newsstands. The most convenient car parks for the central area are:

PARKSÌ
(Villa Borghese)
Viale del Galoppatoio 33
☎ 06 322 5934
⊙ 24 hours
⛽ €1.15 per hour for up to three hours, 90c for 4th to 15th hour; €14.45 per day.

TERMINAL PARK (Termini)
Via Marsala 30
☎ 06 444 1067
⊙ 6am–1am
⛽ €5 for first two hours, €1.50 for 3rd to 12th hour; €28 per day; €17 for second day.

PIAZZALE PARTIGIANI
(Stazione Roma-Ostia)

Piazzale dei Partigiani
☎ 06 574 5942
⊙ 6am–11pm
⛽ 77c per hour; €5 per day.

TERMINAL GIANICOLO
Via di Porta Cavalleggeri
☎ 06 684 0331
⊙ 7am–1.30am
⛽ €1.30 per hour for the first four hours, then €1 or €1.10 per hour; €25.90 per day; €51.70 per week.

PARKING DELL'AUDITORIUM,
Viale Pilsudsky 21
☎ 06 808 1646
⊙ 24 hours

⛽ €1 for first two hours, then €1.50 per hour; €2.55 per day 7.30am–9pm; €7.75 all night 9pm–7.30am.

AUTOSILO VIA MANTOVA,
Via Mantova 24
☎ 06 841 3853
⊙ 24 hours
⛽ €2 per hour for first two hours, then €1.03 per hour.

PARKING LUDOVISI
Via Ludovisi 60
☎ 06 474 0632
⊙ 5.30am–1.30am
⛽ €2 per hour for first five hours, then €1 per hour; €18 per day.

TRAVEL WITH A DISABILITY

Rome is a very difficult city for people with physical impairments to get around without able-bodied help. There has been a gradual improvement to accessibility in recent years, although some areas can still cause problems.

BY AIR

You should contact your airline in advance of your date of travel to let them know what assistance you will need. Both Fiumicino and Ciampino have wheelchair access to all airport services, and many signposts are in braille. At Fiumicino, there are also paths with textured surfaces to guide the visually impaired to key places in the airport. The airports have a disabled persons' courtesy shuttle that will take you to your hotel; it can be booked 24 hours ahead by contacting your airline.

BY BUS AND TRAM

Many of Rome's buses and trams have been, or are being, adapted for wheelchair access, with a view to replacing the whole network. The newer buses have lower access platforms for easier entry. For the most up-to-date information, contact ATAC's disabled services on 06 4695 4001 (daily 8–2.30).

BY METRO

The metro system is also being upgraded. At the moment, most stations on line B have lifts and lavatories suitable for people with disabilities. The only exceptions are Circo Massimo, Colosseo and the southbound platform of Cavour. On line A, only Cipro and Valle Aurelia have wheelchair access, but bus No. 590 follows the same route and is, on the whole, wheelchair accessible. Ten stations on line A have textured paths for the visually impaired, although at present only Cipro is useful for sightseeing.

USEFUL CONTACTS

CO.IN SOCIALE
Via Enrico Giglioli 54a
Rome
Tel 06 712 9011, fax 06 7129 0179
www.coinsociale.it
Has useful information on accessible sights in Rome and Lazio. Publish guides, organize guided tours, and have a minibus available for excursions and transfers.

ACROD LIMITED
P. O. Box 60, Curtin, ACT 2605
Australia
Tel 02 6283 3200, fax 02 6281 3488
www.acrod.org.au
The Australian organization set up to respond to the needs of disabled people.

HOLIDAY CARE
7th Floor, Sunley House, 4 Bedford Park, Croydon, Surrey, CR0 2AP
UK
Tel 0845 124 9971, fax 0845 124 9972
www.holidaycare.org.uk
Produces publications and information on accessibility.

SATH (SOCIETY FOR ACCESSIBLE TRAVEL AND HOSPITALITY)
347 Fifth Avenue, Suite 610, New York NY10016, USA
Tel 212-441-7284, fax 212-447-7284
www.sath.org
Lots of tips on how to travel with mobility or vision impairment.

BY TRAIN

Some of Rome's trains have wheelchair access, and this is indicated on the timetable with a wheelchair symbol. You can also get this information from the station where you will be starting your journey (Termini, tel 06 4881726; Tiburtina, tel 06 4730 7184). If you will need assistance, you should call the Ufficio Disabili 24 hours before the start of your journey to fill in a form indicating what kind of help you need. Someone else can do this on your behalf.

BY TAXI

Most taxis can take wheelchairs, but they will need to be folded and stored in the boot (trunk).

For general information about access in Rome, see page 279.

This section is divided into three parts: Sightseeing Areas, consisting of five areas (shown on the map inside the front cover) highlighting what to see; A–Z of Sights, an alphabetcal listing of places to visit in Rome, all marked on the maps on pages 56–59; and Farther Afield, which describes attractions outside the city centre.

The Sights

Vatican City

HOW TO GET THERE

Ⓜ Ottaviano San Pietro (for the Basilica) or Cipro Musei (for museums)

🚌 23, 32, 49, 81, 590, 982 or tram 19 to Piazza del Risorgimento; 34, 40, 62 to Piazza Pio XII

THE SIGHTS

It is ironic that the world's largest church, museum and piazza should all be contained within the world's smallest independent state, but the Vatican also has a lot of history to support these records.

The Vatican became the smallest independent state in 1929, with the signing of the Lateran Treaty. Until the Risorgimento (unification), Rome had been under Papal rule. With the breaching of the Vatican walls at Porta Pia on 20 September 1870, Pope Pius IX retreated to the Vatican Palace and declared himself a prisoner of the Vatican. He and subsequent popes never recognized

Michelangelo's Last Judgement *in the Sistine Chapel*

the now unified Italy until the signing of the Lateran Treaty nearly 60 years later.

Today, the Vatican has its own shops, postal service, banks, newspapers, radio station—even a helipad. It is still surrounded by the walls that Michelangelo built, and there are only two public entrances: Piazza San Pietro and the museums' entrance. The official language of the Vatican is Latin, but it is more usual to hear Italian.

The first time you visit Basilica di San Pietro, approach it along Via della Conciliazione so you can watch the spectacle of St. Peter's rise in front of you.

THE MAIN SIGHTS

Although, nominally, there are few sights in the Vatican, they are the highlights of most visitors' trips. It would take many years to see everything in the Vatican Museums, and the vast size of St. Peter's is awesome. For most visitors, time is short, so it pays to be selective about what you hope to see.

Capella Sistina

Although the ceiling of Michelangelo's Sistine Chapel is the most famous, don't miss *The Last Judgement* on the end wall. See page 105–106.

Museo Pio-Clementino

Important Greek and Roman statuary, collected by Pius VI and Clement XIV. See page 109.

Michelangelo's *Pietà*

It's difficult to believe that Michelangelo was only 24 when he completed this sensitive portrayal of the Virgin Mary with Christ lying across her lap. See pages 68–69.

Pinacoteca

The Vatican's vast collection of art, from the Middle Ages to 1800. See pages 108–109.

St. Peter's cupola

It's a long climb to the top of the cupola, but the views are amazing. See page 71.

Stanze di Raffaello

Julius II's suite of rooms, decorated with frescoes by Raphael. See pages 106–108.

WHERE TO EAT

Apart from the café in the museum, there is nowhere inside the Vatican to eat. If you are heading back towards the *centro storico*, try one of the many places around Piazza Navona. Alternatively, just to the

Get a saint's-eye view from the cupola of St. Peter's

north of the Vatican is the Prati district, where you will find the following restaurants.

DAL TOSCANO

The speciality of this family-run restaurant is its Tuscan dishes. See page 240.

RISTORANTE-PIZZERIA PIACERE MOLISE

Good value, and just a stone's throw from the Vatican Museums. See page 250.

ROOF GARDEN 'LES ETOILES'

A pricey alternative, but the view of St. Peter's from the roof terrace is wonderful. See page 250.

Trastevere

HOW TO GET THERE

H, 23, 44, 280, 630, 780; tram 8

Despite growing popularity, Trastevere has managed to keep its sense of identity.
The name Trastevere means 'across the Tiber', and it is this separation that makes the area different. The Trasteverini celebrate their separateness each year in a festival called Festa de' Noantri, which roughly translates from Roman dialect as 'Our Own Festival'.

The narrow streets and small piazzas, the community spirit and preservation of the old ways all help to explain why the area is so popular, not just with visitors but also with Romans from the other side of the river.

Trastevere is cut in half by Viale di Trastevere. To the west is the Gianicolo—not one of the original seven hills, but it is higher and affords great views. This is also

The beautiful courtyard of Santa Cecilia in Trastevere

where you'll find Santa Maria in Trastevere. To the east is the bend in the river, and the Isola Tiberina (see page 91) and Santa Cecilia in Trastevere (see page 128).

THE MAIN SIGHTS
Trastevere itself is one the main sights here. Spend some time sitting in Piazza Santa Maria in Trastevere, drinking coffee and people-watching. Or, on a fine summer evening, eat in one of the piazza's many restaurants with outside tables, with views of beautifully lit church.

Gianicolo
It's a long climb to Piazzale Giuseppe Garibaldi, but worth it for the view across the city. See page 90.

Santa Maria in Trastevere
One of Rome's few surviving medieval churches, with beautiful apse mosaics. See page 141.

San Pietro in Montorio
Although most famous for Bramante's Tempietto, with its perfect Classical proportions, the church itself is worth visiting for its rose window. See page 137.

Villa Farnesina
Agostino Chigi's Renaissance suburban villa has frescoes by Raphael. See page 146.

One of the four saints on the 18th-century portico of Santa Maria in Trastevere

OTHER PLACES TO VISIT
See the orchids and palm trees at Orto Botanico (see page 110). Palazzo Corsini (see page 111) holds part of the national art collection, including works by Caravaggio and Van Dyck.

Da Agusto is a popular trattoria in Trastevere

WHERE TO EAT

Trastevere is overflowing with eateries, especially around Piazza Santa Maria in Trastevere.

BIBLI
A great place for Sunday brunch, or just for coffee. See page 235.

CASETTA DÈ TRASTEVERE
The inside of this restaurant, not far from Santa Maria in Trastevere, looks like a Roman piazza. See page 237.

DA AGUSTO
A Trastevere institution, as tradtional as they come. See page 239.

THE SIGHTS

Campo Marzio

THE SIGHTS

HOW TO GET THERE

🚌 44, 46, 84, 715, 716, 780, 781, 810, 916 or tram 8 to Largo di Torre Argentina; 30, 70, 81, 87, 116, 116T, 186, 204, 492, 628 to Corso del Rinascimento; 116 also runs (west to east) through Piazza della Minerva

Is it medieval? Renaissance? Baroque? Campo Marzio is all of these and more.

Rome's liveliest area is bound to the west by the curve of the river and runs roughly as far east as the Via del Corso. It takes its name from the Roman Field of Mars (Campus Martius)—the area where the military were put through their paces. The area began to be built up after the destruction of the aqueducts, in around AD600, because the river was the only source of water. The area was further built up when the popes returned from Avignon in 1377, thanks to its proximity to the Vatican.

The bright flower market at Piazza Campo dei Fiori

Today, Campo Marzio is still where Romans live and work, but their numbers are swollen by the visitors who flock here, and by politicians and diplomats from Palazzo Madama, the seat of government.

THE MAIN SIGHTS

As the hub of Rome's history, there's so much to see here that you will want to make more than one visit. Lots of the sights in this area are churches, which often close during the afternoon. Make good use of this time to sit in one of the many cafés in Piazza Navona or Campo dei Fiori and watch the world go by.

Palazzo Altemps

The Ludovisi family's collection of ancient statuary is displayed in beautifully frescoed rooms. See pages 112–113.

Pantheon

Admire this ancient place of worship from the piazza before moving inside to see the vast domed ceiling. See pages 120–121.

Piazza Campo dei Fiori

Whether you go in the morning for the busy market or in the evening for a meal, this piazza is always a hive of activity. See pages 122–123.

Piazza Navona

Fountains, cafés and ice-cream: Piazza Navona is always popular and there's plenty more to see nearby. See pages 124–125.

Santa Maria sopra Minerva

The interior of this rare Gothic church is a riot of blue and gold, while adults and children alike love Bernini's elephant in the piazza outside. See page 140.

OTHER PLACES TO VISIT

Churches abound in Campo Marzio. The most impressive include Sant'Agostino (see page 128), with Sansovino's *Madonna del Parto*, beloved of expectant mothers; Sant'Ivo alla Sapienza (see page 133), with its spiral dome; La Maddalena (see page 91), a baroque masterpiece just around the corner from the Pantheon; and San Luigi dei Francesi (see page 133), home to three paintings of the life of St. Matthew by Caravaggio.

The Gothic interior of Santa Maria sopra Minerva

WHERE TO EAT

There are plenty of places to eat, drink coffee or just have an ice-cream around the piazzas in the *centro storico*. Remember that you pay a premium for sitting at the outdoor tables, so only do so if you want to linger. For a quick refuel, drink your coffee standing up at the bar.

IL CONVIVIO

For a special meal, try this modern restaurant close to the Palazzo Altemps. See page 238.

DAI TRE AMICI

For a true Roman experience, visit this popular trattoria, not far from the Pantheon. See page 240.

DER PALLARO

Enjoy the daily fixed menu at this trattoria, just behind Sant'Andrea della Valle. See page 241.

Northern Rome

HOW TO GET THERE

🚇 Termini, Repubblica or Barberini

🚌 52, 53, 63, 80, 95, 116, 119 to Via Veneto; H, 40, 64, 84, 86, 90, 170, 175, 492, 910 to Repubblica; H, 36, 38, 40, 64, 86, 90, 92, 105, 170, 175, 217, 310, 714, 910 or tram 5, 14 to Termini

Although not strictly speaking a district, the area between Termini station and the Via Veneto covers a wide variety of interesting places to visit. During imperial times, the area around Via Veneto was a suburb where the wealthy had their villas. Following the sack of Rome in AD410, the area fell into disuse and reverted to open countryside. It experienced a rebirth with the building of Palazzo Barberini in the 17th century.

The Quirinale suffered a similar fate. A residential area until the Middle Ages, it had its own Renaissance when it was chosen each other, and the area is well served with public transportation.

Palazzo Barberini

Both Bernini and Borromini worked on Pope Urban VIII's palace. See page 114.

Palazzo Massimo alle Terme

Behind the façade of this 19th-century palazzo is a wealth of coins, jewellery and ancient statuary. Don't miss the guided tour of the mosaics and frescoes. See pages 116–117.

San Carlo alle Quattro Fontane

Borromini's tiny church, with its equally small cloister, is well worth seeking out. See page 128.

Santa Maria della Concezione

This simple church, at the bottom of the Via Veneto, hides a grizzly secret—the Capuchin monks' cemetery, decorated with their bones and skeletons. See page 136.

Santa Maria della Vittoria

Don't miss Bernini's *Ecstasy of St. Teresa of Avila* in the Cornaro Chapel. See page 137.

OTHER PLACES TO VISIT

Close to Piazza della Repubblica (see page 119), famous for its Fountain of the Naiads, is Terme di Diocleziano (see page 143), the largest baths complex ever built in Rome. Sant'Andrea al Quirinale (see page 128), close to the Palazzo del Quirinale, was Bernini's best-loved church. The palazzo itself (see page 111), home to the Italian president, is open to the public, but its gardens are open only once a year, on 2 June—the anniversary of the founding of the Italian republic.

The grand staircase at Palazzo Barberini, designed by Bernini

as the site for the new papal palace, Palazzo Quirinale, in 1542. It is now home to the Italian president.

Moving up to date, Termini station is a wonderful piece of modern architecture, with a cantilevered roof over the ticket hall and taxi stand. However, this is not a good area to hang around: It's popular with pickpockets (and worse), so head straight for the church or gallery that you are interested in.

THE MAIN SIGHTS

Although slightly off the main tourist track, the sights here are still within walking distance of

The ruins of Terme di Diocleziano

WHERE TO EAT

There is a wealth of restaurants along Via Veneto, but they can be pricey. For a less expensive alternative, try the side streets.

EST! EST! EST!

This pizzeria, close to San Carlino, has been in business for over 100 years. See page 241.

PIZZARÈ

A popular pizzeria, not far off Via Veneto. See page 248.

TRATTORIA ABRUZZESE

Close to busy Via Nazionale, with cooking from the Abruzzo region. See page 253.

THE SIGHTS

Ancient Rome

HOW TO GET THERE

🚌 60, 75, 85, 87, 175, 810, 850 to Colosseo; 40, 60, 64, 86, 88, 492, 590, 715, 716 to Piazza Venezia
Ⓜ Colosseo

According to legend, this is where Rome began, when Romulus built his city on the Capitoline Hill in 753BC. Since then, the area around the Capitoline Hill has remained important. The Forum was the focus of political life in ancient times, and when the city outgrew the site of what we know as Foro Romano, Julius Caesar began a new one at the nearby Fori Imperiali in 46BC, which was added to by subsequent emperors. The area is still central to political life today: Palazzo Senatorio, in Piazza del Campidoglio, is home to the city council.

For many years, the Palatine Hill was the most desirable of

The Colosseum, although now a ruin, still draws in the crowds

addresses: Augustus and Domitian both had homes here. In fact, the name Palatine gives us the word palace.

THE MAIN SIGHTS
Today, this area ranges from the historic, including Vespasian's Colosseo, through Michelangelo's Piazza del Campidoglio to the bustling Piazza Venezia and the early 20th-century Monumento a Vittorio Emanuele II. Most of it, however, is dominated by ancient ruins, and sometimes is can take a leap of imagination to make sense of it all.

Colosseo
Vespasian's amphitheatre is recognized throughout the world. See pages 74–77.

Fori Imperiali
Take the guided tour around this working archaeological site. See pages 82–83.

Foro Romano
Site of the great temples and basilicas of ancient Rome. See pages 84–89.

Musei Capitolini
Two palaces full of works of art, joined by an underground passageway with views across the Foro Romano. See pages 98–103.

OTHER PLACES TO VISIT
If you haven't had your fill of ancient Rome, Nero's Domus Aurea (see page 79) is next to the Colosseo, as is access to the Palatine Hill (see page 110–111). Emperor Trajan built his shopping complex, Mercati Traianei (see page 91), next to the Fori Imperiali.

Santa Maria in Aracoeli (see page 133), next to the steps leading up to Piazza del Campidoglio, is famous for its wooden statue of Christ as a child, while you can see St. Peter's chains at San Pietro in Vincoli (see page 137). Finally, for panoramic views over the whole city, climb to the top of Monumento a Vittorio Emanuele II in Piazza Venezia (see page 119).

WHERE TO EAT
The area around the Fora has few restaurants. For a quick snack, you could try one of the many outlets in Piazza Venezia.

BAR CAPITOLINA
Whether you are visiting the museums or not, the café at the Musei Capitolini is a great place to refuel. See page 234.

NERONE
Abruzzese cooking close to Colle Oppio park. See page 245.

PASQUALINO AL COLOSSEO
Sample dishes from the Mediterranean, with just a touch of Sicily, around the corner from the Colosseo. See page 247.

Constantine's hand, in the courtyard of the Musei Capitolini

THE SIGHTS

Detail from Ara Pacis Augustae, Augustus' Altar of Peace

The Arco di Costantino, in the shadow of the Colosseo

Warhol's painting of Goethe, at the entrance to Casa di Goethe

ARA PACIS AUGUSTAE

⊞ 57 E3 • Lungotevere in Augusta
☎ 06 6880 6848 🕐 Closed for
restoration until 2005 🚇 Spagna
🚌 30, 70, 81, 91, 186, 204, 224, 492,
590, 628, 913

The Altar of Peace is the best
example of Augustan monumental sculpture in Rome, and is a
major work from the Augustan
Golden Age.

The altar, decorated with bas-
reliefs carved in 9BC, was built to
celebrate Augustus' triumphal
return to Rome after campaigns
in Spain and Gaul, and to commemorate the peace he had
established throughout the
Roman world. Over the centuries
the altar became buried, and was
lost until the first fragments were
rediscovered in 1568. It was not
until 1938 that the monument
recovered its ancient beauty,
when the Fascist regime sponsored its reconstruction.

The outside of the enclosure is
decorated with mythological
scenes and grand processional
friezes in which life-size figures
portray Augustus, the imperial
family, officials and other nota-
bles. The 1930s glass pavilion is
being removed, and when the
altar reopens to the public it will
be within a new building.

ARCO DI COSTANTINO

⊞ 58 F6 • Piazza del Colosseo 🆓 Free
🚇 Colosseo 🚌 60, 75, 81, 85, 117,
175, 204, 673, 810, 850

One of Rome's best-preserved
imperial monuments, the Arch of
Constantine stands proudly on
the ancient triumphal way where
victorious armies once marched.

The Senate and people of
Rome built the arch in AD315 to
commemorate the victory of
Constantine the Great over
Maxentius, the last pagan
emperor of Rome, in the battle of
Ponte Milvio (AD312), after which

Constantine granted freedom of
worship to the Christians.

The highly decorated structure
stands nearly 25m (80ft) high
and consists of a large arch
flanked by two smaller ones. It
carries an inscription, repeated
on both sides, celebrating
Constantine's coming to power.
Many of the arch's sculptures
were actually taken from other
monuments: The bas-reliefs
between the statues originally
showed episodes in Marcus
Aurelius' life, but his features
were altered to resemble those
of Constantine.

AVENTINO

⊞ 57 E6 • Circo Massimo 🚌 3, 44, 60,
73 to Viale Aventino, 75, 81, 95, 118,
160, 175, 204, 231, 628, 715

The Aventine is one of the most
beautiful quarters of Rome. Here,
the traffic and chaos of the city
are left far behind, replaced by
peaceful churches, charming
cloisters, beautiful gardens and
panoramic views over the
Trastevere and St. Peter's.

This is the most southerly of
Rome's seven hills. Trajan lived
here before he became emperor,
and his friend Licinius Sura built
his private baths here. It became
such an affluent area that the
Visigoths destroyed it when they
sacked Rome in AD410.

From the Circo Massimo (see
page 78) at the foot of the hill
there is a delightful walk up to
the churches of Santa Sabina
(see page 142) and Sant'Alessio.

One of the finest views of
Rome can be had from the
Giardino degli Aranci (Garden of
Orange Trees), which extends
over the site of the Savelli family's stronghold in the Middle
Ages. The orange trees were
planted here in 1932 to commemorate the first orange tree
planted in Italy, brought from
Spain by St. Dominic early in the

13th century. Legend has it that
the tree still exists and can be
seen in the cloister of the
Dominican monastery of Santa
Sabina.
Don't miss one of Rome's most
popular 'secret' views—St. Peter's
seen through the keyhole in the
main entrance to the Priory of
the Knights of Malta.

BASILICA DI SAN PIETRO

See pages 66–71.

CAPITOLINO

See page 72.

CASA DI GOETHE

⊞ 57 E3 • Via del Corso 18 ☎ 06
3265 0412 🕐 Tue–Sun 10–6 🎟 Adult
€3, child (under 18) €2 🚇 Flaminio
🚌 52, 53, 61, 71, 80, 85, 117, 119, 160,
590, 850
www.casadigoethe.it

Casa Moscatelli was just a small
boarding house when German
poet and dramatist Johann
Wolfgang von Goethe lived here
from 1786 to 1788, and it has
changed little since that time.

In the 1990s, the second floor
of the house, where Goethe
spent one of the happiest and
most productive periods of his
life, was purchased and renovated to house the Goethe
Museum, the only German
museum outside Germany, and
it has developed into a lively
cultural meeting place. The
museum has a permanent exhibition, Goethe in Rome, which
documents the poet's time in
Italy and the influence this had
on his work, and includes pictures, drawings, manuscripts,
prints and books.

The German painter J. H.
Tischbein, who also lived here,
portrayed Goethe in a famous
work known as *Goethe in the
Roman Countryside*; you can see
Andy Warhol's adaptation of it at
the entrance to the exhibition.

Basilica di San Pietro

The Roman Catholic Church's principal shrine and the spiritual focus for millions of believers.
One of the world's largest churches, covering 22,067sq m (237,535sq ft)
and capable of holding a congregation of 60,000.
Incorporates architecture by the greatest High Renaissance and baroque masters.

The interior of the basilica (above left). Michelangelo's Pietà *(above middle). The colonnaded arms around the piazza (above right).*

SEEING THE BASILICA DI SAN PIETRO

The best approach to St. Peter's is by way of Via della Conciliazione. You cross into the Vatican State on entering Piazza San Pietro. It is a good idea to pause frequently while exploring the basilica and its surroundings: Everything is on a huge scale, but the proportions are so perfect that you need time to appreciate the actual size. Once inside, the best way to see St. Peter's is to start by making a circuit of the entire basilica and its artworks, then to visit the treasury, followed by the crypt. Most visitors leave the ascent to the roof and cupola till the end of the visit.

HIGHLIGHTS

PIAZZA SAN PIETRO AND THE COLONNADE

Few buildings are approached through such a superb space as that in front of St. Peter's. The elliptical piazza, folded within the curving wings of the colonnade, is considered Gian Lorenzo Bernini's architectural masterpiece. It was conceived and built between 1655 and 1667, during the pontificate of Pope Alexander VII.

The obelisk in the middle is the oldest monument. It was brought to Rome from Egypt in AD36 by the Emperor Caligula and moved to its present site in 1586; it acts as a sundial, the obelisk's shadow marking noon as it touches the white marble disc. Two beautiful fountains flank the obelisk. That on the right is the work of Carlo Maderno, dating from 1613, while the left-hand fountain, by Carlo Fontana, was erected in 1677. Between the fountains and the obelisk are two stone slabs set in the paving; stand on either one of these to see the colonnade's four rows of columns merge into one. There are 284 columns in four rows, their proportions calculated to enhance the height of the basilica's façade. Bernini designed the colonnade to enable coaches to drive through it, while the side aisles were for people on foot. The main entrance to the Vatican Palace is reached through the right-hand end of the colonnade, via the Portone di Bronzo. Look through here to get a glimpse of Bernini's famous *trompe l'oeil* Scala Regia, where columns of diminishing size are used to add greatness to what is in reality a steep and irregular staircase.

The basilica seen from Via della Conciliazione (left). Piazza San Pietro seen from the air (inset)

☎ Information: 06 6988 4676

🕐 Basilica: daily 7–7, Apr–Sep; 7–6, rest of year. Cupola: daily 8–6, Apr–Sep; 8–5, rest of year; if visiting 1 hour before closing, entrance is via elevator only. Treasury Museum: daily 9–6.30, Apr–Sep; 9–5.30, rest of year. Crypt: daily 9–5. Closed during major religious ceremonies

💶 Basilica: free. Cupola: €5 with elevator, €4 on foot. Treasury Museum: €5. Crypt: free. Necropoli tour €9

🚇 Ottaviano-San Pietro; 🚌 34, 46, 64, 98, 881, 916, 982

🚗 The Necropoli can only be visited by guided tour, which must be booked at least two weeks in advance. Send a fax to 06 6987 3017, stating preferred dates, number of people and which language.

📖 Wide selection of official guidebooks from Vatican Bookshop in 12+ languages €5; unofficial guidebooks from souvenir stands and religious shops on Via della Conciliazione

🏪 Shop inside tourist information point. Also official Vatican shop well stocked with guidebooks, postcards, religious souvenirs, posters, videos, CDs, cassettes, slides, candles, religious statues and church furnishings; multilingual assistants; wide range of prices to cater for pilgrims from all over the world, but quality immensely variable, ranging from top-of-the-range to cheap and tacky. Vatican Post Office is behind right-hand colonnade for Vatican stamps and albums, Mon–Fri 8.30–7, Sat 8.30–8

🚻 In the piazza

www.vatican.va
This is the official website for the Vatican State and Catholic Church. It has no specific information about St. Peter's

THE BALDACCHINO, CONFESSIO AND CATTEDRA

The interior of St. Peter's is dominated by Bernini's great altar canopy, the Baldacchino, which stands directly above the traditional site of the tomb of St. Peter the Apostle, with the Cattedra, the great papal throne, behind. The Baldacchino's twisted bronze columns and massive lantern rise above the high altar, where only the pope may celebrate Mass. Standing 29m (95ft) high, it took over ten years to erect and was inaugurated in 1633 by Pope Urban VIII, a member of the Barberini family—bees, their heraldic symbol, swarm among the foliage of the decoration. The Baldacchino's construction coined a famous lampoon—*quod non fecerunt barbari, fecerunt barberini* ('what the barbarians failed to do, the Barberini did')—as Urban was said to have used bronze taken from the portico of the Pantheon for the columns.

Piazza San Pietro, with the obelisk erected in 1586

In front of the Baldacchino is Carlo Maderno's sunken U-shaped Confessio—a crypt beneath the high altar—with 99 perpetually burning lamps along the balustrade and two flights of curving stairs. The kneeling statue of Pope Pius VI (1820), who is buried beneath, is by Antonio Canova. In front of this, directly beneath the papal altar and behind a grille, is the sixth-century Niche of the Pallia, a surviving relic of the first basilica and said to have given access directly to St. Peter's tomb. Excavations in the 1940s strengthened the hypothesis that there is a very early Christian tomb here, which could, indeed, be that of the saint.

Behind the Baldacchino, and designed to be viewed through it, is the extraordinary set piece known as the Cattedra. The Cattedra itself is an ancient wooden chair, said to have been St. Peter's when he was bishop of Rome, which is enclosed in a bronze throne designed by Bernini in the 1660s. This is raised above the altar of the central apse and surrounded by bronze statues of the Fathers of the Latin and Greek Churches. Above this rises a great gilded metallic structure of angels, clouds and rays of light, all illuminated by the sunlight that streams through the central window in which is depicted a dove representing the Holy Spirit.

MICHELANGELO'S PIETÀ

Behind glass, in the first chapel in the right-hand aisle, gleams Michelangelo's white marble *Pietà*, a representation of the Virgin holding her dead son across her knees. It is the only work the artist ever signed and the most famous of all the treasures in St. Peter's.

This portrayal of the Virgin as a young, grieving woman is both spiritually moving and artistically ground breaking. The young sculptor had mastered anatomy and the handling of marble drapery perfectly; he also solved the compositional problem of the two figures, one upright and one horizontal, by creating a pyramidal shape rising from the horizontal figure of Christ on his mother's lap to the Virgin's head at the

Swiss guardsmen are recruited from Switzerland's four Roman Catholic cantons

Papal Altar, with
Confessio below

1   Door of the
    Dead, by Manzù
2   Main door, by Filarete
3   Porta Santa, by Consorti
4   Pietà, by Michelangelo
5   Monument to Christina of
    Sweden
6   Chapel of the Blessed Sacrament,
    by Borromini
7   Gregorian Chapel
8   Monument to Clement XIII, by
    Canova
9   Nave of the Cattedra
10 Monument to Urban VIII, by
    Bernini
11 Cattedra
12 Monument to Paul III, by della
    Porta
13 Monument to Alexander VII, by
    Bernini
14 Statue of St. Veronica, by Bernini
15 Statue of St. Helen, by Bernini
16 Statue of St. Longinus, by Bernini

17 Statue of St. Andrew, by Bernini
18 Bronze statue of St. Peter
19 Monument to Pius VII
20 Altar of the Transfiguration
21 Monument to Maria
    Clementina-Sobieski
22 Stuart Monument, by Canova
23 Baptistery
24 Equestrian statue of Constantine
25 Equestrian statue of Charlemagne
26 Sacristy
27 Treasury
28 Chapter
29 Canons' Sacristy

apex. After the unveiling, Rome was astounded, and there was talk
that so young a man could never have produced such a work.
Michelangelo, furious, carved his name on the band across the
Virgin's breast, and added an 'M' in the folds of her right hand. This
Pietà is the first of four on the same theme that Michelangelo was to
sculpt during his long life.

BRONZE STATUE OF ST. PETER
At the base of the last pillar on the right of the nave before the
transept is enthroned a bronze statue of St. Peter holding the keys to
the Kingdom of Heaven. For many years believed to be a fifth-century
work, it is now known to date from the late 1200s and is attributed to

The monument to Pius VII, which
stands over the door to the
sacristy (above)

Arnolfo di Cambio, the original designer of the Duomo (cathedral) in Florence. It is an austere and beautiful work, its simplicity emphasized by its baroque setting. Much of the right foot has been worn away by the touch of the faithful down the centuries. Kissing the foot traditionally gains an indulgence—time taken off the waiting time in Purgatory for admittance to Heaven. On major feast days the statue is bedecked with gold-encrusted robes and a tiara; you can see these in the Treasury.

THE CUPOLA AND ROOF

A gallery, 330 steps up from the roof, encloses the base of the interior of the dome, the perfect place for a bird's-eye view. At a height of 53m (174ft) above the floor of the basilica, it is from here more than anywhere else that you can appreciate the sheer size of St. Peter's;

St. Peter's is 218m (715ft) long (externally) and the height to the top of the cross on the dome is 137m (450ft); it contains 778 columns, 395 statues, 44 altars and 135 mosaics.

Opposite: Bernini's Baldacchino dominates the crossing. Near by is the bronze statue of St. Peter (second right)

figures below appear minuscule. Up here you are close to the vast mosaics of Christ and the apostles, popes and saints, and angels holding instruments of the Passion—the crown of thorns, the scourge and the nails. Designed by Cavaliere d'Arpino and executed between 1589 and 1612, the mosaics are remarkable for their size (St. Mark's pen is 1.5m/5ft long) but are hardly great works of art.

Outside, the undulating roof and breezy air make it seem as though you are on a ship at sea. Views down to the piazza below appear between the huge statues, and all around you are domes and cupolas. The main dome, with its paired columns and garlands, is true to Michelangelo's design, though probably higher than he intended. Climb the exterior of this masterpiece to its crowning lantern for breathtaking panoramas over the city.

BACKGROUND

The first basilica was built by the Emperor Constantine in AD324 on the site of a pagan cemetery, the traditional burial place of the Apostle Peter. Sumptuously decorated with marble, mosaics and gold, it was pillaged during the barbarian invasions, but held its place as the central church of Christendom. Reconstruction was planned in the 1450s, and in 1503 Pope Julius II commissioned the architect Bramante to rebuild the church; it was planned on a Greek-cross layout surmounted by a high dome, and involved the demolition of much of the original basilica. After Bramante's death in 1514 work ceased, and the next 30 years saw no progress as arguments raged about the layout. In 1547 Michelangelo, then aged 72, was appointed architect. Despite later changes, today's basilica, and particularly the ground plan, is largely inspired by Michelangelo's designs. In 1606, with building underway, the nave was once more lengthened and the façade altered by Carlo Maderno. Pope Urban VIII consecrated the new basilica in 1626. Much of the mannerist and baroque decoration is the work of Bernini, who succeeded in unifying the various internal elements. St. Peter's is the world's most important Catholic church and is used daily for Mass, as well as for the Church's most important official religious ceremonies.

The obelisk in the piazza was moved to its present site in 1586. The task, with only man- and horsepower available, was immense. Forty-four windlasses were erected and 900 men and 140 horses put to work. After four months, the crucial moment arrived and the obelisk was gradually pulled upright. It rose, only to halt as the ropes started to give way. The story goes that the Pope ordered complete silence, but a voice called out 'water on the ropes!' A Genoese sailor knew this would shrink and tauten the ropes, and the day was saved. In gratitude, the Pope rewarded the man's family and home town.

For Catholic priests visiting Rome, the opportunity to celebrate Mass in St. Peter's is a lifetime's dream. Every morning, from around 7, priests from all over the world occupy the altars of the chapels within the basilica, saying Mass in dozens of languages. Confessions are heard in different languages; a red light over a confessional indicates that it is 'open for business', and a sign informs the penitents which languages the priest speaks.

CAPITOLINO

Rome's focus of political power over the centuries.

The Capitoline Hill, the smallest of Rome's seven hills, is a good place to start an exploration of the historic city. Take in the wonderful views over the Forum from the top before exploring the rest of the hill, where you'll find one of the most interesting museums in Rome as well as site of Michelangelo's fine trapezoidal Piazza del Campidoglio.

A PLACE IN ROMAN HISTORY

Unlike the Roman Forum, the Capitoline Hill is better known through myth than archaeology. However, there was certainly a Bronze Age settlement here, and remains of Iron Age huts from the ninth to eighth centuries BC have been unearthed. In the Middle Ages, it was called Monte Caprino (Goat Hill), suggesting that goats once grazed on the slopes.

THE HILL'S CRESTS

The hill has two crests: To the north is the Arx or citadel, and to the south, the Capitolium, a high promontory looking out over the Tiber, and now covered by the Palazzo dei Conservatori. Between the two crests is the Piazza del Campidoglio (see page 118).

In ancient times the Arx is thought to have been a place of augury, where priests would read the omens they saw depicted in the flight of birds. The Temple of Juno Moneta (which means 'She who warns') was built here, on the top of what was thought to be the Roman mint (giving the alternative meaning of *moneta*—money). The temple had a statue of silver geese to commemorate the geese that gave the alarm when the Gauls tried to attack the city in 390BC (see page 27). The Arx is now the site of the church of Santa Maria in Aracoeli (see page 133).

THE HILL'S PALAZZI

The Palazzo dei Conservatori and the Palazzo Nuovo, collectively known as the Musei Capitolini (see pages 98–103), flank the Palazzo Senatorio, the seat of Rome's city council. In the sixth century BC, the Etruscan king of Rome, Tarquin the Elder, built the Temple of Jupiter Optimus Maximus (Best and Greatest), the largest of its kind ever built. The temple became the sanctuary for what is known as the Capitoline Triad, the gods Jupiter, Juno and Minerva, with statues of all three standing in the porch. Because of its height and exposed position, the temple was struck by lightning on several occasions but rebuilt each time on the same foundations.

RATINGS

Historic interest	●●●●●
Value for money	●●●●●
Walkability	●●●●

BASICS

✚ 57 E5 Ⓜ Colosseo 🚌 44, 46, 63, 70, 75, 81, 84, 87, 95, 715, 716, 780, 781, 810, 916 👥 Inside the museums

www.museicapitolini.org
www.comune.roma.it

TIPS

● Special art exhibitions are held in the Palazzo Nuovo, and concerts and other events take place elsewhere on the Capitoline Hill. Check the website for information

Michelangelo's Cordonata leads to the Capitoline Hill, still the seat of government, with the city council occupying the Palazzo Senatorio, in the background (top)
Marforio, the river god, in the courtyard of Palazzo Nuovo (inset)

CASTEL SANT'ANGELO

**Mausoleum, later a fortress, papal stronghold and museum.
Ten stone angels on the Ponte Sant'Angelo.**

Emperor Hadrian chose this secluded spot away from the main city as the site for his tomb. From the top of the squat structure is one of the finest views over Rome, looking out across the Tiber. Today, Castel Sant'Angelo houses part of the Museo Nazionale Romano, with an excellent collection of ceramics, weapons and Renaissance paintings.

FROM MAUSOLEUM TO FORTRESS

The mausoleum remained the burial place of the imperial family up to the reign of Caracalla in AD217. Aurelian later built the mausoleum into the city's fortifications and surrounded it with walls and towers, converting it into a fortress.

In AD590 Rome was stricken with the plague and Pope Gregory the Great organized a procession to pray for the city's release (see page 35) As a result of the miracle, the building was renamed Castel Sant'Angelo. In the ninth century, Leo IV linked Castel Sant'Angelo to the nearby Vatican by building a high defensive wall. The *passetto*, a later covered walkway built above the wall, was used by Clement VII in 1527 to escape from Emperor Charles V's troops.

WHAT TO SEE

The spiral ramp inside the castle dates back to the time of Hadrian's mausoleum and a part of it can still be climbed to the main courtyard, where the statue of the Archangel Michael, carved by Raffaello da Montelupo in 1544, stands. Another Archangel Michael, a huge 18th-century statue in bronze, stands at the top of the terrace along with the Bell of Mercy, which in the past pealed to announce executions. The moats and gardens are a 20th-century addition. Inside, along the spiral staircase leading to the upper floors, are the remains of some decorative mosaics.

The route to the fortified Castel Sant'Angelo is watched over by Bernini's angels (below)
There are wonderful views from the top of the castle (inset)

Colosseo

●

**The largest surviving ancient Roman structure in the world.
An arena nearly 2,000 years old that held over 50,000 people.
Purpose-built venue for some of the most spectacular, and barbarous,
gladiatorial games ever held.**

SEEING THE COLOSSEUM

The Colosseo, the Roman Empire's biggest amphitheatre, lies at the west end of the Foro Romano, encircled by the Caelian, Palatine and Esquiline hills. To get a sense of the building's scale and size, approach it down Via dei Fori Imperiali. Walk round the outside before you enter to take in the exterior architectural details. The Colosseum's interior has been severely damaged over the years, so joining the guided tour, or using an audio-guide, is almost essential for understanding what you are seeing.

HIGHLIGHTS

THE EXTERIOR

Only a small part of the Colosseo survives after centuries of pillaging for building stone. What's left is still impressive, and gives a good idea of the original external architecture, although the marble facings, painted stucco and statues have all gone. The Colosseo covers about 2.5ha (6 acres). It was built on marshy ground, which had to be drained, and beneath its visible arches are others sunk in the earth on cores of concrete. The external arches, and arcades behind them, are built of travertine stone, which was hauled 27km (17 miles) from Tivoli, outside Rome. Behind the travertine facing there is a tufa infill, while the upper storeys of the arcades behind the façade are built of brick-faced concrete.

Externally, the Colosseo measures 188m x 156m (615ft x 510ft) and rises to 48.5m (158ft), with a façade of three tiers of arches and an attic level. The tiers are faced with three-quarter columns in the classical architectural orders: Doric on the first floor, Ionic on the second and Corinthian on the third, each more elaborate than the one below. The attic has small square window openings and blank walls between Corinthian pilasters, where bronze shields once hung. At the top were 240 brackets and sockets that anchored the huge *velarium*, a shade and bad-weather canopy that could be pulled right over the interior. The holes all over the walls once housed the metal clamps that held the massive stone blocks together; these, along with huge amounts of stone, were pillaged for building in the Middle Ages and Renaissance times.

THE ARCADES AND SEATING

Behind the façade, on the outside edge of the building, superb arcades run the whole way round the Colosseo on each floor, linking the stairways that connect the different levels. Farther in, 80 walls radiate out from the central arena and support vaults for the access passageways and the tiers of seats. Off the arcades, about 80 entrances—called *vomitoriae*—led into the arena itself, allowing vast numbers of people to pass rapidly through.

Inside, there were tiers of marble benches, some of which can still be seen, where over 50,000 people could be seated. In the later days of the empire, cushions were provided, probably much appreciated since it was normal for the games to last throughout the day. Seating was arranged by rank, with the least important members of the crowd—including women—assigned places nearest the top. Closest to

From close up, the sheer size of the Colosseo is overwhelming

RATINGS	
Good for kids	● ● ●
Historic interest	● ● ● ● ●
Photo stops	● ●
Value for money	● ● ●

TIPS

● The Colosseo's ticket office can be very busy—buy your ticket at the Palatine to avoid them.

● It's hard to work out what's what, so take the guided tour to get the most out of your visit.

● An after-dark visit, when the Colosseo is floodlit, adds an extra dimension.

In places, all four floors of the Colosseo are still intact (opposite)

BASICS

⊞ 58 G6 • Piazza del Colosseo ☎ 06 700 5469

🕐 Mon 9–2, Tue–Sun 9–7.15, Apr–end Sep; Mon 9–2, Tue–Sun 9–6.30, Oct; Mon 9–2, Tue–Sun 9–4.30, Nov–mid-Feb; Mon 9–2, Tue–Sun 9–5, mid-Feb–mid-Mar; Mon 9–2, Tue–Sun 9–5.30, mid-Mar–end Mar Last entrance 1 hour before closing

💶 Adult €10, child (under 18) free. For joint ticket see page 287

Ⓜ Colosseo (line B)

🚌 60, 75, 85, 87, 175, 810, 850

🎧 English-language tours at 9.30, 10.15, 11.15, 12.30 and 3: €3.50. Audioguides available in Italian, English, French, German, Spanish and Japanese: €4

📖 Official guidebook in English published by Sovrintendenza dei Beni Culturali; unoffical guidebooks in English available at stands all over Rome

🏪 Two well-stocked souvenir and book shops selling guidebooks, postcards and souvenirs

🚻 Inside the Colosseum and outside on the south side (9–6)

www.archeorm.arti.beniculturali.it

The most famous view of the Colosseo (below)

Looking out over the wide sweep of the arena (above)

the arena was a special box for the emperor, his family and the Vestal Virgins. Senators were also allotted ringside seats, and the rest of the tickets were distributed through the heads of families, with better-born citizens getting the better seats.

The tickets themselves were wooden plaques, carved with the relevant entrance, aisle number, row and seat number. Spectators found the right entrance by looking for the numbers over the exterior arches, and you can still see traces of these. The system was supremely efficient, capable of moving up to 70,000 people in or out in a matter of minutes. The design has never been bettered; in essence, the Colosseo is the prototype for every modern sports stadium.

THE ARENA

Right in the middle of the Colosseo is a jumble of ruins, all that's left of the labyrinthine passages beneath the arena itself. In Roman times, this area was covered by wooden flooring, topped with a waterproof layer of canvas and overlaid with sand—the word arena comes from the Latin word for sand. The four principal entrances were mainly used by the gladiators and corpse removers, but far more dramatic entrances were made through the floor itself, and you can see outlines of the stone rims of trapdoors among the ruins.

During the Colosseo's history, tens of thousands of animals were slaughtered, sent to Rome from all over the empire by specialist animal collectors. Such vast numbers were needed that elephants disappeared from North Africa, hippos from Numibia and lions from Mesopotamia as the Roman appetite for ever more extravagant spectacles grew. Once in Rome, the animals were transported in cages to the Colosseo, then harried through underground passages onto lifts (elevators) that rose up to arena level through the trapdoors. With this in mind, the maze of ruins begins to make sense.

Not all the channels were used for men and beasts. Some were water conduits, and the arena was regularly flooded for entertainments known as *naumachia*, when criminals fought to the death in re-enactments of naval battles in scaled-down galleys. Gladiatorial games began in the morning with an elaborate procession led by the games' sponsor, the prelude to a morning of staged hunts with wild animals pitted against each other or pursued by *bestiarii*, gladiators specializing in animal slaughter. The lunch break was accompanied by executions of the worst criminals, a taster for the climax of the day—the individual gladiatorial combats.

The ruins of the area under the arena are complex (above)

BACKGROUND

The Flavian Amphitheatre, known since the eighth century as the Colosseo, was built by the three emperors from the Flavian family. Construction started under Vespasian in AD72, and the inaugural games, held in a partially completed building, took place during the reign of his son Titus in AD80. The Colosseo was completed by Titus' brother Domitian. It was the first permanent amphitheatre to be built in Rome and one of the first buildings to combine a vast and grandiose design with immense practicality. Games and fights were held here right up until the end of the empire, with the last recorded exhibition of wild beasts under the barbarian ruler Theodoric in the sixth century. During the Middle Ages, the Colosseo was used as a fortress, and from the 15th century as a quarry, providing the stone for some of Rome's finest palazzi. By the late 1700s the crumbling structure was a romantic and overgrown ruin, dedicated since 1750 to the Christian martyrs who had been killed in its arena. Serious conservation started in the 19th century and continues still.

WHAT'S IN A NAME?

The name Colosseum first appeared in the writings of English monk, the Venerable Bede, in the eighth century. Despite the fact that Bede had never been to Rome, it was soon accepted that he derived the name either from the size of the structure, or because of the huge statue of Nero that once stood nearby. Another theory is that it may once have been called *amphitheatrum ad Colle Isaeum*—'the amphitheatre near the Iseum Hill'. Constant use would have led to the dropping of *amphitheatrum*, and as initial vowels elide in Latin the resultant word would have been very close to Colosseum. Whatever the derivation, English travellers may then have taken the name back from Rome to Bede.

The Protestant Cemetery is the final resting place of English poet John Keats

St. Paul looks out from the top of the Column of Marcus Aurelius in Piazza Colonna

CIMITERO PROTESTANTE

🕂 310 E8 • Via Caio Cestio 6
🕐 Tue–Sat 9–5, Sun 9–2 🎟 Free; contribution welcome 📖 Guidebook €4, in English, Italian, German and Swedish
🚇 Piramide 🚌 118

As an oasis of peace and tranquillity, Rome has nowhere better than this well-kept cemetery, last resting place of many a famous name. More than 4,000 non-Roman Catholics who have died in Rome since the late 18th century lie in the shade of cypress and pine trees.

The ashes of the Romantic poet Percy Bysshe Shelley, drowned in 1822 at the age of 29 while sailing in the Gulf of Spezia, are buried here. They were brought to Rome by his friend, Trelawny, who had been present at his cremation.

The tomb of his fellow poet John Keats bears a poignant epitaph: 'This Grave contains all that was Mortal of a young English poet, who on his death bed, in the Bitterness of his Heart, at the Malicious Power of his enemies, desired these words to be engraved on his Tomb Stone: Here lies One Whose Name was writ in Water.'

A simple marble tomb marks the grave of Julius, only son of Johann Wolfgang von Goethe (see page 65), born from the German writer's relationship with Christiane Vulpius, who later became his wife. The grave bears no name, only the inscription 'Goethe filius'.

CIRCO MASSIMO

🕂 57 F6 • Viale Aventino 🚇 Circo Massimo 🚌 81, 160, 204, 628, 715

Even if there is no longer much to see, the Circo Massimo has kept its magical atmosphere and the feeling of past glories. Wandering around the huge elliptical track, now a peaceful garden (if you can ignore the noise of the traffic beyond its boundaries), it is not difficult to imagine the cheers of 300,000 spectators watching the chariot races organized for the emperors of Imperial Rome.

Nestling in a hollow between the Aventine and Palatine hills, the Great Circus was more than 600m (1,970ft) long and 140m (460ft) wide, and was probably built as early as 326BC. Mainly used for two- and four-horse chariot races, it remained in use until AD549.

Emperor Augustus erected the obelisk of the Pharaoh Rameses II (now in Piazza del Popolo) on the *spina,* the dividing wall running down the middle of the track; Constantine also put up an obelisk, later moved to Piazza di San Giovanni in Laterano. The ruins of Porta Capena were part of the circus during Trajan's period. In 1145 the circus was granted to the Frangipani family—the tower at the end towards the FAO building is what remains of their fortress. Excavation and restoration works started in the 1930s.

COLONNA DI MARCO AURELIO

🕂 57 E4 • Piazza Colonna 🚇 Spagna 🚌 52, 53, 61, 85, 117, 119, 175, 160, 492, 628, 630, 850

The Column of Marcus Aurelius stands in the paved and pedestrianized Piazza Colonna, an area that has always been the hub of political power and is now home to the Italian government.

It is made from Luni marble, is 29.5m (96ft) high and 3.5m (11ft) wide, and was erected between AD180 and AD193. A frieze runs in a continuous spiral round the column, with beautiful bas-reliefs depicting significant episodes in the wars conducted by the Emperor Marcus Aurelius against various Danubian tribes in the second century AD. The frieze gives a wealth of information about military and social history for this period.

A statue of Marcus Aurelius and his wife, Faustina, once stood on top of the column, but was lost; in its place, Pope Sixtus V erected a bronze statue of St. Paul (1589) by Domenico Fontana. A spiral staircase of some 200 steps inside the shaft of the column leads up to a little terrace on the top, but it is no longer possible for visitors to go inside.

COLONNA TRAIANA

🕂 57 F5 • Via dei Fori Imperiali 🚇 Colosseo 🚌 117, 810, 850, 175, 84, 85, 87, 60

Trajan's Column is one of the oldest and most intact ancient monuments in present-day Rome. It is an exquisite work of art, with over 100 bas-relief scenes of the Dacian wars (waged in the region of present-day Romania) conducted by Emperor Trajan during the second century AD. More than 2,500 figures decorate 25 great blocks of marble, each one about 3.5m (11ft) wide. These magnificent carvings were probably originally painted in brilliant hues. It stands in Trajan's Forum, part of the Fori Imperiali (see pages 82–83), where you can also see the Mercati Traianei—Trajan's Market (see page 91).

From the base of the column, which is decorated with war trophies, there is a spiral staircase leading up. A statue of St. Peter on top, by Tommaso della Porta, replaces the original statue of Trajan, which looked out over the forum until 1587. The inside of the column can only be visited as part of an organized tour.

The marble blocks vary in diameter from the base to the

Running in a continuous spiral, the frieze on Colonna Traiana shows episodes from the wars with the Dacians

Conca's Allegory of Fame from the Galleria dell'Accademia di San Luca

top of the column. So that the 40m (130ft) column appears straight, the diameter increases gradually from about two-thirds of the way up. Look also for the windows cut in the decorative panels: Barely noticeable from the outside, they allow light to enter the staircase area.

COLOSSEO

See pages 74–77.

CRYPTA BALBI

57 E5 • Via delle Botteghe Oscure 31 ☎ Call centre: 06 399 6700 ⏰ Tue–Sun 9–7.45 💰 Adult €4, child (under 18) free. For joint ticket, see page 287 🚌 30, 40, 46, 62, 63, 64, 70, 81, 492, 628, 630, 780, 787, 916 stopping at Largo di Torre Argentina www.beniculurali.it

This museum, part of the Museo Nazionale Romano, focuses on how the city has changed throughout the centuries, with a rich collection of objects to illustrate social, economic and urban planning changes from ancient times, through the Middle Ages up to the present day. This display is at entrance level.

Two other sections have displays of vases, glass items, mosaics, a bone chessboard and other items dating from between the fifth and eighth centuries. The museum also has ancient coins and finds from the Foro Romano, including works from Palazzo Venezia and the Musei Capitolini.

DOMUS AUREA

58 G6 • Via della Domus Aurea/Giardini di Colle Oppio ☎ Call centre/guided tours: 06 3996 7700 Wed–Mon 9–6 ⏰ Wed–Mon 9–7.45 💰 Adult €6, child (under 18) free 🚶 Guided tour, booked in advance: in Italian, 9.40, 12.20, 4.40 and 6); in English, 10, 3.20. Audioguide €2 in English, Spanish, Italian, French and German 🚌 Colosseo 🚌 60, 64,

75, 84, 85, 87, 117, 175, 810, 850 www.ticketclic.it (to book a guided tour)

Nero's Golden House was a majestic urban villa built in the middle of the city following the great fire of Rome in AD64. It stretched over the Palatine, Caelian and Oppian hills, with pavilions and, in the area where the Colosseo now stands, an enormous artificial lake and gardens. Today, 32 out of the 140 original rooms of this well-preserved site can be visited. It is worth taking a guided tour to gain a better understanding of the structure of the ancient palace.

When trying to imagine the sheer size of this magnificent house, remember that the vestibule held a 35m (115ft) bronze sculpture of the Sun with Nero's face; this colossal statue may have provided the name for the later Colosseo (see page 77). One of the highlights of the house is the octagonal hall, an ingenious banqueting room covered with a rotating dome; the ivory ceiling was pierced so that guests could be showered with flowers and perfume.

Following Nero's suicide in AD68, the house was used as the foundations for the baths of Titus and of Trajan. It then remained hidden until the 1490s, when the section on the Oppian Hill was discovered. Its beautiful frescoes of geometric shapes, animals, faces and landscapes influenced Renaissance artists such as Raphael, who drew inspiration for a new pictorial trend called 'grotesque' from the grotto rooms of the frescoes.

The ruins are inside Colle Oppio. This local park gives a welcome area of greenery in this otherwise monument heavy-area. However, you should avoid the park after nightfall.

FONTANA DI TREVI

See pages 80–81.

FORI IMPERIALI

See pages 82–83.

FORO ROMANO

See pages 84–89.

GALLERIA DELL'ACCADEMIA DI SAN LUCA

57 F4 • Piazza dell'Accademia di San Luca 77 ☎ 06 679 8850 ⏰ Mon–Sat 10–12.30. Closed Jul and Aug 💰 Free 🚇 Barberini 🚌 52, 53, 60, 61, 62, 63, 71, 80, 85, 160, 850 stopping at Piazza San Silvestro

This gallery, one of Rome's most prestigious, was initially founded to promote the training of artists in Renaissance techniques. From 1633, every artist member of the academy had to donate a work of art, resulting in a wonderful collection that includes paintings by Raphael, Antonio Canova, Sir Anthony Van Dyck, Titian, Peter Paul Rubens, Il Guercino, Il Sassoferrato, Guido Reni and Pietro da Cortona.

When its original home was demolished in the 1930s to make way for the Via dei Fori Imperiali, the academy moved to Giacomo della Porta's 16th-century palazzo.

Works of particular interest include Portrait of Clement IX by Baciccia, the famous St. Luke Painting the Virgin, attributed to Raphael, Judith and Holophernes by Piazzetta, and the Virgin and Angels by Van Dyck. There are almost 400 portraits of all the artists of the academy from its inception to the 20th century (although not all of them are on display). Look out for the spiral staircase leading to the upper floors, based on a design by the 17th-century architect Francesco Borromini.

Fontana di Trevi

Rome's most spectacular and popular fountain.
Nicola Salvi's baroque masterpiece.
Uses water from one of the few original Roman water canals still in use.
Immortalized in Fellini's film, *La Dolce Vita*.

RATINGS

Good for kids	● ● ●
Historic interest	● ●
Photo stops	● ● ●
Value for money	● ● ● ● ●

BASICS

✚ 57 F4 • Piazza Trevi, 00187
Ⓜ Barberini
🚌 52, 53, 61, 62, 63, 71, 80, 116, 119, 175, 204, 492, 590, 630, 850 stopping at Piazza San Silvestro
📖 Available in souvenir shops
🏪 Many souvenir shops

From the air, you can see the Fontana di Trevi's theatrical aspect (above)
The sculptures on the fountain are full of symbolism; for example, the agitated horse to the left of Neptune (as you face him) respresents the stormy sea, while the figure blowing into a conch on the other side is the calm sea (right)
Throwing a coin into the fountain ensures your return to Rome and helps a good cause too (right inset)

SEEING THE FONTANA TREVI

Not far from the busy Via del Corso, down Via del Tritone and Via della Stamperia, is the most photographed fountain in Rome, the Trevi. As you step out of the shadows of the surrounding narrow streets into the small Piazza di Trevi, you are met by an overwhelming sight: The fountain, with its theatrical setting, baroque architecture, cascading water, faded rocks and wide basin, cannot fail to impress.

HIGHLIGHTS

THE BACKDROP

The story of the fountain is told in two bas-reliefs, above the two figures flanking the large central statue of Neptune. On the right, a young girl shows Agrippa's thirsty soldiers the way to a freshwater spring (by G. B. Grossi), and on the left, a panel by Andrea Bergondi shows Agrippa approving the plans for the 19km (12-mile) aqueduct from the Salone Spring to Rome.

THE FOUNTAIN

The imposing figure of Neptune, with his fluttering mantle, sits in the middle of this compelling stage, riding in his shell-shaped chariot pulled by two spirited sea horses that are steered by giant tritons. The tall niche that he stands in gives balance and symmetry to the composition. There are various animals, both mythological and real, in the basin, which represents the sea. In the niches to the right and left are the statues of Plenty (left) and Health (right) carved by Filippo della Valle.

THE RITUAL

There is one very important ritual to complete before leaving this magnificent scene behind. Legend has it that visitors should make a wish and toss two coins over their shoulder into the fountain; one coin ensures a return to Rome and the other makes the wish come true. The huge number of coins thrown into the fountain are collected daily and given to CARITAS, an Italian religious charity.

BACKGROUND

Long before the Fontana di Trevi was built, water was brought through the aqueduct designed by Augustus' adviser and friend General Agrippa in 19BC. The water that supplies the Fontana di Trevi runs underground, and it is one of the few original Roman water canals still in use. The aqueduct worked well for many centuries until it was reduced to a trickle in the Middle Ages, mostly due to lack of maintenance. In 1732, Pope Clement XII held a competition to design a new fountain to revive the splendour of ancient Rome. Salvi emerged the winner and was given the delicate task of carrying out this ambitious project. The fountain was completed after his death and finally inaugurated in 1762 by Clement XIII. A thorough restoration project was completed in 1991, returning the fountain to its original grandeur.

Fori Imperiali

**A huge area of ruins that once embodied the power of imperial Rome.
Series of fora built by succeeding emperors as symbols
of self-aggrandizement.
One of the potentially most exciting excavations still remaining in Rome.**

SEEING THE FORI IMPERIALI

The five colonnaded areas just down the road from the Colosseo were once the imperial fora, built as commercial and political meeting places by succeeding emperors. Plundered remorselessly over the centuries, today's ruins seem at first glance little more than a jumble of columns and tumbled stone, so take time to get your bearings. Excavations here are still ongoing, and over 15,000sq m (160,000sq ft) have been unearthed, representing more than half the original fora—and there's still more to discover.

HIGHLIGHTS

TRAJAN'S FORUM

After the wonderfully preserved covered markets of the Mercati Traianei (see page 91), the adjoining Trajan's Forum needs a leap of imagination to visualize its original appearance, when this huge forum was one of the wonders of the world. The last and most opulent forum to be built, it was an enormous public space, constructed to commemorate the conquest of Dacia (modern Romania) in AD106. The rectangular form is still traceable, and you can see the forest of broken columns that was once the Basilica Ulpia. Once the size of San Paolo fuori le Mura (see pages 148–149), it virtually masked the magnificent Trajan's Column (see pages 78–79), which stands behind it.

The Fori Imperiali (above) are made up from fora dedicated to the great and the good of Rome, including Trajan (right)

FORUM OF NERVA

Once a monumental drain and now used as a tunnel, the Chiavicone runs underneath the Via dei Fori Imperiali and leads to the long, narrow Forum of Nerva. On emerging in the forum, you'll be able to make out the ruined podium of the Temple of Minerva, the goddess of household tasks. This was largely intact up to the 17th century, when Pope Paul V plundered the stone to build a fountain. It was also known as the Forum Transitorium (Passageway Forum) because it incorporated the Argiletum, a road linking the old Roman forum with the Subura, the popular district.

THE FORUM OF AUGUSTUS, THE TEMPLUM PACIS AND THE FORUM OF CAESAR

The Subura is adjacent to the Forum of Augustus (2BC), site of the ruins of the Temple of Mars Ultor, built to commemorate Augustus' victory at Philippi and the

RATINGS		
Good for kids	● ●	
Historic interest	● ● ● ●	
Photo stops	● ● ●	
Walkability	● ● ● ●	

BASICS

✚ 57 F5 • Via dei Fori Imperiali ☎ 06 679 7786. Visitor centre 06 6797702 (Tue–Sun 10–12, 3–6.30)
ℹ Fori Imperiali is a working archaeological site, and you can only visit as part of a guided tour. Contact the tourist office for details: 06 3600 4399
Ⓜ Colosseo
🚌 60, 75, 84, 85, 87, 117, 175, 810, 850
🎧 Available at visitor centre €18
🏪 At visitor centre
🚻 At visitor centre

www.beniculturali.it

deaths of Caesar's assassins. Don't miss the African marble columns—all that remains of the Temple of Peace (AD75) in nearby Vespasian's Forum—or the three columns that were once part of Caesar's temple of Venus Genitrix in his forum. The Julia family claimed the goddess as their ancestress and Caesar adorned the temple's statue with pearls from far-off Britain.

BACKGROUND

This entire vast area was constructed between 50BC, when Julius Caesar, aware that the old republican forum had become too small for all its activities, commenced building, and AD113, when Trojan finished his forum. Succeeding fora were built by Augustus, Vespasian, Domitian and Trajan; they all ostensibly commemorate peace and treaties, but were ultimately expressions of the individual emperors' power and prestige, envisioned as fitting monuments to their personal glory.

Foro Romano

**The heart of ancient Rome—the political, economic, religious and commercial hub of the city during Republican times.
One of Rome's most evocative sites.
Buildings and ruins spanning almost a thousand years.**

A view across the Forum, with the Colosseo in the background (left). The Arch of Septimius Severus in the foreground (above left). The remains of the Tempio di Saturno (above right)

SEEING THE FORO ROMANO

The ruins of the Roman Forum lie in what is still the heart of Rome, just behind the looming 'wedding cake' of the Victor Emmanuel monument in Piazza Venezia (see page 119), and below the Capitoline and Palatine hills. There are several access points: The best is through the entrance on Via dei Fori Imperiali, which leads you straight on to the Via Sacra, the sacred way, running through the heart of the complex. It is bounded to the right by the Arco di Settimio Severo, and to the left by the Arco di Tito, with most of the interesting remains lying between these two triumphal arches. At first sight, the Forum appears little more than a jumbled collection of ruins, dotted with upright columns and a few complete buildings, so take time to get your bearings.

HIGHLIGHTS

TEMPLE AND HOUSE OF THE VESTAL VIRGINS

Overlooking the Via Sacra rise the ruins of a circular white temple. This is the Temple of Vesta, goddess of the hearth, where the Vestal Virgins tended an ever-burning fire symbolizing the perpetuity of the Roman state. A Temple of Vesta stood here from the earliest times; the existing ruin and its columns are composed of fragments of the version dating from AD191, built by Septimius Severus after a fire. It was reconstructed in the 1930s.

The cult of Vesta was one of the cornerstones of Roman belief. In primitive times, fire was of such importance it attained an almost sacred significance. Difficult to kindle, it was vital that it should not go out, so the custom evolved of keeping the communal fire in a separate hut. Young girls, with few other responsibilities, were the appointed guardians; thus through the centuries a practice that originated in good sense became imbued with religious symbolism. The temple itself was always circular, in imitation of the round huts of ancient Rome, and everything connected with Vesta and her worship was charged with archaic significance. The fire had to be kept burning at all costs, a difficult task when the winds blew and rain poured through the vent in the roof.

RATINGS	
Good for kids	●●
Historic interest	●●●●●
Value for money	●●●●●
Walkability	●●●●

TIPS

● Making sense of the Forum is quite a challenge—take a guided tour to get more out of your visit.

● Take something to drink with you. There are no bars in the Forum area.

ENTRANCE TO THE ROMAN FORUM

ENTRANCE TO THE ROMAN FORUM

Via Sacra

THE SIGHTS

BASICS

✚ 57 F6 • Via dei Fori Imperiali, Via di San Teodoro, Via di San Gregorio, Piazza Santa Maria 53; Largo Romolo e Remo 5–6

☎ 06 3996 7700 or 800 991199 (free)

🕐 daily 9–7.30

💷 Free

Ⓜ Colosseo

🚌 75, 85, 87, 117, 175, 186, 810, 850

🎫 10.30 daily, adult €3.50, child (under 12) free. Ticket office at Arco di Tito

🚻 Several on site

www.capitolium.org
Although mainly devoted to the ongoing excavations in the Fori Imperiali, there's plenty of information on the Foro Romano too. Excellent virtual reconstructions of what the buildings looked like in Roman times to compare with what you see now. Easy and fast to navigate, with an English option.

www.comune.roma.it
This is a good Italian-language site about the Forum area, its archaeological history and future development. Clear maps and a virtual tour. Run by Rome City Council.

There were six Vestal Virgins, working a rota system to tend the fire. They were recruited at an early age from impeccable families and appointed for 30 years by the emperor. The first ten years were spent learning their duties, the second practising them and the last passing on their knowledge. At the end of their service, Vestals were released from their vows and were free to marry, though few did. In return for their service, they had immense privileges (in a society where women had few rights)—wealth, land ownership, the right to pardon criminals, and access to the emperor. If they broke their vows of chastity, however, the penalties were harsh—some were buried alive. The order survived into the Christian era, being finally disbanded in AD394.

Vestal Virgins lived in the Atrium Vestae, the sprawling site next to the temple. This was built, as were all patrician houses, round an elongated court, whose ruins survive. It was constructed in the second century AD, to replace an earlier building, and must have been immensely grand. Today, the central courtyard with its three pools, lined with statues of the Virgins in their long white robes, is the most striking thing to be seen. Behind lie the tumbled ruins of the Vestals' once-magnificent palace.

THE CURIA

Set back from the open space of the Forum proper is a wonderfully complete, austere, red building. This is the Curia, home to the Senate, the most important civil body during the days of the Republic. According to Roman legend, Romulus, father of Rome, summoned a hundred family heads to meet regularly for consultation. These so-called *patres* (fathers), were the first senators; their role evolved into that of decision-makers on Rome's policies at home and abroad. During the Republic, the Curia was politically the most important place in the Roman world, where famous orators and statesmen

Via Sacra

Via Nova

ENTRANCE
TO THE ROMAN FORUM

spoke, major legal affairs were disputed, and policies shaped. But as the role of the single ruler evolved, its influence waned, and by the second century AD the Senate had no control over affairs, although it continued as an institution right up to the fall of Rome.

The Curia was rebuilt several times over the centuries, and the present building was reconstructed after a fire during the reign of Diocletian (AD285–305). In AD630 it was incorporated into the church of Sant'Adriano, and thus survived to emerge virtually intact when the church was demolished in 1937. It is by no means grand or huge, being built to hold about 300 senators. The height of the Curia is half the sum of its length and breadth, a ratio prescribed by the great first-century BC architect Vitruvius as providing ideal acoustics— important in a building used for debate. Inside, three shallow tiers of marble seats face each other across the central space, with a low dais for the presiding magistrate at the far end, and a statue of a senator in the middle. Grey marble originally covered the walls—you can see

SITE GUIDE

1	Tempio di Saturno
2	Tempio di Vespasiano
3	Tempio di Concordio
4	Rostra
5	Arco di Settimio Severo
6	Mamertine Prison
7	Santi Luca e Martina
8	Lapis Niger
9	Curia
10	Basilica Aemilia
11	Basilica Julia
12	Tempio di Castore e Polluce
13	Tempio di Cesare
14	Tempio di Vesta
15	Atrium Vestae
16	Tempio di Antonio e Faustina
17	Tempio di Romolo
18	Santi Cosma e Damiano
19	Basilica di Massenzio
20	Santa Francesca Romana
21	Tempio di Venere e Roma
22	Arco di Tito

A view across the Forum, with the Temple of Antonius and Faustina in the foreground (left)

The House of the Vestal Virgins

All over the empire, free-born Romans wore the toga. It was a sign of citizenship and the privileges that went with it; it proclaimed that the wearer was protected by Roman law and could not be mistreated, flogged or crucified. The emperors issued edicts about the toga, decreeing that citizens entering the Forum or attending the games had to wear it. It was an elegant but cumbersome garment, with folds that took time to arrange; it had to be re-pleated after every wearing, and it needed constant washing. Citizens disliked putting on the toga, and avoided doing so if possible—it was difficult to do more than stroll about slowly while wearing it.

There were several types of toga: the plain white worn by ordinary citizens; a garment with a red hem for certain priests; and the *toga praetexta*, edged with purple and worn by the 600 senators. Grandest of all was the *toga picta*, woven of purple cloth, worn by the emperor on state occasions.

some surviving sections facing each side of the platform. The floor is a most beautiful example of a technique called *opus sectile*, in which large pieces of stone in different hues are fitted together in figured patterns—a harmonious blend of red, yellow, green and white marble, laid out in rosettes and cornucopias. Only the doors are replacements; the originals were removed in the 17th century, by Pope Alexander VII, to the basilica of San Giovanni in Laterano.

The senate house was a consecrated building with the status of a temple; the first act of each senator on entering was to throw incense grains on to the brazier beside the goddess of victory, whose golden statue stood on an altar at one end. Speakers addressed the Senate from their seats, and voted by division, with those in agreement moving to one side and those against to the other.

The area outside the Curia is the Comitium. Here, during the early Republic, stood the Rostra, from which orators addressed the people. Its name comes from the *rostra*—the prows or beaks—of ships captured at the Battle of Anzio in 338BC, which once decorated it. The fenced-off flat, black marble slab is the Lapis Niger, which the Romans believed marked the burial place of Romulus. A stele dating from the sixth century BC was found here; the inscription engraved on it is believed to be the earliest written form of Latin.

ARCO DI SETTIMIO SEVERO
Next to the Curia, on the triumphal route that led to the Capitoline Hill, stands the Arch of Septimius Severus, a fine example of this peculiarly Roman form of monument. It was built, in AD203, on the orders of the Senate, to commemorate the tenth anniversary of the Emperor Septimius Severus' defeat of the Parthians (in what is now Iran), and to glorify his sons, Caracalla and Geta. Being the first major architectural addition to the Forum area for 80 years, it was suitably grandiose. The central arch is flanked by two lower ones, and faced with four splendid Corinthian columns, surrounded by reliefs with reclining gods and scenes from Severus' career. Originally, it was topped with a statue of Severus and his two sons riding in a chariot drawn by six horses. This has gone, but the inscriptions along the entablature are still clear. In AD212, after he became emperor, Caracalla murdered his brother Geta, co-emperor with him, and removed his name. Look at the fourth line of the inscription and you can see the missing words '*et Gatae nobilissimo cesari*' outlined by the holes left by the clamps that once held the letters.

ARCO DI TITO

At the opposite end of the Forum from Severus' Arch, the Arch of Titus was erected in AD81 in homage to Flavian Emperor Titus and his capture of Jerusalem 11 years previously. This restrained and sober monument, heavily restored, is today most significant for its unique representations, on the inner jambs of the arch, of the sacred furnishings of the great Jewish temple in Jerusalem. On the south side is the triumphant procession entering Rome with the trophies from the temple—the silver trumpets, the sacred altar and the seven-branched candlestick. On the opposite jamb is Titus, crowned with laurel by Nike (goddess of victory), standing in his horse-drawn chariot, surrounded by senators and plebs. For centuries the arch has been a symbol of shame to Jews, and even today, many refuse to pass through it.

The lone columns, fallen masonry and occasional statue in the Roman Forum give few clues to its former impressiveness

VIA SACRA

The Via Sacra runs right through the core of the Forum, from the Palatine Hill to the Capitoline. It was the most famous street in ancient Rome, its name deriving from the sanctuaries that lined it and the victorious processions of generals and emperors that walked

along it. Scholars and archaeologists have argued for years over the precise function of some of the buildings along the Via Sacra, but many are well known, as they were among the most important in the city. Just by the main entrance to the Forum site are the steps of the Regia, the house of kings, probably dating from the seventh century BC. Opposite is the best-preserved temple in the Forum, that of Antoninus and Faustina, which owes its survival to its conversion into a Christian church in the seventh century. Farther along, the huge area of broken columns was once the Basilica Aemilia, built in the second century BC to house the law courts. The Via Sacra curves left from here, with the Forum proper to the right. To the left are the long steps of the ruins of the Basilica Julia, built by Julius Caesar in the 50s BC on his return from the Gallic Wars. The romantic theory that the ruts in the stones were made by Roman chariots is unlikely to be correct, as none was allowed along the Via Sacra; they were probably gouged out by the carts of medieval builders using the Forum as a quarry.

BACKGROUND

The origins of the Forum lie in the eighth century BC when the inhabitants of what was then a small pastoral settlement began to construct a cluster of religious and civic buildings. Over the next centuries the Forum and its associated buildings became the heart of the expanding city of Rome, with ever more magnificent basilicas, temples and commercial premises. It was the venue for religious ceremonies, military triumphs, sacrifices and important funerals, the home of the law courts and banking, trading and commercial activities. It was also the city's main meeting place, fulfilling much the same purpose in Roman life as the piazza does in 21st-century Italian towns. By the second century BC the space was too constricted for Rome's ever-expanding public needs and activities, and in 54BC the first of a series of new administrative centres, the Fori Imperiali, was built by Julius Caesar. With Rome's decline, the original Forum area steadily declined, its buildings either transformed into Christian churches, or abandoned. After AD800 the Forum became little more than a convenient stone quarry for medieval and Renaissance builders. Excavation started in the 19th century, and has continued ever since.

BASILICAS

The Romans invented the architectural form of the basilica, a great hall where the central, higher space, lit by clerestory windows, was divided from the side aisles by rows of columns. Basilicas, with their exterior porticoes and colonnades, were practical buildings where crowds could gather in comfort, and they were used as meeting places for business and as law courts. They were cool and airy during stifling summer months, making it no surprise that the early Christian church adopted the design—and the name. The Christian basilica of San Paolo fuori le Mura is a good place to get an idea of how the basilicas in the Forum must have looked in their heyday (see pages 148–149).

Bacaccia's trompe l'oeil *ceiling in Il Gesù*

From Gianicolo (the Janiculum Hill), the panorama of Rome opens up before you

IL GESÙ

➕ 57 E5 • Piazza del Gesu/Via degli Astalli 16 ☎ 06 697 001
🕐 6.30–12.30, 4–6.15 💶 Free 🚌 30, 40, 46, 62, 63, 64, 70, 81, 492, 628, 630, 780, 787, 916 stopping at Largo di Torre Argentina; tram 8

The inside of this church, dedicated to the Holy Name of Jesus, was undecorated when it was completed in 1584. However, at the end of the 17th century, exquisite marble decorations, stuccowork and baroque frescoes, masterpieces of illusionism, were added to make the Jesuits' principal church one of the most beautiful in Rome.

The façade of the church is divided in two: At the top, a triangular tympanum includes a large central window and two lateral niches; below is a line of pilasters with Corinthian capitals. The interior consists of a central nave with side chapels. The chapel on the left, dedicated to St. Ignatius Loyola, adorned with stuccowork, golden bronzes, sculptures and precious stones, is the work of the Jesuit architect Andrea Pozzo. Pietro da Cortona added the right-hand chapel, and on the altar there is a painting by Carlo Maratta. On the ceiling, above the central nave, a remarkable *trompe l'oeil* fresco of 1679 by Baciccia depicts the *Triumph of the Name of Jesus*: Light descends through a fake window in the sky, colossal figures representing the races and vocations of humankind float in clouds, while others, representing the cardinal sins, fall into darkness.

GHETTO AND SYNAGOGUE

➕ 57 E5 🚌 23, 63, 280, 630, 780; tram 8 ☎ Synagogue: 06 6400 0661
🕐 Mon–Thu 9–7.30, Fri 9–2, Sun 9–12.30 💶 €6 🎫 Tours of Ghetto in English, lasting up to 1 hour, at 12.15 and 5.50. Meet at the Synagogue

The Ghetto is a picturesque place today, its narrow, bustling streets full of Jewish restaurants, pastry shops and workshops—despite its unhappy history, the area is still a meeting point for the Roman-Jewish community.

In 1555, Pope Paul IV created the Ghetto to segregate Rome's Jewish population. They were confined in bad sanitary conditions within the Ghetto walls, where three gates were opened in the morning and closed at dusk, and they were limited in their rights to worship and to trade. In 1888 Pope Pius IX opened the gates for the final time; the walls and houses of the Ghetto were demolished, and Rome's Jewish population were free to leave the area and given the same civil rights as they had formerly enjoyed.

The monumental Synagogue, built in 1904, overlooks the Tiber, its great dome visible from all over the city. It houses the Jewish Museum. Behind runs Via del Portico d'Ottavia, named after the ruins of the portico built in the first century BC by Augustus and his sister. Inside is the church of Sant'Angelo in Pescheria, which owes its name to the open-air fish market held nearby. The stone tablet for measuring the length of the fish is still there. This was one of the four Christian churches Jews were forced to attend every Sunday.

GIANICOLO

➕ 56 C6 • Passeggiata del Gianicolo
🚌 870

Although not one of Rome's original seven hills, the best view over Rome and its monuments has to be from the Janiculum Hill, especially at sunset. Its terrace is the city's largest, but there are spectacular views all the way up from the Passeggiata del Gianicolo, a fine avenue that runs all around the hill, beginning at Ponte Amedeo di Savoia. To save time and energy, take a bus to the top and return to Ponte Amedeo di Savoia on foot.

On the terrace is a huge equestrian monument to Giuseppe Garibaldi, who in 1849 fought a battle nearby to defend the Roman Republic. Eighty busts displayed along the promenade represent famous artists and heroes from Garibaldi's campaign.

The church of Sant'Onofrio has beautiful frescoes by Antoniazzo Romano and Baldassare Peruzzi, together with the remains of the 16th-century Italian poet Torquato Tasso. The adjoining convent, where Tasso spent his last years, has frescoes by Domenichino.

GIARDINO DEL PINCIO

➕ 57 E3 🕐 Closes at sunset
🚇 Spagna or Flaminio 🚌 88, 95, 117, 119, 204, 231, 490, 491, 495

The gardens on the Pincio Hill are Rome's first and most famous public gardens. Designed around 1810 by Giuseppe Valadier, they stretch from Trinità dei Monti to Piazza del Popolo, adjoining Villa Borghese park.

The fashionable gardens occupied part of the area where the Horti Lucilliani once stood. This was the villa and terraced gardens built by the politician (and epicure) Lucullus in the first century BC, and which extended for about 20ha (50 acres) between Trinità dei Monti and Villa Medici. After the sack of Rome, in the fifth century AD, the Pincii family bought the estate, along with most of the hill, and the gardens still bear their name.

If you climb the Rampa del Pincio from Piazza del Popolo, you reach the Pincio Terrace, dedicated to Napoleon I, which

The Synagoge, still at the heart of the Ghetto

The Giardino del Pincio gives welcome respite from the city

Boat-shaped Isola Tiberina from the air

has a spectacular view over the city. Nearby is the lovely Casina Valadier, built by Valadier between 1813 and 1817 as a coffee house. Inside are some noteworthy frescoes and tempera decorations discovered during recent restorations. A fashionable café, the building is still a meeting place for Roman aristocrats, although currently it is closed for restoration.

ISOLA TIBERINA

🕂 57 E6 🚌 23, 63, 280; tram 8

This small island in the Tiber, with its medieval buildings and Roman bridges, feels like a safe harbour, protected from the chaos of the city.

The island is erected on a volcanic rock and its shape resembles that of a ship. There are several legends about its origin, one of which concerns Esculapio, the Greek god of medicine: During the third century BC, the Romans sent a boat to Epidaurus in Greece to discover a cure for the plague. On the return journey, Esculapio left the ship in the shape of a serpent and swam to the island, indicating that a temple to the god of healing should be built there (the church of San Bartolomeo now stands where the sanctuary was erected). In the first century BC, the Romans reshaped the island with slabs of travertine to form a 'prow' and 'stern', and erected an obelisk as a mast, to commemorate Esculapio's ship. The island's tradition of healing and medicine has continued over the centuries, enhanced by the belief that the water on the island is particularly healthy. There is still a large hospital there.

Two bridges join Isola Tiberina to the river banks: Ponte Cestius dates back to the first century BC, and leads to Trastevere; while

Ponte Fabricio, built in 62BC, and the only Roman bridge to survive intact, joins the island to the Ghetto. The latter used to be called Ponte dei Giudei, which means the Bridge of the Jews. On the north side of the island is Ponte Rotto (Broken Bridge), the remains of a Roman wooden bridge built in 179BC.

LA MADDALENA

🕂 57 E4 • Piazza della Maddalena 53 🕾 06 797 796 🕐 Daily 8–noon and 5–7.30 🕃 Free, audioguide €2.50 🚌 40, 46, 62, 64, 70, 81, 492, 628, 630, 780, 787, 916; tram 8 to Largo di Torre Argentina or 116 to Via della Palombella

Just a stone's throw away from the Pantheon is the church of La Maddalena, a typical example of the baroque style, sumptuously decorated and furnished according to 18th-century Roman taste.

The church is the work of various 17th- and 18th-century artists: Carlo Fontana was responsible for the dome and the vault, while Giulio Quadrio completed the church in 1699, except for the façade. The latter was finished in 1735 and influenced by the baroque master Francesco Borromini; it is made of plaster and stucco, which are more ductile and cheaper than traditional travertine.

Inside, there is a magnificent gilded wooden organ, enriched with white-stuccoed statues. In the dome and transept are frescoes by Stefano Parracel and Michelangelo Cerruti, with figures of cherubs, saints and the Doctors of the Church. There are confessionals of inlaid briarwood along the central nave. The side chapels are exquisitely decorated with 17th- and 18th-century paintings.

Don't miss the 18th-century sacristy, with its six splendid marbled closets with golden edges and pictorial decorations on the vault.

MERCATI TRAIANEI

🕂 57 F5 • Via IV Novembre 94 🕾 06 679 0048. Information and guided tours: 06 6978 0532 🕐 Tue–Sun 9–7 🕃 Adult €6.20, child (under 18) free. 🎫 Guided tour for Torre delle Milizie only (book in advance) 📖 Guidebook in English €6.45 🚇 Colosseo 🚌 60, 84, 85, 87, 117, 175, 810, 850

Trajan's markets were a group of commercial buildings on six different street levels terraced up the Quirinal Hill. Today, these buildings house various exhibitions of ancient Roman art and history.

The complex was built at the beginning of the first century AD by Trajan's architect, Apollodorus of Damascus, and it remains the best example of what Roman urban architecture could achieve.

There was a covered shopping arcade with a magnificent vaulted ceiling, as well as an apartment block and some 150 shops of different shapes and types—a prototype for the modern shopping mall. It was not only a retail market, but also an administrative hub for the imperial authorities, where supplies were brought in, divided and redistributed.

The ground-floor shops were rather shallow; one has been reconstructed to show the external travertine door-frames, which gave shopkeepers extra space for their goods.

Via Biberatica, with its original paving, still runs round the upper floor of the front of the complex. It may get its name from the inns that stood on the street (*bibere*, to drink), or possibly from the pepper (*piper*) and other spices sold, which could only be afforded by the wealthier citizens. The view from the upper tiers of the complex will help you to understand the layouts of Trajan's and Augustus' fora nearby (see pages 82–83).

Museo e Galleria Borghese

•

**Great art in a beautiful villa set amid parkland.
The best-loved museum of Romans today.**

*The Borghese's sumptuous interiors and lush gardens are the perfect backdrop for works such as
Canova's* Paolina Borghese *(right) and Bernini's* Rape of Proserpine *(opposite)*

SEEING THE MUSEO E GALLERIA BORGHESE

The Museo e Galleria Borghese is housed in a harmonious
17th-century villa standing in green parkland on the eastern
edge of the Pincio Hill. The entrance leads into the lower ground
floor, where you will find the ticket office, shop, café and other
services. The gallery and museum, a series of interconnecting
rooms set around a central hall, occupy the next two floors. The
museum's sculptural highlights are in the first rooms on the
lower floor, as are Caravaggio's paintings. The Pinacoteca, the
main picture gallery, is on the upper floor. The Borghese is relatively small, so you are unlikely to lose your bearings or run out
of time to see everything.

HIGHLIGHTS

PAOLINA BORGHESE

Antonio Canova (1757–1822), the most famous of all neoclassical
sculptors, sculpted this portrait of Napoleon's sister Pauline in 1808.
Dominating room 1, it is acknowledged to be his masterpiece and is
certainly his most famous work. It shows the beautiful 25-year-old
reclining semi-naked on a couch, posing as Venus, with an apple in
her hand. The other hand supports her head, her hair is scooped up
to show her delicate neck and profile, and the line of her body com-
bines classical tranquillity with more than a hint of suggestiveness. It
was Pauline's own idea to commission this openly erotic piece from
Canova. She already had a reputation for beauty and bad conduct
when she was married off to the much older Prince Borghese, and
she visualized her elderly, dull husband using the statue to flaunt the
charms of his young wife in front of his friends. Once unveiled, *Venus*
caused an immediate scandal—how could Pauline have brought herself to pose naked? 'There was a stove in the studio,' she replied.
Years later, separated from the prince, Pauline regretted her nudity,
and forgetting her original motives for posing, begged him to cease
exhibiting the statue to chosen friends. 'It was created only to afford
you pleasure,' she wrote. The statue is carved from finest white
Carrara marble; the sheen on the skin was achieved with candlewax.

TIPS

● Entrance is limited to 360
people every 2 hours, so book
well ahead whatever the time
of year.

● Leave plenty of time for the
Pinacoteca.

● If you're into Italian gardens,
visit the palazzo's secret garden (tours Sat–Sun 9.30 and
10.30. To reserve a place,
phone 06 8207 7304).

BASICS

➕ 58 F2 • Piazzale Scipione Borghese (entrance on Via Pinciana)

☎ 06 854 8577

🕐 Daily 9–7. Advance booking essential, ticket must be collected 30 min before time slot

www.ticketeria.it, ☎ 06 32810, fax 06 3265 1329

💶 Adult €8.50, child (under 18) €2

🚇 Flaminio or Spagna

🚌 52, 53, 910

🎧 Guided tours every 2 hours in Italian and English (2 hours duration); audiotours €5, Italian, English, Spanish, French, German (2 hours duration)

📖 Italian, English, French, German guide to Galleria Borghese €13, TCI guidebook €19

☕ Café with bar

🏛 Shop with good selection of guides, postcards and souvenirs

🚻 On premises

🅿 On Via Pinciana

www.galleriaborghese.it
Informative website, with English option. There's plenty of background detail on the museum's most important works, full practical information and an on-line booking service. The site is clearly presented, well illustrated, fast and easy to navigate

The face of Bernini's David *may be a self portrait*

THE BERNINI SCULPTURES

Cardinal Scipione Borghese, enthused by the vitality of Gian Lorenzo Bernini's work, commissioned three works from the sculptor: *The Rape of Proserpine* (1621–22), *David* (1623) and *Apollo and Daphne* (1624). With his dynamic compositions and mastery of marble as a medium, Bernini was by far the greatest Italian exponent of the baroque style, producing work full of drama and movement.

Apollo and Daphne is a perfect example of Bernini's genius. The myth tells the story of how the pure and chaste nymph Daphne was pursued by Apollo, the god of light. Desperate to escape, Daphne implored the other gods to save her. Her wish was granted and she was turned into a laurel tree, saved from Apollo's clutches by protective bark. Bernini's life-size sculpture shows the moment of her change, bark creeping over her body and her fingers sprouting leaves.

When it was in its original position, the group was seen first from the back left, and there is no doubt that this is the best viewing point. Bernini's virtuosity shines out again in the Sala degli Imperatori with *The Rape of Proserpine*, another piece inspired by pagan legend. Proserpine, the daughter of Ceres, goddess of the harvest, attracted the attention of Pluto, ruler of the underworld. He abducted the girl, bearing her away to Hades, but when her mother intervened Pluto agreed to return her to earth for six months of each year. Pagans believed that during Proserpine's months in Hades, Ceres mourned,

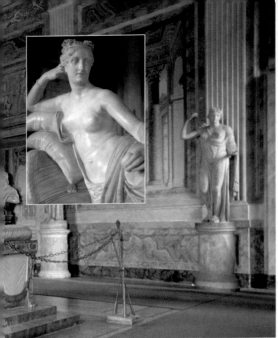

GALLERY GUIDE
GROUND FLOOR
Entrance hall a stunning mix of marble, frescoes and sculpture.
Room 1 *Paolina Borghese*
Room 2 *David*
Room 3 *Apollo and Daphne*
Room 4 Sala degli Imperatori, decorated with busts of Roman emperors and *The Rape of Proserpine*
Room 5 *Sleeping Hermaphrodite*
Room 6 Aenea and Anchises
Room 7 Decorated in Egyptian style with classical sculpture
Room 8 The Room of the Faun, with Caravaggio's paintings

Bernini's Daphne and Apollo captures the moment of the nymph's metamorphosis

Canova's sculpture of Paolina Borghese (above) would once have stood on a revolving base

winter reigned, and the world was cold, barren and overcast. On her return, the earth welcomed Proserpine with a carpet of flowers, and crops grew once more. Bernini shows the moment of abduction: From the left we see Pluto grasping Proserpine, his fingers sinking into her flesh, while she claws at his face. Viewing the group from various angles reveals different aspects of the myth.

THE CARAVAGGIO MASTERPIECES

Michelangelo Merisi, known as Caravaggio (1573–1610), is represented by six dramatic paintings in room 8. This artist is recognized for the extraordinary realism and detail found in his work, but he is known above all for his use of *chiaroscuro*, the balance of light and shade in a painting. The device is judged by the skill with which the artist handles shadows, and the best such artists tend to paint dark pictures illuminated by brilliant shafts of light. You can see this beautifully in Caravaggio's *Madonna dei Palafreni*, painted in 1606. The Virgin holding the child Jesus stands on the left, with her mother, St. Anne, to the right. All three figures are gazing downwards, their attention riveted on a

Above: The Prodigal Son *by Guercino (1591–1666)*
Opposite: The Ecstasy of St. Catherine *by Carracci (1557–1602)*

writhing snake about to strike. Jesus' foot is on the serpent, symbol of sin and heresy, as his mother teaches him how to crush it. Caravaggio painted the picture for the Confraternity of the Palafreni, who hung it in their chapel in St. Peter's basilica. It was there just a month before the reactionary Vatican clique ordered its removal on the grounds of its realism and lack of decorum. Caravaggio had his revenge when the painting was bought by Cardinal Scipione Borghese, preferred nephew of Pope Paul V, and hung it in pride of place in his collection.

The artist's triumph was short-lived, for in the same year, 1606, he was accused of murder and fled Rome, eventually landing up in Malta. It was here that he painted *David with the Head of Goliath*, which he sent to the Papal Court in the hope of pardon. The subject is simple: the boy David holding the head of the slaughtered giant. It is the marvellous play of light on skin and drapery that makes the painting shine; Caravaggio portrayed himself as Goliath.

THE UMBRIAN SCHOOL

Room 9 is crammed with some of the best paintings in the gallery, mainly by Umbrian artists. Perugino and Pinturicchio are both represented, but it is the three Raphaels that shine, in particular the *Deposition*, a picture inspired as much by classical art as religion. It was commissioned in 1507 by Atlanta Baglioni, in memory of her son Grifonetto. The Baglioni were one of the most important families in Perugia, a city where feuds and power struggles were a way of life. The image of a young man's dead body was the perfect subject to commemorate the dead boy. It hung for a century in Perugia, but, with the connivance of the local priest, was spirited away in 1608 and sent to Pope Paul V, who passed it on to his nephew Scipione to adorn the Villa Borghese. Raphael used a relief on a Roman sarcophagus as his inspiration, and the whole composition echoes Michelangelo's sublime *Pietà* in St. Peter's.

TITIAN'S SACRED AND PROFANE LOVE

Of the four paintings by Titian in room 20, *Sacred and Profane Love* stands apart, transfused with warm light and soft hues. It was painted in 1514 to celebrate the marriage of the Venetians Nicolò Aurelio and Laura Baragotto. The meaning of the picture has been hotly debated down the years. It portrays two beautiful women seated on a sarcophagus, which also serves as a fountain, the one on the left clothed in white, while the other is naked except for a few light draperies.

THE SIGHTS

Between them, a putto leans over the water in the fountain; behind, the tranquil landscape is washed with light. This is probably a picture about married love, the woman in white representing the bride, assisted by Venus and Cupid. Venus, with her burning flame, stands for the durability of married love. The picture's present title, coined in the late 18th century, reflects later thinking, and adds a moral dimension that was never intended. In 1899 the Rothschild family offered 4 million lire for the painting, almost half a million lire more than the total value of the rest of the collection and the villa together. The offer was promptly refused.

BACKGROUND

The Villa Borghese was built in 1612–13, designed to be the focal point of the Rome estate of the immensely rich Borghese family. Cardinal Scipione Borghese chose Flaminio Ponzio as his architect, commissioning a building modelled on the villas of ancient Rome and suitable to house his collections. Besides being a passionate and unscrupulous art collector, the Cardinal had interests ranging through music, geology and natural history, and the villa had its own farm, vineyard and zoo. The sculpture and pictures were in place by 1620 and they still form the museum's core collection. The Borgheses were forced to sell up at the end of the 19th century, and both park and villa were acquired by the Italian State in 1902. The villa underwent a lengthy restoration in the 1990s, returning both the exterior and interior to their original appearance.

CARAVAGGIO

Michelangelo Merisi, known as Caravaggio, lived from 1573 to 1610. One of the great baroque painters, he was especially known for his naturalistic style and dramatic use of *chiaroscuro*. His life was as dramatic as his work, full of feuds, plots and flight. In 1606 he was charged with murder and fled Rome to Naples. Pursued again, he went next to Malta, where he was made a knight of the Order of Malta. It seems he fell foul of the knights, who arrested and jailed him in 1608. He escaped and reached Sicily, from where, still in fear for his life, he moved on again to Tuscany, all the time hoping that word of his pardon would come from Rome. But no word came; he was arrested again, contracted a fever, and died on the beach at Porto Ercole.

THE SIGHTS

Musei Capitolini

**The oldest museum collection in the world, with over 1,300 works.
Opulent galleries containing some of Rome's most important
classical sculpture.
A chance to gain a fascinating insight on what lies beneath modern Rome.**

*Ancient statuary, such as the remains of Constantine's giant statue (opposite), Marforio (above left), and
a satyr (middle), and bronzes, such as the Capitoline She-Wolf (right), make up the collection*

SEEING THE MUSEI CAPITOLINI

Rome's civic museum collections occupy two of the three palazzi
around Michelangelo's beautiful Piazza del Campidoglio (see
page 118). Incorporating Roman, medieval and Renaissance elements, the complex of buildings is approached up a graceful
ramp, known as the Cordonata, just off Piazza Venezia. The
museum complex has two entrances, one on each side of the
piazza: The left-hand entrance gives access to the Palazzo Nuovo,
and that on the right to the Palazzo dei Conservatori. These two
buildings are linked by an underground gallery that runs beneath
the Palazzo Senatorio. It's best to start your visit in the Palazzo
Nuovo, although both entrances have ticket offices, cloakrooms
and bookstores. The museum shop proper is on the second floor
of the Palazzo dei Conservatori, next to the bar/restaurant.

HIGHLIGHTS

LOBBY AND COURTYARD OF THE PALAZZO NUOVO

Some of the museum's largest and most exciting pieces of
sculpture are in the lobby and courtyard of the Palazzo Nuovo.
Against the wall at one end of the lobby stands a huge
statue of the goddess Minerva, 3m (10ft) high. Probably a
product of second-century BC Greek craftsmanship and
created for a major temple, she wears a belted chiton
(tunic) and a helmet—the holes in the belt were
intended for metal ornaments that once hung from
it. The eyes are hollow, but would have been filled
with glittering metal and polished stones. At the
far end of the courtyard is *Marforio*, a sculptural
ensemble incorporated into a fountain—typical
of the practical High Renaissance approach to
ancient works of art, which was to use and adapt
them. The reclining bearded figure representing a
river god dates from the first or second century
AD, while the fountain and shells were added in
1594, producing a piece that is an amalgam of

RATINGS	
Good for kids	●
Historic interest	● ● ●
Specialist shopping	●
Value for money	● ● ●

TIPS

● It's worth taking a guided
tour or audioguide as the collection is huge and confusing.

● Allow plenty of time and be
prepared to concentrate—this
is not the easiest museum to
love and is not for the faint-
hearted.

● The piazza and the
interiors look their best
after dark, so go late.

● Some works have
been moved to the
Montemartini
power house on
the Via Ostiense,
but the best
remain here.

BASICS

✚ 57 E5 • Piazza del Campidoglio 1

☎ 06 6710 2071

🕐 Tue Sun 9–8

🎫 Adult €6, child (under 18) free. During temporary exhibitions, the ticket price may be higher and will include entrance to both the exhibition and the museum.

🚇 Colosseo 🚌 40, 60, 64, 86, 88, 492, 590, 715, 716

📖 Short and full guidebooks available in the museum shops

☕ Caffè Caffarelli, with all-day catering service, ice-creams and bar. Lovely rooftop terrace with stunning views. Open outside museum hours in summer.

📚 Libreria Capitolina (2 outlets). Excellent range of guidebooks, postcards, souvenirs and museum merchandise. The shops also sell a large range of other art books and multimedia works.

🚻 Several inside museum

www.museicapitolini.org
Excellent website with English translation, giving a history of the collections and buildings, a virtual tour, and a wealth of practical information. Clearly laid out, fast and well designed.

THE SIGHTS

ancient and modern. During the Renaissance, *Marforio* was used as a place to leave the satirical messages called *pasquinades,* so the figures of satyrs on either side seem appropriate companions. Half-man, half-goat, each balances a basket of grapes on his head; they almost certainly once supported roof beams in a loggia, probably located near the Theatre of Pompey.

A complete contrast to all this pagan revelry is seen in the magnificent and dignified gilded bronze equestrian statue of Marcus Aurelius in a glassed-off room to the right. It was once the focal point of the piazza outside, placed there on a plinth designed by Michelangelo. Threatened by modern pollution, the original has been replaced by a replica. This wonderful piece, once part of a triumphal monument, depicts the Emperor Marcus Aurelius (AD161–180) astride his horse, clad in the toga as a majestic lawgiver. Following the fall of Rome, the statue, with its outstretched hand, was believed to be that of Constantine, the first Christian emperor, and thus survived the Dark Ages when thousands of similar works were destroyed. It stood untouched outside the basilica of San Giovanni in Laterano until it was brought to the Campidoglio.

CLASSICAL SCULPTURE IN PALAZZO NUOVO

Here in the world's oldest public art collection, it is possible to gain a sense of what a museum of the 17th and 18th centuries was like, and scattered among the seemingly endless ranks of statuary in the upstairs rooms of the Palazzo Nuovo are some gems, the city's best Roman copies of Greek sculpture.

Originally, classical statues were brightly painted and acted as focal points in buildings and public spaces. Renaissance restorers mended, replaced and polished, often substituting arms and even heads if they were damaged or missing. The *Discobolos* (discus thrower), in the Gallery, is a prime example. The original was sculpted in Greece around 460BC. Many copies were made, including the powerful torso of the figure here; the rest of the statue was reworked (not very satisfactorily) around 1700. Off the Gallery, the Hall of the Doves contains a beautiful Roman copy of a Hellenistic *Young Girl with a Dove*. The avian theme continues in the room's most famous work, the second-century AD *Mosaic of the Doves*, depicting doves drinking at a fountain, from Hadrian's Villa at Tivoli. Both marble and glass were used for the tesserae, and in the second-century Mosaic of the Theatrical Masks. Also off the Gallery, in a small polygonal room, is the *Capitoline Venus*, discovered in the late 17th century. Slightly larger than life-size, this is a depiction of Venus-Aphrodite, a popular theme of classical sculptors. Beautifully modelled, this version dates from the first century BC.

In rooms IV and V are numerous portrait busts, some of which have surprisingly modern faces. Beyond here is the Great Hall with, among other full-size pieces, the *Apollo of Omphalos*, a fine Roman copy of the fifth-century BC Greek original. The masterpiece in room VII is the *Drunken Faun*, carved in red marble and, although over-restored in the 18th century, a splendid piece, full of *joie de vivre*. Beyond here, in room VIII, is the *Dying Gaul*, one of the most famous and emotive of all Classical statues. Once thought to be a dying gladiator, its true subject is clear from the warrior's weapons, his nudity and his hairstyle—all Celtic attributes.

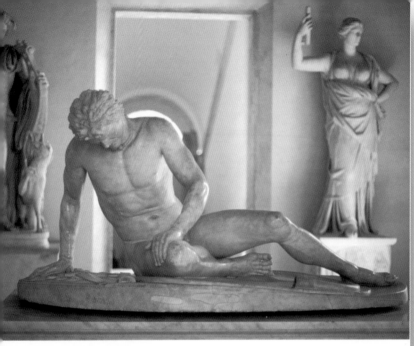

The serene Capitoline Venus *stands in splendid isolation in her own room (opposite, top). The red marble* Drunken Faun *stands out against the rest of the sculptures (opposite, bottom). The* Dying Gaul *is a wonderful example of Classical sculpture (above).* Mosaic of Doves, *from Villa Adriana, gives its name to the Hall of the Doves (left)*

TABULARIUM

The remains of the Tabularium, an imposing building completed in 78BC, lie underneath the Palazzo Senatorio. In Roman times it was where the archives of the Roman State were kept, bronze *tabulae* containing the State laws and official deeds. It is reached via the underground tunnel that connects the two wings of the museum. For classical history enthusiasts this complex is a must, but the attraction for most visitors is the view over the Forum from its arched gallery.

THE PALAZZO DEI CONSERVATORI

The Palazzo dei Conservatori's collection is much larger, spread over two floors. Many of the rooms, originally intended for official civic business, are magnificently frescoed, a fine backdrop for some stunning pieces. The central courtyard, lined with reliefs and inscriptions, contains the surviving fragments of a colossal statue of Constantine the Great, dating from AD313 and discovered in the Forum in 1486. Only the nude parts of the body would have been in marble, with the draperies in gilded bronze covering a supporting frame. Constantine appears again upstairs in the Hall of the Horatii and Curiatii as a superb bronze head. The gilded bronze *Hercules*, a Roman copy of a famous Greek fourth-century BC piece, once stood in a temple.

In room III is one of the museum's best-loved sculptures: The small bronze *Spinario* was one of the first gifts to the museum by its founder Sixtus IV in 1471, and shows a seated boy pulling a thorn from his foot. The pose is unique among ancient statues and it was popular in the Renaissance, inspiring many copies and similar works. Even more inspirational is the *Capitoline She-Wolf* in room IV, the very symbol of Rome. Part of Sixtus IV's gift, it originally stood on the

Spinario, *a first-century BC bronze, is an endearing statue (above)*

GALLERY GUIDE

Palazzo Nuovo
I   Gallery
II   Hall of the Doves
III   Capitoline Venus
IV   Hall of the Emperors
V   Hall of the Philosophers
VI   Large Hall
VII   Room of the Faun
VIII   Hall of the Gladiator

Palazzo dei Conservatori
First floor
I   Room of the Horatii and
      the Curatii
II   Hall of the Captains
III   Hall of the Triumphs
IV   Hall of the Fasti
V   Hall of the Geese
VI   Hall of the Eagles
VII   Green Hall
VIII   Yellow Hall
IX   Pink Hall
X   Hall of the Tapestries
XII   The Chapel
XIII, XIV, XV
      Hall of memorable
      modern events

Second floor
I   Hall 1
II   Painters from Ferrara
III   Painters from Venice
IV   Hall 4
V   Hall 5
VI   Painters from Bologna
VII   Hall of St. Petronilla
VIII   Hall of Pietro da Cortona
IX   Cini Gallery

Palazzo Senatorio
I   Temple of Veiovis
II   Tabularium Gallery
III   Room of the
      Executioner

SECOND FLOOR

FIRST FLOOR

PANORAMIC TERRACE

Horti Borghesiani

Exhibitions and Cafeteria entrance

GROUND FLOOR

ENTRANCE

Courtyard

PALAZZO NUOVO

PIAZZA DEL CAMPIDOGLIO

ENTRANCE

Courtyard

PALAZZO DEI CONSERVATORI

Conjunction Gallery

KEY

Palazzo Nuovo

Palazzo dei Conservatori

Palazzo Senatorio

façade of the Palazzo—without the figures of Romulus and Remus. These were added in 1509 by the Florentine sculptor Pollaiuolo, and the group was brought inside during Michelangelo's revamp of the palace. The statue is Etruscan and dates from the fifth century BC, a wonderfully intelligent portrayal of an animal once common in Italy.

PINACOTECA

The second floor of the Palazzo dei Conservatori houses the Capitoline picture gallery, founded in the 18th century by Pope Benedict XIV. There are far finer collections in Rome, but it does contain a good cross-section of Italian painting, as well as some interesting foreign works. The *Baptism of Christ* is an early Titian, its gentle piety contrasting admirably with the sensual energy of Veronese's *Rape of Europa* in the same room (III). There is a fine Correggio *Madonna* in room V, but some of the best works are in the Hall of St. Petronilla, named after the synonymous picture by Guercino (nickname of Giovanni Francesco Barbieri). Here, there are two splendid Caravaggios and a voluptuous *Romulus and Remus* by Rubens. In the Cini Gallery is *The Brothers de Wael* by another northerner, Anthony van Dyck, painted in Genoa in 1621; here also hangs a *Self-portrait* by Velazquez, painted in 1650 during his second visit to Rome.

BACKGROUND

By the 15th century, civic power in Rome was centred on the Capitoline, where the Palazzo Senatorio and Palazzo dei Conservatori were used for meetings of the magistrates who,

The mosaics in the Capitoline were made using the same processes employed today. Large sheets of glass, or thin slabs of marble, are first shattered into tiny pieces to make the mosaic tiles (tesserae). The surface on which the mosaic will be built is covered with a layer of cement, on which the outline of the image is traced. Next comes a thin layer of mortar; on this, a detailed painting of the final design is made. The pieces of glass and marble, set at fractionally different angles to refract the light, are then pressed into the wet mortar, creating an image that can endure for millennia. The smaller the tesserae, and the more varied the hue, and the more expensive the mosaics.

together with the senators, governed the city. In 1471 Pope Sixtus IV presented the Roman bronzes and statues that formed the nucleus of the museum to the people of Rome, and the Capitoline thus became the world's first public museum. The buildings and piazza were restored and enlarged to Michelangelo's plans in the mid-16th century, and in 1654 Girolamo and Carlo Rainaldi designed the Palazzo Nuovo to complete the architectural ensemble.

The bronze head of Constantine dwarfs the visitors in the Hall of Horatii and Curiatii (above)

Among the exhibits of the Musei Capitolini are figures based on mythology, such as this centaur (left)

Musei Vaticani

The largest, richest, most impressive museum complex in the world with over 1,400 rooms.
Contains sculpture, paintings and objets d'art spanning more than 3,000 years, from every corner of the classical and modern world.

The Galleria delle Carte Geografiche is decorated with 16th-century map frescoes (above left). The giant bronze pine cone in the Cortile della Pigna (above middle). Swiss guards (above right)

SEEING THE MUSEI VATICANI

The once horribly crowded entrance to the Musei Vaticani benefited immensely from a revamp in 2000, the Jubilee Year, although you may still have to wait in high season. The complex includes both museum and gallery complexes and parts of the papal palace, richly decorated by the world's greatest artists. The sheer size of the museum complex is in itself confusing and exhausting, so spend time planning and be aware that it is impossible to see everything in one visit. Various official routes taking in all the main attractions are suggested on leaflets available at the entrance, but these can be very crowded with tour groups, so it is a good idea to plan your own itinerary. The best way to tackle the museums is to focus on the highlights (see below), perhaps taking in one or two other collections; just walking between these will give glimpses of lots more.

HIGHLIGHTS

CAPPELLA SISTINA

The Sistine Chapel was built by Pope Sixtus IV between 1473 and 1481 to serve as both the pontiff's private chapel and as a venue for the gathering of cardinals who elect each new pope—a function it still fulfils. It is a huge structure, with a beautiful cosmatesque mosaic floor and a marble screen by Mino da Fiesole. But it is the frescoes, entirely covering the walls and ceiling, that attract up to 20,000 visitors a day. While the chapel was under construction, Sixtus planned its decoration, settling on scenes from the Old and New Testaments as the subject matter, with the emphasis on the parallels between the lives of Moses and Christ. From Florence, he summoned Sandro Botticelli, together with Domenico Ghirlandaio, Cosimo Rosselli and Perugian artist Perugino. These artists, joined by Pinturicchio, Luca Signorelli and Piero di Cosimo, worked on the walls for 11 months, producing a series of glowing works that should attract thousands of visitors in their own right. The two most important scenes are Perugino's *Christ Giving the Keys to Peter* and Botticelli's *The Punishment of Korah*, each showing the Arch of Constantine in the background.

RATINGS	
Good for kids	●●●
Historic interest	●●●●●
Value for money	●●●●
Walkability	●●●

TIPS

● Don't try to see everything, just choose a few highlights and take breaks.

● Dress respectfully—no shorts or bare upper arms.

● Come when the museum first opens or late in the morning. Wednesday morning can be relatively peaceful as many people are in the Piazza San Pietro for the papal blessing.

● Head straight for what you particularly want to see—then you won't already be exhausted by the time you get there.

● Last admissions are quite early, so arrive in good time.

The impressive 1930s staircase that spirals up to the museums entrance (opposite)

✝ 56 B4 • Viale Vaticano

☎ 06 6988 4676

⏱ Mon–Fri 8.45–4.45 (last admission 3.20), Sat 8.45–1.45 (last admission 12.20), Mar–mid Nov; Mon–Sat 8.45–1.45 (last admission 12.20), rest of year

💶 Adult €10, child €7, under 6 free

Ⓜ Cipro Musei Vaticani, Ottaviano-Vaticano

🚌 19, 32, 49, 81, 98

🎫 Two-hour guided tour €4; book on 06 6988 5100 or at museum information point. Audiotours available in Italian, English, French, German, Spanish, Japanese €5.50

📖 Official guidebook to museum and Vatican State available in Italian, English, French, German, Spanish, Japanese, €7.50

☕ Café and pizzeria inside museum. Expensive, but fine for a quick refill and rest

🛍 Several shops at different points in museum; well stocked with guidebooks, postcards, religious souvenirs, Vatican stamps and museum reproductions

🎟 Many throughout museum complex

www.vatican.va
The official website for the Vatican State, the Vatican Museum and Catholic Church. Lots of pictures from the collections, plus information on the Vatican.

Michelangelo's masterpiece, the ceiling of the Sistine Chapel (above)

These earlier masterpieces, however, tend to be overshadowed by Michelangelo's frescoes on the ceiling and altar wall, arguably Western art's finest achievement and certainly the largest work of painting ever planned and carried out by one man. Julius II commissioned the ceiling in 1508, and Michelangelo completed it in 1512, an artistic tour de force combining narrative scenes, architectural *trompe l'oeil* effects and statuesque figures of immense beauty. The central panels tell the Creation story and that of Noah; these are surrounded by a decorative scheme dominated by the figures of the prophets and sibyls and containing wonderful details, including the famous *ignudi*, nude youths.

Years later, in 1535, Michelangelo was again summoned to the chapel, this time by Paul III, to fresco the altar wall with scenes of the Last Judgement, a huge task that occupied him until 1541. The *Last Judgement* is essentially a celebration of the human body, full of power, potency and movement. Even before it was finished the amount of nudity had offended many, not least the Pope's master of ceremonies. Furious, Michelangelo depicted him in the bottom right-hand corner of Hell as Minos, the doorkeeper, complete with ass's ears and entwined in a serpent. Later, Pius IV objected to the nudity to such an extent he commissioned Daniele da Volterra to clothe the genitals—an exercise that earned him the soubriquet trouser-maker. This overpainting was removed during the extensive, Japanese-funded restoration of the ceiling and *Last Judgment* during the 1980s and '90s, a project said to have cost over $3 million.

STANZE DI RAFFAELLO

Not content with the painting of the Sistine Chapel, in 1508 Julius II embarked on a major decorative scheme in the four nearby rooms of his private apartments, today known as the Stanze di Raffaello (Raphael Rooms). The Stanza della Segnatura, the Pope's study, was Raphael's first major Roman commission, painted between 1508 and 1511. The frescoes are allegories representing the humanist ideals of theology, philosophy, poetry and justice. The *School of Athens* stresses truth acquired through reason, with the great Classical thinkers all represented, the central figures of Plato—probably a portrait of Leonardo da Vinci—and Aristotle dominating the scene. The figure on the left is said to be Michelangelo, added after Raphael had a sneak preview of his work in the Sistine Chapel. Opposite is the *Disputation of the Holy Sacrament*, while the side walls show *Parnassus*, home to the Muses, and the *Cardinal Virtues*.

Chronologically, the next room to be painted was the Stanza di Eliodoro, with its energy-charged *Expulsion of Heliodorus* and serene

Upper floor

10	Museo Gregoriano Etrusco
11	Sala della Biga
12	Galleria dei Candelabri
13	Galleria degli Arazzi
14	Galleria delle Carte Geografiche
15	Cappella di Pio V
16	Sala Sobieski
17	Sala dell'Immacolata
18	Cappella di Urbano VIII
19	Stanze di Raffaello
20	Cappella di Nicolò V
21	Loggia di Raffaello

Lower floor

1	Entrance
2	Staircase
3	Entrance Hall
4	Atrio dei Quattro Cancelli
5	Museo Pio-Clementino
6	Octagonal Courtyard
7	Museo Chiaramonti
8	Galleria Lapidaria
9	Museo Gregoriano Egizio

ENTRANCE

Lower floor (continued)

22	Appartamento Borgia
23	Salette Borgia
24	Collection of modern religious art
25	Cappella Sistina
26	Biblioteca Vaticana
27	Museo Sacro
28	Sala delle Nozze Aldobrandine

Lower floor (continued)

29	Salone Sistino
30	Braccio Nuovo
31	Museo Profano della Biblioteca
32	Courtyard of the Pinacoteca
33	Pinacoteca
34	Museo Gregoriano Profano
35	Museo Pio Cristiano
36	Museo Missionario-Etnologico
37	Museo Storico Vaticano

THE SIGHTS

FRESCO

Fresco painting is a medium in which the pigment becomes permanently part of the wall it covers, thus producing, in the right conditions, an extremely long-lasting image. The artist first draws the scene on paper, then, using a graph, expands the drawing to the desired size to make the working cartoon. The outline of the principal figures and background are then pricked out with tiny holes and the cartoon is attached to the wall surface. Renaissance artists then blew charcoal dust through the holes, leaving the outline of the picture on the wall when the cartoon was removed. As fresco pigments need to be applied to fresh, wet plaster, the artist had to assess the area he would cover that day. Once the plaster was applied, he would follow the charcoal outlines with pigment—a method still used. As the plaster dries, a chemical reaction occurs, binding the pigment and plaster and leaving a permanent image.

The Sistine Gallery (above and right)

Miracle of Bolsena. The latter tells the story of the medieval miracle that occurred in Bolsena, when a priest who doubted the doctrine of transubstantiation (the transformation of the Eucharistic bread and wine into the actual body and blood of Christ) saw the wafer bleed during Mass. The window wall has a superb night scene, showing the *Deliverance of St. Peter from Prison*. The two final rooms were painted to Raphael's designs by his pupils after his death in 1520.

PINACOTECA VATICANA

The Pinacoteca, founded in 1816 by Pius VI, occupies a separate building, erected in 1932, within the museum complex. It is widely considered to be Rome's best picture gallery, with works from the early and High Renaissance to the 19th century. Among these are some of the most remarkable early paintings in Rome, notably Giotto's *Stefaneschi Triptych* (room II). Painted in the early 1300s for the altar of the Confessio in old St. Peter's, it shows the *Martyrdom of SS. Peter and Paul*. The deaths of both saints are shown, with St. Peter crucified upside-down, at his own request, as he felt unworthy to die the same way as Christ. Cardinal Stefaneschi, the donor, is shown on either side of the triptych. The next rooms are devoted to 15th-century Italian art. Look for Fra Angelico's lovely *Madonna and Child with Saints* in room III and the serene Umbrian pictures in room VII, especially Perugino's luminous *Madonna and Child*.

The next room (VIII) is the Pinacoteca's high point, a stunning collection of Raphael's work, including the tapestries that once hung in the Sistine Chapel, woven in Brussels from Raphael's cartoons. Dominating the room is the *Transfiguration*, a sublime work that was unfinished at the artist's death and hung above his coffin at his funeral; his pupils later completed it. The triumphant figure of the ascending Christ pulses with energy amid piercing light and lowering cloud formations, a superb contrast to the artist's *Coronation of the Virgin*, painted when he was only 20 and his first major composition. The gentle *Madonna of Foligno* was commissioned in 1512 as a votive offering, in gratitude for a lucky escape during a siege.

Leonardo da Vinci is represented in room IX by the unfinished and curiously monochrome *St. Jerome*, one of his few works where the authorship has never been disputed. Look out here, too, for the exquisite *Pietà*, by the Venetian painter Giovanni Bellini; the dead Christ lying across his mother's knees was a popular subject for Venetian artists. Venetian painting features again in room X in the shape of two canvases by Titian: a glowing *Madonna with Saints* and the subtle *Portrait of Doge Nicolò Marcello*. There are further psychological insights in Caravaggio's dramatically despairing *Deposition* in room XII, all muted tones and intense *chiaroscuro*.

MUSEO PIO CLEMENTINO

To see the cream of the Vatican's classical sculpture collection, head for the Museo Pio Clementino and its octagonal Court of the Belvedere. The court still contains the two statues that influenced Renaissance sculptors more than any others, both acquired by Julius II: the *Laocöon* and the *Apollo Belvedere*. The *Laocöon* created a sensation on its discovery in 1506 near Nero's Golden House, when it was immediately identified from the description of the first-century Roman scholar Pliny. A Greek second-century BC group from Rhodes, it shows a Trojan priest who, having warned of the dangers of the famous wooden horse, was crushed, along with his sons, by sea serpents sent by Apollo. The *Apollo Belvedere,* a Roman copy of a fourth-century BC Greek statue, more than holds its own beside Canova's *Perseus*. Inside the museum, highlights include a beautiful Hellenistic *Sleeping Ariadne*, superb second-century AD candelabra from Hadrian's Villa at Tivoli, and fine Roman portrait busts, including a splendid one of Julius Caesar.

BACKGROUND

The Musei Vaticani form the oldest 'royal' art museum in Europe, originating as the private collections of the pope in his role as temporal ruler. Innocent III (1179–80) had made an existing palace, near the basilica of St. Peter, into the permanent seat of the papacy, and his successors enlarged and embellished it. Major work was carried out under Nicolas V in the mid-15th century, and in the 1470s Sixtus IV started to build the Sistine Chapel. Although these areas were primarily intended only for the pontiff's own use, the works of art in this part of the papal palace are today the greatest of the Vatican's treasures. It was not until the 18th century that work began on arranging the papal collections as a museum, with proper galleries being built to house sculpture, paintings and objets d'art, a process that continued into the 20th century.

THE VATICAN GARDENS

The Vatican Gardens date back to the early days of the Christian Church and reflect design trends through the centuries. Few tourists get to visit them, but anyone can enjoy glimpses of the parterres and planting from the windows of the Vatican Museums. The overall style of the gardens is very much in the Italian tradition of formal rectangular parterres, with box hedges, cedars and stone pines, underplanted with roses and bedding plants. There are several of these parterres, linked by shady paths, with shrubs framing views of the dome of St. Peter's. Succeeding popes embellished the gardens, adding summer houses and elaborate fountains.

The Vatican Gardens (above)
Sphere With Sphere by Arnaldo
Pomodoro (1990, below)

The Museo Keats-Shelley commemorates the British poets

Museo delle Paste Alimentari celebrates Italy's best-loved food

Ancient ruins and tranquil gardens on the Palatine Hill

THE SIGHTS

MUSEO KEATS-SHELLEY

🗺 57 E4 • Piazza di Spagna 26 ☎ 06 678 4235 🕐 Mon–Fri 9–1, 3–6, Sat 11–2, 3–6 🎫 €3 🚇 Spagna 🚌 117, 119, 530, 590 📷 ♿ www.keats-shelley-house.org

In the delightful Casina Rossa (little red house), at the foot of the Spanish Steps, is the Keats-Shelley Memorial Foundation, which preserves letters, manuscripts and documents associated with a number of English poets, including Byron, Leigh Hunt, Shelley and Keats. In particular, it is a memorial to the last two, both of whom died in Italy.

In 1820–21, John Keats spent the last few months of his life in the Casina Rossa with his friend Joseph Severn.

In 1903, American poet Robert Underwood Johnson set about raising money to acquire the famous Casina Rossa on behalf of the Keats-Shelley Foundation. The house is now a museum with a rich collection of manuscripts, prints and memorabilia illustrating the life and works of the Romantic poets.

Don't miss the portrait of Keats painted by Severn.

MUSEO NAZIONALE DELLE PASTE ALIMENTARI

🗺 57 F4 • Piazza Scanderberg 117 ☎ 06 6991119 🕐 Daily 9.30–5.30 🎫 €9 🚇 Barberini 🚌 52, 53, 61, 62, 63, 71, 80, 85, 160, 850 stopping at Piazza San Silvestro

Not far from the Trevi Fountain is an unusual museum dedicated to Italy's best-loved and best-known food—pasta. It traces the history and evolution of pasta and of the manufacturing processes, from early grindstones for milling the wheat to modern industrial pasta machinery. Visitors discover how pasta is made, mixed and dried. (Dried pasta goes back to the

12th century, when it was invented to allow the food to be kept for months or even years.)

MUSEI VATICANI

See pages 104–109.

ORTO BOTANICO

🗺 56 C6 • Largo Cristina di Svezia ☎ 06 4991 7107 🕐 Tue–Sat 9.30–6.30, Apr–Oct; 9.30–5.30, rest of year. Closed Sun–Mon except when there are exhibitions 🎫 Adult €2.07, child (under 12) €1.04 🚌 H 780, 630; tram 8

In a peaceful corner of Trastevere (see pages 144–145) is the Botanical Garden, a wonderful place to escape the bustle of the area. It was the garden of the imposing Palazzo Corsini (see opposite) until 1883, and now contains a vast collection of plants, which began with the medicinal plants cultivated in the Vatican by Pope Nicholas III in the 13th century.

As you enter, a central path leads to the Tritons Fountain, built in 1570 by the architect Ferdinando Fuga and surrounded by the garden's famous palms. Farther up, on the hill, the rose garden contains species that have been cultivated in Rome since the 17th and 18th centuries. There are wonderful views of the city from the Japanese garden. Descending the slope, you will see a 400-year-old plane tree, one of the oldest in Rome, some spectacular Mediterranean conifers, pine trees, oaks, huge sequoia trees and a *ginkgo biloba* (maidenhair tree). The garden of medicinal herbs, with more than 300 species cultivated since the 15th century, is of great interest. There is an aromatic herb garden specially planted for visitors with visual impairment, and in the various greenhouses there are collections of orchids, and tropical plants.

PALATINO

🗺 57 F6 • Entrances on Via dei Fori Imperiali, Via Sacra, Via di San Teodoro and Via di San Gregorio ☎ 06 3996 7700 🕐 Tue–Sun 9–7, Apr–Sep; 9–3.30, rest of year 🎫 Adult €10, child (under 18) free. Ticket also valid for Palatine museum and Colosseo 🚇 Colosseo 🚌 60, 75, 81, 175, 673 to Via di San Gregorio; 60, 84, 85, 87, 117, 175, 810, 850; tram 3 to Via dei Fori Imperiali

The Palatine Hill offers a delightful walk through gardens and shaded areas, where time seems to have stood still. One of the seven hills of Rome and rich in archaeology, the Palatine is considered the cradle of the city.

Emperors preferred the Palatine for their palaces (as the site of sumptuous residences, the area in fact gave rise to the word 'palace'). Augustus set the trend by enlarging his house after it was damaged by fire; Tiberius followed (his palace is now largely beneath the Farnese gardens), as did Nero with part of the Golden House (Domus Aurea—see page 79). But what remains today consists mainly of Domitian's vast imperial palace.

Among the ruins excavated on the hill are temples to Cybele, goddess of fertility, and to Apollo and Victory, and the first-century BC House of Livia. The remains of Domitian's palace include the Domus Flavia (the seat of government), the Domus Augustana (the Emperor's private quarters) and the House of the Griffins, with frescoes depicting those winged mythological beasts. The Palatine museum houses fragments of frescoes, statues, bas-reliefs and objects found in the Palatine buildings.

The Orti Farnesiani (Farnese Gardens) were designed for Cardinal Alessandro Farnese in the mid-16th century by Giacomo da Vignola and

The Palazzo del Quirinale, once a papal palace and royal residence, is now a presidential palace

Palazzo Spada is home to the Galleria Spada's collection

Girolamo Rainaldi. They were laid out on the site of the Domus Tiberiana, Emperor Tiberius' sumptuous first-century palace.

From Via Nova, the first building encountered when you enter the gardens is the Nymphaeum of Rain, decorated with Renaissance frescoes on the walls and vault. From here, two staircases with ornamental niches lead to the main gardens. At the top, Rainaldi built two pavilions, known as the Aviaries. On the eastern side is the Nymphaeum of Mirrors with beautiful mosaics on the walls; lilies, a symbol of the Farnese family, are grown here. The gardens, as planted today, are largely the work in the 19th century of the archaeologist Giacomo Boni.

PALAZZO ALTEMPS

See pages 112–113.

PALAZZO BARBERINI

See page 114.

PALAZZO CORSINI

🕂 56 D5 • Via della Lungara 10 ☎ 06 6880 2323 🕙 Tue–Sun 8.30–7.30 💶 Adult €4, child (under 18) free 🚌 630, 780; tram 8 🚻 ♿
www.galleriaborghese.it

This majestic 15th-century palace is in a charming corner of Trastevere, opposite Villa Farnesina and opening onto the flourishing botanical gardens (Orto Botanico—see opposite). It contains part of the Galleria Nazionale d'Arte Antica (the rest is in the Palazzo Barberini, see page 114) in the form of a rich collection of 16th- to 17th-century art, both Italian and international, collected since the 18th century and acquired by the Italian State in 1883. Paintings worthy of note include a triptych by Fra Beato Angelico, a portrait of Philip II of Spain by Titian, the

Madonna della Paglia by Van Dyck, Rubens' St. Sebastian and the splendid St. John the Baptist in the Desert by Caravaggio. Of particular interest is the room of Queen Christina of Sweden, who died in the palace in 1689.

PALAZZO-GALLERIA DORIA PAMPHILJ

See page 115.

PALAZZO MASSIMO ALLE TERME

See pages 116–117.

PALAZZO DEL QUIRINALE

🕂 57 F4 • Piazzale del Quirinale ☎ Segreteria Generale Presidenza della Repubblica, for guided tours: 06 46991 🕙 Sun 8.30–12.30, Sep–Jul 💶 Adult €5, child (under 18) free 🚇 Barberini 🚌 H, 40, 60, 64, 70, 71, 117, 170
www.quirinale.it

This luxurious palace looking out over the city stands on the Quirinale and is the seat of the presidency of the Italian Republic.

The palace became the popes' summer home from 1592 because of the healthier air. Later, it was used by the kings of Italy, who decorated the rooms with expensive tapestries.

The architects Domenico Fontana, Carlo Maderno and Gian Lorenzo Bernini all worked on the palace. It has a cycle of frescoes by Guido Reni in the Chapel of the Annunciation, while the Pauline chapel, similar in size to the Sistine Chapel in the Vatican, is decorated with fine stuccowork by Martino Ferrabosco. The courtyard inside, once the reception area for heads of state, is guarded by very tall guards called Corrazzieri and leads to the magnificent staircase of honour built by Flaminio Ponzio. Across from the palace are the papal stables, recently

restored by the Italian architect Gae Aulenti, where important exhibitions are held. The palace gardens are only open to visitors on the 2 June, the anniversary of the Italian Republic.
Don't miss the spectacular view over the city from the coffee shop.

PALAZZO SPADA

🕂 57 D5 • Piazza Capo di Ferro 13/ Vicolo del Polverone ☎ Call centre and ticket bookings: 06 21810 🕙 Tue–Sun 9–7; Borromini perspective: 9.30–6.30 every hour 💶 Adult €5, child (under 18) free 🚌 63, 116, 630, 780; tram 8 🚻 ♿ 🚻
www.galleriaborghese.it
www.beniculturali.it (for guided tours)

The Spada Gallery houses the private collection of 17th-century paintings that once belonged to the wealthy Cardinal Spada, displayed in the palace he acquired in 1632. The gallery consists of four rooms, all frescoed and decorated with statues and friezes.

The collection includes many fine works of art; to get the best from your visit, use one of the information leaflets available in several languages. Look out, in particular, for Guercino Didone's painting of Death in room 3, with its beautiful background, and the canvases by Artemisia Gentileschi and his father Orazio, in room 4. Also in room 4 is the octagonal painting of The Halt at the Inn by the Flemish painter Pieter van Laer (also known as 'Il Bamboccio'), one of Cardinal Spada's best-loved artists.

The palace's courtyard is most interesting for the Borromini perspective, a corridor only 8m (26ft) long, but appearing about four times longer. The columns are not parallel, but converge towards a focal point, and the floor slopes gently upwards. The statue at the end of the corridor is smaller than it appears.

Palazzo Altemps

**One of Rome's finest Renaissance buildings.
Top-class collection of Classical sculpture.
Bears witness to the key role played by Roman nobility in the
16th- and 17th-century re-appreciation of Classical culture.**

SEEING PALAZZO ALTEMPS

The museum is divided between three floors around a courtyard,
with statuary exhibited in arcades, loggias, courtyards and the
beautifully frescoed rooms. Don't try and see everything, but concentrate on what appeals. The exhibits are stunningly lit, and the
best time for a visit is as dusk falls.

HIGHLIGHTS

COURTYARD, GROUND-FLOOR ARCADES AND LOGGIA

The courtyard is probably the most handsome feature of the building.
A fountain made from seashells, pumice stones and vitreous paste
stands to one side; look for the Altemps coat of arms here showing
lightning striking a bridge. Around the courtyard, the arcades are the
perfect setting for larger-than-life-size statues, while the open space is
overlooked by a loggia, its ceiling decorated with cherubs. The room
behind here has *trompe l'oeil* landscapes and views covering the
walls and columns, while nearby is the Sideboard Room, the scene in
1477 of Girolamo Riario's marriage to Caterina Sforza.

THE LUDOVISI THRONE

One of the most beautiful of all surviving Greek sculptures in Rome,
the so-called Ludovisi Throne was thought for years to have been part
of a 5th-century BC altar. More probably it was the throne for a statue
of the goddess Aphrodite of Eryx, whose ancient cult is associated
with Erice in Sicily. She was the patron goddess of mariners and love,
revered throughout the Mediterranean. The throne portrays the birth
of the goddess from the sea foam; she rises between two nymphs,
her draperies clinging to her body and drops of water falling from her
hair, supremely delicate, the embodiment of all that was finest in the
Greek world. Find it in the Tales of Moses Room on the upper floor.

THE FIREPLACE SALON

The Roman copy of the Greek *Gaul and His Wife Committing Suicide*
has been admired for centuries for its realism and pathos; it was
probably commissioned by Julius Caesar as a memento of his time in
Gaul. If you've seen the *Dying Gaul* in the Musei Capitolini (see page
101), it's easy to see that these two pieces were part of a group,
erected in 197–159BC to celebrate a Greek victory. The room's highlight though, is the action-packed relief on the side of the so-called
Ludovisi Sarcophagus. Carved from a single block of marble, it's full of
life and movement, and shows Roman soldiery giving a thorough
beating to some hapless barbarians.

THE CHURCH OF SANT'ANICETO

Leading off the Fireplace Salon is this highly decorated church, which
was commissioned in 1603 by Giovanni Angelo Altemps to house
the relics of St. Aniceto. Altemps invented a story of Aniceto's martyrdom by beheading, which mirrors his own father's death and is
shown in painted cycles around the church.
Don't miss the mother of pearl-decorated ceiling in the confessio,
behind the altar.

BASICS

✚ 57 D4 • Piazza Sant'Apollinare 44
☎ 06 683 3759
🕐 Tue–Sun 9–7 (exit 7.45)
💶 Adult €5, child (under 18) free
🚌 70, 81, 87, 116, 186, 492, 628, 916
🎧 Audiotours: English, Italian, €4
📖 Available in museum shop: brief
guide €7.75, full catalogue €30.95
🏛 Sells guides and souvenirs 🛍

GALLERY GUIDE

Ground floor: Roman copies of
ancient Greek statues; remains of
ancient Roman buildings (Tower
Room); portraits from the
Ludovisi collection (Portrait
Room); Teatro Goldini (16th-cen-
tury private theatre).
Upper floor: Frescoed rooms
(particularly the Painted Views
Room and the Painted Loggia);
Roman copies of ancient Greek
statues, including the *Ludovisi
Throne* (Tales of Moses Room),
the *Ludovisi Sarcophagus* and
*Gaul and His Wife Committing
Suicide* (both in the Fireplace
Salon) and *Aphrodite bathing*
(Duchess's Room); Church of
Sant'Aniceto; Octagonal Chapel

*The Ludovisi Throne shows the
birth of Venus (above)*

BACKGROUND

This beautifully restored 15th-century palace was closed for many years, before being finally reopened to the public in 1997 as part of the Museo Nazionale Romano. The site of a Roman warehouse, the area of the palazzo became part of a fortification dividing two rival Roman families, the Orsinis and the Colonnas. The building as we know it today dates back to 1477 when Girolamo Riario, a nephew of Pope Sixtus IV, commissioned the palace. It was extended by the Altemps family in 1568; they added the courtyard, designed by Martino Longhi the Elder, with its portico and loggias. Between 1621 and 1623, Cardinal Ludovico Ludovisi, nephew of Pope Gregory XV, assembled his 500-piece collection, still the core of today's museum. Later owner-collectors included Cardinal Marco Sittico Altemps, who bought the palace and made it a suitable setting for his magnificent collection of books and antique sculptures. The Italian State acquired the Palazzo Altemps in 1982, and restored the building to reflect 16th- and 17th-century taste and display methods.

The painted loggia, on the upper floor (top)
Large statues watch over Palazzo Altemps' peaceful courtyard (above)
The Gaul and His Wife Committing Suicide (left)

BASICS

🔲 57 F4 • Via Barberini 18/Via Quattro
Fontane 13 ☎ 06 32810 (guided tour),
fax: 06 3265 1329 ⏰ Gallery: Tue–Sun
9–7. Apartments: Tue–Sun 9.30–1.15,
2.15–6.45 💶 Apartments: adult € 6.03,
child (under 18) € 1.03. Gallery: free
🚇 Barberini 🚌 61, 62, 175, 492, 530
to Piazza Barberini; 52, 53, 63, 80, 95
116, 119, 204, 590, 630 to Via Veneto
📖 *Capolavori Galleria Nazionale Arte
Antica Palazzo Barberini* in Italian and
English € 12.50, available in gallery
bookshop. 🎫 Apartments: guided
tours only, at 9.30 and 6.30 in English
and Italian, max 25 persons, included in
admission ticket. 20 minutes
☕ Beautiful café with panoramic view
of Via Barberini open until 1am 📚 Arts
bookshop, very well stocked.
www.galleriaborghese.it

THE SIGHTS

PALAZZO BARBERINI E GALLERIA NAZIONALE D'ARTE ANTICA

Baroque magnificence and several Renaissance masterpieces are the hallmarks of this section of the state-owned art collection.

This imposing baroque palace bears witness to the importance of the Barberini family, and highlights the innovative genius of three great artists: Gian Lorenzo Bernini, his great rival Francesco Borromini, and the painter Pietro da Cortona. The building was commissioned in 1623 by Pope Urban VIII to provide a prestigious dwelling for his family. Carlo Maderno was the original architect, but Bernini and Borromini completed the work in 1633. The palace is now home to one of the city's principal art galleries.

INSIDE THE PALACE

On entering you see two remarkable staircases: the small, spiral staircase by Borromini on the right and a wide, monumental structure designed by Bernini on the left, and the . Take the Bernini one to reach the gallery. You can also take a tour of the 18th-century private apartments of the Barberini family on the second floor.

GALLERIA NAZIONALE D'ARTE ANTICA

Since 1949, the palace has housed the Galleria Nazionale d'Arte Antica (shared with the Palazzo Corsini, see page 111). The impressive collection of works from the 12th to 18th centuries represents private collections of some of the aristocratic families of Rome. In the small antechamber to the gallery are displayed a marble bust of Urban VIII, carved by Bernini between 1637 and 1638, and a Virgin

TIPS

● While you are here, buy tickets in advance for the Borghese Gallery, which is always very crowded.

The 18th-century paintings in the Sala delle Battaglie in the Barberini apartments recall the battles of the husband of Cornelia Barberini (above)

Mary with Christ, dating back to the second half of the 12th century. Other works to look for include the lovely *Virgin Mary with the Christ Child* by Filippo Lippi, *Narcissus* and *Judith and Holofernes*, both by Caravaggio, and Titian's *Venus and Adonis*. The gallery's best-known painting is Raphael's portrait of *La Fornarina* (The Baker's Daughter), believed to be the artist's mistress, painted in the year of his death.

Pietro da Cortona painted his finest work, *The Triumph of Divine Providence*, on the vault of the Gran Salone between 1633 and 1639. It is a masterpiece of baroque art, admired for its powerful portrayal of light and shade (*chiaroscuro*). The painting exalts the glory of the Barberinis; Divine Providence, holding a sceptre, stands above the clouds.

PALAZZO–GALLERIA DORIA PAMPHILJ

This magnificently decorated palace houses one of Italy's most important private art collections.

Not far from Piazza Venezia stands one of the largest palaces in Rome, Palazzo Doria Pamphilj, whose art collection is among the city's most prestigious. Owned and inhabited by the same family since the 17th century, the palace has remained untouched through the centuries; as you walk round the magnificently decorated and furnished rooms, it is like stepping back in time.

INSIDE THE PALACE

Four galleries contain a collection of 16th- to 18th-century paintings and sculptures initiated by Pope Innocent X Pamphilj in 1651. Gallery 1 contains works by Tintoretto, Titian, Raphael and Paolo Veronese, as well as Caravaggio's famous *Flight into Egypt*. This painting caused outrage in its day, since the model used for the figure of the Virgin Mary was the one Caravaggio employed for his *Mary Magdalen*, displayed in the same gallery.

Gallery 2 is dedicated to Flemish artists, with paintings by artists such as Peter Paul Rubens and Pieter Brueghel. A painting by Quentin Massys is a caricature of moneylenders, still relevant today. Also noteworthy are paintings by the Maestro della Candela (Master of the Candle), so called because he painted faces under the light of a candle. Gallery 3 is decorated with 18th-century mirrors and gilding. It contains a portrait of Innocent X—a masterpiece by the Spanish painter Diego Velazquez—and a bust of the same pope sculpted by Bernini for the Holy Year of 1650.

Gallery 4 includes two semicircular works by Annibale Carracci, part of a series of paintings for the palace chapel.

THE PRIVATE APARTMENTS

The private apartments were inhabited by the owners of the palace from the 16th to the 18th century and are now open to the public. They include the Andrea Doria Room, in memory of the great 16th-century admiral. Brussels tapestries depicting the Battle of Lepanto (a Christian victory against the Turks in 1571) decorate the walls. The Dining Room's frieze shows the various properties of the Doria Pamphilj family in the 19th century.

In the ballroom is a 17th-century harp with a double row of strings producing a unique, gentle sound.

RATINGS	
Cultural interest	● ●
Good for kids	●
Value for money	● ● ● ●

BASICS

✚ 57 E5 • Piazza del Collegio Romano 2 ☎ 06 679 7323. Information 06 7707 2842 ◉ Daily 10–5 🎫 €8, child (under 18) €5.70 🚌 30, 40, 46, 62, 63, 70, 81, 87, 116, 117, 119, 186, 204, 492, 628, 810, 916 ☛ To book guided tour, ring 06 679 7323. Audiotours: Italian, English, French, included in price, 2 hours. Concerts can be booked 10 days in advance, Fri–Wed 10–4, and from 7.30 on concert days 📖 Free guide, *Breve Guida della Galleria Doria Pamphilj*, available in several languages ☕ Tea room 🚻 www.doriapamphilj.it

TIPS

● Take the audioguide, which is included in the price and helps you make sense of what you're seeing.

● The paintings are not well lit so it is better to visit during daylight hours.

The sumptuous interior of the Palazzo-Galleria Doria Pamphilj (above)

Palazzo Massimo
alle Terme

Superb national collection of Greek and Roman sculpture.
Outstanding and unique displays of ancient Roman wall paintings and mosaics.

SEEING PALAZZO MASSIMO ALLE TERME

This beautifully restored and well-organized museum is part of the Museo Nazionale Romano. The palace has four floors of museum space, a modern library, a conference room and a computer-based documentation area. The Classical art collection is placed on the first three floors, and includes works of art from the end of the Republican Age (second–first century BC) to the late Imperial Age (fourth century AD), with some original Greek works from the fifth century BC.

HIGHLIGHTS

GROUND FLOOR
Niobid from the Hortus Sallustiani (Room VII)
This superb Greek statue dates from 440BC, and was found on the site of gardens once belonging to Julius Caesar; it was almost certainly once his property. The statue portrays one of Niobe's daughters falling as she tries to remove an arrow embedded in her back—she and her siblings were killed by the gods Apollo and Artemis. The piece probably came from a group decorating the pediment of a Greek temple, later collected by Caesar.

FIRST FLOOR
The Lancellotti Discobolus (Room VI)
One of the most famous copies of the great fifth century BC works, this statue, discovered in the 18th century, was sent to Germany during World War II and returned in 1948. It reproduces an original bronze, showing an athlete throwing a discus, that was probably the work of Myron, a Greek sculptor renowned for his athletic portraits. This very fine marble copy dates from the mid-second century AD.

The Sleeping Hermaphrodite (Room VII)
Dionysian cult statues were popular with both Greeks and Romans—with the Greeks for their religious symbolism, the Romans for their refined sensuality. This lovely example is a second-century AD copy of a second-century BC Hellenistic original. Endowed with the attributes of both sexes, the figure reclines languidly on drapery, the slick polished finish adding to its eroticism.

SECOND FLOOR
The House of Livia (Room II)
Crammed with realistic details, these lovely decorative wall paintings come from a villa belonging to Livia Drusilla, wife of the Emperor Augustus. The panels, moved from the excavations in 1951, decorated the walls of a summer triclinium, a large and airy outside living room, set partially below ground. Look out for the different tree species, flowers, fruit and birds, as fresh now as when they were painted between 20 and 10BC.

BASICS

✚ 58 G4 • Largo di Villa Peretti 1
☎ 06 481 5576. Information 06 3996 7700
🕐 Tue–Sun 9–7.45
💷 Adult €6, child (under 18) free. For joint tickets see page 287
🚇 Repubblica or Termini
🚌 40, 64, 84, 86, 90, 170, 175, 492, 910 to Piazza della Repubblica; 14, 36, 38, 64, 86, 90, 92, 105, 217, 310, 714 or tram 5 to Piazza dei Cinquecento or Termini station
🎧 Sat–Sun 10.30, 3.30 in Italian only €3.50. Audiotours: Italian, English €4
📖 Available from museum shop: brief guide €7.75, full catalogue €38.75
🏪 Very modern and well-stocked bookshop open 9–7
🚻

For online reservations www.pierreci.it

Fresco from Villa Farnesina, in Trastevere (above)
Lancellotti Discobulus (right)

The 19th-century Palazzo Massimo was a Jesuit college until 1960; it has now been lovingly restored (above) This mosaic from Villa Maccarani shows a hippopotamus hunt by the Nile (left)

GALLERY GUIDE

The galleries are arranged thematically.

Basement Coins and jewellery.

Ground floor Power in Republican and early Imperial times. Portrait busts, full statues, mosaics, urns and basins.

First floor Development of different iconographic trends, and copies and reworkings of Hellenistic statuary. Portrait heads, sculpture, bronzes.

Second floor Wall paintings, paintings, frescoes, mosaics and stuccoes of exceptional importance and quality.

The Villa Farnesina (Gallery II, Rooms III–V)

This complete set of frescoes was discovered in 1879 near the Renaissance Villa Farnesina; they can be dated to around 20BC and may have been done to celebrate the wedding of Augustus' daughter Julia. The frescoes are immensely varied, embracing themes such as landscapes, architecture and Egyptian motifs. There are scenes portraying myths, battles and garlands of flowers and leaves: a superb example of the lavishness of upper-class Roman interior decoration.

BACKGROUND

The Palazzo Massimo, designed by Camillo Pistrucci, was built in the late 19th century by the Massimo family to replace an earlier one demolished to make way for the Termini station. In 1981 the palace was acquired by the State, and in the 1990s it was transformed into one of Rome's most attractive museums.

The monument to King Vittorio Emanuele II, Piazza Venezia

The Campidoglio (above)
Fontana delle Api (left)

THE SIGHTS

PALAZZO VENEZIA

57 E5 • Via del Plebiscito 118 ☎ 06 6999 4319 Tue–Sun 8.30–7.30
Adult €4, child (under 18) free
Colosseo 44, 46, 84, 715, 716, 780, 781, 810, 916

The imposing palace dominating Piazza Venezia (see opposite) was one of the first major civil buildings to be erected in Rome during the Renaissance. Today, it houses the Museo del Palazzo Venezia, with collections of paintings and *objets d'art*. Try to time your visit to coincide with one of the temporary art exhibitions the palace hosts.

The Venetian Pietro Barbo started building the palace in 1455 when he became a cardinal, and it was enlarged when he was elected Pope Paul II in 1464. The palace acquired its present name in 1564, when Pope Pius IV gave it to the Republic of Venice as a diplomatic residence. The popes continued to live in a wing of the palace until the 16th century. In the 19th century Napoleon made it the seat of the French administration, and between 1930 and 1944 Mussolini established his government here and used the first floor of the palace for his office.

The permanent museum displays ivory, silver and gold items, 16th- and 17th-century bronze statues, religious works of art, Renaissance models in plaster and terracotta, oriental pottery and 15th-century tapestries.

PANTHEON

See pages 120–121.

PIAZZA BARBERINI

57 F4 Barberini 61, 62, 175, 492, 630 to Piazza Barberini; 52, 53, 63, 80, 95 116, 119, 204, 590 to Via Veneto

This beautiful piazza, named after the powerful Barberini family, showcases the work of the

architect/artist, Gian Lorenzo Bernini, who worked on the family's residential palace (see page 114) and designed the two fountains on the square.

In the heart of the square is the Fontana del Tritone, commissioned in 1643 by Pope Urban VIII: Four dolphins, tails in the air, support a huge scallop shell on which sits a triton blowing a jet of water through a conch. Look for the Barberini coat of arms (the bees) and the papal arms (St. Peter's keys and the papal tiara).

On the corner of Via Veneto is the other Bernini fountain, the Fontana delle Api. The Fountain of the Bees was commissioned to celebrate the 21st anniversary in August 1644 of Urban VIII's accession to the papacy. The fact that Bernini finished it before the actual date was considered a bad omen, borne out when the Pope died eight days before the anniversary. In 1865, the fountain was dismantled and removed from its original site, at the corner with Via Sistina. It was reassembled in its present position in 1916; the only surviving original pieces are the central part of a shell and three bees drinking the water.

PIAZZA DEL CAMPIDOGLIO

57 E5 Colosseo 44, 46, 84, 715, 716, 780, 781, 810, 916
www.museicapitolini.org
www.comune.roma.it

The Piazza del Campidoglio is one of the most spectacular places in Rome, unmissable for the superb view of the Roman Forum and for Michelangelo's wonderful architecture.

Michelangelo designed the square to look out over the city of Rome like an open terrace, and placed on it three magnificent buildings, the Palazzo

Senatorio, Palazzo dei Conservatori and Palazzo Nuovo (Musei Capitolini—see pages 98–103). Much of the work on the palaces was in fact carried out after his death by other architects. He also designed the Cordonata, a monumental ramp leading up to the square. At the top, on either side, are Roman statues of Castor and Pollux, the twin sons of Jupiter by Leda, standing beside their horses. In the middle of the piazza's beautiful, geometric-patterned paving is a modern copy of the equestrian statue of Marcus Aurelius—the original is in the Palazzo Nuovo (see page 100).

Near the steps leading to the Palazzo Senatorio (Rome's city hall) is a fountain flanked by two enormous bearded statues representing the Nile, represented by a sphinx, and—on the right—the Tiber, with the figures of Romulus and Remus and the she-wolf.

The Palazzo Caffarelli on the far right of the Cordonata now hosts temporary exhibitions.

PIAZZA CAMPO DEI FIORI

See pages 122–123.

PIAZZA FARNESE

57 D5 23, 40, 46, 62, 64, 116, 280, 916; tram 8

Just a stone's throw from Piazza Campo dei Fiori, at the historical heart of the Regola quarter, Piazza Farnese is like an elegant open-air drawing room, furnished by the majestic Renaissance Palazzo Farnese (now the French Embassy) and twin fountains to each side. The lily, emblem of the Farnese family and symbol of France, is the dominant theme in the square, visible on the palace façade and on the fountains. The Palazzo Farnese is the highlight of this lovely square, but

Relaxing in the Piazza
Farnese

One of Valadier's water-spitting lions in
Piazza del Popolo

Fontana delle Naiadi in Piazza
della Repubblica

unfortunately can only be visited by appointment or with a private tour. However, it is pleasant to relax and admire the splendid exterior from one of the many outdoor cafés in the square. Look up at the large central window and you may get a glimpse of frescoed walls inside.

PIAZZA NAVONA

See pages 124–125.

PIAZZA DEL POPOLO

✚ 57 E3 🚇 Flaminio 🚌 95, 117, 119, 491, 495, 590, 628, 926; tram 2

When approaching the square from Via del Corso, pause for a moment to admire it from a distance. Its charm lies in the complete harmony of all the distinct architectural styles within it.

Each end of the oval piazza is adorned with a fountain, with sphinxes and statues depicting the four seasons. At the end of the 16th century, Pope Sixtus V erected an Egyptian obelisk of the Pharaoh Rameses II in the middle of the square, and in 1823, Giuseppe Valadier added the rounded basins and four water-spitting marble lions to the base of the obelisk.

The 17th-century twin churches of Santa Maria dei Miracoli and Santa Maria di Monte Santo stand on either side of Via del Corso. Both churches were started by Carlo Rainaldi and completed by Carlo Fontana (work on Santa Maria di Monte Santo was supervised by Bernini). Inside Santa Maria di Monte Santo are frescoes by Baciccia and a 15th-century painting of the Virgin Mary on the high altar.

On the north side of the square is the grand entrance to the square, Porta del Popolo, erected in 1561. It was reworked by Bernini in 1655 to mark the entry to Rome of Queen

Christina of Sweden after her conversion to Roman Catholicism. The adjoining church of Santa Maria del Popolo contains exceptional works of art by Caravaggio, Raphael, Bernini and Pinturicchio, among others.

PIAZZA DELLA REPUBBLICA

✚ 58 G4 🚇 Repubblica 🚌 H, 40, 64, 84, 86, 90, 170, 175, 492, 910

Piazza della Repubblica, one of Rome's busiest spots, has a theatrical fountain at its heart and two semicircular porticoed buildings at the sides. The huge but rather unappealing church of Santa Maria degli Angeli is the dominant building.

The square was created in the late 19th century to follow the curved line of the *exedra* (a recess with raised seating) of the nearby Terme di Diocleziano (see page 143), hence its popular name—Piazza Esedra.

The large central fountain, the Fontana delle Naiadi (1901), gets its name from the four water nymphs that decorate it, the work of Sicilian artist Mario Rutelli. The naked naiads and the allegorical marine animals with which they are entwined represent water in various forms: rivers, lakes, oceans and underground streams. The city authorities thought the figures too erotic when they were first revealed, and ordered a fence (later removed) to be built to hide them from sight. The original central decoration of the fountain, three tritons, a dolphin and an octopus, was

nicknamed the fish fry, and was moved to the gardens of Piazza Vittorio Emanuele. The present central figure is the minor god Glaucus in combat with a fish.

PIAZZA DI SPAGNA

See pages 126–127.

PIAZZA VENEZIA

✚ 57 E5 🚇 Colosseo 🚌 44, 46, 84, 715, 780, 781, 810, 916

This busy traffic junction owes its name to the Palazzo Venezia (see opposite). Next to it, in fact incorporated in the palace complex, is the church of San Marco (see page 133). With origins in the fourth century, this venerable basilica has been much altered and rebuilt over the centuries. It is worth a visit for a wonderful ninth-century mosaic in the apse. Between the palace and the church, look for *Madama Lucrezia*, one of the six 'talking statues'.

Dominating the square, however, is the white theatrical Monumento a Vittorio Emanuele II, the first king of unified Italy. Built between 1885 and 1911, 'Il Vittoriano' changed the appearance of what had been the medieval and Renaissance quarter where Michelangelo lived until his death. A convent on the Capitol Hill and a wing of the Palazzo Venezia were among the structures that had to be demolished to make way for the vast, dazzlingly white monument. Climb to the top for superb views across the city. Since 1921 it has housed the Monument to the Unknown Soldier.

Pantheon

One of the best-preserved ancient Roman buildings anywhere.
A dome that is a magnificent feat of Roman engineering.
Last resting place of the artist Raphael.

SEEING THE PANTHEON

From Piazza della Rotonda, a single door in the portico leads into this historically and architecturally interesting building, which has been a place of worship for over 2,000 years. If possible, visit the Pantheon during a downpour: The sight of the rain entering the building through the oculus is fascinating.

THE BUILDING

The portico is 14m (46ft) high and consists of 16 Egyptian granite columns with Corinthian capitals. The church is paved with marble and granite, and at one time the ceiling was entirely covered in bronze. When Pope Urban VIII restored the roof in the 17th century, the precious material was removed and used for the altar of St. Peter's and other works. The bronze doors are probably original. Around the interior are seven niches where statues of divinities once stood, with the statue of Jove Ultor, the Avenger, at the middle.

THE DOME

The dome, spanning 43.3m (142ft), is the largest ever built before the introduction of reinforced concrete in the 20th century; its diameter is greater than that of the dome of St. Peter's. As seen from outside, it is actually a cheat—a thick skin of brickwork over the smaller structure of the actual cupola inside. This consists of concrete, cast over a temporary framework, the material being thinner and lighter at the base of the dome than at its apex. The cupola represents the sky, while the great central unglazed opening, the oculus, stands for the sun; the oculus is the only source of natural light for the building.

THE TOMBS

Today, the Pantheon acts as the mausoleum of the royalty of Italy, accommodating the tombs of Vittorio Emanuele II, Humbert I and Queen Margherita of Savoy, and of a few notable Italians. In the first chapel on the right, next to the tomb of Vittorio Emanuele II, is a fresco of the Annunciation by Melozzo da Forlì. The third chapel contains the funerary monument by the Norwegian sculptor Thorvaldsen of Cardinal Consalvi (died 1824), and the third niche on the left holds the remains of Raphael (died 1520). Also in the chapel are a sculpture of the Madonna by Raphael's pupil Lorenzetto and an epitaph to Maria Bibbiena, Raphael's betrothed, who died three months before the artist. The tombs of King Humbert I and Queen Margherita of Savoy are beyond, followed by the tomb of the painter and architect Baldassare Peruzzi (1481–1536).

PIAZZA DELLA ROTONDA

The Pantheon faces Piazza della Rotonda, which resembles in shape the arcade thought to have surrounded the ancient Roman temple. The central fountain was designed by Giacomo della Porta in 1575. Pope Clement XI erected a 13th-century BC Egyptian obelisk dedicated to Rameses II at the centre of the basin in 1711. The granite monolith, 6.43m (21ft) tall, stood in the temple dedicated to Isis and Serapis in the nearby area of Campo Marzio before it was moved here.

RATINGS

Good for kids	●●
Historic interest	●●●
Photo stops	●●●●
Value for money	●●●●●

BASICS

✚ 57 E5 • Piazza della Rotonda
☎ 06 6830 0230
🕐 Mon–Sat 8.30–7.30, Sun 9–6.30, holidays 9–1. Closed to visitors during Mass on Sun at 10.30
💶 Free
🚌 116 to Via dei Palombella; 30, 40, 46, 62, 63, 64, 70, 81, 787, 492, 628, 630, 780, 916 or tram 8 to Largo di Torre Argentina
❓ There is an information/security point inside the building with basic information.
📖 Guidebooks to the Pantheon in several languages are available in souvenir shops on Piazza della Rotonda

Giacomo della Porta's fountain in Piazza della Rotonda (above)

BACKGROUND

The original Pantheon was built in 27BC by Augustus' general and son-in-law, Marcus Agrippa, whose name can still clearly be seen on the inscription on the façade: *'M Agrippa L.F. Cos Tertium fecit'* ('Marcus Agrippa, son of Lucius, built this during his third consulate'). Built in the style of a traditional Greek pagan temple, and dedicated to all the gods, Agrippa's building was entirely destroyed in the great fire of AD80. In the early second century Emperor Hadrian rebuilt it as we see it today, reusing the original inscription. In the sixth century, the Byzantine Emperor Phocas gave the Pantheon to Pope Boniface IV, who transformed it into a Christian church, dedicating it to St. Mary of the Martyrs. To consecrate the church, the Pope is said to have brought 28 cartloads of bones of martyrs from the Roman catacombs and buried them underneath the altar. Legend has it that during the ceremony, as the notes of the Gloria were sung, devils and malign spirits rose up and flew out of the hole in the dome.

TIPS

● The Pantheon is often very crowded, especially at the weekend. To make the most of a visit, go on a weekday or early in the morning.

● Relax in one of Piazza della Rotonda's cafés to enjoy the exterior view of the Pantheon and the atmosphere of the lively piazza.

The sun pours through the opening in the Pantheon's roof, but this church is equally as impressive in the rain (above)

Piazza Campo dei Fiori

**One of Rome's most picturesque and atmospheric squares.
The heart of a lively area.
Scene of Rome's most popular food and flower market.
A great place for people-watching.**

The Campo dei Fiori is home to one of Rome's most atmospheric markets, where the daily trade in fruit, vegetables and flowers still continues

RATINGS	
Photo stops	●●●○
Shopping	●●●●○
Value for money	●●●●○
Walkability	●●●●○

BASICS

✚ 57 D5
🚌 23, 40, 46, 62, 64, 116, 280, 870, 916; tram 8
🍴 Streetside cafés in the square
📖 Souvenir shops in the square sell guidebooks

SEEING PIAZZA CAMPO DEI FIORI

For a slice of real Roman life, head for the Campo dei Fiori during the morning market, when the stalls are in full swing and the surrounding shops busy with people. Around lunchtime, it's a good place to pause for a snack or meal, while evenings see the piazza crowded with locals and visitors relaxing.

HIGHLIGHTS

STATUE OF GIORDANO BRUNO

This statue was erected in 1887 to replace a fountain, the Campo's original focal point. It shows the philosopher Giordano Bruno, who advocated the separation of political and religious power. In 1600, he was condemned for heresy and burned alive by the Inquisition on this very spot, the first of a series of executions here during the 17th century. Ettore Ferrari was the sculptor, and the statue soon became a meeting point for intellectuals and anti-establishment thinkers.

PALAZZO RIGHETTI AND PALAZZO DELLA CANCELLERIA

The Pio Righetti palace, at the east end of the square, was built on the site of an old palazzo, over the remains of the Theatre of Pompey. It was bought in the 18th century by the banker Righetti, from whom it takes its name. If you want to see traces of the Theatre of Pompey, on whose steps Caesar was assassinated, ask at the restaurant San Pancrazio on the east corner of the square, where there are remains of it in the cellar—you don't have to eat there to have a look. The late 15th-century Palazzo della Cancelleria is attributed to Bramante, though the interior courtyard is his sole contribution.

THE SURROUNDING STREETS

The Campo is part of the Regola district, traditionally famous for its craftsmen. Many nearby streets owe their names to the artisan work-shops that once stood there: Via dei Giubbonari (jacket-makers) and Via dei Cappellari (hat-makers). These streets are still crammed with tiny shops, great trawling ground for local goods. In Via del Pellegrino, look for a charming old interior courtyard—it's through a gate just round the corner of the west side of the square. Via di Monserrato, father on, is home to the English College, where young British men train for the priesthood.

BACKGROUND

In ancient times the square was used as grazing land for cattle, hence the name Campo dei Fiori, Field of Flowers. In those days, buildings stood on one side of the square only, with a spacious view over the Tiber on the other. By the 12th century the Palazzo Orsini, where the Palazzo Righetti now stands, dominated the scene, and the Campo became the heart of an exclusive residential and business district. It was also an important crossing point, as papal processions and pilgrims on their way to Rome's basilicas had to pass through Via del Pellegrino. Once it had been used for executions it lost its cachet, and became the heart of one of Rome's most vibrant working-class areas.

Piazza Navona

•

A superb baroque city space.
One of Rome's most popular meeting places.
The setting of three magnificent fountains.

SEEING PIAZZA NAVONA

Visitors to Rome are drawn time and again to this beautiful piazza, so plan several visits to appreciate the square at different times of day. You could spend your first visit sightseeing, but be sure to return to relax, sit at a café table, take in the street performers and local worthies, or eat one of Rome's best ice-creams, the wicked chocolate *tartufo* at I Tre Scalini.

HIGHLIGHTS

THE PIAZZA

Harmonious, regularly shaped Piazza Navona is one of the most remarkable examples of town planning in Rome. Notable buildings include the Palazzo Braschi, renovated by Antonio da Sangallo in 1793 and now hosting exhibitions, and the elegant Palazzo Pamphilj, the largest building in the piazza. Built between 1644 and 1650 by Girolamo Rainaldi and Francesco Borromini, the palace is now home to the Brazilian Embassy.

RATINGS		
Good for kids	● ● ●	
Historic interest	● ●	
Shopping	● ● ●	
Walkability	● ● ● ● ●	

BASICS
✚ 57 D5
☎ Church of Sant'Agnese in Agone: 06 329 2326/06 6819 2134. Domitian's Stadium: 06 6710 3819 for guided tours
◷ Church of Sant'Agnese in Agone: Tue–Sat 9–12, 4–7, Sun 10–1, 4–7. Domitian's Stadium: Mon–Fri 9–1, 2–5
🚌 23, 30, 62, 64, 70, 81, 87, 116, 280, 492, 628, 810, 916

Fontana del Moro (above)
The piazza is a popular place to meet for a chat (below)

FONTANA DEI FIUMI

You'll be drawn at once to the famous Fountain of the Four Rivers, designed by Gian Lorenzo Bernini in 1651, which gained him the admiration and protection of Pope Innocent X. The fountain shows the main rivers of the four then known continents: the Danube in Europe, the Ganges in Asia, the Nile in Africa and the Rio de la Plata in the New World. An obelisk (from the Circus of Maxentius) rears boldly into the air surrounded by animals. Legend has it that the fountain symbolizes the rivalry between Bernini and Borromini. Innocent X asked Borromini to do the work, but Bernini obtained the commission by flattering the Pope's sister. According to popular belief, Borromini built the church of Sant'Agnese in Agone in front of Bernini's fountain out of revenge, and the statue of the Nile seems to cover its face to shield its eyes from Borromini's work. Sadly, this is purely apocryphal, since the fountain pre-dates the church—the Nile's face is covered because its source was as yet unknown.

SANT'AGNESE IN AGONE

The church of Sant'Agnese in Agone stands where, according to tradition, 12-year-old Agnes was martyred by the Emperor Diocletian. Exposed naked, the saint was miraculously covered by the prodigious growth of her own hair. Pope Innocent X commissioned the church in 1652 and Borromini took control of the project, radically changing the design of the façade and building the twin bell towers.

THE FONTANA DEL MORO AND THE FONTANA DEL NETTUNO

The Fontana del Moro at the southern end of the piazza was commissioned by Pope Gregory XIII and designed by Giacomo della Porta in 1576, with sculptures of tritons, dragons and dolphins. Bernini altered the fountain in the mid-17th century, adding the central figure of the Moor, apparently wrestling with a dolphin. At the northern end of the piazza, the 19th-century Fontana del Nettuno shows Neptune flanked by nymphs as he battles with a sea monster.

DOMITIAN'S STADIUM

To see the remains of Domitian's stadium, you can visit the building at No. 49 at the northern end of the square. A maximum of five people are allowed in at any one time, but it is well worth a visit.

Fontana del Nettuno (above) The elongated piazza follows the shape of Domitian's stadium (inset)

BACKGROUND

The piazza was laid out in the mid-17th century on the ruins of Domitian's stadium (AD86). The stadium was originally called the Circus Agonalis (*Agones* means games in ancient Greek), but in the Middle Ages it became known as Campus Agonis, which was in turn corrupted by Roman dialect to become *n'agnona* and eventually Navona. The arena was used for festivals and sporting events, even jousting until the late 15th century, when it was paved over and transformed into a marketplace and public square.

Piazza di Spagna

**One of Rome's focal piazzas for both locals and visitors.
Site of the city's most beautiful stairway, the Spanish Steps,
and the French church, Trinità dei Monti.
Historic Anglo-Saxon links.**

SEEING PIAZZA DI SPAGNA

Start your explorations in the Piazza di Spagna itself, pausing on the far side of the fountain to take in the full sweep of the magnificent Scalinata della Trinità dei Monti (Spanish Steps). Walk all round the piazza, with its shops and buildings, before tackling the steps, pausing en route. At the top, scale the staircase leading to the church, from where there's a superb view over Rome, with the cupola of St. Peter's in the distance—wonderful at sunset.

HIGHLIGHTS

THE PIAZZA

More butterfly-shaped than square, the Piazza di Spagna contains one of Rome's most unusual fountains, the boat-shaped Fontana della Barcaccia, commissioned by Pope Urban VIII to commemorate the great flood of 1598. It was designed by father and son Bernini to represent a boat that was stranded in the piazza during the flood, and was finished in 1629. Pietro Bernini exploited the low water pressure of the Aqua Virgo at this point to achieve the 'sinking' effect.

At the piazza's southern end is a Roman column topped by a statue of the Virgin Mary, erected in 1856 to commemorate the establishment of the doctrine of the Immaculate Conception. On 8 December a procession, led by the Pope, terminates here to crown the statue with wreaths.

SCALINATA DELLA TRINITÀ DEI MONTI

The supremely elegant Spanish Steps were designed by Francesco de Sanctis and built between 1723 and 1726. Prior to this, the church was separated from the piazza by a wood, a popular hideout for criminals. There are three flights of shallow steps, 138 in all, of various widths and configurations, along with benches from which you can enjoy the increasingly lovely views. The final flight of two symmetrical staircases brings you to the Piazza della Trinità dei Monti.

THE CHURCH OF TRINITÀ DEI MONTI

King Charles VIII of France commissioned this church in 1495 on the request of St. Francis of Paola, who lived in the nearby convent. It was consecrated by Pope Sixtus V in 1585 and restored in 1816 by Louis XVIII after it was looted by Napoleon. The church of Trinità dei Monti is still owned by the French.

BACKGROUND

The Piazza di Spagna gained its name when the Spanish ambassador took up residence here, but the section towards Via del Babuino—to the left as you look up at the Trinità dei Monti—used to be called Piazza di Francia, since the French claimed the right to pass through the square to reach their church. This resulted in fierce rivalry between the two nations. You can see another sign

BASICS

➕ 57 E3
Ⓜ Spagna
🚌 116, 117, 119, 590
📖 Available from souvenir shops on the square
🍴 Plenty in the area

The Fontana della Barcaccia is designed to look like a sinking boat (above)
Today, the steps are a popular meeting place (opposite)

of diplomatic strife on the steps, this time between the French and the Italians, in the confrontation of Conti eagles (from the coat of arms of Pope Innocent XIII) and the fleur-de-lys of France. During the 18th and 19th centuries, so many English visitors came to Rome and stayed in the numerous hotels and lodging houses scattered around piazza that it eventually came to be known as the English ghetto. Poet John Keats was just one of the illustrious visitors to stay near here. He died in the Little Red House at the foot of the Spanish Steps on the right, now the Museo Keats-Shelley (see page 110). Babington's English Tea Rooms, on the left-hand corner of the steps, founded in 1893 by the Misses Babington, is another sign of the square's 19th-century popularity with the English. Today, it is one of the most sophisticated, refined and expensive tearooms in Rome.

A modern-day use of the Spanish Steps is as a backdrop and stage for the annual fashion show, Donne sotto le Stelle (Women in Starlight), when international fashion designers present their latest creations, and glitzy models parade up and down this unique catwalk.

THE SIGHTS

The Madonna del Parto *in the church of Sant'Agostino*

The peaceful little cloister of San Carlo alle Quattro Fontane

Santa Cecilia in Trastevere, with di Cambio's Gothic altar canopy

THE SIGHTS

SANT'AGOSTINO

➕ 57 E4 • Piazza di Sant'Agostino
☎ 06 6880 1962 ⏰ 7.45–noon, 4–7.30 🎟 Free 🚌 116 to Via Zanardelli, 30, 40, 46, 62, 63, 64, 70, 81, 492, 628, 630, 780, 787, 916 or tram 8 to Largo Torre Argentina

One of the first Renaissance churches to be built in Rome, the church of Sant'Agostino still maintains its Latin-cross plan with apse, chapels and dome. Even if 19th-century additions have spoilt the church's elegance, it is still worth visiting to see the works by Caravaggio, Raphael and other fine artists.

The church was dedicated to St. Augustine of Hippo in the late 15th century and enlarged later in the same century thanks to the generosity of Cardinal d'Estouteville, Archbishop of Rouen in France.

To the left of the central portal near the main door is the *Madonna del Parto* (Madonna of Childbirth) by Jacopo Sansovino, a statue much revered by expectant mothers and childless couples. A fresco of the Prophet Isaiah by Raphael adorns the third pillar of the nave on the left, and below it is the sculpture *St. Anne and the Virgin Mary with the Christ Child* by Andrea Sansovino. The first chapel on the left contains Caravaggio's magnificent *Madonna di Loreto*.

SANT'ANDREA AL QUIRINALE

➕ 58 F4 • Via del Quirinale 29
☎ 06 4890 3187 ⏰ Wed–Mon 8–noon, 4–7; closed Sun morning
🎟 Free 🚌 Barberini 🚌 H, 40, 60, 64, 70, 117, 170

Often called the baroque pearl, this church is one of Gian Lorenzo Bernini's best works, and was closest to his own heart. It was here that he asked to be taken towards the end of his life

to admire the effect of the light streaming through the windows, illuminating the rich and beautiful marble, gold and stucco he had used to embellish it.

The design is very unusual. The façade is on the shorter side of the building and is highlighted by elegant steps and a portico. Inside is an elliptical central hall with eight deep rectangular chapels off it, each one lit by a window over the altar. The dome above the altar is richly decorated with gilded stuccowork, marble and stucco angels and cherubs. The sacristy has a beautiful frescoed vault. In the adjacent convent are the rooms of St. Stanislaus, where the 17-year-old Jesuit novice died in 1568; the statue of the saint, is by the 17th-century French sculptor Pierre Legros. Ask in the sacristy for access to these rooms.

SAN CARLO ALLE QUATTRO FONTANE

➕ 58 F4 • Via del Quirinale ☎ 06 488 3261 ⏰ Daily 10–1, 3–6 🎟 Free
🚌 Barberini 🚌 H, 40, 60, 64, 70, 116, 117, 119, 170
www.sancarlino-borromini.it

This minuscule church, also known as San Carlino, is famously smaller than a single one of the piers supporting the dome of St. Peter's.

Designed in 1638, the church was the great Francesco Borromini's first work; it was also his last, as the new façade he began in 1665 was still unfinished when he committed suicide two years later. San Carlino's architecture reflects the tormented and contradictory state of mind of this artist: Every curve has its counter-curve, and concave and convex sections form complicated patterns. A statue of the Counter-Reformation saint, St. Charles Borromeo, is the main focus of the curved façade.

The interior is extremely simple, an oval shape with stuccoed niches. The intricately designed coffered dome adds to the elegant effect the artist managed to create in such a small space.

Borromini's cloister, with two rows of Doric columns and slightly convex corners, is beautifully proportioned.

Outside are four fountains *(quattro fontane)*, one on each corner of the street. They are the work of Domenico Fontana, and date from 1589.

SANTA CECILIA IN TRASTEVERE

➕ 57 E6 • Piazza di Santa Cecilia 22
☎ 06 5899289 ⏰ Daily 9.30–12.30, 5–6.30. Cavallini fresco: Tue, Thu 10–12, Sun 11–12 🎟 Free 🚌 23, 44, 280, 780, tram 8 🎧 Audioguide in Italian, German, Spanish, French, English €1

You enter the church of Santa Cecilia through a delightful courtyard, with a portico supported by old granite columns and a lily garden with a fountain in the centre. Next, you pass an exquisite façade designed by Ferdinando Fuga in 1741.

According to legend, Cecilia, her fiancé Valeriano and his brother were persecuted and killed in AD303 because of their Christian faith. In the fifth century, a church was built over Cecilia's house, and 400 years later Pope Paschal I built a basilica on the site. In the 12th century, a Romanesque campanile and a portico were added.

A remarkable statue of St. Cecilia by Stefano Maderno is under the high altar. The sculptor was present at the opening of the saint's tomb in 1599 and made sketches of her uncorrupted body.

Splendid ninth-century apse mosaics depicting Jesus with saints Paul, Agata, Peter, Paschal, Valeriano and Cecilia are among

Bernini's best-loved church, Sant'Andrea al Quirinale

The beautiful courtyard of Santi Cosma e Damiano

The baroque façade of Santa Croce in Gerusalemme

Santa Cecilia's treasures. Another is the beautiful fresco *Last Judgement* (1293) by Pietro Cavallini, the remains of a medieval masterpiece that once covered the walls of the central nave but was mostly lost in an 18th-century restoration of the church. The fresco was moved to the nun's choir of the adjoining convent where it can be viewed.

SAN CLEMENTE

See pages 130–131.

SANTI COSMA E DAMIANO

✚ 57 F6 • Via dei Fori Imperiali 1 ☎ 06 699 1540 🕐 8–1, 3–6. Nativity: Tue–Sun 9.30–12.30, 3–6 💰 Church: free. Nativity: €1 🚇 Colosseo 🚌 60, 75, 81, 175, 673 to Via di San Gregorio, 84, 85, 87, 60, 117, 175, 810, 850 to Via Fori Imperiali 📻 Audioguide €1 in Italian, French, English, German, Spanish

The origins of this church are rather unusual. It was formed by combining the library of Vespasian's Temple of Peace (see page 83) and part of the Temple of Romulus in the Roman Forum, the remains of which are still visible inside. The church, the first to reuse a building in the Forum, was consecrated in AD526 by Pope Felix IV and dedicated to twin brothers, miraculous healers from Cilicia (southern Turkey).

The church took on its present form in the 17th century, under Pope Urban VIII Barberini. The original Roman church was hidden underground in a sort of crypt, and the present façade of the church and the cloister were erected. The 17th-century coffered ceiling is ornamented with paintings depicting the triumph of the saintly brothers, and with the Barberini coat of arms.

The sixth-century mosaics in the apse, the church's principal treasure, were highly influential. They portray Christ against a sunset background with the apostles Peter and Paul and the saints Cosma and Damiano. The church also houses a remarkable 18th-century Neapolitan *presepio* (nativity scene).

SAN CRISOGONO

✚ 57 D6 • Viale Trastevere ☎ 06 581 8225 🕐 Mon–Sat 7–11.30, 4.30–7.30, Sun 8–1.15, 4.30–7.30 💰 Church: free. Early Christian basement: €2 🚌 H, 23, 280, 780, tram 8

The simple façade of San Crisogono, one of Trastevere's great medieval basilicas, reveals little of its long history and its hidden treasures.

The original church was founded in the fifth century, and a new church was built between 1123 and 1129 over the old building. The bell tower, together with the nave, the aisles and 22 granite columns, are all that remain of the 12th-century church. Inside, there is a very fine 13th-century cosmatesque marble floor, and a late 13th-century mosaic in the vault of the apse, depicting the Virgin and Child with St. James and St. Crisogono, which is attributed to the school of Pietro Cavallini. The Cappella del Santissimo Sacramento is thought to have been designed by Bernini.

The overall appearance of this church, half Mannerist, half baroque, is the work of the architect Giambattista Soria, who restored the church between 1620 and 1626 on the orders of Cardinal Scipione Borghese. Soria kept the ancient pillars, rebuilding their capitals in stucco, opened up windows in the nave to let more light in, and installed a coffered ceiling with the coat of arms of Cardinal Borghese. The baldachin is also his work.

In 1907, archaeologists discovered traces of the original fifth-century Christian church 6m (20ft) below the floor. The remains, which can be visited, include a later relic chamber with eighth-century frescoes.

SANTA CROCE IN GERUSALEMME

✚ 59 J6 • Piazza di Santa Croce in Gerusalemme 12 ☎ 06 7014769 🕐 7–7 💰 Free 🚇 San Giovanni or Manzoni 🚌 117, 186, 218, 649, 650, 850 🚋

St. Helena, mother of the Emperor Constantine, brought back to her palace in Rome a collection of relics of the Passion of Christ, which she amassed on her travels through the Holy Land. In the fourth century, part of the palace became the church of the Holy Cross in Jerusalem, built to house the fragment of the Holy Cross, a nail from the Cross, thorns from the Crown of Thorns, the original inscription over the Cross and other holy items. The church as seen today, built in the 12th century, was restored and altered in the 18th century.

Emperor Charles V's confessor, Cardinal Francesco Quiñones (died 1540) is buried in the apse; his tomb is by Jacopo Sansorino. The vault here is decorated with a Renaissance fresco depicting the discovery of the True Cross by St. Helena, attributed to Antoniazzo Romano. In the Chapel of St. Helena, reached by descending a 15th-century ramp at the end of the south aisle, are beautiful mosaics by Melozzo da Forlì and a statue of the saint adapted from a classical statue of Juno. The Holy Relics are kept in the Chapel of the Relics at the end of the north aisle. The church also contains a beautifully restored 12th-century cosmatesque floor.

San Clemente

Remains of a temple to the Persian god Mithras.
Magnificent mosaics.
Three distinct levels encapsulating the history of Rome.

SEEING SAN CLEMENTE

In a pleasant valley between the Esquiline and Oppio hills stands one of Rome's oldest basilicas, named after St. Clement, a first-century pope. Three levels of building allow more than 2,000 years of history to be pieced together here through study of the cross-sections of the basilica. The lower—earliest—buildings are very well preserved, and although the church appears small from the outside, there is a wealth of interest within. You will be able to make more sense of San Clemente's history if you buy a map showing the outline of the three levels of building.

THE THIRD LEVEL

The best way to see the whole church is to start from the third, under-ground level. Down here is a temple of Mithras (mithraeum) and what may have been a school for initiates into Mithraism, with remains of stuccowork and frescoes. The mithraeum, the focal point of the Mithraic cult, had benches down both sides for ritual banquets and was in use until the fourth century, when the Christians probably destroyed it. The altar of Mithras is still there: On one side it shows the god cutting a bull's throat during initiation rites, and on the other a snake representing regeneration. Ironically, filling in the mithraeum to make the foundations of the first Christian church helped to preserve it. A narrow passage that was once an alley open to the sky leads to various rooms, one of which contains a source of spring water (not drinkable) that once fed an underground watercourse.

THE LOWER BASILICA

Above the temple is the apse of the lower basilica, consisting of a nave and two aisles. There are fragments of its once fine mosaic floor and some eighth-century frescoes, including one in a niche in the north wall that shows the Virgin as queen of heaven with saints. The frescoes decorating the nave show the legend of Sisinius, Prefect of Rome. Sisinius went to arrest his wife, who was attending a secret Mass held by Pope Clement. He was struck blind in the presence of the holy man, as were his servants, who carried out a column instead of the woman. What makes the Sisinius frescoes so unusual is that the accompanying inscription is written in a very early form of Italian. In the 11th–12th century, pilasters were added to reinforce earlier columns. These were decorated with frescoes showing scenes from the life and death of St. Clement and the legend of St. Alexis.

THE UPPER BASILICA

A few decades later, work began on the upper basilica. The new church preserved the plan of the previous structure: one nave and two aisles either side leading up to a triumphal arch and a semi-domed apse, a quiet courtyard, a four-sided portico with Ionic columns and architraves, and a belfry. Just before the arch is the mar-ble-walled medieval choir, the schola cantorum, which survived from the lower basilica. But it is the apse that is the highlight of the upper basilica, decorated with a beautiful gold mosaic portraying the Crucifixion. Twelve doves symbolizing the Apostles adorn the Cross; the Virgin and St. John stand at the side, and God's hand descends from heaven bearing a crown for His Son. The people arriving to drink

The Temple of Mithras, below the church of San Clemente (above)

from the waters of life at the foot of the Cross represent followers of Christ coming for baptism. The cosmatesque (inlaid marble) floor is one of the best-preserved floors of its kind in Rome.

At the beginning of the 18th century, a radical restoration project began. New windows were added, together with the plain baroque façade, and the upper walls of the nave and ceiling were frescoed.

Don't miss In the left aisle, near the entrance, is the Cappella di Santa Caterina, the chapel of St. Catherine, finely decorated in the 15th century with exceptional frescoes by Masolino da Panicale; these depict scenes from the life of St. Catherine.

BACKGROUND

The upper church was built by Pope Paschal II in 1108 after the earlier church was badly damaged during an attack by the Normans in 1084. He followed the original plans as closely as possible. The church on the second level has a similar layout, but is wider. Very little of the original fourth-century building still exists, aside from parts of the north and south walls and some other fragments. It was dedicated to the Christian cult in the fifth century. According to legend, St. Cyril, the apostle of the Slavs, brought St. Clement's relics from the Black Sea (where he drowned) to Rome, placing them in the church in AD869. Down on the third level are two first-century Roman buildings, divided by a narrow passage. One is a huge warehouse of the early Flavian era, built of tufa blocks, which is believed to have been the mint of ancient Rome. The second building can be dated to AD92–96. Built of brick with an underground courtyard, it was the house of a rich family. Later, it was converted to the worship of the Persian god Mithras, a religion widespread throughout the Roman Empire, with some rituals similar to Christianity. Farther down, archaeologists have found buildings that were probably destroyed in Rome's fire of AD64.

From the Mithraic Temple (middle right), through the 12th-century mosaics in the apse (above and top) to the 18th-century courtyard (middle left), San Clemente's history is laid bare

Andrea Pozzo's trompe l'oeil
cupola in Sant'Ignazio di Loyola

Santi Giovanni e Paolo enjoys a peaceful
setting on the Caelian Hill

The spiral dome of
Sant'Ivo alla Sapienza

THE SIGHTS

SAN FRANCESCO A RIPA

✚ 57 D7 • Piazza San Francesco
d'Assisi ☎ 06 588 1331 ⏰ Mon–Sat
7–noon, 4–7, Sun 7–1, 4–7.30 💶 Free
🚌 H, 23, 280, 630, 780, tram 8

The church of San Francesco
a Ripa, founded in the 13th
century but made thoroughly
baroque 400 years later, is in the
heart of Trastevere. Its two treasures are the monastic cell where
St. Francis of Assisi lived when he
was in Rome and a dramatic
statue by Gian Lorenzo Bernini,
one of his last works.

To see Bernini's masterpiece,
the *Blessed Ludovica Albertoni*,
go down the left aisle to the
Albertoni chapel. Bernini captures perfectly Ludovica's
transformation from her final
agony to the ecstasy of her union
with God. The paintings of St.
Anne and the Virgin Mary, behind
the statue, are by Baciccio.

St. Francis' cell is reached from
the sacristy. It contains the saint's
marble pillow and a walnut baldachin. In the convent garden is
a bitter orange tree, supposedly
planted by St. Francis.

SAN GIOVANNI IN LATERANO

See pages 134–135.

SANTI GIOVANNI E PAOLO

✚ 58 G6 • Piazza Santi Giovanni e
Paolo 13 ☎ 06 700 5745
⏰ 8.30–noon, 3.30–6.30 💶 Free
🚇 Circo Massimo 🚌 81, 117, 118, 628,
673

This church is one of the oldest
Christian places of worship. It
was built over a Roman house,
traditionally that of two Christian
martyrs, John and Paul, former
soldiers who died during the
reign of Julian the Apostate
(AD361–363) when they rejected
pagan practices. The church is
opposite Villa Celimontana and

contains magnificent paintings
that once embellished the
Roman house beneath.

The original church was built in
the fourth century by a private
citizen named Pammachius. It
was rebuilt by Pope Paschal II,
who added a campanile and
porch in the 12th century. The
five arches above the remarkable
porch, and the gallery, belong to
the original building.

The interior mostly dates from
the 18th century. Entrance to the
house of John and Paul is down
the steps at the end of the aisle.
There are several rooms to see,
some decorated with wall paintings, most notably a beautiful
third-century marine fresco in the
underground nymphaeum.

The apse of the church is
decorated with a frieze by
Pomarancio and fourth-century
frescoes of the martyrdom of
John and Paul.

SAN GREGORIO MAGNO

✚ 58 F7 • Piazza di San Gregorio
☎ 06 5526 1617 ⏰ Daily 9–1, 3–6
💶 Free 🚇 Circo Massimo 🚌 81, 117,
118, 628, 673

Not far from the Colosseo is the
majestic church of San Gregorio
Magno, set on the beautiful,
quiet Caelian Hill and surrounded by tranquil gardens.

The church stands on the site
of St. Andrew's monastery,
founded by St. Gregory in AD575.
It was restored in 1633 for
Cardinal Scipione Borghese—the
eagle and dragon of his coat of
arms can be seen above the
lower arches. A spectacular staircase and broad portico take you
inside, where there are three
chapels built in the early 17th
century by Cardinal Cesare
Baronio. In St. Barbara's chapel
is a marble table supposedly
used by St. Gregory to feed the
poor. St. Sylvia's chapel, dedicated to Gregory's mother, has a

wonderful fresco by Guido Reni
in the apse showing a concert of
angels. The chapel of St. Andrew
has frescoes of the *Flagellation
of St. Andrew* by Domenichino
and *St. Andrew's Matryrdom* also
by Reni.

In the chapel at the end of
the right aisle is the altar of St.
Gregory the Great, decorated
with bas-reliefs illustrating the
saint's life. To the right, in the
cell of St. Gregory, are the
relics of the saint, his marble
throne and the stone he used
as a pillow.

SANT'IGNAZIO DI LOYOLA

✚ 57 E5 • Piazza di Sant'Ignazio 8
☎ 06 679 4406 ⏰ Daily 7.30–12.30,
3–7.30. Closed to visitors during Sun am
Mass 💶 Free 🚌 116 to Via del
Seminario, 30, 40, 46, 62, 63, 64, 70, 81,
492, 628, 630, 780, 787, 916 to Largo di
Torre Argentina

St. Ignatius of Loyola, founder of
the Jesuit order and of the
nearby Roman College, is the
dedicatee of this lavishly decorated church, designed by the
Jesuit architect Orazio Grassi.

The church was completed in
1685 without a cupola, but
another Jesuit, the painter
Andrea Pozzo, remedied this by
painting a remarkable *trompe
l'oeil* dome above the crossing,
imitating the lighting and depth
of a cupola. Pozzo's work dominates the interior. The corners of
the crossing glorify the Jesuits'
missionary activities, with paintings showing the Glory of St.
Ignatius in each of the four
known continents. In the
middle of the nave Pozzo used
the same technique to give a
three-dimensional effect to the
figures in the fresco of St.
Ignatius bathed in divine light.
Stand on the disc in the centre of
the nave and then move towards
the transept to get the best view.

The basilica of San Marco was named after both St. Mark the Evangelist and Pope Mark

Over 122 marble steps lead to the austere façade of Santa Maria in Aracoeli

THE SIGHTS

SANT'IVO ALLA SAPIENZA

✚ 57 E5 • Corso Rinascimento 40 ☎ 06 686 4987 ⏰ Mon–Sat 9–7, Sun 9–12 🎫 Free 🚌 23, 30, 40, 46, 62, 64, 70, 81, 87, 116, 280, 492, 628, 916; tram 8

The domed church of Sant'Ivo alla Sapienza is one of Francesco Borromini's masterpieces. Built in the grounds of the Palazzo alla Sapienza (Palace of Wisdom), which was the University of Rome until 1935, this church is worth visiting for its extraordinary spiral dome surmounted by a crown of flames. It is dedicated to St. Ives, patron saint of lawyers, who gave his services free to the poor.

The façade is baroque, and has two rows of arches running along the side walls. The unusual hexagonal plan suggests a honeycomb, an allusion to the Barberini bee emblem (Barberini Pope Urban VIII gave Borromini the commission).

The culmination is the extravagant dome with its spiral crown, possibly inspired by the architect's collection of shells.

SAN LUIGI DEI FRANCESI

✚ 57 E4 • Piazza San Luigi dei Francesi ☎ 06 688 271 ⏰ Fri–Wed 8–12.30, 3.30–7, Thu 8–12.30 🎫 Free 🚌 23, 30, 40, 46, 62, 64, 70, 81, 87, 116, 280, 492, 628, 916; tram 8

San Luigi dei Francesi, the national church of the French in Rome, is essential viewing for lovers of Caravaggio's work—it contains no less than three canvases by him.

The church was begun in 1518 by Cardinal Giulio de' Medici, the future Pope Clement VII, and was finally completed in 1589 by Domenico Fontana, with money from France provided by Henri II, Henri III and Catherine de Médicis. On the broad travertine façade, by Giacomo della Porta, is the salamander emblem of François I of France. The French theme continues with statues of Charlemagne and St. Louis in the lower part of the façade, and St. Clotilde and St. Joan of Valois in the upper part.

The church received much embellishment in the baroque period, with marble, paintings, gilding and stucco. Restoration work is currently under way.

There are frescoes by Domenichino in the chapel of St. Cecilia, but the church's main draw—the Caravaggio paintings—are in St. Matthew's chapel. They are dramatic depictions of three episodes from the saint's life: *St. Matthew and the Angel, The Calling of St. Matthew* and *The Martyrdom of St. Matthew*.

SAN MARCO

✚ 57 E5 • Piazza di San Marco ☎ 06 679 5205 ⏰ Daily 8–12.30, 4–8 🎫 Free 🚇 Colosseo 🚌 44, 46, 84, 715, 716, 780, 781, 810, 916

San Marco is well worth visiting for its ninth-century mosaic. It was founded by Pope St. Mark in AD336, and is dedicated to St. Mark the Evangelist, who is believed to have written his gospel in Rome.

Pope Gregory IV rebuilt the church in the ninth century, and the crypt, which contains the relics of the Persian saints Abdon and Senna, dates from the same period. Inside the porch, look for the 16th-century funerary plaque of Vanozza Catanei, who was the mistress of Pope Alexander VI and mother of Cesare and Lucrezia Borgia. The elegant Renaissance façade, with its double row of arches, is attributed to Leon Battista Alberti, who reused materials from the Colosseo and the Theatre of Marcellus.

The interior of the church is a mixture of styles. In the 15th century, a coffered ceiling showing the coat of arms of Pope Paul II was added, and there were baroque additions in the 18th century. The real gem is the gorgeous ninth-century mosaic in the apse, which shows Christ as the central figure, his hand raised in blessing, surrounded by saints. Pope Mark (or St. Gregory) holds a model of the church.

SANTA MARIA IN ARACOELI

✚ 57 F5 • Piazza d'Aracoeli ☎ 06 6798155 ⏰ Daily 9–12.30, 2.30–4.30 🎫 Free 🚇 Colosseo 🚌 44, 46, 84, 715, 716, 780, 781, 810, 916

There has been a church on this site since at least the sixth century, and in the eighth century it was part of a monastery. However, much of what you see today dates from the end of the 13th century.

Inside, the badly worn tomb of Archdeacon Giovanni Crivelli, carved by the Florentine sculptor Donatello in 1432, stands to the right of the entrance. Another tomb (1465), that of Cardinal d'Albret, is one of Andrea Bregno's best works. The decorative frescoes in the chapel of St. Bernardino of Siena are by Pinturricchio and depict the life and death of the saint. The left transept leads to a little chapel dedicated to the Santo Bambino (Holy Child). The jewelled wooden statue of the Christ Child is a modern replica of the 15th-century original—said to have been carved out of olive wood from the Garden of Gethsemane—which was stolen in the 1990s.

From the top of the Scalinata d'Aracoeli on the Capitolino (see page 72) there is a great view over the city. Allow time to take this in before passing behind the austere brick façade.

San Giovanni in Laterano

The cathedral of the city of Rome.
Grandiose basilica rich in interior decoration.
Site of the Scala Santa (Holy Staircase), one of Catholicism's most sacred relics.

SEEING SAN GIOVANNI IN LATERANO

This solemn, peaceful basilica is best approached from the splendid piazza, named—like San Giovanni itself—after the Laterani family, who once owned this land. Inside, take time to appreciate the overall scale before focusing on the individual treasures. The baptistery is near the exit on the left and you can access the cloister from the left aisle. The Scala Santa entrance is outside.

RATINGS	
Good for kids	●
Historic interest	● ● ●
Value for money	● ● ● ● ●
Specialist shopping	● ●

BASICS

✚ 58 H6 • Piazza di San Giovanni in Laterano 4 ☎ 06 6988 6433. Guided tours: 06 6988 6392 or email: mater.caput@org.va. Vatican History Museum: 06 6988 6294

⊙ Basilica: daily 7–6.45. Cloister: daily 9–6; closed Sun morning. Baptistery: daily 7–12.30, 4–7.30. Scala Santa: daily 6.15–noon, 3–6.15. Cappella Sancta Sanctorum: Tue, Thu, Sat 10.30–11.30, 3–5.30. Vatican History Museum: Sat 9.30–2.15, first Sun of the month 8.45–1

🖐 Basilica, Scala Santa and baptistery: free. Cloister: €2. Cappella Sancta Sanctorum: €2.50. Vatican History Museum: €4

⊙ San Giovanni

🚌 16, 85, 87, 117, 186, 218, 650, 850

🎧 For a guided tour of the basilica, cloister, baptistery and Scala Santa, book in advance via contact number or e-mail address above. €5 per head in all languages. Guided tour also of Vatican History Museum. Audiotours: basilica and cloister €2 all languages

📖 San Giovanni Basilica Patriarcale Roma €6.20 in all languages

🏬 Souvenir shop inside the basilica (9–6)

♿ Inside complex

HIGHLIGHTS

EXTERIOR

The severe baroque east façade by Alessandro Galilei (1735) supports a balustrade with 15 gigantic statues representing Christ, the two St. Johns, and the Doctors of the Church. The portico in front of the church, inspired by that of St. Peter's (see pages 66–71), has antique bronze doors from the Senate House in the Foro Romano (see pages 84–89) and a huge statue of Constantine, discovered in the Baths of Constantine on the Quirinale. The last door on the right is the Holy Door, opened most recently in 2000 by the Pope to mark the start of a Holy Year, a once-every-25-years occurrence.

THE NAVE

The present interior of the church was commissioned by Pope Innocent X in 1646 and is mainly the work of Francesco Borromini. He's responsible for the nave and four aisles, while the ornate ceiling is probably by Piero Ligorio. Statues of the 12 Apostles flank the nave, each in its own separate niche and surmounted by bas-reliefs depicting stories from the Bible. On the left-hand pillar in the right aisle, its fragility protected by glass, is a restored fragment of a Giotto fresco of Boniface VIII declaring the Holy Year of 1300, while the Corsini Chapel, designed by Alessandro Galilei, is on the left.

THE TRANSEPT AND APSE

In contrast to the nave, the transept, a fine example of Mannerist decoration, is elaborately decorated in style. Nebbia, Pomarancio and Cavaliere d'Arpino were responsible for the frescoes; the central ceiling, showing Clement VIII's coat of arms, is by Taddeo Landini.

The apse mosaic is a 19th-century restoration of Jacopo Torriti's 13th-century masterpiece. Torriti added figures of the Virgin, Pope Nicholas IV and major saints. The small figure of St. Francis on the left was probably included because Torriti was a Franciscan monk.

THE PAPAL ALTAR

At the heart of the basilica is the Papal Altar, at which only the pope may officiate; it contains a wooden table said to have been used by St. Peter, although it probably dates from the fourth century. Above rises a fine 14th-century Gothic canopy, made of precious marble and decorated with mosaics. Here, too, are copies of the 15th-century reliquaries containing the relics of St. Peter and St. Paul, housed in a tabernacle frescoed with the Good Shepherd, the Crucifixion, the Virgin and various saints. Beneath the altar of the Confessio (the crypt below the Papal Altar) is the tomb slab of Pope Martin V (died 1431).

THE CLOISTERS

The exquisite cloisters, built between 1215 and 1232, are the work of Jacopo and Pietro Vassalletto, two of the most famous artists of the cosmatesque style of mosaic. The sparkling, multi-hued twisted and plain columns have splendid capitals, and the marble mosaic frieze is decorated with bizarre birds and beasts; stand by the ninth-century well in the middle of the garden for the best view. Fragments of the medieval basilica are displayed around the cloister walls.

Vast size is a visitor's first impression of the interior of San Giovanni (far left)
The statues on top of the entrance façade can be seen from afar (second left)
The 13th-century cloisters with close-up of a pillar (third left)
One of the majestic statues inside the church (left)

THE SIGHTS

THE BAPTISTERY

The octagonal baptistery, originally built during the reign of Constantine, has four chapels containing early mosaics. The green basalt urn in the middle is the baptismal font.

THE SCALA SANTA

The Scala Santa (Holy Staircase) is supposedly from the house of Pontius Pilate in Jerusalem, ascended by Christ before his Crucifixion. The 28 marble steps—which believers climb on their knees to earn an indulgence—have covers to protect stains said to be traces of Christ's blood. The staircase leads to the Sancta Sanctorum, once the pope's private chapel and adorned with fine mosaics.

The octagonal baptistery of St. John behind the church dates from the fifth century, though it has been much restored (above)

BACKGROUND

Originally dedicated to Christ the Saviour, and only later to St. John the Evangelist and St. John the Baptist, San Giovanni in Laterano dates from the fourth century. Following his victory over Maxentius in AD312 and the establishment of Christianity as the imperial religion, Constantine built a basilica here on the site of his rival's imperial guard's barracks. This early church represented the victory of Christianity over paganism, and was designated Mother and Head of all churches of the city and the world. In AD314 Pope Sylvester I took up residence in the group of Lateran buildings, which included a palace, a basilica and a baptistery. This became the official papal residence until the popes moved to Avignon in France in the 14th century. After various restorations and rebuildings over the centuries, the church was radically restored in the baroque style in the 17th and 18th centuries.

TIP

● If you visit in the morning, take time to check out Via Sannio, scene of one of Rome's best-known markets (see page 174).

Santa Maria in Cosmedin has beautiful cosmatesque floors

The Capuchin monks' crypt in Santa Maria della Concezione

The Assumption of the Virgin, in Santa Maria in Popolo

SANTA MARIA DELLA CONCEZIONE

✚ 57 F4 ✉ Via Vittorio Veneto 27 ☎ 06 487 1185 🕐 Daily 7–12, 3–7. Capuchin cemetery: Thu 9–12, 3–6 💷 Free (donation for cemetery) Ⓜ Barberini 🚌 52, 53, 63, 80, 95, 116, 119, www.cappucciniviaveneto.it

The original setting of this majestic structure, the church of a Capuchin convent, has been spoiled by the construction of Via Veneto, but even so it attracts many visitors. The church's rather austere exterior gives no clue to the extraordinary sight it contains within—its macabre Capuchin cemetery.

The church was built around 1626, commissioned by Cardinal Antonio Barberini (brother of Pope Urban VIII). His tombstone is on the floor in front of the main altar, with the inscription: 'Hic jacet pulvis, cinis et nihil' ('Here lie dust, ashes and nothing more').

On the right-hand side of the front steps is the entrance to the cemetery in the crypt. Here, the walls and ceilings of five chapels are decorated with the skeletons (some of them clothed) and loose bones of about 4,000 Capuchin monks who died between 1528 and 1870. The floor is scattered with earth brought from the holy sites in Palestine.

SANTA MARIA IN COSMEDIN

✚ 57 E6 • Via Bocca della Verità ☎ 06 678 1419 🕐 9–7.30 💷 Free Ⓜ Circo Massimo 🚌 81, 160, 628, 715

The church of Santa Maria in Cosmedin is best known for the Bocca della Verità (Mouth of Truth) and its associated superstition, rather than for anything inside. But venture in and you will find a rare Roman medieval

church that has been stripped of its later baroque additions.

There were classical temples on the site of the present church, and in the sixth century a deaconry was established here to provide aid for the poor. The church that existed by the eighth century was given to Greek refugees from Byzantium, which was when the word Cosmedin (from the Greek for 'decorated') became part of its name. The church retains its Greek connections; a Greek Orthodox Mass is celebrated here every week.

Inside the church, the 12th-century cosmatesque floors are particularly good, and the frescoes in the apse and the mosaic fragment in the sacristy are well worth a look. The Corinthian columns probably came from the preceding pagan temple.

The Bocca della Verità is a large stone disk carved with the face of a man, found just inside the church porch. According to medieval tradition, a liar risks having his hand bitten off if he dares to put it in the mouth of the image. In fact, the stone was probably nothing more sinister than a Roman drain cover, but it's a popular myth.

SANTA MARIA IN DOMNICA

✚ 58 G7 • Via della Navicella 10 ☎ 06 700 1519 🕐 9–noon, 3.30–6 💷 Free Ⓜ Circo Massimo 🚌 81, 117, 673

The setting of the church of Santa Maria in Domnica, near Villa Celimontana, makes it a popular choice for weddings. It is also known as Santa Maria della Navicella ('little boat'), after the 16th-century fountain incorporating a Roman stone boat in front of the stylish church porch.

Santa Maria in Domnica was built in the ninth century by Pope

Paschal I on the site of an earlier house of worship called a dominicum. Pope Leo X restored the church in the 16th century, and you can see his emblem—the lion—on the keystones.

The interior of the church remains much as it was in the ninth century, with a nave and two aisles separated by ancient columns of grey granite. Beautiful Byzantine mosaics decorate the triumphal arch and apse. The artist has represented the religious scenes with great realism, giving the impression that there is a breeze stirring the angels' clothes. A mosaic at the middle of the vault shows Pope Paschal kneeling before the Virgin; note the square halo, known as a nimbus, indicating that the Pope was still alive at the time.

SANTA MARIA MAGGIORE

See pages 138–139.

SANTA MARIA SOPRA MINERVA

See page 140.

SANTA MARIA DEL POPOLO

✚ 57 E3 • Piazza del Popolo 12 ☎ 06 3610836 🕐 Mon–Sat 7–noon, 4–7, Sun 8–1.30, 4.30–7.30 💷 Free Ⓜ Flaminio or Spagna 🚌 117, 119, 628, 926 🎧 Audioguide €1 in Italian, English, German, French and Spanish

The church of Santa Maria del Popolo is a must for art lovers, with works by some of the great names from the 16th and 17th centuries, including Raphael, Caravaggio and Bernini.

According to legend, Nero's tomb once stood under a walnut tree on the site of this church, and the notorious emperor's ghost used to haunt the place. Pope Paschal II had the tree cut down and built a small chapel in its place. The name, St. Mary of

Bernini's *Ecstasy of St. Teresa of Avila, in the Cornaro Chapel of Santa Maria della Vittoria*

Michelangleo's *imposing statue of Moses, San Pietro in Vincoli*

the People, recalls the fact that the Pope asked the people of Rome to pay for the building of the chapel. In 1472, Sixtus IV commissioned the present church to be built by Andrea Bregno. It was later reworked in baroque style, largely by Gian Lorenzo Bernini.

The sumptuously decorated Chigi Chapel in the left aisle was designed by Raphael for the banker Agostino Chigi, its plain exterior a sharp contrast to the rich interior; Bernini completed the chapel after Raphael's death. The bright red travertine marble Cerasi Chapel, at the end of the same aisle, contains two of Caravaggio's masterpieces: *The Conversion of St. Paul* and *The Crucifixion of St. Peter*.

SANTA MARIA IN TRASTEVERE

See page 141.

SANTA MARIA DELLA VITTORIA

✚ 58 G4 • Largo di Santa Susanna 17 ☎ 06 4274 0571 ◷ Mon–Sat 7–noon, 3.30–7, Sun 8.15–10, 3.30–6 🎫 Free 🚇 Repubblica or Barberini 🚌 60, 61, 62, 84, 90, 175, 492

This church is a monument to the baroque style in all its richness, beauty and harmony. Among its treasures is Bernini's superb *Ecstasy of St. Teresa of Avila*.

Cardinal Scipione Borghese commissioned the church to celebrate the victory of the Catholics over the Protestants at the Battle of the White Mountain near Prague in 1620, which was attributed to the chaplain taking an image of the Virgin Mary into battle. The St. Mary of Victory over the altar is a copy of the one that survived the battle—the original was destroyed by fire in 1833.

The vault is painted with *trompe l'oeil* frescoes of the *Triumph of the Virgin Mary over Heresies* by Andrea and Giuseppe Orazi; Perugino frescoed the ceiling. On the altar is *The Most Holy Trinity* by Giovanni Francesco Barbieri (known as Il Guercino), while in the Chapel of St. Francis of Assisi is *The Virgin Offering the Child to St. Francis* by Domenichino.

The star attraction, however, is Bernini's Cornaro Chapel, the last chapel on the left-hand side. Designed in 1646 for Cardinal Cornaro of Venice, it has carvings of members of his family in side balconies, like a theatre audience, gazing at St. Teresa in her ecstacy. Bernini captures the moment that St. Teresa is pierced by a golden arrow, an experience she described in her autobiography.

SAN PIETRO IN MONTORIO AND TEMPIETTO DEL BRAMANTE

✚ 56 D6 • Piazza di San Pietro in Montorio ☎ 06 581 3940 ◷ 9–noon, 4–6. Tempietto: Tue–Sun 9.30–12.30, 2–4, Nov–end Apr; 9.30–12.30, 4–6, May–end Oct 🎫 Free 🚌 870

In a quiet, picturesque corner on the Janiculum Hill stands the church of San Pietro in Montorio, with a splendid view over the city of Rome. It is best known for the tiny circular building by Donato Bramante in the adjoining cloister, the much admired Tempietto.

Although there may have been an earlier church on this site, the present building dates back only to the end of the 15th century, when the Catholic Monarchs of Spain, Ferdinand and Isabella, commissioned Baccio Pontelli to build it. It was dedicated to St. Peter, who, it was believed, was crucified here.

The church is essentially Renaissance, but has a remarkable Gothic rose window in the façade. The Peruzzi Chapel, the second on the left, was designed by Bernini.

In the middle of the cloister adjoining the church, on what was once thought to be the exact spot of St. Peter's crucifixion, stands one of Rome's most attractive Renaissance buildings. Bramante designed the beautiful Tempietto in around 1500. Its style and perfect proportions hark back to Classical temples such as the Temple of Vesta at Tivoli.

SAN PIETRO IN VINCOLI

✚ 58 G5 • Piazza San Pietro in Vincoli 4 ☎ 06 488 2865 ◷ Daily 7–12.30, 3–7. Closed to visitors during Mass (Sun at 11) 🎫 Free 🚇 Colosseo 🚌 60, 75, 84, 85, 87, 117, 175, 810, 850 🎧 Audioguide €1 in English, French, German, Spanish and Italian

The name of this church, St. Peter in Chains, gives a clue to one of its treasures: the chains that bound St. Peter in prison, which can be seen in a gilt bronze urn under the high altar.

The ceiling of the church is decorated with a fresco showing the miracle of the chains. According to the legend, two sets of chains that were used to bind St. Peter—in Jerusalem and in the Mamertine prison in Rome— miraculously fused together when placed side by side.

The church's main attraction, however, is Michelangelo's tremendous statue of Moses, which was one of the 40 figures that were intended to adorn the mausoleum of Pope Julius II in St. Peter's basilica. The original project was abandoned after Julius' death. The huge seated figure of Moses is sculpted from Carrara marble, and the figures in the niches are Jacob's wives, Leah and Rachel.

Santa Maria Maggiore

One of the four Roman basilicas that belong to the Vatican, and the only surviving example of the four to retain its classical interior. Contains the city's highest bell tower.

SEEING SANTA MARIA MAGGIORE

Spend a moment admiring the 18th-century façade of the basilica, with Rome's tallest campanile rising behind. You may then want to visit the Museum of the Patriarcale Basilica di Santa Maria Maggiore, next to the basilica. If timings are right, visit the Loggia delle Benedizione for the view over the piazza and the 13th-century mosaics by Filippo Rusuti. Pass through the portico, with a bronze statue of Philip IV and the great Holy Door, and, once inside, spend a few moments absorbing everything before you start your tour.

HIGHLIGHTS

THE NAVE AND AISLES CHANCEL

The interior of this immense church is dominated by the long nave, flanked with 40 ancient Roman columns. Above, 36 fifth-century mosaic panels tell Old Testament stories; they're high and hard to see, but perseverance pays off. Higher still, the superb Renaissance coffered ceiling is said to be decorated with the first gold to have been brought from the New World, a gift from Ferdinand and Isabella of Spain. The coats of arms are those of popes Calixtus III and Alexander V. Beneath your feet stretches a beautiful cosmatesque marble pavement, dating from the 12th century.

THE CHANCEL AND APSE

The fifth-century Byzantine-style mosaics glitter from the triumphal arch, whose four sections depict the Annunciation, the Epiphany and other scenes from the early life of Christ. The apse mosaic is later, created in 1295 by Jacopo Torriti; it shows the Coronation of the Virgin, attended by Pope Nicholas IV and Cardinal Iacopo Colonna.

The baldachino, made up of porphyry columns with bronze foliage, is by Fernando Fuga. It stands above the *confessio*, the most sacred spot in the basilica, which contains a silver urn by Giuseppe Valadier supposedly containing fragments of the Christ child's wooden crib.

THE CHAPELS

The Cappella Sistina, to the right of the nave, was commissioned by Pope Sixtus V and built by Domenico Fontana (1585) on a Greek-cross plan, reusing marble from a classical Roman building. The vast chapel, with its dome, frescoes, marbles and monumental tombs, is as large as many churches. Beneath it are the remnants of the Presepio, with exquisite nativity-scene figures by the sculptor Arnolfo di Cambio that once accompanied the holy crib (see above).

The Cappella Paolina, just off the north aisle mirrors the Sistine Chapel, and is perhaps even more beautiful, with mosaics by Cavaliere d'Arpino, frescoes by Guido Reni and an incredibly sumptuous bejewelled altar. It is also known as the Borghese Chapel after the family name of the commissioning Pope Paul V. Nearby, off the left aisle, the Cappella Sforza was probably built by Giacomo della Porta from drawings by Michelangelo.

On the right wall at the end of the nave is the magnificent inlaid marble tomb of Cardinal Consalvo Rodriguez (died 1299), a contrast to the simple, humble tomb of the Bernini family nearby.

RATINGS

Good for kids	●
Historic interest	● ● ● ●
Specialist shopping	● ●
Value for money	● ● ● ●

BASICS

✚ 58 G5 • Piazza Santa Maria Maggiore ☎ 06 483195

🕙 Basilica: daily 7–7. Cappella Sforza: Mon–Fri 9.30–5. Museum: daily 9.30–6.30. Sacristy: daily 7–12.30, 3–6.30

💶 Basilica and Cappella Sforza: free. Museum: Adult €4, child (under 18) €2

🚇 Cavour, Termini or Vittorio Emanuele

🚌 16, 71, 70, 75, 105, 204, 360, 590, 649, 714

🎫 Guided tours of Loggia delle Benedizioni (€2.60) and Presepe di Arnolfo di Cambio (€1.50): Mon–Sat 9.30–1, 4–6 (loggia afternoons only). Ask in the museum. Audiotours: €1. For guided tours contact Patrizia Riccitelli (tel 06 483058 or **www.prtour.it**)

📖 €6.70 in English, Italian, German, Spanish.

🏪 Bookshop inside basilica

THE BAPTISTERY

The baptistery is baroque, the work of Flaminio Ponzio. The porphyry font was decorated by Giuseppe Valadier; the high-relief *Assumption* on the altar is by Pietro Bernini, father of the famous Gian Lorenzo.

BACKGROUND

Legend, sadly now disproved, associates the founding of the original church with Pope Liberius in the fourth century. He dreamed the Virgin instructed him to build it wherever snow fell that night—5 August, the height of summer. In the morning, snow dusted the Equiline Hill, and so here the church was built. The present church was built by Sixtus III in AD432–440. Considerable changes were made in the 12th and 13th centuries, and the chapels were added in the 16th century. The present façade, with its triple-arched loggia, was designed around the original mosaics by Fernando Fuga in 1746.

TIPS

● If you want to see everything properly, call in advance to book a guided tour.

● The area near the basilica, around Termini station, is not one of the safest; watch your belongings.

● Bring binoculars if you're really interested in seeing the mosaics.

Ferdinando Fuga's 18th-century façade (below)
Restoration hides a much earlier church (left and far left)

THE SIGHTS

SANTA MARIA SOPRA MINERVA

A touch of Gothic amid Rome's prevailing Renaissance and baroque.

Behind its Renaissance façade, Santa Maria sopra Minerva is a rarity in being Rome's only Gothic church (although much restored in the 19th century). Some of the most prominent Italian families called upon the celebrated artists of their time to embellish their chapels, so there is plenty inside to interest art lovers.

THE TEMPLE OF MINERVA

The first church was built in the eighth or ninth century on top of (*sopra*) a temple of the pagan goddess Minerva. In 1280, two Dominican friars, Sisto and Ristoro, began reconstructing the church in Gothic style, apparently on the model of Santa Maria Novella in Florence, of which they were also the architects. In the 16th and 17th centuries, the interior was redecorated in baroque style, and in the 1840s, restorers indulged their taste for the Gothic style.

THE CHURCH'S INTERIOR

The interior, divided into a nave and two aisles, has chapels on either side. In the right transept is the splendid Capella Carafa, built and decorated by order of Cardinal Carafa in honour of the philosopher-saint Thomas Aquinas (1224–74). Filippino Lippi frescoed the walls of this chapel in the 1480s with scenes from the life of St. Thomas Aquinas and a beautiful *Assumption of the Virgin*. The tomb of Pope Paul IV (died 1559) is also here.

Near the high altar in the choir is a statue of the *Risen Christ with the Cross* by Michelangelo. The remains of St. Catherine of Siena, one of the patron saints of Italy, lie under the altar. In the apse are the tombs of the Medici popes Leo X and Clement VII, the work of Antonio Sangallo the Younger.

BERNINI'S ELEPHANT

Outside, in Piazza della Minerva, is one of Rome's best-loved oddities: a sixth-century BC Egyptian obelisk on the back of a marble elephant. The work was designed by Bernini and sculpted by his pupil Ercole Ferrata in 1667. The inscription on the base, by Pope Alexander VII, reads: 'A strong mind is necessary to support solid wisdom'—meaning that the obelisk represents the wisdom that grows from, and is supported by, the strong mind of the elephant.

The tomb of St. Catherine of Siena lies under the main altar (above)
The soaring Gothic arches and gilded interior (right)

SANTA MARIA IN TRASTEVERE

A rare medieval church.

On the right bank of the Tiber lies the picturesque quarter of Trastevere (see pages 144–145), at the heart of which is the first church to be dedicated to the veneration of the Virgin Mary, Santa Maria in Trastevere. One of the few medieval churches in Rome, Santa Maria in Trastevere remains a local church, attended by the inhabitants of the quarter.

BUILDING THE CHURCH
Legend has it that in 38BC (or alternatively on the day of Jesus' birth) a fountain of oil suddenly started flowing to announce the coming of God's Son. Pope St. Calixtus (AD217–222) built a sanctuary on this spot, called the Taberna Meritoria, to commemorate the miracle and encourage the worship of the Virgin Mary. The present basilica was built in the 12th century during the pontificate of Innocent II, using material from the Baths of Caracalla.

THE APSE MOSAICS
The mosaics in the apse, which date from the 12th century, illustrate St. Calixtus and Pope Innocent II offering his church to Mary. The Virgin, adorned with gold, is shown in the Byzantine style with a certain oriental rigidity. At the top of the mosaic is *Paradise,* showing the hand of God crowning Jesus. The cities of Jerusalem and Bethlehem are shown, and the lambs represent the 12 Apostles.

Another set of mosaics between the windows, a masterpiece by Pietro Cavallini, represents scenes from the life of the Virgin, including her birth, the Annunciation, the Nativity, the Epiphany, the Presentation in the Temple and the Dormition. The medallion above the throne shows the Virgin and Child between saints. Peter and Paul, along with Cardinal Bertoldo Stefaneschi, who commissioned the work in 1290.

THE ALTEMPS CHAPEL
The Altemps Chapel contains the sixth-century Byzantine painting of *Our Lady of Mercy,* one of the oldest images of the Virgin in existence. The late 16th-century mosaics in this chapel demonstrate the re-emerging interest in religious art during the Counter-Reformation. To the left of the nave is the Avila Chapel, with a cupola by Antonio Gherardi decorated in a baroque *trompe l'oeil* effect.

EXTERIOR
The 12th-century bell tower has a 17th-century mosaic of the *Virgin and Child,* while on the façade there is a beautiful 12th- to 13th-century mosaic showing the Virgin Mary enthroned, with processions of women approaching from both sides. The statues of saints above the porch on the balustrade in front of the façade have stood there since the 17th century.

RATINGS	
Good for kids	●●
Historic interest	●●●
Value for money	●●●●●

BASICS
✚ 57 D6 • Piazza di Santa Maria in Trastevere ☎ 06 5897332 ◷ Daily 7.30–1, 4–7 🚌 H, 23, 280, 630, 780 📖 *Pilgrims in the Heart of Rome: a Journey to Trastevere,* published by the nearby Community of Sant'Egidio €12.91 📖 Small bookshop selling general guides (open 9–5)

TIP
● Visit in the evening, then have a drink in one of the outdoor cafés, from where you can appreciate the beautifully lit piazza and basilica.

The apse mosaics are one of the highlights of this medieval church (top)
Twenty-two columns from ancient monuments divide the nave from the aisles (above)

The mosaic of Christ surrounded by angels in Santa Prassede

The fourth-century Santa Pudenziana

Santa Sabina is lit by ninth-century windows, glazed with the mineral selenite

SANTA PRASSEDE

✚ 58 G5 • Via di Santa Prassede 9/A
☎ 06 488 2456 🕐 Daily 7–12, 4–6.30.
Closed Aug 💷 Free 🚇 Cavour,
Termini or Vittorio Emanuele 🚌 16, 70,
71, 360, 649

An unimposing entrance through an arch supported by pillars leads into the atrium of the church of St. Prassede, worth visiting for its bright Byzantine mosaics, notably those in the Capella di San Zeno, the most important examples in Rome.

A house of worship has stood on this spot since AD489. The present building, with its brick façade, was built in AD822 by Pope Paschal I, who enlarged it to store relics of martyrs from the catacombs. It has been rebuilt and restored many times since.

In the right aisle is the tomb of Bishop Giovanni Battista Santoni, the first work by Gian Lorenzo Bernini. Remarkable ninth-century mosaics embellish the apse and the triumphal arch. The coffered ceiling is a relatively recent 19th-century addition. The Chapel of St Zeno in the right aisle contains beautiful mosaics depicting Christ, saints and the Virgin Mary, all on a brilliant gold background. It also has an excellent ornamental pavement in polychrome marble. In a room to the right of the entrance is a fragment of a column brought from Jerusalem in 1223; according to tradition, it is where Jesus was scourged.

SANTA PUDENZIANA

✚ 58 G5 • Via Urbana 60 ☎ 06 481
4622 🕐 Mon–Sat 8–noon, 3–6, Sun
9–noon, 3–6. Closed to visitors during
during Mass 💷 Free 🚇 Cavour,
Termini or Vittorio Emanuele 🚌 16, 70,
71, 360, 649

This church is said to be on the site of the house of Senator Pudens, father of saints Prassede and Pudenziana, who welcomed St. Peter as a guest. The building was transformed into a church in the late fourth century, making it one of the oldest sites of Christian worship in Rome.

The bell tower dates from the 12th century, as does the elegant door with its fluted columns. The dome was added in the 16th century and the façade was restored in 1870.

The interior of the church was transformed into one nave in 1588 by Francesco da Volterra. He also designed the dome, which was frescoed by Nicolò Circignani.

The apse mosaic, which was probably done under Pope Innocent I in the fifth century, portrays Christ sitting on a throne surrounded by the Apostles and two female figures, who may be Pudenziana and Prassede, or may represent the Church of the Jews and the Church of the Gentiles.

SANTI QUATTRO CORONATI

✚ 58 G6 • Via dei Santi Quattro
Coronati ☎ 06 7047 5427
🕐 8.30–noon, 3–7. Cloister and crypt:
9.30–12.30 💷 Free 🚇 San Giovanni
🚌 117, 186, 218, 650, 850

Like all the churches built on the Caelian Hill, Santi Quattro Coronati (Four Crowned Saints), at the end of a steep, quiet road, is a little gem.

This picturesque church and the adjoining convent are dedicated to four Christian Roman soldiers (or possibly sculptors), martyred because they refused to worship (or make a statue of) the Greek demigod of healing, Esculapio. An earlier church was completely demolished during the sack of Rome of 1084, and 20 years later a new, fortified church was built on the site by Pope Paschal II. This had a larger central nave and a spacious courtyard at the entrance; the aisles were pulled down to make way for the lovely cloister and a dining hall.

Above the entrance is a tower-like belfry. Inside, there is an unusual *matroneum*, or women's gallery. The large apse is beautifully decorated with baroque frescoes illustrating the lives of the Quattro Coronati. **Don't miss** the adjoining cloister and the crypt just below the altar.

SANTA SABINA

✚ 57 E7 • Via di Santa Sabina 2
☎ 06 5794 0660 Ask sacristan to visit
Pope Pius V's room and St. Dominic's
cell 🕐 7–12.30, 3.30–7 💷 Free.
Medieval cloister: €1 🚇 Circo Massimo
🚌 60, 73, 75, 118, tram 3 to Viale
Aventino, 175, 715

The lovely basilica of Santa Sabina, on the Aventine Hill, has kept its original fifth-century early Christian plan almost intact. Next to the church is a beautiful medieval cloister where St. Dominic is said to have planted the first orange tree in Rome, the descendants of which still perfume the monks' garden.

A church dedicated to the martyred Roman matron St. Sabina has stood on this spot on the Aventine Hill since AD425. The basilica has seen many changes over the centuries: It was turned into a fortress in the 10th century, incongruously restored in the 16th century by Domenico Fontana, and restored again in the 19th century, when all its baroque elements were removed and the church was returned to its original plan.

At the entrance, behind a front portico, is one of the church's main treasures. The entrance doors are divided into wooden panels, many of them survivors from the fifth-century church, carved with scenes from the Old

The simple exterior of Santo Stefano Rotondo

The ruins of the finest baths ever built in Rome—Terme di Caracalla

Terme di Diocleziano

and New Testaments. The Crucifixion can be seen high up on the left.

Inside, the church is well proportioned, with light entering through the beautiful ninth-century windows, now restored to their original brilliance.

SANTO STEFANO ROTONDO

🔲 58 G7 • Via di Santo Stefano Rotondo 7 ☎ 06 7049 3717 🕐 9–1, 3.30–6 🔰 Free 🚇 Colosseo, San Giovanni 🚌 81, 117, 673, 714, 850

Santo Stefano, set in a beautiful private park on the Caelian Hill, is one of the oldest and largest round churches anywhere, and has plenty to interest lovers of both art and history.

The church was built in the late fifth century by Pope Simplicius and dedicated to St. Stephen, the first Christian martyr, whose relics are here, and later also to St. Stephen of Hungary. Long before that, there was an ancient sanctuary to the pagan god Mithras on this site. A gold-covered head from a statue was found during excavations below the church.

The walls are frescoed with 34 scenes of Christian martyrs painted by Pomarancio and Antonio Tempesta in the 16th century. The harrowing scenes have inscriptions explaining the action and giving the names of the emperors who ordered the executions. They are not for the faint-hearted.

The church's mosaics and marble decorations, once the most opulent in Rome, date from AD523–530. One shows two fourth-century martyrs, Primus and Felician, with a jewelled cross. Their relics were brought here by Pope Theodore I in the seventh century.

There is ongoing restoration work to the floor, but the church can still be visited.

TERME DI CARACALLA

🔲 311 G7 • Viale delle Terme di Caracalla 52 ☎ 06 575 8626 🕐 Tue–Sun 9–6, Mon 9–1, Apr–Sep; Tue–Sun 9–3, Mon 9–2, rest of year 🔰 Adult €5, child (under 18) free 🚇 Circo Massimo 🚌 67, 90, 118, 160, 613, 714, 715 🛒 www.beniculturali.it

The Baths of Caracalla were the most luxurious of the imperial baths, and are among the most impressive, monumental complexes to have survived from ancient Rome. Designed not only for the care of the body but as a cultural and local meeting place, they also included flourishing gardens.

The baths were opened in AD217 under Emperor Caracalla, but his successors Elegabalus and Alexander Severus completed them. They remained in use until the wars with the Goths, when soldiers destroyed part of the aqueducts supplying water to the baths in AD537 as part of their strategy to conquer Rome.

The complex included pools, rooms for cold, hot and warm baths, porticoes, halls, gymnasiums, fine statues, libraries and even a stadium. There was capacity for 600 people at a time to bathe here. All the rooms were finely decorated with alabaster and granite, with magnificent ceilings and wall mosaics, many of them still intact.

Recent excavations have uncovered an underground mithraeum, a temple dedicated to the cult of the pagan god Mithras (see Basilica di San Clemente, pages 130–131).

TERME DI DIOCLEZIANO

🔲 58 G4 • Piazza dei Cinquecento 78 ☎ 06 4782 6152. Call centre for guided tours: 06 3996 7700 🕐 Museum: Tue–Sun 9–7. Octagonal Hall: closed for restoration 🔰 Museum: Adult €5, child (under 18) free Audioguide €4 in English and Italian 🚇 Termini 🚌 H, 5, 14, 36, 38, 40, 64, 86, 90, 170, 175, 217, 310, 714

This grand baths complex was the largest ever to be built in Rome—it could accommodate 3,000 people. Today, it incorporates the church of Santa Maria degli Angeli and part of the Museo Nazionale Romano, and is the underlying structure of Piazza della Repubblica (see page 119).

The Emperor Diocletian never came to Rome, but in AD298 he commissioned Maximian, who ruled the Western empire under him, to build the most luxurious baths in the city. At the height of their popularity they included libraries, concert halls, gardens, galleries of sculpture and art, and exercise rooms. Like the Terme di Caracalla, Diocletian's were abandoned in the sixth century when the aqueducts were destroyed.

In the 16th century, Pius IV commissioned Michelangelo, then aged 86, to convert the grand central hall of the baths into a church, Santa Maria degli Angeli. His adaptation was not particularly successful and was not improved, after his death, by alterations to the design by Luigi Vanvitelli. In the early 20th century the façade was removed to reveal the unadorned curved wall of the caldarium (hot room) of the baths, while the present atrium of the church corresponds to the tepidarium (warm room). Part of the baths complex beside the church contains some of the collection of the Museo Nazionale Romano, including sarcophagi, decorations from the Aurelian temple. Also here is a cloister by Michelangelo, enclosed by a portico of 100 columns and 100 arcades.

TRASTEVERE

See pages 144–145.

Trastevere

Rome's answer to Paris' Rive Gauche.
A genuine working area with lively atmosphere.
A great place for eating and drinking in the evening.

SEEING TRASTEVERE

The main bridge from Rome proper into Trastevere is the Ponte Garibaldi, which runs into the Viale di Trastevere, a main drag that divides the area neatly into north and south zones. Use this road to keep your bearings while you explore the whole of Trastevere; in particular, don't miss the superb church of Santa Maria in Trastevere (see page 141). Alternatively, approach over the lovely Ponte Sisto footbridge, which brings you into the area south of the viale. Allow half a day for the visit, and aim on eating lunch or dinner at one of the excellent *trattorie* here.

HIGHLIGHTS

SOUTH OF VIALE DI TRASTEVERE

The Torre dell'Anguillara, opposite the Isola Tiberina, is a medieval tower, the sole survivor of the many family-owned fortress-towers that once crowded Trastevere. Alongside is a fountain with a statue of Gioacchino Belli, a popular Roman dialect poet in the 19th century.

Il Chiostro dei Genovesi (Genoan Cloister) stands next to the church of Santa Maria dell'Orto. This flower-filled cloister, with its central well, was part of a 15th-century hospice built for Genoan sailors.

NORTH OF VIALE DI TRASTEVERE

The Gianicolo has breathtaking views over the whole city and is home to the Orto Botanico.

The Via della Lungara, which runs parallel to the river, was built by Sixtus V to link Trastevere with the Vatican City. Halfway along stands the imposing Regina Coeli prison, named after a church that once stood here. At the end of the street, coming back towards Trastevere, is Villa Farnesina, a sumptuous residence commissioned by banker Agostino Chigi in the early 16th century and decorated with frescoes by Raphael and Giulio Romano, among others (see page 146).

RATINGS	
Good for food	● ● ● ● ●
Historic interest	● ● ●
Shopping	● ● ● ●
Walkability	● ● ● ●

BASICS
✚ 57 D6
🚌 H, 23, 44, 280, 780, 630; tram 8

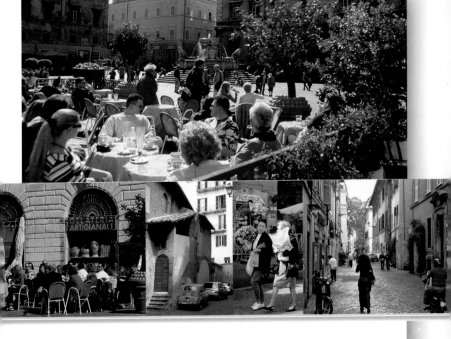

The Porta Settimiana takes you to Via della Scala, with its wine bars, pubs and cafés, leading up to the heart of the area. The Casa della Fornarina stands just inside the Porta Settimiana, at Via di Santa Dorotea 20. This 15th-century house is believed to have been the home of Margherita la Fornarina (the Baker's Daughter), the great love of the painter Raphael's life. Piazza San Callisto has an ancient arch, and is a popular meeting place for young people in the evening.

The Fontana della Botte stands at the corner of Piazza San Callisto and Via della Cisterna. Built in 1927, this curious fountain shows a barrel between two wine measures in celebration of the many popular *osterie* (inns) of the area. The Museo di Roma in Trastevere is in the former monastery of Sant'Egidio. The Municipality of Rome acquired the building in 1875, and it now holds a collection of paintings and drawings of Roman life in the 18th and 19th centuries, along with items that belonged to the Roman dialect poet Trilussa (Carlo Salustri, died 1950).

BACKGROUND

The name Trastevere comes from the Latin expression *trans Tiberim*—'on the other side of the Tiber' and the area was initially populated by immigrants and freed slaves who had come to Rome from all over the empire. During the imperial age, this was an agricultural area, packed with farms and vineyards, and home to country villas and splendid gardens. In the Middle Ages, Trastevere's port of Ripa Grande was used by popes when they journeyed by water, and a shipyard was built there for the construction of the pontifical navy. Strategically positioned for trade, the port was used by ships coming from Ostia on the coast. Syrian and Jewish communities thrived here before they moved across the Tiber to the Ghetto area. In 1870, embankments were built for flood prevention and the port vanished. Trastevere remained a solid working-class area under papal rule, a role that continued well after unification. Today, there's more than a touch of gentrification in evidence, witnessed by the wine bars and expensive restaurants, and by climbing property prices. It still retains much of its charm, and is still a place where you'll hear the native dialect of Rome spoken by its traditional inhabitants, the Trasteverini.

TIPS

● Trastevere is a popular meeting place for young people, but some restaurants can be quite expensive, so check the prices before you go in.

● If you're in Rome at the end of July, take in the traditional and popular *Festa dei Noiantri* (Our Own Festival), celebrated with games and street stands.

Piazza di Santa Maria in Trastevere is a popular place to stop for a snack; at night the church is floodlit and people congregate on the fountain steps (top)
Trastevere is still an area where everyday life goes on much as usual (opposite and above)

The Via Appia Antica—the most important of ancient roads

The Temple of Esculapio, in the Villa Borghese

Agostino Chigi's sumptuous Villa Farnesina

VIA APPIA ANTICA

✚ 312 H9 🚇 Circo Massimo 🚌 118, 160, 628

The Appian Way was the first and most important of the roads built in the fourth century BC. It followed an existing track from Rome south to Capua, a distance of 212km (132 miles). The road was paved with basoli, basalt rock stones of polygonal shape, which survive almost intact. Walking along this ancient surface, with the monuments of the Roman dead at the side of the road and the catacombs of the early Christian martyrs nearby, brings the distant past very close.

The Via Appia proper begins at Porta San Sebastiano; immediately before the ancient gateway, inserted in a modern wall, is the ancient column that marked the first (Roman) mile. Take the bus as far as this in order to avoid the unpleasant section of the road that runs through the city outskirts. Via Appia Antica is closed to cars on Sundays, when it is particularly popular.

At the corner with Via Ardeatina is the church of Domine Quo Vadis ('Lord, where are you going?'), where Jesus is supposed to have shamed Peter into returning to execution in Rome when he was fleeing Nero's persecution. Farther along the road are the basilica and catacombs of San Sebastiano. The catacombs are an atmospheric network of underground tunnels, used as burial places between the second and fifth centuries AD. Because they are so extensive, they can only be visited with a guide.

VILLA BORGHESE

✚ 57 F2 🕐 sunrise–sunset 🚇 Flaminio or Spagna 🚌 52, 53, 88, 95, 116, 117, 119, 490, 495, 491, 910

In the early 17th century, Cardinal Scipione Borghese decided to create a country estate, the Villa Borghese. The extensive grounds now form one of Rome's most important parks. The Cardinal kept his rich art collection in the imposing Villa Pinciana or Casino Borghese (now Museo e Galleria Borghese, see pages 92–97), but there is much else to see in this park, including the Casino della Meridiana and the aviary. The most romantic part is the artificial lake, with a little island in the middle dominated by the temple to Esculapio, erected in the 18th century in Ionian style and adorned with a statue of the Greek god of medicine.

The Piazza di Siena is where Rome's International Horse Show takes place every May (see page 195). Prince Camillo Borghese allowed people to gather here for the Festa delle Ottobrate, celebrated during October with music and dancing. There is also a zoo, Bioparco, which was set up in 1911 (see page 194).

VILLA FARNESINA

✚ 56 D5 • Via della Lungara 230 ☎ 06 6802 7268 🕐 Mon–Sat and first Sun of the month 9–1 💶 Adult €4.50, child (14–18) €3.50 🚌 23, 280, 870

If you are in Trastevere during the morning, it is well worth visiting the beautiful Renaissance Villa Farnesina for its lovely interior or for a walk in the gardens.

In 1508, Agostino Chigi, a wealthy banker from Siena, commissioned Baldassare Peruzzi to build him a suburban villa. Here, Chigi entertained artists, princes and cardinals. His banquets were memorable: After the meal, Chigi would have the gold and silver dishes thrown into the Tiber to impress his guests with his wealth. What they did not know was that the plates were caught

by safety nets and returned to the kitchens. In 1580, the villa was bought by the Farnese family, and it has been know as Villa Farnesina ever since.

On the ground floor are the Loggia of Galatea, with a much admired fresco by Raphael of the Triumph of Galatea, and the Loggia of Cupid and Psyche, frescoed to Raphael's designs by some of his pupils. On the upper floor is the beautiful Salone delle Prospettive, with a fresco by Baldassare Peruzzi of a trompe l'oeil colonnade through which can be seen rural landscapes, villages and a town.

VILLA MEDICI

✚ 57 E3 • Viale Trinità dei Monti 1 ☎ 06 67611 🕐 Gardens only: Sat–Sun 10.30–11.30. Closed Jul–end Aug 💶 €6 🚇 Spagna 🚌 116, 119, 590 www.villamedici.it

The grounds of the Villa Medici are one of the best examples of an Italian Renaissance garden, with rare plants growing amid the pine trees, and elegantly placed fountains and sculptures. The house is not open to the public.

In 1576, Cardinal Ferdinando Medici (later Grand Duke of Tuscany) bought the existing building as a villa-museum, incorporating ancient Roman bas-reliefs in the façade, which has recently been restored.

Look out, too, for the round fountain, topped with a cannon-ball fired, so the legend goes, from Castel Sant'Angelo by eccentric 17th-century Swedish queen Christina to announce to her hosts that she would be arriving for dinner.

Between 1961 and 1977, the French painter Balthus restored the villa to its earlier glory: Statues were placed in the gardens, excavation works unveiled 16th-century frescoes, and an exhibition space was created.

VILLA GIULIA E MUSEO NAZIONALE ETRUSCO

Splendidly housed in the 16th-century Villa Giulia is the National Etruscan Museum, an ideal setting in which to introduce the way of life—and death—of the mysterious Etruscan civilization.

THE VILLA
Commissioned by Pope Julius III, the villa was built between 1551 and 1555 after a design by Giacomo da Vignola. It is set among a series of courtyards, with a beautiful loggia by Bartolomeo Ammannati, and is surrounded by pleasant gardens. The courtyard leads down to an enchanting nymphaeum with false grottoes and a Vasari fountain. The Etruscan museum was founded here in 1889.

THE SARCOPHOGUS OF THE SPOUSES
The most famous piece of Etruscan art is kept in the halls displaying the finds from Cerveteri. The terracotta Sarcophagus of the Spouses represents a husband and wife reclining in an affectionate pose, and vividly demonstrates that the Etruscans believed in the afterlife. It has become an emblem of the Etruscan civilization.

THE COLLECTION
Among the rest of the collection, the Tomb of the Warrior, dating from the sixth century BC, is of particular interest. A reconstruction beneath hall 5 shows what the funeral chambers of the tombs in Cerveteri would have looked like.

Halls 11 to 18 contain a rich collection of domestic objects made from bronze and terracotta, including mirrors, statuettes, candelabra, cinerary urns and, in particular, the bronze Chigi Vase, an exquisitely decorated wine pitcher dating from around 640–625BC (hall 15). In this room is another vase dating from the 6th century BC, decorated with the Etruscan alphabet, revealing its Latin and Greek influences and helping experts to unravel further the Etruscan language.

AN ENIGMATIC PEOPLE
The origins of the Etruscan people are shrouded in mystery. They arrived in Italy in the eighth century BC—from where, nobody knows, although there are several theories—and settled in Etruria (the area of present-day Tuscany and parts of Umbria and Lazio). They were rulers of Italy, with an empire extending from Corsica in the west to the Adriatic, and from Bologna in the north to Capua in the south, until they were conquered by the Romans in the first century BC. Little trace of the Etruscan civilization remains, except for what has been found and pieced together from the tombs.

RATINGS	
Cultural interest	● ● ● ● ●
Good for kids	●
Value for money	● ● ● ●

BASICS
🔡 57 E2 • Piazzale Villa Giulia 9 ☎ 06 3200 562. Reservations: 06 824 529
🕐 Daily 8.30–7.30 💰 Adult €4, child (under 18) free 🚇 Flaminio 🚊 Tram 19 📖 Available in the bookshop, *Museo Etrusco Villa Giulia* in English and Italian, €13 ☕ Caffè dell'Aranceria: beautiful café in the Giardino dell'Aranceria 🎨 Art bookshop, well stocked
www.ticketeria.it
www.beniculturali.it

TIPS
● Stroll among the orange trees in the Giardino dell'Aranceria, and pause for a coffee in the cafeteria.

● Combine the Villa Giulia with the nearby Galleria d'Arte Moderna, worth visiting for the quality of art it displays in a magnificent setting.

The semicircular portico at the back of Vignola's gracious villa (above)

San Paolo fuori le Mura

**Burial place of St. Paul the Apostle.
Grand 19th-century structure containing some fine medieval art.
The farthest flung of the Vatican-ruled basilicas.**

SEEING SAN PAOLO FUORI LE MURA

Allow plenty of time for a visit, as the basilica is some distance from the city—the name literally means 'St. Paul Outside the Walls'. Once there, bear in mind that the present building is only 150 years old and you'll have to track down its medieval treasures. Take time to take in the sheer size of the building before starting your tour.

HIGHLIGHTS

THE FAÇADE

Size and bright hues will be your first impression of the façade, with its 10 huge columns, each 10m (32ft) tall, soaring up towards the glittering mosaic entablature. It's fronted by a portico with a covered arcade, in front of which is a huge 19th-century statue of St. Paul brandishing a sword. Another statue, this time of St. Luke, stands on the right-hand corner of the portico near the Holy Door. Above the portico on the façade is a somewhat garish mosaic showing Christ Giving Benediction between Peter and Paul, the Lamb of God and the Prophets. Statues of saints Peter and Paul guard the central entrance to the church, and silver and bronze doors portray the lives of the two saints. The bronze Holy Door, to the right of the main entrance, survived the 1823 fire; it dates from the 11th century.

THE NAVE, AISLES AND TRANSEPT

Eighty granite columns divide the church into a wide nave and four aisles, the forest of columns and shadowy spaces giving a vivid impression of what the ancient Roman basilicas must have looked like. Above soars the magnificent white and gold coffered ceiling, while light filters through screens of alabaster.

The triumphal arch leading to the chancel has inscriptions recording that the emperors Theodosius and Honorius built the original basilica. It is embellished with a mosaic funded by Galla Placidia, the daughter of Theodosius, which was transferred from the original arch after the fire in the 19th century. The Byzantine-style apse mosaics behind here were made around 1120 by craftsmen specially summoned from Venice by Pope Honorius III. The altars at the head of each arm of the transept are faced with malachite and lapis lazuli, a gift from the Tsar of Russia, Nicholas I, after the 1823 fire, while running around the nave is a mosaic frieze with portraits of all the popes.

THE CIBORIO, PASCHAL CANDLESTICK AND APSE

The triumphal arch frames the beautiful Gothic ciborium, made by Arnolfo di Cambio and Pietri Cavallino in 1285. The canopy is supported by four porphyry columns with gold capitals, while a marble plaque marks the spot where the St. Paul's relics are buried beneath the altar. To the right of the ciborium is the Paschal Candlestick by Nicola di Angelo and Pietro Vasselletto (12th century), a remarkable masterpiece of Romanesque art. Its base depicts monsters, while the shaft has scenes from the life of Jesus. In the Chapel of the Holy Sacrament to the left of the apse are a 14th-century wooden crucifix

San Paolo's 19th-century façade (above left) was built after the fire of 1823, but some of its older treasures, such as the 13th-century Paschal Candlestick (above right), were saved

FARTHER AFIELD

attributed to Pietro Cavallini, who is buried here, a statue of St. Bridget kneeling, by Stefano Maderno, and a wooden statue of St. Paul. To the right between the apse and the Greek-cross baptistery is a decorated stoop sculpted by Pietro Galli in the 19th century, which shows a child threatening a terrified demon with holy water.

THE CLOISTERS

The cloisters are an outstanding example of cosmatesque work by the Vassalletto family, constructed in the first quarter of the 13th century. Richer and better preserved than those of San Giovanni in Laterano (see pages 134–135), they're full of charming detail, sparkling with gold, and are exquisitely worked. It's worth spending time studying the incredible variety of the columns, some straight, some twisted, and some so richly decorated with mosaics the base stone is invisible.

The picture gallery, to one side of the cloisters, displays paintings from the 13th to 19th centuries. The Chapel of Relics next door contains a 15th-century silver reliquary cross.

BACKGROUND

The first church here was built by Constantine over the tomb of the Apostle Paul, and was concentrated in AD324. From AD395 it was extended, so that until the construction of St. Peter's, it was the largest church in

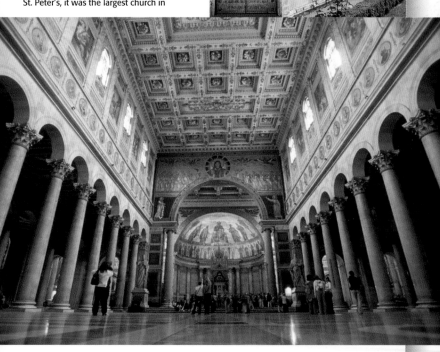

Christendom. In the ninth century, Pope John VIII built fortifications to protect the basilica from Lombard raiders, and a village—called Giovannipoli after the Pope—grew up around it, only to fall derelict as malaria took its toll. Disaster struck on the night of 15 July 1823, when the great basilica, one of the least changed since ancient times, was practically destroyed by fire. Work immediately began on an even more magnificent replacement, based on the original plan and funded by contributions from all over the world. The new San Paolo fuori le Mura was finally completed in 1854 and, in the presence of 185 bishops, was consecrated by Pope Pius IX.

The bronze Holy Door (top left) and the beautiful 13th-century cloisters (top right) survived the 1823 fire, as did the inscription on the triumphal arch (above), which was incorporated into the new church, along with its restored fifth-century mosaics

Palazzo dei Congressi (left), in the EUR complex

EUR AND ITS MUSEUMS

✠ Off 311 G9 ◎ EUR Fermi ◻ 703, 714, 717, 764, 765, 780, 791

The Esposizione Universale di Roma (EUR) was begun in 1936 as an emphatic statement about Fascist ambitions. The construction of this new quarter was interrupted by the outbreak of World War II, and it was not until 1951 that they were completed. Today, the EUR is a focus for a variety of events and art exhibitions, and many shops, cinemas and clubs have opened up. For visitors the main attractions are three excellent museums.

MUSEO DELLA CIVILTÀ ROMANA
Piazza Giovanni Agnelli 10 ☎ 06 5926135 ◎ Tue–Sat 9–6, Sun 9–2 💶 €4, child (under 18) free

The Museum of Roman Culture traces the history of the city of Rome through models and reconstructions. There's a scale model of ancient Rome, showing all the buildings that stood within the Aurelian Walls in the fourth century. There are also moulds taken from Trajan's Column (see pages 78–79), giving you a chance to study the carvings close up.

MUSEO NAZIONALE DELLE ARTI E TRADIZIONI POPOLARI
Piazza Guglielmo Marconi 8/10 ☎ 06 5926148, 06 591 2669 ◎ Tue–Sat 9–2, Sun 9–7.30 💶 Adult €4, child (under 18) free 🎫 👫 www.popolari.arti.beniculturali.it

The collection of the National Museum of Arts and Popular Traditions has objects relating to everyday life from the 18th century to the present day. It was put together in 1911 to celebrate the 50th anniversary of Italian unity, and moved here in 1956.

MUSEO NAZIONALE PREISTORICO ETNOGRAFICO
Piazza Guglielmo Marconi 8/10 ☎ 06 549521 ◎ Daily 9–7.30 💶 Adult €4, child (under 18) free www.pigorini.arti.beniculturali.it

This internationally important ethnographic museum has collections from Africa, Oceania and America. The African display includes around 250 weapons, ivory tools from Nigeria, fabrics, and 17th-century wooden sculptures from the Congo. Inuit, pre-Columbian and Amazonian items make up the American collections. The prehistoric section covers the Stone, Bronze and Iron Ages with displays of archaeological finds, largely from within Italy.

Palazzo della Civiltà del Lavoro, known as the Square Colosseum (above), contains the Museo della Civiltà

SANT'AGNESE FUORI LE MURA AND MAUSOLEO DI SANTA COSTANZA

✠ 307 J1 • Via Nomentana ☎ 06 861 0840 ◎ Church: daily 7.30–12, 4–6. Catacombs and mausoleum: Tue–Sat 9–12, 4–6, Sun 9–12, Mon 4–6 💶 Free ◻ 30, 60, 84, 90, 93, 168 ◻ Guided tour of catacombs €5

Although it is a little way out of the main tourist area, the beautiful group of buildings consisting of Sant'Agnese fuori le Mura, the Catacombs of Sant'Agnese, the remains of a basilica from the time of Constantine and the circular Mausoleum of St. Constantia, should not be missed.

The catacombs were developed between the third and fourth centuries, and hold the remains of the martyred St. Agnes (see page 124). The church above, dedicated to her, was built by Pope Honorius I in the seventh century and is one of the best-preserved Byzantine basilicas in Rome. On the apse is a seventh-century mosaic of St. Agnes with the popes Honorius I and Symmachus, the latter holding a model of the basilica.

Nearby are the huge walls of another basilica, built between AD337 and AD350 by Constantia, daughter of the Emperor Constantine. The Mausoleum of St. Constantia was erected against one side, built by Constantia for herself and her sister. Inside is a beautiful colonnade with 12 pairs of granite columns, above which are 12 windows reaching up into the frescoed dome. The barrel-vaulted ceiling of the corridor is adorned with beautiful fourth-century mosaics. One of the central panels shows Constantia and her husband Annibaliano. In a niche at the rear of the mausoleum is a copy of Constantia's red porphyry sarcophagus; the original is in the Vatican.

THE SIGHTS

FARTHER AFIELD

This chapter gives information on things to do in Rome, other than sightseeing.
Shops and performance venues are shown on the maps at the beginning of each section.

What to Do

SHOPPING

In the Eternal City you can almost literally shop till you drop. More and more shops are now open all day from 9.30am to 8.30pm. Many are also open on Sunday, often from 11am to 1pm and 4pm to 7.30pm.

Traditionally, shops have closed for the sacrosanct lunch and siesta time from 1pm to 4pm, but even this is becoming less common. During winter, they tend to open earlier in the afternoon, while to avoid the summer heat (and enjoy a long lunch) later opening around 5pm is more usual. Throughout these listing, we have indicated where shops open outside these standard hours.

August is holiday time in Rome, when many small businesses traditionally take their two-week annual break, and almost everything closes around Ferragosto, the public holiday on 15 August. Many shops are also closed on Monday mornings, and food stores tend to close on Saturday afternoons in summer and Thursday afternoons in winter.

CREDIT CARDS

Although Italy is traditionally known as a cash society, credit cards are widely accepted in Rome, with the main exceptions of small grocery shops and delicatessens. You should always get a receipt (ricevuta fiscale) as the law requires all shopkeepers and restaurateurs to provide this, and they can be fined if they don't. In practice, this is rare, but it's useful if you have bought high-value goods and need proof for Customs—or if you need to make an insurance claim.

SMALL IS BEAUTIFUL

The shopping malls and department stores so beloved of other countries are in their infancy in Rome, although there are exceptions such as the Cinecittà Due mall (see page 171) and the popular La Rinascente (see page 171). Small, specialized shops are the way to a Roman heart and when in Rome…!

Conveniently, different areas tend to specialize in different goods. The most famous designers have taken over the streets around the Piazza di Spagna, especially the very chic Via dei Condotti, where galaxies of starry names such as Valentino, Gucci, Bulgari and Prada are clustered. Here the Italian art form of la bella figura is at its height. Near Piazza Navona, the Via del Governo Vecchio has less expensive independent designer boutiques, while the Via dei Giubbonari, near Campo dei Fiori, has inexpensive fashion. But in stylish Rome, cheaper clothes tend to be of good quality as well as being well-cut.

The roads down from Via dei Condotti have some gorgeous shoes, bags, belts and every other kind of accessory, while Via Nazionale, Via del Tritone and Via del Corso are good places to seek out beautiful, reasonably priced must-haves.

The Via Margutta is full of artists' studios, while Via dei Coronari showcases some of Rome's finest antiques. Trastevere is full of artisan workshops selling hand-made jewellery and ceramics.

Near the Vatican, the Via Cola di Rienzo is fashion central, with some of the big names and all the mid-market chains, as well as newcomers from overseas, such as Mango. This is also a good place to visit some of Rome's popular delis, where the aromas will make you think you're in gourmet heaven.

SOUVENIRS

Pasta in every shape and size; greenest extra virgin olive oil; funghi porcini (dried mushrooms); truffle oil and spices all make durable food buys. Hand-made ceramics, kitchen gadgets, espresso coffee pots and individually designed cups, kettles, salt and pepper grinders—especially those with the Alessi mark—are all Italian style at their best. There is a long tradition of artisan silver- and goldsmithing in Rome. Herbalists and shops specializing in lotions and potions have tempting arrays of fragrant delicacies.

The souvenir shops around the Vatican do a healthy trade in religious statues, crosses, rosaries and plenty of St. Peter's in snowstorms. Around the tourist honeypots are plenty of sourvenirs from figures of thonged Roman centurions and gladiators to models of the Colosseo and the Trevi Fountain.

If you are not an EU resident, you can claim back the tax on your shopping once you get home (see page 281)

TAX FREE REFUND

20%

CASHMERE & WOOL
EU.145

WOOL 120'S
EU.275

Tridente and Via del Corso

HOW TO GET THERE

🚇 Spagna

🚌 62, 63, 116, 117, 119, 492, 590

The area around Piazza di Spagna (known as the Tridente after the trio of roads built off Piazza del Popolo to relieve congestion in the 16th century) is the smartest and most expensive shopping area in Rome, while Via del Corso sells cheaper versions of the latest styles.

VIA DEI CONDOTTI

Rome's version of Bond Street or 5th Avenue is Via dei Condotti. Start here forthe best in Italian fashion: **Gucci** (No. 8), **Valentino** (No. 13), **Max Mara** (No. 17– 19/a), **Trussardi** (No. 49–50), **& Gabbana** (No. 51–52), **Armani** (No. 77) and **Prada** (No. 95). You will find the **Versace** store for women on Via Bocca di Leone (No. 26–27), a

The great fashion houses on Via dei Condotti—Gucci at No. 8...

street that intersects with Via dei Condotti. Just to the south, the quieter Via Borgognona runs parallel to Via dei Condotti and holds just as much to tempt the fashion-crazed: **Gianfranco Ferré** (No. 6), **Roberto Cavalli** (No. 7/a), **Moschino** (32/a), **Fendi** store (No. 36-7) and **Laura Biagiotti** (No. 43-44), **Tod's** (No. 45) and **Hogan** (No. 46). For edgier fashions try **Galassia** on Via Frattina (No. 20-1).

VIA DEL BABUINO

Welcome respite from the hordes of Prada-hungry tourists on Via dei Condotti try Via del Babuino with its fashion options

(**Armani Jeans** at No. 70a; **Etro** at No. 102), antique collectors, jewellers and trendy specialist shops. Down towards Piazza del Popolo on the left is **Tad** (No. 155a), a so-called concept store with a fabulous selection of clothing and shoes, the Aussie Aesop range of cosmetics, a hairdresser, a flower shop and a fabrics and furniture section. It even has its own café. A few doors further down is **Fabriano** (No. 173), a pen and stationery shop to die for with writing paper, photo albums, wallets and travel diaries. The streets that connect Via del Babuino and Via del Corso are well worth exploring too. On one of the most animated, Via della Croce, you will find some good delis and one-off clothing boutiques like that of Rome designer Vanessa Foglia, **abitart** (No. 46-7), whose bright and flowing clothes are displayed like works of art. On Via Mario de' Fiori make a beeline for **C.u.c.i.n.a.** (No. 65), one of the best kitchenware stores in Rome for choice, and a mix of cheap and more expensive brands.

VIA DEL CORSO

Avoid the part of Via del Corso from Piazza Venezia until Largo Chigi as the cheap clothing stores and traffic are uninspiring. Start instead at one of Rome's oldest department stores, **La Rinascente** (Piazza Colonna). Heading towards Piazza del Popolo you will pass huge **Diesel** (No. 186), **Energie** (No. 510) and **Benetton** (No. 426), all big Italian mid-market success stories. Keeping in teenager and surf

dude mode try also **Energie** (No. 407-8, 486-7), which stocks brands like O'Neill, Puma, Adidas, Converse and Camper. **Messaggerie Musicali** (No. 472) sells an enormous selection of cds and dvds, as well as books, travel books and magazines in English.

...and Prada at No. 95

WHERE TO STOP

ANTICA VINERIA DI VIA DELLA CROCE
Via della Croce 76b, 00187
Tel 06 679 0896
🕐 Daily 10am-1am
A delightful wine bar that also serves light meals.

AU PAIN QUOTIDIEN
Via Tomacelli 24, 00187
Tel 06 6880 7727
🕐 Tue-Sun 9am- midnight, closed Mon
Great for stone-ground bread and French-style buttery croissants and pains au chocolat. Huge garnished salads (rare in Italy), soups and quiches served all day long.

Via Nazionale and the Monti district

Long, wide and traffic-ridden, Via Nazionale has many affordable mainstream fashion options, a handful of genuinely cool clothing

Browsing for paintings at a street stall

boutiques and a wide selection of mid-priced shops selling handbags, luggage and footwear. Off to the southeast is the village-like Monti district, with its appealing selection of artisan shops and one-off clothing and jewellery emporia.

VIA NAZIONALE

Come out at Repubblica metro station and start walking down Via Nazionale. On your right after Mel Bookstore head in to **Fiorucci** (No. 236), a store for women who want to express their girlie side. Outfits by Dolce and Gabbana, Moschino Jeans,

Kookai, Diesel, Killah and Liu Jo range from the feminine to the grungy and are undeniably fun.

Regal (No. 234) is one shop down and stocks a wide variety of mid-priced bags, umbrellas and purses. Brands vary from Eastpak to Nannini, Armani and Mandarina Duck, passing by those eminently practical, bright, foldable bags by Longchamp. Cross the street and at No. 55 (after Via Genova) you will spot **Furla** with its simple but varied range of leather bags and accessories in shades that cover the spectrum from classic to loud. By the time you've left Rome you will have seen so many branches you will start to wonder if they are a little too popular for comfort, yet the suppleness and quality of their leather, and their highly affordable prices, have assured them a huge following.

Staying on this side of the street and heading down Via Nazionale turn left up Via Milano for the classic looks of **Sorelle D'Italia** (No. 31), with clothes by Patrizia Pepe, Marithé & François Girbaud and Luciana Conti. The shop is cheerful and decorated with original art works and ornaments. Back on Via Nazionale, chic women in the know come to **LEI** (No. 88). Party dresses and feminine fashions are by a mix of Belgian and British designers, patterned T-shirts are by Barcelona designer Custo; all are complemented by delicate shoes by Kallisté and Katharine Hamnett. For original gift items and Rome souvenirs, including untacky T shirts, pop into **Museum Shop** (No. 185).

MONTI

Bohemian Monti's main drags are Via del Boschetto, Via Panisperna and Via dei Serpenti (which leads straight to the Colosseum); its most atmospheric piazza is Santa Madonna dei Monti (just off the map). Starting with Via del Boschetto you should make a beeline for the sheer originality of **Le Gallinelle** (No. 76), a former butcher's shop with original designs and customized vintage garments of Wilma Silvestri. On the same street you will find a selection of enticing one-off interior design and antique stores, as well as the Japanese inspired **Linn-Sui** (No. 78/a) which offers so-called ecological beds and futons, slippers, rugs and tableware, as well as a range of pillows, pouffes and bags made with Designer Guild fabrics.

WHERE TO STOP

DAGNINO
Galleria Esedra
Via Vittorio Emanuele Orlando 75, 00185
Tel 06 481 8660
🕐 Mon-Sun 7.30am–10.30pm.
www.pasticceriadagnino.com
Fortify yourself before shopping in this café, bar and restaurant. Dagnino's has an immaculate 1950s interior, and an incredible array of Sicilian sweets and savoury goodies.

F.I.S.H.
This minimalist restaurant serving fine fusion food actually looks and tastes the part. Great for Mediterranean-cum-Oriental cuisine, or sushi at the bar. See page 242.

Trastevere

HOW TO GET THERE
🚇 H, 23, 280, 780, tram 8

Across the river, Trastevere feels like a city within a city. Though very touristy in parts, its shops, many of them artisan or boutiques, reflect its local atmosphere and separateness—and are open late, too.

VIA DELLA LUNGARETTA AND PIAZZA SANTA MARIA IN TRASTEVERE

Enter Via della Lungaretta from Viale Trastevere on the right-hand side and head straight for **Roma Store** (No. 63) which may not sound promising but has a vast selection of refined and hard-to-find perfumes and cosmetics, from Artisan Parfumeur, L'Occitane, Acqua di Parma, Vetiver, Etro, Comptoir Sud Pacifique and Penhaligon's. Don't come here looking for J-Lo's

Trastevere is known for its lively markets, especially Porta Portese

Glow! Now walk straight into the atmospheric Piazza Santa Maria in Trastevere. **Pandora** at No. 6 is open late and is crammed with attractive and moderately priced jewellery (including some lovely glass items by the Sent sisters and other contemporary Venetian artists), and well-chosen handmade ceramics, stoneware and glass ornaments.

VIA SAN FRANCESCO A RIPA AND VIA NATALE DEL GRANDE

Turn left out of the piazza and head to Via San Francesco a Ripa for two clothing boutiques worth the detour: **Victory** (No. 19) and

Verso Sud (No. 168). The former stocks dressier clothes by Marithé and François Girbaud, and Pinko, and the second hip-thinking women's clothes by Isabel Marant, BP Studio, Comme des Garçons, Vivienne Westwood and Alberta Ferretti. Both have a deservedly loyal following.

Next turn right at Via Natale del Grande, a street filled with delis and stores selling fresh pasta, pastry and fish, all with a local feel and quality goods. One of the most characterful food shops in Rome is **Innocenzi** at No. 31, which stocks regional products such as olive oils, breads, pastas and sauces from all over Italy, but also the staples for Indian, Thai, Japanese and Mexican cooking. They have a good range of organic products and sell sweets loose from jars, and pulses and rice from large bags on the floor. Delightfully old-fashioned. **Piazza San Cosimato** hosts a small but lively food market every morning except Sunday.

VICOLO DEL CINQUE AND PIAZZA TRILUSSA

Walking straight ahead turn right at Piazza Sant'Egidio (where artisans sell their wares most evenings of the week) and down Vicolo del Cinque. Here you will find restaurants and artisans aplenty, including handmade jewellery, using a glass-fusion technique and a store dedicated to antique lamps (No. 48), as well as mad sculptural footwear creations by **Joseph Debach** (No. 19). Farther down on the left is **Jacche Calzature** (No. 24/b) which sells shoes for men and

women all priced at €36.

Amid the unexceptional there are always some finds to be had. Once in Piazza Trilussa turn left past the fountain into Via di Ponte Sisto. Here in a tiny atelier you will find the larger than life **Ivano Langella** (No. 73a) and his jewellery creations, with

Hat stall at Porta Portese market, held on Sunday mornings

lots of pearl, semi-precious stones, horn and chunky silver. He has counted Kylie Minogue among his clients.

WHERE TO STOP

TRASTÈ
An informal café where you can choose from a huge range of herbal teas, as well as *frullati* (fruit shakes) and alcoholic beverages. See page 253.

LA RENELLA
Via del Moro 19, 00153
Tel 06 581 7265
🕐 Mon–Sun 9am–9pm
Freshly baked bread and thick, tasty slices of pizza.

Campo dei Fiori and Piazza Navona

HOW TO GET THERE
🚌 40, 46, 62, 64, 70, 81, 87, 571, 916

Campo dei Fiori has one of Rome's best-known local markets every morning except Sunday. In the medieval streets off it are multitude of antique stores, artisan shops and fashionable clothing stores. The streets north of Piazza Navona attract Rome's more refined and wealthy shoppers, the streets west of it are where to hunt for unique fashions, both first and second hand.

CAMPO DEI FIORI AND AROUND

Head southeast out of Campo dei Fiori along Via dei Giubbonari for a vast selection of unusual, and in some cases, cutting-edge fashions to fit all budgets. From

Tempting fruit and vegetables at Campo dei Fiori market

Levi's to hip streetwear store **Prototype**, through **Ethnic**, Italy's version of H&M, this is the place to come for trendy but original outfits. Back on Campo dei Fiori turn right down Via dei Baullari for **Loco** (No. 22) and its mad, expensive fashions for the feet. Turn right again on Piazza Pollarola for a Carrie Bradshaw slice of shoe heaven at **Nuyorica** (No. 36–7) where the latest by Marc Jacobs, Pierre Hardy and Rodolphe Menudier await you. Off the north-west of Campo dei Fiori you will find Via del Pellegrino and various potters, jewellers and offbeat optician's **Mondello Ottica** (No. 98) with

local artists' installations in the windows. Turn off briefly on to Vicolo del Bollo for delightfully patterned hand-made children's dungarees, jackets and skirts by Swedish-born **Rachele** (No. 6). Back on Via del Pellegrino pop in to **Regola 71** (at the corner with Via dei Cappellari) for original fashions by Belgian and French designers that make any woman feel distinctly stylish, regardless of body shape and size. Via dei Banchi Vecchi, and the wide leafy Via Giulia to the northwest, are home to some refined antique shops and interior design stores.

PIAZZA NAVONA AND AROUND

On the northern tip of Piazza Navona is renowned toy store **Al Sogno** (No. 53) which has been going strong since 1945. Leave the piazza and turn left for Via dei Coronari, the street par excellence for antiques in Rome. Or, cross the street and walk straight until you reach Via dell'Orso and the surrounding alleys, a refined and quiet area with lots of jewellers. **Massimo Maria Melis** (Via dell'Orso 57) creates new jewels using ancient Roman coins in gold and silver settings. Off the south-western end of Piazza Navona lies Via del Governo Vecchio where bazaar-like second hand clothing shops and high fashion temples dedicated to foreign and local *stilisti* (designers) reign supreme. Running parallel to the east of Piazza Navona is Corso Rinascimento where a branch of Florence's famous **Officina di**

Santa Maria Novella (No. 47) sells creams and perfumes from original recipes by Dominican friars. In the same vein, **Ai Monasteri** at No. 72 sells teas, honeys, liqueurs, and potions made by monks from all over Italy.

Come to Via dei Coronari to browse the antique shops

WHERE TO STOP
WINE TIME
This vibrant spot is just the place for a light snack (pasta, salads, veggie and meat burgers). The kitchen is open all day. See page 254.

CAFFÈ NOVECENTO
Via del Governo Vecchio 12, 00186
Tel 06 686 5242
🕐 Mon-Thu 11.30am-8.30pm, Fri, Sat 11.30-8.30pm, summer; Mon 12.30pm-8.30pm, Wed–Sun 12.30pm–12.30am, rest of year
Vegetarian brunches, light meals and salads, and an array of teas, fruit juices, *frullati* (fruit shakes) and home-made cakes.

Shopping Directory

This selection of retail outlets, arranged by theme, covers some of Rome's top fashion stores, plus markets and shops selling gifts, food, books and art.
• See pages 152–155 for shopping locator maps
• See pages 172–173 for chain stores chart
• See page 278 for clothing sizes

BOOKS

ALMOST CORNER BOOKSHOP
Map 153 D6
Via del Moro 45, 00153
Tel 06 583 6942
Interesting and unusual selection of books, especially considering the shop's small size. Competitively priced and particularly good on biography and history, with a strong emphasis on Rome and Italy. Extensive children's section, from toddlers to teenagers. Special orders at no extra charge. Over 5,000 titles on display. Helpful and knowledgeable owner.
◉ Mon–Sat 9.30–1.30, 3.30–8, Sun 11–1.30, 3.30–8; closed Sun in Aug
🚌 H, 8, 23, 280 to Trastevere; tram 8

ANGLO AMERICAN BOOK CO.
Map 153 E4
Via della Vite 102, 00187
Tel 06 679 5222
www.aab.it
This is one of the better English bookshops in the city. It is a short distance from the Spanish Steps, going towards Piazza del Popolo, and in a 19th-century building. The excellent selection includes music, cinema, philosophy, religion and science, as well as fiction and children's books. It also sells travel guides to Rome, Italy and most world destinations.
◉ Tue–Sun 10–7.30, Mon 3.30–7.30, Sep–end Jun; Mon–Fri 10–7.30, Sat 10–2, rest of year 🚌 40, 62, 64, 116

ANTICA LIBRERIA CROCE
Map 153 D5
Corso Vittorio Emanuele II 156, 00186
Tel 06 6880 2269
This primarily Italian bookshop, with some titles in English, specializes in books on all aspects of classical and contemporary art and photography. It has an extensive selection on two floors, and from time to time art exhibitions are held here.
◉ Tue–Sat 10–8, Sun 10–1.30, 4–8, Oct–end May; Sun 10–midnight, rest of year 🚌 40, 62, 64, 116

FELTRINELLI INTERNATIONAL
Map 154 G4
Via V. E. Orlando 84, 00184
Tel 06 4827878
www.lafeltrinelli.it
Come here for novels and books in English, French, Spanish, Portuguese, German and Japanese, including probably the widest selection of travel guides in English. There's also a good section dedicated to learning Italian. Feltrinelli has more than 100,000 books, at generally more competitive prices than most other bookstores selling foreign books.
◉ Mon–Sat 9–8, Sun 10–1.30, 4-7.30
🚇 Repubblica G40, 64, 170, H

FINE IDEAS
Map 154 G4
Via Torino 136, 00184
Tel 06 474 6877
www.fineideas.it
A bookshop with a difference. Every Saturday between 10.30

and noon, parents can leave their children, free of charge, while they browse the shelves. Kids are entertained and in safe hands. Excellent travel section, plus videos, DVDs, second-hand books and English greetings cards. Prices are somewhat on the high side.
◉ Mon–Sat 9–8 🚇 Repubblica 🚌 64, 70, 170

MEL BOOKSTORE
Map 154 G4
Via Nazionale 254–255, 00184
Tel 06 488 5405
www.melbookstore.it
Mel Bookstore takes up two floors of an appealingly spacious art deco interior with wide marble staircases. Sofas are dotted everywhere, allowing you to peruse before purchase in comfort. Other highlights include a small but interesting selection of second-hand books and CDs, a good number of English paperbacks, guides relating to current and recent art exhibitions in Rome, and a café.
◉ Daily 9–7.30, Sun 10–1.30, 4–8
🚇 Repubblica 🚌 H, 40, 60, 64, 70, 117, 170

OPEN DOOR BOOKSHOP
Map 153 E6
Via della Lungaretta 23, 00153
Tel 06 589 6478
www.books-in-italy.com
An eccentric little bookshop that is a real find. The building dates from the 16th century while the shop started life in 1965. The American owner stocks mainly second-hand books, including rare and out-of-print volumes. He also publishes his own satirical political review on current events in Italy and the world, which are well worth browsing through.
◉ Tue–Sat 10.30–2.30, 4.30–8.30, Mon 4.30–8.30 🚌 Tram 8

MUSIC

RICORDI MEDIA STORE
Map 153 E5
Via Cesari Battisti 120, 00187
Tel 06 679 8022/3
www.lafeltrinelli.it
Attractively designed and popular music store in a building that once housed the Verdi archives. It has the largest classical DVD/CD collection in Rome, plus an extensive Italian music section. Sheet music and musical instruments are also on sale. Four other outlets are at Termini, Viale Guilio Cesare, Piazza della Repubblica and Via del Corso.
⚙ Mon–Sat 9.30–8, Sun 3.30–8; closed Sun Jul–end Aug 🚌 40, 62, 64, 117 to Piazza Venezia

ART AND ANTIQUES

COMIC'S BAZAR
Map 152 D5
Via dei Banchi Vecchi 127–128, 00186
Tel 06 6880 2923
A veritable Aladdin's cave specializing in early 20th-century Viennese Thonet lamps and furniture from the 1800s to the 1920s. One of two entrances is just beyond Via Sforza Cesarini, on your left going towards Campo dei Fiori, while the other is a little farther down. Their more contemporary and ethnic-inspired store is close by at Via Giulia 140/e.
⚙ Tue–Sat 9.30–7.30, Mon 3–7.30 🚌 46, 62, 64, 116, 492, 571, or any bus to Corso Vittorio Emanuele II

LUMIÈRES
Map 153 D6
Vicolo del Cinque 48, 00153
Tel 06 580 3614
Unassuming shop crammed with goods. If an interesting lamp from the French art deco or Italian Liberty periods is what you're after, this is the place to come. Choose from dozens of antique lamps, all fully restored. Or bring your own lamp to be restored by an artisan.
⚙ Mon–Sat 10–1, 4–8.30 🚌 H, 780; tram 8

MARIA GRAZIA LUFFARELLI
Map 152 D5
Via dei Banchi Vecchi 29, 00186
Tel 06 683 2494
www.mgluffarelli.com
Bright watercolour landscapes of hills, sea and sun. Prices

range from very low to moderate for original works by the eponymous artist. Also on sale is a beautiful range of Rome watercolour reproductions in postcard format, as well as prints of Luffarelli's work mounted on tables of brightly painted wood.
⚙ Mon–Sat noon–8 🚌 40, 64, 116, 492, 571, or any bus to Corso Vittorio Emanuele II

MATHERIA FARNESE
Map 152 D6
Via G. Garibaldi 53–55/a, 00153
Tel 06 581 7566
www.farnese.it
This is the showroom of an internationally renowned group of architects and artisans who create stunning, handcrafted ceramic floor tiles inspired by Roman villas and 18th-century patrician houses. They also restore antique tiles, plates and jugs. This kind of craftsmanship comes at a price, however.
⚙ Mon–Fri 10–7, Sat–Sun by appointment only 🚌 23, 280

NATOLLI
Map 153 D5
Corso del Rinascimento 55, 00186
Tel 06 6830 1170
www.muranopiumadeinitaly.com
Natolli is on a street that runs parallel with Piazza Navona and sells exquisitely crafted

Murano glass, with items ranging from chandeliers to mirrors, glasses and even sculptures. All items are sold with a certificate of authenticity and signed in limited editions. Up the road, at No. 43, is another shop selling smaller items. Shipping is possible worldwide.
⚙ Daily 9–8 🚌 64, 87, 116, 492

LE TERRE DI AT
Map 155 J5
Via degli Ausoni 13, 00185
Tel 06 491748
The Sicilian-born potter who sells her work here likes to give an innovative, often ethnic twist to her ceramics. She produces tableware, mugs and vases, as well as exquisite jewellery, which she plates with gold and platinum.
⚙ Tue–Sat 10–1, 4–8, Mon 4–8 🚌 71, 492; tram 3, 19

LE TRE GHINEE
Map 153 D5
Via del Pellegrino 53/a, 00186
Tel 06 687 2739
A mother and daughter design team making jewellery and objets d'art using Tiffany glass and pottery techniques. The mother deals in glass and the daughter is a pottery wizard. Items range from expensive vases to very reasonable cups and goblets. Pottery nativity scenes are on sale at Christmas. Evening classes offered.
⚙ Mon–Sat 10–8 🚌 46, 62, 64, 116, 492, 571, or any bus to Corso Vittorio Emanuele II

TOYS

AL SOGNO
Map 153 D4
Piazza Navona 53, 00186
Tel 06 686 4198
www.alsogno.com
This veritable box of treats will enthrall adults and children alike. Packed with beautifully made toy animals, from pandas to poodles, miniature and life size. Exquisite Italian handmade

SPECIAL

LA CITTÀ DEL SOLE
Map 153 E4
Via della Scrofa 65, 00186
Tel 06 6880 3805
www.cittadelsole.com
Between Piazza Navona and the Pantheon. This is a toy store for the progressive parent, crammed with educational toys, puzzles, games and books. Divided into sections for children aged 0–14, with a focus on creative playing and learning. All the best toys in safe plastics and wood.
🕐 Mon–Sat 10–7.30, Sun 11–7.30 🚌 116

dolls and wooden Pinocchios, Venetian masks and handcrafted chess sets. There's even a *Lord of the Rings* room.
🕐 Daily 10–8 🚌 64, 87, 116, 492

BABE
Map 153 E5
Via della Palombella 22, 00186
Tel 06 6830 1875
The idea in this inspired store, just behind the Pantheon, is that anything kids up to 12 will like goes: toys, gadgets, drawing pens, soft toys, bags, party decorations and some clothing items. They also organize children's birthday parties in a special room downstairs, and the staff are very friendly.
🕐 Mon–Fri 10–8,Sat 10–2, Oct–end May; Mon–Fri 10–8, rest of year 🚌 116 to Pantheon, or 30, 40, 64, 492, 916 (plus several others) to Largo di Torre Argentina

BARTOLUCCI
Map 153 E4
Via dei Pastini 98, 00186
Tel 06 6919 0894
www.bartolucci.com
Not far from the Pantheon is this master craftsman's workshop—all articles are handmade, the result of the most skilled and patient work. More than a hundred different animal clocks with moving eyes, wooden marionettes, horses and much more. Prices start at just a few euros.
🕐 Daily 10–8 🚌 116

GIFTS AND SOUVENIRS

CANDLE HOUSE
Map 153 E4
Via della Maddalena 41, 00186
Tel 06 679 5633
www.candlehouse.it
The Candle House is just along from the baroque Maddalena church in a 14th-century palazzo with beamed ceilings and wooden floors. Its glass shelves are full of candles for every occasion, and it carries on the long Roman tradition of quality candle-making. All are supremely handcrafted and, considering the quality, prices are reasonable.
🕐 Tue–Sun 12–8, Sep–end Jun; Tue–Thu 12–8, Fri–Sun 12–3, 4–midnight, rest of year 🚌 116, 175 to Piazza di Montecitorio

CASA DEL ROSARIO
Map 154 G5
Via Esquilino 33–34, 00185
Tel 06 486991
Large, rambling emporium of religious memorabilia. It needs renovating, but don't let that put you off. Covers the spectrum from tacky to serious: candles, rosaries, certificates of papal blessing and kitsch souvenirs all abound. Inexplicably, there is also a roomful of reasonably priced suitcases.
🕐 Mon–Fri 9–1, 3–7.30, Sat 9–1 🚇 Termini or Cavour 🚌 75, 84, 105, 204, 360, 590, 714; tram 5, 14

CENTRO RAKU
Map 153 E4
Via dei Pastini 20, 00186
Tel 06 678 7682
www.raku.it
The raku ceramic technique of glazed earthenware originated in 16th-century Japan, where it is mainly reserved for the tea ceremony. The word raku

means 'to celebrate the day', or 'to live in harmony'. Here, in one of the most beautiful areas of Rome, near the Pantheon, are hundreds of handmade raku clocks (from €25 to €100).
🕐 Mon–Sat 11–9 (sometimes closed Sat pm) 🚌 116

D CUBE
Map 153 D4
Via della Pace 38, 00186
Tel 06 686 1218
D Cube is packed with design objects from around the planet, each labelled with its country of provenance. The range includes everything from tableware, kitchenware, candles and bags to quirkier items such as ecological radios, either clockwork or powered by solar energy. What's on offer is very original, with something for every budget. There's another branch at Piazza Mignanelli 24.
🕐 Daily 11–10 🚌 40, 64, 116, 492, 571, or any bus to Corso Vittorio Emanuele II

FABRIANO
Map 153 E3
Via del Babuino 173, 00187
Tel 06 3260 0361
Minimalist in design, this store sells stacks of paper goods and stationery such as notepads and address books, laid out tantalizingly from the brightest to the most muted. The paper, of the highest quality, has been made by the same technique for 800 years, and prices are high. Pens and briefcases are also sold.
Mon–Sat 10–7.30 Spagna or Flaminio 81, 117, 119, 590, 628

MUSEUM SHOP
Map 153 F5
Via Nazionale 185, 00184
Tel 06 474 6872
One of Rome's more tasteful and original sources of gifts and souvenirs. Good selection of espresso cups, photograph albums, notepads, posters, watches and pens. Also some highly entertaining but very wearable T-shirts with messages about Rome, Italy and life in general.
Mon–Sat 10–8, Sun 12–8 Repubblica H, 40, 60, 64, 70, 117, 170

PANDORA
Map 153 D6
Piazza Santa Maria in Trastevere 6, 00153
Tel 06 5817145
This is an unusual but tasteful store, with a great selection of contemporary Venetian glass items (some by the well-known Sent sisters from Murano), Italian handmade ceramics, ethnic and hand-made jewellery, small antique pieces and accessories, such as scarves and bags.
Daily, all day H, 780; tram 8

FOOD AND DRINK
ANDREOTTI
Map off 153 E7
Via Ostiense 54/b, 0054
Tel 06 5750773
Just along from the white marble pyramid at Ostiense is this patisserie-cum-café. You

can sit and try one of their delectable choux pastries filled with a *limoncello* or rum cream, accompanied by a frothy cappuccino, before choosing from the many other pastries to take out. There are ice creams and a few savouries, too.
Daily 7.30am–10pm Piramide

ANTICA PESCHERIA GALLUZZI 1894
Map 154 G4
Via Venezia 26/28, 00184
Tel 06 474 4444
This most noble of fishmongers, on a side street off the Via Nazionale, has been supplying Romans for well over 100 years. In a lovely old palace with brick arches you'll find quality fish and shellfish caught from all over the Mediterranean. Their anchovies are said to be the best in town.
Tue–Sat 6–1.30; closed last 2 weeks in Aug Repubblica 64, 70

AVENATI
Map 154 F5
Via Milano 44, 00184
Tel 06 488 2681
Like nearly every other delicatessen in Rome, this one is satisfyingly old-fashioned. It's a gem, guaranteed to make your mouth water. Packed with traditional Italian foods not found in the local markets: quality salamis, olive oils from Tuscany, Umbria and Puglia, special pastas, wines and cheeses, including handmade, buffalo-milk mozzarella.
Daily 8–8; closed Sun and 2nd half of Aug Repubblica 40, 64, 71, 75, 117

LA BOTTEGA DEL CIOCCOLATO
Map 154 G5
Via Leonina 82, 00184
Tel 06 4821473
A blissful little Italian chocolate shop. Most goodies are produced from a 19th-century Piedmont recipe; others are 'secrets of old masters'. Period

SPECIAL
CASTRONI
Map 152 C3
Via Ottaviano 55, 00192
Tel 06 3972 3279
This deli brings a slice of the 1950s to modern-day Rome—the date the shop first started trading. All manner of produce from Italy and the world over. Particularly impressive selection of jams, boiled sweets and coffee beans. It's a treat for the eyes and palate, with a beautiful wood-panelled interior stocked from floor to ceiling with goodies. The assistants in red jackets are ready to lend a hand. Espresso bar also on site.
Mon–Sat 7.30–8 Ottaviano 70, 81, 492

cupboards and shelves, and a large mirror reflecting the chocolate creations along the walls and in jars behind the counter. The pralines are made on the premises, and a selection of special chocolates for all festive occasions is sold. From €6 per 100g (4oz).
Mon–Sat 9.30–7.30; closed Sun and mid-Jun–end Aug Cavour 117

IL FORNO DI CAMPO DE' FIORI
Map 153 D5
Campo dei Fiori 22/22A, 00186
Tel 06 6880 6662
www.campodefiori.com
This tiny bakery has been on the Campo dei Fiori since 1850 and is always packed. There is no discernible order in which people are served, but hang on in there—all is forgiven with one bite of their *pizza bianca*, fresh from the oven, with a hint of rosemary, olive oil and sea salt, served as bread. Also home-made biscuits and cakes. Credit cards are not accepted.
Mon–Fri 7.30–2.30, 4.30–8, Sat 7.30–2.30 46, 64, 116

IL GIARDINO DEL TÈ

Map 154 F5
Via del Boschetto 112, 00184
Tel 06 474 6888
www.ilgiardinodelte.it

There is no garden, but there are over 100 teas from all over the world. Soothing classical music helps you select from a staggering collection, neatly packaged in cellophane bags with instructions attached. The teas conjure up whole other worlds, with names like Jasmine Dragon Eyes. Biscuits, jams and spiced coffees are also on sale. Tea starts at €5 per 100g (4oz).

🕐 Mon–Sat 10.30–1.30, 4–7.30; closed Aug 🅜 Cavour 🚌 117

GRAN CAFFÈ DAGNINO

Map 154 G4
Via V. E. Orlando 75 (Galleria Esedra), 00185
Tel 06 481 8660
www.pasticceriadagnino.com

Restaurant, café and bar in the unremarkable Galleria Esedra. However, once inside this Sicilian emporium of all things gastronomic, all else will be forgotten: mouth-watering ricotta, candied fruit-filled Sicilian sweets and succulent savoury delicacies. Also plenty of attractive foodstuffs you can take with you, from jams and cakes to wines, sauces and preserves.

🕐 Daily 7am–1am 🅜 Repubblica 🚌 H, 40, 60, 64, 70, 117, 170 to last stop on Via Nazionale

INNOCENZI

Map 153 D6
Via Natale del Grande 31, 00153
Tel 06 581 2725

Old-fashioned store in a street known for its food, with sweets in open jars, and rice and pulses spilling out of sacks on the floor. Foods from all over the world and some of Italy's best regional items can be bought, such as breads from Sardinia and honey biscuits from Calabria, as well as organic products. Credit cards are not accepted.

🕐 Mon–Wed, Fri–Sat 7–1.30, 5.30–8, Thu 7–1.30 🚌 H, 780; tram 8

PANELLA

Map 154 G5
Via Merulana 54–55, 00185
Tel 06 487 2344

For over a century, Panella has sold dozens of varieties of bread and cakes, and it has the largest selection of home-made *grissini* (breadsticks) in Rome. The three back rooms are packed with hard-to-find ingredients and spices, plus organic pastas, flours, honeys, jams and pulses.

🕐 Mon–Fri 8–2, 5–8, Sat–Sun 8–2 🅜 Vittorio Emanuele 🚌 16, 204, 714, 850; tram 3

LA RENELLA

Map 153 D6
Via del Moro 15, 00153
Tel 06 581 7265

Wonderfully fresh bread and pizza all day, every day. This also means it is crowded at all hours. Try freshly baked, thick, unctuous slices of simple *pizza bianca,* topped with olive oil and rosemary, or opt for a number of different fresh toppings. They also make excellent cakes.

🕐 Daily 7am–12.30am 🚌 H, 780; tram 8

VALZANI

Map 153 D6
Via del Moro 37/b, 00153
Tel 06 580 3792

Going strong since the mid-1920s, this *pasticceria* (cake shop) is an institution in the Trastevere district. One of the best German-style cakes, *torrone* (a kind of nougat), chocolates and spicy Roman *pangiallo* fruitcake (called *panpepato* when covered in chocolate) are all made on the premises. *Diavoletti al peperoncino,* chocolates laced with chilli, will make your tongue tingle. Credit cards are not accepted.

🕐 Wed–Sun 10–8.30 (daily 9–9 in month before Easter) closed Jun–15 Sep 🚌 H, 630; tram 8

VOLPETTI

Map off 153 E7
Via Marmorata 47, 00153
Tel 06 574 2352
www.volpetti.com

Probably the best (though not the cheapest) deli in Rome. Astounding variety of breads, cheeses, hams, salamis, fresh pasta and ready-made dishes. Service is professional and cheerful. Staff let you sample the cheese to help you decide. Whatever happens, you will not come out empty-handed. It is also a good place for gifts.

🕐 Mon–Sat 8–2, 5–8.15; closed Tue pm Jul–end Aug 🅜 Piramide 🚌 23, 30, 60, 75, 280, 716, or any bus to Piramide or Via Marmorata; tram 3

VOLPETTI

Map 153 E4
Via della Scrofa 21/32, 00186
Tel 06 686 1940
www.volpetti.it

Related to the more famous branch in Testaccio (see above). Prices are high, but quality is higher. Delicacies include truffles, 100 varieties of cheese, home-made salamis and pâtés, and a good selection of wines, all under a 16th-century copper ceiling. Try their sliced *porchetta* (roast suckling pig), which is among the best in the world.

🕐 Mon–Sat 10–3.30, 6–9.30 🚌 62, 64, 87, 116, 492 to Piazza Navona

WHAT TO DO

FASHION AND LINGERIE

ABITART
Map 153 E4
Via della Croce 46–47, 00187
Tel 06 6992 4077
www.abitartworld.com

Rome designer Vanessa Foglia makes vivid, flowing separates and dresses, which look like works of art both on and off the body. Unusual shapes, forms and combinations of patterns and hues, combined with some quirky accessories, ensure an individual look.
🕐 Mon–Sat 10–8, Sun 11–8
🚇 Spagna 🚌 81, 117, 119, 590, 628

BRIONI
Map 154 F4
Via Barberini 79, 00187
Tel 06 484517
www.brioniroma.com
Brioni has dressed royalty and celebrities since 1945, and has a well-deserved reputation as one of Italy's top tailors. Leave your measurements and you can call up for a suit anytime, anywhere. This, the oldest and largest Brioni store, also stocks women's ready-to-wear items. Others branches are at Via dei Condotti 21a and Via Vittorio Veneto 129.
🕐 Mon–Sat 10–1.30, 3.30–7.30
🚇 Barberini 🚌 63, 116, 175, 492, 590, 630

DAVIDE CENCI
Map 153 E4
Via Campo Marzio 1–7, 00186
Tel 06 699 0681
Calm and sophisticated preserve of those who prefer old-fashioned class over ephemeral fashion. The names

to be found here include Burberry, Ralph Lauren, Tod's, Hogan, Ballantyne, Brooks Brothers and Church's. Everything required to dress both men and women for work and play, with an emphasis on timeless, unprovocative style.
🕐 Mon–Sat 9.30–1.30, Tue–Sat 5–8, Jun–Oct; 3.30–7.30, rest of year
🚌 116, or any bus to Largo Argentina

IL DISCOUNT DELL'ALTA MODA
Map 153 E3
Via Gesù e Maria 14 and 16/a, 00187
Tel 06 361 3796
These two shops, standing side by side, are tucked away in a little side street opposite Rome's Anglican church. One sells menswear, the other women's clothes. They both have a good selection of top designer labels (end of stock) at knockdown prices. They don't exactly advertise themselves, but the shops are bright, neat and compact inside.
🕐 Tue–Sat 10–7.30, Mon 2.30–7.30
🚇 Spagna or Popolo

FIORUCCI
Map 154 G4
Via Nazionale 236, 00184
Tel 06 488 3175
Fiorucci's signature angels on T-shirts are sold here to the delight of teenagers—and women who are still girls at heart. Downstairs are dresses, skirts and blouses by the likes of Fiorucci, Kenzo, Gaultier Soleil, Kookai and D&G, as well as jeans. Upstairs are kitsch shoes, Hello Kitty gadgets and more T-shirts.
🕐 Mon–Sat 9.30–8 🚇 Repubblica
🚌 H, 40, 60, 64, 70, 117, 170

LE GALLINELLE
Map 154 F5
Via del Boschetto 76, 00184
Tel 06 488 1017
www.legallinelle.it
Tiny and unusual boutique in a former butcher's shop. Vintage, ethnic and contemporary fab-

rics are transformed into inspired retro clothing with a modern twist. There is also a great selection of vintage accessories and garments. Prices are reasonable and there's a small men's section, with trousers and overcoats.
🕐 Tue–Sat 10–1, 3.30–8, Mon 3.30–8, Aug–end Apr; Mon–Sat 10–1, 4–8, rest of year 🚌 H, 40, 60, 64, 70, 117, 170

INTIMISSIMI
Map 155 G4
Via Nazionale 227, 00184
Tel 06 485914
www.intimissimi.it
Intimissimi branches have proliferated all over Rome, but don't be put off by this. They have some of the cutest lingerie, T-shirts and nightwear around, plus items for men. Not the most durable clothing, and fabrics are often synthetic, but they are comfortable, inexpensive, pretty and sexy.
🕐 Mon–Sat 9.30–8 🚇 Repubblica
🚌 H, 40, 60, 64, 70, 117, 170

LEAM
Map 154 H7
Via Appia Nuova 26, 00183
Tel 06 7720 7204
www.leam.com
Near San Giovanni in Laterano, Leam has two stores within a few doors of each other, selling top designer fashion and accessories for both sexes. It has the best of Italian design: Armani, Gucci, Prada, Dolce & Gabbana and even Philippe Starck dresses. Shop assistants can be over attentive, which is a common complaint in Rome. There is a roof terrace and bar in the women's store.
🕐 Tue–Sat 9.30–8, Mon 4–8 🚇 San Giovanni 🚌 87, 360

LEI
Map 154 F5
Via Nazionale 88, 00184
Tel 06 482 1700
The name on the shop window is understated in small letters, but it's well known to young Rome-based socialites and women of fash-

WHAT TO DO

ion. They come here for their D&G staples, Romeo Gigli ready-to-wear, and a dazzling selection of party dresses and delicate slip-on shoes by French designers such as Stephane Kélian.

🕐 Mon–Sat 10–8 (also Sun 10–2, 4–7.30, Jul and Dec) 🚌 H, 40, 60, 64, 70, 117, 170

MAGA MORGANA

Map 153 D5
Via del Governo Vecchio 27 and 98, 00186
Tel 06 687 9995

Two shops selling clothes by designer Luciana Iannace. The shop at No. 27 has mostly hand-knitted jumpers, skirts and dresses. At No. 98 (on the other side of the road), delve into designs for the evening or for special occasions, even weddings. Prices are high, but you can still pick up a bargain.

🕐 Mon–Sat 10–8 🚌 40, 64, 116, 492, 571, or any bus to Corso Vittorio Emanuele II

SCHOSTAL

Map 153 E4
Via del Corso 158, 00186
Tel 06 679 1240

A shop with a long tradition of selling good-quality lingerie. You can also find shirts, ties and socks for both sexes. It is family-run, friendly and reasonably priced. The shop is remembered for giving every client a free shirt when it reopened after World War II, and photographs from its long history adorn the walls.

🕐 Mon–Sat 9.30–6.30, Sep–end Jun; Mon–Fri 9.30–6.30, Sat 9.30–1 rest of year 🚇 Spagna or Popolo

STEFANEL

Map 153 E4
Via del Corso 122–125, 00187
Tel 06 6992 5783
www.stefanel.it

This shop deals in classic, easy-to-wear separates, plus pieces that are contemporary, but not overly so. Moderately priced and of decent quality, with a few items that show some really creative touches and emulate high fashion at a fraction of the price. It's a good place to come if you are looking for better than average high-street fashions. Also at Via Nazionale 57–59.

🕐 Mon–Sat 10–8, Sun noon–8
🚇 Spagna 🚌 81, 117, 119, 590, 628

TREPPIEDI

Map 153 E5
Via del Teatro Valle 55/D, 00186
Tel 06 6880 6268

Two minutes from Piazza Navona is this most specific of shops. Quaintly old fashioned, it has been famous for years in Rome for its women's lingerie and made-to-measure swimwear. Prices are high but so is the quality. Large sizes are kept in stock.

🕐 Tue–Fri 9.30–1, 4–7.30, Sat 9.30–1
🚌 40, 62, 64, 116

VERSO SUD

Map 153 D6
Via S. Francesco a Ripa 168, 00153
Tel 06 5833 3668

On first sight Verso Sud looks minimalist and forbidding, with limited stock and a stark

layout. In fact, it is a really informal place where you can feel comfortable looking without buying. Clothes range from the expensive but still affordable (Comme des Garçons) to the affordable and fashionable (Diesel Style Lab).

🕐 Tue–Sat 10–2, 5–8, Mon 5–8 🚌 H, 780; tram 8

CHILDREN'S CLOTHES

LA CICOGNA

Map 154 H7
Piazzale Appia 2, 00183
Tel 06 7049 2554

Just along from San Giovanni in Laterano, this shop is part of a chain of nine dealing exclusively in children's clothes and fancy dress, up to the age of 14. The clothes are well made and the prices moderate. They also have a good selection of toddlers' shoes.

🕐 Tue–Sat 9.30–1, 4–8, Mon 4–8.30
🚇 San Giovanni

MESSI MAI

Map 154 G2
Via Salaria 91, 00198
Tel 06 8424 1541

With its memorabilia and posters on the walls, the Messi Mai feels like an American sports bar. It has an exceptional mix of new and good-condition second-hand clothes for kids. Used jeans by Levi and dungarees by OshKosh B'Gosh look brand new. New clothes and shoes from Abercrombie, Converse, Gap, Kookai and more.

🕐 Tue–Sat 9.30–1.30, 4–8, Mon 4–8
🚌 38, 53, 63, 86, 92, 217, 360, 630, or any bus to Piazza Fiume or Via Salaria

RACHELE

Map 153 D5
Vicolo del Bollo 6–7, 00186
Tel 06 686 4975

Delightful shop tucked down a side alley close to Campo dei Fiori. Clothes, from classic and retro to the latest kids' fashions, are all handmade by the Swedish owner in high-quality, durable cottons and wools. Stock items are for children up to age 6; special orders up to age 12. There is a good line of amusing accessories, including a range of hats inspired by animals and fruits.

🕐 Tue–Sat 11–2, 4–8 🚌 46, 62, 64, 116, 492, 571, or any bus to Corso Vittorio Emanuele II

RAPHAEL JUNIOR

Map 153 F3
Via Veneto 96–98, 00187
Tel 06 488 5692

Children's clothing by over 40 Italian designer names. Helpful and knowledgeable staff will show you all the latest trends in garments and shoes for little ones by the likes of Armani, Versace, Byblos, Les Copains and Blumarine. Customers are the sort who don't bat an eyelid at the price tag.

🕐 Mon–Sat 9.30–1.30, 3.30–7.30
🚇 Barberini 🚌 52, 53, 63, 95, 116, 119, 204, 630

WHAT TO DO

ACCESSORIES

BARRILÀ BOUTIQUE

Map 153 E3
Via del Babuino 33a, 00187
Tel 06 3600 1726

Women's shoes and boots in an unchanged 1960s interior. In the best Italian tradition, all are classic in style. Not the most up-to-date models, but

each is available in at least 26 colours—something to match any bag, which you can also buy here. Prices range from €50 to €200.

🕐 Mon–Sat 9.30–8, Sun 10–7.30
🚇 Popolo or Spagna 🚌 117

BORSE SCULTURA

Map 155 J5
Largo degli Osci 67/a, 00185
Tel 06 446 9284

Exquisitely handcrafted and hand-stitched bags adorned with spirals, lips, and feminine curves and shapes. Briefcases with a keyhole or mouth shape cut out of one side stand cheek by jowl with bags of

more classic form. As good to look at on the arm as off. Prices start at €110.

🕐 Tue–Sat 10–1, 4–8 🚌 71, 492 to stop nearest Largo degli Osci; tram 3, 19

CALZATURE BOCCANERA

Map off 153 E7
Via Luca della Robbia 36, 00153
Tel 06 575 6804

This place is a Roman classic for wearable designer shoes. Brands such as Camper, Hogan, Tod's, Prada and Sergio Rossi are all packed together under one roof at uninflated prices. The good service is a bonus.

🕐 Daily 9–1, 4–8 🚇 Piramide 🚌 23, 30, 60, 75, 280, 716, or any bus to Piramide or Via Marmorata; tram 3

CAPPELLERIA TRONCARELLI

Map 153 D5
Via della Cuccagna 15, 00186
Tel 06 687 9320
www.troncarelli.it

This family-run hat shop close to Piazza Navona, catering predominantly to men, is a pleasant throwback to a bygone age. Every conceivable hat is here, from panamas and Florentine straw hats to trilbies (felt hats with an indented crown) and flat caps, all hand-crafted and to suit every occasion. Prices range from €50 to €180.

🕐 Mon–Sat 10–1.30, 2.30–8 Jun–end Oct; Mon–Sat 10–1.30, 2.30–7.30 rest of year 🚌 46, 62, 64, 70, 87, 116, 492

FABINDIA

Map 152 D4
Via del Banco di Santo Spirito 40, 00186
Tel 06 6889 1230
www.fabindia.com

Facing the Ponte Sant'Angelo is this delightful emporium selling Indian fabrics, scarves and garments, all hand-woven and made in Indian villages. The company is devoted to developing fair and equitable relationships with the producers. The style is both traditional and more contemporary. Also stocks bags, pillows and photograph albums, made with, or

SPECIAL

GIORGIO SERMONETA

Map 153 E3
Piazza di Spagna 61, 00187
Tel 06 679 1960
www.sermonetagloves.com

The shop front is fairly small and it may feel cramped, but there's a surprise in store—just look up. The gloves are the real decor of this shop, literally thousands of them, women's and men's, in a terrific array of shades and styles. Top quality. Price range €23–€100.

🕐 Mon–Sat 9.30–8 🚇 Spagna
🚌 116, 117

covered in, Indian cottons and silks.

🕐 Tue–Sat 10–1.30, 3–5.30, Mon 3–5.30 🚌 40, 64, 116, 492, 571, or any bus to Corso Vittorio Emanuele II

FURLA

Map 153 E4
Piazza di Spagna 22, 00187
Tel 06 6920 0363
www.furla.it

Purveyors of chic bags and practical totes in cheerful tones, along with scarves,

shoes and jewellery. Prices are moderate compared with other big-name accessory designers. Wild combinations and original touches add a twist. The company has several other branches in Rome.

🕐 Daily 10–8 🚇 Spagna 🚌 116, 117, 119, 590

MONDELLO OTTICA
Map 153 D5
Via del Pellegrino 98, 00186
Tel 06 686 1955
Eyewear with a difference: This minimalist boutique has regular installations by local artists. Prices may be higher than average, but the glasses are superlative in quality and sheer chic. All have that little extra something special that makes the price worth paying. Friendly owners will provide repairs with a smile whenever they are required.
🕐 Tue–Sat 9.30–1, 4–7.30, Mon 4–7.30
🚌 46, 62, 64, 116, 492, 571, or any bus to Corso Vittorio Emanuele II

OXUS
Map 154 G3
Via Bergamo 14, 00198
Tel 06 8535 6310
www.oxus.it
Milan-based designer of striking, hand-sewn bags, some inspired by artists such as Catalan Joan Mirò. Also makes items under licence for designers, including Sonia Rykiel, Laura Biagiotti and the eccentrically brilliant Castelbajac. All bags are well finished, with inspired touches, such as internal pockets for mobile phones, and zips that button shut once closed. There's another branch at Via Borgognona 2a/b.
🕐 Mon–Fri 9.30–7.30, Sat 9.30–1
🚌 38, 53, 63, 86, 92, 217, 360, 630, or any bus to Piazza Fiume

JEWELLERY
AUREA AETAS VALLICELLA
Map 153 D5
Vicolo del Governo Vecchio 53, 00186
Tel 06 686 1840
zz9@interfree.it
Under the arch in a side street off Corso Vittorio Emanuele II are two linked shops, the workshops of three master goldsmiths. Pieces are designed to your specifications, or you can choose from the catalogue. Good value for money, consiering what you get. Orders can be made by email, and worldwide shipping

is possible. Items from €80. English spoken. Credit cards are not accepted in the shop.
🕐 Tue–Sat 9.30–7, Sun 4–7, Mon 9.30–1 🚌 40, 62, 64

LA GRANDE OFFICINA
Map 155 J5
Via dei Sabelli 165b, 00185
Tel 06 445 0348
A husband and wife team creates each item from scratch. Precious and semi-precious stones and pearls are set to maximum effect, using inventive or retro-inspired mountings—for example, ball bearings studded with diamonds, old Balinese coins or a large black pearl on a simple gold band. Items for all budgets.
🕐 Mon–Fri 10–1, 4–7, summer; 10–7.30, winter, plus Sun Nov–Dec
🚌 71, 492; tram 3, 19

IVANO LANGELLA– LABORATORIO ARTIGIANO
Map 153 D6
Via di Ponte Sisto 73/a, 00153
Tel 333 420 9100
Ivano Langella makes intricate jewellery, fashioning silver, gold and bronze with pearl, horn and even plants, to create eye-catching rings and necklaces. Custom-made pieces will be ready in 3–5 days. His loyal clientele includes a number of celebrities. Credit cards are not accepted.
🕐 Daily 10.30–1, 4–11; sometimes closed Sun in winter 🚌 H, 780; tram 8

HEALTH AND BEAUTY
AI MONASTERI
Map 153 D4
Corso del Rinascimento 72, 00186
Tel 06 6880 2783
www.monasteri.it
This late 19th-century pharmacy has a fascinating array of edible goods (chocolate, honeys and jams) and cosmetics, made in monasteries throughout Italy from natural ingredients to traditional recipes. For ladies of a certain age, there's *olio alla trigonella* (fenugreek oil) to firm up the

bust and smooth neck wrinkles. You can order online.
🕐 Tue–Fri 9–1, 5–8, Sat 9–1 🚌 40, 64, 116, 492, 571, or any bus that goes along Corso Vittorio Emanuele II, or 30, 70, 81, 87, 186, 628 to Corso del Rinascimento

MUZIO
Map 154 G4
Via Vittorio Emanuele Orlando 77, 00185
Tel 06 488 3529
Every kind of shaving implement, manicure set, mirror, hair accessory and penknife under the sun can be found in this traditional store with old-fashioned service. The goods are of high quality, and they stock lesser known aftershaves, shaving creams, toothpastes and soaps. There is another branch at Via del Tritone 50.
🕐 Mon–Sat 9.30–8 🚇 Repubblica
🚌 H, 40, 60, 64, 70, 117, 170 to last stop on Via Nazionale

OFFICINA PROFUMO— FARMACEUTICA DI SANTA MARIA NOVELLA
Map 153 D5
Corso Rinascimento 47, 00186
Tel 06 6879608
www.smnovella.com
This elegant branch of the pharmacy in Florence's Via della Scala, founded in 1612,

sells creams, soaps and perfumes from original recipes by Dominican friars. Some of the recipes go back to medieval times. Their signature and extremely fragrant potpourri is made with herbs from the Florentine hills.

Mon–Sat 9.30–7.30, (also Sun in run-up to Christmas) 40, 64, 116, 492, 571 to Corso Vittorio Emanuele II, or 30, 70, 81, 87, 186, 628 to Corso Rinascimento

ROMA STORE
Map 153 D6
Via della Lungaretta 63, 00153
Tel 06 581 8789
Despite the unpromising name, this Trastevere shop stocks an incredibly tantalizing selection of hard-to-find and sophisticated British and French perfumes, including L'Artisan Parfumeur, Creed, Etro, Penhaligon's, L'Occitane, Vetiver and Comptoir Sud Pacifique. Creams and imported US and UK brands of soap and toothpaste complete the almost infinite stock.
 Daily 9.30–9 H, 780; tram 8

HOME AND SOFT FURNISHINGS

ARCHIVIA
Map 154 F5
Via del Boschetto 15/a, 00184
Tel 06 474 1503
A profusion of beautiful glass and furnishings. Reasonably priced gifts, from signed hand-made glasses to vases, Italian pottery, unusually framed mirrors, rugs, cushions and gorgeous curtains in natural materials and a vast array of hues. It will come as no surprise that the owner is an interior designer.
 Tue–Sun 10–2.30, 3.30–7.30, Mon 3.30–7.30; closed Aug Repubblica 40, 64, 71, 75, 117

IL BIANCO DI ELLEPI
Map 153 E3
Via della Croce 3/4, 00187
Tel 06 679 6835
Delightful shop in a 16th-century building on the north side of Piazza di Spagna, just across from the Spanish Steps. You will find all sorts of towels, bathrobes and bathmats, which can be personalized. A shipping service is available to anywhere in the world. Prices start at €180.

FRETTE
Map 153 E5
Piazza di Spagna 11, 00187
Tel 06 679 0673
www.frette.it
Beautiful sleepwear and household linens in stylish prints are what Frette is all about. You'll find only the best fabrics—cottons, linens, cashmeres and silks—as well as a range of beautiful accessories and some shoes and clothing. Old-style glamour, but in step with modern design. There is another branch at Via Nazionale 84.
 Tue–Sat 10.30–1.30, 2.30–7.30, Mon 1.30–7.30 Spagna 116, 117, 119, 590

 Mon–Sat 9.30–7.30 Spagna 116, 117

C.U.C.I.N.A.
Map 153 E3
Via Mario de' Fiori 65, 00187
Tel 06 6791275
www.cucinastore.com
Opened in the 1980s, and still the place to come for the most complete selection (more than 20,000 items) of kitchen utensils in steel, porcelain and wood. Prices to suit all budgets. Culinary heaven for cooks of all levels.
 Tue–Sat 10.30–7.30, Mon 3.30–7.30 Spagna 81, 117, 119, 590, 628

JOY
Map 153 D4
Via del Governo Vecchio 4, 00186
Tel 06 6833495
If leopard skin prints or cow hides are your thing, Joy is where to get your fill. From the kitsch (cow-inspired mugs resting on pink udders instead of feet) to the zany (a leopard-print umbrella). It also has the craziest assortment of crockery and pillows around.
 Mon–Sat 11–8, Sep–end May; Mon 4.30–8, Tue–Sat 11–2, 4.30–8, Jun–end Jul; closed Aug 40, 64, 116, 492, 571, or any bus to Corso Vittorio Emanuele II

LEONE LIMENTANI
Map 153 E5
Via del Portico d'Ottavia 47, 00186
Tel 06 6880 6686
Every possible cooking utensil, plus the finest porcelain and crystal, are to be found in this rambling, basement warehouse-style store. Everything is 10–20 per cent less expensive than in smarter stores in the city. Take a numbered wooden plaque at the entrance, and wait for an assistant.
 Tue–Sat 9–1, 4–8, Mon 4–8 H, 23, 63, 280, 630, 780 to Lungotevere dei Cenci, or any bus to Largo di Torre Argentina or Piazza Venezia, then walk

LINN-SUI
Map 152 D4
Via dei Banchi Nuovi 37–38, 00186
Tel 06 683 3406
www.linn-sui.it
Bio-ecological beds and accessories, mainly Japanese in inspiration, such as futons and tatami. Also, a range of pillows and cushions (some from vintage fabrics in animal shapes), duvets, wall hangings and portable beds for children
 Mon–Fri 10–1, 4.30–8, Sat 10–1 40, 64, 116, 492, 571, or any bus to Corso Vittorio Emanuele II

SPAZIO SETTE
Map 153 E5
Via dei Barbieri 7, 00186
Tel 06 6880 4261
Housed in a 17th-century cardinal's palace, this is one of the few stores in Rome that will make even the most hardened shopper salivate over furnishings for the kitchen, living room and bathroom. The range includes vases, lamps and various other ornaments from the biggest names in Italian and international design.
 Tue–Sat 9.30–1, 3–7.30, Mon 3–7.30 30, 40, 46, 62, 64, 81, 87, 186, 492, 628, 916; tram 8 to terminus

WHAT TO DO

DEPARTMENT STORES AND SHOPPING CENTRES

CINECITTÀ DUE
Map 155 J7
Via Palmiro Togliatti 2, 00173
www.cinecittadue.com
You can't actually tour the studios of 'Hollywood on the Tiber', where all those spaghetti westerns were filmed, but you can shop with the stars in the Cinecittà Due shopping mall. All the shops you might need under one roof, plus good parking facilities.
Ⓒ Mon–Fri 9.30–8, Sat 9.30–8.30
Ⓢ Subaugtsa Ⓑ 341, 409, 451

MAS
Map 154 H5
Via dello Statuto 11, 00185
Tel 06 446 8078
Rome's first department store opened its doors in 1882. Its five floors, totalling 8,000sq m (86,000sq ft), are filled floor to ceiling with clothing, shoes and houseware. The discounted brands and inexpensive copies of branded goods compensate for the lack of glamour.
Ⓒ Daily 9–1, 4–7.30 Ⓢ Vittorio

MITSUKOSHI
Map 154 G4
Via Nazionale 259, 00184
Tel 06 482 7828
Prices are given in euros and yen, and most of the customers here are Japanese: You may wonder if you are still in Rome, but all the goods are indeed made in Italy. Accessories and some clothing items from the major Italian names, plus, in the bazaar-style basement, food, wine and kitchenware.
Ⓒ Tue–Sat 10.30–7.30, Mon 12–7.30
Ⓢ Repubblica Ⓑ H, 40, 60, 64, 70, 117, 170

LA RINASCENTE
Map 154 G3
Piazza Fiume, 00198
Tel 06 7679691
www.rinascente.it
More modern and with a better selection than the

SPECIAL

COIN
Map 154 H7
Piazzale Appio 7, 00183
Tel 06 708 0020
www.coin.it
One of Rome's most popular department stores, well laid out over five floors, is close to San Giovanni in Laterano. A modern, bright, predominantly glass building with cosmetics, home furnishings, kitchenware, toys, and fashions for men, women and children. The top floor is dedicated to home exhibitions. Prices are higher than in the average store; there is a snack bar on the fourth floor.
Ⓒ Mon–Sat 9.30–8.55 Ⓢ San Giovanni

original Via del Corso store. Six floors with upmarket cosmetics and accessories, some of the better diffusion lines (a designer's second and less expensive range) such as Versace Classic and Trussardi Sport, and mid-range brands like Esprit, Diesel and Calvin Klein. It also has a good line for teenagers. Top-floor restaurant/café and hairdresser.
Ⓒ Mon–Sat 9.30–8, Sun 10.30–8
Ⓑ 38, 53, 63, 86, 92, 217, 360, 630, or any bus to Piazza Fiume

TAD
Map 153 E3
Via del Babuino 155a, 00187
Tel 06 3269 5122
www.taditaly.com
Very smart store selling a bit of anything as long as it's cool,

exotic and expensive. Beautiful flowers, including orchids, plus magazines and books, fabrics, candles, furniture, tableware, clothing, shoes, cosmetics—you name it and (if it's the latest thing) it's here. Also, an exclusive hair salon and café/restaurant.
Ⓒ Mon–Sat 10–8, Sun 4–8 Ⓢ Spagna or Flaminio Ⓑ 81, 117, 119, 590, 628

SUPERMARKETS

AUCHAN
Map 155 L5
Via A. Pollio 50, 00159
Tel 06 432 071
www.gallerie-auchan.it
The big French hypermarket has arrived in Rome. With nursery facilities and French produce such as cheeses, wines and pâtés, this is an easy store in which to spend time. Good deli and fish counters, but the prices are higher than in Italian supermarkets.
Ⓒ Mon–Sat 9am–9.30pm Ⓢ Tiburtina Station Ⓑ 545, 409 to Ipermercato

MUSEUM DRUGSTORE
Map off 153 D7
Via Portuense 313, 00149
Tel 06 559 3633
This 24-hour drugstore is built over a Roman necropolis, part of which is on display inside. It is a fair distance from town, but there are good public transportation connections. There is a café, pub and pizzeria in the same complex.
Ⓒ Daily 24 hours Ⓢ Trastevere
Ⓑ 791 to Hospital San Camillo

CHAIN STORES

NAME	Menswear	Womenswear	For children	Shoes	Cosmetics and toiletries	Sports equipment and clothes	Accessories	Household	Books, music and DVDs	Perfume	HEAD OFFICE
Beauty Point					✓					✓	06 9040631
Benetton	✓	✓	✓								0422 519111
BluNauta	✓	✓					✓				06 696421
Brioni	✓	✓									06 4620161
Calzedonia						✓	✓				
Camper				✓							06 6992 5678
Cisalfa						✓					035 4556111
Coin	✓	✓	✓	✓	✓		✓	✓		✓	041 2398000
Confalone								✓			06 6500 3137
C.u.c.i.n.a.								✓			06 6791275
D Cube								✓			06 6789054
Diesel	✓	✓	✓	✓			✓				06 6783933
Energie	✓	✓		✓							0871 5891
Etam	✓	✓	✓				✓				33 1 5590 7575
Ethic		✓									06 4120 0621
Expensive		✓									800 311678
Feltrinelli									✓		02 725721
Foot Locker				✓		✓					02 45281314
Frette		✓						✓			039 60461
Furla				✓			✓				051 6202711
Gente	✓	✓					✓				06 3207671
Geox				✓							0423 282529
Intimissimi	✓	✓									06 68301784
Laltramoda		✓									06 882991
Mandarina Duck							✓				51 764411
Mariella Burani		✓									0522 373131
Miss Sixty		✓									0871 5891
Officina Profumo Farmaceutica di Santa Maria					✓					✓	055 216276
Onyx	✓	✓	✓				✓				06 4050 1243
Oviesse	✓	✓	✓	✓	✓	✓	✓	✓		✓	041 2398000
Pandemonium	✓	✓									06 6868061
Prénatal			✓								039 651638
Pro Fumum					✓					✓	06 6795982
Replay	✓	✓	✓								0423 9251
Ricordi Media Store									✓		02 725721
La Rinascente	✓	✓	✓	✓	✓	✓	✓	✓		✓	06 6797691
Sephora					✓					✓	06 4782 3445
Sisley	✓	✓									0422 519111
Stefanel		✓									0422 8191
Upim	✓	✓	✓	✓	✓	✓	✓	✓		✓	06 4465579

Rome is a great city for shopping. As well as a wide range of individual specialist stores, it has its share of chain stores, including a number of internationally known names, such as Italy's greatest export, Benetton. The numbers of stores shown in the table below are those in Rome, but you will usually find branches in other Italian cities too.

NUMBER OF STORES	DESCRIPTION	SHOP WEBSITE
33	Glossy cosmetics store, selling all the best-known brands at bargain prices.	www.beautypoint.it
	Some of the best and most affordable casualwear in Italy.	www.benetton.com
11	Simple designs, quality fabrics and good all-round value.	www.blunauta.it
3	Classic cuts and designer fabrics—popular with the stars.	www.brioni.it
32	Swimwear and anything that goes on your feet and legs.	www.calzedonia.it
1	Unconventional footwear from Spain that is made to last.	www.camper.com
15	All the well-known brands of sportswear, sports equipment and trainers.	www.cisalfa.com
4	A department store selling mid-range to elegant stock.	www.coin.it
6	Beautiful handmade furniture and sofas.	none
3	This shop sells everything you need in the kitchen, and much more.	www.cucinastore.com
3	Buy innovative or sleek-looking gifts and souvenirs at this design store.	none
3	Urban trendsetters who embrace innovative fabrics and bright shades.	www.diesel.com
5	Store selling the hippest brands for surf dudes and beach babes.	www.energie.it
4	French version of H&M; less hip, but affordable and imaginative.	www.etam.com
11	Cool, cheap and original, with a focus on vintage looks and ethnic fabrics.	www.ethic.it
8	Not expensive as the name suggests, but affordable and wearable.	www.expensive-fashion.it
4	One of the best bookshops in Italy, with regular guest writer appearances.	www.lafeltrinelli.it
8	All the trainers you could ever want under one roof.	www.footlocker-europe.com
4	Beautifully crafted linens for the home, plus enticing nightwear.	www.frette.it
13	Handcrafted leather bags and footwear with an ultra-modern twist.	www.furla.it
3	Accessories, denim, dresses and eveningwear by hip designers.	none
5	Modern styles with soles that keep water out, but let your feet breathe.	www.geox.com
31	Cute and glamorous underwear at affordable prices.	www.intimissimi.it
9	Well-made versatile and stylish clothes that won't break the bank.	www.laltramoda.it
5	Functional, high-tech leather bags and leisurewear.	www.mandarinaduck.com
1	Well-tailored womenswear—from romantic and retro to sexy and revealing.	www.mariellaburani.it
4	Casualwear and jeans for funky teens and twentysomethings.	www.misssixty.com
1	Founded by monks in the early 17th century, this store sells beautifully packaged soaps, perfumes and creams made from plants and herbs.	www.smnovella.com
4	A teenager's dream come true; a vast selection of bright trendy gear.	www.onyx.it
25	Low-end to medium-priced clothes (including swimwear) and homewares.	www.oviesse.it
9	Sassy streetwear that mixes Dolce & Gabanna with Calvin Klein.	www.pandemonium.it
10	Everything for your baby or toddler in one store.	www.prenatal.it
3	An exclusive store selling harder-to-find ranges such as Kiehl's and Aesop.	none
3	The place to come for jeans and funky accessories.	www.replay.it
5	Established and reasonably priced music store that sells concerts tickets.	www.lafeltrinelli.it
2	Jewellery, cosmetics, accessories and designer clothes (also in larger sizes).	www.larimascente.it
1	A minimalist, glossy cosmetics superstore with its own affordable range.	www.sephora.com
15	Cool and up-to-date fashions.	www.sisley.com
14	Affordable but modern styles for women that stand the test of time.	www.stefanel.it
16	Department store selling cheap but sturdy fashions and household items.	www.upim.it

WHAT TO DO

MARKETS

CAMPO DEI FIORI
Map 153 D5
Campo dei Fiori, 00186
This field of flowers hosts Rome's liveliest produce market. Traders hawk vibrant

vegetables, seafood, meat, household goods and flowers. Order small items by the *etto* (100g/4oz). Art fair on Sun. Credit cards are not accepted.
🕐 Mon–Sat am 🚌 46, 62, 64, 87, 116, 492

MERCATO DEI FIORI
Map 152 B2
Via Trionfale 47–9
This wholesale flower market to the north of the Vatican is usually only open to the trade, but on Tuesday mornings the public can come in to wander among the two floors of bargain cut flowers, potted plants and exotic Mediterranean blooms. Credit cards are not accepted.
🕐 Tue 10.30–1 Ⓜ Cipro-Musei Vaticani 🚌 490, 492, 913, 990, 991

PIAZZA DELLE COPPELLE
Map 153 E4
Piazza delle Coppelle
This tiny but very scenic food market wedged in among the cars and tourists just north of the Pantheon makes a welcome respite from a tiring morning's sightseeing. There are fresh flowers as well as food. Credit cards are not accepted.
🕐 Mon–Sat 7–1 🚌 23, 30, 75, 280, 716 or buses to Via Marmorata; tram 3

PIAZZA SAN COSIMATO
Map 153 D6
Piazza San Cosimato
Trastevere's liveliest food and produce market, which, despite the area's tourist attraction, is still mainly visited by local people. All types of produce are on sale but the cheeses are especially good.
🕐 Mon–Sat 7–1 🚌 H, 23, 280, 780; tram 8

PIAZZA VITTORIO MARKET
Map 154 H5
Via Principe Amadeo, 00185
The former Piazza Vittorio market has moved indoors, and has been officially renamed Nuovo Mercato Esquilino, but most still refer to it by its old name. The move has not dented its popularity and continues to attract thousands of Romans every day. The area has a large Asian population, which is reflected in the produce sold: everything from exotic fruits to clothing and suitcases—all at least a third less expensive than anywhere else. Credit cards are not accepted.
🕐 Mon–Thu 7am–3pm, Fri–Sat 7am–4pm Ⓜ Vittorio

PORTA PORTESE
Map 153 E7
Piazza Porta Portese and around, 00153
Rome's most famous flea market is home to nearly 2km (1 mile) of bargains. The whole of Via Portuense from

the Porta Portese to Trastevere station is flanked by stands and teeming with people—and there's more in the side streets. Fashionable clothes to antiques and downright junk. Be early for the best buys and beware of pickpockets. Credit cards are not accepted.
🕐 Sun 6.30–1 Ⓜ Porta Portese 🚋 Tram 3

SOFFITTA SOTTO I PORTICI
Map 153 E3
Piazza Augusto Imperatore, 00186
Tel 06 3600 5345
Approximately 100 stands where anybody can come once a month to sell all the curious heirlooms and other objects hidden in their attic. The focus is on antiques and rare items, and the setting—under the porticoes around the piazza—is very pleasant, especially in the summer. Credit cards are not accepted.
🕐 3rd Sun of month 9–8; closed Aug 🚌 71, 81, 117, 119, 224, 913

UNDERGROUND
Map 153 F3
Via Francesco Crispi 96, 00187
Tel 06 3600 5345
One of the best established, this antiques and collector's market is in the Ludovisi underground car park. More than 100 stands selling prints, small antiques, frames, comics, lace and old vases. Also some kids' stalls for the sale and exchange of toys. Credit cards are not accepted.
🕐 1st Sun of month 9–7, Oct–Jan and Mar–Apr Ⓜ Spagna 🚌 116, 119, 204, 630, 910, or any bus to Via Veneto

VIA SANNIO
Map 154 H7
Via Sannio, 00183
The market, based in one street and with an indoor section, starts at the side of the Coin department store. Saturday has most stalls and the best atmosphere. All sorts of clothes, new and second-hand, in a wide range of styles for both sexes. Credit cards are not accepted.
🕐 Mon–Fri 8am–2pm, Sat 8am–5pm Ⓜ San Giovanni

PERFORMANCE

Rome is often likened to an outdoor theatre and its 'actors' have an innate sense of style. A night at the opera, concert or theatre is certainly a showcase for visual display and it would be almost a sin not to dress suitably for the occasion. So don your finery in the certainty you will not be overdressed!

CLASSICAL MUSIC

For classical music, the Accademia Nazionale di Santa Cecilia (see page 180) is the jewel in the crown. Founded in the 16th century, it attracts some of the world's best-known conductors and its schedule also includes non-classical music. The winter season is held at the giant Auditorium, Parco della Musica (see page 181).

Other main companies include the Accademia Filarmonica Romana (tel 06 320 1752; www.filarmonicaromana.org), which can claim Verdi, Donizetti, Paganini and Rossini among its founders. Its varied offerings include chamber music, opera, ballet and ancient music. This Accademia uses the Teatro Olimpico (see page 182), in the northern suburbs, for its Thursday concerts and also acts as a venue for many of the events in the trendy RomaEuropa Festival (see page 182), running from September to November.

In the listings that follow, the opening times refer to the box office and the dates to when the season runs. Credit cards are accepted at most venues; we have stated only when they are not. Smoking is not permitted, but at events held outdoors, it is usually allowed.

THEATRE

The main theatres include Teatro di Roma-Argentina (see page 185), which is Rome's most prestigious and has its own resident company. The little Teatro Valle (see page 185), in the remains of the Teatro di Pompei, is a theatrical jewel and is managed and sponsored by the Italian Drama Board—the Ente Teatrale Italiano (ETI). Also managed by the ETI, the Teatro Quirino (Via Mario Minghetti, tel 06 679 4585) stages productions by well-known playwrights. There are around 80 theatres in and around the city, and there are many experimental and avant-garde performances to see as well as classical offerings.

The Teatro dell'Opera (see page 182) has almost perfect acoustics. The season runs from November to June and during the summer, at different open-air venues. The resident classical ballet company, Corpo di Ballo, also performs at the Teatro dell'Opera and in the summer at alternating other venues (www.opera.roma.it). For contemporary ballet and modern dance try the Teatro Olimpico, Teatro Vascello (see page 182), or the Teatro Greco in the northern suburbs (Via R. Leoncavallo 16, tel 06 860 7513; www.teatrogreco.it).

Smoking is not permitted in auditoriums.

CINEMA

Cinema is alive and flourishing in Rome, and it's a great city for viewing both locally made and foreign films. Although foreign films tend to be dubbed into Italian there are more and more cinemas showing them in their *versione originale—* (original version). The Nuovo Olimpia (see page 180) often dedicates one of its screens to original-language films. The Cineporto (held in summer) has become one of the most popular summer festivals.

Smoking is not permitted in cinemas, and generally credit cards are not accepted.

CONCERTS

The new Auditorium Parco della Musica is Rome's long-awaited venue for big concerts, not only classical music but rock and pop, too. There are also some stunning venues that play host to international stars—such as the Villa Borghese and Ostia Antica's Roman theatre.

Most smaller concert venues do not take credit cards.

WHAT'S ON

For listings of what's on where, the weekly *Roma C'è* covers music, theatre, dance, cinema and nightlife, and has an English-language section. *Trovaroma* is published on Thursdays (free with *La Repubblica*); it covers the week's major happenings on the cultural scene, and has an English-language section. The monthly *WHERE Rome* is available from any APT tourist information point. For daily information about events, buy a copy of Rome's newspaper, *Il Messaggero*.

TICKETS

For one-stop ticket booking, the following agencies are useful. They charge a commission for making your booking, usually about 10 per cent:
● Orbis (Piazza dell'Esquino 37, tel 06 4827403) sells tickets for most theatres, concerts and sporting events.
● Hello Ticket (tel 06 8088352 or freephone 800 907080) is a call centre where you can book most events with a credit card.
● Chartanet is an online booking service (www.chartanet.it), where you can buy tickets for the opera and some theatrical productions and concerts. It also sells tickets through several banks, including branches of Banca di Roma and Credito Bergasamo, among others.

D

PTE DEL
RISORGIMENTO

Auditorium, Parco
della Musica
Teatro Olimpico

E

DELLE BE

Gramsci

Mangili

ULISS

VIA S. MERCADANTE

PARIO

VIA G. Donizetti

G

VIA G. Verdi

VIA G. Pierluigi

VIA G Allegri

Villa
Strohl-
Fern

Villa Giulia

Villa Giulia

Bioparco

Viale del Giardino Zoologico

Viale dei Daini

VIA Pietro Raimon

Piazza della
Marina

Viale
Viale

Villa

VIA PINCIANA

2

Viale M. Metizia

Piazza
di Siena

Uccelliera

Pupazzi

Viale dei

VIA Liv

Viale dell'Aranciera

Viale San Paolo del Brasile

Borghese

Cavalli

Viale del Museo Borghese

VIA Marini

VIA Isc

VIA PINCIANA

D'ITAL

Giardino
del
Pincio

Galoppatoio

VIA PINCIANA

CORSO

3

Metropolitan

VIALE DEL MURO TORTO

VIA VITTORIO VENETO

Sardegna

Abruzzi

BONCOMPAGNI

AGIMUS

Gusto

Spagna

VIA SICILIA

Piemonte

Sallustiana

Accademia
Nazionale
di Santa Cecilia

Piazza
Augusto
imperatore

Belsima

VIA L. BISSOLATI

VIA G. Carducci

Nuovo Olimpia

Gregory's

**Teatro
Sistina**

Barberini

VIA XX Settembre

4

Piazza
Cavour

PONTE
CAVOUR

Tritone

VIA delle Quattro
Fontane

VIA Fire

Piazza
Colonna

Palazzo delle
Esposizioni

VIA NAZIONALE

Piazza del
Viminale

Locale

Piazza
del Quirinale

Quirinale

Teatro
Eliseo

**Teatro
Valle**

**Teatro
Rossini**

Piazza
del Santi
Apostoli

Piazza
Venezia

Panisperna

5

VIA CAVO

Cavour

VIA

**Teatro di Roma-
Argentina**

VIA DI SAN MARCO

VIA IV NOVEMBRE

CAVOUR

Gloss

Piazza
del
Campidoglio

VIA DEI

FORI

GHETTO

Concerti del
Tempietto

IMPERIALI

Colosseo

VIA N SALVI

Pasquino

Piazza del

Colosseo

6

Stazione
Ouagadougou

TRASTEVERE

Alcázar

Orti
Farnesiani

VIA CELIO VIBENNA

Parco
del Celio

Villa
Celimontana

Big Mama

Parco di
Sant'Alessio

VIA DEL CIRCO MASSIMO

7

**Nuovo
Sacher**

AVENTINO

Akab
Caffè Latino
Caruso
Coro della Scuola Popolare
di Musica di Testaccio
Izgud
No Stress Brasil
Radio Londra Caffè
Villaggio Globale

Alpheus
Be Bop
Ex-Magazzini

Palacisalfa
Palalottomatica
Terme di Caracalla

177

D

E

F

Brancaleone
Horus Club

Villa Mirafiori

Villa Massimo

Villa
orlonia

Piazza Bologna

BARI

CATANIA

Piazza di Porta Maggiore

PRENESTINA

Aula Magna dell'Università la Sapienza

Bebo do Samba

Cimitero Campo Verano

CIRCONVALLAZIONE

Forte Prenestino

PRENESTINA

Via del Pigneto

Piazza Lodi

Circolo degli Artisti

Piazza di villa Fiorelli

Piazza Lugo

Cinema

ALCAZAR
Map 177 D6
Via Cardinale Merry del Val 14, 00153
Tel 06 588 0099
One of the first to show blockbusters in English (Mon only) with a decadent velvet interior. Frequented by students and expatriates. Bar with coffee and popcorn.
⊙ Daily, screenings 5, 8 and 10.30
⚡ €4.50–7 🚌 H, 23, 44,56, 75, 280 to Viale Trastevere; tram 8

INTRASTEVERE
Map 177 D6
Vicolo Moroni 3a, 00153
Tel 06 588 4230
Housed in a 17th-century building, this is Rome's most celebrated independent cinema. The three-screen complex sometimes shows movies in English on Mon night.
⊙ Daily, 3 screenings ⚡ €4.50–7
🚌 H, 23, 44, 56, 75, 280 to Viale Trastevere; tram 8

METROPOLITAN
Map 177 E3
Via del Corso 7, 00187
Tel 06 320 0933
Four screens and maximum comfort in a cinema with bar, air-conditioning and ticket machines where you can pay by credit card. One screen is dedicated to original-version films from Sep to Jun.
⊙ Daily screenings from 4pm
⚡ Varies 🚇 Spagna 🚌 81, 117, 119, 590, 628

NUOVO OLIMPIA
Map 177 E4
Via in Lucina 16/b, 00186
Tel 06 6861068
A two-screen cinema with an interesting choice of art-house and more mainstream Italian and foreign films, most of which are not dubbed. Often the only cinema in town to screen certain films.
⊙ Daily screenings from 4pm; closed Jun–Sep ⚡ €4–7
🚌 81, 628 to Via del Corso

NUOVO SACHER
Map 177 D7
Largo Ascianghi 1, 00153
Tel 06 581 8116
Trastevere cinema owned by iconic Italian film director Nanni Moretti. It screens a number of independent films from abroad. English-language movies shown Mon and Tue. In the summer, there is also an open-air screen. Large snack bar with drinks and food.
⊙ Daily, screenings 5, 8 and 10.30
⚡ €5.50–7 🚌 H, 23, 44, 56, 75, 280 to Viale Trastevere; tram 8

PASQUINO
Map 177 D6
Piazza Sant'Egidio 10, 00158
Tel 06 580 3622
A Roman institution near Santa Maria in Trastevere. All films are in English, shown on three screens, so is popular with the English-speaking expatriate community here. Crowded espresso bar before screenings.
⊙ Daily, screenings 5, 8 and 10.30; closed Jun–Sep ⚡ €7 🚌 H, 23, 44, 56, 75, 280 to Viale Trastevere; tram 8

QUIRINALE
Map 177 F5
Via Nazionale 190
Tel 06 488 2653
An older cinema, so is not the largest or most modern of venues. Nevertheless the Quirinale often shows films in their original version on one of its two screens and also shows films after most other cinemas have made way for newer, more commerical blockbusters. There is no bar and the seats are not excessively comfortable.
⊙ First show at 6pm ⚡ €6.20 (€4.15 Wed) 🚌 H, 40, 64, 70, 71, 170

WARNER VILLAGE MODERNO
Map 178 G4
Piazza della Repubblica 45, 00184
Tel 06 477 791
www.warnervillage.it
A recent addition to the Roman cinema scene, this venue is large, airy and hi-tech. Decent popcorn and comfortable seats with plenty of leg room make it a pleasant experience all round. The schedule is commercial but one of the five screens shows blockbusters and big romantic comedies in the original language.
⊙ Daily screenings from 2:30pm
⚡ €7.50, €5.50 before 6pm and Wed
🚇 Repubblica 🚌 H, 40, 64, 170, 492

Classical music, dance and opera

ACCADEMIA NAZIONALE DI SANTA CECILIA
Map 177 E3
Via Vittoria 6, 00187. Box office: Biglieteria Auditorium, Parco della Musica, Viale Pietro de Coubertin 15
Tel 06 328171. Box office 06 808 2058
www.santacecilia.it
The Music Academy of Rome attracts the best professors and students. A beautifully put together menu of musical events is staged in different locations throughout the city.

The offical season means that it is closed in Jul, but the Accademia stages a number of outdoor concerts. Check the website for more details.
⊙ Thu–Tue 11–6, Oct–Jun ⚡ €8–40
🚌 Bus to Piazza del Popolo

AGIMUS (ASSOCIAZIONE GIOVANILE MUSICALE)
Map 177 E3
Via dei Greci 18, 00187
Tel 06 3211 1001
www.agimus.it
Organized by the Associazione Giovanile Musicale, Rome's biggest youth choir stages performances at venues such as churches and parks.

◉ Mon–Sat 3–7, Sep–end Jul 💶 €10
🚇 Termini 🚌 53, 217, 231, 910

ASSOCIAZIONE MUSICALE ROMANA ALL'ORTO BOTANICO
Map 176 D5
Via dei Banchi Vecchi 61, 00186
Botanical gardens: Largo Cristina di Svezia 23b, 00186
Tel 06 686 8441
www.uniroma.it
Rome's botanical gardens provide a much-loved venue for music events, mainly hosted by the Roman Music Association. From Gershwin to classical, plus a harpsichord festival.
◉ Box office open 1 hour before concert, no advance tickets. Season: Mar–Sep 💶 €10–25 🚌 H, 780, 630

AUDITORIO PIO
Map 176 C4
Via della Conciliazione 4, 00186
Tel 06 6880 1044
Part of the Vatican complex. The new Auditorium, Parco della Musica (see below) now puts on concerts that would previously have been heard here, but this is still a good venue for symphony orchestras. It also hosts a range of rock or pop artists.
◉ Daily 10.30–1.30, 3–6. Season: Oct–Jun 💶 €10–50 🚌 23, 40, 62, 64

AUDITORIUM, PARCO DELLA MUSICA
Map off 177 D2
Viale Pietro de Coubertin 30, 00197
Tel 06 8024 1206
www.musicaperroma.it
Architect Renzo Piano has finally given Rome the concert hall it deserves. Opened in

2002 near Stadio Flaminio, this three-auditorium complex is the city's biggest music venue, with a capacity for 4,600.
◉ Daily 11–6, 8–start of performance, all year 💶 From €8 🚇 Flaminio, then tram 2 🚌 53, 217, 231, 910 to Auditorio

AULA MAGNA DELL'UNIVERSITÀ LA SAPIENZA
Map 179 J4
Piazzale Aldo Moro 5, 00185. Box office: Lungotevere Flaminio 50, 00185
Tel 06 361 0051
www.uniroma1.it
This is the concert hall of the University of Rome, playing mostly classical music but occasionally some jazz, too. It is always packed with student audiences. A great venue, with some of Rome's best futuristic architecture.
◉ Mon, Wed–Fri 10–1, 3–6, Tue and Sat 10–noon, Oct–end Apr
💶 €12–33 🚇 Policlinico
🚌 Trams 3, 19

CONCERTI DEL TEMPIETTO AL TEATRO DI MARCELLO
Map 177 E6
Teatro di Marcello, Via del Teatro di Marcello 44, 00186. Box office: Via Rodolfo Morandi 3, 00139
Tel 06 8713 1590
www.tempietto.it
In winter, the Associazione Musicale 'Il Tempietto' stages concerts at the Sala Baldini in Piazza Campitelli and in the Basilica di San Nicola. In summer, the music is performed alfresco in the stunning, ancient Teatro Marcello.
◉ Season: Jun–end Sep 💶 €15
🚌 81, 160, 204, 628 to Via del Teatro Marcello, or 40, 64, 87, 628 to Piazza Venezia, then walk

CORO ROMANI CANTORES
Via Franco Sacchetti 78, 00137
Tel 06 8713 9264
www.spmtestaccio.it
This choir specializes in early Renaissance music, which is often played on period and antique instruments. Performances take place in various venues around the city,

the most impressive of which is Santa Maria Maggiore.
◉ Season: Sep–end Jun 💶 Free

CORO DELLA SCUOLA POPOLARE DI MUSICA DI TESTACCIO
Map off 177 E7
Via Monte Testaccio 91, 00153
Tel 06 575 0376
www.bandatestaccio.it
The choir of the well-known Testaccio music school has its seat in Rome's charming Testaccio district. Patrons benefit from a series of concerts and choral events. The school also has a brass band.
◉ Season Sep–Jun 💶 Free
🚌 75, 280

NEW CHAMBER SINGERS
Map 178 G4
Chiesa di San Paolo entro le Mura, Via Napoli 58, 00186
Tel 06 3600 1881
This amateur choir, previously directed by members of Rome's Episcopalian church, is now in the hands of the rival Anglican church, All Saints.
◉ All year 💶 Free 🚇 Repubblica
🚌 H, 40, 64, 70, 71, 170

OPERA ALLA TERME DI CARACALLA
Map off 178 G7
Terme di Caracalla. Box office: Teatro dell'Opera, Via Firenze 72, 00184
Tel 06 481 601

Lavish productions with real elephants used to take place here, but the practice ended in 1995 when archaeologists decreed that the shows endangered the monuments. Smaller music concerts are still

WHAT TO DO

held here in the summer: bring a cushion to sit on.

⊙ Tue–Sat 9–5, Sun 9–1.30, Jul 🎵 €20–50 🚇 Circo Massimo 🚌 67, 90, 118, 160, 714, 715

ORATORIUM IL GONFALONE
Map 176 D5
Via del Gonfalone 32a, 00186. Box office: Vicolo della Scimmia 1b, 00186
Tel 06 687 5952
Specializing in chamber music, Il Gonfalone hosts excellent groups from around the world. Events are held in the 16th-century Oratorio del Gonfalone, complete with frescoes and a gilded ceiling.

⊙ Mon–Fri 9.30–4, Oct–end May 🎵 From €13 🚌 116, or 46, 62, 64, 87, 492 to Campo dei Fiori, then walk

ROMAEUROPA FESTIVAL
Via XX Settembre 3, 00186
(box office at Via del Teatro Valle 21)
Tel 06 4229 6300 or 0800-795525 (free)
www.romaeuropa.net

A series of concerts in spectacular theatre settings, all close to the city. Organized in collaboration with the French Academy at Villa Medici, the German Academy at Villa Massimo and the Rome International Cultural Centre.

⊙ Daily 10–1, 3–7, 20 Sep–30 Nov 🎵 €5–38

SANTA MARIA DELLA PACE
Map 177 D4
Box office: Chiostro del Bramante, Vicolo della Pace 2
Tel 06 7807695,
www.millenunanote.org)
Piano recitals and ensembles take place in the church in summer on various days.

Adjacent to the famous Bar della Pace, the perfect place for a post-concert espresso.
⊙ August 🎵 €11–€15 🚌 46, 62, 64, 87, 116, 492 to Piazza Navona

TEATRO GHIONE
Map 176 C4
Via delle Fornaci 37, 00186
Tel 06 4781 8485, 06 637 2294
www.ghione.it
Close to Piazza San Pietro, Teatro Ghione is dedicated to up and coming stars, big-name pianists and other soloists. The lively audience gives the place a more relaxed feel.
⊙ Mon–Fri 10–1, 4–8, all year 🎵 €9–21 🚌 46, 64, 571, 916

TEATRO OLIMPICO
Map off 177 D2
Piazza Gentile da Fabriano 17, 00196
Tel 06 326 5991, 0800-907080 (free)
www.teatroolimpico.it
Very comfortable venue for music lovers, although upstaged of late by the new Auditorium (see page 181). Owned by the Accademia Filarmonica. Acoustics and concerts are always excellent.
⊙ Mon–Fri 10–1, 3–5.30, or after 8 for same-day tickets, Sep–end May
🎵 €20–35 🚌 32, 168, 186, 280, or any bus to Piazza Mancini then cross river; tram 2

TEATRO DELL'OPERA DI ROMA
Map 178 G4
Via Firenze 72, 00186
Tel 06 481 7517
www.opera.roma.it
One of Italy's top opera houses and also an official venue for ballet. The interior of the theatre is adorned with all the trimmings expected of a true opera house, including velvet boxes. When closed over the summer, performances are run through Opera alla Terme di Caracalla.
⊙ Mon–Fri 9.30–2pm, Nov–end May
🎵 €8–120 🚌 30X, 64

TEATRO VASCELLO
Map 176 C7
Via Giacinto Carini 72, 00165
Tel 06 588 1021
www.enteteatrale.it
On the edge of Trastevere, this is a small but good venue for experimental dance and some classic ballet. Also organizes workshops and conferences dedicated to the arts.
⊙ Tue–Sat 5.30–9, Sun 3–5, Sep–end Jun 🎵 €12 🚌 44, 75, 115, 710, 870

Contemporary live music

AKAB
See Clubs, page 189

ALEXANDERPLATZ
Map 176 B3
Via Ostia 9, 00193
Tel 06 3974 2171
Rome's most famous jazz venue also holds outdoor concerts at Villa Celimontana in summer and jazz festivals all year round. American bands often feature. Creole cooking is served up in the restaurant.
⊙ Mon–Sat 9pm–1.30am; closed first 2 weeks in Aug 🎵 €6.50 🚌 23, 30, 31, 70, 495

WHAT TO DO

ALPHEUS
Map off 177 F7
Via del Commercio 36, 00153
Tel 06 574 7826
Many huge rooms for large music events and live bands, with dancing to close the night. You can hop from room to room, changing musical genre as you please.
🕐 Tue–Sun 10pm–4am 🎫 €7
🚇 Piramide 🚌 60, 95, 118, 175, 280, 719

BE BOP
Map off 177 F7
Via Giulietti 14, 00153
Tel 06 5728 8959
www.bebopmusicclub.it
Large, comfortable 100-seat venue playing exclusively jazz and blues. The live acts are mainly Italian, although international guests are often invited.
🕐 Tue–Sun 10.30–2am 🎫 Free; €4 to join club as one-off payment
🚇 Piramide 🚌 30

BEBA DO SAMBA
Map 179 J5
Piazza dei Campani 12, 00185
Tel 339 878 5214
www.bebadosamba.it
African and Central American sounds predominate at this popular two-room venue in the studenty San Lorenzo district, but there is room for anything as long as it is not mainstream. There are sofas and cushions in one room, and stage and bar in the other.
🕐 Daily 9pm-2.30am 🎫 Compulsory annual membership €3
🚌 71, 491; tram 3, 19

BIG MAMA
Map 177 D6
Vicolo San Francesco a Ripa 18, 00158
Tel 06 581 2551
www.bigmama.it
Trastevere jazz joint where local and international bands play in a cavernous, smoke-filled underground room. The audience sits close to the band and dancing on tabletops is not uncommon.

🕐 Daily 9pm-1.30am; closed Jul–end Oct 🎫 €6–13 🚌 H, 23, 44, 56, 75, 280 to Viale Trastevere, or any bus to Piazza Mastai; tram 8

BRANCALEONE
Map 179 J2
Via Levanna 11, 00162
Tel 06 8200 0959
www.brancaleone.it
Italy is flooded with *centri sociali*, unofficial underground youth centres. Brancaleone, however, has been authorized by the town hall because of its socially useful activities. This non-profit group is one of Rome's best *centri sociali*, holding live concerts and serving draft beer. There are also live radio broadcasts Thu–Sat, midnight–6am.
🕐 Thu–Sun 10.30pm–5am
🎫 €5 donation 🚌 60, 211, 311, 343

CAFFÉ LATINO
Map off 177 E7
Via Monte Testaccio 96, 00153
Tel 06 5728 8556
Once *the* place for live music, this place still draws a crowd in a city that loves Latin and jazz. Live acts Monday to Wednesday, followed by dancing. Sunday is gay night.
🕐 Daily 11pm–3am 🎫 €5–€10
🚌 Piramide 🚌 75, 280

CARUSO
Map off 177 E7
Via Monte Testaccio 36, 00153
Tel 06 574 5019
Best bet for Latin sounds, ranging from salsa to hip hop. Mix of live bands and Rome's best DJs. Always packed, especially on Sun, which is disco night. Arabic music nights, too.

🕐 Tue–Sun 10.30pm–3am 🎫 €8–10
🚇 Piramide 🚌 75, 280

CIRCOLO DEGLI ARTISTI
See Clubs, page 189

DOME ROCK CAFÉ
Map 178 H6
Via D. Fontana 18, 00185
Tel 06 7045 2436
This recent addition to Rome's music scene has become very popular in a short space of time, thanks to good beer and great dance music.
🕐 Daily 10pm–3am 🎫 Free 🚌 87, 117, 218 to Piazza San Giovanni

EX-MAGAZZINI
Map off 177 F7
Via dei Magazzini Generali 8, 00153
Tel 06 575 8040
A Rome classic in the Testaccio/Ostiense area. Live music and dancing inside a former greengrocer's premises. The acts come from Rome's underground music scene and range from Italian rap to jazz. It also holds art exhibitions.
🕐 Tue–Sun 9pm–4.30am 🎫 €8, includes one drink 🚇 Piramide 🚌 60, 95, 118, 175, 280, 719

FONCLEA
Map 176 C3
Via Crescenzio 82a, 00197
Tel 06 689 6302
This is a restaurant and pub that also hosts a mixture of funk, Latin and other live music acts. The food and drink (including 200 different cocktails) are great. This audience is always ready to move to the music.
🕐 Daily noon–3, 8.30–2 🎫 Free; except Sat, €5 🚇 Ottaviano 🚌 23, 271, 280, 492, 990

FORTE PRENESTINO
Map 179 M5
Via Federico Delpino, 00175
Tel 06 2180 7855
www.forteprenestino.net
This *centro sociale* (underground youth centre) lies outside the city in a 15th-century fortress complete with moat and underground

tunnels. Students, hippies and political activists screen films and hold parties. There are also a number of live band performances, but for specific details please call ahead.
🕐 Daily, usually 11pm–late 🎟 €5 donation 🚃 Tram 5, 19 to Via Prenestina, or take a taxi

GLOSS
Map 178 F5
Via del Cardello 13a, 00184
Tel 06 487 2558
www.sigilloweb.com
Gloss's three rooms host a fun restaurant and winebar and put on light and quintessentially Roman cabaret shows or plays. After the performance there is 70s and 80s music until the small hours.
🕐 Daily 7pm–4am 🎟 Varies; €13–16 for cabaret or theatre. Disco free after 12.45. If you have dinner with a show you pay €8 on top of the meal
🚇 Colosseo 🚌 81, 87, 117, 571

GREGORY'S
Map 177 F4
Via Gregoriana 54d, 00186
Tel 06 679 6386
www.gregorysjazzclub.com

John Bull and Guinness are washed down to the sound of live jazz at this nightspot. There is a jam session every Wed and the fans who come here take their jazz very seriously.
🕐 Tue–Sun 8pm–3.30am; closed Aug 🎟 Free 🚇 Barberini 🚌 52, 53, 61, 62, 63, 80, 95, 116, 117

GUSTO
See Restaurants, page 244

HORUS CLUB
Map 179 J2
Corso Sempione 21, 00141
Tel 06 8689 9181
Once a cinema, Horus has now been revamped to include a high-tech music-mixing stage and lighting for concerts. It holds a wonderfully varied selection of concerts—expect to see some real talent, such as Sicily's Carmen Consoli.
🕐 Wed–Sat 9pm–3am 🎟 From €10 🚌 60, 211, 311, 343 to Piazza Sempione

IZGUD
Map 177 E7
Via Mastro Giorgio 19, 00153
Tel 06 5728 8794
www.izgud.it
Minimal decor, vintage seating and tables and cool eclectic sounds (live jazz and lounge sounds that range from bossa nova to electro) accompanied by dishes from Egypt, the US, France, China and Japan, make this one of the most appealing new entries in lively Testaccio. Friday is jazz night, while on Thursdays the music comes from the same place as the evening's menu: a combined feast for the ears and palate!
🕐 Tue–Sun 7.30pm–2am 🎟 Free 🚌 Piramide 🚌 23, 30, 75, 280, 673, 716, 719; tram 3

JIVE
Map off 177 F7
Via Giuseppe Libetta 7, 00154
Tel 06 574 5989
An exciting venue for some of the newest sounds to hit Rome. One special feature is the outdoor area, where concerts are staged in the summer.
🕐 Thu–Sat 9pm–4am 🎟 Free 🚇 Garbatella 🚌 23, 702 to Via Ostiense

IL LOCALE
Map 177 D4
Vicolo del Fico 3, 00186
Tel 06 687 9075
Great rock-music venue and you can't beat the location, near the Piazza Navona. The downside is it sometimes

closes early when locals complain about the noise.
🕐 10pm–3am; closed Aug 🎟 €5 🚌 46, 62, 64, 87, 116, 492 to Piazza Navona

NO STRESS BRASIL
Map 177 E7
Via degli Stradivari 35, 00153
Tel 06 5833 5015
www.nostressbrasil.net
This is actually a *churrascaria*, where you can eat some of the best steak in town imported directly from Argentina and Brazil. Live music by Brazilian bands and blues concerts accompany you every evening and are followed by DJ sets and partying till dawn.
🕐 Daily 8.30pm–3.30am 🎟 Free Mon–Thu & Sun, €10 Fri–Sat 🚌 Piramide G23, 30, 75, 280, 673, 716, 719; tram 3

PALACISALFA
Map off 178 G7
Viale dell'Oceano Atlantico 271, 00144
Tel 06 5728 8018
www.palacisalfa.com
When music fans complained that the Palalottomatica (see below) was not ideal for smaller concerts, city officials built the Palacisalfa. It is a more friendly venue with good sound quality and atmosphere.
🕐 Performances usually at 8pm 🎟 €12–40 depending on artist 🚇 EUR Fermi 🚌 706, 779

PALALOTTOMATICA
Map off 177 F7
Piazzale dello Sport, Viale dell'Umanesimo, 00144
Tel 06 540901
www.palalottomatica (schedule)
www.ticketweb.it (tickets)
The biggest venue in the city hosts all the top international acts—everyone from Sting to the Rolling Stones has played in this sports stadium-turned-concert hall.
🕐 Performances usually at 8pm 🎟 €20–40 depending on artist 🚇 EUR Palasport

RADIO LONDRA CAFFÈ
Map off 177 E7
Via Monte Testaccio 65b, 00153
Tel 06 575 0044
At the heart of clubbers' row in Testaccio, this is the place to go for classic rock, 80s music, good dancing and live bands. It serves beer and snacks, and has a laid-back attitude.
🕐 Mon–Sat 9pm–3am 💶 Free
🚇 Piramide 🚌 75, 280

STAZIONE OUAGADOUGOU
Map 177 D6
Via della Lungaretta 75, 00158
Tel 06 659 0030
One of the only places in town for African music, African snacks and even African beer. It is decorated with funky black and white photography from Africa. Both staff and clientele are very friendly.
🕐 Tue–Sun 8.30pm–2am; closed mid-Jul–mid-Aug 💶 Free 🚌 H, 23, 44, 56, 75, 280 to Viale Trastevere; tram 8

VILLAGGIO GLOBALE
Map off 177 E7
Lungotevere Testaccio, 00153
Tel 06 575 7233
Rome's most popular music venue is in a former slaughter-house (the Mattatoio). Huge outdoor courtyard for concerts and dancing. During larger events, food stands are set up inside.
🕐 Varies, usually 6pm–3am
💶 Maximum €10 🚌 75, 280, or bus to Lungotevere Testaccio

Theatre

AMBRA JOVINELLI
Map 178 H5
Via Guglielmo Pepe 43–7, 00185
Tel 06 4434 0262
www.ambrajovinelli.com
Built at the turn of the 20th century this was once Rome's foremost variety venue but was almost knocked down in the 1990s after a period of steady decline. It was entirely renovated and reopened in January 2001 and now pulls in some of the best comic actors in Italy, and puts on some of

the best comic plays and one-man shows too. It also hosts jazz concerts.
🕐 Sep–end May, with one-off events in Jun and Jul. Box office Mon–Sat 10–7, Sun 11–1.30, Oct–Jun; Mon–Sat 10–1, 2–6 Jul, Sep; closed Aug 💶 €11.50–27.50 🚇 Termini 🚌 70, 71; tram 5, 14

PALAZZO DELLE ESPOSIZIONI
Map 178 F4
Via Nazionale 194, 00184
Tel 06 482 8757
www.palazzoesposizioni.it
Dating from the 1870s, this is Rome's all-round cultural gathering place where theatre, film showings, and art and photography exhibitions are staged under one roof.
🕐 Wed–Mon 10–9 💶 Varies 🚌 Bus to Via Nazionale

TEATRO COLOSSEO
Map 178 G6
Via Capo d'Africa 5, 00184
Tel 06 700 4932
www.teatrocolosseo.com
In the shadow of the mighty Colosseo, this venue is a rarity for Rome—a theatre staging English-language plays. It is a good showcase for young directors and actors, and the small stage suits one-man shows.
🕐 Mon–Sat 10–1, 3–7, Sep–end Jun 💶 €10–20 🚇 Colosseo 🚌 30

TEATRO ELISEO
Map 177 F5
Via Nazionale 183, 00184
Tel 06 488 2114
www.teatroeliseo.it
Large, modern and popular, the Eliseo puts on plays by major and established Italian and international playwrights, while the smaller Piccolo Eliseo next door pays more attention to contemporary and fringe theatre.
🕐 Sep–end May. Box office Mon–Sat 9.30–2.30, 3.30–7; closed Aug, and Sat in Jun and Jul 💶 €8–27 🚌 40, 64, 70, 71, 170

TEATRO DI ROMA—ARGENTINA
Map 177 E5
Largo Argentina 52, 00186
Tel 06 6880 4601
www.teatrodiroma.net
One of Rome's most historic theatres, a leading venue for beautifully staged productions. A performance here is a night out and the audience dresses up accordingly. There is a cocktail bar.
🕐 Box office: Mon–Sat 10–2, 3–7 💶 €12–27 🚌 64, 87, 492 to Largo Argentina; tram 8

TEATRO ROSSINI
Map 177 E5
Piazza Santa Chiara 14, 00186
Tel 06 6880 2770
Run by Alfiero Alfieri, with performaces dedicated to comedy, local dialect and the traditional characters of popular and traditional Roman theatre.
🕐 Daily 10am–8pm 💶 €15–18 🚌 64, 87, 492 to Largo Argentina; tram 8

TEATRO SISTINA
Map 177 F4
Via Sistina 129, 00186
Tel 06 420 0711
www.ilsistina.com
This theatre stages largely dramatic productions and some musicals, including international extravaganzas. The informal atmosphere draws a young audience, which tends to participate vocally.
🕐 Daily 10–7, Oct–end May 💶 €20–40 🚇 Spagna

TEATRO VALLE
Map 177 E5
Via del Teatro Valle 21a, 00186 Rome
Tel 06 6880 3794
www.teatrovalle.it
Charming little theatre with excellent dramatic performances, including the classics, all produced with great attention to detail. This also makes it popular with students.
🕐 Tue–Sat 10–7 💶 €11–29 🚇 Barberini 🚌 64, 87, 492 to Largo Argentina, or any bus to Corso Vittorio Emanuele; tram 8

NIGHTLIFE

Whether it's a quiet drink in an atmospheric *enoteca* or dancing until dawn in a smoke-filled club, there's something for everyone in Rome. Choose from lounge, house, retro, electronica, cheesy Euro sounds, hip hop, R&B, cigar rooms, speed-dating, high tech, cool sounds with attitude, hot South American, reggae—the list is endless. Most clubs don't get going until around 1am, so a visit to a couple of bars and a late pizza is the Roman way to kick off proceedings.

The Campo dei Fiori is the place for posing and pubbing, Trastevere bristles with buzzing bars, and the university quarter, San Lorenzo, is always a happening scene with lots of cheap bars and pubs. But the heart of hip Roman life is Testaccio—the old slaughterhouse area. This hilly area, just south of the Aventine Hill is out of the *centro storico*. If you're using public transportation, there is a *servizio notturno* (night bus service), identified by the letter N. It covers most of the city from midnight to 5.30am, after which normal daytime service is resumed. But traditionally, all-night revellers round off a night on the tiles with a cappuccino and fresh *cornetti caldi* (hot croissants) at one of the bars, such as the Bar del Mattatolo in Testaccio. Once the drinking spot for the slaughterhouse workers from across the road, it now has an early morning clientele that includes largely revellers from clubland.

Clubs and discobars can be expensive. In addition to the entrance fee, they often make you pay for a membership card *(tessera)*. Admission often includes one free drink, but from then on you pay full price. Prepare to wait for entry to the hottest clubs. It pays to dress up. Cool clothes, vampire garb, black leather goth style, scanty and flimsy—any number of variations are de rigueur in the hippest spots. There are plenty of alternative, gay and transgressive hang-outs—especially in Testaccio. The Alibi was one of the first scene-setters to put Testaccio on the club map and it's still just as popular today.

Bars and Pubs

ALIBI
Via Monte Testaccio 69, 00153
Tel 06 574 3448
This cellar was dug into an old Roman rubbish dump, Monte Testaccio, a hill made of broken pottery. Today, its vaulted arches throb with music. Popular with the gay crowd in summer, when the large terrace comes into use, the bar is more mixed in winter. Credit cards are not accepted.
🕐 Wed–Sun midnight–5 💶 €10–15
🚇 Piramide 🚌 75, 280

ANIMA
Via di Santa Maria dell'Anima 57, 00186
Tel 338-1767166 (mobile phone)
In the heart of Rome's nightlife district, west of Piazza Navona. Popular with visitors and English-speakers. It serves excellent fresh fruit cocktails, ultra-modern in style and has competent resident DJs. Credit cards are not accepted.
🕐 Tue–Sun 9.30–2 💶 Free 🚌 46, 62, 64, 81, 87, 116, 492

ANTICA BIRRERIA
Via di San Marcello 19, 00187
Tel 06 679 5310
Art nouveau beer hall near Piazza Venezia. German beer is served in big steins. Inexpensive and brimming with alcohol-fuelled cheer.
🕐 Mon–Sat noon–midnight 💶 Free 🚌 40, 46, 62, 64, 916

ANTICA ENOTECA DI VIA DELLA CROCE
Via della Croce 76/b, 00187
Tel 06 679 0896
Old-fashioned style at its most enticing: frescoed walls, enamelled tabletops and wooden ceilings. Good wine, plus cheese and light snacks, too. Some outdoor seating is available in summer.
🕐 Daily 11.30am–1am 💶 Free
🚇 Spagna 🚌 116, 117, 119

ANTICA VINERIA
Via Monte della Farina 38, 00186
Tel 06 6880 6989
Just off the crowded and expensive Campo dei Fiori. Run on typically Roman terms—somewhat flexible opening hours, but a good glass of wine at some of the best prices in the city. Credit cards are not accepted.
🕐 Daily 8.30–2, 6.30–9 💶 Free
🚌 40, 46, 62, 64, 492, 630; tram 8

ANTICO CAFFÈ DELLA PACE
See Restaurants, page 233

ASSIZE OF ALE
Via della Vite 96, 00187
Tel 06 6920 2391
www.assizeofale.it
Wine and cocktail bar in an ancient building not far from Piazza di Spagna. The theme is medieval and yet the feel is of an exclusive men's club. Food is available, and the happy hour is usually 6–7.
🕐 Tue–Sun 11am–2am 💶 Free
🚇 Spagna

BARBAR
Via Crescenzio 18, 00193
Tel 06 6830 8435
Just behind Castel Sant'Angelo is this cavernous and sophisticated minimalist lounge bar, with a cigar room. It plays good music to its 30- to 40-something crowd. Venue for Rome's first spate of speed-dating meetings.
🕐 Tue–Sat 7pm–3am 💶 Free except on special theme nights 🚌 30, 40, 62, 280, 492, 990; tram 19

BARFLY

Vícolo del Bologna 74, 00153
Tel 338 494 5483
Wood-furnished Irish pub in Trastevere, with a good variety of beers and ales, as well as live music almost every night. Happy hour Fri–Sat, 5.30–10.
🕐 Tue–Sun 5.30pm–4am 💶 Free
🚇 H, 175; tram 8 to Piazza Sonnino

BARTARUGA

Piazza Mattei 7, 00186
Tel 06 6892299
This retro kitsch venue has it all: a grand piano, Murano crystal, comfortable sofas and suffused lighting. In summer, it spills out onto one of the most beautiful little piazzas in Rome. Occasional live music and cabaret nights. Credit cards are not accepted.
🕐 Daily 3pm–2am 💶 Free 🚇 Largo Argentina

IL CENTRALE

Via Celsa 6, 00186
Tel 06 6780501
www.centraleristotheatre.it
Il Centrale is a *ristotheatre*, taking its name from the fact that it is based in a former theatre dating from the 1920s. It has a bar with a DJ, a lounge area, and a restaurant where you can eat while watching a live cabaret or music show that makes use of the old stage. *Aperitivo* time is 6–10pm, and for €8 you can have a drink and all you can eat from a buffet of pasta salads.
🕐 Thu–Sun 6pm–3am (closed Jul–mid-Sept 💶 From €8 🚇 30, 40, 46, 64 or any bus to Piazza Venezia or Largo Argentina

CHARITY CAFÉ

Via Panisperna 68, 00184
Tel 06 4782 5881
www.charitycafe.it
Intimate bar playing live jazz and blues at night, when it serves wine, cheeses and salami. In the afternoons, it becomes a tearoom offering 25 types of herbal teas. Happy hour 4–10pm every evening.

Credit cards are not accepted. Free membership entry form to be completed, which can be re-used for future visits.
🕐 Daily 4pm–3am 💶 Free
🚇 Colosseo

CUL DE SAC

See Restaurants, page 239

THE DRUNKEN SHIP

Campo dei Fiori 20–21, 00186
Tel 06 6830 0535
One of Campo dei Fiori's many lively drinking spots. Caters to a mainly British and Anglo-friendly student crowd. Has DJ sets most evenings and a popular happy hour from 5 to 8pm.
🕐 Daily 4pm–2am 💶 Free 🚇 46, 62, 64, 492 to Corso Vittorio Emanuele II (ask for Campo dei Fiori), or 116 to Campo dei Fiori

EDOARDO II

See Restaurants, page 241

ENOTECA TRASTEVERE

Via della Lungaretta 86, 00153
Tel 06 588 5659
Tavern-like wine bar with more than 900 wines, in addition to salads, soups and home-made desserts. During weekends, a pianist plays soft jazz and swing. Outdoor tables in summer make for great people-watching.
🕐 Daily 5pm–2am 💶 Entry free; D €20, Wine €15 🚇 H, 175; tram 8 to Piazza Sonnino

ESCOPAZZO

Via d'Aracoeli 41, 00186
Tel 06 6920 0422
www.escopazzo.it
This wine and cocktail bar, very near Piazza Venezia, Rome's central hub, is a warm, intimate place perfect for a romantic soirée. The music is live most days, the atmosphere relaxed and relaxing. Credit cards are not accepted.
🕐 Daily 8.30–3 💶 Free 🚇 40, 64, 170, 175 to Piazza Venezia

FRIENDS ART CAFÉ

See Restaurants, page 242

GARBO

Vícolo Santa Margherita 1/a, 00153
Tel 06 5832 0782
www.garbobar.com
For those who prefer quiet conversation and a chance to speak to some locals about the gay scene. Small, candlelit bar tucked on a side street in Trastevere. Tasteful and elegant. Credit cards are not accepted.
🕐 Tue–Sun 10pm–3am 💶 Free, but membership of Arcigay, national gay organization, is required (€13) 🚇 H; tram 8 to Piazza Sonnino

HANGAR

Via in Selci 69, 00184 Rome
Tel 06 488 1397
Rome's oldest gay establishment is an American-style pick-up bar for men. Layout is long, narrow and crowded, with bars playing music videos on either side of a central corridor. Credit cards are not accepted.
🕐 Wed–Mon 10.30pm–2.30am; closed Aug 💶 Free; Arcigay membership required (€13) 🚇 Colosseo 🚌 75, 84 to Via Cavour

THE HIGHLANDER PUB

Vícolo San Biagio 9, 00186
Tel 06 6880 5368
Scottish pub off the north end of Via del Corso, with a disco and three rooms for carousing until the early morning. Lots of beer and noise. Local acts perform live music. Credit cards are not accepted.
🕐 Tue–Sun 5pm–3am 💶 Free 🚇 63, 117

JONATHAN'S ANGELS

Via della Fossa 16, 00186
Tel 06 689 3426
Quirky portraits of the bar's charismatic owner and children feature amid the decorations of this popular haunt, a must for both casual visitors and hardened night-owls. The music is cheesy (bad Italian or French retro), which matches the decoration. Credit cards are not accepted.

Ⓒ Tue–Sun 8pm–3.30am 🎫 Free
🚌 46, 62, 64, 492 to Corso Vittorio
Emanuele II (ask for Campo dei Fiori),
116 to Campo dei Fiori

MAD JACK'S
Via Arenula 20, 00186 Rome
Tel 06 6880 8223
www.madjacks.com
This Irish pub will suit those
looking for a festive place in
which to pass the night hours.
The music is loud and drinks
are flowing.
Ⓒ Daily 10am–3am 🎫 Free 🚌 40, 64
to Largo Argentina; tram 8

MAX'S BAR
Via A. Grandi 7a, 00185 Rome
Tel 06 7030 1599
www.maxbar.net
Very popular gay bar for men
of all ages, not far from Termini
station. It is literally underground, so can become quite
hot and crowded. Consists of
two bars, a dance floor, and a
large sitting/socializing area.
Credit cards are not accepted.
Ⓒ Thu–Tue 10.30am–3.30am
🎫 Thu–Sun €8–11, includes one drink;
Mon free 🚇 Manzoni

OMBRE ROSSE
Piazza Sant'Egidio 12, 00153
Tel 06 5884155
www.ombrerosse.com

In Trastevere, next door to the
popular Pasquino English-
language cinema (see page
180). Everything from full
breakfast to afternoon tea, and
from aperitifs to nightcaps. Live
jazz or blues on Thu or Sun
nights.

Ⓒ Mon–Sat 7.30am–2am, Sun
5pm–2am 🎫 Free 🚌 H, 23, 44, 56,
75, 280 to Viale Trastevere; tram 8 to
Piazza Sonnino

OPPIO CAFFÈ
Via delle Terme di Tito 72, 00184
Tel 06 474 5262
www.oppiocaffe.it
High-tech meets ancient
history: glass and steel bar
fixtures, Plexiglas seats and
plasma video screens, all
underneath imperial Roman
brickwork. There is an amazing
view of the Colosseo from the
terrace. Live music Thursday
and Friday.
Ⓒ Tue–Sun 7am–2am, Sun–Mon
7am–8pm 🎫 Free 🚇 Colosseo

LA PALMA
Via Giuseppe Mirri 35, 00159
Tel 06 4359 9029
www.lapalmaclub.it
A long way from the city, but
with the newest and most
interesting in jazz and ethnic
sounds. Able to woo some of
the classiest names on the
international music scene.
Credit cards are not accepted.
Ⓒ Daily 8.30–12.30 🎫 €12–25
🚌 71, 168, 204, 492, 649

IL POSTO DELLE FRAGOLE
Via Carlo Botta 51, 00184
Tel 06 4782 4868
www.ilpostodellefragole.org
Named for an Ingmar Bergman
film, this bar/club promotes
Scandinavian culture in Rome.
Nightly events include films
and live music, from
Scandinavian to blues. Credit
cards are not accepted
Ⓒ Tue–Sun 5pm–2am; closed Jun–Sep
🎫 Varies depending on events held;
membership required (free) 🚇 Vittorio
Emanuele 🚌 85, 87, 810

SHAKI
Via Mario de' Fiori 29/a, 00187
Tel 06 679 1694
This elongated stylish bar, with
a faintly oriental, minimalist
design in the chic Tridente
area is ultra-cool. The food is
tantalizingly fresh, the wine
expensive.

Ⓒ Daily 10am–midnight 🎫 Free
🚇 Spagna 🚌 116, 117, 119

SIDE MEETING POINT
Via Labicana 50, 00184
Tel 348 692 9472
A popular gay bar with retro-
kitsch interior, and is one of
the few exclusively gay
nightspots in Rome. It spills
out onto the street in summer.
Has stood the test of time.
Ⓒ Daily noon–2am 🎫 Free
🚇 Colosseo

STARDUST LOUNGE
Vicolo de' Renzi 4, 00153 Rome
Tel 06 5832 0875
Small, smoky club in Trastevere
full of atmosphere. Although it
no longer has live music, the
setting retains a jazz club feel
in a soulful way rare in Rome.
Credit cards are not accepted.
Ⓒ Daily 7pm–2am 🎫 Free 🚌 H, 175;
tram 8 to Piazza Sonnino

LA TAVERNA DEL CAMPO
Campo dei Fiori 16, 00186
Tel 06 6874402
www.pierluigi.it
This tavern, on Campo dei
Fiori, is always full, both inside
and out, and has reasonably-
priced food and loud music.
There are tables to be had on
the piazza.
Ⓒ Daily 9am–2am, summer; Tue–Sun
9am–2am, rest of year 🎫 Free 🚌 46,
62, 64, 87, 116, 492

TRASTE'
Via della Lungaretta 76, 00153 Rome
Tel 06 589 4430
Casual bar in the heart of
Trastevere, popular with a
younger crowd. Simple setting,
with large cushions for seating
and trendy design. Very wide
drinks selection, both alcoholic
and non-alcoholic. Credit cards
are not accepted.
Ⓒ Daily 5–2 🎫 Free 🚌 H, 175; tram
8 to Piazza Sonnino

TRINITY COLLEGE
Via del Collegio Romano 6, 00186
Tel 06 678 6472
www.trinity-rome.com

This Gothic-looking building houses one of Rome's most reliable Irish pubs. Found in the well-heeled area between the Pantheon and Via del Corso, and not far from Galleria Doria Pamphilj.
🕐 Daily noon–3am 💶 Free
🚌 62, 63, 81, 85, 95, 117, 119, 175

WINETIME WINE BAR
See Restaurants, page 254

Clubs

AKAB
Via Monte Testaccio 69, 00153
Tel 06 5730 5177
One of Rome's oldest nightclubs, but still very much in style. The music theme changes throughout the week to cover electronica, hip-hop, R&B, pop and house music. Plays host to international DJs, rock bands and even occasional cabaret acts. Two floors with a secluded courtyard. Credit cards are not accepted.
🕐 Tue–Sun 11pm–4.30am 💶 €15
🚇 Piramide 🚌 75, 280

ALIEN
Via Velletri 13–19, 00198
Tel 06 841 2112
Large disco with three dance floors in different styles: black and white for the Rock Room, carpets and incense for the India Room, and deep blues for the Main Room. Credit cards are not accepted.
🕐 Tue–Sun 11pm–5am 💶 €13
🚌 490, 495 to Piazza Fiume

BAJA
Lungotevere Arnaldo da Brescia, 00196
Tel 06 3260 0118
One of Rome's few waterborne offerings—a moored boat near Piazza del Popolo. Judicious mix of high-tech and ethnic design. Cool dub, house and lounge sounds downstairs. The cocktails are fantastic, and food is served upstairs.
🕐 Tue–Sun 8pm–3am 💶 Free to resturant; €10 for men, €5 for women to piano bar 🚇 Flaminio 🚌 95, 117, 119, 491, 590, 926; tram 2

BLOOM
Via del Teatro Pace 29–30, 00186
Tel 06 6880 2029
Sushi upstairs and cool sounds in a futuristic setting downstairs. It is the trendiest of the Roman *fashionista* hangouts, so you may well have trouble getting in—but it's worth a go.
🕐 Daily 7pm–2am; closed Jul–end Aug 💶 Free 🚌 46, 62, 64, 87, 116, 916

BUSH
Via Galvani 46, 00153
Tel 06 5728 8691
Probably Testaccio's most frequented nightclub, mainly by a 30-something crowd. Arty yet high-tech feel: black and white photographs and big-screen TVs on the walls. Latest house music. Tue is gay night.
🕐 Tue–Sat 10pm–4am 💶 up to €15; Thu free 🚇 Piramide 🚌 23, 30, 75, 280, 673, 716, 719; tram 3

CAFFÈ LATINO
See Contemporary Live Music, page 183

CIRCOLO DEGLI ARTISTI
Via Casilina Vecchia 42, 00182
Tel 06 7030 5684
www.circoloartisti.it
This large venue is more of a social meeting place than a nightclub. Two dance floors are supplemented with a large outdoor area, including bars, food stands, and even an outdoor cinema. Live music from acid jazz and funk to reggae-rap. There is a gay night on Fri. Credit cards are not accepted.

🕐 Tue–Sun 10pm–4am 💶 Free
🚌 105

CLASSICO VILLAGE
Via G. Libetta 3, 00154
Tel 06 3751 8615
The most coolest of Rome's many once-a-week gay dance events. The crowd, of both sexes, typifies *la bella figura*—cutting a fine figure on the dance floor. Warehouse-style premises, with three dance floors and two courtyards. Credit cards are not accepted.
🕐 Sat 11.30pm–4am 💶 €15
🚇 Garbatella 🚌 23, 702 to Via Ostiense

THE GALLERY
Via della Maddalena 12, 00186
Tel 06 687 2316
www.thegallery.it
Created by English artists, this modern, elegant bar behind the Pantheon is pumping with energy. Music ranges from hip-hop and R&B to 70s/80s revival, and draws a crowd that's ready to party.
🕐 Tue–Fri 8.30pm–3am, Sat–Sun 8.30–4 💶 €10 🚌 116 to Pantheon

GILDA
Via Mario de' Fiori 97, 00187
Tel 06 678 4838
www.gildabar.it
The place to see and be seen: It's all about attitude and who you know. A night here is a must if you want to see Rome's people of the moment. Live music on weekends.
🕐 Daily 11.30pm–4.30am, Oct–end May 💶 €15 🚇 Spagna

GOA
Via G. Libetta 3, 00154
Tel 06 574 8277
Chic club in the Ostiense district that attracts a stylish, but not too pretentious, crowd. One large room in a bright ethnic/industrial style consists of various nooks for dancing, drinking or just hanging out. Credit cards are not accepted.
🕐 Tue–Sun 11pm–3am 💶 From €10, depending on artist 🚌 23, 702 to Via Ostiense

JUNGLE CLUB ROMA
Via di Monte Testaccio 95, 00153 Roma
Tel 333 720 8694
www.jungleclubroma.com
This dark, gloomy and popular Goth venue (some of the DJs have names like Transmuter and Gothfather) is embellished with decoration reminiscent of Central America and industrial lighting effects. One room is for drinking and the other for dancing. The music ranges from live to DJ sets that cater especially to the Italian 'dark' scene: post-punk, Goth, indutrial and heavy metal sounds. You'll need plenty of black eyeliner.
◎ Sat 10.30pm–4am ▣ €8, free before 11 ▣ Piramide ▣ 30, 118, 160, 175, 280; tram 3

LA MAISON
Vicolo dei Granari 4, 00186
Tel 06 683 3312
Fashionable, multi-room venue where stars of the small and big screens mingle with more humble beings. The interior design is opulent with chandeliers and comfortable divans, and the music is varied.
◎ Tue–Sun 10.30pm–4am ▣ €10–15 ▣ 40, 46, 62, 64 to Corso Vittorio Emanuele II, or 30, 70, 81, 204, 628 to Corso Rinascimento

PIPER CLUB
Via Tagliamento 9, 00198
Tel 06 8555398
One of Rome's first discos and still very popular after several decades. High-tech effects complement the dance music play-list. Many intimate seating areas allow you to see but not seen. Well north of central Rome.
◎ Sat–Sun 10.30pm–4.30am ▣ Sat €18, Sun varies ▣ 53, 63, 86, 92, 168, 630; tram 3, 19

QUBE
Via di Portonaccio 212, 00159
Tel 06 438 5445
Young bodies dance till they drop in Rome's biggest underground disco. Fri night is Muccassassina night, the name

given to the once gay and transgressive night, now more straight than gay and more mainstream than alternative.
◎ Thu–Sat 11pm–4am ▣ varies ▣ 168, 204, 409, 545, 649, or 71, 492 to Tiburtina station, then walk

SIENA ART CAFÉ
Viale del Galoppatoio 33, 00197
Tel 06 3600 6578
A vast, minimalist New York-style venue under Villa Borghese, which has only been around for a couple of years but has fast become a must for trend-seekers. Celebrity-spotters will be happy, too.
◎ Tue–Sat: restaurant 9–1am; disco 11.30–4am ▣ €20–25 ▣ 116

SPEEDY GONZALEZ
Via G. Libetta 13, 00154
Tel 06 5728 7338
Whimsical re-creation of a Mexican village in the Ostiense district. It serves a large

selection of South American cocktails as well as typical Mexican dishes. The atmosphere is noisy and fun, with music ranging from '70s to the latest hits. Credit cards are not accepted.
◎ Tue–Sun 8.30pm–3am; closed Aug ▣ Sat €6; free all other nights ▣ 23, 702 to Via Ostiense

SUITE
Via degli Orti di Trastevere 1, 00153
Tel 06 586 1888
Futuristic lounge bar catering to Rome's super-cool crowd. Large, open space divided into a dance floor, bar and sitting areas, the latter with plastic couches. Music varies nightly from lounge to house and retro. Credit cards are not accepted.
◎ Tue–Sat midnight–4 ▣ €10–20 ▣ H; tram 8 to Piazza Bernardo da Feltre

GAY AND LESBIAN ROME
The year 2000 was a milestone for gays and lesbians in Rome. It was the year of the city's first Gay Pride March and, although disapproved of by the Vatican, it was attended by tens of thousands of people. Gay Pride now takes place each year, usually in early July.
The following places are either gay or have one gay night each week. See the main listings for more information.

BARS AND PUBS
Alibi (summer only—see page 186)
Garbo (see page 187)
Hangar (see page 187)
Max's Bar (see page 188)
Side Meeting Point (see page 188)

CLUBS
Bush (Tuesdays only—see page 189)
Circolo degli Artisti (Fridays only—see page 189)
Classico Village (once a week—see page 189)

RESTAURANT
Edoardo II (see page 241)

For more information, pick up a copy of *Babilonia*, a monthly gay magazine which has comprehensive listings for the whole of Italy (€5.20 at newsstands), or log on to www.archigay.it, the official site of Italy's foremost gay and lesbian network (Italian and English), or www.mariomieli.org, an important Rome-based gay and lesbian group (Italian only).

WHAT TO DO

SPORTS AND ACTIVITIES

Life in this city is enacted on an outdoor stage. When in Rome, and it all becomes too overwhelming, the best thing to do is to imitate the Romans and their art of *far niente*—literally doing nothing—and just soak up the atmosphere. Chill out over a cold glass of Frascati in the midst of a fountain-splashed piazza, feigning oblivion to the layers of history around and below you, which has given the world more than two millennia of artistic achievement.

SOCCER

Generally, the Romans tend to prefer to watch rather than participate in sports. But the great national passion is soccer, and Rome's two teams, Lazio and Roma, are hero-worshipped. Lazio play in blue and white with an eagle as the mascot, while Roma wear red and yellow with a wolf. One team plays at home almost every Sunday from September until June at the Stadio Olimpico. Tickets for big matches tend to sell out quickly, and expect to pay prices up to around €85. Tickets are also available from ticket agencies such as Orbis (*tel 06 4620 4310*).

OTHER SPORTS

There are few tennis courts in the city, but the Italian Open Tennis tournament in May is a very popular, stylish event, held at the Foro Italico. The International Horse Show comes to town in April and May at the Villa Borghese, and other equestrian events, including flat racing, steeplechases and show jumping, take place at the Ippodromo delle Capanelle, (*Via Appia Nuova, tel 06 718 8750*). Should you want to experience Rome on horseback you could try the Centro Ippico di Villa Borghese (*Vicolo del Galoppatoio 23, tel 06 320 1667*) or the Cavalieri dell'Appia Antica (*Via dei Cerceni 15, tel 06 780 1214*).

OTHER ACTIVITIES

And, kitsch as it might sound, a stroll around the edge of the Forum, a cool drink overlooking the Colosseo, or a visit to the Fontana di Trevi, especially at moonlight, are magical. Don't forget to toss your coins over your shoulder to ensure your return to the Eternal City.

Spectator Sports

EQUESTRIAN
CONCORSO IPPICO INTERNAZIONALE DI PIAZZA DI SIENA
Piazza di Siena, Villa Borghese, 00186
Tel 06 327 9939
www.piazzadisiena.com
It is not well known that Rome is host to an important annual equestrian event, with show-jumping at the heart of the action.
🕑 End Apr–early May 💶 Adult €10–44, child €6–7 🚌 116, 231, 491, 495

MARATHON
ROME CITY MARATHON
Via dei Fori Imperiali, 00186
Tel 06 3018 3022/06 3018 3016
www.maratonadiroma.it
Each spring runners flock to participate in this event, which is slowly reaching the level of those in London and New York. It starts and finishes on the Via dei Fori Imperiali.
🕑 3rd Sun in Mar 🚇 Colosseo 🚌 60, 75, 85, 117, 175, 186, 271, 571, 810, 850

RUGBY
STADIO FLAMINIO
Stadio Flaminio, Viale Tiziano, 00196
Tel 06 3685 7832
www.federugby.it

Don't think that Italians only go mad for soccer. The national team competes in the Six Nations tournament (with England, France, Ireland, Scotland and Wales). The country has 24 rugby clubs, and the best games are in the capital when RDS Roma hits the field. Credit cards are not accepted.
🕑 Season Oct–May 💶 €10–30
🚌 204, 231, 910; tram 2

SOCCER

STADIO OLIMPICO
Viale dello Stadio Olimpico, 00194
Tel 06 323 7333
www.stadioolimpico.it
No spectator sport is more important to Romans than soccer. The city has two rival teams that share the stadium and play at home on alternate days. When Roma fans are in, they sit on the south side of the stadium; when Lazio is playing, their fans sit on the north side.
🕑 Sun, end Aug–early Jun 💶 €15–85
🚌 32, 168, 186, 280 to Piazza Mancini then cross river

TENNIS
CAMPIONATO INTERNAZIONALE DI TENNIS
Foro Italico, Viale dei Gladiatori, 00194
Tel 06 323 3807
Every May, Rome hosts the Italian Open tennis tournament, Europe's most important tennis event outside the Grand Slam. There are events for both men and women.
🕑 1–15 May 💶 €8–55 🚌 32, 168, 186, 280 to Piazza Mancini then cross river

WHAT TO DO

Activities

WHAT TO DO

EQUESTRIAN

CENTRO IPPICO DI VILLA BORGHESE
Via del Galoppatoio 25, 00186
Tel 06 322 6797
Rome's equestrian club has classes for horse enthusiasts year round, which last one hour and are tailor-made to suit all levels. The school is happy to let you ride one of its horses from its own stables.
🕐 Tue–Sat 8.30–6, Sun 8.30–2; closed Aug 💰 Expensive, cost depends on courses required 🚌 95, 116, 119, 204, 490, 491, 495

GOLF

CIRCOLO DEL GOLF DI ROMA
Via Appia Nuova 716/a, 00178
Tel 06 780 3407
www.golfroma.it
This lovely 18-hole course is surrounded by umbrella pines and Roman ruins. Non-members may play in competitions on Sundays. There is a great restaurant.
🕐 Tue–Sun 8–sunset 💰 Green fees start at €20 🚇 Colli Albani, then a taxi

GREEN SPACES

GIANICOLO HILL
Piazzale Aurelio, 00152
Join families and lovers strolling the ridge overlooking Rome. There is a bar, carousel, puppet show and summer evening theatre, plus miniature pony rides on weekends. The nearby Villa Doria Pamphilj is the city's largest park.
💰 Free 🚌 44 to corner Via Giacinto Carini and Via Fratelli Bonnet,or 31, 791, 982

VILLA BORGHESE
Villa Borghese, 00186

Rome's green oasis is all about hiring rollerblades and bicycles, or rowing boats on the tree-lined lake. A very popular park with locals at weekends.
🕐 Daily 24 hours 💰 Free 🚌 95, 116, 119, 204, 490, 491, 495

VILLA DORIA PAMPHILJ
Villa Doria Pamphili, 00152
One of the most beautiful parks in Rome, with ancient villas, ponds and green woods. City officials have installed workout stations for stretching and muscle toning.
🕐 Daily dawn–dusk 💰 Free 🚃 Tram 8

ROMAN EXPERIENCES

CLIMBING THE MONUMENTO VITTORIO EMANUELE
Piazza Venezia, 00187
Tel 06 699 1718
Mussolini built this much-ridiculed monument—often called the Wedding Cake—in homage to Italian unification. The white marble edifice dominates the area, but the view from the top is superb.
🕐 Daily 9–6; last entrance 5.30 in summer; 4.30 in winter 💰 Free 🚇 Colosseo 🚌 44, 46, 84, 715, 716, 780, 781, 810, 916

PAPAL AUDIENCE
Piazza di San Pietro, 00120 Città del Vaticano
Tel 06 6988 3017. General information: 06 6988 2019
www.vatican.va
Mass audiences take place in Basilica di San Pietro or Aula Paolo VI. Request tickets by post (Prefettura della Casa Ponteficia, 00120 Città del Vaticano) or in person (north side of piazza, Mon–Tue 9–1). Confirm reservations and dress modestly.
🕐 Usually Wed at 11 💰 Free 🚇 Ottaviano 🚌 34, 46, 64, 98, 881, 916, 982

SQUASH

AS AGONISTICA SQUASH ROMAN SC
Viale del Galoppatoio 33, 00197
Tel 06 321 8096
Squash is a popular sport in Rome, and tournaments are staged throughout the year involve participants from all over Italy. You can join the club to play or watch competitions. Credit cards are not accepted.
🕐 Mon–Sat 9am–10pm, Sun 9–3 💰 €7.75 for 45 minutes 🚌 95, 116, 119, 204, 490, 491, 495

SPORTS VENUES

ROMAN SPORTS CENTER
Villa Borghese, Viale del Galoppatoio 33, 00186
Tel 06 320 1667/06 3218096
Rome's smartest sports venue is just a stone's throw from the Spanish Steps. This facility has three aerobics rooms, saunas, two weights rooms, and an Olympic-sized swimming pool. Day membership available.

Mon–Sat 9am–10pm, Sun 11–5
Daily pass €25 95, 116, 119, 204, 490, 491, 495

SWIMMING

CAVALIERI HILTON
Via Cadlolo 101, 00136
Tel 06 3509 2950
www.cavalierihilton.it
The pool at this hotel in the northwest of the city is part of an impressive suite of spa facilities. It is among Rome's cleanest and least crowded. There is a good restaurant and bar on site.
Daily 9–7, May–Sep Mon–Fri €40, Sat–Sun €65 (for all spa facilities) 46, 912

PISCINA DELLE ROSE
Viale America 20, 00144
Tel 06 592 6717
Rome's largest open-air pool, at the heart of the ultra-sleek Palasport sports facility built by Mussolini. A great place to bring the kids on weekends. Credit cards are not accepted.
Daily 9–10 €10 EUR Palasport

TENNIS

CIRCOLO DELLA STAMPA
Piazza Mancini 19, 00196
Tel 06 323 2452
Owned by the professional body for Italian journalists, this tennis club has both clay and synthetic-grass courts at reasonable prices. Friendly atmosphere, with tennis lessons available for all levels.
Mon–Fri 9am–11pm, Sat–Sun 9–8 €12 per hour 48, 53, 231, 280, 910; tram 2

TENPIN BOWLING

THE BRUNSWICK
Lungotevere dell'Acqua Acetosa 10, 00196
Tel 06 808 6147
The Brunswick has bowling lanes, games rooms and mini-golf. On special occasions the bowling balls are fluorescent and disco lights shine overhead. Open for tournaments and amusement. Credit cards are not accepted.

Sun–Thu 10am–2am, Fri–Sat 10am–4am €2 before 2pm, €6 after 2pm 231

Health & Beauty

AQUAVIRGO
Via Fioravanti 90, 00189
Tel 06 2244 0336
This giant health/spa complex lies half an hour from the heart of the city. Treatments include Shiatsu massage, herbal baths, ayurvedic rubs, manicures, Finnish sauna and hydrotherapy. Bach flower remedies, aloe treatments and temple massages are also available.
Wed–Fri 9.30–6.30, Sat–Sun 9–6.30 massage: €45 Take exit 16 towards Palestrina from the Grande Raccordo Anulare autoroute. Travel for 6km (4 miles); turn left down Via Della Riserva Nuova, left again down Via Don Primo Mazzaolari, then onto Via Fioravanti

AVEDA SALON
Rampa Mignanelli 9, 00187
Tel 06 6992 4886
www.aveda.com
Salon of Aveda, Europe's leading potions and lotions brand. You can try plant steam inhalation, skin hydration or mild aromatherapy, plus facial treatments, manicures, pedicures and waxing. Aveda beauty products are is on sale.
Tue–Sat 10–8, Mon 3.30–8 Manicure: €25, plant steam inhalation: €31 Spagna

BOSCOLO GRAND HOTEL
Via Vittorio Veneto 70, 00187
Tel 06 478719
A wealth of pampering services can be had at the Boscolo's

Dibi Beauty Centre. Beautiful swimming pool, plus solarium, giant Turkish bath and Jacuzzi. Massages last for over an hour. There's also a manicure salon and fitness centre.
Tue–Fri 11–7, Aug; Mon–Sat 10–8, rest of year massage: €50, facial: €35 Barberini

GRAND HOTEL TIBERIO
51 Via Lattanzio, 00136
Tel 06 399629
www.ghtiberio.com
Relax in the intense heat of this four-star hotel's sauna, or tone up your muscles in its gymnasium facilities by purchasing a reasonably priced day pass. Within walking distance of Vatican City.
Daily 7.30am–9.30pm all day use of sauna and fitness centre: €15 Proba Petronia-Appiano

HOTEL DE RUSSIE
9 Via del Babuino, 00187
Tel 06 328881
Top hotel with a huge range of holistic techniques including Shiatsu, reflexology and aromatherapy, as well as massage, saunas and facials. Masks, body wraps and personal training also available.
Daily 9–8 Aromatherapy session: €75 Spagna

TERME DEI PAPI
12 Strada Bagni, 01100 Viterbo
Tel 0761 3501
www.termedeipapi.it
In the province of Lazio, 75km (45 miles) north of Rome, this spa is in beautiful grounds. There are mud baths, herbal inhalations, facials, organic treatments and a sumptuous wooden-decked swimming pool. There's pleasant walking in the nearby hills. Advance booking is advised.
Mon–Sat 7–7, Sun 9–7pm mud bath: €25–90 Take the Orte exit from A1 Rome–Florence autoroute. Head for Viterbo on S204; the Terme dei Papi is 5km (3 miles) past the town

WHAT TO DO

CHILDREN'S ROME

There are few attractions specifically aimed at children in Rome, but there are also few other destinations where they can act out fantasies of chariot races, relive the stage set of *Gladiator*, clamber over ruins, cool off in fountains and be treated like miniature adults. And, if all else fails, there's always a delicious ice-cream—the Italians are still the masters of glorious *gelato*.

Children's menus don't really exist, but pizza and pasta are aplenty and, in all but the smartest establishments, restaurateurs will generally give children a warm welcome; menus are easily adaptable. Rome is also the perfect place for picnics. Stock up on goodies at the Campo dei Fiori and take your picnic to the Villa Borghese gardens; on the northern side is the recently renovated Bioparco zoo, always very popular. Or picnic on the Palatine Hill, the legendary birthplace of Rome. Here the cooler air is refreshing and the views over the Forum and Colosseo are superb.

The Colosseo is free for under 18s, and is probably the top attraction. See the pens where animals and gladiators were winched up to do the ultimate battle. Your family can pose with a Roman centurion for memorable photographs. Visit the Circo Massimo, the oldest and largest ancient arena where charitot races were held, as seen in *Ben Hur*.

Water, water is everywhere in Rome. The city is positively awash with fountains—there are over 4,000 in total—always popular with kids. Encourage them to toss a coin into the Trevi Fountain, but don't let them take a dip as this will incur a hefty fine for you.

EXPLORA—IL MUSEO DEI BAMBINI
Via Flaminia 82, 00192
Tel 06 361 3776
www.mdbr.it
Rome's first and only children's museum, and particularly good for children aged eight and under. Four sections are dedicated to humankind, the environment, communications and society. On-site restaurant. Advance reservations required for Sat–Sun; tours last 1 hour 45 mins.
🕐 Tue–Sun 9.30, 11.30, 3 and 5; 3, 5 (and at 9 in Aug); closed 2 weeks in mid-Aug 🎟 Adult €6, under-3s free 🚇 Flaminio 🚌 95, 117, 119, 204, 231, 490, 495, 618, 916; tram 2, 3, 19

LUNEUR PARK
Via delle Tre Fontane, 00144
Tel 06 5925933
www.luneur.it
Built in 1953, the oldest fun park in Italy has kept up with the times. Activities and rides range from the traditional to the adrenalin-pumping, with a puppet theatre, several haunted houses, bumper cars, a lake with motor boats and rides with names like Flipper, Thriller and Space Kickers. Suitable for children and teenagers.
🕐 Mon, Wed–Thu 3–7, Fri 3–midnight, Sat 3–2, Sun 10–1, 3–10 🎟 Rides €1–6, half-day visit €15–25 🚇 Magliana, Palasport or EUR Fermi 🚌 706, 707, 714, 717, 765, 771

MUSEO CRIMINOLOGICO DI ROMA
Via del Gonfalone 29, 00186
Tel 06 6830 0234
www.polizia-penitenziaria.it/struttura/museo1931.html
A criminological museum covering the history of the Italian prison system, solving of crimes and punishment of criminals. Instruments of torture, and engravings depicting various forms of punishment are guaranteed to interest most kids. Credit cards are not accepted.
🕐 Tue–Sat 9–1 (also Tue, Thu 2.30–6.30) 🎟 Adult €2, under-18s free 🚌 40, 46, 62, 64, 517 to Chiesa Nuova on Corso Vittorio Emanuele II

MUSEO DEL PRESEPE TIPOLOGICO INTERNAZIONALE
Via Tor de' Conti 31/a, 00184
Tel 06 6796146
This tiny museum is entirely dedicated to *presepe*, the representation of the Nativity. There are over 3,000 statuettes from all over the world, made of all sorts of materials, including terracotta, hay, glass and marzipan, and assembled in all sorts of ways.
🕐 Mon–Sat 4–8, Sun 10–1, 4–8, 24 Dec–Jan 6; Wed, Sat 5–8, 7 Jan–end Jun, Sep–23 Dec; closed Jul–Aug; 🎟 Free 🚇 Colosseo 🚌 75, 87, 175

TIME ELEVATOR
Via S.S. Apostoli 20, 00186
Tel 06 6990053
www.time-elevator.it
A multimedia experience illustrating the history of Rome from its founding in 753BC to the present day. Armed with headphones, a screen, a moving platform and other surprise special effects, this is a fun (if occasionally factually weak) introduction to the city. Watch it burn and see Caesar killed.
🕐 Daily 10am–10.30pm 🎟 Adult €11, child (under 12) €9.20 🚌 40, 62, 63, 64, 916 to Via del Corso or Piazza Venezia

VILLA BORGHESE
Porta Pinciana
Tel 06 3600 4399
Rambling park extending for 6.5km (4 miles) through the heart of the city. Rent bikes or a boat, ride a trolley train, hop on an old-fashioned carousel or visit the Bioparco zoo. Credit cards are not accepted.
🕐 Bioparco: daily 9.30–7, Apr–end Sep; 9.30–5, Oct–end Mar 🎟 Park: free. Bioparco: adult €4.13, under-18s free 🚇 Flaminio or Spagna 🚌 95, 116, 119, 204, 495

FESTIVALS AND EVENTS

Today's celebrations are less extravagant than they were in the days of ancient Rome, but there are still many festivals and exhibitions held in the city throughout the year

SAN SILVESTRO AND CAPODANNO
31 December–1 January
Crowds throng to Piazza del Popolo to see out the old year and welcome in the new with a free disco, concert and spectacular firework display. New Year's Day is a public holiday.
✉ Piazza del Popolo
🚇 Flaminio 🚌 88, 95, 117, 119, 490, 491, 495; tram 2

EPIFANIA–LA BEFANA
6 January (public holiday)
The Feast of the Epiphany is celebrated in a Mass said by the Pope at St. Peter's. The Romans know Epiphany better as La Befana–the old witch–who, according to legend, brought presents for good children and lumps of coal for bad ones. Piazza Navona is full of market stalls from mid-December to Epiphany–the highlight of which is when La Befana arrives in the piazza late on 5 January.
✉ Basilica di San Pietro, Piazza San Pietro
🚇 Ottaviano 🚌 46, 64, 98, 916, 982
✉ Piazza Navona
🚌 23, 30, 62, 64, 70, 81, 87, 116, 280, 492, 628, 810, 916

SANT'EUSEBIO ANIMAL BLESSING
17 January
The congregation of the little church of Sant'Eusebio all'Esquilino consists of animals with their doting owners, keen to get them blessed.
✉ Via Napoleone 111
🚇 Vittorio 🚌 70, 71, 105; tram 5, 14

CARNEVALE
February–March (the week before Lent)
There are street celebrations and masked revellers throughout the city during the traditional pagan festival of Carnevale—meaning 'farewell to meat'.

FESTA DI SANTA FRANCESCA ROMANA
9 March
Santa Francesca Romana is the patron saint of motorists. Her church is the venue for Roman drivers to bring their cars to be blessed.
✉ Eastern (Colosseo) end of the Foro Romano
🚇 Colosseo 🚌 60, 75, 85, 87, 117, 175, 810, 850

ROME CITY MARATHON
Third Sunday in March
The race begins and ends in the Via dei Fori Imperiali.
☎ 06 4065064 (information line)
www.maratonadiroma.it

SETTIMANA SANTA E PASQUA
Mid-March to mid-April (date varies)
The open-air mass in St. Peter's Square on the Saturday before Palm Sunday marks the beginning of Holy Week. Events draw to their climax on Good Friday when the Pope's Stations of the Cross (Via Crucis) and Mass take place at the Colosseo late in the evening. On Easter Sunday there is a papal blessing at St. Peter's. Easter Monday is a public holiday.
✉ Piazza del Colosseo
🚇 Colosseo 🚌 60, 75, 85, 87, 117, 175, 810, 850
✉ Vatican
🚌 34, 46, 64, 98, 881, 916, 982

NATALE DI ROMA
21 April
Celebrations of Rome's official birthday focus on the torchlit Campidoglio, with spectacular firework displays.
✉ Piazza del Campidoglio
🚌 44, 46, 84, 715, 780, 781, 810, 916

FIERA D'ARTE DI VIA MARGUTTA
Late April–May (also in October/November)
The street is full of art galleries that burst into life in these two open-air exhibitions.
✉ Via Margutta
☎ 06 8123340
🚇 Spagna 🚌 88, 95, 117, 119, 628, 926; tram 2

CONCORSO IPPICO INTERNAZIONALE
End April/beginning May
The International Horse Show is a very smart show-jumping event, attracting the stylish and the glitterati.
✉ Piazza di Siena, Villa Borghese
☎ 06 3279939
🚇 Spagna or Flaminio 🚌 52, 53, 88, 95, 116, 117, 119, 490, 491, 495, 910
www.fise.it

PRIMO MAGGIO
1 May (public holiday)
Open-air rock concert traditionally held in front of the San Giovanni in Laterano basilica to celebrate May Day.
✉ Piazza di San Giovanni
🚇 San Giovanni 🚌 16, 85, 87, 117, 218, 650, 850

MOSTRA DELL'ANTIQUARIATO
May (also late October)
During the two-week-long fair, held in Via de'Coronari—the heart of the antiques trade—the street is lit with candles and shops stay open late.
✉ Via de'Coronari
☎ 06 3612322/06 6880 6052
🚌 30, 40, 46, 70, 81, 87, 116
www.assviadeicoronari.it

CAMPIONATO INTERNAZIONALE DI TENNIS
May
The Italian Open tennis championships are among the first big events in the European season.
✉ Foro Italico, Viale dei Gladiatori
🚌 32, 224, 280; tram 2
www.wtatour.com;
www.masters-series.com/roma

WHAT TO DO

ESTATE ROMANA
June–September
Outdoor film screenings, music, ballet and theatre are among hundreds of events throughout the Roman Summer Festival in venues from parks to palazzi.
www.estateromana.it

FESTA DI SAN GIOVANNI
23 June
The Festival of St. John involves much consumption of snails (lumache in umido) and roast suckling pig (porchetta), plus a fair and a fireworks display in the Piazza di San Giovanni in Laterano. A candlelit procession at night is usually led by the Pope to the church.
✉ San Giovanni in Laterano, Piazza di San Giovanni in Laterano
🚇 San Giovanni 🚌 16, 85, 87, 117, 218, 650, 850

FESTA DI SANTI PIETRO E PAOLO
29 June
Rome's patron saints, Peter and Paul, are honoured in this annual festival. At St. Peter's there is a Mass, while at St. Paul's there is an all-night street fair outside the church.
✉ Basilica di San Pietro, Piazza San Pietro
🚇 Ottaviano 🚌 34, 46, 64, 98, 881, 916, 982
✉ San Paolo fuori le Mura, Piazzale San Paolo 1c
🚇 Basilica di San Paolo 🚌 4, 23, 128, 761, 769, 770

CINEPORTO
July–August
Two large screens showing dubbed films have made this into a hugely popular summer festival in the park. In between screenings there are frequent live concerts.
✉ Parco della Farnesina, north suburbs by the Stadio Olimpico
☎ 06 3600 5556
www.cineporto.com

TEATRO ROMANO DI OSTIA ANTICA
Mid-July–mid August

Concerts, and Greek and Roman classics are performed in this beautifully preserved open-air theatre, southwest of the city. Take a cushion.
✉ Scavi di Ostia Antica, Viale dei Romagnoli 117
☎ 06 6880 4601

FESTIVAL EUROMEDITERRANEO
July–August
The stunning Villa Adriana is the setting for a wide range of events, from concerts and opera to drama and flamenco dancing—all with a Mediterranean feel.
✉ Villa Adriana, Via di Villa Adriana
☎ 06 6880 9107/8/9/10
🚌 Cotral bus from Metro Ponte Mammolo.

FESTA DEI NOIANTRI
Last two weeks in July
This Peoples' Festival is an open-air party with music, markets, feasting, processions and every kind of entertainment in Trastevere, one of Rome's oldest quarters.
✉ Piazza Santa Maria in Trastevere, Piazza Mastai
🚌 23, 44, 280, 630, 780; tram 8

FESTA DELLE CATENE
1 August
The chains with which St. Peter was said to have been bound are displayed at a special Mass in the church to celebrate the Festival of the Chains.
✉ San Pietro in Vincoli, Piazza San Pietro in Vincoli
☎ 06 4882865
🚇 Cavour 🚌 60, 75, 84, 85, 87, 117, 175, 810, 850

FESTA DELLA MADONNA DELLA NEVE
5 August
To commemorate the legend of snow falling on the Esquiline Hill on this day in AD352, petals are showered onto the congregation celebrating Mass in the basilica.
✉ Basilica di Santa Maria Maggiore, Piazza Santa Maria Maggiore
☎ 06 483195

🚌 16, 70, 71, 75, 105, 204, 360, 590, 649, 714; tram 5, 14

FERRAGOSTO
15 August (public holiday)
This is the main midsummer holiday, when just about everything closes down.

ROMAEUROPA FESTIVAL
September–November
This is Rome's major arts festival, with something for every taste offered by performers of international calibre. The venues are no less starry, including some of Rome's most glorious monuments.
✉ Festival Office: Via XX Settembre 3
☎ 06 4890 4024 (information line); 06 4742308 (booking line)
www.romaeuropa.net

OGNISSANT
1 November (public holiday)
All Saints' Day, also known as Day of the Dead, is marked by Romans visiting family graves and a Mass celebrated by the Pope at the Verano cemetery.
✉ Cimitero del Verano, Piazzale del Verano
🚌 71, 163, 492; tram 3, 19

FESTA DELL'IMMACOLATA CONCEZIONE
8 December (public holiday)
Religious service in the piazza to celebrate the Festival of the Immaculate Conception, where the focal point is the statue of the Madonna, decorated with flowers.
✉ Piazza di Spagna
🚇 Spagna 🚌 116, 117, 119, 590

NATALE & SANTO STEFANO
25–26 December (public holidays)
During the Christmas period, ornate cribs (presepi) decorate many of Rome's churches—the largest is in St. Peter's Square along with a towering Christmas tree. If you want to celebrate Midnight Mass in St. Peter's, put your request in months in advance.
✉ Prefettura Office: Piazza San Pietro
☎ 06 6988 3273.
🚌 34, 46, 64, 98, 881, 916, 982

Rome is compact enough to explore on foot, and this section describes six walks that take in some of the most interesting parts of the city. The areas covered by the walks are marked on the map on the inside front cover of the book. This chapter also gives suggestions for excursions outside the city (see map on page 210)

Out and About

GHETTO TO TRASTEVERE

This walk passes through two of Rome's less explored areas, the Ghetto and the Isola Tiberina, before crossing the Tiber to the popular but unspoilt Trastevere quarter.

THE WALK

Length: 4.25km (2.5 miles)
Allow: 3 hours minimum
Start: Piazza del Campidoglio
End: Campo dei Fiori

HOW TO GET THERE

For Piazza del Campidoglio, the nearest metro station is Colosseo (line B). Alternatively, several buses will take you nearby: nos. 44, 46, 84, 715, 716, 780, 781, 810 and 916.

From Piazza del Campidoglio, with the Palazzo Senatorio straight in front of you, take the lane on the right-hand side, which leads down to the Foro Romano. At the bottom, turn right onto Via della Consolazione, cross the piazza and turn down Via San Giovanni Decollato, passing San Giorgio in Velabro.

❶ San Giorgio in Velabro is named after the area where Rome's founding twins, Romulus and Remus, were discovered. The interior of the church is beautifully simple, and reuses marble and granite columns from ancient buildings. The façade of the church was severely damaged in a bomb blast in 1993, but sympathetic renovation has restored it to its former glory.

Retrace your steps past two ancient arches: Arco degli Argentari (Arch of the Moneychangers) adjoins the church, while the second, Arco di Giano, is on the opposite side of the road. Continue to the large Piazza della Bocca della Verità. On your right, look for two surprisingly well-preserved second-century BC temples, the circular Tempio di Vesta and the rectangular Tempio di Fortuna Virilis. Across the piazza is the 12th-century church of Santa Maria in Cosmedin ❷ (see page

136)—look for the large stone face called Bocca della Verità (Mouth of Truth) in the porch. According to legend, the mouth clamps shut on the hands of liars. With your back to the church, walk straight across the square and then right to join Lungotevere dei Pierleoni. Pass through Piazza Monte Savello, where the road becomes Lungotevere dei Cenci. Just ahead of you is the synagogue. Turn right onto Via del Portico d'Ottavia, leading to the Portico d'Ottavia.

❸ The Portico d'Ottavia is a fragment of a Roman building begun in 146BC and dedicated to Octavia, Augustus' sister. It now forms part of the 12th-century Sant'Angelo in Pescheria (Angel of the Fishmarket), a reminder of the area's long fishing history in the nearby river.

Turn left at the top of the street, onto Via dei Funari, which leads to Piazza Mattei and the heart of the old Ghetto ❹ (see page 90). Although the walls have long been demolished, many Jewish families and businesses are still based in the area. The piazza is best known for the Fontana delle Tartarughe (Fountain of the Tortoises), one of the most charming in the city. Turn left onto Via della Reginella, which leads back to Via Portico d'Ottavia. Turn right then left through Piazza delle Cinque Scole to rejoin Lungotevere dei Cenci. Turn left, then right onto the Ponte Fabricio, Rome's oldest bridge, which crosses the Tiber to the Isola Tiberina ❺ (see page 91).

Put your hand in the Bocca della Verità

The shape of Tiber Island resembles a boat, and the ancient Romans erected an obelisk as a mast, adding travertine panels to make a prow and stern, remains of which can still be seen. The island has a tradition of healing, begun in 291BC when a temple was dedicated to Esculapio, the god of healing. Today, in keeping with this tradition, much of the island is given over to a hospital.

Leave the island, on the opposite side, by Ponte Cestio. This leads you directly into Trastevere (see pages 144–145), another district well worth exploring. Cross the busy Lungotevere dell'Anguillara and carry straight on to Piazza in Piscinula. Turn right onto Via della Lungaretta. Continue straight on until you come to Piazza di Santa Maria in Trastevere and the church of the same name (see page 141). Facing the church, take the right-hand road out of the piazza: Via della Scala. When you reach the junction with Via Garibaldi, turn right onto Via di San Dorotea, which leads to Piazza Trilussa, a small piazza right beside the Tiber. From here, cross the river by the traffic-free Ponte Sisto. Turn left, and follow the right fork into Via Giulia, through a pretty archway draped with vines.

❻ Via Giulia, one of Rome's most elegant streets, was laid out for Pope Julius II in 1508 and formed the main approach to St. Peter's. There are now many interesting buildings lining this street, including the church of Santa Maria dell'Orazione e Morte ❼, ghoulishly decorated with skulls.

As Via Giulia opens out onto a piazza, turn right onto Vicolo della Moretta, which soon leads on to Via del Pellegrino. Take the first right onto Via dei Cappellari, with its traditional artisans' workshops. At the end of the street is Campo dei Fiori ❽ (see pages 122–123).

OUT AND ABOUT

Palazzo Senatorio, in Michelangelo's Piazza del Campidoglio (left)

The Mattei family commissioned the Tortoise Fountain for 'their' square (above)

The boat shape of Isola Tiberina has given rise to many legends about its origin (left)

OUT AND ABOUT

WHEN TO GO

Any time, but remember that many churches will be closed during the afternoon.

WHERE TO EAT

There are many restaurants and cafés in Trastevere and Campo dei Fiori, or for traditional Jewish fare, try Giggetto al Portico d'Ottavia (see page 243).

WHERE TO GO

San Giorgio in Velabro
Via del Velabro 19
☎ 06 6920 4534
🕒 Daily 8.30–12.30, 4–6.30

Sant'Angelo in Pescheria
Via Tribuna di Campitelli 6
☎ 06 6880 1819
🕒 Wed 5.30, Sat 5

The church of Santa Maria in Trastevere dominates the piazza that shares its name (above)

Bramante's Via Giulia cuts a straight line through Rome's winding medieval streets (left)

AROUND PIAZZA NAVONA

Leading from Piazza Navona to the Piazza di Spagna and back, via the Fontana di Trevi, this walk takes in some of Rome's best-known sights.

THE WALK

Length: 2.5km (1.5 miles)
Allow: 3 hours
Start: Piazza Navona
End: Piazza Navona

HOW TO GET THERE

Take a bus to Piazza Navona: nos. 23, 46, 64, 87, 119 and others all pass nearby.

Leave Piazza Navona from the northern end (near the Fontana del Nettuno—pictured below). From Via Agonale, turn right onto Piazza Sant' Agostino. On your left is the church of Sant'Agostino (see page 128).

1 Sant'Agostino is known for its works of art, including Caravaggio's *Madonna di Loreto* (or Madonna of the Pilgrims, 1605) in the first chapel off the left aisle. The painting caused a scandal when it was first unveiled because of its realism—the Virgin was depicted with dirty feet and some of the pilgrims shown as old and sick.

Having crossed the piazza, bear left on Via della Scrofa, which becomes Via di Ripetta, until you reach Via Tomacelli. Turn right onto Via Tomacelli and then bear left onto Piazza Augusto Imperatore. Cross the piazza, then turn right onto Via dei Pontefici. At the end of the street is the Accademia Nazionale di Santa Cecilia (see page 180).

2 L'Accademia Nazionale di Santa Cecilia is the national school of music, founded in 1585. It has an orchestra of 90 members and has performed more than 14,000 concerts.

Turn right onto Via del Corso, a busy street, lined with shops. A short way along the street, turn left onto Via della Croce, renowned for its food shops and cafés; at number 76 is Antica Enoteca, an old wine bar. Follow the road until it opens out into lively Piazza di Spagna **3** (see pages 126–127). Turn right to reach the bottom of the Spanish Steps, usually busy with both locals and visitors chatting or simply taking in the atmosphere and the view. With your back to the steps, cross the piazza onto Via dei Condotti. Spend some time window-shopping along this, one of Rome's most exclusive shopping streets before bearing left onto Via Belsiana just before you reach Via del Corso again. Continue as far as Piazza San Silvestro, crossing Via Frattina and Via della Vite, and go diagonally across the square to turn down a little street called Via del Pozzetto. Take the first right, Via Poli, which crosses Via del Tritone and takes you to Piazza di Trevi and Nicola Salvi's theatrical Fontana di Trevi (see pages 80–81).

4 Opposite the Trevi Fountain is the church of Santi Vincenzo e Anastasio, notable for its grisly relics: Between 1590 and 1903, the hearts and lungs of 22 popes, preserved in urns, were interred in the crypt.

Facing the Trevi Fountain, take the traffic-free street to the left, Via delle Muratte, which leads back to Via del Corso. Turn right onto the Corso, towards Piazza Colonna, named after Marcus Aurelius' column, which stands in the middle of the square. Erected between AD180 and 193, the monument illustrates victorious episodes in the Emperor's war campaigns. With your back to the Corso, take Via dei Bergamaschi, the narrow street in the far

left-hand corner of the piazza, which leads to Piazza di Pietra.

5 On the right-hand side of the Piazza di Pietra, you can see the last remaining columns of Hadrian's temple, now incorporated into the 17th-century Borsa, the stock exchange. These 15m (50ft) columns formed part of a temple built and dedicated to the Emperor Hadrian in AD145 by his successor Antoninus Pius.

Carry straight on along Via de' Burro to reach the rococo Piazza di Sant'Ignazio, with its beautiful church (see page 132). Step inside to admire the magnificent *trompe l'oeil* dome by the Jesuit architect Andrea Pozzo. Continue down Via di Sant'Ignazio—the Jesuit Collegio Romano is on your left—until you emerge onto Piazza del Collegio Romano. Turn right onto Via Piè di Marmo, which leads to Piazza della Minerva and the church of Santa Maria sopra Minerva **6** (see page 140), with Bernini's delightful statue of an elephant outside. On the right-hand side of the church's façade are several plaques showing the water levels when the Tiber flooded between 1598 and 1870.

With the church on your right, continue down Via della Minerva to Piazza della Rotonda and the Pantheon **7** (see pages 120–121), one of Rome's best-preserved ancient monuments. Facing the Pantheon, take Via della Rotonda, the road that runs up the right-hand side of the building, then take the first right, Via della Palombella, which leads onto Piazza Sant'Eustachio. Here you will find Sant'Eustachio il Caffè where, some say, they serve the best coffee in Rome (see page 251). Leave the square on the opposite side, down Via dei Staderari. This takes you along the side of the church of Sant'Ivo alla Sapienza **8** (entrance on Corso del Rinascimento—see page 133). Via dei Sediari, opposite the church's entrance, will take you back to Piazza Navona.

OUT AND ABOUT

Delicatessens and cafés line Via della Croce

Via dei Condotti is the best place to shop for designer fashions

E3

Via di San Giacomo
Via A Canova
Via della Frezza
Via dei Greci
2 **L'Accademia Naz di Santa Cecilia**
Via Vittoria
Mausoleo di Augusto
Via della Croce
Spagna
Piazza di Spagna
Trinità dei Monti
3

Ara Pacis Augusta
Via V Colonna
PONTE CAVOUR
Piazza Augusto Imperatore
Via Tomacelli
Via dell' Arancio
Via Belsiana
Via di Campo Marzio
Via Bocca di Leone
Via di Condotti
Via Mario de'Fiori
Museo Keats-Shelley
Via Crespina
Via del d'Due Macelli
V Francesco Crispi
Sistina
Via Zucchelli

LUNGO PRATI
Tevere
LUNGOTEVERE MARZIO
Via di Ripetta
Via della Scrofa
Via della Lupa
Via Frattina
Via della Vite
Via della Mercede
Traforo Umberto I

D4
PONTE UMBERTO
Via G Zanardelli
Via dell'Orso
Via di M Brianzo
Via della Maddalena
Piazza San Silvestro
Via della
Tritone
Galleria dell' Accademia di San Luca
F4

Palazzo Altemps
1 Sant'Agostino
Via delle Coppelle
La Maddalena
Piazza Colonna
Colonna di Marco Aurelio
Via del Corso
Via del Poli
Fontana di Trevi 4
Museo N delle Paste Alimentari

Via delle Sant Luigi dei Francesi
Via Giustiniani
7
Piazza di Pietra
5
SS Vincenzo e Anastasio
Palazzo Quirinale
Via d Dataria

Piazza della Rotonda
Borsa
Sant'Ignazio di Loyola
Via dell'Umiltà
Piazza del Quirinal

Pantheon
Piazza S.Eustacio
6
Collegio Romano
Via della Pilotta

Piazza Navona
Sant'Ivo alla Sapienza
8
Santa Maria sopra Minerva
Piazza del Santi Apostoli

D5
Corso del Rinascimento
Via di Torre Argentina
Via del Gesù
Palazzo Doria Pamphilj
Piazza Venezia
Palazzo Venezia

Via del Sudario
VIA DEL PLEBISCITO
Il Gesù
San Marco
VIA DI SAN MARCO

0   200 m
0   200 yds

E5

OUT AND ABOUT

WHEN TO GO
Any time is fine, but remember that many churches are closed in the afternoon.

WHERE TO EAT
Antica Enoteca
Via della Croce 76b
☎ 06 679 0896
⏰ Daily 11.30–11; restaurant daily 12.30–midnight
Order wine by the bottle or by the glass in this traditional winebar. Restaurant at the rear.

WHERE TO GO
Santi Vincenzo e Anastasio
Vicolo dei Modelli 73
☎ 06 678 3098
⏰ Daily 7.30–12, 4–7

Bernini chose an elephant, the ancient symbol of piety and intelligence, to support the obelisk in Piazza della Minerva

IN THE FOOTSTEPS OF THE ANCIENT ROMANS

From Michelangelo's Piazza del Campidoglio, you plunge down into the pedestrian lanes of the Foro Romano to lose yourself in the ancient ruins of imperial Rome.

THE WALK

Length: 2km (1.2 miles)
Allow: 2 hours
Start: Piazza del Campidoglio
End: Piazza del Campidoglio

HOW TO GET THERE

For Piazza del Campidoglio, the nearest metro station is Colosseo. Alternatively, several buses will take you nearby: nos. 44, 46, 84, 715, 716, 780, 781, 810 and 916.

From Piazza del Campidoglio take the lane to the left of Palazzo Senatorio, the middle palace. Look up at the corner of the building to see a statue of the legendary she-wolf with Romulus and Remus, the twins credited with the foundation of Rome. At the back of the building, the whole of the Foro Romano ❶ (see pages 84–89) opens up in front of you. Take in the view from this elevated position before descending the steps to the Forum.

Before passing through the Arco di Settimio Severo, look to your right. The columns here belong to the Tempio di Saturno.

❷ The Tempio di Saturno is one of the oldest buildings in the Forum, dating from 479BC, although what remains today is from reconstructions in 42BC and AD284, As the god of agriculture, Saturn was extremely important. The Saturnalia, a festival in his honour that took place in December, lasted a whole week, during which time slaves were given temporary liberty and a huge public banquet took place in the Forum.

Pass through the Arch of Septimius Severus, with the red-brick Curia ❸ on your left. Continue along the Via Sacra, the main route through the Forum, passing the Basilica Aemilia on your left, until you come to the area covered by a green roof. This is the Tempio di Cesare ❹.

Despite laws banning burials in the Forum, Mark Antony appealed to the Romans to allow Caesar's body to be cremated here. Augustus built a temple in Caesar's honour in 29BC, and a column marks the place where he was cremated.

With the temple on your left, look straight ahead. What you see is the temple of the twin brothers of Helen of Troy, Castor and Pollux, the Dioscuri, whose statues stand in the Piazza del Campidoglio. To the left of the temple is the Basilica Giulia. Although very little remains, it is clear that this was a large and important building. It was built as a courthouse and a meeting place for the city's civic tribunals. Rejoin the Via Sacra. The next building on your left, surprisingly intact, is the Tempio di Antonino e Faustina ❺.

Built by Emperor Antoninus Pius in AD141, the temple was dedicated to his wife Faustina, in honour of her virtue. However, the contemporary gossip was that the Emperor was the only one who did not know about his wife's numerous affairs. The building was converted to a church in the 11th century, which ensured its survival.

Next to the temple is the church of Santi Cosma and Damiano ❻ (see page 129), whose entrance is on Via dei Fori Imperiali. The small, round building on the Forum side of the church is the fourth-century AD Tempio de Divo Romolo, dedicated to the son of Emperor Maxentius rather than the mythical founder of Rome. With your back to the temple, the large complex ahead of you is the Atrium Vestae, house of the Vestal Virgins ❼. Continue along the Via Sacra; the vast, triple-arched building on the right is the Basilica di Massenzio.

❽The basilica was begun during the reign of Maxentius in AD306 and continued by his successor, Constantine, the building was designed as a hub for business and justice. Maxentius designed the building to be entered from the right-hand, shorter side, with a nave and aisles running its 100m (330ft) length. Constantine moved the entrance to the longer side (facing you), which produced three shorter (65m/215ft), broader aisles, each ending in the barrel-vaulted room that is seen today.

The next building along the Via Sacra is the Tempio di Venere e Roma. There is no public access, but you get a good view of the building as you leave the Forum. Walk through the Arco di Tito, and leave the Forum along the last stretch of the Via Sacra. At the end is the Meta Sudans, the remains of a large fountain built at the same time as the Colosseo. Turn right to walk around the Arco di Costantino (see page 65), then go around the outside of the Colosseo (see pages 74–77—the entrance is on the south side of the amphitheatre).

Walk up Via dei Fori Imperiali towards the Fori Imperiali (see pages 82–83) before turning right onto the traffic-free Via del Foro di Traiano. On the right is the Foro di Augusto, of which very little remains. On the left, on the opposite side of Via dei Fori Imperiali, is the Foro di Cesare, the first to be built outside the old Forum. The greater part of these forums is buried under Via dei Fori Imperiali, built by Mussolini in 1932. At the end of the traffic-free street, turn right, and then left onto Via Alessandrina. This road leads you to Mercati Traianei (see page 91—entrance on Via Quattro Novembre) on the right and, on the left, Foro Traiano. The broken columns do little to suggest that this was once one of the city's finest monuments, but Colonna Traiana (see pages 78–79), at the top of the site, remains largely intact (although the statue of Trajan on top was replaced in the 16th century with one of St. Peter). Follow the road around to the left to arrive at Piazza Venezia, just around the corner from Piazza del Campidoglio.

OUT AND ABOUT

Rome's founding twins, Romulus and Remus, were suckled by a she-wolf

Take in an elevated view of the Foro Romano before you descend the steps

F5

Via XXIV Maggio
VIA NAZIONALE
VIA IV NOVEMBRE
Via Mazzarino
Via del
Via Panisperna
Via Cimarra
Boschett
serpenti

0   200 m
0   200 yds

Cavour

G5

Piazza Venezia
San Marco
VIA DI SAN MARCO
d'Aracoeli
Santa Maria in Aracoeli

Mercati Traianei
Colonna Traiana
Foro di Cesare
Foro Traiano
V Alessandrina
VIA DEI FORI
Foro di Augusto
Via Tor de'
Conti
Via della M dei Monti
Via
Baccina
Via Leonina
Via del S dei Cori
VIA
CAVOUR

E5

Piazza del Campidoglio
Capitolino
Musei Capitolini
Palazzo dei Conservatori
Palazzo Nuovo
Palazzo Senatorio

Arco di Settimio Severo
Tempio di Saturno
Curia
Basilica Julia

① ② ③ ④ ⑤ ⑥ ⑦ ⑧

Tempio di Antonio e Faustina
Santi Cosma e Damiano
Basilica di Massenzio
Via dei Colosseo
VIA DEGLI ANNIBALDI
San Pietro in Vincoli
Via L Crenona

Atrium Vestae
Via Sacra
Via S Teodoro
Palatino
Orti Farnesiani

S Teodoro

Domus Aurea

VIA N SALVI

Colosseo
Piazza del Colosseo
Colosseo
S Francesca Romana
Meta Sudans
Arco di Costantino
VIA CELIO VIBENNA

E6
VIA L PETROSELLI
Via di S Decollato
Via de Fienili
Via di S Teodoro
Via del Velabro

Domus Flavia
S Anastasia
Via dei Cerchi
Stadio

Parco del Celio

F6
G6

OUT AND ABOUT

Any time is suitable, but in summer the Colosseo is floodlit at night, and the fora are open until late

Although there is nowhere to eat in the Forum, there are many places nearby, such as Gran Caffè Martini e Rossi (see page 243) or the Musei Capitolini's Bar Capitolina (see page 234).

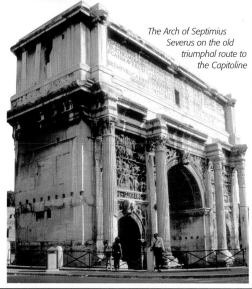

The Arch of Septimius Severus on the old triumphal route to the Capitoline

PIAZZA DI SPAGNA TO PIAZZA SAN PIETRO

Some of Rome's best shopping streets form the route to one of the city's main attractions, the Basilica di San Pietro.

THE WALK

Length: 2.5km (1.5 miles)
Allow: 3 hours
Start: Piazza di Spagna
End: Piazza San Pietro

HOW TO GET THERE

For Piazza di Spagna, take the metro to Spagna.

Allow some time to look at the many shops in the grid of streets surrounding Piazza di Spagna ❶ (see pages 126–127) before taking Via Frattina (to the left if you have your back to the Spanish Steps). This is a great place to shop for designer labels. On emerging onto Via del Corso, cross the road into Piazza San Lorenzo in Lucina, a charming square with outdoor cafés, and a church of the same name.

❷ San Lorenzo in Lucina is one of Rome's earliest churches, and in typical medieval style reuses ancient columns in its façade. Inside is a 19th-century memorial to the French painter Nicolas Poussin (died 1665), who is buried in the church.

Cross the square and take Via del Leone on the right. This leads to Largo Fontanella Borghese, which takes its name from the elegant

Look through the archways of Palazzo Borghese to glimpse the grandeur within

Palazzo Borghese ❸ on the right, once the city residence of the Borghese, one of Rome's most powerful families.

Both Cardinal Scipione Borghese, whose art collection is housed in the Museo e Galleria Borghese, and Napoleon's sister Paolina Borghese, the subject of one of the museum's best-known sculptures, lived here. The

palace is closed to the public, but a glance into the courtyard gives an idea of its elegance.

Cross the square, and leave it by Via del Clementino, passing through Piazza Nicosia and along Via di Monte Brianzo. Take the last small lane on your left, Via dei Soldati, then go left onto Via dell'Orso, lined with charming shops. Turn right at the church of Sant'Antonio dei Portoghesi onto Via dei Pianellari which leads to Piazza Sant'Apollinare, where you will see Palazzo Altemps ❹ (see pages 112–113).

With your back to the museum, Piazza Navona ❺ (see pages 124–125) is straight ahead. Midway down, on the right-hand side, take Via di Sant'Agnese in Agone. On the corner of Via della Pace is Bar della Pace, a great place for a drink. A short distance away, on Vicolo dell'Arco della Pace, is the church of Santa Maria della Pace ❻.

Legend has it that, during a 15th-century war with Florence, a painting of the Virgin bled when it was pierced by a soldier's sword. Pope Sixtus IV made a vow that he would build a church if the Virgin interceded to bring peace. She obliged, and Santa

OUT AND ABOUT

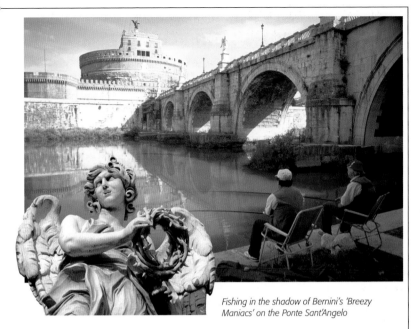

Fishing in the shadow of Bernini's 'Breezy Maniacs' on the Ponte Sant'Angelo

Maria della Pace was begun around 1480. The Cappella Chigi contains frescoes by Raphael, and the adjacent cloister is by Bramante—his first work in Rome.

Return to the bar, turn right and then go straight on along Vicolo delle Vacche and Vicolo della Vetrina. On your left is a charming café, Bar del Fico, in a square of the same name. From Vicolo della Vetrina turn left onto Via dei Coronari, where there are a great number of antique and furniture shops. The church of

San Salvatore in Lauro is on your right. Continue straight on, down the small Vicolo del Curato, as far as Via del Banco di Santo Spirito. Turn right and head straight for Ponte Sant'Angelo **7**.

There has been a bridge here since AD134, when it was built to connect with Hadrian's mausoleum (now within Castel Sant'Angelo). Bernini's stone angels line the bridge, watching over the traditional pilgrims' route to San Pietro. With their flowing robes and outstretched wings, they

appear to be struggling to keep their balance in the wind, which has earned them the nickname 'Breezy Maniacs'.

Cross the bridge to Castel Sant'Angelo **8** (see page 73). Turn left onto Via della Conciliazione, which leads you straight to Bernini's majestic Piazza San Pietro. Facing the basilica, follow the right-hand colonnade to Via di Porta Angelica, which leads up to Piazza del Risorgimento. From here frequent buses run back to the city centre.

OUT AND ABOUT

WHEN TO GO

Go in the morning or late afternoon to catch the churches open. Sunset from Ponte Sant'Angelo is a spectacular sight.

WHERE TO EAT

In addition to the bars mentioned here, there are plenty of restaurants and cafés around Piazza Navona. Try Antico Caffè della Pace (see page 233), Il Capriccio (see page 237) or Da Francesco (see page 239).

Bar della Pace
Via della Pace 3–7
☎ 06 686 1216
🕐 daily 9am–2am (Mon from 4pm)
Popular with locals and visitors alike. The bar also owns the pizzeria next door.

WHERE TO GO

San Lorenzo in Lucina
Via in Lucina 16a
☎ 06 687 1494
🕐 Daily 8–12, 3–8

Santa Maria della Pace
Vicolo dell'Arco della Pace 5
☎ 06 686 1156
🕐 Mon–Fri 10–12.45

[Map showing area from Piazza di Spagna to surrounding streets, with grid references E4, F4, F5, E6, F6, and labels including Spagna, Piazza di Spagna, Trinita dei Monti, Museo Keats-Shelley, Via della Croce, Via Bocca di Leone, Via dei Condotti, Via Frattina, Via della Vite, Via della Mercede, San Lorenzo in Lucina, Galleria dell'Accademia di San Luca, Colonna di Marco Aurelio, Piazza Colonna, Fontana di Trevi, Sant'Ignazio di Loyola, Via dell'Umiltà]

ROME'S CHURCHES

In busy squares redolent of history, or dreaming peacefully in quiet, romantic little streets, the churches that punctuate this walk offer both interest and variety.

THE WALK

Length: 2km (1.2 miles)
Allow: 2.5 hours
Start: Piazza di Santa Maria Maggiore
End: Piazza di Santa Maria Maggiore

HOW TO GET THERE

The nearest metro stations for Piazza di Santa Maria Maggiore are Cavour (line B) and Vittorio Emanuele (line A). Bus nos. 16, 70, 71, 360 and 649 also stop nearby

With your back to the basilica of Santa Maria Maggiore (see pages 138–139), take Via Merulana, a major thoroughfare on the right. Take the first narrow street on the right to visit the church of Santa Prassede ❶ (see page 142) and its beautiful mosaics. Follow the road around to the left to rejoin Via Merulana, lined with lively shops. Cross Viale Manzoni and climb up to Piazza di Porta San Giovanni in Laterano ❷ (see pages 134–135). The entrance to the church is on the opposite side of the building from here. Take time to admire the basilica, the Lateran Palace, and the Egyptian obelisk, which was originally erected in Thebes during the 15th century BC. Almost opposite the entrance to San Giovanni is the Scala Santa.

❸ This Holy Staircase is said to be the steps from Pilate's palace in Jerusalem climbed by Jesus at his trial. They were brought to Rome by St. Helena, mother of the Emperor Constantine. Wood now protects the marble steps, and glass panels show what are claimed to be Christ's bloodstains. The devout climb the steps on their knees to earn indulgences (remission from temporal sins).

After returning to the square, leave by Via di San Giovanni in Laterano, then take the road on the left, Via di Santo Stefano Rotondo, which runs alongside the Ospedale San Giovanni. Almost at the end of the road on your left is the church of Santo Stefano Rotondo ❹ (see page 143), with its beautiful circular

This obelisk, near Santa Maria Maggiore, was erected in 1587 as a landmark for visiting pilgrims

plan. At the end of the road, turn right onto Via della Navicella, right again to Piazza Celimontana past the Opedale del Celio, and then another sharp right onto Via Annia. Carry straight on, turning left near the end onto Via dei Querceti. Walk down the steps and you'll see the back of the church of Santi Quattro Coronati ❺ (see page 142)—the

entrance is in the next street, the charming and quiet Via dei Santi Quattro Coronati.

The Santi Quattro Coronati is named after four early Christians, possibly soldiers, who refused to worship pagan idols. They were killed by having an iron crown (corona), driven into their heads.

At the end of Via dei Querceti, bear left onto Via di San Giovanni in Laterano; the basilica of San Clemente ❻ (see pages 130–131) is in front of you. This 12th-century church hides a much older history, having been built over a fourth-century AD church and a much earlier pagan temple. Just past the basilica, turn right onto Via Celimontana. At the junction with Via Labicana, cross the road and turn left, heading towards the Colosseo. Keeping on the right-hand side of the road, climb up to Via Nicola Salvi, which leads to the Colle Oppio. Turn right onto Via delle Terme di Tito, and left onto Via Eudossiana at the end of the street. On your right is the entrance gate to Colle Oppio.

❼ Colle Oppio, on the slopes of the Esquiline Hill, is a charming mix of grass, trees and archaeological ruins. It is popular with Romans, but should be avoided after dark.

Follow Via Eudossiana down past the University School of Engineering until you reach the beautiful Piazza San Pietro in Vincoli ❽. Allow some time to visit the church (see page 137), which contains Michelangelo's mighty sculpture of Moses. Facing the church, there is a tiny passageway on your left; go down the steps and you'll find yourself on Via Cavour. Head towards the right, then, at Largo Visconti Venosta, take Via Urbana, which leads to the church of Santa Pudenziana ❾ (see page 142). At the end of the road, turn right and cross Piazza d'Esquilino to return to Santa Maria Maggiore.

Colle Oppio is Rome's most central park (left)

Santa Pudenziana's façade was restored in 1870, but parts of the church date from the 12th century

9 **Santa Pudenziana**

Santa Maria Maggiore

1 **Santa Prassede**

F5

8 **San Pietro in Vincoli**

Piazza S Pietro in Vincoli

Parco del Colle Oppio 7

H5

Domus Aurea

Colosseo

6 **San Clemente**

Arco di Costantino

Colosseo

Parco del Celio

Santi Giovanni e Paolo

5 **Santi Quattro Coronati**

Ospedale San Giovanni

Piazza San Giovanni in Laterano 2

San Giovanni in Laterano

3 H6

Scala Santa

Villa Wolkonsky

Santa Maria in Domnica

4 **Santo Stefano Rotondo**

Villa Celimontana

0   250 m
0   250 yds

G7   H7

WHERE TO GO

Scala Santa
Piazza di San Giovanni in Laterano 14
☎ 06 6988 6433
🕐 daily 6.30–12, 3–6

Surrounded by decorative leaves, this macabre skull is set into the plaster of the wall at the Church of Santa Prassede

San Giovanni in Laterano is the cathedral of the city of Rome

VILLA BORGHESE

A walk through this popular park, once the private estate of Cardinal Scipione Borghese, is the perfect antidote to the turmoil of Rome's busy streets.

THE WALK

Length: 2km (1.2 miles)
Allow: 2 hours
Start: Piazza del Popolo
End: Piazzale Flaminio

HOW TO GET THERE

The most convenient metro stations are Flaminio or Spagna. Alternatively, take a bus: Nos. 117, 119, 628 and 926 all serve the area.

Piazza del Popolo was the city's northern focal point (see page 119). Two important Roman roads, Via Cassia and Via Flaminia, entered the city through the Porta del Popolo before making their way to the Capitolini and the forums. Today's traffic-free square is the site of two almost identical churches, Santa Maria dei Miracoli and Santa Maria di Monte Santo ❶, which stand on the corners of Via di Ripetta and Via del Babuino.

These two churches were designed by Carlo Rainaldi (and others) in 1679. His brief was to build identical churches, but the land available was not of equal size. What he built is an optical illusion: When viewed from the piazza, the churches appear the same, but Santa Maria di Monte Santo, on the left, has an oval dome while that of Santa Maria dei Miracoli, on the right, is round.

With your back to the churches, take Viale G. d'Annunzio, on the right-hand side of the square. Follow the road as it snakes up, turning left onto Viale Mickievicz for the last leg into the Giardino del Pincio ❷ (see page 90). Continue to Piazzale Napoleone I for a panoramic view over the *centro storico*. Retrace your steps as far as Viale dell'Obelisco and turn left. Don't miss the Casina Valadier, an elegant coffee house on your right, which is currently closed. Carry straight on, crossing Viale dell'Orologio, with its fascinating water-clock, until you reach Piazzale dei Martiri and the entrance to the Villa Borghese

park (see page 146). Keep walking straight on, along Viale delle Magnolie, until you reach Via de Casina di Raffaello, the first right after busy Piazza delle Canestre. Just ahead is a small house, said to have belonged to Raphael ❸. Follow this road up to the Tempietto di Diana ❹.

This 18th-century Classical temple is dedicated to Diana, goddess of hunting. The ceiling is decorated with blue medallions: The central motif is of Diana, accompanied by one of her hunting dogs; the rest are all hunting motifs.

Turn left at the temple, onto Viale dei Pupazzi. From here there is a good view, to the left, of the stadium-shaped Piazza di Siena, where Rome's International Horse Show is held in May ❺. When you reach Piazzale dei Cavalli Marini, continue straight on to the end of the path. To your right is the Museo e Galleria Borghese ❻ (see pages 92–97). Turn to your left and head towards Piazzale del Giardino Zoologico and the entrance to Bioparco ❼.

There has been a zoo on this site since 1911, but it was updated in 1997 and now concentrates on conservation. The zoo arranges many activities for children.

An Egyptian obelisk surrounded by marble lions spouting water dominates Piazza del Popolo

Keep left, walking down Viale del Giardino Zoologico until you reach Largo P. Picasso. Climb the steps up to the Tempio di Esculapio, which is almost surrounded by a lake where rowing boats can be hired. Take the next lane on the right (at the side of the temple) to emerge onto Piazza Paolina Borghese. From here it is just a short walk to the Galleria Nazionale d'Arte Moderna, where you could stop for a coffee in the Café degli Arti.

❽ **The Galleria Nazionale d'Arte Moderna displays work by Italian and foreign artists, from 1800 to the present day. It is also used for major exhibitions. Alternatively, farther along Viale delle Belle Arti is the Museo Nazionale Etrusco ❾ (see page 147).**

To leave the park, retrace your steps to Piazza Paolina Borghese and take the road in front of you, Via Bernadotte, which leads you down to Piazzale Fiocco and the Esculapio Fountain. Continue straight down to Viale Washington, which ends with the spectacular gate in Piazzale Flaminio. On your left is the gate leading back to the busy Piazza del Popolo.

OUT AND ABOUT

The tree-lined avenues of the Villa Borghese are ideal for a weekend walk

E2
VIALE BRUNO BUOZZI
VIALE DELLE BELLE ARTI
F2

Via Michele Mercati
Via C Linnei
Via C de Notaris
Via Giuseppe Manguii
Via A Vesalii
Via ULISSE
ALDROVANDI

9 Villa Giulia Museo Nazionale Etrusco
8 Galleria Naz d'Arte Moderna
7 Bioparco

Via del G Zoologico

Villa Strohl-Fern
Piazza Paolina Borghese
Villa
Viale del Giardino Zoologico
Viale dei Daini
Via M Fortuny

Via Giulia
Villa
Viale del Museo

Museo e Galleria Borghese **6**

Fontana di Esculapio
Tempio di Esculapio
5 Piazza di Siena

Viale dell'Aranciera
Viale G Washington
Viale F La Guardia
Via di Casina di Raffaele

Flaminio
3
4 Tempietto di Diana

Via Cesare Beccaria
Via Flaminia

VIALE DEL MURO TORTO
Piazzale Napoleone I
Viale delle Magnolie
Viale San Paolo del Brasile
Borghese

Piazza del Popolo
S Maria del Popolo
Giardino del Pincio **2**
Piazzale dei Martiri

S Maria dei Miracoli
1 S Maria di Monte Santo

Galoppatoio

VIA PINCIANA

Casa di Goethe
Via Laurina
Via Margutta
Via della Trinità dei Monti
VIALE DEL MURO TORTO

Villa Medici

Via di Porta Pinciana
VIA VITTORIO VENETO

Via A Brunetti
Via di San Giacomo
Via A Canova
Via della Frezza
Via Vittoria
Spagna
Via del Babuino
Via dei Greci
Via del Corso

Mausoleo di Augusto
Via Bocca di Leone
Via Mario de' Fiori
Via della Croce
Piazza di Spagna
Via di Propaganda
Via Lazio
Via Emilia
Via Ludovisi
Via V Veneto
Via Liguria

E3

Trinità dei Monti

Museo Keats-Shelley
Via Sistina
Via Gregoriana

F4

0 ——— 250 m
0 ——— 250 yds

OUT AND ABOUT (vertical, right margin)

WHEN TO GO

Villa Borghese is open from dawn to dusk, so visit at any time during the day. It is popular with Roman families on Saturdays and Sundays.

WHERE TO EAT

With the Casina Valadier closed, the only places to stop for refreshment are the museum cafés. However, there are plenty of choices between Piazza del Popolo and Piazza di Spagna, such as Il Brillo Parlante (see page 236) or Il Margutta (see page 245).

WHERE TO GO

Bioparco
Viale del Giardino Zoologico
☎ 06 360 8211
🕐 Mon–Fri 9–6, Sat–Sun 9–7

Galleria Nazionale d'Arte Moderna
Viale delle Belle Arti 131
☎ 06 322981
🕐 Tue–Sun 8.30–7.30. Closed 1 May
www.gnam.arti.beniculturali.it

Bioparco, in Villa Borghese, is a popular zoo where the main emphasis is on conservation

EXCURSIONS

There may come a point in your stay when you tire of Rome's endless museums and churches, particularly if you visit during the oppressively hot summer months. The countryside of Lazio and beyond is a refreshing change from the city's heat, and much of it is accessible by public transportation, making it an easy day's escape. Whenever possible, avoid visiting on Saturday and Sunday: The Romans enjoy getting out of the city, too, and the popular places will be crowded. Plan your visit for a weekday and you might even have the place to yourself. So why not do as the Romans do: Pack up a picnic and head for *la campagna*.

EXCURSION 1

VITERBO

Lazio's most historic town, with fine medieval and Renaissance buildings, an unspoilt atmosphere and the bonus of a world-class 16th-century garden nearby.

OUT AND ABOUT

BASICS

Tourist Information Office
Piazza San Carluccio 5
☎ 0761 304795

Museo Nazionale Archeologico
Rocca Albornoz, Piazza della Rocca
☎ 0761 325929
🕐 Tue–Sun 9–2, Apr–Oct; 9–1 rest of year

Museo Civico
Piazza F. Crispi
☎ 0761 340810
🕐 Tue–Sun 9–7, Apr–Oct; 9–6 rest of year

Villa Lante
Via Iacopo Barozzi 71
Bagnaia
☎ 0761 288008
🕐 Tue–Sun 8.30–6.30
💶 Adult €2, child (under 18) free

www.viterboonline.com
Excellent multi-language site covering Viterbo and the surrounding area, with full information on everything there is to see, as well as good listings, travel hints, and information about what's on. Good links, an efficient search facility and plenty of maps and photos

HOW TO GET THERE

Trains: every 20 minutes from Termini, Roma Ostiense or Stazione Flaminio; journey time approximately 1.5–2 hours. The town is a 10–15-minute walk.
Cotral bus: from Saxa Rubra (Via Flaminia) every 30 minutes; journey time approximately 1.5 hours.
By car: 1.5 hours; take A1 (E35) north to GRA, then exit at Orte onto S204 signed to Viterbo (110km/68 miles).
Villa Lante is 5km (3 miles) east of Viterbo. Bus No. 6 hourly from Piazza Martini dei Ungheria; by car, east of town at Bagnaia, follow signs off S204.

OVERVIEW

The largest town in northern Lazio and a quietly prosperous provincial capital, Viterbo has a long history. It's this legacy of the past, in the shape of intact medieval walls, a maze of narrow streets and its stately palazzi, that gives the town its appeal today. Viterbo was originally an Etruscan settlement, absorbed by Rome in AD310. Its heyday was the Middle Ages, when a succession of popes scuttled here to live away from trouble in Rome, making it their capital in 1257. It was during this period that the magnificent walls went up, civic buildings and churches were constructed and the town took on its present form.

THE HEART OF TOWN

After the decidedly unattractive approach to the town, it's a relief to see the battlemented walls that encircle the old town. Once inside, spend time getting your bearings in the Piazza del Plebiscito, a fine square surrounded by 15th- and 16th-century palaces, still home to the town's council. The main, arcaded building is the

Renaissance Mannerist gardens. The villa is easily reached from Viterbo, and you should certainly leave time to fit in a visit.

Spreading over a series of five terraces, the gardens are perfectly proportioned and richly detailed, the planting enhancing the importance of water in the overall design. It's a lovely place on a hot summer's day.

Don't Miss Walk up the Via San Pellegrino to the Piazza San Pellegrino; it's Viterbo's main street and has an example of just about everything that makes the area special.
Villa Lante has 16th-century water jokes— ask the guide to activate them.

15th-century Palazzo dei Priori, decorated, like many others, with lions and palm trees, symbols of Viterbo. The palazzo's council chamber, reached through a lovely courtyard overlooking the river valley, is decorated with a series of murals telling the town's history. From here, head down Via San Lorenzo to the Romanesque church of Santa Maria Nuova— where St. Thomas Aquinas preached for peace in 1266— before heading through a couple of pretty piazzas to the Quartiere San Pellegrino, Viterbo's oldest area. It's tangle of narrow alleys is decidedly picturesque, with outside staircases, fountains and flower-drenched balconies.

PIAZZA SAN LORENZO
For a bit more culture, retract to the Piazza del Plebiscito and head in the opposite direction, towards Piazza San Lorenzo. The square was built on the original Etruscan town and is flanked by the 13th-century Palazzo Papale and the Duomo. The Great Hall in the Papal Palace was once the scene of half a dozen or so papal elections, but for most visitors it's the view from the open Gothic loggia that slices into the green gorge that's truly memorable. Memorable, too is the serene beauty of the Romanesque Duomo, with its elegant striped cosmatesque floor and stately campanile.

The loggia of Palazzo Papale (top)
San Pellegrino quarter (above)
The gardens of Villa Lante (right)
Piazza del Plebiscito (far left)

CHURCHES AND MUSEUMS
Santa Maria Nuova, built in 1080, and the Duomo are the pick of the town's churches, but it's worth tracking down the 19th-century building dedicated to Santa Rosa, at the far end of Corso Italia. Inside a chapel in the south aisle is the saint's body, still dressed in nun's clothing; macabre, but fascinating.

The Museo Nazionale Archeologico, up the hill in Piazza della Rocca, focuses on archaeological finds from the Stone Age to the Middle Ages, with the emphasis firmly on the Etruscan finds from the area around Viterbo. There are more local treasures in the Museo Civico, outside the walls and next to the 12th-century church of Santa Maria della Verità, including Roman sarcophagi found nearby, but it's the paintings on the upper floors that shine.

THE VILLA LANTE
To the east of Viterbo is the small town of Bagnaia, completely dominated by the 16th-century palace of the Villa Lante, whose gardens are considered one of the finest of all the existing

WHERE TO EAT
Ristorante Il Portico
Via Cardinal La Fontaine 28
Tel 0761 321143
In summer you can eat outside this charming restaurant, close to Santa Maria Nuova, which serves local dishes and seafood.

Enoteca la Torre
Via della Torre 5
Tel 0761 226467
🕐 Mon–Sat 1–2.45, 8–10.30
Right in the heart of town, this *enoteca* has an excellent choice of wines.

OSTIA ANTICA

Ancient Rome's port is one of the top three best-preserved Roman towns in Italy, and is a haven of romantic ruins and soothing greenery.

BASICS

Ostia Antica
Viale dei Romagnoli 717
☎ 06 5635 8099; fax 06 5651500
🕐 Tue–Sun 8.30–7.30, May–Sep; 9–6, Apr; 9–5, Mar and Oct; 8.30–4, rest of year
🎫 Adult €4, child (under 18) free. Includes entry to Museo Ostiense nearby
🚶 Guided tours in Italian only, Sun 11 €3.50 extra. Audioguides in Italian, English, French, Spanish and German €5
🅿 available (fee)
☕ 🚻 Both on site
📖 Bookshop with guide books, maps and plans, postcards and souvenirs

Borgo
🕐 Castello: Tue–Sun 9–1; also Tue, Thu 2.30–4.30

www.ostia-antica.org
This superlative English-language site is aimed at tourists and academics alike, so there's an immense range of information at every level. Lots of plans, photos, 3-D reconstructions, practical advice and links to a huge number of related sites.

www.ostiaantica.net
An enthusiastic site crammed with his-tory, information and photos. You can take a virtual tour and bone up on what you'll want to see. Only the main headings are in English, so you'll need to read Italian to get the most out of it.

HOW TO GET THERE

Train: from Stazione Ostiense to Ostia Antica (metro to Piramide); journey time 30 minutes. Metro from Termini; journey time 30 minutes
By car: 35–40 minutes if the traffic's not bad. Take Via del Mare (SS8) from Porta San Paolo

OVERVIEW

Roman legend puts Ostia's founding in the seventh century BC; factual dating of the ruins points to the fourth century BC. From then, a small port and trading community established itself, getting a boost from its military role during the First Punic War. The second century BC was boom time, with the commercial harbour growing in importance as Rome flourished and Ostia's own population reached half a million. The port was soon a victim of its own success, unable to handle the vast quantity of trade generated by the empire and, initiated by Claudius, a second port—close to the modern airport—was constructed in the first to second centuries AD. This Portus Romae attracted more and more shipping, and Ostia became largely a residential town. By the fifth century and the fall of Rome, it was largely abandoned, the sea retreated and the harbour silted up. Malaria and pirates did the rest, and by the 17th century, Ostia Antica was all but forgotten.

EXCAVATIONS

Archaeological excavations began in the 19th century, and today about half the town has been uncovered, with some low-key excavations still continuing. For visitors, Ostia is a quintessentially

romantic Classical ruin, complete with elegant umbrella pines, grassy slopes and spreads of wildflowers. These certainly contribute to its evocative allure, but they make its preservation a nightmare, damaging walls and foundations: the old Italian story of too much to preserve and not enough money to do it.

DECUMANUS MAXIMUS

Like all Roman towns, Ostia was bisected by a dead-straight main street, the Decumanus Maximus, and its cobbled length is the first thing you see as you enter the site through the Porta Romana. On either side of this there's a confusing jumble of streets and ruins, admittedly evocative, but you'll need a plan to make sense of it all. A city this size needed civic buildings, temples, administrative offices, entertainment complexes and shops, as well as housing for a population covering the full social spectrum. Some of these you should certainly track down, so head down the Decumanus towards the town. The first big building on the right is the Terme di Nettuno, the public baths, built by Hadrian, and wonderfully decorated with mosaics aptly showing Neptune himself and his wife Amphitrite, goddess of the sea. Next to the baths is the amphitheatre, a semi-circular building that went up in AD196; its tiers of seats for 4,000 have been restored and it is used for summer concerts. Ostian citizens could move through the back of the theatre directly into the Piazzale delle Corporazioni.

PIAZZALE DELLE CORPORAZIONI

This is the mercantile heart of the city. Here, the shipping agents had their offices, many of them identified by the black and white mosaics in front of their doors— chandlers, grain-merchants, rope-makers and others. Their

Follow the Decumanus Maximus to see the sights of Ostia Antica

warehouses, known as *horrea*, are scattered all over Ostia. To get some idea of the scale of commerce in ancient times, spend a few moments simply taking in the sheer numbers of these *horrea* and their impressive proportions.

Near the piazzale, there are a couple of private houses you should see: the Casa di Apulius and the Casa di Diana. The former's owner splashed out on an atrium and mosaic-decorated rooms, interior design that was unusual this far north—you're more likely to see it in Pompeii. He was a devotee of the slightly sinister god Mithras, and there's a Mithraic temple next to the

Fragment of wall decoration (top)
Terme di Nettuno (above)
The amphitheatre (left)

house. The owners of the nearby Casa di Diana worshipped the same god and had a *mithraeum* at the back of their grand house, with its central courtyard.

THE INSULAE AND FORUM

Not all Ostians lived in villas, and it's the blocks of workers' flats that really speak to us across the centuries. These *insulae* (islands) rose to four or five floors, had running water, heating and plumbing and often shared a communal garden—the Casa di Giardino is a fine example. Citizens of all classes flocked to the Forum, with its Capitol, baths and basilicas, but just as many doubtless spent time in the Thermopolium, near the Casa di Diana. This ancient café, with its high counter, outside seats, display shelves and wall paintings of the day's special, tells us more about the Romans than a thousand broken columns.

To flesh out the bones of what you've seen, head for the museum, which is devoted to finds from the site. There's a fine statue of Mithras killing a bull (the god's symbol), sarcophagi from all over the town and wall paintings with touching scenes of everyday life.

THE BORGO

It's worth a detour across the road to the Borgo, Ostia's medieval village. It's dominated by the Castello, built for Pope Julius II in 1483–86 by Pontelli. Once the customs house for ships sailing up the Tiber to Rome, it lost its usefulness when the river changed course in 1587.

Don't Miss The size and scale of Ostia are more impressive by far than the capital's Forum, and it gives a far better idea of ancient Roman life.
The combination of pine trees, greenery and spring wildflowers within the ruins themselves make a lovely picture.

TIPS

● Allow a whole day for the site; perhaps bring a picnic.

● In summer, take water with you, and rest in the shade during the early afternoon.

● Buy a plan of the site (available at the museum shop) and spend time when you arrive planning your visit.

WHERE TO EAT

Ristorante il Monumento
Piazza Umberto I 8
Tel 06 565 0021
🌑 Closed Mon
At the entrance to the beautiful medieval Borgo you can enjoy reasonably priced local dishes on the veranda here.

There are plenty of seafood restaurants in Ostia Lido along the Lungomare. Take a train or metro to Ostia Lido C. Colombo (the last stop on the line you arrived on).

TIVOLI

A hill town that's home to one of Europe's greatest Renaissance water gardens, a gorge complete with crashing waterfalls and tempting restaurants for alfresco dining.

Cardinal d'Este's 16th-century gardens descend on a series of terraces

OUT AND ABOUT

BASICS

Tourist Information Office
Piazza Garibaldi
☎ 0774 311249

Villa d'Este
Piazza Trento
☎ 0774 333404
🕐 Tue–Sun 8.30–6.30, Apr–Sep;
Tue–Sun 8.30–5, Mar; Tue–Sun 8.30–4,
rest of year
🎫 Adult €6.50, child (under 18) free
🖥 🍴 🛍
📖 Guidebook €6 and €5

Villa Gregoriana
This is currently closed for restoration,
but is planned to reopen in 2004.
Contact the tourist information office for
more details.

HOW TO GET THERE

Train: from Stazione Tiburtina; journey
time approximately 35–60 minutes

Cotral bus: from Stazione Tiburtina and
Ponte Mammolo (Via Prenestina) every
15 minutes; journey time 1 hour

By car: take A24 northeast, then Tivoli
exit

OVERVIEW

Perched among olive groves on a ridge of the Monti Tiburtini, Tivoli has always been an escape for Romans from the heat of the city—it's amazing what a bit of height can do to the freshness of the air. In Classical times it was a retirement town and summer retreat for wealthy Romans, including the emperor—Hadrian's enormous Villa Adriana is just outside the town (see pages 216–217). Later, Renaissance nobility built country villas throughout the town and surrounding area. The most famous of these is the Villa d'Este, whose world-famous gardens are a symphony of lush greenery and thundering water.

The town has other delights. It's enfolded in an oxbow formed by the River Aniene, and retains its picturesque medieval streets, fine churches and a general air of prosperity, wealth derived from the travertine stone quarries you'll see lining the road on the way into town.

THE VILLA D'ESTE

The Villa d'Este is Tivoli's main draw, a stunning garden where cascading water is combined with lush cool greenery and landscaped around a Renaissance villa, converted from a former Benedictine convent by Pirro Ligorio for Cardinal Ippolito d'Este in 1550. The Cardinal was the son of Lucrezia Borgia and the Duke of Ferrara, and had grown up in a rich and sophisticated court, a background that is reflected in both the villa and gardens. Ten rooms on the ground floor of the villa have been restored; these are vividly frescoed with scenes of the history of Tivoli and mythology by Girolamo Muziano and Federico Zuccari.

The frescoes were executed between 1550 and 1560. There's a great view over the garden's symmetrical terraces from the loggia.

The Villa's Gardens

Below the villa stretch the gardens, some of the most spectacular and theatrical ever designed. They represent the full flowering of Renaissance culture and had a huge influence on garden design throughout Europe. Laid out around a central axis, the design is strictly formal, based on the combination of static lines of greenery, sculpture and statuary with living water. It's this contrast between the sombre planting and the exuberance of the myriad fountains and water features that gives the Villa d'Este gardens their appeal.

The Fountains

Fountain-wise, the stupendous Organ Fountain takes top prize. Fully restored, it sends millions of litres of water thundering into the air against a spectacular decorative stone background. Visitors have always loved the Via delle 100 Fontane, a wooded walkway flanked by a hundred cooling spouts of water, whose focal point is the splendid Fontana dei Draghi—a dragon that was the emblem of its builder, Pope Gregory XIII. The Fontana dell'Ovata is fringed with statues and set against a shadowy arcade, and the great Gian Lorenzo Bernini was responsible for the graceful shell-shaped Fontana del Bicchierone. Another stunner is the Fontana della Rometta, little Rome, with reproductions of Rome's main classical monuments.

These set-pieces are scattered throughout the gardens, but wherever you go you'll be surrounded by the sound of water and find a surprise round every corner. Originally, the surprises included the watery jokes found in every great Renaissance garden—jets that drenched visitors at the touch of a hidden button, benches that flooded when sat upon, curtains of water to trap the unwary, owls that whistled and chirruped during the day. These no longer work, but remember that such conceits were as much part of the gardens as the beauty of the fountains and cascades.

VILLA GREGORIANA

Tivoli's other garden, the Villa Gregoriana, was created much later. The River Aniene was prone to flood the town, and in 1831 Pope Gregory XVI solved the problem by diverting the flow of water over an artificial waterfall, the Cascata Grande. Bernini had

Tivoli's watery gardens were designed to provided respite from the city's heat, and they continue to do so today

a hand in the plan, designing a smaller cascade at the neck of the 60m-deep (200ft) gorge. The park and gorge are a wonderfully luxuriant habitat, overgrown and wild, and a good contrast to the formal style of the Villa d'Este.

The Waterfalls

From the deafening vantage point overlooking the Cascata Grande, there's a path, noisy and cool with the rush of water, zigzagging down to the bottom of the gorge. It passes two smaller waterfalls before retracking to the main falls and continuing past two grottoes; water rushes straight down past the Grotto della Sirena, and the Grotta di Nettuno is heavily and picturesquely covered with mineral deposits. It's a steep climb back up the other side but worth it for the views from the top and the close-up of the little Tempio di Vesta. The temple is in the grounds of a restaurant, but you can go in and peer out from the belvedere.

THE TOWN

It's worth a quick wander round the town, particularly along the Via del Duomo, where there's a high percentage of late-medieval houses. Fans of the Romanesque should take in some of the churches: San Pietro alla Carità has a lovely façade and Classical columns. The Duomo, founded in the fifth century, has a Romanesque campanile, though its portico dates from 1650. To see an earlier portico, head for San Silvestro—its columns are Roman, and there are 13th-century frescoes in the apse.

TIPS

● Allow all day to visit Tivoli, particularly if you're going to visit both the Villa d'Este and the Villa Adriana.

● Be prepared to find some fountains at Villa d'Este out of action owing to continuing restoration.

● Don't be tempted to drink the water, or even splash around in it—it's basically sewage from the town above. Some fountains are labelled *acqua potabile*; these are safe.

WHERE TO EAT

Antica Hostaria de' Carrettieri
Via D. Giuliami 65
Tel 0774 330159
The Sardinian owner serves dishes from home in a warm, friendly atmosphere. Close to the medieval heart of town.

Ristorante Sibilla
Via della Sibilla 50
Tel 0774 335281
An enviable location, with tables set around the temples of Vesta and Sibilla, overlooking the famous cascades of Villa Gregoriana.

VILLA ADRIANA

The epitome of a romantic ruin, the remains of the largest and most elaborate villa ever constructed during the Roman Empire, set in a peaceful and beautiful landscape.

BASICS

Tourist Information Office
Piazza Garibaldi
Tivoli
☎ 0774 311249

Villa Adriana
☎ 0774 382733
🕙 Daily 9–6, Mar–Oct; 9–3.30 rest of year
🎫 Adult €6.50, child (under 18) free
🏛 🚻 🛒

HOW TO GET THERE

Train: from Stazione Tiburtina to Tivoli; journey time approx 30 minutes
Cotral bus: from Ponte Mammolo (Via Prenestina) to Tivoli; journey time 50 minutes, or from Tivoli, take bus No. 4/4X from Piazza Garibaldi out to Villa Adriana
By car: take A24 northeast, then Tivoli exit; Villa Adriana is signed from here

OVERVIEW

The Villa Adriana, just outside Tivoli, was built by Hadrian, emperor from AD118 to 138. As a provincial, Hadrian was viewed with suspicion by both the Senate and the aristocracy. It was partly for this reason that Hadrian made this grandiose villa his main residence when he was in Rome, rather than taking over one of the existing imperial palaces. He also kept away from the power struggles in Rome by travelling throughout the empire, and probably hoped eventually to make this sumptuous villa his

retirement home. Sadly, ill-health forced him south and he only had a few years to enjoy the completed villa. His travels had played a large part in the planning; an enthusiastic sight-seer, Hadrian dotted his creation with reconstructions of buildings that had impressed him throughout the Roman world—a sort of second-century theme park. Building started in AD125 and continued for 10 years. Tivoli, with its famous travertine quarries and abundant water, was an ideal place for such a vast project, as there was plenty of tufa and lime available to mix the tonnes of cement needed.

The Villa eventually sprawled more than at least 100ha (250 acres), with over 30 buildings, some of which have still to be excavated. After Hadrian's death,

the whole vast complex fell rapidly into disrepair, was plundered and forgotten, until early Renaissance enthusiasts rediscovered it in 1450.

WHAT TO SEE

You'll need plenty of imagination to visualize the ancient glory of the site; all the upper parts of the buildings are gone, making the complex seem much more open that it was originally. What now appear to be open spaces were once covered walkways connecting the various buildings, which were several floors high, embellished with domes and faced with marble and other precious stones. It must once have looked like an enclosed city—it's worth remembering that the villa covered an area as large as the area of imperial Rome itself. Archaeologists still haven't discovered the original purpose of many of the structures, so it makes sense to concentrate on the best and save some energy to soak up the atmosphere.

THE PECILE

Kick off at the Pecile, the huge colonnade near the entrance. Once surrounded by gardens, its focus point is the central pool.

The subterranean Cryptoportico (left)
Hadrian's Teatro Marittimo (below)

Once flanked with statues, the Canopus is the highlight of a visit to Villa Adriana

Hadrian based its design on the Stoa Poikile of Athens, which he admired on his travels. It was probably used as a gymnasium and it's thought it also served as an after-dinner promenade during the summer. Along the west side you'll see the Cento Camerelle, a warren of small rooms probably used as storage space and slave quarters.

TEATRO MARITTIMO

In the northeast corner of the Pecile there's access through the ruins of a large hall (the niches once held statues of Greek philosophers) to the Teatro Marittimo, one of the villa's highlights and one of the few places where there's a real impression of the original appearance. An Ionic-columned portico rings a circular canal, once crossed by movable bridges leading to a little round island. This was Hadrian's own retreat, where he withdrew to read, paint and relax in the miniature *domus*, complete with peristyle, that stood on the islet.

THE BATHS

Just south of here is a modestly sized set of baths, with a *heliocaminus*, a round pool used for sunbathing where you baked before bravely plunging into the nearby *frigidarium*, the cold-water pool. Far grander are the *terme* proper, a vast bath complex with open-air pools, hot baths heated by an elaborate system and courtyards for relaxing. By contrast to this hedonism, there's a bit of cultural stimulus near here in the shape of the Canopus, modelled on an Egyptian site that had much

impressed the Emperor. It's a replica of the Temple of Serapis at Canopus, which was linked to the Nile by a canal; here, an artificial waterway runs down a man-made valley to the temple replica—it's fringed with statues and fragments of columns, including four serene caryatids. It must have been a wonderful backdrop for late-night dining, which was probably its purpose. Have a look at the nearby Pretorio, the barracks, then visit the underground portico, deliciously cool and shady, where the Emperor took his summertime strolls.

PALAZZO IMPERIALE

Winter would have seen Hadrian making full use of the Palazzo Imperiale itself, a complex that covered 50,000sq m (180,000sq ft) and came complete with an efficient underground heating system. The palace was made up of three complexes set round their own peristyles, which housed both residential and official rooms. The Piazza d'Oro, in the southeast, has yielded some

fabulous archaeological treasures; like so much else from here, they're now dispersed to museums in Rome and all over the world. The library building is another thought-provoking area—two originally multi-floor buildings that housed works in Greek and Latin. One side of the library courtyard was occupied by 10 guest rooms, perhaps for visiting scholars, paved with black and white mosaic floors and complete wth three sleeping niches in each room.

There's much more beside, best enjoyed as part of the overall scene. There's also an entire underground series of roads, passage and store rooms, from where the infrastructure needed to run this huge palace operated. The small museum has some statues, portraits and mosaics (though all the best are elsewhere), and is also the place to see the latest discoveries, sometimes exhibited here.

OUT AND ABOUT

PARCO NAZIONALE DEL CIRCEO

A national park with a wide variety of wildlife habitats, wonderful coastal scenery, great beaches and a couple of pretty villages.

BASICS

Centro d'Informazione Parco
Nazionale del Circeo
Via Carlo Alberto 107
Sabaudia
☎ 0773 511386
Main park information centre with exhibitions, audio-visual show, natural history museum and picnic area

Tourist Information Office
Sabaudia
☎ 0773 515046

Tourist Information Office
San Felice Circeo
☎ 0773 547770

www.parks.it/parco.nazionale.circeo
This wonderful site, beautifully laid out and packed with information and photographs, tells you everything you'll want to know about Circeo and its habitats, flora and fauna. There's practical information, news of what's happening and links to all of Italy's national and regional parks. In English.

HOW TO GET THERE

Cotral bus: from Laurentina to San Felice Circeo/Sabaudia; journey time 2.25 hours

By car: take S148 south via Latina, then follow signs east to Sabaudia; journey time 1.5–2 hours

OVERVIEW

South of Rome, the Pontine Marshes, malaria-ridden, unproductive and unhealthy, once stretched along the coast below Anzio. In 1928 Mussolini embarked on a massive drainage project, transforming the region into a productive agricultural area, complete with the new towns of Latina and Sabaudia. As early as the late 1920s, conservationists realized the threat the scheme might cause to this sensitive and classic coastal environment, and in 1934 the Parco Nazionale del Circeo was founded. Covering an area of 8,500ha (21,000 acres), it's the smallest of Italy's national parks, but despite its diminutive size, the park embraces a superb variety of natural environments, ranging from dunes, wetlands, sea caves and beaches to thick deciduous woods and limestone

maquis. Roads, tracks and paths thread through the park and link the different zones, making the whole area accessible and enjoyable to every type of visitor. Circeo is the perfect antidote to the noise and heat of Rome, a green oasis with immensely varied scenery and a mixed flora and fauna that's unique in this part of Italy.

WHAT TO SEE

Circeo has superb woods of deciduous oaks, holm- and cork oaks, but it's the dunes, maquis and wetlands that draw naturalists and birdwatchers to the park. The dunes are backed by four lakes, drawing a wide variety of both resident and migratory birds, so there should be no problem spotting something interesting—over 230 species have been recorded. You may see the turned-over earth that signals wild boar, or get a glimpse of fallow and roe deer, foxes or even a pine marten. Wildflower lovers will find spring the best time to come, when the maquis—the typical scrubby Mediterranean habitat—is at its best, burgeoning with brilliant cistus, rosemary and broom. The park has man-made attractions, too, in the shape of a rich archaeological heritage—Domitian's Villa is the best known.

EXPLORING THE PARK

Explore the park by heading south from Sabaudia, taking in the dunes and wetlands on the way to Monte Circeo, at 541m (1,775ft) the highest point. The drive south covers the quintessential Mediterranean

coastline of the promontory—white-sand beaches, rocky coves and aromatic pines running down to the sea. From Monte Circeo there are fabulous views north over the beaches and lagoons. Monte Circeo is the legendary island of Circe mentioned in Homer's *Odyssey*, and the whole promontory resembles the sorceress's reclining figure. From the top, the road exits the park into the picturesque, and distinctly trendy, coastal village of San Felice Circeo. In summer, it's crowded with flashy cars and yachts, but any other time should be high on the sightseeing list.

Don't Miss The view over the dunes from the summit of Monte Circeo is superb—and you can drive up to the top. If you're here during spring or autumn migration, try birdwatching in the wetlands.

TIPS

● Spend time at the visitor centre in Sabaudia to learn about the park.

● Take a boat trip around the lagoon from Sabaudia, or up and down the coast or to Circe's grotto from San Felice Circeo.

● If you want to stay the night, try one of the moderately priced hotels in San Felice, which are busy only in high season.

WHERE TO EAT

Il Grottino
Piazza Vittorio Veneto 3, San Felice Circeo
Tel 0773 548446
This seafood restaurant, just outside the old town, has a panoramic terrace overlooking the attractive Golfo di San Felice.

Ristorante Lo Scolglio
Via Caterattino 38, Sabaudia
Tel 0773 515581
Enjoy excellent seafood and wines, set off by the view of the beach from the terrace.

FRASCATI

The loveliest of the Castelli Romani towns of the Colli Albani hills, famous for its wine and dominated by a majestic villa and its gardens.

BASICS

Tourist Information Office
Piazza Marconi 1
☎ 06 9420331

Villa Aldobrandini
Via Cardinale Massaia 12
🕙 9–noon (for visits call at the tourist information office)

For *cantine* visits, ask at the tourist information office or enjoy a tour and tasting at one of the local restaurants

HOW TO GET THERE

Train: from Stazione Termini every 15–30 minutes; journey time approximately 30 minutes

Cotral bus: from Anagnina metro station to all the Castelli Romani towns; journey time approximately 30 minutes

By car: take S215 south (exit Tuscalano on GRA), then S216 to Frascati; journey time approximately 50 minutes

OVERVIEW

South of Rome stretches a ridge of volcanic hills, the Colli Albani, famed for the light and aromatic white wines produced from the rich soil. The hills are home to a group of 13 towns, the Castelli Romani, so called because they developed around the feudal castles built by the popes and the Roman aristocracy. Despite the sprawling post-World War II development around them, each has its own charm, with Frascati leading the field.

WHAT TO SEE

The grandest of Frascati's villas is the Villa Aldobrandini, designed by Giacomo della Porta in 1598 for Cardinal Aldobrandini, a 'nephew' (a tactful euphemism for an illegitimate son) of Pope Clement VII. The vast palace, all faded majesty, dominates the town, and is surrounded by a superb example of an early baroque garden, laid out between 1598 and 1603. Head first for the terrace with its fabulous views towards Rome, then explore the other terraces, avenues and follies, including the water theatre.

The view back towards Rome (above)
Villa Aldobrandini (bottom)

The town is scattered with other gently decaying palaces, like the Villa Falconieri and the Villa Mondragone. Villa Torlonia, among the grandest, was destroyed during World War II, but its gardens are now the town's park—don't miss the fountain, designed by Carlo Maderno.

The baroque cathedral is worth a look, as are some of the other churches, particularly the Gesù, but do leave time to get to grips with the wine. Made here since the third century BC, Frascati is a worldwide hot seller, and it's a revelation to drink it in its birthplace. Light, floral and aromatic, it's made from both Trebbiano and Malvasio grapes, two varieties that thrive in the porous volcanic soils.

Don't Miss Sip a glass of the famous wine in the place it's made.
Come in late afternoon for the best views across the Campagna towards Rome.

TIPS

● Avoid weekends, when Frascati is packed with Romans out for the day, so it's hard to get a trattoria table.

● The fountains in the gardens of the Villa Aldobrandini are often switched off, so be prepared.

You can pick up a *panino* from one of the *porchetta* (whole roast suckling pig) stands on Piazza del Mercato and eat it in one of the *cantine* while you sample the wine.

WHERE TO EAT

Al Fico
Via Anagnina 86
Tel 06 9431 5390
The local dishes are excellent in this central restaurant. Sit outside, on the terrace or in the garden, or go downstairs for wine tasting in the cellar.

Ristorante Cacciani
Via Diaz 15
Tel 06 942 0378
Enjoy excellent local cuisine on the terrace of this elegant restaurant. There's a great wine list, too.

OUT AND ABOUT

There are many organized tours in and around Rome and beyond. Choices range from escorted walking tours around the city's streets and museums to personalized tours with your own guide. Most tours are available in a number of languages.

GUIDED WALKS

Walking tours are a great way of getting into the heart of the city. There are lots of companies offering walking tours of Rome, so you are sure to find something that appeals.

ENJOY ROME
Via Marghera 8a
Tel 06 445 1843 /06 445 0734
www.enjoyrome.com
A wide selection of city itineraries (in English only), including special tours of Bernini's Rome or Fascist Rome. Most tours cost €20, or €14 for under-26s, and last for three hours. They run every day except Christmas Day and 6 January.

ROME(ING) TOURS
Tel 349 671 0823
www.romeingtours.com
Lively tours of the city, including an evening walk ending with a pub crawl. Daytime walks last 3.5 or 4.5 hours and cost €18, or €15 for students. The evening walk costs €15.

THROUGH ETERNITY
Tel 06 700 9336
www.througheternity.com
Archaeologists, art historians and other experts on ancient Rome offer the usual, popular tours, plus an interactive one, where audience participation is essential. Prices vary according to the length of time, but start at €20 for a 2.5-hour tour.

SELF-GUIDED WALKS

If you prefer to go your own way, why not use an audioguide?

ROMEWALKS
www.audiowalks.com
These audio tapes can be ordered from most bookshops before you leave home, quoting ISBN 1-89-048903-4. They cost around £11.50 ($18.99) for two 90-minute cassettes.

CYCLING TOURS

ENJOY ROME
Via Marghera 8a
Tel 06 445 1843 /06 445 0734
www.enjoyrome.com
Three-and-a-half-hour cycling tours of the city for €25 (€20 for under-26s), which includes bicycle rental.

BUS TOURS

There are many companies providing a range of bus tours of Rome and beyond.

ATAC
Piazza dei Cinquecento
Tel 06 4695 2252
Rome's public transportation company runs the 110 City Tour, which leaves from Termini station. You can either buy a Stop and Go ticket for €12.91, which allows you to hop on and off the bus all day, or there is a Non-Stop ticket at €7.75, which covers you for one complete circuit. The service runs every half-hour between 9am and 8pm from April to September (10–6, rest of year) and makes 10 stops. You can book in advance at the ticket office or buy your tickets on the bus for €13.94 and €8.26 respectively.

Other bus companies run tours around the city and to popular places farther afield, such as Tivoli and Ostia Antica. These include **Appian Line** (Piazza Esquilino 6/7, tel 06 4878 6604), **Green Line Tours** (Via del Viminale, tel 06 462 0651/ 06 482 8647/ 06 4877 2253, www.greenlinetours.com) and **Stop 'n' go** (tel 06 4782 6379, www.romecitytours.com).

BOAT TOURS

BATTELLI DI ROMA
www.battellidiroma.it
Cruises along the Tiber, with a commentary, leaving from Ponte Castel Sant'Angelo. Tickets can be bought in advance from the Hotel Reservations desk at Termini station or on board the boat. Daytime cruises cost €10 and leave at 9, 10.30, 3.30 and 5. Evening cruises, at 8pm, include dinner and cost €43.

FLIGHTS

CITYFLY SPA
Rome Urbe Airport
Via Salaria 825
Tel 06 88333
www.cityfly.com
Get a bird's-eye view of Rome in a nine-seater, two-engine plane. This 20-minute tour costs €70 per person (minimum two people), with a 30 per cent discount for children under 10.

PERSONAL GUIDES

CENTRO GUIDE TURISTICHE DI ROMA
Via di Santa Maria alle Fornaci 8d
Tel 06 6390409
www.centroguideroma.org
Personal guided tours for up to 20 people.

OUT AND ABOUT

Eating

A
B
C

2
VIALE DELLE MEDAGLIE D'ORO
VIA MARZIALE
Clivio di Cinna
Baldina
Platone
Fedro
Cornelio Nepote
Andronico
Cordio
Piazzale Clodio
VIA CLODIA
VIALE
VIA C Mirabello
VIA M Amato
CIRCON
Via Premuda
Via Emilio Faà di Bruno
VIA DELLA TRIONFALE
Via Cunfida
Via Rodi
VIALE
GIUSEPPE
MAZZINI
Via Col di Lana
Piazza Giuseppe Mazzini

3
VIALE DEGLI AMMIRAGLI
Piazzale degli Eroi
Cipro Musei Vaticani
V PISANI
CIPRO
CIRCE
Ristorante-Pizzeria Piacere Molise
Dal Toscano
Ottaviano San Pietro
Lepanto
Cesare

4
ANASTASIO II
Via Angelo Emo
CITTÀ DEL VATICANO
Giardini Vaticani
VATICANO
Piazza del Risorgimento
Roof Garden 'les Etoiles'
Taverna Angelica
Parco Adriano

5
VIA GREGORIO VII
Via Aurelia
GAL PRINCIPE A SAVOIA AOSTA
SAN PIETRO
VIA AURELIA
VIA DI PORTA CAVALLEGGERI
Piazza San Pietro
Piazza del Sant'Uffizio
Borgo Santo
Spirito
Conciliazione
Winetime
Taverna da Giovanni
Il Goccetto
Pierlui
Da Giovanni

6
ANT
VIA BETANIA
VIA DI VILLA
Via Aurelia Antica
Villa Floridi
Villa Abamelek
VIA DELLE FORNACI
VIA NUOVA DELLE FORNACI
Parco Gianicolense
Romolo 'Nel Giardino di Raffaello e della Fornarina
Dar Poe
VIA GARIBALDI

7
Villa Doria Pamphilj
Antico Arco
Bar Gianicolo
VIA DI SAN PANCRAZIO
Lumière di Sicilia
VIA NICOLA FABRIZI
Il Cortile

222

A
B
C

This is a map page showing the area around Termini and the surrounding neighborhoods of Rome.

Grid references (top): **F**, **G**, **H**

Left margin numbers: 2, **3**, **4**, **5**, **6**, **7**

224 **F** **G** **H**

Labels and locations:

- Bioparco
- Giardino Zoologico
- Villa
- Villa Borghese
- Piazza di Siena
- Borghese
- Galoppatoio
- Villa Albani
- Villa Paganini
- Villa Torlonia
- Ambasciata d'Abruzzo
- Un Cochon dans mon Jardin
- Al Ceppo
- Piazza Trasimeno
- Piazza Buenos Aires
- Il Pomodorino
- Ristorante Giovanni
- Pizzarè
- Hard Rock Café
- La Terrazza
- Trimani 'Il Winebar'
- Piazza del Indipendenza
- Castro Pretorio
- Bone ation
- The Albert
- Il Gelato di San Crispino
- Bruschetteria Nonna Papera
- Piazza del Quirinale
- Piazza del Viminale
- Est! Est! Est !
- Trattoria Abruzzése
- Ristorante Nuova Stella
- Ristorante da Nazzareno
- Roma Termini
- Termini
- La Barrique
- Café Renault
- Il Guru
- Antica Locanda
- Il Trono dei Pazzi
- Agata e Romeo
- F.I.S.H.
- Offside Café
- Sitar
- Piazza Vittorio Emanuele II
- Fassi-Palazzo del Freddo
- Nerone
- Colosseo
- Gran Caffè Martini e Rossi
- Pizza Forum
- Café Café
- San Clemente
- Pasqualino al Colosseo
- Charly's Saucière
- I Buoni Amici
- Osaka
- Orti Farnesiani
- Parco del Celio
- Villa Wolkonsky
- Piazza di Porta San Giovanni
- San Giovanni
- Villa Celimontana
- Circo Massimo

EATING OUT IN ROME

When in Rome prepare yourself for rich, sun-drenched tastes where more than 5,000 eateries cater for every budget and dining experience. The feasts of ancient Rome may have long since disappeared, but eating is so much a social way of life that is far from uncommon to spend hours over a meal. Traditionally, many establishments are family-run, where the owners pride themselves on fresh and home-made delicacies.

Pasta, salami and locally produced wine all help to produce a memorable meal

CUCINA ROMANA

Authentic Roman cuisine, *cucina romana,* uses the often discarded parts of the animals and originates from the area of Testaccio, near the old slaughterhouse where many locals once worked. The butchers were paid partly in cash, partly in offal—known as the fifth quarter—including liver, heart, intestines and brains. Slow cooking with herbs and spices, transformed these cuts into high-protein, low-cost dishes that can still be found in many of Rome's top restaurants today. *Coda alla vaccinara,* literally tail in the style of the slaughterhouse worker, is a famous signature dish of braised oxtail that was created at Rome's oldest and most famous restaurant in Testaccio, Checchino dal 1887 (see page 238).

The fertile countryside around Rome in the Lazio region is rich in herbs, exquisite vegetables and pungent garlic and onions. Tender, plump globe artichokes, fried whole in olive oil until crispy, are served to perfection by the Romans. Known as *carciofi alla giudia,* this is a typical and delicious dish of the atmospheric Ghetto area, whose origins date back over 400 years and are reflected in the *cucina romana* and Jewish dishes in the local restaurants.

Fishy delights are plentiful, too, with a bountiful harvest of seafood from the shores just 24km (15 miles) from the city. Many of the city's starriest restaurants are temples to the best of seafood, including Alberto Ciarla (see page 232), Quinzi e Gabrieli (see page 249) and La Rosetta (see page 251).

As in other Italian regions, pasta is still the mainstay of the Roman meal. *Spaghetti alle vongole* (with clams and tomatoes) is one of the best-known Roman pasta dishes, while *spaghetti alla carbonara,* made with cured bacon, egg yolk and cheese, is equally famous and Roman to the core. The ever-popular pizza comes in every variety, from the authentic thin, crisp *pizza romana* to the thicker, puffier Neapolitan version.

WHEN TO EAT

If you are eating breakfast in a bar, as many Romans do, you will find that most of them open at around 7–7.30am for cappuccino and a *cornetto* (croissant). In hotels, breakfast usually starts at 8am, and includes cereal, cold meat and cheeses.

Restaurants open for lunch at 12.30 or 1pm, and serve until around 3pm. Romans generally eat late, so many establishments open for evening meals from 8pm, although you will find those that open earlier. Some places, especially cafés and bars, stay open all day

WHERE TO EAT

Perhaps confusingly, there are several different types of eating establishment in Rome. A *ristorante* tends to be the most expensive with pristine table linen and equally pristine waiters. The *trattoria* is less formal, less expensive and often still family-run. An *osteria* or *hostaria* can be basic, sometimes with paper tablecloths and no written menu, but can often serve some of the best food in the city. Interestingly, some of Rome's trendiest and most glamorous establishments have adopted the name *osteria,* echoing the shabby chic fashion. A *rosticceria* or *tavola calda* is a fast-food outlet serving mostly cold foods that you can eat then and there or take away for a picnic. A take-away pizzeria is advertised as *pizzeria rustica* or *a taglio* (by the slice). If you want to sit down to enjoy your pizza, always look for the sign, *pizzeria forno a legno* to make sure that it is traditionally cooked in a wood-fired brick oven.

WHAT'S ON THE MENU

A traditional full meal begins with *antipasti* (starters/hors d'oeuvres). This is followed by *primi*—the first pasta courses, such as *spaghetti alle vongole,* best on Tuesdays and Fridays when the clams are guaranteed to be fresh; or try perhaps *gnocchi alla romana*—little dumplings made in the traditional Roman way in different sauces—Thursday is gnocchi day. The second course, *secondo,* is usually a meat, fish or vegetarian dish, accompanied by *contorni*—vegetables, which are

day and night, getting their quick fix of caffeine. It is also normal to drink the heady brew standing up, even in the most famous cafés, such as the Sant Eustachio (see page 251), which, many say, serves the best espresso in Rome.

The line between café and bar is very blurred, but generally a bar is good for a quick drink, while a café is where you sit and people-watch while enjoying your coffee, or meal, or long, cool drink—or all three. You will certainly pay at least double if

Pizza, ice-cream and an espresso are Rome's version of fast food; waiter service adds to the cost

served as side dishes. Finally, you come to the *formaggio* (cheese) and/or *dolci* (puddings), the espresso and perhaps a drink to aid digestion—*digestivo.* If this quantity of food seems daunting, do not despair. Locals rarely eat such gargantuan meals and pick and mix their courses. However, while it may be acceptable to order *antipasti* alone for lunch, it is not the done thing for dinner and, should you miss out the pasta course, you may be given a sad-eyed look—not for nothing is it known as *il primo.* Very smart restaurants will sometimes offer a *gourmet menu degustazione,* not to be confused with a *menu turistico.* With the latter you usually pay for quantity rather than quality and it is unlikely to give you an authentic Roman dining experience. If you see yellowing photographs of the various dishes displayed outside a restaurant, just don't even go there!

PRICE MATTERS/IL CONTO

Although in theory restaurants are no longer allowed to add a bread and cover (*pane e coperto*) charge, many feign oblivion to this and just charge for the bread anyway, usually between €1-€2 per head. Bottled water is automatically served and charged to your bill. Normally, service is not included, although a minority do still add it as a fixed item. In everyday establishments, a tip of 5 per cent is perfectly adequate, but in *ristoranti,* if the service has been good, 10 per cent would be acceptable. You should always be given a receipt (*ricevuta fiscale*) after paying the bill (*il conto*) as, theoretically, the restaurant could be fined if they don't issue one.

CAFFÈ SOCIETY

Drinking coffee is a ritual in Rome—some would say it is an addiction. It is quite normal to see people at the cash desk (*cassa*) at every time of

you elect to be waited upon rather than consume your drink at the bar.

The type of coffee you drink is also important. Romans wouldn't dream of drinking milky cappuccinos after breakfast, opting instead for the quick caffeine fix of an espresso or a caffè macchiato, with just a drop of milk.

Another variation on the theme is the *enoteca,* or wine bar. These are extremely popular and keep popping up all over the city. Some are self-consciously chic, others are dark and atmospheric, yet others serve excellent food, but all are united in their love of their carefully selected wine. You can drink by the glass or bottle, usually with cold and hot snacks.

GELATERIE

The *gelato* is an indispensable part of Roman life. Some view it as an art form, such as the Gelateria San Crispino (see page 242), just behind the Trevi Fountain, which many regard as the best ice-cream maker in town. Here, the choices are distinctively seasonal, ranging from summer raspberry to nougat, *tiramisù* and countless others. Glorious *gelato* is almost a fashion accessory during the evening *passeggiata* and, even if you don't want to take time to sit and enjoy it, there are kiosks at the corner of almost every street. Look out for the sign *produzione artigianale,* meaning that it is home-made, and avoid the most lurid, which probably means it contains synthetic additives. Other variations include a *gratachecca,* a water ice grated by hand and topped with fruit syrup.

But for the truly sublime, do try a *tartufo* ice-cream. Named after its resemblance to the shape of an exotic truffle, this chocolate-studded ice-cream is utterly delicious, expensive and not just a little decadent.

Eating is one of Rome's great pleasures. To appreciate its cuisine fully you will need an adventurous spirit and at least a smattering of Italian. If you don't speak the language, menus can be a daunting prospect, but knowledge of a few key words will help you to work out what's on offer, order what you want and avoid any embarrassing blunders. This menu reader is designed to help you translate common words and familiarize yourself with dishes that you are likely to come across on a Roman menu.

Cured hams and salami, lemons, chillis and aubergines (eggplants)

EATING OUT

Piatti–Courses
antipasti starter
stuzzichini appetizers
primi piatti first course
secondi piatti main course
contorni vegetables/side dishes
dolci desserts
spuntini snacks

Carne–Meat
agnello lamb
cacciagione game
coniglio rabbit
cuore heart
fegato liver
maiale pork
manzo beef
pancetta bacon
pollame poultry
pollo chicken
prosciutto Parma ham
prosciutto cotto cooked ham
rognoni kidneys
salsiccia sausage
tacchino turkey
vitello veal

Pesce–Fish
alici anchovies
baccalà dried salt cod
branzino sea bass
dorate bream
fritto misto mixed fried fish
merluzzo cod
pesce spada swordfish
sarde sardines
sogliola sole
tonno tuna

triglia mullet
trota trout

Frutti di Mare–Seafood
aragoste lobster
calamari squid
canestrelli scallops
cozze mussels
gamberetti prawns
granceola spiny spider crab
molluschi shellfish
ostriche oysters
seppia cuttlefish
vongole clams

Verdure–Vegetables
asparagi asparagus
carote carrots
carciofo artichoke
cavolfiore cauliflower
cavolo cabbage
cetriolino gherkin
cetriolo cucumber
cicoria chicory
cipolla onion
fagioli beans
fagiolini green beans
fave broad beans
finocchio fennel
lattuga lettuce
melanzane aubergines (eggplant)
patate potatoes
peperone red/green pepper (capsicum)
piselli peas
pomodori tomatoes
spinaci spinach

verdure cotte cooked greens
zucchini courgettes (zucchinis)

Metodi di Cucina–Cooking Methods
affumicato smoked
al forno baked
alla griglia grilled
arrosto roasted
bollito boiled
casalingo home-made
crudo raw
fritto fried
frulatto whisked
ripieno stuffed
stufato stewed

La Pasta–Pasta
cannelloni baked meat- or cheese-filled tubes
conchiglie shell shapes
farfalle butterfly shapes
fettucine wide strips
fusilli spiral shapes
lasagne sheets of pasta, layered with meat sauce and béchamel sauce to make *lasagne al forno*
linguine thin strips
pappardelle rippled strips
penne quill shapes
ravioli pasta cushions filled with meat, cheese or spinach
rigatoni short, fat tubes
tagliatelle thin ribbons or strips
tortellini little 'hats' with meat or cheese filling
trenette long narrow strips

Salsi/Sugi–Sauces

amatriciana bacon, tomato and onion
arrabbiata tomato and hot chilli
brodo broth
cacciatore sauce for meat: tomato, onion, garlic, wine
carbonara smoked bacon, egg, cream and black pepper
passata sieved tomatoes
pesto basil, garlic, pinenuts, olive oil and pecorino cheese
puttanesca tomato, garlic, hot chilli, anchovies, capers

brodetto fish soup
frittata omelette
gnocchi small dumplings made from potato and flour or semolina
minestra soup
risotto rice cooked in stock
risotto ai funghi mushroom rissoto
risotto alla Milanese risotto with saffron
strufolone rolled pizza
uovo egg
zuppa soup

Bevande–Drinks

acqua minerale mineral water
birra beer
caffè corretto coffee with liqueur/spirit
caffè freddo iced coffee
caffè latte milky coffee
caffè lungo weak coffee
caffè macchiato coffee with a drop of milk
caffè ristretto strong coffee
digestivo after-dinner liqueur
dolce sweet
frizzante fizzy

Wild mushrooms, olive oil, fresh fish and yellow peppers

ragù minced meat, tomato and garlic
salsa di pomodoro tomato
salsa verde piquant/ vinaigrette

Specialità–Special Dishes

carpaccio thin-sliced raw beef served with a cold vinaigrette
coda alla vaccinara oxtail stew
osso bucco veal stewed with tomatoes, onions and garlic
pastiera Neapolitan Easter grain pie, filled with ricotta and flavoured with orange
peperonata sweet pepper (capsicum) and tomato stew
polpetti meatballs
saltimbocca veal escalopes with ham, sage and white wine
scaloppini thinly sliced veal cooked in white wine
stracotto beef stew
timballo baked meat and vegetable pie

Contorni–Side Dishes

insalata mista mixed salad
insalata tricolore mozzarella, tomato and fresh basil
insalata verde green salad
pane bread
patate fritte chips (french fries)
polenta maize-meal dish
riso rice

Altri Piatti–Other Dishes

antipasto misto mixed cold meats: salami, ham etc.

Dolci–Cakes/Desserts

cassata Sicilian fruit ice-cream
cioccolata chocolate
crema custard
macedonia fruit salad
panna cream
una pasta a cake/pastry
semifreddo chilled dessert made with ice cream
tiramisù chocolate/coffee sponge dessert
torta tart
zabaglione egg, sugar and Marsala dessert
zabaione di Verduzzo custard pudding with Friuli wine
zuccotto ice-cream sponge
zuppa inglese trifle

Frutti–Fruits

arancia orange
fragola strawberry
lampone raspberry
mela apple
melone melon
pera pear
pesca peach
pesca noci nectarine
uve grapes

Formagi–Cheeses

formaggio di capra goat's cheese
formaggio dolce mild cheese
formaggio nostrano local cheese
parmigiano Parmesan
pecorino Roman hard cheese, like Parmesan

ghiaccio ice
liquore liqueur
porto port wine
secco dry
spumante sparkling wine
succo di arancia orange juice
té tea
té al latte freddo tea with milk
té freddo iced tea
vini pregiati quality wines
vino bianco white wine
vino rosato rosé wine
vino rosso red wine
vino di tavalo house wine

Condimenti–Seasonings

aceto vinegar
aglio garlic
aromatiche herbs
basilico basil
capperi capers
pepe pepper
peperoncino chilli
prezzemolo parsley
rosemarino rosemary
sale salt
salvia sage
senape mustard
timo thyme
zucchero sugar

Il Conto–The Bill

coperto cover charge
IVA value-added tax (sales tax)
servizio compreso service charge included
servizio non compreso service charge not included

	LOCATION		LOCATION
Bruschetterie		**Jewish/Kosher**	
Bruschetteria degli Angeli	Campo dei Fiori	Da Paris	Trastevere
Bruschetteria Nonna Papera	Trevi	Giggetto al Portico d'Ottavia	Ghetto
		La Taverna del Ghetto	Ghetto
Cafés			
Antico Caffè della Pace	Piazza Navona	**Roman**	
Antico Caffe Greco	Piazza di Spagna	Agata e Romeo	S. Maria Maggiore
Babington's Tea Rooms	Piazza di Spagna	Al 34 (Tretaquattro)	Piazza di Spagna
Bar Capitolina	Campidoglio		
Bar Gianicolo	Monteverde		
Bar San Calisto	Trastevere		
Bibli	Trastevere		
Café Café	Colosseo		
Café dell'Arancia	Trastevere		
Café di Marzio	Trastevere		
Café Renault	Via Nazionale		
Da Benito	Ghetto		
Friends Art Café	Trastevere		
Non Solo Bevi	Colonna		
Offside Café	Monti		
Open Music Café	Via Latina		
Sant'Eustachio il Caffè	Pantheon		
Tazza d'Oro	Pantheon		
Trastè	Trastevere		

		Antonio al Pantheon *(above)*	Pantheon
Enoteche		Casetta de Trastevere	Trastevere
The Albert	Trevi	Checchino dal 1887	Testaccio
Antica Locanda	Monti	Pasqualino al Colosseo	Colosseo
La Barrique	Via Nazionale	Renato e Luisa	Campo dei Fiori
Cul de Sac	Piazza Navona	Sora Lella	Isola Tiberina
Il Goccetto	Campo dei Fiori	Otello alla Concordia	Via del Corso
Il Piccolo	Piazza Navona	Taverna 'Da Giovanni'	Castel S. Angelo
Trimani 'Il Winebar'	Termini	Taverna Parione	Piazza Navona
Vinarium	San Lorenzo	Tram Tram	San Lorenzo

		Pizzerie	
		Acqua, Farina e…	Trieste
		Almacrì	Trastevere
		Il Capriccio	Piazza Navona
		Corallo	Piazza Navona
		Da Baffetto	Piazza Navona
		Da Vittorio	Trastevere
		Dar Poeta	Trastevere
		Est! Est! Est!	Quirinale/Viminale
		Good Good	San Giovanni
		Ivo a Trastevere	Trastevere
		Leoncino	
		Panattoni (I Marmi) *(below)*	Trastevere

Vineria Reggio *(above)*	Campo dei Fiori	Pizza Ciro	Piazza S. Silvestro
Winetime	Corso Vittorio	Pizzarè	Via Veneto
		Pizzeria Popi Popi	Trastevere
Fish Restaurants		San Clemente	Colosseo
Alberto Ciarla	Trastevere	San Marino	Trieste
La Caraffa	Appio-Latina	Gran Caffè Martini e Rossi	Colosseo
F.I.S.H.	Monti	Pastarito Pizzarito	Trastevere
Grotte del Teatro di Pompeo	Campo dei Fiori	Pizzeria La Montecarlo	Piazza Navona
Pierluigi	Campo dei Fiori	Pizza Forum	Colosseo
Quinzi e Gabrieli	Piazza Navona		
Taverna Angelica	Vatican		

Gelaterie	
Da Quinto	Piazza Navona
Fassi – Palazzo del Freddo	Piazza Vittorio
Gelateria della Palma	Pantheon
Il Gelato di San Crispino	Trevi
Giolitti	Montecitorio
Tre Scalini	Piazza Navona

EATING OUT

Italian

	LOCATION
Al Bric	Campo dei Fiori
Al Ceppo	Parioli
Alfredo a Via Gabi	San Giovanni
Ambasciata d'Abruzzo	Parioli
Antico Arco	Monteverde
L'Archeologia	Via Appia Antica
Il Bacaro	Pantheon
Il Boom	Trastevere
Bramante	Piazza Navona
Il Brillo Parlante	Popolo
Cibus	Trastevere
Il Convivio	Piazza Navona
Il Cortile	Monteverde
Da Agusto	Trastevere
Da Settimio	Pantheon
Dal Toscano	Vatican
Edoardo II	Piazza Venezia
El Toulà	Augusto Imperatore
Evangelista	Ghetto
Gusto	Augusto Imperatore
Lumière di Sicilia	Monteverde
Maccheroni	Pantheon
Myosotis	Pantheon
Navona Notte	Piazza Navona
Nerone	Colosseo
Osteria dell'Anima	Piazza Navona
Il Pomodorino	Via Veneto
La Proposta	Giovanni
Il Pulcino Ballerino	San Lorenzo
Ristorante Da Nazzareno	Termini
Ristorante Giovanni	Via Veneto
Ristorante Nuova Stella	S. Maria Maggiore
Ristorante Papa Giulio	Via Giulia
Ristorante-Pizzeria Piacere Molise	Prati
Roof Garden 'Les Etoiles'	Prati
Romolo 'Nel Giardino di Raffaello el della Fornarina'	Trastevere
La Rosetta	Pantheon
Trattoria Abruzzese	Equilino/Viminale
Vecchia Roma	Musei Capitolini

Mediterranean

	LOCATION
La Terrazza	Via Veneto

Salads

Insalata Ricca	Campo dei Fiori

Spaghetterie

L'Archetto	Trevi
I Primi della Classe	Piazza Navona
T-Bone Station	Piazza Barberini, Piazza di Spagna
Il Trono dei Pazzi	S. Maria Maggiore

Roof Garden 'Les Etoiles'

Trattorie

Da Tre Amici	Pantheon
Ditirambo	Campo dei Fiori
Grappolo d'Oro/Zampanò	Castel Sant'Angelo
I Buoni Amici	San Giovanni
Da Francesco	Piazza Navona
Da Giovanni	Trastevere
Der Pallaro	Campo dei Fiori
Fiaschetteria Beltramme	Piazza di Spagna

Vegetarian

Il Margutta	Popolo
Il Tiepolo	Flaminio

International	LOCATION	TYPE
Hard Rock Café	Via Veneto	American
Baires	Piazza Navona	Argentinian
Ketumbar	Testaccio	Asian
Lowenhaus	Popolo	Bavarian
Un Cochon dans Mon Jardin	Parioli	French
L'Eau Vive	Piazza Navona	French
Charly's Saucière	San Giovanni	French
Ouzerie	Trastevere	Greek
Il Guru	Monti	Indian
Sitar	Colosseo	Indian
Osaka	San Giovanni	Japanese
Tapa Loca	Piazza Navona	Spanish
Thai Inn	Monteverde	Thai

Restaurants

The prices given are for a two-course lunch (L) for two people and a three-course dinner (D) for two people, without drinks. The wine price is the starting price for a bottle of wine.

ACQUA, FARINA E...
Map off 225 J2
Via Tripolitania 105–109, 00198
Tel 06 8632 4853
The speciality of this pizzeria is *strufoloni*—rolled pizza with traditional fillings, including mozzarella, courgette (zucchini) flowers and anchovies. Mozzarella with fried chicory is also superb. For dessert try *strufolone* spread with chocolate and sprinkled with coconut. It's outside central Rome, but the bus connections are good.
🕐 Daily 7.30–11.30; closed 8–25 Aug
🍴 D €24, Wine €11
Ⓢ Section
🚌 38, 60X to Viale Libia

AGATA E ROMEO
Map 224 H5
Via Carlo Alberto 45,
Tel 06 446 6115
Enjoy Roman and southern Italian dishes in this intimate and elegant restaurant. *Baccalà* (salt cod), smoked and cooked with an orange sauce, is just one of the delights on the menu, and is best accompanied by an Italian wine from their great wine list. Reservations essential.
🕐 Mon–Fri 1–2.30, 8–10.30; closed Aug and 2 weeks in Jan
🍴 L €80, D €130, Wine €25
Ⓢ
Ⓜ Vittorio Emanuele
🚌 4, 70, 71

AL 34 (TRENTAQUATTRO)
Map 223 E3
Via Mario de'Fiori
Tel 06 679 5091
This comfortable, intimate restaurant produces Roman and southern Italian meat and fish dishes using seasonal vegetables and herbs. The service is fast and efficient, great for those in a hurry. Al 34 is very popular, which means that reservations are essential.
🕐 Tue–Sun 12.30–3, 7.30–11; closed Aug
🍴 L €40, D €60, Wine €10
Ⓜ Spagna
🚌 116, 119

AL BRIC
Map 223 D5
Via del Pellegrino 51, 00186
Tel 06 687 9533
Very stylish *osteria* and wine bar with many small tables in a large room overlooking Via del Pellegrino, near Campo dei Fiori. The wine list is huge, with more than a thousand labels. The menu has a wide selection of creative dishes matched perfectly with wine suggestions. Try spaghetti with anchovies and pecorino cheese or pears with Gorgonzola cheese and the homemade bread. Among the desserts, don't miss the strudel with cinnamon ice cream.
🕐 Daily 7.30–11.30, Oct–end May; Tue–Sun 7.30–11.30, rest of year
🍴 D €80, Wine €8
🚌 64, 87, 492 to Largo Argentina; tram 8

AL CEPPO
Map 224 G2
Via Panama 2/4, 00198
Tel 06 841 9696
www.ristorantealceppo.it
In the residential Parioli district a few kilometres from central Rome is this fine restaurant specializing in grilled foods. There are three rooms, one of which is a lounge for your *aperitivo*. Dining rooms are furnished with chestnut benches, tasteful linen and lights made of Murano glass. The menu, which changes daily, places a special emphasis on the Marches region of Italy, although fish is served on Tue and Fri. The chargrilled ribeye steak with juniper berries, bay leaves and oregano is a real treat. Extensive wine cellar.
🕐 Tue–Sun 1–3, 8–11; closed Aug
🍴 L €38, D €98, Wine €13
Ⓢ Section
🚌 53, 360; tram 3, 19 to Piazza Ungheria

THE ALBERT
Map 223 F4
Via del Traforo 132, 00187
Tel 06 481 8795
This well-established English pub between the Spanish Steps and the Trevi Fountain is ideal for a break from sightseeing. Family run and with

ALBERTO CIARLA
Map 223 D6
Piazza San Cosimato 40, 00153
Tel 06 581 8668
www.albertociarla.com

Internationally reputed fish restaurant on the market piazza of San Cosimato in the district of Trastevere. Its rather retro and formal red and black, mirrored interior is being transformed into something more minimalist in style, but the innovative menu and supreme skills of master chef Alberto Ciarla remain. Bean soup with seafood, and lentils from Ponza with lobster are but two pearls in this sea. Six different tasting menus available if you simply can't choose. Vast wine cellar.
🕐 Mon–Sat 8–12.30
🍴 D €120, Wine €13
Ⓢ Section
🚌 H to Piazza Santa Maria in Trastevere, 115; tram 3, 8

friendly service, it provides a step back in time: The furniture is Victorian, and there is a fireplace and stained-glass ceilings. Well worth the stop for a proper pint or a lunch buffet at good prices. Afternoon tea, too. Credit cards are not accepted.
🕐 Mon–Fri 11am–2am, Sat 5pm–2am, Sun 7pm–2am
🍴 Salad bar €6, pint €5, spirits €4.50

EATING

⊖ Barberini
🚌 116, 117, or any bus to Piazza San Silvestro

ALFREDO A VIA GABI
Map 224 H7
Via Gabi 36/38, 00183
Tel 06 7720 6792
www.alfredoaviagabi.it

It is well worth venturing out of the *centro storico* for this one. Only 1.5km (1 mile) from the basilica of San Giovanni in Laterano, it's the perfect retreat after a day of looking around churches. It retains a smart 1950s ambience: handsome, dark wood panelling and carved screens, crisp white linen, brass candelabras and a profusion of fresh flowers. The Italian cuisine is refreshingly original, such as pasta with wild mushroom sauce, a baked dish of anchovy and artichoke, and zabaglione mousse.

🕐 Wed–Mon noon–3, 8–11; closed Aug
🍽 L €40, D €50, Wine €5
Ⓢ Section
Ⓜ Re di Roma
🚌 87, 360

ALMACRÌ
Map 223 D7
Via F. Benaglia 3, 00153
Tel 06 589 5651
www.almacri.it

Don't be misled by its stylish furniture and popularity—this Trastevere restaurant is excellent value whether you choose pizza, pasta or meat. Pizzas are huge, with traditional or creative toppings. The *tagliata di pollo* (grilled chicken) served with salad and cherry tomatoes is recommended. Roast potatoes are rich on garlic, salads vast and crisp, and the desserts good. The wine list is negligible—it's better to choose from the 26 bottled beers. Reservations are essential.

🕐 Tue–Sun 7.30–2
🍽 D €48, Wine €4
Ⓢ Section
🚌 H, 23, 44, 56, 75, 280; tram 8 to Viale Trastevere

AMBASCIATA D'ABRUZZO
Map 224 G2
Via Pietro Tacchini 26, 00197
Tel 06 807 8256
www.ambasciata-di-abruzzo.it

This restaurant in smart Parioli district is well known for its dishes from the Abruzzo. The region (east of Lazio) is renowned for its hams and cheeses, hence the astounding antipasti here, a meal in itself: salamis, fresh sheep's milk ricotta, buffalo mozzarella, a plate of Abruzzo cured ham, fried vegetables, a soufflé of potatoes and jellied veal's head. They also do a sampler of practically everything on the menu for €30. Seating available outside in summer.

🕐 Daily 12–4, 7–midnight
🍽 L €40, D €65, Wine €7
Ⓢ Section
🚌 56, 910 to Via Antonelli and Viale Bruno Buozzi

ANTICA LOCANDA
Map 223 F5
Via del Boschetto 85, 00184
Tel 06 4788 1729
www.antica-locanda.com

Brick walls, oak beams and candlelight make this a delightful place in which to spend an evening sampling fine wines from all over Italy. Just a 10-minute walk from the Forum in the heart of one of the city's oldest quarters. A limited but good selection of

food: pasta, mixed vegetables and daily specials. Two good Chardonnays to try are the Tenuta Santa Anna and the Prinè Chardonnay Barrique. For reds, try the Cabernet Bosco del Merlo. Wines are sold by the glass or bottle.

🕐 Tue–Sun 11am–1am, Mon 11am–8pm
🍽 L €24, D €40, Wine €10
Ⓜ Cavour
🚌 117, or any bus to Via Nazionale

ANTICO ARCO
Map 222 C6
Piazzale Aurelio 7, 00152
Tel 06 581 5274

Sample modern cuisine inside an 18th-century palazzo on the Gianicolo Hill. Antico Arco attracts international accolades for dishes such as pheasant

ANTICO CAFFÈ DELLA PACE
Map 223 D4
Via della Pace 3/7, 00186
Tel 06 686 1216

A real Roman institution just off Piazza Navona—a Liberty-style (art nouveau) café, with marble interior and wrought-iron tables under an ivy cascade outside. Attracts the showbiz crowd when they are in Rome, including Robert De Niro, Mel Gibson, Sophia Loren and Madonna. Possibly the last stronghold of *la dolce vita*. Good for light meals or an *aperitivo*. Credit cards are not accepted.

🕐 Daily 8am–midnight
🍽 Cocktail from €10, sandwich from €7
Ⓢ
🚌 46, 62, 64, 87, 116, 492 to Piazza Navona

breast with truffles on a potato tart, spaghetti with cheese, pepper and courgette (zucchini) flowers, and Sicilian cassata made from ricotta cheese. The extensive wine list contains over 400 labels.

🕐 Mon–Sat 12.30–3, 7.30–midnight; closed Aug
🍽 L €30, D €75, Wine €9
Ⓢ Section
🚌 44, 870

EATING

ANTICO CAFFÈ GRECO

Map 223 E4
Via dei Condotti 86
Tel 06 679 1700

This famous old café was founded in 1767 by a Greek, hence the name. It has always been popular with the rich and famous, and numbered Keats, Byron and Goethe among its clientele. Look for pictures of some of the café's well-known past customers in the back room.

🕒 Daily 8–8
🍴 Coffee from €4.75, cake €6.20 (table service only)
🚇 Spagna
🚌 119 to Piazza di Spagna, or 52, 58, 61, 71, 85, 160 to Piazza San Silvestro

ANTONIO AL PANTHEON

Map 223 E4
Via dei Pastini 12, 00186
Tel 06 679 0798

Family-run restaurant in a pedestrian street near the Pantheon. Large, brick-vaulted room with 1960s paintings adorning the walls. The food is quintessentially Roman and

the clientele local. Try the fresh fettuccine with creamy walnut sauce and, for a main course, the calves liver cooked in chilli, olive oil and wine. The portions are very generous and the service is a joy.

🕒 Mon–Sat noon–3, 7–11; closed 2 weeks in Aug
🍴 L €20, D €30, Wine €8
🚌 40, 62, 64, or any bus to Piazza Navona and Corso Vittorio Emanuele II

L'ARCHEOLOGIA

Map 224 G7
Via Appia Antica 139, 00178
Tel 06 788 0494
www.larcheologia.it

Near the catacombs on the Appian Way, this elegant restaurant has three dining rooms and a garden full of ancient statues. Open fires and warm hues make for a luxuriant setting. Dishes from the

Lazio region are served: roast veal stuffed with pancetta and a black truffle sauce, and *fettuccine alla catullo* (seafood pasta) are two winners. Try the Virtu Romane white wine—at €11 it's worth twice the price. Finish off with a visit to the medieval wine cellar.

🕒 Wed–Mon 12.30–3, 8–11
🍴 L €60, D €80, Wine €6
🚇 Section
🚌 218 to Catacombe di San Callisto

L'ARCHETTO

Map 223 E4
Via dell'Archetto 26, 00186
Tel 06 678 9064

Serves pizza and grilled meat, but, most of all, spaghetti— there are more than 100 different kinds to choose from and portions are always generous. Dishes range from traditional recipes such as carbonara and *spaghetti alle vongole* (with clams) to more creative incarnations: The lemon spaghetti is especially good. There area a few tables outside, plus vaulted ceilings and arches inside. Excellent fruit salad.

🕒 Daily 12–3, 7–1
🍴 L €32, D €50, Wine €4
🚇
🚌 117, 119, or any bus to Piazza Venezia or Via del Corso

BABINGTON'S TEA ROOMS

Map 223 E3
Piazza di Spagna 23, 00186
Tel 06 678 6027

The area around the Spanish Steps has been a magnet for

BAR CAPITOLINA

Map 223 E5
Piazzale Caffarelli 4, 00186

What many don't know is that you can access the bar of the Musei Capitolini without actually visiting the museum. It's worth having a drink or lunch here because, apart from reasonable prices, it has a large terrace with stunning views of the Tarpeian Rock and ancient Rome. Guests with disabilities should ask for lift access, as it is quite a climb up. The way in to the bar is via the museum exit on Piazzale Caffarelli (look carefully: there are no signs outside).

🕒 Tue–Sun 9–8; closed 1 Jan, 1 May, 25 Dec
🍴 Roll, sandwich and salad: inside €19 (terrace €28), wine €7.75, Coffee €1.30 (terrace €4)
🚇 Section
🚌 40, 64, 87, 628 to Piazza Venezia, or 40, 62, 63, 64, 492, 571, 628, 916 to Teatro di Marcello

British visitors since the days of the Grand Tour. This very British tearoom was opened by two spinsters in 1896 to cater for homesick visitors. Today, you can still enjoy a pot of Earl Grey with your afternoon tea, but you will also see American food, such as pancakes and maple syrup. Brunch is served all day.

🕒 Wed–Mon 9–8.15
🍴 Brunch €68
🚇 Spagna
🚌 116, 119

IL BACARO

Map 223 E4
Via degli Spagnoli 27, 00186
Tel 06 686 4110

Near the Pantheon, this restaurant is ideal for a romantic dinner, especially in summer when you can dine outdoors under a roof of ivy vines. The creative cuisine is strongly based on seasonal products, including rigatoni pasta with blue Stilton and Brussels sprouts, and beef fillet cooked with Merlot wine. Among the home-made pastries, the flaky, creamy *millefoglie sbriciolato con crema pasticcera* (millefoglie crumble with a creamy sauce) is sublime. Excellent

EATING

wine and cheese lists. Reservations recommended.

🕐 Mon–Fri 1–3.30, 7.30–11.30, Sat 7.30–11.30; closed 1 week in Aug

🍷 L €60, D €84, Wine €8

Ⓢ Section

🚌 64, 87, 492 to Largo Argentina; tram 8

BAIRES

Map 223 E5
Corso Rinascimento 1, 00186
Tel 06 686 1293
www.baires.it

The bright walls and floors, as well as the sounds of tango, create a South American atmosphere just behind Piazza Navona. Argentinian grilled meat served with various

sauces form the menu. Starters include marinated chicken (pollo all'escabeche), and there's a wide choice of salads and soups. Unsurprisingly, the wine list focuses on Argentina; the house red and white are organic.

🕐 Daily 12–3.30, 7.30–midnight

🍷 L €40, D €60, Wine €12

🚌 87, 116, 492

BAR GIANICOLO

Map 222 C6
Piazzale Aurelio 5, 00152
Tel 06 580 6275

This coffee shop is a Roman institution. Families flock here after weekend excursions in the Gianicolo park. At night, young people buzz in and out, but visitors may feel more welcome in the afternoon than later on. The menu includes fresh apple and carrot juice,

small pizzas and light sandwiches. The blasé staff do wait on the tables, but may need some prompting; opt for bar service if you're in a hurry. Credit cards are not accepted.

🕐 Tue–Sun 6am–1am

🍷 Espresso 75c; fresh juice 50c

🚌 44

BAR SAN CALISTO

Map 223 D6
Piazza San Calisto 4, 00153
Tel 06 583 5869

Join the rowdy night-time crowd in Piazza San Calisto and sample Bar San Calisto's famous affogato (ice-cream drizzled with liqueur). The vodka-lemon sorbet is especially sought after. The scene is calmer during the day. The bar, nicknamed Marcello's, serves inexpensive coffee, beer and ice-cream from cramped, utilitarian premises. It's glamorous in a gritty way: a true slice of old Trastevere. Credit cards are not accepted.

🕐 Daily 5.30am–2am; closed end Aug

🍷 Coffee 80c, ice cream €1–2

🚌 H, 63, 75

LA BARRIQUE

Map 224 F5
Via del Boschetto 41/b, 00184
Tel 06 4782 5953

A wine bar, particularly loved by theatregoers, just off Via Nazionale. Ideal for a light but sophisticated dinner; for a romantic evening, reserve the tiny mezzanine floor with the

sofa. Creative cooking, with every dish designed for a perfectly matched wine. Desserts change daily, but the mousses are always mouth-watering. The ample wine list includes a good choice of wine by the glass.

🕐 Mon–Fri 11–3, 6–2, Sat 6pm–2am

🍷 L €20, D €40 Wine €2 (by the glass)

Ⓜ Repubblica or Cavour

🚌 30X, 64

BIBLI

Map 223 D6
Via dei Fienaroli 28, 00153
Tel 06 588 4097
www.bibli.it

This Trastevere bookshop-cum-cafeteria is particularly popular for Sun brunch. A selection of pastas, quiches, couscous with vegetables and other vegetarian dishes are served buffet

style. Among the homemade cakes, poppy seed is very popular. The wine list is limited, but the choice of teas and herbal infusions is so vast as to make this a perfect place for an afternoon reviver. There is also a tiny courtyard for hot summer nights.

🕐 Daily 11am–midnight (café and Sat–Sun brunch); Mon 7.30–11.30 buffet-style dinner

🍷 Brunch €32, D €40, tea €5

🚌 H, 23, 44, 56, 75, 280; tram 8 to Viale Trastevere or Piazza Sonnino

IL BOOM

Map 223 D6
Via dei Fienaroli 30a, 00153
Tel 06 5897196
www.ilboom.it

Italian 1960s atmosphere, with an original jukebox and photos of la dolce vita celebrities hanging on the walls of this Trastevere ristorante. The granmisto is a selection of different starters, from fried vegetables to creative bruschette (toasted bread). Gnocchetti sardi pasta with rocket (arugula) and ricotta is a speciality. The wine list focuses on southern Italy, but there are also Passiti and Malvasie to complement the homemade desserts.

🕐 Mon–Sat 7.30–midnight

🍷 D €50, Wine €8

Ⓢ

🚌 H, 44, 780; tram 3, 8

BRAMANTE

Map 223 D4
Via della Pace 25, 00186
Tel 06 6880 3916

The setting of this chic bar/restaurant, complete with an art nouveau window, could scarcely be bettered: It's on one of the city's most prestigious and beautiful baroque squares, Piazza Navona. Inside, you could be in a Tuscan-style villa, softly lit with oil lamps; the walls are frescoed with

local scenes and classical music plays. Unfortunately, the cuisine is not the most imaginative, especially for the above average prices. But the service is first class.

🕐 Mon–Sat 6.30am–2pm, Sun 12.30–2
🍴 L €25, D €50, Wine €11
🚌 46, 62, 64, 87, 116, 492 to Piazza Navona

IL BRILLO PARLANTE

Map 223 E3
Via della Fontanella 12, 00186
Tel 06 324 3334
www.ilbrilloparlante.com

Wine bar with a selection of cheeses and salami served on the wood counter upstairs, and restaurant with vaulted ceilings and five small rooms below. Popular among the locals. Excellent grilled Danish meat and also fish. The pizzas are

good but not memorable. Among the homemade desserts, the chocolate tart and tiramisu are great, but it's

worth coming for the pear mousse alone. Excellent wine list—a choice of 300 for every budget. Tables outside during the summer.

🕐 Tue–Sun 12.30–3.30, 7.30–1; closed 1 week in Aug
🍴 L €30, D €50, Wine €12
Ⓜ Flaminio
🚌 117, 119

BRUSCHETTERIA DEGLI ANGELI

Map 223 E5
Piazza B. Cairoli 2/a, 00186
Tel 06 6880 5789

Just behind Campo dei Fiori, this eatery offers an alternative to pizza. Huge *bruschette* (toasted breads) are served with over 50 different toppings, from tomatoes and rocket (arugula) salad to Asiago cheese and *speck* (bacon), plus pasta dishes and huge salads. The international

beer list is ample. Tables are available outside during the summer. Paper tablecloths and warm wooden furniture contribute to the rustic image.

🕐 Mon–Sat noon–3, 7–1, Sun 7pm–1am, Sep–end Jun; daily 7pm–1am, rest of year
🍴 *Bruschette* from €16, beer from €2.50
Ⓢ Section
🚌 64, 87, 492 to Largo Argentina; tram 8

BRUSCHETTERIA NONNA PAPERA

Map 223 F4
Via dei Modelli 60, 00186
Tel 06 678 3510

In a tiny alley behind the Trevi Fountain is this eatery, with country-style wooden furniture, cherry tomatoes hanging from the ceiling, and ceramic decorative tiles. Huge *bruschette* with all sorts of toppings, including a lovely version with ham and chicory, plus savoury crêpes with artichoke cream or salmon: A good idea for a light lunch.

🕐 Tue–Sun noon–3, 7–10
🍴 *Bruschette* €6.50, D €40, Wine €9
Ⓢ
🚌 40, 64, 87, 628 to Piazza Venezia, or any bus through Via del Corso

I BUONI AMICI

Map 224 H6
Via Aleardo Aleardi 4, 00185
Tel 06 7049 1993

This trattoria near San Giovanni in Laterano is one of the best-value restaurants in Rome, despite its celebrity clientele. Traditional interior design, with red-and-white checked tablecloths. Delicious antipasti include aubergines (eggplant), courgettes (zucchini), spinach and squid salad. Try the fresh pasta with lobster and some chargrilled fish to follow, or the roast lamb. Leave room for the home-made tiramisu and *pannacotta*. The Cannonau red from Sardinia is a bargain at only €8 a bottle.

🕐 Mon–Sat 12.30–3, 7.30–11
🍴 L €24, D €45, Wine €4
Ⓜ Manzoni
🚌 16, 81, 87, 117, 714

CAFÉ CAFÉ

Map 224 G6
Via dei SS. Quattro 44, 00184
Tel 06 700 8743

Escape the tourist traps encircling the Colosseum and relax in bohemian elegance at this café/restaurant. The Swedish owner serves up coffee, cakes, fresh juice, homemade ice-cream and light Italian fare. Expect hand-lettered menus, bright walls and soft jazz. The tiny place fills up quickly for Sun brunch, a €12 buffet of crunchy salads, *bruschette*, cheese and prosciutto. Highly recommended for vegetarians and vegans, plus for visitors on their own, who will delight in the generous pile of newspapers.

🕐 Tue–Sun 10am–2am; closed Aug
🍴 L €10, D €15, Wine €12.50

CAFÉ DI MARZIO

Map 223 D6
Piazza Santa Maria in Trastevere 15, 00153
Tel 06 581 6095

Sip exquisite coffee or hot chocolate facing the golden façade of Santa Maria in Trastevere. Of course, the see-and-be-seen outdoor tables are costly; visitors on a budget should go inside and enjoy an espresso at the bar, then soak in the view from the fountain steps. Di Marzio is also popular enough to be able to accept large notes (bills)—a lifesaver here in the land of correct change.

🕐 Tue–Sun 7am–2am
🍺 Coffee from 75c inside (€2 outside)
🚌 H, 63, 75 to Via Trastevere

🚇
🚇 Colosseo

CAFÉ DELL'ARANCIA

Map 223 D6
Piazza Santa Maria in Trastevere 2, 00153
Tel 338 110 8064

There's a good reason this café/gelateria/cocktail bar is called the café of oranges: Sitting out under the canopy, you are surrounded by baskets of the fruit. It's the perfect place to pass an hour or two people-watching in the Piazza di Santa Maria in Trastevere,

and what better way to enjoy the square than with the house special, a Campari citrus cocktail served in a giant crystal flute? A range of citrus cocktails, as well as coffee and ice-cream are available. Credit cards are not accepted.

🕐 Daily 10am–1.30am; closed Dec–Jan
🍺 Cocktails €8, ice cream €8
🚌 23; tram 8

CAFÉ RENAULT

Map 223 F5
Via Nazionale 183/b, 00184
Tel 06 4782 4452
www.cafe-renault.it

A vast, high-tech café right in front of Banca d'Italia on Via Nazionale, with metal chairs, leather sofas and holograms on the tabletops. Self-service cafeteria with light lunches

during the day and great cocktails (their mojito is made with mint, lime, rum and tonic water) and also a full restaurant menu in the evenings. Occasional live music (especially lounge-style) and multimedia events connected with the car manufacturer that gives the café its name.

🕐 Mon–Sun 8am–2am
🍺 L €16, D €60, Wine €12
🚇 Section
🚇 Repubblica or Termini
🚌 30X, 64

IL CAPRICCIO

Map 223 D5
Via della Pace 27/a, 00186
Tel 06 6880 4458

Pizza a taglio (cut pizza) to go is a Roman institution. This establishment is just along from Piazza Navona. You decide how much they should slice off the large rectangular tray-baked pizzas and then pay by weight—no slice is too small. Other tasty morsels are the olives *ascolane* (large green olives, stuffed with meat and herbs and deep fried), or

suppli, which are deep-fried tomato risotto and cheese balls. Credit cards are not accepted.

🕐 Tue–Sun midday–2am; closed 2 weeks in Feb, end Aug
🍕 Pizza slice approx. €1.50 per 100g/4oz, beer €3.50
🚇
🚌 46, 62, 64, 87, 116, 492 to Piazza Navona

LA CARAFFA

Map off 225 J7
Via Giovanni Villani 44, 00179
Tel 06 786 513

This fish restaurant bordering the archaeological park of the Appian Way is one of Rome's best-kept secrets. People come to sample its simple, inexpensive but excellent fish dishes, served in two dining rooms and on a covered terrace. The huge seafood and vegetable buffet immediately catches the eye. Best known for its *spaghetti alla scogliera*, a mountain of seafood on a bed of spaghetti, served on a silver platter—easily enough for two. Visa only accepted.

🕐 Daily 12.30–3, 7.30–1; closed 1 week in Aug
🍺 L €28, D €50, Wine €5
🚇 Section
🚇 Furio Camillo
🚌 87, 628

CASETTA DÈ TRASTEVERE

Map 223 D6
Piazza Dé Renzi 31/a–32, 00153
Tel 06 580 0158
www.casettaditrastevere.com

Enter this ordinary-looking restaurant on a quiet little piazza, and inside is another piazza bright with red-and-white checked tablecloths and washing hanging from lines—a life-size re-creation of a Roman square. It's on two levels—you can sit in the house balconies and watch the piazza below. Unsurprising but remarkably inexpensive menu: *Rigatoni della casetta* is nicely al dente,

EATING

and incorporates porcini mushrooms, sausage and cheese. Vegetarian dishes available. There are tables outside on the real piazza, too.

🕐 Daily noon–3, 7.30–11
🍽 L €30, D €50, Wine €6
Ⓢ Section outside
🚌 H, 23, 280, 780 to Lungotevere Ponte Sisto; tram 8

CHARLY'S SAUCIÈRE
Map 224 H6
Via di San Giovanni in Laterano 270, 00184
Tel 06 7049 5666
This well-established restaurant specializes in French and Swiss cuisine, which is served by professional, attentive staff. As you might expect, French wine is prominent on the carefully selected wine list.

🕐 Mon–Sat 12.45–2.15, 8–midnight; closed 1 week in Aug
🍽 L €40, D €70, Wine €12
Ⓜ Mazzini
🚌 85, 117, 850

CHECCHINO DAL 1887
Map off 223 E7
Via di Monte Testaccio 30, 00153
Tel 06 574 6318
www.checchino-dal-1887.com
Although it lies outside central Rome, the Checchino dal 1887 is well worth the trip. In the cool, vaulted restaurant you can sample traditional Roman cuisine, including *bue garofolato*, a rustic dish of beef, which is exclusive to this establishment. All this can be accompanied by a choice from Rome's best wine list. Reservations are essential.

🕐 Tue–Sat 12.30–3, 8–midnight; closed 1 week in Aug plus Christmas and New Year
🍽 L €50, D €80, Wine €14
Ⓜ Piramide
🚌 23, 75, 280, 716 to Piramide or Via Marmorata

CIBUS
Map 223 D6
Via della Scala 8, 00153
Tel 06 581 6317
www.delicious.it
Right in the heart of Trastevere, this little restaurant serves traditional cuisine with a creative touch. Under the arches, jazz and lounge music plays in the background. Try the *paccheri* pasta with truffle and duck ragoût or with aubergine (eggplant) and oregano. Fish dishes are a speciality; pasta,

IL CONVIVIO
Map 223 D4
Vicolo dei Soldati 31, 00186
Tel 06 686 9432
www.ilconviviotroiani.com

The interior of this restaurant, down a narrow cobbled street behind Palazzo Altemps in the heart of Rome, is high-tech and gloriously spacious. Service is excellent. The *degustazione* (tasting) menu includes a bit of everything. While the creative regional menu changes frequently. If available, try the courgette (zucchini) flowers filled with porcini mushrooms and goat's cheese, or the rabbit stuffed with olives and sausage with a fennel sauce. Choice wine list—more than 2,000 different bottles.

🕐 Tue–Sat 1–2.30, 8–10.30, Mon 8–10.30
🍽 L €50, D €150, Wine €30
Ⓢ Section
🚌 46, 62, 64, 87, 116, 492 to Piazza Navona

desserts and some of the bread are home-made. The wine list comprises more than 100 different labels, plus a large selection of distillates and liqueurs. Tables outside during the summer.

🕐 Mon–Sat 7.30–11.30; closed first half of Aug
🍽 D €80, Wine €15
Ⓢ
🚌 23, 280 to Piazza Trilussa; tram 3, 8

UN COCHON DANS MON JARDIN
Map off 224 G2
Via G. Antonelli 30, 00199
Tel 06 807 3968
www.uncochon.it
In the Parioli district (north of Villa Borghese). The two floors are decorated with frescoes representing country life, but in

spite of the name, no French cuisine is served here. Starters are creative and delicious: spinach and cheese flan, for instance, or fried artichokes with potatoes. Grilled meat, imported from Argentina, is the speciality. Pasta and rice are also very good, especially risotto with chicory and Barolo red wine. Excellent wine list but the house wines are good.

🕐 Sun–Fri 12.30–3, 7.30–midnight, Oct–end May; Sat–Sun 7.30–midnight, rest of year
🍽 L €14, D €30, Wine €8
Ⓢ Section
🚌 56, 910 to Piazza Euclide

CORALLO
Map 223 D4
Via del Corallo 10, 00186
Tel 06 6830 7703
This restaurant/pizzeria is divided into different rooms, all with a maritime theme and a quiet atmosphere ideal for a calm meal. Very thin pizza baked in a wood oven is the house special, and the focaccia is very popular. The beef filet is also delicious and perfectly cooked, and there's fresh fish on Tuesday and Friday. Reservations advised. Tables outside in summer.

🕐 Daily 7.30–1, Oct–end Apr
🍽 D €40, Wine €8
🚌 64, 87, 492 to Largo Argentina; tram 8

IL CORTILE
Map off 222 C7
Via Felice Cavallotti 46, 00152
Tel 06 580 3433
The antipasto buffet here is legendary: plump button mushrooms, marinated bell peppers, grilled aubergines (eggplant), bean salad, caramelized onions and breaded courgette (zucchini) strips are just a few of the delights. The first and second courses don't compare, so load up on starters and skip to the desserts. The atmosphere is elegant yet congenial, especially at the candlelit outdoor tables of this Monteverde restaurant.

🕐 Tue–Sat noon–3, 8–11, Sun noon–3; closed Aug
🍽 L €40, D €80, Wine €5
Ⓢ Section
🚌 44

DA AGUSTO

Map 223 D6
Piazza de' Renzi 15, 00153
Tel 06 580 3798

This is what cheap and cheerful Roman dining is all about. Sit outside in summer at folding wooden tables with paper tablecloths, on which your bill will be scribbled at the end of the evening. Inside is rather cramped and a little chilly in winter. Spontaneous singing often breaks out and a carafe of the house wine aids appreciation. The *pasta e fagioli* (thick borlotti bean soup with pasta) and gnocchi are well worth crossing the Tiber for. Credit cards are not accepted.

🕐 Mon–Fri 12.30–3, 8–11, Sat 12.30–3; closed mid-Aug–mid-Sep

🍴 L €16, D €30, Wine €5

Ⓢ Section

🚌 H, 23, 280, 780 to Lungotevere Ponte Sisto; tram 8

CUL DE SAC

Map 223 D5
Piazza Pasquino 73, 00186
Tel 06 6880 1094

Very close to Piazza Navona, Cul de Sac was originally just a wine bar but has gradually

built a reputation for food as well, with skilfully suggested food/wine combos. It's well known for its pâtés: Two fine

examples are the sweet and sour wild boar pâté and the veal and tabasco pâté; all are served with toasted bread (€8). The interior is reminiscent of a 1950s train, furnished in beautiful solid white wood. Thirty-five wines are available by the glass and over 1,400 varieties are in stock.

🕐 Daily noon–4, 7–12.30

🍴 L €25, D €37, Wine €8

🚌 46, 62, 64, 87, 116, 492 to Piazza Navona

DA BAFFETTO

Map 223 D5
Via del Governo Vecchio 114, 00186
Tel 06 686 1617

Eat early, or if you come later be prepared to wait like a Roman, joining the exuberant mob outside one of the capital's best pizzerias. Sixties radicals frequented Da Baffetto; now the whole world vies for a seat at this straightforward establishment. Don't miss the savoury *bruschetta al*

pomodoro (toasted bread topped with tomato, basil and olive oil). Be prepared for more genial jostling at the outdoor tables, and long waits for the superb pizzas. Credit cards are not accepted.

🕐 Daily 6.30pm–1am

🍴 D €30, Wine €5

🚌 46, 62, 64, 87, 116, 492 to Campo dei Fiori

DA BENITO

Map 223 E5
Via dei Falegnami 14, 00186
Tel 06 686 1508

Very friendly, family-run spot in a quiet, cobblestone side street near Largo Argentina. Serves hot and cold food cafeteria style; just choose and point, then take it to your table. When you've finished, simply tell the cashier what you had. There are always a couple of fresh specials of the day, including homemade

pasta. A plateful of assorted mixed vegetables with olive oil dribbled over, together with *polpette* (meatballs), makes a perfect quick lunch. Credit cards are not accepted.

🕐 Mon–Sat 6.30am–7.30pm

🍴 L €16, D €20, Wine €5

Ⓢ Between 12pm and 3pm

🚌 64, 87, 492 to Largo Argentina; tram 8

DA FRANCESCO

Map 223 D4
Piazza del Fico 29, 00186
Tel 06 686 4009

Set on a jewel of a square just a few minutes from Piazza Navona, this trattoria is very popular with locals (expect to wait if you come after 8pm). With paper tablecloths and no frills, the best tables are outside. Try their fantastic focaccia with Parma ham, which is served alongside the vegetable and fish buffet. Shellfish pastas are good (Tuesday and Friday), as is the porcini mushroom pasta. Pizzas are available evenings only (from €5). Good draught beer and house wine. Credit cards are not accepted.

🕐 Wed–Mon noon–3, 7–1, Tue 7pm–1am

🍴 L €30, D €60, Wine €7

🚌 46, 62, 64, 87, 116, 492 to Piazza Navona

DA GIOVANNI

Map 222 C5
Via della Lungara 41/a, 00165
Tel 06 686 1514

Artists' hangout on the edge of Trastevere. Prices are unbelievably low and the cooking is good, plain Roman fare. It's tiny and you can't make reservations, so come as close to opening time as possible. The menu changes daily but *fettuccine al sugo* (pasta with simple tomato sauce) is always there. Try the pasta with chickpeas or borlotti beans if you can. House wine doesn't cost much more than water.

EATING

🕐 Mon–Sat noon–3, 7–10; closed Aug
🍴 L €20, D €30, Wine €8
🚌 23, 280 to Ponte Mazzini

DA PARIS
Map 223 D6
Piazza San Callisto 7a
Tel 06 581 5378

This great restaurant serving Jewish food near Santa Maria in Trastevere, is known for its fish and pasta, are particularly for the traditional Roman dish of *trippa alla romano* (tripe in the Roman style). All this is accompanied by an excellent wine list. There is a small terrace in front, where meals are served in warm weather. Reservations essential.

🕐 Tue–Sat noon–3, 7.30–11, Sun noon–3
🍴 L €40, D €80, Wine €10
🚌 75, tram 8

DA QUINTO
Map 223 D4
Via di Tor Millina 15, 00186
Tel 06 686 5657

Five siblings run this small, idiosyncratic *gelateria* just beside Piazza Navona. Family photos plaster the walls, alongside foreign currency and soccer pennants. The ice-creams are light and icy, especially the fruit ones (try

the lemon and pistachio), and the scoops are generous. Served alongside smoothies, banana splits and fruit cups. Mainly takeaway, as seating is limited to a narrow wooden bench. Credit cards are not accepted.

🕐 Daily 11am–2am; occasionally closed Wed in winter
🍴 Ice cream from €1.50
🚫
🚌 62, 64, 87, 116, 492 to Piazza Navona

DAI TRE AMICI
Map 223 E5
Via della Rotonda 8, 00186
Tel 06 687 5239

Unpretentious trattoria in a 16th-century building just behind the magnificent Pantheon. Epitomizes the Roman spirit of dining—lots of noise and organized chaos. Waiters weave their way through the packed tables with dishes such as *farfalle alla calabrese* (pasta with garlic, butter and cheese) followed by wafer-thin beef with porcini mushrooms. Beamed ceilings, wicker chairs and simple wooden tables. The antipasto buffet is extensive and great for vegetarians. Fresh fish Tuesday and Friday. Best to make a reservation or go before 8pm.

🕐 Daily noon–3, 7–midnight
🍴 L €20, D €44, Wine €8
🚫
🚌 116, or any bus to Largo Argentina, such as 64, 87, 492

DA SETTIMIO
Map 223 E4
Via delle Colonnelle 14, 00186
Tel 06 678 9651

Wrought-iron flourishes and sprawling piles of fruit greet you at this vivid gem of a restaurant by the Pantheon. Graffiti covers the walls, old beams and terracotta tiles. The fare is simple but spot on,

---

including the best *penne all'arrabiata* (pasta with fiery chilli, tomato and garlic sauce) in town, and superb truffles and game dishes. Reserve a table for dinner, as both tiny rooms quickly overflow with cheerful customers.

🕐 Tue–Sat noon–3, 7.30–11.30; closed Aug
🍴 L €60, D €60, Wine €8
🚫 Section
🚌 116, or any bus to Largo Argentina, such as 64, 87, 492

DA VITTORIO
Map 223 D6
Via di San Cosimato 14, 00153
Tel 06 580 0353

Pizzeria serving endearingly heart-shaped and incredibly tasty Neapolitan pizzas. Start with the mixed antipasti and oil-drenched crust called *pizza bianca*. Many dishes have this as a base, sprinkled only with mozzarella, but Vittorio will also indulge customers craving a sauce, as with the festive bouquet of rocket (arugula) and cherry tomatoes on the pizza Margherita. Reservations are crucial, as the tiny, blue-lit nook fills quickly. Look for sultry Sophia Loren among the celebrity gallery on the walls. Credit cards are not accepted.

🕐 Mon–Sat 7.30–midnight
🍴 D €20, Wine €4
🚌 H, 63, 75

DAL TOSCANO
Map 222 C3
Via Germanico 58, 00192
Tel 06 3972 5717
www.ristorantedaltoscano.it

Family-run restaurant in the Prati district, close to the Vatican, serving Tuscan cuisine. Efficient service in a pleasant, vaulted room with traditional wooden furniture; shaded terrace in summer. The pappardelle pasta with wild boar sauce is a Tuscan treat, as are the huge chargrilled Fiorentina steaks or the thinly sliced beef cooked with wine and salad leaves. Accompany it all with a glass of superb Chianti.

🕐 Tue–Sun 12.30–3, 8–11; closed Aug
🍴 L €30, D €70, Wine €11
Ⓜ Ottaviano

DER PALLARO

Map 223 D5
Largo der Pallaro 15, 00186
Tel 06 6880 1488

Traditional Roman cooking in a timeless trattoria right behind Campo dei Fiori. No need to choose from a menu, as the waiter will bring you everything that's on that day, from starter to dessert, for the price of €19, including house wine. The cooking is simple but good, and the portions generous. Excellent choice for late dinners. In summer you can eat outside in the square. Credit cards are not accepted.

🕐 Tue–Sun 12–4, 7.30–1; closed 2 weeks in Aug

🍴 L€38 D €38 (includes house wine)

🚌 64, 87, 492 to Largo Argentina; tram 8

DAR POETA

Map 223 D6
Vicolo del Bologna 45, 00153
Tel 06 588 0516

Be sure to maintain your place in line at this casual pizzeria, undisputedly one of the city's best. It serves up traditional toppings, as well as eccentric

combinations such as apple and Grand Marnier. The chefs shun the typical Roman thin crust, preferring soft, dripping pizza on a slow-risen base. Dar Poeta skips the frills (no

reservations, and the bill is scrawled on the tablecloth), and concentrates on a jovial atmosphere and great food.

🕐 Daily 7.30–1, Jun–end Sep; 7.30–midnight, rest of year

🍴 D €30, Wine €6.50

🚫

🚌 H, 23, 280, 780 to Lungotevere Ponte Sisto; tram 8

DITIRAMBO

Map 223 D5
Piazza della Cancelleria 74, 00186
Tel 06 687 1626
www.ristoranteditirambo.it

Downtown trattoria (one block south of Corso Vittorio Emanuele) that far transcends the tourist menu, even satisfying the difficult-to-please *bel mondo* of Rome. The kitchen

uses organic ingredients, and produces homemade bread (often with olives or pumpkin seeds), pasta (including its showcase dish with courgette flowers) and desserts. Furnishings lean towards country chic: their mellow charm compensates for the somewhat harrassed staff. The wine list, supplied by vinter Cavour, is legendary. Reservations essential.

🕐 Tue–Sun 1–3, 8–11.30, Mon 8–11.30; closed Aug

🍴 L €25, D €80, Wine €12

🚫

🚌 46, 62, 64, 87, 116, 492 to Campo dei Fiori

L'EAU VIVE

Map 223 E5
Via Monterone 85, 00186
Tel 06 6880 2101/06 6880 1095

Unusual restaurant run by an international sisterhood of nuns, in a Renaissance building with frescoed vaulted ceilings. Cuisine is international, mainly French, and includes soups, main courses and desserts. Classical music plays in the background. Excellent wine list. The

restaurant helps the nuns raise funds for missions to developing countries. You can join the sisters for evening prayers at 10pm.

🕐 Mon–Sat 12.30–4, 7.30–11; closed Aug

🍴 L €50, D €80, Wine €8

🚫

🚌 64, 87, 492 to Largo Argentina; tram 8

EDOARDO II

Map 223 E5
Vicolo Margana 14, 00187
Tel 06 6994 2419
www.edoardosecondo.it

Sophisticated gay restaurant very close to the Jewish quarter and Piazza Venezia. Candles and soft lighting complement pale stucco walls with modern paintings and photographs. It has been transformed from one of Rome's most popular gay bars into a comfortable place to dine as well. Mainly Mediterranean cuisine—meat and fish, plus delicious vegetable pies and a vast assortment of cakes and pastries. Good selection of more than 100 wines.

🕐 Wed–Mon 7.30–2; closed 1 week in Aug

🍴 D €50, Wine €10

🚫 Section

🚌 40, 64, 87, 628 to Piazza Venezia

EL TOULÀ

Map 223 E4
Via della Lupa 29b
Tel 06 6873498
www.toula.it

Considered to be one of Rome's best restaurants, El Toulà is a great place to look for the rich and famous. The service is exceptional, the Venetian and international cuisine divine and the wine list superb.

🕐 Tue–Fri 1–3, 8–11, Sat, Mon 8–11; closed Aug

🍴 L €44, D €140, Wine €15

Ⓜ Spagna

🚌 81, 117, 119, 492 to Via del Corso or Largo Carlo Goldini

EST! EST! EST!

Map 224 G4
Via Genova 32, 00185
Tel 06 488 1107

At a hundred years old, this is one of Rome's most long-established pizzerias. It stays with the tried and tested combination of excellent pizza and Italian wines, served in a simple room with wooden tables.

- ⏰ Tue–Sun 7–midnight
- 🍕 Pizza €15, Wine €6
- Ⓜ Repubblica
- 🚌 H, 64, 170

EVANGELISTA
Map 223 D6
Via delle Zoccolette 11a, 00186
Tel 06 687 5810

In this genteel restaurant near the Tiber, ideal for long, intimate meals, the stars of the rich menu are its artichoke dishes. Try them *alla giudia* (Roman-Jewish style, fried

whole in batter) or *al mattone* (crushed between two bricks, then baked). Also recommended is the pasta with aubergines (eggplant), almonds and ricotta. The interior design is elegant and the service gracious.

- ⏰ Mon–Sat 8–11.30; closed Aug
- 🍴 D €90, Wine €15
- Ⓢ Section
- 🚌 H, 23, 280, 780 to Lungotevere Ponte Sisto; tram 8

FASSI–PALAZZO DEL FREDDO
Map 224 H5
Via Principe Eugenio 65, 00185
Tel 06 446 4740

One of the very best ice-cream shops in Rome. The location, close to the Basilica of Santa Maria Maggiore and Termini station, is not one of the most salubrious these days, but it's fine during the day, and the ice-cream makes it all worthwhile. You can sit inside and be impressed by the incredibly high ceilings, or in a little internal garden. Credit cards are not accepted.

- ⏰ Tue–Sun noon–midnight
- 🍨 Ice creams from €1.30
- Ⓢ
- Ⓜ Vittorio

FIASCHETTERIA BELTRAMME
Map 223 E3
Via della Croce 39

Known to locals as Cesaretto, and very easy to miss in the narrow Via della Croce, this traditional trattoria is wonderfully understated. Locals, artists and shopkeepers, together with a few visitors in the know, sit down to simple but well-prepared food, including pasta and salads. They do not accept bookings—there's no telephone, anyway—so arrive early for the chance of a shared table in this popular eatery. Credit cards are not accepted.

- ⏰ Mon–Sat, noon–3, 7.30–10.30
- Ⓜ Spagna
- 🚌 117, 119

F.I.S.H.
Map 224 F5
Via dei Serpenti 16, 00184
Tel 06 4782 4962
www.f-i-s-h.it

Australian-inspired sushi restaurant near the Colosseo that recalls the Sydney waterfront. After an *aperitivo* with oysters at the bar, head into the restaurant. The back room

has a view of the cooking area. Oak wood is alternated with glass and iron seats and tables. Select from three menus: Mediterranean, oriental and Antipodean. Finish with the crème brûlée with coconut and dates or a sashimi of exotic fruits.

- ⏰ Tue–Sun 1–3, 8–2; closed 10 Aug–2 Sep
- 🍴 L €70, D €80, Wine €12
- Ⓢ Section
- Ⓜ Cavour or Colosseo
- 🚌 117

FRIENDS ART CAFÉ
Map 223 D6
Piazza Trilussa 34, 00153
Tel 06 581 6111

Excellent place near the Tiber for an *aperitivo*; great value. Snacks set out on the counter

are included in the price of a drink. Behind the bar there's a dining area decorated with modern paintings that serves salads, vegetable pies and a small selection of pastas and meat dishes, plus desserts.

- ⏰ Mon–Sat 7am–2am, Sun 6pm–2am
- 🍴 L €20, cocktails €8
- Ⓢ Section
- 🚌 23; tram 8

GELATERIA DELLA PALMA
Map 223 E4
Via della Maddalena 20, 00186
Tel 06 6880 6752

Close to the Pantheon, this ice-cream shop offers a huge variety, including no less than 20 different kinds of chocolate, plus mousses and ice-cream with meringues. For those who prefer the taste of fruit, the raspberry is simply unforget-

table. There are two wooden benches inside, but the place gets extremely crowded. The best idea is to buy your ice cream, then stroll down to Piazza della Rotonda in front of the Pantheon. Credit cards are not accepted.

- ⏰ Daily 8am–2am
- 🍨 Ice creams from €2
- Ⓢ
- 🚌 64, 87, 492 to Largo Argentina; tram 8

IL GELATO DI SAN CRISPINO
Map 223 F4
Via della Panetteria 42, 00187
Tel 06 679 3924
www.ilgelatodisancrispino.com

This has to be the best ice-cream shop in Rome. Attention to detail has made other offerings pale in comparison. The ice-creams are rich and creamy, without additives. The signature (*gelato di San Crispino*) is made with wild Sardinian honey. The zabaglione ice-cream is made with marsala wine aged for thirty years in oak barrels. The shop can be hard to find as it has a very discreet entrance

without a real sign. Facing the Trevi Fountain, head right down Via Lavatore then take the second left down Via Panetteria; San Crispino is halfway down on your right.
🕐 Mon, Wed–Thu 12–12.30am, Fri–Sat 12–1.30am
🍴 €2–€6 per cup
🚌 61, 62, 116, 175, 492, 630

GIGGETTO AL PORTICO D'OTTAVIA
Map 223 E5
Via del Portico d'Ottavia 21/a, 00186
Tel 06 686 1105
www.giggettoalportico.com
Family-run restaurant in the heart of the Ghetto district. For more than 80 years, they have specialized in traditional Roman-Jewish cuisine. Original brick-vaulted ceilings and beams decorated with strings of garlic, chillies and laurel. Without a doubt the pièce de résistance is the *carciofi alla giudia* (Jewish artichoke), and you should try the unusual salad featuring wild chicory shoots with an anchovy dressing—all prepared to perfection. Wine cellar with over 500 labels, and exceptional desserts, too.
🕐 Tue–Sun 12.30–3, 7.30–11; closed last 2 weeks in Jul
🍴 L €25, D €70, Wine €12
Ⓢ Section
🚌 62, 64, 87, 492, 628 to Largo Argentina

GIOLITTI
Map 223 E4
Via degli Uffici del Vicario 40, 00186
Tel 06 699 1243
www.giolitti.it
This family-run *gelateria* has been making delicious ice-creams since 1900. Ever popular with Roman families, the Liberty-style (art nouveau) room, with olive-green ceilings and marble floors is the perfect setting in which to linger over an ice-cream (over 60 varieties), or a home-made pastry with a cup of tea. For pure indulgence, ask for *panna* (whipped cream) on top of your ice-cream. There is also a takeaway counter.
🕐 Daily 7am–1am
🍴 Ice creams €5–9 (to take away €1.50–8)
Ⓢ Section
🚌 52, 53, 61, 71, 80, 85, 160, 850

IL GOCCETTO
Map 222 D5
Via dei Banchi Vecchi 14, 00186
Tel 06 686 4268
Wine bar in a medieval bishop's house between Corso Vittorio Emanuele and the Tiber. Frescoes on the walls, and bottles and glasses stored on the shelves and in open cupboards, create a relaxed atmosphere. Not only is there a vast wine list (800 different labels), but there's also an extensive cheese list and other regional delicacies, including various kinds of salami and ham.
🕐 Mon–Sat 11.30–2, 6–11.30
🍴 Selection of salami/cheese from €8, desserts from €5, Wine €3 (by the glass)
Ⓢ
🚌 64, 87, 492 to Largo Argentina; tram 8

GOOD GOOD
Map off 225 J7
Via Latina 103, 00179
Tel 06 780 0855
Restaurant-pizzeria serving some of the best pizzas in town. Experience the hustle and bustle of Roman family life, especially on Sunday, traditionally pizza night. Make a reservation or you could be in for a long wait. Good antipasto table and 40 varieties of pizza. For the finishing touch, accompany your meal with excellent draught beer or a carafe of the sparkling house wine.
🕐 Tue–Sun 7–midnight; closed 2nd half of Aug
🍴 D €45, Wine €4.50
Ⓜ Furio Camillo
🚌 87, 628

GRAN CAFFÈ MARTINI E ROSSI
Map 224 G6
Piazza del Colosseo 3/a, 00184
Tel 06.700 4431
Bar/restaurant/pizzeria popular with locals, and what better location could it have than looking across to the Palatine

Hill, with the Colosseo just across the road? Friendly staff and early 1900s feel to the interior. Serves food all day and has an extensive wine cellar. There are good-value all-inclusive menus, plus vegetarian dishes and pizzas, or if a snack is all you want, try one of the *panini* (hot and cold filled rolls) on offer. Pizzas from €7.
🕐 Daily 8am–1am; closed Jan
🍴 L €50, D €72, Wine €18
Ⓢ Section
Ⓜ Colosseo
🚌 85, 87, 117; tram 3

GRAPPOLO D'ORO/ ZAMPANÒ
Map 223 D5
Piazza della Cancelleria 80
Tel 06 689 7080
One of the best-priced places near Campo dei Fiori, this unspoiled trattoria has remained unchanged for years. Traditional Italian dishes are always good here, and the *ravioli alla Gorgonzola* is divine. This place is popular with locals, so arrive early to be sure of a table.
🕐 Daily 12.30–2.30, 7.30–10.30 (closed Tue lunch)
🍴 L €20, D €70, Wine €7
🚌 46, 62, 64 to Corso Vittorio Emanuele II

GROTTE DEL TEATRO DI POMPEO
Map 223 D5
Via del Biscione 73, 00186
Tel 06 6880 3686
www.ristorantidiroma.com/grotteteatropompeo.it
The back rooms of this restaurant, which is just behind the spot where Julius Caesar was assassinated, are carved out of the first stone theatre in Roman history. Some of the best fish dishes around are served here: Spaghetti with seafood, oven-baked turbot with potatoes, or grilled scampi are all excellent. Good wine list. In summer, sit outside and try the Prosecco Mionetto (€13), a sparkling wine perfect with fish.
🕐 Tue–Sun noon–3, 7–11; closed Aug
🍴 L €30, D €40, Wine €6
🚌 64, 87, 492 to Largo Argentina; tram 8

EATING

IL GURU

Map 224 F5

Via Cimarra 456, 00184

Tel 06 474 4110

Excellent Indian food in the heart of Rione Monti, near the Colosseo. Every detail of the ethnic interior is designed to

re-create a little corner of India in Rome. House specials are tandooris and curries of varying strengths. You can choose one of three fixed menus—vegetarian, meat or fish—or order à la carte. Traditional desserts and Indian beer. Welcoming staff.

⚙ Daily 7.30–1

🍴 D €40, Wine €6

🔘 Section

🚇 Cavour

🚌 68

GUSTO

Map 223 E3

Piazza Augusto Imperatore 9, 00186

Tel 06 322 6273

www.gusto.it

Very trendy, state-of-the-art restaurant, pizzeria and wine bar behind the Mausoleum of Augustus. Exposed brickwork, industrial lighting and hugely inflated prices, so you won't find many locals here. Pizzas

(from €6) and salads are decent. A slight twist is given to some traditional recipes. However, this place is about ambience and there's plenty of that. Live jazz on Tuesday and Thursday at 11pm. There's also a kitchen shop.

⚙ Daily 12.45–3, 7.30–12

🍴 L €16 (buffet), D €36, Wine €18

🚇 Spagna

🚌 81, 116, 117, 628, 913

HARD ROCK CAFÉ

Map 223 F3

Via Vittorio Veneto 62/a, 00187

Tel 06 420 3051

www.hardrock.com

Yes, there's one in Rome, and on the exclusive Via Veneto. The interior is standard Hard Rock: wooden floors and a litter of 1950s paraphernalia, the only exception being the frescoed angels on the ceiling. Seats over 260, with lots of nooks and crannies to hide in. The menu is the same as

always, with burgers and chips. And there's a shop where you can add another Hard Rock t-shirt to your collection.

⚙ Daily noon–2am

🍴 L €28, D €48, Wine €9

🔘 Section

🚇 Barberini

🚌 52, 53, 56, 58b, 95, 116

INSALATA RICCA

Map 223 D5

Largo de' Chiavari 85, 00186

Tel 06 6880 3656

This Italian chain concentrates on salads and *bruschette* (toasted bread with toppings) to marvellous effect. Start with artichoke pâté or sesame goat's cheese on seared bread. Then tuck into a massive salad, ranging from mozzarella and tomato to greens drizzled in honey, and topped with walnuts and slivers of Parmesan. The interior incorporates exposed brick and sponge-painted walls, but most prefer the crowded outdoor tables. Its bilingual staff are famous for making visitors welcome.

⚙ Daily 12.30–3.30, 7–midnight

🍴 L €20, D €32, Wine €6

🔘 Section

🚌 46, 62, 64, 87, 116, 492 to Campo dei Fiori

IVO A TRASTEVERE

Map 223 D6

Via San Francesco a Ripa 158

Tel 06 581 7082

A Roman institution. The classic pizza is always good, but the owners also come up with interesting and unusual toppings. It's busy and bustling, so arrive early or be prepared to wait for a table. However, the turnover is quick and the service efficient.

⚙ Wed–Mon 5.30pm–2am

🍴 Pizza €6, Wine €5.78

🚌 8, 44, 75, 780 to Viale Trastevere

KETUMBAR

Map off 223 E7

Via Galvani 24, 00154

Tel 06 5730 5338

Ethnic food is very belatedly beginning to make its mark in Rome. The name of this very stylish Asian restaurant/bar, with sleek Indonesian furnishings and vaulted ceilings means coriander (cilantro) in Malay. There's a fusion of Asian influences in the kitchen. Sushi is their special—and it's very good. So, too, is the *nasi goreng* (Indonesian fried rice). Try the triple chocolate dessert to finish. All a bit pricey, but worth it.

⚙ Daily 8–midnight, Sep–end Jun; Tue–Sun 8–midnight, Jul; closed Aug

🍴 D €90, Wine €18

🚇 Piramide

LEONCINO

Map 223 E4

Via del Leoncino 28, 00186

Tel 06 687 6306

For great pizza, baked in a wood-fired oven, you can't beat Leoncino, where you can eat inside, where the interior has remained unchanged for over 30 years, or on the terrace outside. It's popular with locals, so expect to wait. Credit cards are not accepted.

⚙ Mon–Fri 1–2.30, 7–midnight, Sat, Sun 7–midnight

🍴 L €11, D €20, Wine €5.20

🔘

🚇 Spagna

🚌 81, 119 to Via del Corso or Via Tomacelli

LOWENHAUS

Map 223 E3

Via della Fontanella 168, 00186

Tel 06 323 0410

Why eat Bavarian food in Rome? For the answer, try Lowenhaus's superb *stinco di*

EATING

maiale al forno (roast pork shin with roast potatoes and cabbage). Also a great place if you have a taste for good German beer; the list is endless and includes some very idiosyncratic ones. Also serves cakes such as strudel and *Sachertorte* (chocolate cake). The restaurant is divided into several rooms, and there are tables outside in summer.

🕒 Daily 11am–2am
🍴 L €30, D €60, Wine €10
🚬 Section
🚇 Flaminio
🚌 116, 117

LUMIÈRE DI SICILIA
Map 222 C7
Via Fratelli Bonnet 41, 00152
Tel 06 581 3287
Popular local restaurant, serving up the best Sicilian cuisine north of Palermo. Start with the mixed antipasti or *caponata*, an aromatic mélange of aubergine (eggplant), bell pepper, basil and pine nuts. First courses include mouth-watering pistachio pesto, ravioli crammed with orange and ricotta, and squid-ink risotto. The staff are courteous, humorous and warm, even if your children get underfoot. Worth straying off the beaten track for (it's out towards Villa Doria Pamphilj).

🕒 Tue–Sun 8–11; closed Aug
🍴 D €50, Wine €9
🚌 44

MACCHERONI
Map 223 E4
Piazza delle Coppelle 44, 00186
Tel 06 6830 7895
This is a funky place, which is popular more for its lively atmosphere and young staff than its food. The pasta dishes are very good, but the rest is average.

🕒 Mon–Sat 1–3, 8–12
🍴 €25 without wine
🚬 Section
🚌 23, 30, 75, 280, 716 or any bus to Via Marmorata; tram 3

IL MARGUTTA
Map 223 D3
Via Margutta 118, 00187
Tel 06 3265 0577
www.ilmargutta.it
The only real vegetarian restaurant in the city is in this famous artists' street from the film *Roman Holiday*. Large,

futuristic space with traditional touches, with art exhibited on the walls. There is a buffet at lunchtime, but it is more intimate in the evening. Over 40 vegetarian dishes (mostly organic) available. There are 120 wines on offer, some organic, all at reasonable prices. Very good dessert wine list, too.

🕒 Daily 12.30–3.30, 7.30–11; closed 2 weeks in Aug
🍴 L €30, D €60, Wine €15
🚬 Section
🚇 Flaminio or Spagna
🚌 116, 117

MYOSOTIS
Map 223 E4
Vicolo della Vaccarella 3–5, 00186
Tel 06 686 5554
www.myosotis.it
Despite being so near the Pantheon, lively Myosotis is great value for money. The chef uses only the freshest ingredients to make sure that everything on the menu is of the highest standard. The fresh pasta dishes are particularly good; try the carbonara or seafood sauces.

🕒 Tue–Sat 12.30–3, 7.30–11.30, Mon 7.30–11.30; closed Aug and first week in Jan
🍴 L €40, D €80, Wine €7.50
🚬 Section
🚇 Spagna
🚌 30, 40, 64, 70

NAVONA NOTTE
Map 223 D5
Via del Teatro Pace 44, 00186
Tel 06 686 9278
This pizzeria/restaurant near Piazza Navona is one of the few in the *centro storico* that does a tourist menu. For €5, you can have mussels with focaccia, followed by either spaghetti, such as *spaghetti alla amatriciana*, or a pizza and a glass of wine. The typical Roman thin-crust pizzas are made in a wood-burning oven. Good honest fare and simple

style. Get a seat outside if you can, and enjoy the buzz and bustle in the heart of Rome.

🕒 Wed–Mon 5.30–1; closed Jan
🍴 D €12, Wine €6.50
🚌 62, 64, 87, 116, 492

NERONE
Map 224 G6
Via delle Terme di Tito 96
Tel 06 481 7952
This small, friendly trattoria, close to the Colosseo, is famous for its Abruzzese cooking—the antipasti buffet is particularly good. In warm weather there are table outside, opposite the Colle Oppio.

🕒 Mon–Sat noon–3, 7–11; closed Aug
🍴 L €24, D €50, Wine €8
🚌 30b, 75, 85, 87, 117, 175, 196 to Piazza del Colosseo
🚇 Colosseo

NON SOLO BEVI
Map 223 E4
Piazza di Pietra 64, 00186
Tel 06 679 4519
www.nonsolobevi.it
The name means 'not just drinks', which is true enough as this trendy cafeteria serves a vast assortment of salads. The Brunello di Montalcino salad (named for the fine red wine from Tuscany) heaps on rocket (arugula), cherry tomatoes, Gorgonzola, Brie and *stracchino* (soft) cheese, Indian corn, olives, courgettes (zucchini) and mozzarella. Have a seat outside or try the vaulted cellar. Great location just a few steps from the Temple of Hadrian.

🕒 Daily 7am–midnight, summer; 7am–9pm, rest of year
🍴 Coffee €2.50, wine €10, beer €4.50
🚬
🚇 Spagna
🚌 116

EATING

OFFSIDE CAFÉ

Map 224 F5
Piazza della Madonna dei Monti 5, 00184
Tel 06 9761 8094

Take a break at this cocktail-cum-snack bar in a lovely piazza, close to the Forum. Four-centuries-old exposed beams, and walls painted in a pleasing yellow and claret. Flip through one of the 100 or so books on display and try the famed *bruschette*: The Three Musketeers is topped with wild boar, wild hare and venison, and is enough for two. In the evening, sit outside. Free buffet appetizers 7.30–8.30pm.

⏰ Daily 7am–2am
🍴 Set menu €3–€5, Wine €8
Ⓢ Cavour or Colosseo
🚌 117

OPEN MUSIC CAFÉ

Map off 224 H7
Piazza Galeria 14, 00179
Tel 06 7049 2512
www.tiscalinet.it/openmusiccafe

Very popular 24-hour café, but with limited indoor seating. Rock and pop music is bearably loud in the evening, but outside seating is also available. The interior design is sleek—stainless steel, glass and mirrored walls, mosaic floors, TV monitors and a wavy bar. Most evenings, at about 7pm, they dish out free snacks, such as prawns, salmon and olives, and even pizza and pasta. Credit cards are not accepted.

⏰ Daily 24 hours
🍴 L €8, Wine €11
🚌 360 to Termini station

OSAKA

Map 224 H6
Viale Carlo Felice 29/31, 00185
Tel 06 700 1821

Japanese restaurant in front of the basilica of San Giovanni in Laterano. Lovely interior in black and dark red, with low tatami-covered tables furnishing half the room. The freshly

prepared sushi is very good, but if you don't know what to choose, try one of their very reasonably priced fixed menus, either the Snake Bento (€15) or the Sashimi Bento (€13). Included in both menus are soup, rice, sushi and fruit. Individual sushi from €1.75.

⏰ Tue–Sun 11–3, 7–midnight; Mon 7–midnight
🍴 L €34, D €50, Wine €9
Ⓢ Section
🇸 San Giovanni
🚌 87, 117, 218

OSTERIA DELL'ANIMA

Map 223 D4
Via Santa Maria dell'Anima 8, 00186
Tel 06 686 4661

Refined restaurant behind Piazza Navona, with a refreshingly different look (seascape frescoes in pastel tones). With seasonal menus, the young chef invests a great deal of thought into the cuisine and its presentation. Prices are surprisingly reasonable. Try the ravioli filled with scampi and artichokes in a tomato and cream sauce, or thinly sliced beef alternated with *caciotta* (ewe's milk) cheese, tomatoes from Pachinio and salad leaves. All the bread is home baked. Over 150 wines, many from Tuscany.

⏰ Daily 7–midnight, May–end Oct; Tue–Sun noon–3, 7–midnight, rest of year
🍴 L €46, D €62, Wine €6.50
Ⓢ Section
🚌 40, 62, 64, or any other bus to Piazza Navona or Corso Vittorio Emanuele II

OTELLO ALLA CONCORDIA

Map 223 E3
Via della Croce 81, 00187
Tel 06 679 1178

Take refuge from the shopping madness of Via del Corso in this magnificent 18th-century courtyard, laden with plants, fruit, amphorae, hanging vines and an ancient bath fountain. Family run for over 50 years, the restaurant serves typically Roman fare. The antipasto of meats and salamis is a nice varied selection to start with, and the baked aubergine (eggplant) *parmigiana* is divine. Try a local Castelli Romani (Frascati) wine with your meal.

⏰ Mon–Sat 12.30–3, 7.30–11; closed 3 weeks in Jan
🍴 L €25, D €80, Wine €7.50

Ⓢ Section
🇸 Spagna
🚌 116, 117, 492

OUZERIE

Map 223 E6
Via dei Salumi 2, 00153
Tel 06 581 6378
www.clubgrecia.bbk.org

This restaurant/club in Trastevere is practically the only place in Rome where you can find Greek food and be spontaneously entertained. Authentic taverna setting with fishing nets and bouzoukis,

serving taramasalata, calamari, Greek salads, prawns baked with feta cheese and tomato, delicious kebabs, baklava, and yogurts with a variety of toppings. Live entertainment Friday and Saturday (reservations essential at weekends). Nominal membership (€1.50) payable on your first visit. Credit cards are not accepted.

⏰ Mon–Sat 8.30–2; closed 2 weeks in Aug
🍴 D €13, Wine €9
🚌 H to Viale Trastevere or Piazza Mastai; tram 3, 8

PANATTONI (I MARMI)

Map 223 D6
Viale Trastevere 53/59, 00153
Tel 06 580 0919

Huge marble-slab tables earn this classic Trastevere pizzeria two nicknames: *I Marmi* (The Marbles) and the less appetizing *l'Obitorio* (The Morgue). Somehow the grim association

EATING

doesn't succeed in scaring off customers, and neither does the poor service. Crabby waiters bang down vast pizzas, chilled Peroni beer and passable house red. Stark and cranky, but endearing. Credit cards are not accepted.

🕐 Thu–Tue 6.30–2.30; closed Aug
🍴 D €25, Wine €5.20
🚌 H, 63, 75

PASQUALINO AL COLOSSEO
Map 224 G6
Via SS. Quatro Coronati 66, 00184
Tel 06 700 4576
www.pasqualinoalcolosseo.com
In view of the Colosseo, on a quiet side street, is this trattoria with dining on two levels. Downstairs is wonderfully 1960s, with mock-wood lino walls and huge rotating fans, while the upper level more classic in style. The cuisine is

essentially Mediterranean (fresh fish daily) with a touch of Sicilian. Pasta with mushrooms, peas and sausage, and *carpaccio* (thinly sliced raw, dressed fish) of sea bass and tuna are both exceptional. Swordfish steak with capers and olives is nicely original and the tiramisu is first class.

🕐 Tue–Sun noon–3, 6.30–11; closed Aug
🍴 L €30, D €50, Wine €8
Ⓢ Section
Ⓜ Colosseo
🚌 85, 87, 117; tram 3

PASTARITO PIZZARITO
Map 223 D6
Via Roma Libera 19, 00153
Tel 06 588 3863
www.pastarito.it
Restaurant/pizzeria, part of the Pastarito chain found throughout Italy that gives good quality and service. Great location, on the market square of San Cosimato in Trastevere. If you can't find a table outside, or if you want to watch your pizza being made, head inside.

Pasta and pizzas are the order of the day. The tourist menu for €9 consists of a pasta dish, salad, wine and coffee. Pizzas from €4.

🕐 Daily 11–3.30, 6.30–midnight
🍴 L €20, D €20, Wine €10
🚌 H, 44, 78; tram 3, 8

IL PICCOLO
Map 223 D5
Via del Governo Vecchio 74, 00186
Tel 06 6880 1746
A lovely wine bar near the beginning of Via del Governo Vecchio where bottles of wine are stored up to the ceiling. A few tables outside, plus just a couple inside that add to the intimate atmosphere. The

ample wine list includes white *fragolino* (a sweet wine with strawberry aroma) and blackberry and raspberry sangria. There's a selection of different cheeses and meats: Try the *bresaola*—dried fillet of beef— or delicious sun-dried tomatoes from Calabria. Credit cards are not accepted.

🕐 Daily 10.30–3.30, 5.30–2
🍴 L €14 (selection of salami/cheeses from €7), Wine €3 (by the glass)
Ⓢ
🚌 87, 492 to Largo Argentina; tram 8

PIERLUIGI
Map 223 D5
Piazza dei Ricci 144, 00186
Tel 06 686 1302
www.pierluigi.it
Fish restaurant par excellence, and reasonably priced considering its setting and quality. It's on a gem of a piazza, with plenty of tables outside. Inside, cool terracotta floors, brick arches and chunky medieval beams are beautifully spotlit. Scampi risotto is a good choice, as is the *carpaccio* (thinly sliced raw, dressed fish) of tuna or swordfish. Fresh fish of the day is displayed behind in glass cabinet. Ask to see the wine cellar. Good service.

🕐 Tue–Sun noon–3, 7.30–midnight
🍴 L €42, D €80, Wine €14
🚌 46, 62, 64, 87, 116, 492 to Campo dei Fiori

PIZZA CIRO
Map 223 E4
Via della Mercede 43–45, 00186
Tel 06 678 6015
Pizzeria behind Piazza San Silvestro and not too far from Piazza Navona. The checked tablecloths may be a little banal, but the patio at the back is just perfect on a warm summer night. Serves Neapolitan-style pizzas (large

and thick), but you can also ask for a thinner Roman one. The starters are exceptional, especially the *antipasto sfizioso* of typical Neapolitan fried savouries. *Pizza bufalina doc*, with buffalo mozzarella, is the most popular.

🕐 Daily 12.30pm–2.30am
🍴 L €11, D €20, Wine €9
Ⓢ Section
🚌 117, 119, 175, 492, or any bus to Piazza San Silvestro

PIZZA FORUM
Map 224 G6
Via San Giovanni in Laterano 34–38, 00184
Tel 06 700 2515
www.pizzaforum.it
Large pizzeria behind the Colosseo. An entrance hall with Roman cobblestones brings you alongside the pizza ovens and invites you to enter the spacious dining room, which is furnished with stained

glass. Possibly the best pizzeria in Rome serving proper Neapolitan pizza (thicker than Roman pizza). Choice of over 35 pizzas and excellent salads. Service is neat and friendly. Pizzas from €4.

🕓 Daily noon–3, 7.30–midnight
🍴 L €20, D €26, Wine €5
Ⓢ Section
Ⓜ Colosseo
🚌 85, 87, 117; tram 3

PIZZARÉ
Map 224 G3
Via Lucullo 20, 00187
Tel 06 4201 3075

In a 1920s-style building surrounded by palm trees, just a short walk from Via Veneto, this is probably the most popular pizzeria in the heart of Rome. Real Neapolitan pizza with buffalo mozzarella, bought fresh daily. Try *ripieno fritto*, a folded and fried pizza with tomato, mozzarella, ham and ricotta filling, or *pizza re*, with tomato sauce, fresh Sicilian cherry tomatoes and buffalo mozzarella. Also homemade traditional Neapolitan cakes, including the famous *pastiera* (filled with ricotta, egg yolks and candied peel). Reservations are essential.

🕓 Daily 12.30–2.30, 7.30–midnight
🍴 L €15, D €20, Wine €6; special lunch meals for €8
Ⓢ Section
Ⓜ Barberini

IL POMODORINO
Map 224 F3
Via Campania 45, 00187
Tel 06 4201 1356

Pizzeria/*ristorante* with the best value available in the extortionately priced Via Veneto. Indoor and outdoor seating for up to 400 people. Inside is Neapolitan terracotta with a white, beamed ceiling, pastel walls and red-and-white table linen. Huge central buffet, packed with vegetables. Pizza chefs work on one side

PIZZERIA LA MONTECARLO
Map 223 D5
Vicolo Savelli 11A–12–13, 00186
Tel 06 686 1877

Typical Roman pizzeria in a medieval quarter near Piazza Navona, with simple, unfussy food and service. Arrive before 8.30pm. The walls are totally covered with photographs of more or less famous diners. Thirty different pizzas baked in wood ovens. The house special is the *pizza montecarlo*: tomato, mozzarella, mushrooms, artichokes, sausage, eggs, peppers, onion and olives. One pizza is made with seasonal vegetables. Credit cards are not accepted.

🕓 Tue–Sat noon–3, 6.30–1; closed 2 weeks in Aug
🍴 L €6, D €10, Wine €5
Ⓢ Section
🚌 40, 62, 64, or any other bus to Piazza Navona or Corso Vittorio Emanuele II

of the room, and the 13 other chefs in the open kitchen. A superb dish is the veal *mille-foglie*, a mountain of thinly sliced meat layered with crisply fried artichokes.

🕓 Daily 12.30–3.30, 7.30–midnight, Sat 7.30–midnight
🍴 L €20, D €50, Wine €6
Ⓢ Section
Ⓜ Veneto
🚌 52, 53, 56, 58, 58b, 95, 116

PIZZERIA POPI POPI
Map 223 D6
Via delle Fratte di Trastevere 45, 00153
Tel 06 589 5167

On one of the little alleys that join Viale Trastevere to the basilica of Santa Maria in Trastevere, Popi Popi is excellent for both its pizzas and its prices. Very popular with young Romans, especially in summer, when you can sit outside and enjoy Trastevere's bustle. There's a selection of traditional dishes in addition to pizzas.

🕓 Daily 7–1
🍴 D €24, Wine €5
Ⓢ Section
🚌 H, 23, 44, 56, 75, 280 to Viale Trastevere; tram 8

I PRIMI DELLA CLASSE
Map 223 D5
Via del Governo Vecchio 86/87, 00186
Tel 06 687 2529

Behind Piazza Navona, and with *trompe l'oeil* panoramic windows on Rome, this restaurant is known for its pasta—there are 130 different kinds from all over Italy. The best are the filled fresh pastas, such as ravioli, tortelli and

pansotti. If you can't make up your mind, there's also a *menu degustazione*, with your choice of six small portions. The salads are also tasty.

🕓 Tue–Sun 12.30–2, 7.30–midnight
🍴 L €40, D €50, Wine €5
Ⓢ Section
🚌 64, 87, 492 to Largo Argentina; tram 8 or any bus to Corso Vittorio Emanuele II

EATING

LA PROPOSTA

Map 225 J7
Via Terni 13, 00182
Tel 06 701 5615

A 10-minute walk from the basilica of San Giovanni in Laterano. Low-ceilinged vaulted room, painted in shades of ochre and white, with waist-high partitions separating the tables. Chef's recommendations are faultless, such as *fettuccine alla carlofortina* (pasta in a red pesto sauce), or stuffed rabbit with a blueberry sauce. The wine recommendations are excellent, too, with the vast majority under €25. Such harmonious suggestions are difficult to refuse.

🕐 Mon–Sat 7.30–midnight; closed Aug
🍽 D €60, Wine €10
Ⓢ Section
Ⓜ Re di Roma
🚌 16, 85, 87, 117; tram 3, 19

IL PULCINO BALLERINO

Map 225 J5
Via degli Equi 66/68, 00185
Tel 06 494 1255
www.ristorantidiroma.com/ilpulcinoballerino

Bright paper tablecloths and a lively atmosphere. Diners can cook their own food (meat, vegetables or cheese) on a *pietra ollare*, a searingly hot

stone. There is also a selection of pastas served ready to eat, and appetizing vegetable and cheese pies *(tortini)*. Homemade cakes include a luscious chocolate 'salami'. Ample wine list, mostly Italian but a couple of Chilean and French ones, too.

🕐 Mon–Fri 12.30–3.30, 8–midnight, Sat 7.30–midnight; closed last 2 weeks in Aug
🍽 L €24, D €40, Wine €6
Ⓢ
🚌 492

QUINZI E GABRIELI

Map 223 E4
Via delle Coppelle 5, 00186
Tel 06 687 9389

Well-established, if pricey, fish restaurant in a splendid 15th-century palazzo not far from Piazza Navona. Three wonderfully camp dining rooms with murals of exotic beaches, stone columns and a wooden canopy (a cross between

South Pacific and *Carousel*) created by a film-set designer. Service is efficient, with Italian flair. A house special is the raw fish platter, with bass, crayfish, tuna and squid. Try the spaghetti with lobster, which is the best in Rome and well worth splurging on.

🕐 Mon–Sat 7.30–11.30
🍽 D €200, Wine €20
🚌 116, 492

RENATO E LUISA

Map 223 E5
Via dei Barbieri 25, 00186
Tel 06 686 9660

Tiny restaurant (only 10–15 tables) behind Largo di Torre Argentina. Traditional Roman cuisine with a touch of creativity. Starters include mozzarella cheese with pesto or truffles, grilled or au gratin vegetables and focaccia (pizza

crust with olive oil). Among the pastas, the special is fettuccine with cherry tomatoes and ricotta cheese. Good house wine. Credit cards are not accepted.

🕐 Tue–Fri 12.20–2.30, 7.30–11.30, Sat–Sun 7.30–11.30
🍽 L €24, D €45, Wine €4
Ⓢ
🚌 64, 492 to Largo Argentina; tram 8

RISTORANTE DA NAZZARENO

Map 224 H4
Via Magenta 35, 00185
Tel 06 495 7782

Great-value restaurant in the busy Termini station area. Especially good antipasto buffet for vegetarians, and a fish buffet as well. The interior, dominated by the enticing central buffet table, is large, with white walls, stone floors and wooden chairs. *Bucatini* pasta with tomatoes and pancetta, and *ossobuco* (veal stew in tomato sauce) are popular with the locals. Try the local Castelli Romani house wine.

🕐 Thu–Tue noon–3.30, 6.30–11
🍽 L €30, D €60, Wine €6
Ⓢ Section
Ⓜ Termini
🚌 40, 64

RISTORANTE GIOVANNI

Map 223 F3
Via Marche 64, 00187
Tel 06 482 1834

Family-run restaurant close to Via Veneto. The dining room has terracotta floor tiles, beams, pristine white walls and traditional wooden chairs. Home-made gnocchi with pheasant sauce is a satisfying, if heavy, starter. The *ossobuco*

(veal stew in tomato sauce) with rice is a house recommendation, as is the fresh squid cooked on an open fire. The wine cellar contains 175 labels to choose from; the house wine is a crisp white Verdicchio from the Marche region.

🕐 Sun–Fri 12.30–3, 7.30–11; closed Aug
🍽 L €30, D €80, Wine €10
Ⓢ
Ⓜ Veneto
🚌 52, 53, 56, 58, 58b, 95, 116

EATING

RISTORANTE NUOVA STELLA

Map 224 G4
Via Manin 50–52–54, 00184
Tel 06 4897 6140
www.nuovastella.it

Unpretentious spot between Termini and Santa Maria Maggiore. The two large dining areas have white linen table-cloths and and eye-catching buffet; fresh fish is available

Tuesday and Friday. Specials include spaghetti with prawn, courgettes (zucchini) and tomato sauce, fettuccine with hare, and the classic *saltim-bocca romana* (veal with ham, cooked in white wine and butter), served with delicious rosemary roast potatoes. In warmer weather the tables spill out onto the pavement.

🕐 Mon–Sat noon–3, 6.30–11
🍴 L €24, D €50, Wine €8
🚫 Section
Ⓜ Termini
🚌 40, 64

RISTORANTE PAPA GIULIO

Map 223 D5
Via Giulia 14, 00186
Tel 06 6813 5920

Dim old mirrors and leather banquettes line the walls of this local restaurant. The interior—all crisp linen, candles and crystal—has a mellow elegance, like a 1930s film set.

The outdoor tables nestle in a secret garden, unspoilt by the Tiber highway bustling a few steps away. Menu highlights include seafood and innovative

dishes such as smoked salmon and champagne risotto.

🕐 Wed–Mon 11.30–3, 7.30–12.30
🍴 L €30, D €5, Wine €8
🚌 46, 62, 64, 87, 116, 492 to Campo dei Fiori

RISTORANTE-PIZZERIA PIACERE MOLISE

Map 222 B3
Via Candia 60, 00195
Tel 06 3974 3553

In a shopping street just minutes away from Musei Vaticani. Fresh flowers, damask linen and pale walls create an intimate setting in this elegant

family-run restaurant. Pasta with aubergines (eggplant), tomatoes and olives, and roast lamb cutlets with rosemary potatoes are dishes to savour. Good selection of fresh fish and decent house wine. A bottle of Banfi-Brunello di Montalcino is cheaper to buy here than in the shops.

🕐 Daily noon–3, 7–midnight
🍴 L €24, D €40, Wine €7
🚫 Section
Ⓜ Cipro Musei Vaticani
🚌 23,70, 99, 492

ROMOLO 'NEL GIARDINO DI RAFFAELLO E DELLA FORNARINA'

Map 222 D5
Via di Porta Settimiana 8, 00153
Tel 06 581 8284

Next to the ancient gateway of Settimiano, this is where Raphael's lover, 'La Fornarina', once lived, and where the popular poet Trilussa used to

ROOF GARDEN 'LES ETOILES'

Map 222 C4
Via dei Bastioni 1, 00193
Tel 06 687 3233
www.atlantehotels.com

For unparalleled views of St. Peter's, and food to match, this roof-terrace restaurant is a must if you can afford it— the dining room is one level down. High-backed upholstered dining chairs, candlelit tables and St. Peter's illuminated beyond. Sumptuous Mediterranean cuisine includes a raw tuna and tomato pasta, and château filet with foie gras and sliced truffle. Imaginative wine list that includes one of Umbria's best-kept secrets—the Sagrantino di Montefalco red.

🕐 Daily 12.30–2.30, 7.30–10
🍴 L €60, D €145, Wine €15
🚫
Ⓜ Ottaviano
🚌 70, 492

wine and dine. Divided into four rustic dining rooms, with wonderful oak-beamed ceilings, stone floors and original fireplace. But the garden is the place to be. For starters, try the fried mozzarella rolled with Parma ham and a hint of anchovy. As a main course, how about chicken breast with mozzarella and Parma ham, artichoke and a creamy tomato sauce?

🕐 Tue–Sun 12–3, 7–11; closed Aug
🍴 L €60, D €80, Wine €9
🚫 Section
🚌 23 to Ponte Sisto or Viale di Trastevere; tram 8

EATING

LA ROSETTA

Map 223 E4
Via della Rosetta 8–9
Tel 06 686 1002/06 6830 8841
www.larosetta.com
Wonderful fish and seafood, brought in daily from Sicily, form the basis of La Rosetta's menu. Cooked in the simplest ways to enhance its quality, it is best accompanied by a Sicilian white wine. The restaurant is always popular, so reservations are essential.
🕐 Mon–Fri 1–3, 8–11.30, Sat 8–11.30; closed 3 weeks in Aug.
🍽 L €50, D €200, Wine €30
Ⓢ Section
🚌 119 to Piazza della Rotonda, or 70, 81, 87, 90 to Corso del Rinascimento

SAN CLEMENTE

Map 224 G6
Via San Giovanni in Laterano 124, 00184
Tel 06 7045 0944
www.sanclemente.it
This bar/pizzeria/pub is a great place to refuel between the Colosseo and the basilica of San Giovanni in Laterano. It has three vaulted rooms and a terrace, 15 different beers and decent, inexpensive food. The

tourist menu, available for lunch and dinner, consists of cannelloni followed by roast chicken and potatoes, plus coffee, with wine or beer, plus coffee, and all for €12.90—with a free lithograph of the Colosseo thrown in.
🕐 Daily 7am–1am
🍽 L €20, D €30, Wine €8
Ⓢ Section
Ⓜ Colosseo or San Giovanni
🚌 85, 87, 117; tram 3

SAN MARINO

Map off 225 K2
Via San Marino 52, 00198
Tel 06 855 8439
Lively pizzeria well off the tourist trail, particularly popular with students, but not too chaotic. Among the starters,

SANT'EUSTACHIO IL CAFFÈ

Map 223 E5
Piazza Sant'Eustachio 82, 00186
Tel 06 6880 2048
www.santeustachioilcaffe.it

The scent of pure Arabian coffee hangs in the air here, in a square with a view of the church of Sant'Eustachio and the Senate buildings. Connoisseurs come from far and wide to this café, which has been here since 1938 (the mosaic floor dates from the 1930s), to try what is generally regarded as the best coffee there is. All the blends are roasted on the premises in wood-fired ovens—hence the glorious aroma. Credit cards are not accepted.
🕐 Daily 8.30am–1am
🍽 Coffee from €1
🚌 40, 62, 64, 85, 87, 117, 492 to Corso Rinascimento

the *bruschetta* with tomatoes is unforgettable, and the fried courgette (zucchini) flowers and *suppli* (fried rice balls with tomato sauce and mozzarella) are very good. Ample choice of thin-crust pizzas, including sausage, mushroom and mozzarella, and cherry tomato. Place your order by drawing a cross on the menu. Credit cards are not accepted.
🕐 Mon–Sat 7.30–midnight
🍽 D €24, Wine €4
Ⓢ
🚌 38, 60X to Piazza Istria

SITAR

Map 224 G5
Via Cavour 256/a, 00184
Tel 06 488 4004
An oasis of tranquillity on busy Via Cavour. Superior Indian cuisine from the northern regions of the country, with

excellent service and presentation. The interior design is subtle and welcoming, with vaulted bricked ceilings, tiled floors and the eponymous sitar hanging on the wall. The friendly owner is on hand to help you decide, but the chicken tikka followed by butter chicken is recommended; as for dessert, try *gulab jamun* (fried dough balls in a delicate syrup). The Indian wine is a revelation, full bodied and with a great bouquet.
🕐 Daily noon–3, 7–11.30
🍽 L €30, D €50, Wine €8
Ⓢ Section
Ⓜ Cavour
🚌 75, 84

SORA LELLA

Map 223 E6
Via di Ponte Quattro Capi 16, 00153
Tel 06 686 1601
A family-run restaurant established in 1943 by the sister of the then famous actor Aldo Fabrizi. It is on Isola Tiberina, in the Tiber, near Trastevere—arguably one of the most special locations in Rome. Roman cuisine is at its best here, and if you're lucky enough to sit near the window, you'll have a river view. All the

typical dishes, from oxtail with cinnamon, cloves, raisins and pine nuts to some memorable *carciofi alla Giudia* (fried artichokes). There is an ample wine list. Reservations recommended.
🕐 Mon–Sat 12.45–2.30, 8–11; closed Aug
🍽 L €40, D €100, Wine €13
Ⓢ
🚌 23; tram 8

EATING

TAPA LOCA

Map 223 D4
Via di Tor Millina 4/5, 00186
Tel 06 683 2266

Between Piazza Navona and the beautiful Piazza della Pace is a real rarity: a Spanish restaurant in Rome. The comfortable, large dining area, with chunky tables and chairs, lies within a 16th-century palazzo. Four different paellas, including vegetarian, and a wide variety of meat, fish and vegetarian tapas. Also a good selection of Torres wines.

🕐 Daily 6.30–2
🍷 D €40, Wine €11.50
🚌 46, 64, 87, 116, 492 to Piazza Navona

TAVERNA ANGELICA

Map 222 C4
Piazza Amerigo Capponi 6, 00193
Tel 06 687 4514

This popular restaurant is the best mid-priced option near the Vatican. Don't be misled by the name—the interior is minimalist and the cooking delicate and innovative. Most of the dishes are fish or seafood based, and accompanied by a carefully selected wine list. Reservations essential.

🕐 Mon–Sat 7.30–midnight, Sun 12.30–2.30, 7.30–midnight. Closed 2 weeks in Aug
🍷 L €50, D €70, Wine €10
🚇 Section
🚌 19, 23, 34, 51, 64, 81, 492, 982
Ⓜ Ottaviano

TAVERNA 'DA GIOVANNI'

Map 222 D4
Via Banco Santo Spirito 58, 00186
Tel 06 686 4116

This restaurant serves good, no-frills Roman food across the river from the Castel Sant'Angelo. Better to dine here than on the overpriced St. Peter's side of the river. It has three rooms and a terrace, the walls are covered with canvases and copper pots hang from the 15th-century wooden

TAZZA D'ORO

Map 223 E4
Via degli Orfani 84, 00186
Tel 06 678 9792
www.torrefazionetazzadoro.com

This bustling bar/coffee shop near the Pantheon sparks major arguments: Is it the city's best coffee or merely a contender? The standard blend is creamy and fragrant, but the Jamaican Blue Mountain provides the smoothest buzz. Seasonal choices include *granita di caffè* (coffee sorbet) and *cioccolata calda con panna* (hot chocolate with whipped cream). Take home a bag of beans or Aroma di Roma coffee liqueur from the gift shop. Bar service only, no seating.

🕐 Mon–Sat 7am–8pm
🍷 Coffee from 75c, *granita* €1.30
🚌 40, 62, 64, or any bus to Piazza Navona or Corso Vittorio Emanuele II

ceiling. Extremely good-value three-course menu with wine and bottled water for €15, or an upgraded version with a large antipasto and coffee added for €18. The pasta starters are very generous.

🕐 Tue–Sun noon–2.30, 7–11
🍷 L €32, D €40, Wine €6
🚌 46, 62, 64, 98, 280

LA TAVERNA DEL GHETTO

Map 223 E5
Via del Portico d'Ottavia 8, 00186
Tel 06 6880 9771
www.latavernadelghetto.com

A kosher restaurant just along the street from the Portico d'Ottavia in the heart of the Ghetto district. The dining area, within a 14th-century building, is an attractive brick-pointed room with an arched Gothic ceiling. Kosher kitchen serving

Roman-Jewish dishes, and the menu changes every two weeks. Chicory and anchovy pie and baked salted cod with pine nuts, raisins and cherry tomatoes are two typical dishes. Good wine list, including Israeli selections.

🕐 Sat–Thu noon–3, 7–11; Fri noon–3
🍷 L €50, D €65, Wine €15.50
🚫
🚌 62, 64, 87, 628, or any other bus to Largo Argentina

TAVERNA PARIONE

Map 223 D5
Via dei Parione 38–39
Tel 06 686 9545

There has been a restaurant in this 15th-century palazzo, near Piazza Navona, for over 60 years. This spacious, simple

place, with artwork on the walls, serves wholesome Roman food, including pizzas, accompanied by wine from its own cellar. Popular with local celebrities—look for their pictures on the photo board. Tables outside in warm weather.

🕐 Daily noon–3, 7–midnight
🍷 L €28, D €40, Wine €10
Ⓜ Spagna
🚌 46, 64

EATING

T-BONE STATION

Map 223 F4

Via Francesco Crispi 29/31, 00186

Tel 06 678 7650

Between Piazza di Spagna and Piazza Barberini is the trendiest steakhouse in Rome. The theme is based around black and white movie stills and high-tech design. Steaks are the obvious choice, but the salads are huge and appetizing, especially the fresh crispy spinach and the classic chicken Caesar with parmesan topping (make sure the cheese is slivered, *a scaglie*, not grated). The cocktails are also excellent.

🕐 Daily 12.30–3, 7.30–1.30; closed 1 week in mid-Aug

🍴 L €20, D €60, Wine €12

🚭

Ⓜ Barberini

🚌 52, 53, 61, 62, 63, 80, 95, 116, 117, 119, 175, 492, 590

LA TERRAZZA

Map 223 F3

Via Ludovisi 49

Tel 06 478121

The formal atmosphere of the Hotel Eden's Michelin-starred restaurant is a good excuse to dress up. The food is predominently modern Mediterranean, and is always excellent—try smoked scallops with asparagus, or sea bass with black olives and oregano. And as if this wasn't enough, the view is fantastic.

🕐 Daily 12.30–2.30, 7.45–9.30

🍴 L €50, D €200, Wine €40

🚭 Section

🚌 116, 119

Ⓜ Spagna or Barberini

THAI INN

Map off 222 B7

Via Federico Ozanam 94, 00152

Tel 06 5820 3145

Fairy lights, blue lanterns, bamboo matting, fake flowers and butterflies create a tranquil Asian atmosphere in the Monteverde district of the city. The waiters—who generally speak better English than Italian—are attentive, and the Thai chefs would make a name for themselves in any city. The menu includes vast coconut soups, grilled fish with banana leaves, '18 Buddhist Warriors' (delicately steamed vegetables), and crisp Thai beer.

🕐 Daily 7.30–11.30

🍴 D €40, Wine €6.50

🚌 44

IL TIEPOLO

Map off 222 D2

Via G. B. Tiepolo 3, 00199

Tel 06 322 7449

Between Stadio Flaminio and the Tiber, this little bistro serves light meals—mostly vegetarian dishes, including rich salads, pastas and pies—and the menu changes daily. Stuffed potatoes are the house special, and fillings range from artichokes to truffles and Gorgonzola. Reservations are advised as the place is tiny, but there are tables outside in the summer.

🕐 Daily 12.30–3, 7.30–midnight; closed 1 week in Aug

🍴 L €20, D €30, Wine €8

🚭

Ⓜ Flaminio

🚋 Tram 2

TRAM TRAM

Map 225 J5

Via dei Reti 44, 00185

Tel 06 4470 2585

This restaurant, in the heart of San Lorenzo (one of the liveliest districts of Rome, near the university), serves a mixture of Apulian and Roman cuisine. There's also a choice of vegetarian dishes, including delicious vegetable lasagne.

There are tables outside in summer, next to the tram tracks that give the restaurant its name. The wine list is excellent, but the waiters are little help if you have difficulty choosing. Reservations are advised.

🕐 Tue–Sun 12.30–3.30, 7.30–midnight; closed 2 weeks in Aug

🍴 L €40, D €50, Wine €9

🚭

🚌 492

TRASTÈ

Map 223 D6

Via della Lungaretta 76, 00153

Tel 06 589 4430

By day, a chic but informal café in Trastevere where you can

choose from a huge range of herbal teas, as well as *frullati* (fruit shakes), milkshakes and alcoholic drinks. In the evening, it's becomes a pub, and light meals are available.

🕐 Mon–Sun 5pm–2am

🍴 D €20, Wine €10

🚭 Section

🚌 780; tram 8

TRATTORIA ABRUZZESE

Map 224 G4

Via Napoli 4, 00185

Tel 06 482 5556

Cuisine from Abruzzo, the mountainous region to the east of Lazio, famous for its wild boar and rich, heavy pasta. After passing through an entrance shrouded with plants, you find yourself in this welcoming trattoria, spread over four rooms, two of them non-smoking. Photographs of rich and famous patrons cover the walls. Try the *pasta alla amatriciana* (with bacon, tomato and onion) or one of their divine chargrilled veal chops.

🕐 Mon–Sat noon–3, 6–11.30

🍴 L €30, D €40, Wine €6

🚭 Section

Ⓜ Repubblica

🚌 64, 70, 117

TRE SCALINI

Map 223 D4

Piazza Navona 28–32, 00100

Tel 06 6880 1996

You cannot visit Piazza Navona without sampling Tre Scalini's tartufo ice-cream. There are tables outside where you can sit and enjoy your gelato, but at a premium. Why not take your ice-cream away to eat in the piazza in the shade of Bernini's fountain?

🕐 Sun–Fri 10am–midnight, Sat 10am–3am

🍴 €2.50 (small ice-cream to take away)

🚌 63, 492 or any bus to Largo Argentina

TRIMANI 'IL WINEBAR'

Map 224 G3

Via Cernaia 37/b, 00185

Tel 06 446 9630

www.trimani.com

Great wine bar/restaurant just along from Termini station in a leafy piazza. The original, 120-year-old Carrara marble counter has survived renovations, and the plain wooden tables and striking basaltic slab floor harmonize perfectly with

EATING

VECCHIA ROMA
Map 223 E5
Piazza Campitelli 18
Tel 06 686 4604
A great restaurant, which has remained unspoiled despite its popularity. In summer, salads can be eaten outside in the pretty piazza, while in winter diners move to the 18th-century interior for more substantial meals, based around polenta. Reservations are recommended. Only American Express and Diners Club accepted.
🕐 Mon–Tue, Thu–Sun 1–3, 8–11
🍴 L €60, D €80, Wine €8
🚌 44, 46, 56, 60, 75, 85, 87, 95

VINARIUM
Map 225 J4
Via dei Volsci 103/107, 00185
Tel 06 446 2110
This restaurant and wine bar in San Lorenzo has its shelves stacked right up to the ceiling, and bottles are extracted with

a long gripping tool. The excellent list includes wines by the glass, among which Primitivo di Manduria is specially recommended. Pastas and meat dishes change daily: Try *tagliere misto* (a selection of salami, prosciutto and cheeses), plus honey and apple jam, to complement your wine. Impeccable wine presentation, though service can be very slow at the weekend.
🕐 Tue–Sun 12.30–3, 7.30–1, Oct–end Jul; 7.30pm–1am, rest of year
🍴 L €32, D €50, Wine €3 (by the glass)
🚭
🚌 492

VINERIA REGGIO
Map 223 D5
Piazza Campo dei Fiori 15, 00186
Tel 06 6880 3268
Wine bar on the market square of Campo dei Fiori in an original 16th-century building, with

the bottles lining the walls. All dishes include a wine suggestion—for instance, *bresaola* (thinly sliced dried fillet of beef) with Gorgonzola, walnuts and pear, or pâté de foie gras, are recommended with the Schiaffo Colacicci Anagni 2000, one of more than 600 wines, all of which are served by the glass. The platter of Italian cheeses is easily shared. The bar is open all day.
🕐 Mon–Sat 11.30–3, 7–midnight
🍴 L €40, D €58, Wine €10
🚭 Section
🚇 Repubblica or Castro Pretorio

IL TRONO DEI PAZZI
Map 224 G5
Via Carlo Alberti 6/c, 00185
Tel 06 445 3764
This is a rarity in Rome: a steakhouse. It is very close to the basilica of Santa Maria Maggiore, and sits 5m (16ft) below ground in five vaulted cellars decorated with frescoes and copies of the weird works of Flemish artist Hieronymus Bosch. It's good for children, too, as they do hot dogs, pizzas and hamburgers, but their mainstay, the 250g (9oz).

Florentine chargrilled steaks, are mouth-wateringly good. Steaks are presented on large platters and flambéed at your table.
🕐 Wed–Mon 11–3.30, 6–11.30
🍴 L €20, D €40, Wine €7.50
🚭
🚇 Vittorio
🚌 70, 71, 105, 360, 649; tram 5

exposed beams, terracotta floors and a marble bar. Have a light lunch and a glass of wine among locals after a visit to the market. The wine selection is vast, with fine choices from all over Italy. In the evening, the atmosphere is vibrant, with people spilling out onto the piazza. Wines per glass start at €2.10 and go up to €10.50.
🕐 Mon–Sat 8.30am–2am, Sun 4pm–2am; closed 2 weeks in Aug
🍴 L €30, Wine €4
🚌 46, 62, 64, 87, 116, 492 to Campo dei Fiori

WINETIME
Map 222 C4
Piazza Pasquale Paoli 15, 00186
Tel 06 687 5706
www.winetime.it
Panoramic wine bar with a view of Castel Sant'Angelo and an ample wine list of about 300 labels, mainly Italian. Glossy wood tables, open cupboards displaying bottles and glasses, and a 10m (33ft) wooden counter running through the main room give a stylish yet warm touch. All dishes are coupled with a suitable wine, from the creative

starters (roasted Piedmont cheese, smoked ham with vegetables) to the salads and meat dishes. Reservations are advised.
🕐 Mon–Sat noon–2 am
🍴 L €15, D €40, Wine €8
🚭
🚌 64 to Corso Vittorio Emanuele II

Staying

STAYING IN ROME

Following Rome's renaissance in the wake of the Jubilee Year in 2000, there are now more luxury hotels than ever. Previously crumbling palazzi have been restored and many of the longer established hotels have been completely renovated. The number of five-star hotels in the city is now 20—almost double what it was before the millennium celebrations.

STAYING

LOCATION, LOCATION

As in any city, Rome has a wide range of accomodation types, from small, low-budget *pensioni* around Termini to grand, five-star luxury hotels on the Via Veneto. What to expect, in terms of price and quality, depends largely on whereabouts your hotel is in the city (see table opposite).

Staying in the *centro storico* means that you are close to all of Rome's sights, but also to its sounds. Rome is a noisy city that goes to bed late and gets up early. Narrow streets and tall buildings tend to amplify the sounds of traffic and late-night revellers. Quiet places can be found, on the edge of the popular areas or in hotels with double or even triple glazing. Some of the more expensive hotels have soundproofing. When booking a hotel, ask for a quiet room, which will either be at the back of the building or overlooking a central courtyard.

If you really value your sleep, book a hotel in the quieter Aventino, Celio or Prati districts. The disadvantage here is that you will have to spend time on buses or trams, commuting into the *centro storico*. However, public transportation is inexpensive and reliable, and hotels here are often cheaper than similarly rated establishments in the heart of the city.

WHAT YOU GET FOR YOUR EUROS

The familiar star system operates in Italy, with five stars denoting the highest standard of comfort, luxury and facilities. A one-star hotel or *pensione* has few facilities and frequently does not include a private bathroom. Normally both television and telephone will be downstairs in the lobby. These establishments tend to have an early curfew, do not accept credit cards and do not have a 24-hour desk service. You should expect to pay up to around €110 for a double room per night, although some are substantially cheaper.

Prices in a two-star rise to around €160 for a double room. Three stars go from about €80 to €310, four stars from €220 to around €620, while five-star de luxe properties start at around €420 and keep on soaring upwards.

Some hotels charge extra for breakfast and as, a general rule of thumb, the more expensive the establishment, the less likely it is that breakfast is included. In the listings that follow, breakfast is included unless stated otherwise. In the more moderately-priced hotels, most rooms will have telephones and a mini-bar, and prices here tend to include breakfast, tax and service charges. The smaller boutique hotels are extremely popular and tend to be in lovely, old historic buildings tucked away from the main streets. These do not come cheap, but offer many services and usually include breakfast, tax and service. The larger, de luxe hotels usually have full business facilities and access to the internet, as well as health spas and pools. The cost of a stay here is usually exclusive of both breakfast and service.

BOOKING

As Rome is an eternally popular destination, it pays to reserve well in advance, especially if your stay is over the peak periods, which, nowadays, tend to be the greater part of the year. However, January to March and August are the least popular months of the tourist calendar and you should be able to find some good deals at this time. Do consult hotels' websites for details of special offers, and remember that specialist tour operators usually have a fixed allocation in some of the best hotels and can include your flights and transfers at very competitive prices for an all-in package. If you arrive without a reservation, do ask to see the room first before you commit yourself. Information and accommodation agencies are always a useful resource.

Il Tridente The chic shopping area around the Piazza di Spagna has traditional hotels in the upper price range

Via Veneto Rome's top-end hotels are here, although it is no longer the heart of la *dolce vita*

The Pantheon and Piazza Navona Upper to mid-price hotels in an area buzzing with life

The Ghetto and Campo dei Fiori Low- to medium-price hotels with bags of character

Monti and Esquillino Traditionally an area of low-budget accommodation

Prati, Aventino and Celio Peaceful, quietly charming mid- to high-price hotels, away from the activity of the *centro storico*

Trastevere Better known for its bars and nightlife, but has added to its quota of accommodation

The Vatican From spartan pilgrim hostels to comfortable hotels in bustling medieval lanes

ACCOMMODATION SERVICES

The APT (Azienda di Promozione Turistica di Roma) tourist office at Via Parigi 5, Esquilino (tel 06 3600 4399, www.romaturismo.com) provides an independent list of accommodation, although you are responsible for making your own booking. The office is open Mon–Sat 9–7, while the phoneline is open daily 9–7.30. There is also a branch at Fiumicino airport (tel 06 3600 4399). Also at Rome's Fiumicino airport, The **Hotel Reservation Service** (arrivals halls, Terminal A, B and C; open daily from around 7.30am to 10.30pm—times do vary) with English operators and details of availability of accommodation in every price range. The service also has branches at Ciampino airport Apr–Nov and at Termini (platform heads 2–3 and 20). The telephone number for Hotel Reservation Service is 06 6991000, www.hotelreservation.it. Credit cards are not accepted.

Termini—the area around the station—is full of 'officials' who are keen to direct you to a hotel. Some are appointed by the tourist office, others are impostors, so be wary. To avoid any misunderstanding it is always better to go direct to the tourist information point (PIT—Punti Informativi Turistici, instantly recognizable by the green-painted kiosk) at Termini (daily 8am–9pm). There are other information points around the city.

A very useful service is run by **Enjoy Rome**, which is a private English-speaking agency that can give helpful advice and also provides a free accommodation booking service. Its main office is just by Termini station (take the north exit from the station at Via Marsala, walk straight along for three blocks and it is on the left) at Via Marghera 8A (tel 06 4451843, www.enjoyrome.com) It is open Mon–Fri 8.30–7, Sat 8.30–2, summer; Mon–Fri 8,30–6.30, Sat 8.30–2, winter. Credit cards are not accepted.

OTHER OPTIONS

Camping The Touring Club Italiano publishes an annual directory *Campeggi in Italia*, which covers sites throughout the country and is available in bookstores (around €12).

Bed-and-Breakfast Bed-and-breakfast is a relatively new concept in Rome, but it is booming. More than a thousand are now registered, from spare bedrooms in out of town family flats to rooms in opulent palazzi. They are the new shabby chic trend and some are a great deal more chic than shabby.

The **Bed and Breakfast Italia** agency, (Corso Vittorio Emanuele 284, tel 06 6878618, www.bbitalia.it) lists around 250 properties, including luxury four-crown accommodation in palazzi. Prices start from around €60 per room in this category, descending to around €25 in a two-crown establishment.

Rent an apartment If you want to rent an apartment, the peak times for availability tend to be in July, August and December, when the owners traditionally take their own holidays. Agencies specializing in apartment and villa rentals include:

Homes International, Via L. Bissolati 20, tel 06 4881800, www.homesenint.@tin.it. The service covers short- and long-term rentals for apartments and villas, and English is spoken. The office is open from Mon–Fri 9–6, Sat 9–1.

Rome Property Network, Via dei Gesu e Maria 25 (near Piazza del Popolo), tel 06 3212341. English is also spoken in this agency, where they specialize in apartments and villas in the *centro storico* and Trastevere. Open Mon–Fri 9.30–6, Sat 10–2.

Useful websites include **Flat in Rome**: www.flatinrome.com and **Romeguide**: www.romeguide.it.

STAYING

Hotels

The hotels below are listed alphabetically and cover a range of budgets. The prices given are for a double room and include breakfast, unless otherwise stated.

ABRUZZI
Map 257 E4
Piazza della Rotonda 69, 00186
Tel 06 6792021
www.hotelabruzzi.it
Although its prices have increased in recent years, this hotel still represents one of the best deals in the city, considering what you get: The most dramatic view of the Pantheon that Rome has to offer. Most rooms have en suite bathrooms, and all have double-glazing and air-conditioning.
€90–195
25

116

ADRIATIC
Map 256 C4
Via Vitelleschi 25, 00193
Tel 06 6880 8080
www.adriatichotel.com
A family-run hotel, just three blocks from St. Peter's. The reception has a pleasant interior of reds and golds, plus an old-style wooden desk. Rooms

are moderately spacious with patterned carpets and reproduction furniture. Not all guest rooms have private bathrooms, but they do have satellite TV and air conditioning (€15 extra per day). There is 24-hour bar service but no breakfast.
€75–105, excluding breakfast
42

Ottaviano San Pietro
40 81, 62, 64

ALBERGO DEL 'SOLE' AL BISCIONE
Map 257 D5
Via del Biscione 76, 00186
Tel 06 6880 6873
www.solealbiscione.it

In a little side street just off bustling Campo dei Fiori. Competitively priced for a hotel in the heart of medieval Rome, although in need of a little updating. Rooms are clean, if on the small side, with old furniture. All have TV and bathroom with shower. Staff are friendly and there is a gem of a roof terrace for viewing the surrounding skyline. There is no access for visitors in a wheelchair. Paid parking, but credit cards are not accepted.
€110–140, excluding breakfast
62
20 rooms
40, 62, 64, 87, 116, 492

ALBERGO DE SOLE AL PANTHEON
Map 257 E4
Piazza della Rotonda 63
Tel 06 6780441
www.hotelsolealpantheon.com
This chic hotel claims to be the oldest in Rome, and with a history stretching back to 1467 they could be right. It has an enviable location in the same square as the Pantheon, with stunning views from the windows at the front of the building. Some rooms have painted ceilings or tiled floors, and more than half have jacuzzis; all have satellite TV.
In warm weather, breakfast is served in the attractive courtyard.
€280–340
25

Spagna
119 to Piazza della Rotonda, 70, 81, 87 to Corso del Rinascimento, or any bus to Largo di Torre Argentina

ALIMANDI
Map 256 B3
Via Tunesi 8, 00192
Tel 06 3972 3948
www.alimandi.org
Superior three-star, family-run hotel that is very good value for money. The 19th-century building, close to the Vatican Museums, retains some original features, including elegant Venetian stuccowork. Rooms

are spacious, with modern furnishings and pastel shades; all have satellite and pay TV, and roomy bathrooms with hairdryers. There is an internet computer point for guests to use, and a free airport shuttle, plus parking. Continental buffet breakfast on the roof terrace or in the dining room.
Closed 10 Jan–10 Feb
€130–150
35

Cipro Musei Vaticani or Ottaviano San Pietro
81, 492, 495

ANGLO AMERICANO
Map 257 F4
Via Quattro Fontane 12, 00184
Tel 06 472941
www.hotelangloamericano.it
This distinguished hotel has a genteel, belle époque atmosphere, from the cool, blue and white striped wallpaper in the lounge to the solemn busts guarding the door. The 18th-century palazzo has well-ordered and well-appointed rooms, all with private bath, hairdryer, satellite TV and internet connection. The hotel is near the Piazza di Spagna, Fontana di Trevi, Via Veneto and Parliament, making it popular with politicians.
€150–180
122

Spagna

ANNE AND MARY

Map 258 F5

Via Cavour 325, 00184

Tel 06 6994 1187

www.anne-mary.com

This welcoming bed-and-breakfast occupies an elegant 19th-century building near the Colosseo. Rooms are simple but dramatic, with clean lines and swooping curtains. Each has a small private bathroom with enclosed shower, TV, mini bar, safe and hairdryer. The wood parquetry on the hall floors is especially handsome. Via Cavour is a large, somewhat frantic, artery, but the convenience for sites and shops is worth the muted noise.

🛏 €100–125

🛌 3 (all non-smoking)

💲

🚇 Cavour

🚌 75, 81, 85, 87, 116, 117

ANTICA LOCANDA

Map 258 F5

Via del Boschetto 84, 00184

Tel 06 4788 1729

www.antica-locanda.com

In the oldest part of Rome, not far from the Colosseo, is this quaint, inexpensive, family-run hotel. Check in at the 15th-century wine bar of the same name next door. There is no lift

(elevator) up the four floors, but a porter service is provided. Rooms have beamed ceilings, wooden floors with rugs, and Italian reproduction furniture, plus TV, minibar, shower and hairdryer. There is a large flower-filled roof terrace (and on request the use of a barbecue) overlooking this medieval part of the city. The continental breakfast is served in the wine bar.

🛏 €104–155

🛌 18

💲

🚇 Cavour

🚌 117, or any bus to Via Nazionale

ATLANTE STAR

Map 256 C4

Via G. Vitelleschi 34, 00193

Tel 06 687 3233

www.atlantehotels.com

This luxury hotel between Vatican City and the Castel Sant'Angelo exudes class and elegance. Richly upholstered sofas, heavy drapes, stuccoed ceilings and plush carpets, all in of gold, reds and blues, plus antiques and 18th-century paintings. The rooms are equally lush and spacious; half

have whirlpool baths. There is a bar and a renowned gourmet restaurant, plus a free airport shuttle. There are astounding views of St. Peter's from the breakfast room.

🛏 €170–299

🛌 80

💲

🚇 Ottaviano San Pietro

🚌 32, 81, 492

BAROCCO

Map 257 F4

Via della Purificazione 4, 00187

Tel 06 487 2001

www.hotelbarocco.com

Three historic buildings have been merged to form this intimate, elegant hotel. The newer wing has jacuzzi tubs in some rooms, while the older part is rich with cherrywood-framed mirrors, opulent drapes and precious marble. Although it overlooks Piazza Barberini, the hotel is well soundproofed, muting Rome's constant roar. Visitors praise the Barocco's fresh flowers, extra towels, courtesy kits and efficient staff. Guests in the suites also get dressing gowns.

🛏 €232–284

🛌 37 rooms (all non-smoking), 5 suites

💲

🚇 Barberini

BBROMA

Map 256 B3

Via Sebastiano Veniero 78, 00192

Tel 06 6821 0776

www.bbroma.com

This is a collection of bed-and-breakfasts put together on a website by a group of friends. Some of these rooms are near the Vatican, and reservations

are handled centrally by Signora Erminia Pascucci. Rooms are generally spacious and nicely furnished, mostly in a late 19th-century style. All have telephone, TV and bathroom. The organization also arranges for stays in rooms in houses with communal kitchen and in apartments. Be sure to check the website for conditions. Credit cards are not accepted.

🛏 €75–95

🛌 3 near the Vatican, plus 50 more around the city

🚇 Cipro Musei Vaticani

🚌 19, 23, 70, 492, 495

BERNINI BRISTOL

Map 257 F4

Piazza Barberini 23, 00187

Tel 06 488 3051

www.berninibristol.com

This *grande dame* has always been popular with aristocrats and royalty. The 1874 palazzo is refurbished, but antiques and vintage tapestries maintain the tone. Both restaurants are renowned, especially the rooftop panorama of L'Olimpo, with its impressive views. Once the heart of *la dolce vita*, the Bernini's nightclub and lounges remain chic. Facilities include babysitting, car rental, valet parking, private garage, secretarial service, sauna and hot tub. Pets are welcome.

🛏 €464–675, excluding breakfast

🛌 127, 100 non-smoking

📺 💲

🚇 Barberini

🚌 61, 62, 116, 119, 175, 492, 590

CAMPING FLAMINIO VILLAGE DI VITTORIO CANTELLA E FIGLI SRL

Map off 257 D1
Via Flaminia Nuova 821, 00189
Tel 06 333 2604
www.villageflaminio.com

Only a few kilometres from the city, these bungalows are well served by public transportation. They are also well furnished with bath, shower and private garden. Many have kitchens and living rooms, plus satellite TV, garden furniture, barbecue and parking, and a weekly maid service. There is also a shaded campsite in the peaceful urban oasis of Parco di Veio. Services here include pool, laundry, restaurant/bar/pizzeria, safe deposit and internet. A riverside cycle path leads all the way into the city. Car and scooter rental.

🛏 Bungalows €58–91, campsite €23–28 including tent
ℹ 90 bungalows, 300 tent plots
🏊 ♿
🚌 200 from Piazza Mancini
🚆 Flaminio to Due Ponti

CAPO D'AFRICA

Map 258 G6
Via Capo d'Africa 54, 00184
Tel 06 772801
www.hotelcapodafrica.com

Handsome 19th-century building close to the Colosseo in a fashionable district. It is a fusion of contemporary and classic, with a hint of Japanese design. The beautiful rooms are in warm ochre and saffron tones, and the perfectly fitted

bathrooms are in marble and wood. The American buffet breakfast is served on the roof with views of the Colosseo. Large, well-equipped gym and solarium.

🛏 €265–280
ℹ 65 (20 non-smoking)
🍴 ♿
Ⓜ Colosseo
🚌 81, 85, 87, 117; tram 3

IL CASTELLO

Map 258 H6
Via Vittorio Amedeo II 9, 00185
Tel 06 7720 4036
www.ilcastello.com

Il Castello is a rare gem: a Roman budget hotel that accepts credit cards and has 24-hour desk service rather than the usual early curfew normally typical of this class. It even has room service, laundry, telephone and fax. Breakfast is the usual minimal Italian fare, of cornflakes, toast and *cornetti* (croissants). Termini is one of the less salubrious areas after dark, but this keeps rates low, and Il Castello is certainly a safe oasis. As an extra bonus, the staff are multilingual.

🛏 €52–93
ℹ 18 (12 non-smoking)
Ⓜ Manzoni
🚌 70, 105; tram 5, 14

CILICIA

Map off 258 H7
Via Cilicia 7, 00179
Tel 06 700 5554
www.hotelcilicia.it

A 1950s-built hotel justa 5-minute walk from the city end of the Via Appia. The interiors have an old-world feel, with an austere cherrywood reception desk and Austrian blinds. The lounge has a studded-leather bar counter, and the dining room has some grandeur, but is comfortable enough. Ample-sized rooms all with bath, satellite TV, minibar and electronic safe. Parking available.

🛏 €130–150
ℹ 62 (5 non-smoking)
♿
Ⓜ San Giovanni
🚌 360

COLONNA PALACE HOTEL

Map 257 E4
Piazza Montecitorio 12, 00186
Tel 06 675191
www.itihotels.it

Overlooking the Parliament buildings in the hub of 16th-century Rome, the Colonna is a superb base for discovering the eternal city. It is fairly chintzy throughout—pink walls, bright floral upholstered chairs and drapes, and neo-Grecian columns. Rooms are spacious, with bathroom, TV and minibar. The breakfast room, serving a Continental buffet

breakfast, overlooks the Presidential Palace. There is also a roof terrace bar and solarium.

🛏 €265–350
ℹ 102
♿
🚌 46, 62, 116

COLUMBIA

Map 258 G4
Via del Viminale 15, 00184
Tel 06 4744289
www.hotelcolumbia.com

This charming hotel is just a stone's throw away from Termini station, just around the corner from Teatro dell'Opera, and its friendly, efficient staff are always happy to help. All the rooms are simply furnished and have satellite TV. Breakfast is served on the roof terrace—a great way to start the day—and as the day wears on, you can relax in the bar or lounge. Ask for a quiet room, as those near the road can be noisy.

🛏 €133–149
ℹ 45
♿
Ⓜ Termini
🚌 40, 64 or any bus to Termini

THE DUKE

Map off 257 E1
Via Archimede 69, 00197
Tel 06 367221
www.thedukehotel.com

In the heart of the well-heeled Parioli district, between the parks of the Villa Borghese and the Villa Gloria. Beautiful English country house interiors with a classical influence. Delightful art nouveau glass cupola in the Polo Lounge. The guest rooms are luxurious and intimate, spacious and light, in warm hues, with fresh flowers, minibar, safe, satellite TV and games console. There are also large marble bathrooms. Children get a welcome pack and free tickets to the zoo.

STAYING

€285–380

78

Flaminio

52, 53, 168, 217, 230, 231, 910

HOTEL EDEN

Map 257 F3
Via Ludovisi 49
Tel 06 478121
www.hotel-eden.it
Just off the Via Veneto is the
Eden, one of Rome's top
hotels. Its relaxed, old-
fashioned luxury makes it a
popular choice with visiting
celebrities and European royalty. All the rooms are very
tasteful and furnished with
antiques, and have marble
bathrooms, satellite TV and
internet access. After dinner in
La Terrazza restaurant, relax in
the piano bar.

€645–745, excluding breakfast

121

Barberini

63, 116 or any bus to Via Veneto

EXEDRA

Map 258 G4
Piazza della Repubblica 47, 00185
Tel 06 489381
www.boscolo.com
True luxury, built over the
remains of Diocletian's third-
century baths, on Piazza della
Repubblica. Carrara marble
and Venetian glass are used to
stunning effect in the lobby.
The two restaurants were created by architect Adam Tihany.
Guest rooms are equally lush,
in Regency style with marble
bathrooms, satellite TV and

safe. There is contemporary
artwork throughout. Solarium,
spa, and roof terrace with
swimming pool and bar.

€275–800, excluding breakfast

240 (96 non-smoking)

Repubblica

40, 64 to Via Nazionale

FAWLTY TOWERS HOTEL AND HOSTEL

Map 258 H4
Via Magenta 39, 00187
Tel 06 445 0374
www.fawltytowers.org
Decent inexpensive hotel/
hostel accommodation near
Termini station, with both private and shared rooms. When
you arrive, take the lift (elevator) up to the fifth floor. This
certainly isn't dormitory bunk-
bed accommodation; instead,
you get a bed for the night in a
four-person room. The place
has a clubby feel; there are
wood floors and a theme of
cheerful orange and zany
stripes, with bouquets of
sunflowers and an odd papier-
mâché puppet head. It is
slightly eccentric in a fun and
functional way. There is a communal kitchen and free
internet access, and no curfew.
Credit cards are not accepted.

€58–66, excluding breakfast

16 (all are non-smoking)

6 rooms

Termini

40, 64 or any bus to Termini

GABRIELLA

Map 258 H4
Via Palestro 88, 00185
Tel 06 445 0120
www.gabriellahotel.com
This first-floor hotel with lift
(elevator) is near Termini station and the main bus
terminal. There is a comfortable feel about the place: it
has a welcoming lobby and
small reading/TV lounge with
sofas and coffee tables.
Medium-sized rooms with

ceramic floors, Tuscan-style
matching coverlets and curtains, double-glazed windows,
safe, minibar and satellite TV.
The white-tiled bathrooms
have showers (some have
baths) and hairdryers. There is
a spacious breakfast room/bar
serving a Continental breakfast, and the staff speak
English.

€80–135

23 (all non-smoking)

Castro Pretorio

492, or any bus to Termini

GENIO

Map 257 D4
Via G. Zanardelli 28, 00186
Tel 06 683 2191
www.leonardihotels.com
This hotel has a nice touch of
the old world about it. Antique
furniture and rich red carpets
throughout give it a regal air.
Good-sized, high-ceilinged
rooms with embroidered
armchairs and marble-fitted

bathrooms. Bar and roof
terrace have fine views of
nearby St. Peter's and Castel
Sant'Angelo. It is a wonderful
base for exploring for the
Renaissance quarter of Rome
and is just seconds away from
Piazza Navona. A free airport
shuttle service is available, as
is private parking.

€200–232

60

70, 81, 87,116, 492

STAYING

GRAND HOTEL DE LA MINERVE

Map 257 E5
Piazza della Minerva 69, 00186
Tel 06 695201
www.hotel-invest.com

This historic 17th-century hotel is close to the Pantheon. The classically furnished lobby has Roman statues, palm trees, marble flooring and an art nouveau glass cupola. Guest rooms are elegantly furnished and painted in soft pastel blues and ochre; some have exposed beams or frescoed ceilings. All have marble bathrooms, satellite/pay TV, coffee-maker, trouser press, safe and internet access. Amenities include restaurant, bar, roof garden, sauna and fitness facilities. The staff are always ready to help.

€400–515
135
116, or any bus to Via del Corso

HILTON ROME AIRPORT

Map off 257 D7
Via Arturo Ferrarin, 00050 Fiumicino
Tel 06 65258
www.hilton.com
The Hilton is the only hotel on or near the airport grounds, right in front of the departure hall. The rooms are spacious and the hotel has a number of comforts, such as all-day dining in the buffet-style restaurant, as well as a café with pizza and pasta. Other amenities include fitness facilities with indoor pool, gym, two outdoor floodlit tennis courts, sauna, steam room and massage—plenty to help guests get over jet lag. Train or free shuttle to the city, 35 minutes away.

€255–€335
517, 204 non-smoking

HASSLER

Map 257 E3
Via Trinità dei Monti 6, 00187
Tel 06 699340
www.hotelhasslerroma.com
The *bel mondo* gather at the Hassler to be cosseted by Roberto Wirth (of the Swiss hotel dynasty) and his impeccable staff. The hotel sits at the top of the Spanish Steps, surveying St. Peter's, the Villa Medici and the Vittorio Emanuele monument. The interior is lavish, rich with marble, frescoed walls, hand-painted tiles, fringed curtains and glass-roofed lounge. Big spenders prefer the penthouse, though corner room 403 is also coveted. Facilities include a restaurant, bar, hair salon, massage, babysitting, laundry, room service, tennis court and the use of bicycles free of charge.

€450–795
100 rooms, 15 suites

Spagna

Fiumicino Airport

HOLIDAY INN ROME-WEST

Map off 256 A6
Via Aurelia Km 8.400, 00163
Tel 06 6641 1200
www.sixcontinentshotels.com
If Rome's chaos and excitement become overwhelming, you can retreat to the Holiday Inn 8km (5 miles) west of the city, on the Via Aurelia highway. It is ideal for frazzled executives, with 14 meeting rooms, secretarial and translation services, and private limousine hire, plus a gym and pool to unwind. There is also free internet access, a restaurant, cocktail lounge, garden, snooker tables and children's playground. Pets cost an extra €6 per night. Park free or in the guarded lot (€5). Free shuttle service to city from the hotel.

€104–250, excluding breakfast
196 rooms, 102 non-smoking, 8 suites

Cornelia, then bus 246

HOTEL CELIO

Map 258 G6
Via dei Santi Quattro 35c
Tel 06 7049 5333
www.hotelcelio.com
The simple façade of this elegant hotel, just a short walk from the Colosseo, belies its stunning interior. All bedrooms have frescoes, inspired by Renaissance painters, and include satellite TV and VCRs with a selection of films in English and Italian. Rooms on the upper floors have jacuzzis.

€150–290
20
Colosseum
116, 117

HOTEL CESARI

Map 257 E4
Via di Pietra 89a, 00186
Tel 06 674 9701
www.venere.it/roma/cesari
The quiet but central position of this charming, friendly hotel means that it has a loyal client base, and so early booking is recommended. Built in 1787, close to the Pantheon, it has 11 pillars from the second-century AD Temple of Hadrian incorporated into its structure. Its large rooms all have satellite TV.

€170–228
47 (21 non-smoking)
60, 62, 85, 117, 119, 160 to Via del Corso

HOTEL D'ESTE

Map 258 G5
Via Carlo Alberto 4b, 00135
Tel 06 446 5607
www.hotel-deste.com
This early 19th-century hotel is in a tree-lined street, directly across from the basilica of Santa Maria Maggiore and a few minutes away from Termini station. There is a charming reception hall with a cobbled floor and beamed ceiling. The bar and restaurant are on the first floor, making the hotel unsuitable for

STAYING

wheelchair users. Guest rooms are simple, clean and spacious, with parquet floors and reproduction furniture. All have TV and bathroom with hairdryer. Alfresco dining in summer.

€45–166
37
Vittorio
70, 360

HOTEL D'INGHILTERRA
Map 257 E4
Via Bocca di Leone 14, 00187
Tel 06 69981

The wealthy Torlonia family built this palazzo, now a sumptuous hotel, near the boutique-lined Via Condotti. Outside it has an imposing golden façade, supported by arches, while beyond the entrance a black and white carpet runs through the lobby, punctuated by delicate antiques and plump red sofas. The guest rooms, though less dramatic, are pleasant, with thick carpeting, carved bed frames, and carefully chosen paintings and prints. There is 24-hour room service.

€325–445, excluding breakfast
98 (20 non-smoking)
Spagna

HOTEL DELLE MUSE
Map off 258 F1
Via T. Salvini 18, 00197
Tel 06 808 8333
www.hoteldellemuse.com

Hilltop Parioli is one of Rome's most élite areas, and a cool oasis in summer months. It is worth venturing off the beaten track to find this pleasant hotel, particularly if you have special requirements. The management is sensitive towards vegetarian, kosher and halal diets. They also have family discounts and and an internet booking discount of 5 per cent, and pets are welcome. There is free email and internet access, a restaurant, bar and outdoor garden. Tours depart from the hotel.

€113–150
60
360 to Piazza delle Muse

HOTEL NAVONA
Map 257 E5
Via dei Sediari 8
Tel 06 6864203
www.hotelnavona.com

HOTEL DE RUSSIE
Map 257 E3
Via del Babuino 9, 00187
Tel 06 328881
www.roccofortehotels.com

Near Piazza del Popolo in the heart of the city, amid all the top designer shops, this is arguably Rome's top hotel. It is a historic palazzo, where the contemporary and classic are blended. Guest rooms have high ceilings and are lovingly furnished, and the bathrooms are works of art. Amenities include spa with hydropool, sauna, Turkish baths and beauty treatments. The first-class restaurant is elegant and, when its doors are opened onto the gardens, the most romantic spot in Rome.

€572–798
129 (37 non-smoking)
Flaminio
117

The Italio-Australian owners create a friendly atmosphere in this hotel, close to the Piazza Navona and Pantheon in a quiet side street, which makes it very popular. The history of the place is interesting, as some parts of the building date from the first century AD, and were built over the Baths of Aggripa; Keats and Shelley once stayed on the top floor. The rooms are basic and simple, most have bathrooms, and air conditioning is available at a €15 supplement. The breakfast isn't the best, but there are plenty of places to eat nearby. Credit cards are not accepted.

€120–€130
35
31 rooms
30, 70, 86, 87, 116

INTERNAZIONALE
Map 257 F4
Via Sistina 79, 00187
Tel 06 6994 1823
www.hotelinternazionale.com

Wisteria winds up the front of this palazzo—a faint echo perhaps of the ancient Roman gardens that once stood here. The building evolved over the years, serving as a convent in the 16th–17th centuries. Today, the breakfast lounge is in soothing pastel blues and purples, and this tranquil scheme continues throughout, from the cupids in the cupola to the silk wall coverings in the bedrooms. There is 24-hour room service, a bar, currency exchange, babysitting and parking, and pets are welcome.

€212–235
42
Spagna
62

ITALIA
Map 257 G4
Via Venezia 18, 00184
Tel 06 487 0919
www.hotelitaliaroma.com

Inexpensive, family-run hotel in a 19th-century building just off Via Nazionale, the second-largest shopping street in the city. Reception is on the first floor. Both public and guest rooms are very clean and simple throughout, and the guest

rooms have TV, minibar, air conditioning (€8 extra per day), bathroom and hairdryer. All are spacious, with parquet floors, functional furniture and cream walls. The hotel has a bar and a safe at reception.

€75–114
32 (15 non-smoking)
21 rooms (€8 extra)
Repubblica
64

THE KENNEDY HOTEL
Map 258 H5
Via Filippo Turati 62–64, 00185
Tel 06 446 5373
www.hotelkennedy.net

This three-star hotel is between Termini station and the basilica of Santa Maria Maggiore. Half of the guest rooms overlook the

archaeological park of the Roman Aquarium. Rooms are spacious, with fitted wardrobes, double glazed windows, satellite TV, and small but well-equipped bathrooms. The public areas are warmly lit, and there is a small reading room with some books and guides in English. The three small breakfast rooms with a bar serve a buffet breakfast.

🛏 €70–160
🛌 51
♿
🚇 Termini
🚌 40, 64, 70

LANCELOT
Map 258 G6
Via Capo d'Africa 47, 00184
Tel 06 7045 0615, 06 7045 0616
www.lancelothotel.com

This welcoming, family-run hotel is just around the corner from the Colosseo. The entrance hall and dining room

have period furniture and Murano glass chandeliers. Other public spaces are the bar, the library and a delightful courtyard. Rooms are spacious, and most have wooden floors,

pastel walls and individual charm. All have a safe, satellite TV and bathroom with shower. Some guest rooms have their own terraces, but there's also a lovely roof terrace

🛏 €145
🛌 60
♿
🚇 Colosseo or Manzoni
🚌 81, 85, 87, 117; tram 3

LAURENTIA
Map 259 J5
Largo degli Osci 63, 00185
Tel 06 445 0218
www.hotellaurentia.com

Classic, refined hotel in the heart of the university district, taking its name from the goddess of ancient Rome. Comfortable guest rooms, with free internet access in the lounge. Continental buffet breakfast served in the Piranesi room, which was formerly a bakery and is named for a famous local bread. There are also plenty of good places to eat locally.

🛏 €90–130
🛌 41
♿
🚌 71 from Piazza San Silvestro, or 492

LOCARNO
Map 257 E3
Via della Penna 22, 00186
Tel 06 361 0841
www.hotellocarno.com

Artists and intellectuals, including Umberto Eco (author of The Name of the Rose), opt for this art deco refuge on a sleepy street near Piazza del Popolo. The 1925 building retains original features, including a cast-iron lift (elevator). The interiors have been skilfully designed, using period lamps and furnishings, and each room is individually decorated. Guests have free use of the business and internet facilities, and vintage bicycles.

🛏 €190–310
🛌 66 (6 non-smoking)
♿
🚇 Flaminio
🚌 117

LUCE
Map 258 H4
Via Magenta 34, 00185
Tel 06 446 9277
www.sebraeli.it

Modern, light, three-star hotel close to Termini station and the shops. All public areas

LORD BYRON HOTEL
Map 257 E1
Via Giuseppe de Notaris 5, 00197
Tel 06 3220404
www.lordbyronhotel.com

In the leafy Parioli district, overlooking the Villa Borghese is the Lord Byron, which, true to its name, is a romantic hideaway. The art deco villa has scarlet sofas, lacquered furniture, gilded mirrors and marble bathrooms. There is a piano bar for relaxation, where servings of port and petits fours can lull you to sleep each night. The hotel's restaurant, Sapori del Lord Byron, is considered one of Italy's finest. Ask for rooms 503, 602 or 603, as they have spectacular views. Parking is available.

🛏 €300–440
🛌 36, 6 non-smoking
♿
🚇 Flaminio
🚌 117

have attractive inlaid marble floors and comfortable sofas. The breakfast room is elegant, with upholstered spoon-back chairs and gold-braided tablecloths. Guest rooms are stylish and spacious, with draped curtains, fitted wooden furniture and good spot lighting. All rooms have bathroom, TV and minibar. Parking available.

STAYING

€104
68
[icon]
Termini
40, 64

MERCURE DELTA COLOSSEO
Map 258 G6
Via Labicana 144, 00184
Tel 06 770021
www.mercure.com
One of the last developments (1975) allowed in this part of the old city, the Mercure is in view of the Colosseo and beside Nero's Domus Aurea (Golden House). It has a beautifully marbled, spacious reception with internet access,

a high-tech minimalist bar and a piano bar. Medium-sized rooms with marble bath, comfortable sofas, satellite and pay TV, safe and minibar. There is also a bar on the roof with a 360-degree view of the city.
€147–247
160, 40 non-smoking
Outdoor
[icon]
Colosseo or Manzoni
87, 117; tram 3

NAZIONALE A MONTECITORIO
Map 257 E4
Piazza Montecitorio 131, 00186
Tel 06 695001
www.nazionaleroma.it
Next to the Parliament buildings, and close to the Fontana di Trevi and Piazza di Spagna. Charming, old world feel, with dark wood panelling,

marble floors and columns in lobby. Medium-sized rooms with high ceilings, period furniture, and decorated in gold and brown tones, all with bathroom, satellite/pay TV, minibar and safe. Old-fashioned bar and restaurant with marble floors and a wooden Renaissance-style ceiling; Italian and Continental cuisine served.
€321–500
92
[icon]
46, 62, 116

NOVA DOMUS
Map 256 B3
Via G. Savonarola 38, 00195
Tel 06 399511
www.novadomushotel.it
In a quiet location near St. Peter's, this four-star hotel has a distinct touch of the 1950s.

Good-sized, traditionally furnished rooms in warm hues, with satellite TV and private bathroom. The good restaurant compensates for a notable lack of eating places in the area. The staff are friendly and knowledgeable, and exceptional private city guides are provided at a modest prices.
€90–336
117, 40 non-smoking
[icon]
Cipro Musei Vaticani
492

ORAZIA
Map 258 H5
Via Buonarroti 51, 00185
Tel 06 4467202
www.hotelorazia.com
The Orazia is on the firth floor of a building on the Colle Esquilino, just one street away from the Colosseo. Guest rooms are furnished in classic Italian 19th-century style, including marble floors. All have private bath or shower, hairdryer, telephone, minibar

and satellite TV. The same Italian style is found in the breakfast room, where evening meals can be served on request.
€120–220
33
[icon]
Vittorio Emanuele
70, 360

PAVIA
Map 258 G4
Via Gaeta 83, 00185
Tel 06 4880379
www.hotelpavia.it
Small, simple three-star hotel in the Termini station area, overlooking the ancient remains of Terme di Diocleziano. The interior design of the rooms is not

exciting and there is functional plywood furniture. However, the rooms do have satellite/pay TV, minibar, electronic safe, internet access points and basic showers. There is a pleasant bar/lounge area open 24 hours. The hotel is based on two floors, but there is no lift (elevator).
€85–€150
25
[icon]
Castro Pretorio
492, 495

STAYING

PICCADILLY

Map off 258 H7
Via Magna Grecia 122, 00183
Tel 06 7047 4858, 06 7046 4859
www.bestwestern.it/piccadilly_rm
Part of the Best Western chain
and extremely good value for
money. It is south of the city,
near the basilica of San
Giovanni, in a busy shopping
street. Elegant, modern, first-
floor lobby, and light, quiet and

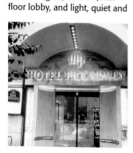

moderately spacious guest
rooms. All have TV, minibar
and safe. The bathrooms are
on the small side, but are fitted
with showers and hairdryers.
There are panoramic views
from the breakfast room on
the ninth floor, which has red
marble floors and leather sofas.
🛏 €120–165
ⓘ 55 (20 non-smoking)
🅂
🚇 San Giovanni or Re di Roma
🚌 87, 360

PONTE SISTO

Map 257 D5
Via dei Pettinari 64, 00186
Tel 06 686310
www.hotelpontesisto.it
This grand hotel is in Rome's
famed jewellers' row, just
along from the River Tiber and
the bridge from which it takes
its name. The interior is truly
splendid: marble floors, glass
foyers and ample reception
space, with a fine courtyard
decked with contemporary
wrought-iron furniture and
palm trees, creating an oasis
for its guests. The guest rooms

are tastefully furnished with
cherrywood suites and all-
marble bathrooms; satellite TV
with the option of internet
access is also available. The
roof terrace has a breathtaking
360-degree view of baroque
Rome.
🛏 €310
ⓘ 103, 50 non-smoking
🅂
🚌 116, 280

PORTOGHESI

Map 257 E4
Via dei Portoghesi 1, 00186
Tel 06 686 4231
www.hotelportoghesi.com
A gem of a hotel, tucked into
the labyrinth of the Tor di Nona
area, north of Piazza Navona.
This is a far cry from tourist
Rome—you can feel the city's
heartbeat, as mopeds sputter
and passers-by chatter. It's
easy to miss the unassuming
entrance, flanked by potted
evergreens: Keep an eye out
for the row of dainty flags.
Highlights include the breakfast solarium and inevitable
roof terrace, which overflows
with flowers.
🛏 €170–190
ⓘ 28
🅂
🚇 Spagna
🚌 116, 280

PRESIDENT

Map 258 H6
Via Emanuele Filiberto 173, 00185
Tel 06 770121
www.rosciolihotels.com
Built in the 1960s, the
President has an unappealing
façade and grey, functional
lobby. But the guest rooms all
have bright wooden furniture,
TV/pay TV and well-equipped
bathrooms (but no minibar). It

is next to a metro station and
only a short walk to the
Colosseo. Ask for a room with
a window facing the internal
courtyard, as the street side

RAPHAEL

Map 257 D4
Largo Febo 2, 00186
Tel 06 682831
www.raphaelhotel.com

Day or night, the ivy-covered
façade of this hotel, a few
steps away from Piazza
Navona, always looks a
dream. There is a period feel
to the antique-filled lobby,
with its golden velvet sofas
and gilt tables. The guest
rooms are littered with objets
d'art and are beautifully furnished, mixing patterns and
faux-marble. Facilities in the
rooms include satellite TV,
safe and minibar. The restaurant is of international repute
and the roof terrace has
unparalleled views of the city.
There is also a sauna and
fitness facilities.
🛏 €390–420, excluding breakfast
ⓘ 47 (5 non-smoking)
🗪 🅂
🚌 40, 62, 64, 87, 116, 492, 628 to
Piazza Navona

can be very noisy. Larger
rooms are available on
request. The breakfast room
serves an inexpensive lunch.
🛏 €240–280
ⓘ 192 (6 non-smoking)
🅂
🚇 Manzoni
🚌 55, 360, 590

PRINCIPESSA TEA

Map 258 G3
Via Sardegna 149, 00187
Tel 06 474 4243
www.hoteltea.com
The Principessa Tea presides
over the Via Veneto and Villa
Borghese. This is true old
world elegance—traditional
and elaborate without being
fussy. Oriental carpets, gilt mirrors and mauve upholstery add
to the genteel atmosphere.

STAYING

The Ludovici Group deserves high praise for preserving the style of this *grande dame* hotel. There is an American bar, traditional trattoria and four suites, plus indoor parking on request.

€90–140
35

Spagna

REAL ROME

Office: Via delle Cese, 00040 Ariccia
Tel 339 827 1285
www.realrome.com
Why not do the real Roman thing and stay in a stylish apartment in the *centro storico*? Browse the selection of apartments online, then contact this friendly agency. The coordinator is Tim Pearson; most owners speak English. Don't be surprised if the kitchen—well stocked with staples such as olive oil and coffee—also comes with a gift of fresh pastries. Highly recommended for those craving privacy and a slightly different experience of the Eternal City. There is a three-day minimum stay, and credit cards are not accepted.

€70–95
54 apartments
40 apartments

RESIDENCE BARBERINI

Map 257 F4
Via Quattro Fontane 171–172, 00184
Tel 06 420 3341
www.residencebarberini.com
These sleek suites are packed with modern gadgets: All have a king-sized bed, marble bathroom, TV with DVD, personal computer, internet access, printer, webcam, fax, microwave oven and refrigerator. The penthouse includes a large roof garden with wicker loungers, dining table and pavilion. Furnishings are simple and elegant, including snowy-white quilts and

wrought-iron bed frames. Breakfasts are served in the guest rooms or on the terrace. Contemporary art is exhibited in the communal areas.

€319–455, excluding breakfast
12 suites (5 non-smoking)

Barberini

RESIDENCE PALAZZO AL VELABRO

Map 257 E6
Via del Velabro 16, 00186
Tel 06 6792758, 06 6792985
www.velabro.it
Surrounded by ancient monuments and just across from the River Tiber, this is self-sufficiency in a dream setting. The apartments are light and very spacious, with a living/dining room with folding door concealing a gallery

kitchen, plus bedroom and bathroom. Lemon walls, satellite TV and comfortable sofa beds all make for a relaxed atmosphere. There is a bar and two terraces for enjoying the stunning views. Ideal for families.

€166–202, excluding breakfast
35

81, 160, 204, 628, then 15-min walk

ROMA PARK

Map off 258 H7
Via della Caffarelletta 112/114, 00179
Tel 06 7835 9552
www.romapark.com
Originally a villa, this hotel in a leafy suburb, overlooking the archaeological park of Caffarella maintains the atmosphere of a large country house. Rooms have a light, spacious feel, pastel walls and cherrywood furnishings. All have bathroom and satellite TV. The cheeful breakfast room, furnished in bamboo, serves a buffet breakfast, while the adjoining roof garden is the perfect spot for

an evening *aperitivo*. There is private parking, and some very good inexpensive trattorias nearby.

€95–115
42

Furio Camillo
628

SANT'ANSELMO

Map of 257 E7
Piazza S. Anselmo 2, 00153
Tel 06 578 3214
www.aventinohotels.com
Serene setting high on the Aventino (one of Rome's seven hills) and just minutes from the Circo Massimo. The predominant style is 19th-century, but the furnishings have overtones of Napoleonic grandeur. The extremely elegant rooms have marble floors, embroi-

dered bedspreads and gilt-edged furniture, plus satellite TV, electronic safes and stylish bathrooms. A Continental breakfast is served in a garden shaded by orange trees in summer, and there is a roof terrace.

€104–166
46

23, 75, 175, 715, 716; tram 3

SAN PIETRO ROOMS

Map 256 C3
Viale Giulio Cesare 62, 00192
Tel 06 372 5528
www.italmarket.it/rm/sanpietrorooms
Despite the name, this establishment is a good 20-minute walk away from St. Peter's, and is certainly not exceptionally economical. It is, however, very close to shopping areas and transportation links, and not too far from the Castel Sant'Angelo. Set within a typical palazzo, most of the rooms have blue wallpaper, tiled floors and sparse furnishings. Only some have private bathrooms, but all have TV.

STAYING

🕭 €70–120
🏠 13
💲 2 rooms
Ⓜ Ottaviano San Pietro
🚌 23, 70, 81, 492

SANTA MARIA
Map 257 D6
Vicolo del Piede 2, 00100
Tel 06 5894626, 06 5895474
www.htlsantamaria.com
In the heart of Trastevere, and close to the church of the same name, is this charming little hotel. The former 15th-century cloister is now a private, tranquil garden with orange trees, and all the rooms bar one open onto it. The guest rooms are large, and all have satellite TV, safe, minibar and hairdryer, plus internet connection. There is also private parking.
🕭 €145–207
🏠 19
💲
🚌 H, 780; tram 8

SANTA PRASSEDE
Map 258 G5
Via di Santa Prassede 25, 00184
Tel 06 481 4850
www.hotelsantaprassede.it
The street and hotel take their name from the church of Santa Prassede, known for its early Christian mosaics; Santa Maria Maggiore is just around the corner. The 27 quiet guest rooms, all in typically Roman

shades and with dark wooden floors, have private bathroom, central heating and safe

deposit box. There is a bar and a TV lounge as part of the communal areas. Laundry service available.
🕭 €80–130
🏠 25
💲
Ⓜ Termini or Cavour
🚌 64, 70, 71

SCALINATA DI SPAGNA
Map 257 F3
Piazza Trinità dei Monti 17, 00187
Tel 06 679 3006
www.hotelscalinata.com
You need to reserve months—if not years—in advance at this boutique hotel at the top of the Spanish Steps. La Scalinata's 16 rooms are highly coveted (especially those with the best views). The breakfast terrace, overlooking the red-tiled roofs and cupolas, has wrought-iron chairs and riots of blossom. Active visitors

enjoy jogging in the nearby Villa Borghese park, which also has a modern underground gym. The less active can plug in a laptop, or use the free internet TV with email service.
🕭 €160–350
🏠 16 (5 non-smoking)
💲
Ⓜ Spagna
🚌 116

SIRACUSA
Map 258 H4
Via Marsala 50, 00185
Tel 06 490 191
www.sebraeli.it
The Siracusa is directly opposite Termini station, so rooms facing it can be very noisy. The reception area is small and functional, and the breakfast room on the first floor is light and airy. Half the rooms have private bathrooms and are generally on the small side. The walls are covered with Venetian stucco and the furniture has 1950s styling. All rooms have TV, minibar and

electronic safe, but there is no room service. Excellent area for shopping, and cultural activities.
🕭 €93–104
🏠 142
💲
Ⓜ Termini
🚌 40, 64, 70

STARGATE HOSTEL & HOTEL
Map 258 H4
Via Palestra 88, 00185
Tel 06 445 7164
www.stargatehotels.com
Very clean and efficient hostel/hotel near Termini station, and it's extremely good value. The first option is to stay at the hostel, which has dormitory rooms sleeping four to six people. These are spacious, with bunk-beds, desks, chairs, wardrobe, washbasin, TV and internet access. The hostel also has its own internet lounge

and kitchen. Some rooms come with own shower, and there is a communal shower on each floor. Towels and linen are provided and there's a launderette. No curfew is imposed. The hotel rooms are similar but more private, catering for one or two people. An Italian breakfast of coffee and brioche is included.
🕭 Hostel €10–20, hotel €40–90
🏠 Hostel 20, hotel 20
Ⓜ Castro Pretorio or Termini
🚌 492

STELLA

Map 258 H4

Via Castelfidardo 51, 00185

Tel 06 444 1078

www.travel.it/roma/hotelstella

This hotel is very close to Termini station, so is handy if you're arriving by train. All the rooms are clean and comfortable, but some are quite small and can be noisy as there is a bar nearby. Remember to ask for a quiet room when booking. Air conditioning is available at a supplement.

€45–90

27

Termini

16, 75

SWEET HOME

Map 258 G4

Via Principe Amedeo 47, 00185

Tel 06 488 0954

www.hotelsweethome.it

Near Termini station, Sweet Home is a two-star hotel with a late 19th-century feel to it. It has high ceilings and spacious rooms with simple, painted wooden tables, TV,

comfortable sofas and bright design; half the rooms have a bath, half a shower. The breakfast room has a bar, which is open throughout the day and there is a charming, private room with chandelier available for meetings. Internet access point. Hotel staff are friendly and helpful.

€82–103

20, 5 non-smoking

Termini

40, 64, 70

TEATRO DI POMPEO

Map 257 D5

Largo del Pallaro 8, 00186

Tel 06 6830 0170

www.hotelteatrodipompeo.it

The Theatre of Pompey—site of Caesar's assassination in 44BC—was absorbed into a medieval palazzo, where this

boutique hotel can now be found. It is just steps away from the Campo dei Fiori, but insulated from its noise. Breakfast is taken in an archaeological site, a cavern dotted with palms. All rooms are double or twin, with private bath and simple interiors: turquoise coverlets, terracotta tiles and wood-beam ceilings stained dark with age. Avoid the less charming annexe. Other facilities include room service, babysitting and laundry.

€170–190

13

46, 62, 64, 87, 116, 492 to Campo dei Fiori

TRASTEVERE

Map 257 D6

Via Luciano Manara 24, 00153

Tel 06 581 4713

www.hoteltrastevere.it

Very small, family-run hotel overlooking the lively market of San Cosimato and just a few

minutes from Piazza di Santa Maria in Trastevere. The charming entrance hall is painted in pastels, with the occasional garland adorning the walls. Rooms are plainly furnished in light tones, have bath and hairdryer, and all look out onto the delightful square. The Continental buffet breakfast is served on the ground floor next to the entrance hall. A lift (elevator) is available.

€98–103

23

10

44, 780, H; tram 3, 8

TRITONE

Map 257 E4

Via del Tritone 210, 00187

Tel 06 6992 2575

www.tritonehotel.com

This hotel has a great location, just 100m (110yd) from the Trevi Fountain, making it ideal for exploring the *centro storico*

of the city. Breakfast is served on the roof terrace, from which there are fabulous views. The rooms are clean and simply furnished, and all are sound-proofed.

€150–228

43

Barberini

175, 204, 492, 590

VICTORIA

Map 258 F3

Via Campania 41, 00187

Tel 06 473931

www.hotelvictoriaroma.com

Efficiently run by its Swiss management, the Victoria is just inside the Aurelian Walls, at the top of Via Veneto and within striking distance of the area's restaurants. The bedrooms are large, as are the bathrooms, and all rooms have satellite TV. In the summer months, the buffet breakfast is served on the roof garden. The hotel also has a bar and restaurant, and private parking is available.

€180–350

113

Spagna

95, 116, 116T, 119, 204

VILLA SAN PIO

Map off 257 E7

Via S. Melania 19, 00153

Tel 06 574 5174

www.aventinohotels.com

This hotel is in a peaceful location on the exclusive Aventine Hill. The entrance hall is bright with an inlaid marble floor, and antiques are scattered throughout the hotel. Guest rooms are sumptuously furnished in late 18th-century style—elaborate bed furnishings, parquet floors, rich gold and red hues—and come with satellite TV and an electronic safe. Luxurious bathrooms, some with whirlpool baths and power showers. Helpful staff and 24-hour bar.

€140–197

76

Piramide

23, 30, 60, 75, 673, 716; tram 3

STAYING

HOTEL CHAINS

Name of hotel chain	Description	Hotels in Rome	Website and phone number
Best Western	The world's largest group, with 4,000 independently owned hotels in 80 countries.	8	www.bestwestern.it
Boscolo Hotels	Seventeen luxury hotels in some of the most sophisticated cities in Italy and beyond.	3	www.boscolohotels.com
Charming Hotels	The Charming Hotels group was founded only in 1995, but it already has 60 luxury hotels worldwide.	5	www.charminghotels.it
The Giannetti Hotels Group	Italian chain of stylish three- and four-star hotels.	1	www.thegiannettihotelsgroup.com
Golden Tulip (inc Tulip Inns)	This Netherlands-based company has around 440 hotels in 51 countries, branded as either Golden Tulip (four-star hotels) or Tulip Inns (three stars).	5	www.goldentulip.com
Hilton	This American-based chain of top-class hotels has almost 500 branches throughout the world.	1	www.hilton.com
Ibis	Part of the French Accor group, Ibis is a fast-growing chain, with more than 670 hotels worldwide.	1	www.ibishotel.com
ITI Hotels	A group of 30 hotels, mostly in Sardinia, but also in Rome, South, Central and North America.	1	www.itihotels.it
Jolly Hotels	Jolly has been running hotels in Italy since 1949, and now has establishments in 26 cities there.	4	www.jollyhotels.it
Mercure	Part of the French group Accor, Mercure has 715 hotels in 45 countries, at various price levels.	3	www.mercure.com
Le Meridien	Le Meridien is a global hotel group with over 135 luxury hotels in 56 countries.	1	www.lemeridien.com
Novotel	Part of the French group Accor, Novotel has 373 hotels in 63 countries.	1	www.novotel.com
Quality Inn Comfort Inn	Quality Inns offer mid-priced accommodation, while Comfort Inns are a limited-service chain.	2 1	www3.choice hotels.com
Rocco Forte Hotels	Rocco Forte Hotels is a collection of nine individual, luxury hotels in key locations around the world.	1	www.roccofortehotels.com
Roscioli Hotels	A family-owned chain of prestigious four-star hotels, all in the heart of Rome.	4	www.rosciolihotels.it
Sina Hotels	Founded by the Bocca family in 1959, Sina Hotels now has six four- and five-star hotels in key cities Italian cities.	1	www.sinahotels
Sofitel	Part of the French group Accor, Sofitel is the company's premium brand, with 160 hotels worldwide.	1	www. sofitel.com
Sol Meliá	Spain's leading hotel company has over 350 hotels in 30 countries.	1	www.solmelia.com
Starwood Hotels	Starwood is the name behind such prestigious hotel chains as Sheraton, Westin and St. Regis, owning, leasing or managing almost 750 hotels in 79 countries.	2	www.starwood.com

Planning

BEFORE YOU GO

CLIMATE
Rome's weather can be unpredictable. Rainfall can be high, even in the warmer, summer months but, equally, you can experience bright, clear days in winter. The charts below show what you are likely to find, but it best to pack for all eventualities.

WHEN TO GO
The best time to visit Rome is in spring or autumn (fall), when the temperature should be pleasantly warm. There is less risk of rain than in the winter months, but you might still catch the occasional shower. The downside of visiting at this time of year is that everyone else does too. Easter, especially, is popular, with high numbers of tourists swollen by visiting pilgrims to the Holy City. The summer, particularly July and August, can be oppressively hot, with temperatures of up to 40°C (105°F) broken by sudden and dramatic thunderstorms. Many Romans take their holidays in August, and it is not unusual for shops and restaurants to be closed for between two weeks and a month. Winters are generally mild and damp, and snow is rare.

WEATHER REPORTS
Weather reports are given during each news bulletin on Italian channels, as well as English-language channels shown on satellite TV, such as CNN or BBC World.

You can also check the website of your local news network station, such as the BBC (www.bbc.co.uk) or CNN (www.CNN.com), or a specialist website like the Weather Channel (www.weather.com).

WHAT TO TAKE

La bella figura is alive and well, and living in Rome. Romans tend to dress smartly at all times, and anyone appearing scruffy is likely to be stared at—although you won't be refused admission to most places.
● Bring clothes that cover your shoulders and knees for visiting churches. A lightweight raincoat is useful for the summer showers, as is a folding umbrella.
● A small bag is handy for daily use, such as a shoulder bag that can be worn across the body, or a money belt, and finally, but most importantly, comfortable shoes. You will probably do a lot of walking, either through the streets, or around museums or archaeological sites—very tiring on the feet.
● Your address book, for emergency contacts or postcards.
● Photocopies of all important documents, such as your passport and insurance details.
● A torch (flashlight) for viewing works of art in dark churches. You may also find binoculars useful for a closer look.
● First aid kit, including plasters (Band Aids), antiseptic cream, painkillers and any prescription medicine.
● An Italian phrasebook. Although most people you meet will speak English, any attempt at Italian is always appreciated.
● Earplugs are useful if you are a light sleeper, or if your hotel doesn't have double glazing. Rome is a noisy city.

PASSPORTS
British citizens will need a passport to enter Italy, but visitors arriving from other EU countries only need a national identity card. All other foreign visitors to Italy will need a passport, which should be valid for at least another six months from the date of entry into the country.

If you intend to work or study in Italy, make sure your passport

TIMES ZONES
Italy is on Central European Time (CET), one hour ahead of GMT (Greenwich Mean Time, measured from London) during the winter. In April, the clocks are put forward by one hour, and then put back a gain in October.

City	Time difference	Time at 12 noon GMT
Amsterdam	0	noon
Auckland	+11	11pm
Berlin	0	noon
Brussels	0	noon
Chicago	-7	5am
Dublin	-1	11am
Johannesburg	+1	1pm
London	-1	11am
Madrid	0	noon
Montréal	-6	6am
New York	-6	6am
Paris	0	noon
Perth, Australia	+7	7pm
San Francisco	-9	3am
Sydney	+9	9pm
Tokyo	+8	8pm

TEMPERATURE

Average temperature per day
per night

°C / °F
30 / 86
20 / 68
10 / 50
0 / 32

J F M A M J J A S O N D

Average no. of days above 18°C
below 0°C

30
20
10
0

J F M A M J J A S O N D

RAINFALL

Average rainfall

mm / in
120 / 4.5
80 / 3
40 / 1.5
0 / 0

J F M A M J J A S O N D

PLANNING

is stamped with your date of entry. You will need it to apply for a *Permesso di Soggiorno*.

VISAS

If you are an EU national, or are from Australia, Canada, New Zealand or the United States, you do not need a visa for stays of up to 90 days. To extend your visit for a further 90 days, you can, one time only, apply to any police station. This extension cannot be used for studying or employment, and you must prove that you can support yourself financially.

If you are a citizen of a country not mentioned above, you should contact the Italian Embassy in your home country to check visa requirements. These differ depending on your nationality and are also subject to change without notice. Check prior to a visit and follow news events that may affect your situation.

DUTY-FREE AND DUTY-PAID GUIDELINES

Anything that is clearly for personal use can be taken into Italy free of duty. However, it is worth carrying receipts for valuable items in case you need to prove on your return home that they haven't been bought while you are in Italy.

For the most up-to-date information on duty-free and duty-paid allowance, see either the US Department of Homeland Security's website (www.customs.treas.gov) or that of H. M. Customs and Excise (www.hmce.gov.uk). You cannot buy goods duty-free if you are journeying within the EU.

Whatever your entitlement, you cannot bring home goods for payment (including payment in kind) or for resale. These goods are considered for commercial use, and duty is payable.

CUSTOMS

Importing wildlife souvenirs from rare or endangered species may be either illegal or require a special permit. Check customs regulations before you buy.

HEALTH ISSUES

No vaccinations are necessary, unless you are coming from an infected area. If you have any doubts, contact your doctor before your trip. Take out your insurance as soon as your book your journey. If you leave it too

---

DUTY-FREE ALLOWANCES FOR NON-EU CITIZENS

US citizens can bring home up to $800 of duty-paid goods, provided they have been out of the country for at least 48 hours and haven't made another international trip in the past 30 days. This limit applies to all members of the family, regardless of age, and exemptions may be pooled.

200 cigarettes; or	1 litre of spirits or strong liquors
100 cigarillos; or	2 litres still table wine
50 cigars; or	2 litres of fortified wine, sparkling wine
250g smoking tobacco	or other liquors
	60cc/ml of perfume
	250cc/ml of toilet water

DUTY-PAID GUIDELINES FOR EU CITIZENS

European citizens can take home unlimited amounts of duty paid goods, as long as they are for personal use. H. M. Customs and Excise consider anything over the following guidelines as for commercial use.

3200 cigarettes; or	90 litres of wine
400 cigarillos; or	(of which only 60 litres can be sparkling
200 cigars; or	wine)
3kg of tobacco	20 litres of fortified wine
	(such as port or sherry)
110 litres of beer	
10 litres of spirits	

The EU countries are: Austria, Belgium, Denmark, Finland, France, Germany, Greece, Irish Republic, Italy, Luxembourg, Netherlands, Portugal, Spain (but not the Canary Islands), Sweden and the United Kingdom (but not the Channel Islands)

ITALIAN EMBASSIES ABROAD

Australia
12 Grey Street, Deakin,
ACT 2600, tel 02 6273
3333, ww.ambitalia.org.au

Canada
275 Slater Street,
21st Floor, Ottawa (ON)
K1P 5H9, tel 613 232 2401,
www.italyincanada.com

Ireland
63/65 Northumberland
Road, Dublin 4,
tel 01 6601744,
www.italianembassy.ie

New Zealand
34-38 Grant Road,
P. O. Box 463, Thorndon,
Wellington,
tel 04 4735 339,
www.italy-embassy.org.nz

South Africa
796 George Avenue,
Arcadia 0083 Pretoria,
tel 430 5541/2/3/4,
www.ambital.org.za

UK
14 Three Kings Yard,
London W1K 4EH,
tel 020 7312 2200,
www.embitaly.org.uk

USA
3000 Whitehaven Street
NW, Washington DC20008,
tel 202 612 4400,
www.italyemb.org

---

close to your departure date you may not be covered for delays.

Make sure your insurance policy is valid for the duration of your visit. Most policies cover cancellation, medical expenses, accident compensation, personal liability, and personal belongings (including money). Your policy should cover the cost of getting you home in a medical emergency.

If you have private medical cover, check your policy, as you may be covered while you are away. Also, check your home contents insurance: It may cover loss of money and personal belongings away from home.

As well as health insurance, European citizens should carry an E111 form, available from post offices, health centres and social security offices. This entitles you to free healthcare. Health insurance often doesn't cover treatment you could have got with an E111. One form covers the whole family for an indefinite period. You will need to get it stamped in your home country.

For up-to-date information, see the Department of Health's website on www.doh.gov.uk (in the UK), or the National Center for Infectious Diseases on www.cdc.gov/travel in the US.

PRACTICALITIES

ELECTRICITY
- The power supply is 240 volts.
- Plugs have two round pins. It is a good idea to bring an adaptor with you, although these are readily available in the city.
- Visitors from North America should also bring a transformer for appliances operating on 110/120 volts; these are hard to find, so bring one with you.

LAUNDRY
- Most visitors trust their laundry to their hotel, where your clothes are returned to your room and the charge added to your bill. However, there are alternatives.
- Rome's old-style cleaners (*tintorie*) are still plentiful in the city. Charges start at around €2, but check the rate for any additional services, such as pressing pleats. A *tintoria* will also provide a dry-cleaning service.
- Self-service launderettes are few and far between. One of the most central is Punto Blu at Via Cavour 168, tel 06 4817857 (open daily 8am–10pm).

MEASUREMENTS
- Italy uses the metric system, with all foodstuffs sold by the kilogram or litre. Italians also use the *ettogramme* (hectogram—100g or just under 4oz), usually abbreviated to *etto*.
- Fuel is sold by the litre, and distances are measured in kilometres.

LAVATORIES
- You will find public lavatories at railway stations and in larger museums, but otherwise they are few and far between. There are lavatories in Piazza San Pietro, either side of the square, and others at the Colosseo.
- In other parts of the town you will need to use the toilet in a bar or café. Although they are obliged to let you use their facilities, staff prefer you to buy something.
- Facilities can be basic, to say the least. Toilet paper may or may not be provided, and sometimes there is only one toilet for both men and women.
- In some places there will be a dish for gratuities—you should tip around 25c.

CONVERSION CHART

FROM	TO	MULTIPLY BY
Inches	Centimetres	2.54
Centimetres	Inches	0.3937
Feet	Metres	0.3048
Metres	Feet	3.2810
Yards	Metres	0.9144
Metres	Yards	1.0940
Miles	Kilometres	1.6090
Kilometres	Miles	0.6214
Acres	Hectares	0.4047
Hectares	Acres	2.4710
Gallons	Litres	4.5460
Litres	Gallons	0.2200
Ounces	Grams	28.35
Grams	Ounces	0.0353
Pounds	Grams	453.6
Grams	Pounds	0.0022
Pounds	Kilograms	0.4536
Kilograms	Pounds	2.205
Tons	Tonnes	1.0160
Tonnes	Tons	0.9842

- Where separate facilities exist, make sure you recognize the difference between *signori* (men) and *signore* (women).

SMOKING
- Smoking is still very popular in Italy, and is permitted in most hotels and restaurants, although there should be no-smoking areas available.
- A new law, prohibiting smoking in all public areas, is on the table, but no date has been set for its implementation.
- Smoking is already banned on public transportation, inside the airport buildings and in most public offices, such as post offices and police stations.
- Cigarettes and other tobacco products can only legally be sold in *tabacchi* (tobacconists) and only to those over 16. The stand-alone *tabacchi* are only open during normal shop hours (usually 8–1, 3.30–8), but others are attached to bars, so stay open longer.

Italian is as much about gestures as it is about words

CLOTHING SIZES
Clothing sizes in Italy are in metric. Use the chart below to convert the size you use at home into metric.

UK	Metric	USA	
36	46	36	SUITS
38	48	38	
40	50	40	
42	52	42	
44	54	44	
46	56	46	
48	58	48	
7	41	8	SHOES
7.5	42	8.5	
8.5	43	9.5	
9.5	44	10.5	
10.5	45	11.5	
11	46	12	
14.5	37	14.5	SHIRTS
15	38	15	
15.5	39/40	15.5	
16	41	16	
16.5	42	16.5	
17	43	17	
8	36	6	DRESSES
10	38	8	
12	40	10	
14	42	12	
16	44	14	
18	46	16	
20	46	18	
4.5	37.5	6	SHOES
5	38	6.5	
5.5	38.5	7	
6	39	7.5	
6.5	40	8	
7	41	8.5	

LOCAL WAYS
- A few words of Italian will always go down well (see pages 291–296), even if you can only manage hello and goodbye.
- Italians tend to use please and thank you less frequently than in other nationalities.
- Use *buongiorno* up to midday, and *buonasera* in the afternoon and evening.

PLANNING

- Show respect and dress appropriately when visiting places of worship. Cover your shoulders and knees. St. Peter's in particular has a strict dress and conduct code.
- Don't intrude on religious services unless you wish to take part.
- Always check before taking photographs in churches and museums.
- Italians tend to drink only with meals, and public drunkeness is frowned upon.
- In cafés, never pay bar prices, then attempt to use the tables.
- If you only want a one-course meal, eat in a pizzeria. It's considered bad form to eat less than two courses in a restaurant.
- Be polite but assertive when waiting to be served. Although it may look disorganized, everyone knows who is in front of them. (See page 13.)

VISITING ROME WITH CHILDREN

- Children are welcomed at most restaurants. Although children's menus are rare, most places will serve up small portions, and will often produce simple meals of pasta in tomato sauce or pizza.
- Disposable nappies (diapers) and baby foods are available in many food shops, but changing faclities are hard to find. Museums and restaurants with the most modern facilities are your best option.

- A lack of public lavatories, most of which will not be as clean as you'd like (see above), can make things difficult for people with very young children. Always carry tissues or wipes, as not all establishments will supply toilet paper.
- Rome has few attractions specifically aimed at children, many of whom will get bored visiting museums and galleries. As a compromise, look out for things that will interest your child, such as animals in paintings or as part of sculptures.
- Admission to most of Rome's museums and galleries is free for under 18s. Where there is a charge, it is usually reduced for children.
- Children under age 10 travel free on Rome's public transport system. Some of Rome's metro stations are not accessible with prams (baby carriages).
- See page 194 for suggested attractions for children.

VISITORS WITH DISABILITIES

- Wheelchair access in Rome is improving, but very slowly. It is always worth checking with individual establishments what their access is like. The narrow, cobbled streets and lack of pavements can prove difficult for people with mobility issues.
- All the major hotels, as well as the newer ones, should have wheelchair access. In older buildings, it is not always possible to make the changes needed, and you should contact the

USEFUL CONTACTS

CO.IN Sociale Via Enrico Giglioli 54a, Rome, tel 06 7129011, fax 06 7129 0179, www.coinsociale.it (in English and Italian)
Useful information on accessible sights. Publish guides, organize guided tours; minibus available for excursions and transfers.
Holiday Care 7th Floor, Sunley House, 4 Bedford Park, Croydon, Surrey CR0 2AP, tel 0845 124 9971, fax 0845 124 9972, www.holidaycare.org.uk
Publications and information on accessibility.
SATH (Society for Accessible Travel and Hospitality), 347 Fifth Avenue, Suite 610, New York NY10016, tel 212-441-7284, fax 212-447-7284, www.sath.org
Lots of tips on how to travel with mobility impairment or with blindness.

individual hotels to ask about your specific needs.
- Rome's public transportation system has improved in recent years, and around half the stations are accessible by wheelchairs. Most new buses have ramps that can be lowered for access. See page 54 for more information.

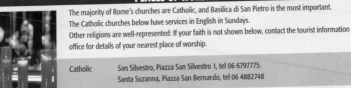

PLACES OF WORSHIP

The majority of Rome's churches are Catholic, and Basilica di San Pietro is the most important. The Catholic churches below have services in English in Sundays.
Other religions are well-represented: If your faith is not shown below, contact the tourist information office for details of your nearest place of worship.

Catholic	San Silvestro, Piazza San Silvestro 1, tel 06 6797775. Santa Suzanna, Piazza San Bernardo, tel 06 4882748
Jewish	Lungotevere Cenci, tel 06 655051
Muslim	Moschea di Roma, Viale della Moschea, tel 06 8082167
Protestant	St. Paul's Episcopal, Chiesa Americana di San Paolo, Via Napoli 58, tel 06 4883339 Anglican Church of England, All Saints', Via del Babuino 153/b, tel 06 3600 1881 Presbyterian Church of Scotland, Chiesa di Scozia, Via XX Settembre 7, tel 06 4827627
Greek Orthodox	Chiesa Ortodossa Greca, Via Sardegna, tel 06 4818820

Italy is one of 12 European countries that have adopted the euro as their official currency. Euro notes and coins were introduced in January 2002, replacing the former currency, the lira.

BEFORE YOU GO

● It's advisable to use a combination of cash, travellers' cheques and credit cards, rather than relying on one means of payment during your trip.
● Check with your bank and/or credit card company that you can withdraw cash from ATMs. You should also check what fee will be charged and what number you should call if your card is lost or stolen.
● Notify your credit card company that you will be using your card abroad. Some place blocks on use overseas for security reasons.
● Remember to keep a separate note of your travellers' cheque numbers, with a note of the number to call if they are stolen.

LOST/STOLEN CREDIT CARDS

American Express
06 7228 0371
Diners Club
800 864064
CartaSi including MasterCard and Visa
800 151616
MasterCard
800 870866
Visa
800 877232

EXCHANGE RATES

● The euro exchange rate for visitors is subject to daily fluctuation, but at the time of printing €1 is approximately £0.70, US$1.10 and C$1.50.

CREDIT CARDS

● Italians have traditionally used cash, but this is changing and credit and debit cards are now more widely accepted, but not for small sums. Look for the credit card symbols in the shop window or check with the staff.

● Food bills are usually paid for in cash. Market traders and smaller establishments will often only take cash.

TRAVELLERS' CHEQUES

● Travellers' cheques are accepted almost everywhere. To avoid additional exchange rate charges, take travellers' cheques in euros, pounds sterling or US dollars.
● There is a branch of Thomas Cook at Piazza Barberini, and a branch of American Express in Piazza di Spagna. They will cash travellers' cheques issued by their company without charging commission.

BANKNOTES AND COINS

One euro is made up of 100 cents. Euro notes come in denominations of 5, 10, 20, 50, 100, 200 and 500 euros.

Coins come in denominations of 1 and 2 euros and 1, 2, 5, 10, 20, and 50 cents.

LOST AND STOLEN CARDS AND TRAVELLERS' CHEQUES

● If your credit card or bank card is stolen, report it to the police and the appropriate emergency number. All are open 24 hours a day and have English-speaking staff.
● If your travellers' cheques are stolen, notify the police, then follow the instructions given with the cheques. You can contact the Rome office of American Express or Thomas Cook, or telephone the following toll free numbers:
● For American Express travellers' cheques, call 800 872000
● For Thomas Cook travellers' cheques, call 800 872050

ATMS

● Cash machines, called Bancomats in Italy, are plentiful in Rome, and many are accessible 24 hours a day.
● Most have instructions in English (and other languages) as well as Italian.
● Check with your bank before leaving home that you will be able to access your account from Italy.

BANKS

● There are no shortage of banks in Rome, most of which have cash machines and exchange facilities, although there are often long queues for this as they offer the best rates.
● Banks are usually open from 8.30 until 1 or 1.30, and again for an hour or so in the afternoon. Some now open on Saturdays.

BUREAUX DE CHANGE

● There are bureaux de change (cambio) all over the city, usually open throughout the day, until around 7.30. They often offer 'commission free' exchange, but the exchange rates are not usually as good as those from banks.

DISCOUNTS

● Over 65s can often get discounted admission charges to museums and galleries—use your passport or driver's licence as proof of age.
● Children's admission charges are usually available up to 18 years of age, and reductions on the full adult rate are sometimes made for 18–26 year olds.
● Students sometimes qualify for discounts. You should apply for a Student Identity Card from the ISIC (see page 50).
● Sometimes, these discounts are only available for European citizens.

WIRING MONEY

● Wiring money is a lengthy process and the bureaucracy involved means that it is probably not worthwhile unless you are planning to be in Rome for a while.
● Ask your bank at home for a list of affiliated banks. You can get money wired to any bank from home, but if your bank already has a connection with certain banks in Italy, it will make the process a lot easier.
● If you have a bank account in Italy and at home, you can transfer money directly if both banks are part of the Swift system of international transfers. Again, it takes about 5–7 days, if not longer.

● Always ask for a separate letter, telex or fax to be sent to Swift, confirming that the money has been sent. It can take up to a week for the money to transfer.
● American Express, Moneygram and Western Union Money Transfers are faster from the US, but more expensive. Citibank has a service where you can transfer money for a flat fee of $10 to anywhere in the world.

TAX REFUNDS

● Sales tax, known as IVA, is added to all goods and services in Italy.
● Visitors from non-EU countries are entitled to reimbursement of the tax paid on major purchases.
● The store must provide a properly completed invoice (una fattura), itemizing all goods, the price paid for them and the tax charged, as well as full address details of both the vendor and the purchaser.
● The goods must be taken out of the EU within three months of the date of purchase.
● When leaving Italy, present the fattura to customs for stamping. You may need to show the goods, so make sure they are easy to reach.
● When you get home, send the stamped receipt to the shop. Your refund will either be made by cheque or directly back to your credit card account.

TIPPING

Italians do not tip heavily. Service is often included in your hotel or restaurant bill, although a little extra is appreciated, if the service has been good. The following is a general guide:
Pizzerias/trattorias: round up to the nearest euro
Smart restaurants: 10%
Bar service: up to 25c, or 5–10% for table service
Taxis: round up to nearest 50c
Porters: 50c–€1 per bag
Chambermaids: 50c–€1 per day
Cloakroom attendants: 50c
Lavatories: 25c

10 EVERYDAY ITEMS AND HOW MUCH THEY COST	
Takeaway sandwich	€3
Bottle of water	75c
Cup of coffee (outside/inside)	€1.50/€5
Beer—half a litre (outside/inside)	€3.50/€7
Glass of house wine (outside/inside)	€1/€50
Daily newspaper (Italian)	€1
Roll of camera film	€5
20 cigarettes	€2.50
Ice-cream (takeaway)	€2.50
Litre of petrol	€1.25

HEALTH

All visitors are entitled to free emergency health treatment through Italy's national health system, both from doctors and hospitals.

BEFORE YOU GO

● No vaccinations are required, but it is a good idea to check when you last had a tetanus injection and, if more than 10 years ago, have a booster before you travel.

● Italy has a standard agreement with other EU countries entitling EU citizens to a certain amount of free health care, including hospital treatment. In the UK, you should ask for an E111 form before you leave home. See page 277.

● If will you need treatment for a pre-exisiting condition while you are away, such as injections, you should apply to your department of health for an E112.

● Despite this reciprical arrangement, you are strongly advised to take out travel insurance. For non-EU visitors this is esssential.

● Vistors from the US and Canada may find that their existing health policy covers them while they are abroad. Check with your insurance company before you travel, and remember to bring your policy identification card.

● Check with your doctor or pharmacist for the chemical name of any prescription drugs you need, in case you have to replace them while you are away. The brand name will often change from country to country.

● It is a good idea to take photocopies of all important documentation, such as travel insurance and your E111 (for EU citizens), which should be kept separate from the originals. You could scan the photocopies, and send them to an email address that can be accessed anywhere in the world.

HOW TO GET A DOCTOR (UN MEDICO)

● To get in touch with a doctor, ask at your hotel reception or consult the Yellow Pages (Pagine Gialle) under Unita Sanitaria Locale (USL).

● Visitors to Italy from as far as the US, Australia or New Zealand may be concerned about the effect of long-haul flights on their health. The most widely publicized concern is Deep Vein Thrombosis, or DVT. Misleadingly called 'economy class syndrome', DVT is the forming of a blood clot in the body's deep veins, particularly in the legs. The clot can move around the bloodstream and could be fatal.

● Those most at risk include pregnant women, the elderly, and those using the contraceptive pill, smokers and the overweight. If you are at increased risk of DVT see your doctor before departing. Flying increases the likelihood of DVT because passengers are often seated in a cramped position for long periods of time and may become dehydrated.

To minimize risk:

• drink water (not alcohol)
• don't stay immobile for hours at a time
• stretch and exercise your legs periodically
• do wear elastic flight socks, which support veins and reduce the chances of a clot forming
• a small dose of aspirin may be recommended; this thins the blood before the flight.

EXERCISES

1 ANKLE ROTATIONS **2 CALF STRETCHES** **3 KNEE LIFTS**

Lift feet off the floor. Draw a circle with the toes, moving one foot clockwise and the other counterclockwise.

Start with heel on the floor and point foot upward as high as you can. Then lift heels high keeping balls of feet on the floor.

Lift leg with knee bent while contracting your thigh muscle. Then staighten leg pressing foot flat to the floor.

Other health hazards for flyers are airborne diseases and bugs spread by the plane's air-conditioning system. These are largely unavoidable but if you have a serious medical condition seek advice from a doctor before flying.

HOW TO GET TREATMENT WITH YOUR E111

● If you are taken ill while you are away, take your E111 to the USL office (see this page), who will give you a certificate of entitlement. Take this to any doctor or dentist on the USL list to received free treatment.

● If you are referred to a hospital, you will be given a certificate that entitles you to free treatment. If you go to hospital without being referred by a doctor, you should give the E111 to the hospital.

● If you do not have a USL certificate, you will have to pay for treatment and may have difficulty getting the money back afterwards, and then probably only a partial refund.

● If you are charged in full for medicines, keep the price tags— you will not get a refund without them.

● It is advisable to carry a photocopy of your E111, as some doctors and hospitals keep the form. If they do, you can pick up another form when you get home.

- If you want to avoid all this bureaucracy, make sure you have adequate medical cover as part of your travel insurance.

HOW TO GET TREATMENT WITH TRAVEL INSURANCE
- Take a copy of your travel insurance documents to the doctor or hospital—they may be able to bill your insurance company direct.
- If you pay for treatment, keep all of your receipts as you won't be able to make an insurance claim without them.

DENTISTS *(DENTISTI)*
- For emergency dental treatment with an E111, contact the USL, as above.
- If you do not have an E111, you should contact a private dentist (in the Yellow Pages under *dentisti*). Again, take a copy of your insurance details, and keep your receipts.

PHARMACIES *(FARMACIE)*
- Rome's pharmacies sell toiletries as well as a wide range of over-the-counter medicines.
- Pharmacists are well-trained and can give advice or deal with minor ailments.
- Most pharmacies are open from 8.30 to 1 and again from 4 until 8, but they operate a rota system so that there is at least one open at all times—there will be a list displayed in the window or published in the newspaper.
- If the pharmacy do not have the medicine that you need, try the pharmacy at the Vatican.

OPTICIANS *(OTTICHI)*
- Opticians can usually carry out minor repairs to your glasses, such as replacing screws, on the spot, for little or no charge.
- Lenses can often be replaced overnight.
- If you really cannot survive without your glasses or contact lenses, bring a copy of your prescription with you so that

FOR EMERGENCY TREATMENT

If you need emergency treatment, you can go directly to the *pronto soccorso* (casualty department or emergency room) at the following hospitals:

Bambino Gesù (children's hospital), Piazza San Onofrio 4, tel 06 68591

Fatebenefratelli, Isola Tiberina, tel 06 68371

Policlinico Gemelli, Largo Gemelli 8, tel 06 30151

Policlinico Umberto I, Viale del Policlinico 155, tel 06 49971

San Camillo, Circonvallazione Gianicolense 87, tel 06 58701

San'Eugenio, Piazzale dell'Umanesimon 10 (at EUR), tel 06 51001

San Filippo Neri, Via Martinotti 20, tel 06 33061

San Giacomo, Via Canova 29, tel 06 36261

San Giovanni, Via Ambra Aradam 8, tel 06 77051

If you prefer to be treated at a private hospital, contact: **Salvator Mundi International Hospital**, Viale delle Mura Gianicolensi 66/67, tel: 06 588961

Not your average pharmacy—the elegant Officino Profumo

you can have replacements made up, or better still, bring spares.

ALTERNATIVE TREATMENTS
- You can buy homeopathic remedies is most pharmacies.
- For information on acupuncture, contact the following association for practitioners in your area: Italian Medical Association of Acupuncture (AMIA) Piazza Navona 49, 00186 Rome, tel 06 6868556

TAP WATER
- Yes, you can drink the water. Rome's tap water is completely safe, as is the water in the city's drinking fountains.

For an ambulance, call 118
For the Italian Red Cross call 06 5510

- However, you should look out for signs that say *acqua non potabile*, indicating that the water is not drinkable.

SUMMER HAZARDS
- The sun can be strong between May and September, and a high-factor sun block is recommended. Your sunglasses will make a stylish accessory.
- There are few biting insects as such in Rome, but if you plan to visit the surrounding area, you might like to take an insect repellant, although insect bites are more irritating than dangerous.

COMMUNICATION

TELEPHONES
CALL CHARGES
● There are three call bands for telephone charges. Peak time is between 8am and 1pm, off-peak is between 1pm and midnight, and cheaper international rates between 6.30pm and 8am (in two price bands—up to midnight and after) and at weekends.

PAYING FOR CALLS
Public telephones
● Most payphones now take phonecards, rather than cash. You can buy cards for calls within Italy in denominations of €1, €2.50 and €5 at tobacconists, newsstands and some bars. You need to tear off the top right-hand corner of the card before you use it.
● For overseas calls, buy an Interglobal Card 5, which can be used with public, private and mobile phones. They are like a scratch card, with a hidden number.

Telefono a scatti
● There are now a number of places around Rome where you can make a metered call from a sound-proofed booth. Locations include Fiumicino Airport and Termini station. At the end of your call, you just pay the cashier.
● There is no additional charge for this service, but you will find that most of them are not open late enough to take advantage of the cheaper rates in the evening. The only exception is the Palazzo delle Poste at Piazza San Silvestro, which is open 24 hours a day.

COLLECT OR CREDIT CARD CALLS
● To make collect or credit card calls you will need to call the operator in the country you are calling:

Australia (OPTUS) 800 172 611
Australia (TELSTRA) 800 172 601
Canada 800 172 213
Ireland 800 172 256
New Zealand 800 172 641
UK 800 172 440
USA (AT&T) 800 172 444
USA (MCI) 800 905 825
USA (SPRINT) 800 172 405

COUNTRY CODES FROM ITALY
To call abroad from Italy, first dial 00, followed by your country code (see below), the area code (sometimes minus the first zero) and then the telephone number.

Australia 61	Germany 49	Netherlands 31	UK 44
Belgium 32	France 33	New Zealand 64	USA 1
Canada 1	Ireland 353	Spain 34	

To call Italy from home, the country code is 39:
You need to keep the zero of the code.

USEFUL NUMBERS
Operator 170
Post/telegram enquiries 160
Time 161
Italian directory enquiries and operator 12
International directory enquiries 176

SPECIAL PREFIXES
● The area code for Rome is 06, and you need to dial this as part of the telephone number, even if you are calling from within Rome.
● Numbers beginning 800 are free, known as *numeri verdi*, and those that start with 840 or 848 will only be charged at one unit.
● Italian mobile phone numbers start with 3, although you might still see them written as 03, their old format. Just drop the zero and dial the rest of the number as usual.

Remember you need to tear off the corner of your phonecard

MOBILE PHONES
● British, Australian and New Zealand mobile phones can be used in Italy without any problems. You may need to unbar your telephone for use overseas: Contact your service operator for details.
● American mobile phones can only be used if they are triband, because of the different frequency.

PLANNING

- It can be very expensive to use your mobile phone abroad, as you will often be charged to receive calls as well as to make them. If you travel frequently, consider swapping your SIM card for one from an alternative provider—either a network based in the country you are visiting or a dedicated provider of international mobile phone services. You can buy these at mobile phone stores before you leave home or when you are in Rome.
- Another alternative is to rent a mobile phone while you are in Rome. Phones can be rented from HLC (Via Zoe Fontana 220, tel 06 4190600, info@hlc.it). The shop is open Monday to Friday 9–6, and rental charges are €10 per day or €35 per week, plus the cost of calls.
- Text messages are often a cheaper alternative to voice calls, but check the charges with your service provider.
- Remember to add the international dialling code to the numbers you wish to call at home. Add + and the international code (see panel).

INTERNET ACCESS

- The internet is a great way of keeping in touch while you are away from home. Increasing numbers of hotels are offering internet access, and internet cafés are springing up all over the city.
- One of the biggest venues is EasyEverything (Via Barberini 2, tel 06 4290 3388; www.easyeverything.com), with 250 terminals. It is open 24 hours a day, seven days a week.
- Thenetgate (www.thenetgate.it) currently has five branches in Rome: Piazza Firenze 25, Via delle Grazie 4, inside the drugstore at Termini, Hotel Palatino in Via Cavour and Via Cluniacensi 26–30 in Tiburtina.
- The netcafe.com (www.netcafe.com/countries.italy .htm) has an impressive searchable directory of internet cafés in Rome, and indeed the rest of the world.

POST OFFICES

- The main post office is the Ufficio Postale Centrale at Piazza San Silvestro. It is open Mon–Fri 9–6 and Sat 9–2.
- The city's other post offices open Mon–Fri 8.25–2 or 2.30 and Sat 8.25–noon.

The central offices have a currency exchange, which is sometimes open throughout the day until 6.30.

MAIL
Postage rates (national and international)

The Vatican's Swiss-run postal service uses blue or yellow mailboxes (left and middle) in contrast to the red boxes elsewhere in the city

- Rome's notoriously bad postal service is gradually improving. Letters can now be sent by posta prioritaria, similar to first class post in the UK.
- The postage rate for Europe also applies to letters send within Italy.
- You can buy postage stamps (francobolli) from post offices, although they are always very busy. You can also buy them from tobacconists, where there will be less of a wait.
- Registered letters or parcels are sent by Raccomandata. The cost varies considerably, depending on the size and weight of the package.
- Post boxes are red and have two slots: Per la città is for Rome,

and Tutte le altre destinazione for everywhere else, including international destinations.
- The Vatican operates its own postal service, which is more efficient than the Roman one. There is a post office is outside Basilica di San Pietro, in Piazza San Pietro, where you can buy stamps, and there is a post box outside. Both are on the left as you face the basilica.
- Roman stamps cannot be used in the Vatican post box, and vice versa.

POSTCARDS

- These are classed as low priority post, so if you want them to arrive at their destination before your trip becomes a distant memory, put them inside an envelope and they will be dealt with like a letter and take around two weeks.
- Alternatively, you can send your postcard by prioritaria. This faster service should only take around three days, and is only a little more expensive. (See table below).

POSTAGE RATES

Airmail (via aerea)	Letter (20g)		Delivery time
Europe	41c		up to 2 weeks
USA and rest of World	77c		up to 2 weeks
Posta Prioritaria	Letter (20g)	Letter (21–100g)	Delivery time
Europe	62c	€1.25	3 days
USA and rest of World	77c	€1.55	4–8 days

FINDING HELP

PERSONAL SECURITY

Rome is basically a safe city and instances of serious crime against visitors are rare. The main problems for visitors are likely to be pickpockets or bag snatchers. By taking a few sensible precautions, you can minimize the risk of becoming a victim.

- Never carry money or valuables in your back pocket—always keep them secure in a money belt, pouch or similar.
- Don't flaunt your valuables.
- Never put your camera or bag

down on a café table, where it could be snatched.

- Groups of gypsy children have perfected a scam where they show you a piece of cardboard—while you try to read what is written on it, they use its cover to steal from your pocket or handbag.
- Carry bags or cameras on your side that is away from the road, to minimize the risk from bag snatchers on scooters.
- Keep a close eye on your possessions while on crowded buses or metros, particularly in areas popular with visitors.
- Leave valuable jewellery in the hotel safe
- Women should note how the Roman women wear their handbags—across their bodies, rather than just over one

shoulder where they could be easily snatched.

- If you have a codeable safe in your hotel room, don't use your date of birth as the code. It is on your passport and your hotel registration.
- After dark, avoid parks, the area around Termini or on the edge of Trastevere.
- You should report any theft to a police station, where you will need to make a statement. Although it is unlikely that you will get your belongings back, you will need the statement (denuncia) to make a claim on your insurance. The main police station is Questura, Via San Vitale 15 (tel: 06 46861).

LOST PROPERTY

- The main lost property office (Ufficio Oggetti Rinvenuti) is at Via Niccolò Bettoni 1 (open Mon, Wed, Thu 8–5.45, 8–1 rest of week, tel 06 5816040).
- The ATAC lost property office, for articles left on buses or trams, is at Via Volturno 65 (open Mon–Fri 9–1, 2–5, tel: 06 5810583).
- For anything lost on any FS trains, try the office on platform

24 of Termini (open daily 7am–midnight, tel: 06 4782 5543).

- If you will be making an insurance claim, you will need to report the loss to the police to get a statement (denuncia).
- If your passport is lost or stolen, report it to the police and your embassy (see below).
- If your credit card or travellers' cheques are stolen, report them to the issuing company (see page 280).

WHAT TO DO IF YOU ARE ARRESTED

If you are taken into custody by the police, you could be held for up to 48 hours without appearing before a magistrate. You can also be interviewed without a lawyer present. You do, however, have the right to contact your consul, who is based at your country's embassy.

Your consul will not be able to get you out of prison, but they can put you in touch with English-speaking lawyers and interpreters, and contact your family on your behalf.

WHAT TO DO IF YOU LOSE YOUR PASSPORT

If you lose your passport, contact your embassy in Rome. It helps if you have a note of your passport number, so either keep a note of it or carry a photocopy of the information page separately from your passport. Alternatively, you could scan the page and email it to an account that can be accessed anywhere.

POLICE

There are three branches of the police in Italy, any of whom should be able to help you if you are in difficulty.

- The carabinieri are military police, easily recognizable by the white sash they wear across their bodies. They deal with general crime, including drug control.
- The polizia is the state police force, who wear blue uniforms. They, too, deal with general crime, and if you are unfortunate enough to be robbed (or worse), they are the ones you will need to see.
- The vigili urbani, in dark blue uniforms and white hats, are traffic police.

PLANNING

OPENING TIMES AND TICKETS

PUBLIC HOLIDAYS

Shops and banks generally close on public holidays, and roads and railways are usually very busy. However, with the exception of Labour Day, Assumption and Christmas Day, most bars and restaurants will still be open. There is a limited public transportation service on Labour Day and the afternoon of Christmas Day.

If a public holiday falls on a weekend, it is not celebrated on the next working day, as it is in the UK and the USA. However, if the holiday falls on a Tuesday or Thursday, many people take the Monday or Friday off to make a *ponte* (bridge) to the weekend.

Roman Holidays	
1 Jan	New Year's Day
6 Jan	Epiphany
Mar/Apr	Easter Monday
25 Apr	Liberation Day
1 May	Labour Day
2 Jun	Republic Day
29 Jun	St. Peter and St. Paul Day (or St. Peter's Day)
15 Aug	Assumption of the Virgin (Ferragosto)
1 Nov	All Saints' Day
8 Dec	Feast of the Immaculate Conception
25 Dec	Christmas Day
26 Dec	San Silvestro

SHOPS

Traditionally, shops open between 8 and 9, closing for lunch at around 1. They reopen at 3.30 or 4 and close at 8. Most are closed all day Sunday plus Monday morning.

However, Rome's shops are increasingly staying open all day—look for the sign *orario continuato*.

BANKS

Mon–Fri 8.30–1.30. Some larger branches might open on Sat.

POST OFFICES

Mon–Fri 8.15–2, Sat 8.15–noon or 2.

DOCTORS & PHARMACISTS

Pharmacists are usually open the same hours as shops, but take it in turns to stay open during the afternoon and late into the evening. Look for the list posted in the window for the nearest pharmacy that will be open.

TICKETS

Generally in Rome you will find that most churches do not charge admission (although often a donation is expected). There is sometimes a charge made at churches where there is a special architectural feature or work of art.

Most Roman establishments operate separately, each charging their own admission fee. The only exception is the Roma Archeologica Card, which is valid for seven days and gives admission to nine different places of interest (Colosseo, Palatino, Terme di Caracalla, Terme di Diocleziano, Palazzo Altemps, Palazzo Massimo alle Terme, Crypta Balbi, Villa dei Quintili and the tomb of Cecilia Metella). The card costs €20 and is available from any of the participating sights.

Tickets for popular museums and galleries can be booked in advance through a number of agencies, who charge a booking fee on top of the normal admission price.

Ticketclic (www.ticketclic.it)
Colosseo
Crypta Balbi
Domus Aurea
Musei Capitolini
Palazzo Altemps
Palazzo Massimo alle Terme
Terme di Caracalla
Terme di Diocleziano
Villa Adriana (Tivoli)

Beneculturali (www.beneculturali.it)
Galleria Borghese
Galleria Corsini
Galleria Barberini
Galleria Spada
Museo Nazionale Etrusco
Scavi (Ostia Antica)
Museo Archeologico
Necropoli dei Monterozzi (both at Tarquinia)

Ticketeria (www.ticketeria.it)
Galleria Borghese
Palazzo Barberini
Palazzo-Galleria Doria Pamphilj
Galleria Spada
Galleria Corsini
Palazzo Venezia
Museo Nazionale Etrusco
Museo Etrusco
Necropoli dei Monterozzi (both at Tarquinia)

MUSEUMS AND GALLERIES

The opening times for museums and galleries vary greatly. Some are open all day, while others close at lunchtime. Many close one day each week, usually Monday. Check the Sights section of this book (see pages 65–150), or contact the museum or gallery concerned for the most up to date information.

CHURCHES

Most churches open early in the morning for Mass, often around 7. They close at lunchtime, opening again around 4 and closing at 7. Some of the larger churches are open all day, and some are closed to non-worshippers during services. Check the Sights section of this book (see pages 65–150) or contact the church to check.

Many restaurants are open late for alfresco summer eating

CAFÉS AND BARS

The hours kept by Rome's cafés and bars vary considerably from establishment to establishment and according to season. Some are open for breakfast, others open in time for lunch and some are only open in the evenings. Winebars usually close at midnight or later.

RESTAURANTS

Restaurants that serve lunch open at around 12.30 and usually close during the afternoon. They reopen, along with those that only serve dinner, sometime after 7pm and stay open late. Pizzerias are usually only open in the evening. Many restaurants close for the whole of August—look for the sign *chiuso per ferie*.

TOURIST OFFICES

The main tourist office in Rome is at Via Parigi 5, near Terme di Diocleziano (06 48891, open daily 9–7.30). The best number for tourist information is 06 3600 4399, where they speak good English. There are smaller, information points (open daily 9.30–7.30), in green, pagodas, dotted around the city, who can supply you with maps and other information (in English).

- Aeroporto Leonardo da Vinci (in arrivals, Terminal B)
- Stazione Termini, platform 4
- Largo Goldoni, Via del Corso
- Piazza San Giovanni in Laterano
- Palazzo delle Esposizioni, Via Nazionale
- Piazza delle Cinque Lune, near Piazza Navona
- Piazza Pia, near Castel Sant'Angelo
- Piazza del Tempio della Pace, near Fori Imperiali
- Piazza Sonnino, Trastevere
- Via dell'Olmata, near Santa Maria Maggiore
- Piazza dei Cinquecento, outside Termini
- Via Marco Minghetti, near Trevi Fountain
- Via San Pietro (left-hand side of Basilica's façade, for information on St. Peter's)

ITALIAN GOVERNMENT TOURIST OFFICES

Level 26, 44 Market Street, NW 2000 Sydney, tel: 92 621666	175 Bloor Street East, Suite 907 South Tower, Toronto, Ontario M4W 3R8, tel: 416 925-4882, fax: 416 925-4799; www.italiantourism.com	1 Princes Street, London W1B 2AY, tel: 020 7489 1254/020 7355 1557, fax: 020 7499 3567; www.enit.it	630 Fifth Avenue, Suite 1565, New York NY 10111, tel: 212 245-5618 / 245-4822, fax 212 586-9249; www.italiantourism.com Also offices in Chicago and Los Angeles

USEFUL WEBSITES

TOURISM

www.romaturismo.it
The city of Rome's official website is packed with useful information, such as hotel and restaurant listings, suggested itineraries and events. You can also request brochures. In English and Italian.

www.enjoyrome.com
This independent website, staffed by English-speakers, is great for organized tours, accommodation and information on life in Rome. In English only.

www.vatican.va
Information on the Vatican state, including the museums, but not much on St. Peter's. In six languages, including English.

www.comune.roma.it
The city council's website, has details of tourism and events. In English.

www.romaclick.com
This English-language website is good for booking online accommodation.

www.romeguide.it
Information on exhibitions and attractions, plus online ticket booking. In English.

TRANSPORT

www.atac.roma.it
Details of routes, fares and tickets for buses, trams and the metro. In English and Italian.

www.trenitalia.it
Information on getting around the country by Italy's train service. In English and Italian.

www.adr.it
Covers both of Rome's airports. Includes airport services and flight information.

NEWS

www.bbc.co.uk
For UK, regional and world news, plus weather reports. You can also listen to certain radio stations via the website.

www.cnn.com
For US and world news, plus weather reports.

www.ilmessaggero.it
Rome's newspaper online, with news, sport and events. In Italian only.

KEY SIGHTS QUICK WEBSITE FINDER		
Sight	**Website**	**Page**
Basilica di San Pietro	www.vatican.it	66–71
Casa di Goethe	www.casadigoethe.it	65
Colosseo	www.archeor.arti.beniculturali.it	74–77
Fori Imperiali	www.capitolium.org	82–83
Foro Romano	www.capitolium.org	84–89
Galleria Borghese	www.galleriaborghese.it	93–97
Galleria Spada	www.galleriaborghese.it	111
Musei Capitolini	www.museicapitolini.org	98–103
Musei Vaticani	www.vatican.va	104–109
Palazzo Barberini	www.galleriaborghese.it	114
Palazzo Corsini	www.galleriaborghese.it	111
Palazzo-Galleria Doria Pamphilj	www.doriapamphilj.it	115
Palazzo Quirinale	www.quirinale.it	111
San Carlo alle Quattro Fontane	www.sancarlino-borromini.it	128
Santa Maria della Concezione	www.cappucciniviaveneto.it	136
Santa Maria sopra Minerva	www.basilicaminerva.it	140
Villa Farnesina	www.lincei.it	146
Villa Medici	www.villamedici.it	146

PLANNING

MEDIA

TELEVISION
- Italy has three state-run television stations (RAI-1, -2 and -3), three stations run by Berlusconi's Mediaset group (Italia Uno, Rete Quattro and Canale Cinque), plus a number of local channels. RAI-3 has an international news programme, which includes an English-language section. It starts at 1.15am.
- Italian television shows are almost always accompanied by scantily-clad women. Moves are underway to change this, with a view to making respectful references to the image of women, but with the role of 'game show girl' as popular as ever, how successful this will be remains to be seen.
- Most hotels, from mid-range upwards, have satellite television, which means you can keep up to date with the news on BBC World or CNN.

RADIO
- RAI Radio 1, 2 and 3 (89.7FM, 91.7FM and 93.7FM respectively), the state run stations, have a mixture of light music, chat shows and news—all in Italian.
- Radio Vaticano (93.3FM) broadcasts news in a number of languages. There are English-language broadcasts at 5.10pm and 9.50pm daily.
- Some of the local radio stations play American and British music, so if you are feeling homesick, try Radio Centro Suono (101.3FM) for music from the 1960s up to the present day. Radio Antenna 1 (107.1FM) play American and British hits from the 1970s, 80s and early 90s. For light classical music, try 100.3FM, or if Latin-American is your thing, tune into Radio Mambo (106.85FM).
- The BBC World Service frequencies are MHz 12.10, 9.410, 6.195 and 0.648.

NEWSPAPERS
English-language newspapers
- You can often buy major international newspapers on the day of publication, from about 2pm, at larger newsstands. Titles include *The Times, The Guardian, The Financial Times,*

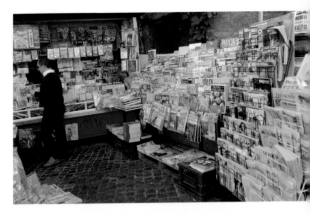

The European, The New York Times, The Wall Street Journal and the *International Herald Tribune.*
- There are also some Italian newspapers available in English, namely *Italy Daily* (produced jointly by *Corriere della Sera* and *International Herald Tribune*) and *Il Sole/24 Ore* (economic and financial news from FT.com).

Italian-language newspapers
- *Il Messaggero* is the local paper, popular with Romans. *La Repubblica, Corriere della Sera, La Stampa* and *Il Sole/24 Ore* are the main national dailies. *La Repubbica* and *Corriere della Sera* both have local editions for Rome. *La Repubblica* has a good what's-on section on Thursdays and a glossy magazine supplement on Saturdays called *La Repubblica delle Donne*, with excellent articles reflecting all aspects of Italian life and society.

Search out the English-language magazines at newsstands

- There are two daily sports papers published in Italy: *La Gazzetta dello Sport* and the *Corriere dello Sport* are mainly dominated by soccer and motor sport news. *La Gazzetta dello Sport* also publishes a supplement on Saturdays called *Sport Week*, which tends to cover a wider range of sports, and contains excellent colour photos and features on the week's events.

MAGAZINES
- English-speakers will see many familiar looking magazines on the newsstands. Italian versions of well-known publications such as *Vogue* and *Marie Claire* are very popular.
- Many Italian magazines on sale in Rome are adorned with pictures of scantily-clad women, but this isn't necessarily a reflection of their content (although it can be).
- English language magazines are few and far between, but if you read a little Italian, magazines such as *Panorama* and *L'Espresso* are good for news, while *Sette* (Thursdays) and *Venerdì* (Fridays) are colour supplements with lots of pictures.
- *Roma C'è* (Fridays) and *Time Out Roma* (monthly) both have English-language sections. *Wanted in Rome* is aimed at resident English-speakers, but also has what's-on listings.

Relaxing in the Giardino del Pincio with a good book

BOOKS, FILMS AND MAPS

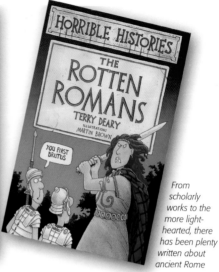

From scholarly works to the more light-hearted, there has been plenty written about ancient Rome

BOOKS

Apart from your guidebook, there are any number of books dealing with Rome's long and eventful history. By far the most in-depth is Edward Gibbon's 19th-century *The History of the Decline and Fall of the Roman Empire*, published in six volumes (although abridged versions are available from publishers such as Penguin). *The Battle for Rome*, by Robert Katz, recounts the German occupation of Rome and the fall of Mussolini.

For history in novel form, try *I, Claudius*, by Robert Graves, or Irvine Stone's *The Agony and the Ecstasy*. More light-hearted is Lindsey Davis' series of detective stories, based around the Roman Empire, but mostly set in Rome.

Anyone interested in Italian politics should read *The Dark Heart of Italy* by Tobias Jones, which discusses Berlusconi's administration (see page 18).

As an accompaniment to your guidebook, try John Varrinao's *A Literary Companion*, which is full of quotes from major writers who spent time in Rome. Another good companion is *City Secrets Rome*, by Robert Kahn, which gives you an insight into how today's Romans see their city.

For younger readers, *The Rotten Romans*, part of the popular Horrible Histories series, takes a more light-hearted look at this fascinating period of history. It is aimed at 9–12-year olds.

FILMS

Mussolini's Cinecittà studios didn't really come into their own until after World War II, when they began to make neorealist films, like *Ladri di Biciclette* (Bicycle Thieves—1948). A winner of both a BAFTA and a Golden Globe, it was shot entirely in Rome, using non-actors.

The 1950s saw a resurgence in film-making in Rome, with the much-acclaimed *Roman Holiday* (1953), which thrust Audrey Hepburn into the limelight. You'll recognize many of the landmarks she and Gregory Peck visit, including the Bocca della Verità (see page 136). *Three Coins in a Fountain* (1954) followed closely behind, and although the storyline now seems old fashioned, it's still a great travelog for Rome. Probably the most famous image of Rome is Anita Ekberg's dip in the Trevi Fountain in *La Dolce Vita* (1960), which was also filmed in Tivoli and Viterbo (see pages 214 and 210).

The Agony and the Ecstasy (1965) is one of a great number of historical epics set in Rome, with Charlton Heston as a tortured Michelangelo painting the Sistine Chapel's ceiling for Julius II (Rex Harrison).

Roma (1972) is a typical piece of Felliniesque film making. This plotless film shows Fellini's Rome, which he voices over in the English-language version.

More recently, *The Talented Mr. Ripley* (1999) was filmed all over Italy, including Rome, and *Gladiator* (2000) is set, in part, in Rome, although much of it was filmed elsewhere.

MAPS

There is a central street map at the back of this guide (see pages 298–313) and a metro and tram map in the inside back cover. All the tourist information points have free street maps if you want to pick up something else while you are out there. There are free metro and bus maps available from the information office at Termini (see page 46).

ITALIAN WORDS AND PHRASES

Once you have mastered a few basic rules, Italian is an easy language to speak: It is phonetic, and unlike English, particular combinations of letters are always pronounced the same way. The stress is usually on the penultimate syllable, but if the word has an accent, this is where the stress falls.

Vowels are pronouned as follows:

a	casa	as in	mat short 'a'
e	vero closed	as in	base
e	sette open	as in	vet short 'e'
i	vino	as in	mean
o	dove closed	as in	bowl
o	otto open	as in	not
u	uva	as in	book

Consonants as in English except:

c before i or e becomes ch as in church
ch before i or e becomes c as in cat
g before i or e becomes j as in Julia
gh before i or e becomes g as in good
gn as in onion
gli as in million
h is rare in Italian words, and is always silent
r usually rolled
z is pronounced tz when it falls in the middle of a word

All Italian nouns are either masculine (usually ending in o when singular or i when plural) or feminine (usually ending in a when singular or e when plural). Some nouns, which may be masculine or feminine, end in e (which changes to i when plural). An adjective's ending changes to match the ending of the noun.

CONVERSATION

What is the time?
Che ore sono?

When do you open/close?
A che ora apre/chiude?

I don't speak Italian
Non parlo italiano

I only speak a little Italian
Parlo solo un poco italiano

Do you speak English?
Parla inglese?

I don't understand
Non capisco

Please repeat that
Può ripetere?

Please speak more slowly
Può parlare più lentamente?

What does this mean?
Cosa significa questo?

Write that down for me, please
Lo scriva, per piacere

Please spell that
Come si scrive?

I'll look that up
Lo cerco

My name is
Mi chiamo

What's your name?
Come si chiama?

Hello, pleased to meet you
Piacere

This is my friend
Le presento il mio amico/la mia amica

This is my wife/husband/daughter/son
Le presento mia moglie/mio marito/mia figlia/mio figlio

Where do you live?
Dove abiti?

I live in …
Vivo in …

I'm here on holiday
Sono qui in vacanza

Good morning
Buongiorno

Good afternoon/evening
Buonosera

Goodbye
Arrivederci

See you later
A più tardi

See you tomorrow
A domani

See you soon
A presto

How are you?
Come sta?

Fine, thank you
Bene, grazie

I'm sorry
Mi dispiace

That's alright
Si figuri

USEFUL WORDS

yes **sì**	thank you **grazie**	where **dove**	when **quando**	why **perchè**
no **no**	you're welcome **prego**	here **qui**	now **adesso**	who **chi**
please **per piacere**	excuse me! **scusi!**	there **là**	later **più tardi**	may I/can I **posso**

Could you help me, please?
Può aiutarmi, per favore?

How much is this?
Quanto costa questo?

I'm looking for …
Cerco …

Where can I buy…?
Dove posso comprare…?

How much is this/that?
Quanto costa questo/quello?

When does the shop open/close?
Quando apre/chiude il negozio?

I'm just looking, thank you
Sto solo dando un'occhiata

This isn't what I want
Non è quel che cerco

I'll take this
Prendo questo

Do you have anything less expensive/smaller/larger?
Ha qualcosa di meno caro/più piccolo/più grande?

Are the instructions included?
Ci sono anche le istruzioni?

Do you have a bag for this?
Può darmi una busta?

I'm looking for a present
Cerco un regalo

Can you gift wrap this please?
Può farmi un pacco regalo?

Do you accept credit cards?
Accettate carte di credito?

I'd like a kilo of …
Vorrei un chilo di …

Do you have shoes to match this?
Ha delle scarpe che vadano con questo?

This is the right size
Questa è la taglia (misura— for shoes) giusta

Can you measure me please?
Può prendermi la misura, per favore?

This doesn't suit me
Questo non mi sta bene

Do you have this in …?
Avete questo in …?

Should this be dry cleaned?
Questo è da lavare a secco?

Is there a market?
C'è un mercato?

NUMBERS

0 zero	6 sei	12 dodici	18 diciotto	40 quaranta	100 cento
1 uno	7 sette	13 tredici	19 diciannove	50 cinquanta	1000 mille
2 due	8 otto	14 quattordici	20 venti	60 sessanta	million milione
3 tre	9 nove	15 quindici	21 ventuno	70 settanta	quarter quarto
4 quattro	10 dieci	16 sedici	22 ventidue	80 ottanta	half mezza
5 cinque	11 undici	17 diciassette	30 trenta	90 novanta	three quarters tre quarti

MONEY

Is there a bank/currency exchange office nearby?
C'è una banca/un ufficio di cambio qui vicino?

Can I cash this here?
Posso incassare questo?

I'd like to change sterling/ dollars into euros
Vorrei cambiare sterline/ dollari in euro

Can I use my credit card to withdraw cash?
Posso usare la mia carta di credito per prelevare contanti?

What is the exchange rate today?
Quant'è il cambio oggi?

I'd like to cash this travellers' cheque
Vorrei incassare questo travellers cheque

POST AND TELEPHONES

Where is the nearest post office/mail box?
Dov'è l'ufficio postale più vicino/la cassetta delle lettere più vicina?

What is the postage to…?
Quando costa spedire una lettera a…?

One stamp, please
Un francobollo, per favore

I'd like to send this by air mail/ registered mail
Vorrei spedire questo per posta aerea/posta raccomandata

Can you direct me to a public phone?
Dov'è il telefono pubblico più vicino?

What is the charge per minute?
Quanto si paga al minuto?

Can I dial direct to …?
Posso chiamare … in teleselezione?

Do I need to dial 0 first?
Devo comporre prima lo zero?

Where can I find a phone directory?
Dove posso trovare un elenco telefonico?

Where can I buy a phone card?
Dove posso comprare una carta telefonica?

What is the number for directory enquiries?
Qual è il numero del servizio informazioni?

Please put me through to…
Mi passi …

Have there been any calls for me?
Ci sono state telefonate per me?

Hello, this is …
Pronto, sono …

Who is this speaking please?
Con chi parlo?

I'd like to speak to …
Vorrei parlare con …

Extension … please
Interno … per piacere

Please ask him/her to call me back
Puo dirgli/dirle di richiamarmi?

COLOURS

black **nero**	light blue **celeste**
brown **marrone**	sky blue **azzuro**
pink **rosa**	purple **viola**
red **rosso**	white **bianco**
orange **arancia**	gold **oro**
yellow **giallo**	silver **argento**
green **verde**	grey **grigio**
blue **blu**	turquoise **turchese**

SHOPS

Baker's **Panetteria**	Fishmonger's **Pescheria**	Lingerie shop **Biancheria intima**
Bookshop **Libreria**	Florist **Fiorista**	Newsagent's **Giornalaio**
Butcher's **Macelleria**	Gift shop **Regali**	Perfume shop **Profumeria**
Cake shop **Pasticceria**	Grocer's **Alimentare**	Photographic shop **Fotografo**
Clothes shop **Abbigliamento**	Hairdresser's **Parrucchiere**	Shoe shop **Calzature**
Delicatessan **Salumeria**	Jeweller's **Gioielleria**	Sports shop **Articoli sportivi**
Dry-cleaner's **Lavasecco**	Launderette **Lavanderia**	Tobacconist's **Tabaccheria**

GETTING AROUND

Where is the train/bus station?
Dov'è la stazione ferroviaria/ degli autobus (dei pullman – long distance)?

Does this train/bus go to …?
È questo il treno/l'autobus (il pullman–long distance) per…?

Does this train/bus stop at …?
Questo treno/autobus (pullman–long distance) ferma a…?

Please stop at the next stop
La prossima fermata, per favore

Where are we?
Dove siamo?

Do I have to get off here?
Devo scendere qui?

Where can I buy a ticket?
Dove si comprano i biglietti?

Is this seat taken?
È occupato?

Where can I reserve a seat?
Dove si prenotano i posti?

Please can I have a single/ return ticket to …
Un biglietto di andata/andata e ritorno per …

When is the first/last bus to …?
Quando c'è il primo/l'ultimo autobus per …?

I would like a standard/first class ticket to…
Un biglietto di seconda/ prima classe per…

Where is the information desk?
Dov'è il banco informazioni?

Where is the timetable?
Dov'è l'orario?

Do you have a subway/bus map?
Ha una piantina della metropolitana/degli autobus?

Where can I find a taxi?
Dove sono i tassì?

Please take me to …
Per favore, mi porti a …

How much is the journey?
Quanto costerà il viaggio?

Please turn on the meter
Accenda il tassametro, per favore

I'd like to get out here please
Vorrei scendere qui, per favore

Could you wait for me, please?
Mi può aspettare, per favore?

Is this the way to…?
È questa la strada per…?

Excuse me, I think I am lost
Mi scusi, penso di essermi perduto/a

Monday **lunedì**	morning **mattina**	today **oggi**	May **maggio**	December **dicembre**	Epiphany **Epifania**
Tuesday **martedì**	afternoon **pomeriggio**	yesterday **ieri**	June **giugno**	spring **primavera**	Easter **Pasqua**
Wednesday **mercoledì**	evening **sera**	tomorrow **domani**	July **luglio**	summer **estate**	Assumption **Ferragosto**
Thursday **giovedì**	night **notte**	January **gennaio**	August **agosto**	autumn **autunno**	All Saints' Day **Ognissanti**
Friday **venerdì**	day **giorno**	February **febbraio**	September **settembre**	winter **inverno**	Christmas **Natale**
Saturday **sabato**	month **mese**	March **marzo**	October **ottobre**	New Year's Day **Capodanno**	26 December **Santo Stefano**
Sunday **domenica**	year **anno**	April **aprile**	November **novembre**		New Year's Eve **San Silvestro**

IN TROUBLE

Help!
Aiuto!

Stop, thief!
Al ladro!

Can you help me, please?
Può aiutarmi, per favore?

Call the fire brigade/police/an ambulance
Chiami i pompieri/la polizia/un'ambulanza

I have lost my passport/ wallet/purse/handbag
Ho perso il passaporto/il portafogllio/il borsellino/la borsa

Is there a lost property office?
C'è un ufficio oggetti smarriti?

Where is the police station?
Dov'è il commissariato?

I have been robbed
Sono stato/a derubato/a

I have had an accident
Ho avuto un incidente

Here is my name and address
Ecco il mio nome e indirizzo

Did you see the accident?
Ho visto l'incidente?

Are you insured?
È assicurato/a?

Please can I have your name and address?
Mi dà il suo nome e indirizzo?

I need information for my insurance company
Ho bisogno d'informazioni per la mia compagnia d'assicurazione

ILLNESS

I don't feel well
Non mi sento bene

Could you call a doctor please
Può chiamare un medico, per favore

Is there a doctor/pharmacist on duty?
C'è un medico/farmacista di turno?

I need to see a doctor/dentist
Ho bisogno di un medico/ dentista

Where is the hospital?
Dov'è l'ospedale?

When is the surgery open?
Quando apre l'ambulatorio

I need to make an emergency appointment
Ho bisogno di un appunta- mento di emergenza

Do I need to make an appointment?
Ho bisogno di un appuntamento?

I feel sick
Mi sento male

I am allergic to …
Sono allergico/a a…

I have a heart condition
Ho disturbi cardiaci

I am diabetic
Sono diabetico/a

I'm asthmatic
Ho l'asma

I've been stung by a wasp/bee
Mi ha punto una vespa/ un'ape

Can I have a painkiller?
Posso avere un analgesico?

How many tablets a day should I take?
Quante pillole al giorno devo prendere?

How long will I have to stay in bed/hospital?
Per quanto tempo dovrò rimanere a letto/in ospedale?

I have bad toothache
Mi fanno molto male i denti

I have broken my tooth/ crown
Mi sono rotto un dente/una corona

A filling has come out
Ho perso un'otturazione

Can you repair my dentures?
Può ripararmi la dentiera?

Waiter/waitress
Cameriere/cameriera

What time does the restaurant open?
A che ora apre il ristorante?

I'd like to reserve a table for … people at …
Vorrei prenotare un tavolo per … persone a …

A table for …, please
Un tavolo per …, per favore

We have/haven't booked
Abbiamo/non abbiamo prenotato

Could we sit there?
Possiamo sederci qui?

Is this table taken?
Questo tavolo è occupato?

Are there tables outside?
Ci sono tavoli all'aperto?

Where are the lavatories?
Dove sono i gabinetti?

We would like to wait for a table
Aspettiamo che si liberi un tavolo

Could you warm this up for me?
Mi può riscaldare questo, per piacere?

We'd like something to drink
Vorremo qualcosa da bere

Could we see the menu/wine list?
Possiamo vedere il menù/la lista dei vini?

Do you have a menu/wine list in English?
Avete un menù/una lista dei vini in inglese?

What do you recommend?
Cosa consiglia?

Is there a dish of the day?
C'è un piatto del giorno?

What is the house special?
Qual è la specialità della casa?

I can't eat wheat/sugar/salt/pork/beef/dairy
Non posso mangiare grano/zucchero/sale/maiale/manzo/latticini

I am a vegetarian
Sono vegetariano/a

I'd like…
Vorrei…

May I have an ashtray?
Può portare un portacenere?

I ordered …
Ho ordinato …

Could I have bottled still/sparkling water?
Vorrei acqua minerale naturale/gassata?

Could we have some more bread?
Può portare ancora pane?

Could we have some salt and pepper?
Può portare del sale e del pepe?

The food is cold
Il cibo è freddo

The meat is overcooked/too rare
La carne è troppo cotta/non è abbastanza cotta

This is not what I ordered
Non ho ordinato questo

Can I have the bill, please?
Il conto, per favore?

Is service included?
Il servizio è compreso?

The bill is not right
Il conto è sbagliato

We didn't have this
Non abbiamo avuto questo

How much is this dish?
Quanto costa questo piatto?

I'd like to speak to the manager, please
Vorrei parlare con il direttore

The food was excellent
Abbiamo mangiato benissimo

I have made a reservation for … nights
Ho prenotato per … notti

Do you have a room?
Avete camere libere?

How much per night?
Quanto costa una notte?

Double/single room
Camera doppia/singola

Twin room
Camera a due letti

With bath/shower
Con bagno/doccia

May I see the room?
Posso vedere la camera?

I'll take this room
Prendo questa camera

Could I have another room?
Vorrei cambiare camera

Is there a lift in the hotel?
C'è un ascensore nell'albergo?

Is the room air-conditioned/heated?
C'è aria condizionata/riscaldamento nella camera?

Is breakfast included in the price?
La colazione è compreso?

Do you have room service?
C'è servizio in camera?

When is breakfast served?
A che ora è servita la colazione?

I need an alarm call at…
Potete svegliarmi alle …

The room is too hot/too cold/dirty
La camera è troppo calda/troppo fredda/sporca

I am leaving this morning
Parto stamattina

Please can I pay my bill?
Posso pagare il conto?

Please order a taxi for me
Mi chiama un tassì, per favore

Where is the tourist information office/tourist information desk, please?
Dov'è l'ufficio turistico/il banco informazioni turistiche?

What can we visit in the area?
Che cosa c'è da vedere in questa zona?

Do you have a city map?
Avete una cartina della città?

Can you give me some information about…?
Puo darmi delle informazioni su …?

What sights/hotels/restaurants can you recommend?
Quali monumenti/alberghi/ristoranti mi consiglia?

Please could you point them out on the map?
Me li può indicare sulla cartina?

What is the admission price?
Quant'è il biglietto d'ingresso?

Is there a discount for senior citizens/students?
Ci sono riduzioni per anziani/studenti?

Are there guided tours?
Ci sono visite guidate?

Are there boat trips?
Ci sono gite in barca?

Where do they go?
Dove vanno?

Is there an English-speaking guide?
C'è una guida di lingue inglese?

Are there organized excursions?
Ci sono escursioni organizzate?

Can we make reservations here?
Possiamo prenotare qui?

What time does it open/close?
A che ora apre/chiude?

Is photography allowed?
Si possono fare fotografie?

Do you have a brochure in English?
Avete un opuscolo in inglese?

What's on at the cinema?
Cosa danno al cinema?

Where can I find a good nightclub?
Mi può consigliare un buon nightclub?

What time does the show start?
A che ora comincia lo spettacolo?

Could you reserve tickets for me?
Mi può prenotare dei biglietti?

How much is a ticket?
Quanto costa un biglietto?

Should we dress smartly?
È necessario l'abito da sera?

on/to the right **a destra**	in front of **davanti**	closed **chiuso**	town **città**	lake **lago**
on/to the left **a sinistra**	behind **dietro**	daily **giornalmente**	old town **centro storico**	bridge **ponte**
around the corner **all'angolo**	north **nord**	cathedral **cattedrale**	town hall **municipio**	no entry **vietato l'accesso**
opposite **di fronte a...**	south **sud**	church **chiesa**	boulevard **corso**	push **spingere**
at the bottom (of) **in fondo (a)**	east **est**	castle **castello**	square **piazza**	pull **tirare**
straight on **sempre dritto**	west **ovest**	museum **museo**	street **via**	entrance **ingresso**
near **vincino a**	free **gratis**	monument **monumento**	avenue **viale**	exit **uscita**
cross over **attraversi**	donation **donazione**	palace **palazzo**	island **isola**	lavatories – men/women **gabinetti – uomini/donne**
	open **aperto**	gallery **galleria**	river **fiume**	

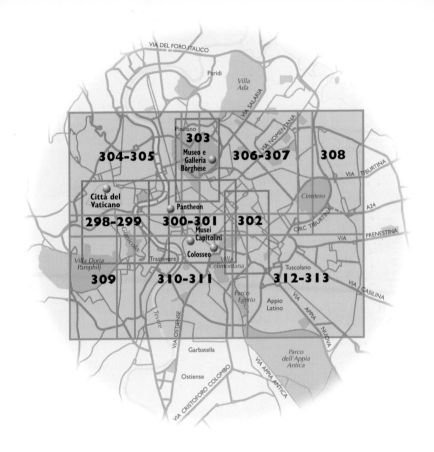

	Main road
	Other road
	Minor road/path
	Railway
	City wall
	Park
	Important building
	Featured place of interest
	Metro station
	Railway station
	Car park

298-303

| 0 | | | | 250 m |
| 0 | | | | 250 yds |

304-313

| 0 | | | | 500 m |
| 0 | | | | 500 yds |

Maps

Trinità dei
Monti

Via di Po
Via Cadore
Via Ludovisi
Via Emilia
Via Sallustiana
Via Luciulo
Via Quintino Sella
Via Flavia
Via Aureliana

F

Via Sistina
Via XX SETTEMBRE
3
G

Via L BISSOLATI
Via G Carducci
Via Umbria
Via XX

ata della
dei Monti

303

Via Gregoriana
Via di Purificazione
Via del Due Macelli
Santa Maria
della Concezione

Santa Maria
della Vittoria

Via Antonio Salandra

P

Terme di
Diocleziano

CERNAIA

Via V E ORLANDO
Via Parigi

VIALE
4
AUDI

Barberini
Piazza
Barberini
Palazzo
Barberini

Via del Tritone
Via F Crispi
Via Zucchelli
Salita di S N da
Via di S N Tolentino
Via Barberini
Via XX Settembre
Via Firenze
Via Modena
Via Torino

Repubblica
Fontana
delle Naiadi
Piazza della
Repubblica
Palazzo Massimo
alle Terme

Via G A M

Largo
del
Tritone
Via del Tritone
Via d'Avignonese
Via Rasella
Via dei Giardini

Galleria
dell'Accademia
di San Luca

Via del Scuderie
Traforo Umberto I
Giardini del
Quirinale
Quirinale
Via delle Quattro Fontane
San Carlo alle
Quattro Fontane
Sant'Andrea
al Quirinale
Via di San Vitale

VIA NAZIONALE
Via Napoli
Teatro
dell'Opera
Viminale
TORINO
Via d'Azeglio

Museo Naz
delle Paste
Alimentari
Via d Dakaria
Palazzo del
Quirinale
Via del Quirinale
Piacenza
Via Genova

Piazza
del Quirinale
Palazzo
Consulta
VIo Mazzarino
Piazza
del Quirinale

Via Parma
Palermo
Piazza del
Viminale

VIA AGOSTINO DEPRETIS
Cesare
Balbo
Santa
Pudenziana
Urbana
Piazza
d'Esquilino
Santa Maria
Maggiore
VIA LIBERIANA
Via Paolina
Via di Quattro Leoni
Il Olmata

302
5
Santa
Prassede

ostoli
Palazzo
Colonna
Via della Pilotta
Via XXIV Maggio
NAZIONALE
Milano
Panisperna

VIA IV NOVEMBRE
Via di S Eufemia
Colonna
Traiana
Piazza
del Grillo
Via Mazzarino
Via del
Via Cimarra
Boschetto
Serpenti
Via Capocci
Via Sforza
VIA CAVOUR

Fori
Imperiali
Mercati
Traianei
Via Alessandrina
de Tor
de Conti
Via Baccina
Via d Zingari
Via Leonina
Cavour
VIA GIOVANNI LANZA
Via In Selci
S Martino
ai Monti
Oppi

Santa Maria
in Aracoeli
Palazzo
Nuovo
VIA DEI
Via Sal Vecchia
Via della M dei Monti
CAVOUR
Frangipane
VIA DEGLI
Colosseo
San Pietro
in Vincoli
Via d
Polveriera
Via Cremona
delle
Sette
Sale
Parco
di
Traiano
Monte
Via delle Terme
Esquilino

Palazzo
Senatorio
FORI
Via del Foraggi
IMPERIALI
Santi Cosma
e Damiano
Santa
Francesca
Romana
ANNIBALDI
Viale
Domus
Aurea
Viale della Domus Aurea

Fienili
Foro
Romano
Via sacra
Colosseo
Piazza dei
VIA N SALVI
VIA LABICANA
Via G
6

S Teodoro
Via di san Teodoro
Orti
Farnesiani
Palatino
Domus
Flavia
Arco
di Costantino
Colosseo
Colosseo
San Clemente
Via Ostilia
Via Capo
Via dei
Cellimontana
Via d'Africa
Santi Quattro
Coronati

S Anastasia
Stadio
VIA CELIO VIBENNA
VIA DI SAN GREGORIO
Viale del Parco del Celio
Parco
del Celio
Via Claudia
Via Marco Aurelio
Via Annia
301

Circo
Via del Cerchi
F
G

A   B   C

Via Friggeri
Via Festo
Via T Macrobio
Via C Stazio
Via Lucilio
Via Aviano
Via
Seneca
Via F M Tocci
Via Cadiolo
Via Alberto
Via
Via
Via F Nicolai
della
VIALE DELLE MEDAGLIE D'ORO
Balduina
Civio di Cinna
Via
Fedro
Via Cornelio Nepote
Via Platone
Viale
VIA MARZIALE
Via L Andronico
Via C Cordo
Via P de Cristoforo
VIALE DEGLI AMMIRAGLI
VIA ANASTASIO II
Via Angelo Emo
Via Richelmo
Via Pietro

Via Trionfale
Via Romeo Romei
Via Antonio Varisco
Via M Amato
CIRCON
VIA
Via Premuda
Via Cunfida
Via G Bovio
Via Trionfale
Via Rodi
Via Buccari
DELLA
GIULIANA
Via Emilio Faa di Bruno
Via Riccardo G Lante
Via C Morin
TRIONFALE
Via San Tommaso d'Aquino
CIRCNE
Via C Passaglia
Via A Labriola
Via B G Telesio
Via Tommaso
Via R di Laura
Via R Fiore
VIA
Via Simone Simoni
Via Luigi Rizzo
Via Sebastiano Ziani
Via Giorgio Scalia
CIPRO
Via Angelo Emo
Viale Vaticano
Andrea
Via Savonarola
Campanella
Doria
Via Moccenigo
Via Candia
Tunisi
Via Ptolemaide
Via Santamaura
Via Sebastiano Veniero
Viale   Vaticano
Piazzale degli Eroi
Cipro
Musei Vaticani
Via F Albenzio
VIA V PISANI

P
Piazzale Clodio
Via U Novaro
Via Fasana
Via Teulada
Via Muggia
Via Dardanelli
Via C Mirabello
CLODIA
Viale
CIRCONVALLAZIONE
CLODIA
VIALE   GIUSEPPE   MAZZINI
Via Comenizza
Via Durazzo
Via Filippo
Via E Turba
ANGELICO
Via M Pertica
Via M Nero
Via Monte Sabotino
Via Vodice
Via Montelli
VIALE ANGELICO
VIALE   BARLETTA
Via G Bettolo
Viale
Via de Bettolo
Via G Camozzi
Via S Pellico
Via G B Bazzoni
Via A Balamonti
Via P Borsieri
Via A Brofferio
delle
Via C A della Chiesa
Giulio
Via Fabio Massimo
Germanico
Via Silla
Gracchi
VIA
Via del
Via degli Scipioni
Vespasiano
Via Ottaviano
Via Otranto
Via Famagosta
Via Leone IV
Ottaviano San Pietro
Via G
Corridori
Via M
Via Carso
Via Asiago
Oslavia
Santo
Via Timavo

CITTÀ DEL VATICANO
Giardini Vaticani
Musei Vaticani
VATICANO
Basilica di San Pietro
Piazza San Pietro
Piazza del Risorgimento
Via di Porta Angelica
Borgo
Angelico
Via di Porta Angelica
Via dei Mascherino
Borgo
Borgo
Vittorio
Pio
Borgo Sant
Via dei Corridori
Via della Conciliazione
Borgo   Santo   Spirito
Via S Porcari
Via G Vitelleschi
VIA
Via Properzio
Via Tibullo
P
LUNGO IN SAC

Piazza del Sant'Uffizio
VIA AURELIA
VIA DI PORTA CAVALLEGGERI
Via Nicolo V
Via Aurelia
Via Aurelia
Via Paolo III
Viale
Vaticano
GAL PRINCIPE A SAVOIA AOSTA
Via del Gianicolo
Piazza della Rovere
Viale
FORNACI
Gianicolo
Passeggiata del

GREGORIO VII
VIA
VIA
GREGORI VII
Via del Cottolengo
Via della Stazione di S Pietro
VIA D CROCIFISSO
Via D Silveri
Via Paolo
Via Nicolo III
VIA DELLE FORNACI
SAN PIETRO
Vlo del Gelsomino
Vlo della Cava
Fati
Damaso

309

304   A   B   C

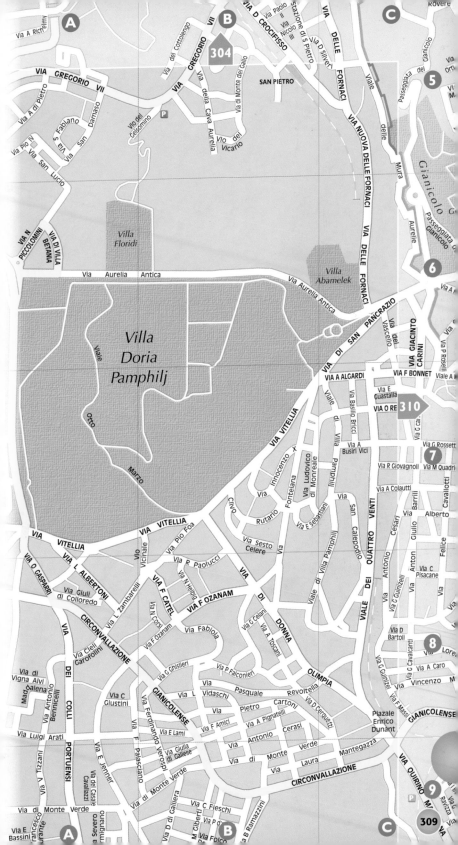

Via A. Richielmy
Via del Cottolengo
VIA GREGORIO VII
VIA D. CROCIFISSO
Via P. Paolo II
Stazione di S Pietro
Via Nicolò III
Via D Silveri
VIA
DELLE
FORNACI
Rovere

304

VIA GREGORIO VII
Via della Cava Aurelia
Via di Monte del Gallo
SAN PIETRO
Passeggiata del Gianicolo
Via Ortigara
Via M.

Via A. di Pietro
Via S. Fabiano
Via S. Damaso
San
Vio del Celsomino
Vio del Vicario
Via VIA NUOVA DELLE FORNACI

5

Via Pio IV
Via S. Lucio
Vio dei Vicario
Mura

Gianicolo
Ge

Via N. PICCOLOMINI
VIA DI VILLA BETANIA
Villa Floridi
Via Aurelia Antica
Villa Abamelek
Via Aurelia Antica
VIA DELLE FORNACI
Aurelie
Passeggiata Gianicolo
Via A

6

Via
Viale
Villa Doria Pamphilj
Orto
Marzo
Via Aurelia Antica
VIA DI SAN PANCRAZIO
Via del Vascello
VIA GIACINTO CARINI
Via P Roselli
Via A

VIA A. ALGARDI
VIA F BONNET
Viale A
Viale
Via E Guastalla
Via Basilio Bricci
VIA O RE **310**
Via C Car

Via A Busiri Vici
Via G Rossetti
Via della Villa Pamphilj
Via A
Via R Giovagnoli
Via M Quadri

7

VIA VITELLIA
Via Innocenzo X
Via Fonteiana
Via Ludovico di Monreale
Via A Colautti
Via R Giovagnoli
Cavallotti

Via
Rutario
Via E Sebastiani
Via San Calepodio
Via Barrili
Via Cesari
Via Alberto
Via Giulio
Via Anton
Via Felice

VIA VITELLIA
Via Pio Foa
Via Sesto Celere
VIALE DEI QUATTRO VENTI
Via Antonio
Via C Guinizelli
Via C Pisacane

VIA VITELLIA
Vio Vicinale
Via R Paolucci
Via di Villa Pamphilj
Via Antonio
Via C Guinizelli

VIA L. ALBERTONI
Via L Zambarelli
Via N Halpig
Via N Corsi
VIA F CATEL
VIA F OZANAM
VIA DI
Via D Bartoli

8

VIA O GASPARRI
Via Giuli di Colloredo
Via F Ozanam
Via Fabiola
Via C Celani
Via A Toscani
DONNA
Via G Cavalcanti
Via G Guinizel
Via A Caro
Via Lore

CIRCONVALLAZIONE
Via Cieli Garofolini
Via G Ghislieri
OLIMPIA
Via F Massi
Via Vincenzo
M

Via di Vigna Alvi Salena Mad
Via Antonio Bennicelli
Via C Giustini
Via L Vidaschi
Via P Falconieri
Via Pasquale Cartoni
Via Revoltella
Via D Cerquetti
Piazale Enrico Dunant
GIANICOLENSE

DEI COLLI
GIANICOLENSE
Via Pietro
Via A Pignatelli
Via Antonio Cerasi
Via F Amici
Via di Monte Verde
Via Giulia di Galliese

Via Luigi Arati
Via E Lami
Via di Monte Verde
Via Laura
Mantegazza
VIA QUIRINO M

PORTUENSI
Via V Tizzani
Via A Jenner
Via F Palasciano
CIRCONVALLAZIONE

9

Via di Monte Verde
Via E Bassini
Via F Galliera
Via C Fieschi
Via D Severo
Via M Gilberti
Via P di
Via B Ramazzini
Via Folco

309

Principe Umberto, Via 302 H5

Prisco, Via T 313 K8

Procida, Via Giovanni da 308 K2

Properzio, Via 299 C4

Provincie, Viale delle 307 K3

Publicii, Clivo dei 311 E7

Puglie, Via 306 G3

Pupazzi, Viale dei 303 F2

Purificazione, Via 301 F4

Rizzo, Via Luigi 304 A3

Rocca, Via Morozzo della 308 L5

Roccapriora, Via 313 L9

Rodi, Via 304 B3

Rogazionisti, Via dei 313 K7

Rolli, Via Ettore 310 D8

Romagna, Via 306 G3

Romania, Viale 306 G1

Romei, Via Romeo 304 B2

Rosazza, Via F 310 D8

Roselli, Via P 310 C6

Rossetti, Via G 310 C7

Rossini, Viale G 303 F1

Rotonda, Via di 300 E5

Rovere, Piazza della 304 C5

Rovereto, Via 307 J1

Rovigo, Via 307 J3

Rubattino, Via 310 D7

Rubicone, Via 306 G1

Ruga, Via P 313 M7

Ruspoli, Via F 306 G1

Rutario, Clivo 309 B7

San Tommaso d'Aquino, Via 304 B2

San Vitale, Via di 301 F4

San Vito, Via di 302 G5

Sangallo, Lungotevere dei 305 C5

Sanguigna, Via della Pietra 308 M2

Sannio, Via 302 H7

Sant'Alberto Magno, Via 311 E7

Sant'Angela Merici, Via di 308 K1

Sant'Angelo, Ponte 299 D4

Santa Ciriaca, Via 307 K3

Santa Costanza, Via di 307 J1

Santa Croce in Gerusalemme, Via di 312 H6

Santa Lucia Filippini, Lungotevere di 300 E5

Santa Maria delle Grazie, Piazza 298 B3

Santa Maria in Trastevere, Piazza di 299 D6

Santa Maria Maggiore, Piazza 302 G5

Santa Melania, Via di 311 E7

Santa Prisca, Via di 311 F7

Santa Sabina, Via di 311 E7

Sant'Agnese, Via di 307 J1

Sant'Alessio, Piazza di 310 E7

Sant'Alessio, Via di 311 E7

Santamaura, Via 304 B3

Sant'Angelo, Borgo 299 C4

Sant'Anselmo, Via di 311 E7

Sant'Erasmo, Via di 311 G7

Sant'Eustachio, Piazza 300 E5

Santi Apostoli, Piazza del 300 E5

Sant'Ippolito, Via di 308 K3

Santissimi Quattro, Via dei 302 G6

Santo Spirito, Borgo 298 C4

Santo Stefano di Rotondo, Via 302 G6

Sant'Orsola, Via di 308 K2

Sant'Uffizio, Piazza del 298 C4

Sanudo, Via Marin 313 L6

Sanzio, Lungotevere Raffaello 299 D6

Sapri, Via 307 H3

Sardegna, Via 303 F3

Sardi, Via dei 307 J5

Sassia, Lungotevere in 299 C4

Sassoferrato, Via 305 E1

Satrico, Via 312 H8

Saturnia, Via 312 H7

Savelli, Vicolo 299 D5

Savoia, Via 306 G2

Savoia, Via L di 312 J6

Savonarola, Via G 304 B3

Savorgnan, Via dei 313 M8

Scala, Via della 299 D6

Scalia, Via Giorgio 298 A3

Scalinata della Trinita dei Monte 303 F4

Scalo San Lorenzo, Viale dello 312 J5

Scarfoglio, Via E 308 M3

Scarpa, Via Antonio 307 J3

Scauro, Clivo di 311 F6

Schiaparelli, Via G 303 E1

Scialoja, Via degli 305 D2

Scienze, Viale delle 307 J4

Scipioni, Via degli 304 C3

Scolari, Via F 313 L6

Scrofa, Via della 300 E4

Scuderie, Via dei 301 F4

Seato Celere, Via 309 B7

Sebastiani, Via E 309 B7

Sebino, Via 307 H1

Secchi, Via A 306 F1

Segesta, Via 312 J8

Seguenza, Via G 308 L1

Selci, Via in 301 G5

Selle Sale, Via delle 301 G5

Seminario, Via del 300 E4

Seneca, Via 304 A1

Sensini, Via Pietro 313 L7

Sequestre, Via Vibio 313 L7

Serbelloni, Via Gabrio 313 M7

Sergio III, Via 298 B5

Serpenti, Via dei 301 F5

Sessoriana, Via 312 J6

Settembrini, Via Luigi 305 D2

Severano, Via Giovanni 307 J2

Sforza, Via 301 G5

Siacci, Via Francesco 303 F1

Sibari, Via 312 H7

Sicilia, Via 303 F3

Siena, Piazza di 303 F2

Siezia, Via la 312 J6

Sigonio, Via C 313 K8

Silla, Via 304 C3

Silveri, Via D 298 B5

Simeto, Via 306 G2

Simoni, Via Simone 304 A3

Siracusa, Via 307 J3

Siria, Via 312 J8

Sistina, Via 303 F4

Sisto V, Piazzale 302 H5

Sisto, Ponte 299 D5

Soana, Via 312 H7

Soluntto, Via 312 J8

Sommeiller, Via G 312 J6

Sonnino, Piazza 300 E6

Spada, Via G 312 K9

Spalato, Via 307 J1

Spallanzani, Via Lazzaro 307 J2

Specchi, Via degli 300 E5

Spello, Via 313 L8

Spezia, Via la 312 J6

Squarcialupo, Via G L 308 K2

Statilia, Via 302 H6

Statuto, Via dello 302 G5

Stazio, Via 312 J8

Stazione di San Pietro, Via della 298 B5

Stazione Ostense, Via di 311 E8

ARCHITECTURAL GLOSSARY

Aisle: the interior corridors of a church, running either side of the nave

Alabaster: a fine grained limestone, often red and white or yellow and white. Thinly cut, it was used to glaze church windows in the Middle Ages

Allegory: a painting, sculpture or story where the meaning is shown through symbols

Apse: the semi-circular end of a church or chapel

Arcade: a range of arches, supported by pillars

Architrave: a moulded frame around a door or window

Atrium: an inner courtyard, open to the sky

Baldacchino/baldacchin: a canopy, usually over a throne or altar

Balustrade: a series of short pillars, or balusters, supporting a rail

Baroque: architectural style popular in 17th-century Rome. It is characterized by its elaborate decoration of convex and concave curves

Basalt: dark volcanic rock

Basilica: originally, in ancient Rome, a public hall, but the building shape and the name were later used for early Christian churches. A basilica has no transepts

Bas-relief: a carving showing a three-dimensional scene, whose surface is relatively shallow

Belvedere: a small tower on the roof of a building

Byzantine: architectural style developed after AD330, when Byzantium became capital of the Eastern Empire. It is characterized by its Eastern influences and highly decorated style

Campanile: a bell tower, often separate from the main building

Cartoon: a full-size preliminary sketch for a painting, mosaic or tapestry

Caryatid: a column, sculpted as a female figure

Casina: literally 'little house', used by 18th-century gentry for dancing, entertainment and gambling

Catacomb: an underground cemetery, usually Christian

Cattedra: the bishop's throne usually in the apse of the cathedral church

Chancel: the eastern end of a church, where the high altar is found

Chiaroscuro: the treatment of light and shade in painting

Cinerary urn: used to hold ashes after cremation

Circus: in ancient Roman architecture, an elongated rectangular structure with rounded ends used for horseracing; in 18th-century architecture, a row of houses in a circular pattern

Classical: architectural style characterized by its use of elements from Ancient Greece or Rome, including finely proportioned, simple shapes, and which has its roots in the 5th century BC. Classicism has seen many revivals from the 15th century to the present day, including Renaissance in the 16th century and Neoclassicism, which was popular between the late 18th and early 19th centuries

Cloister: a courtyard, often in a monastic building, surrounded by a covered passageway with an open arcade or colonnade on the interior side

Coffering: ceiling decoration made up from patterns of recessed squares or other shapes

Colonnade: a row of columns supporting a beam

Column: an upright, usually used as a decorative support, but sometimes freestanding as a monument. The design and proportions of columns vary, depending on their order (see Orders of columns, below)

Confessio: an underground area of a church, usually below the altar, which houses relics

Cosmatesque: decorative flooring of marble, glass and stones

Crossing: the area of a church where the transepts, nave and chancel intersect

Cruciform: cross-shaped, usually refers to a church

Crypt: area below the main church, usually for graves

Cupola: a domed roof

Etruscans: a race of people who inhabited Rome from around the 8th century BC. Their architecture was similar in style to that of Greek architecture of the same period

Exedra: in ancient Rome, a recess with raised seating

Fascist era: the extreme right-wing nationalist movement of 1922–43

Flavian era: the period of rule of Emperor Vespasian and his sons, Titus and Domitian, from 69–96AD

Forum: in ancient Rome, a large open space surrounded by public buildings

Fresco: a painting made directly onto damp plaster so that the image becomes permanent

Frieze: a decorated band, often along the top of a wall

Gothic: architectural style popular between the late 12th century and the mid-16th century, recognizable by its pointed arches and ribbed vaulting on the ceiling

Greek cross: a church layout, whose ground plan resembles a cross with four equal arms (see also Latin cross)

Grotesque: style based on ancient Roman decoration found in underground ruins

Holy Door: a door in a major basilica, which is only opened in a Jubilee Year (every 25 years—the last Jubilee Year was 2000). The devout can earn an indulgence by passing through the door

Imperial age: the age of the emperors, from 27BC to 284AD

Lantern: a small roofed tower with windows all around

Lapis lazuli: a blue mineral used as a gemstone. In Renaissance Italy, it was ground to make a bright blue pigment

Latin cross: a church layout, whose ground plan resembles a cross with three short arms and one longer one

Loggia: a room or gallery that is open on one or more sides

Malachite: a bright green mineral, often used as a gemstone

Mannerism: an architectural style, popular between 1530 and 1590, characterized by breaking the rules of Classicism and using Classical forms in a way other than is traditionally be acceptable

Medallion: a round decorative panel

Medieval period: between 1000 and 1453

Nave: the long arm of a Latin cross church; the opposite end to the apse

Nymphaeum: in ancient Rome, a temple of the nymphs (semi-divine female river spirits)

Oculus: a circular opening, usually in a wall, but also at the top of a dome

Orders of columns: the style of the column. In classical architecture there are four main orders of column: Doric, Tuscan, Ionic and Corinthian. All have a base, a shaft (the main part of the column) and a capital (the decorative top part). Doric columns have fluted shafts and a simple two-part capital. Tuscan columns are similar, but with a smooth shaft. Ionic columns are usually slimmer and taller, and their capitals have two large curls (sometimes two on each face), called volutes. Corinthian columns are slimmer again, with a very elaborate capital, decorated with leaves and curls. A final order, the Composite column, has a capital similar to a Corinthian one, but topped with the volutes of an Ionic capital

Papal altar: an altar at which only the pope can say Mass

Pediment: in classical architecture, a low gable and entableture forming a triangular shape. Usually on the outside of a building, but also above doorways and fireplaces

Peristyle: columns ranged around a building or courtyard

Pier: a supporting pillar; the solid wall between two windows or other openings, or; certain types of Gothic column that appear to be made of many shafts (when viewed in cross-section)

Pilaster: a decorative column, protruding only slightly from a wall. It will always correspond to one of the orders of column (see above)

Porphyry: a hard rock, flecked with white or red crystals

Portico: a roofed area, usually the focus of a building's façade, supported by columns and topped with a pediment (see above)

Reliquary: an elaborate container holding part of a deceased holy person's body

Renaissance (High Renaissance): a period of Classical revival, popular in 16th-century Italy, where it is sometimes called the *Rinascimento*

Republican age: from the declaration of the republic in 509BC to 27BC

Rococo: architectural style popular in the 18th century, characterized by low-relief decoration, usually in white and gold

Romanesque: an architectural style popular in the 11th–12th centuries, combining Classicism with influences from Byzantium and Islam

Rose window: large, circular window, usually in a church

Sacristy: in a church, where the vestments and sacred vessels are kept

Sarcophagus: a stone coffin

Satyr: a mythological woodland god with an animal's ears and tail

Sepulchre: a tomb cut from rock, or built from stone or brick

Stucco/stuccowork: a slow setting plaster, used to form intricate decoration

Tabernacle: in a church, an ornamental container for the consecrated host

Tempietto: literally, a small temple

Tesserae: small squares of glass, marble or stone, used to make mosaics

Transept: the short arms of a Latin cross church

Travertine stone: a white or light calcium carbonate-based rock, used for building

Triptych: a picture or carving on three panels, often used as an altarpiece

Trompe l'oeil: paintings that appear to show a room or landscape by use of perspective

Tufa: a porous rock found around mineral springs

Tympanum: between the lintel over a door and the arch above it. Also used to describe the flat area inside a pediment (see above)

Vaulting: an arched ceiling or roof

Villa: in Renaissance architecture, a country residence. Sometime used to describe the surrounding parkland

ACKNOWLEDGMENTS

Abbreviations for the credits are as follows:
AA = AA World Travel Library, t (top), b (bottom), c (centre), l (left), r (right), bg (background)

UNDERSTANDING ROME

5cl AA/A Kouprianoff; 5c AA/J Holmes; 5cr AA/P Wilson; 8tr AA/C Sawyer; 8tc AA/S McBride; 8tcr AA/P Wilson; 8bcr AA/C Sawyer; 8br Brand X Pictures; 9tl AA/C Sawyer; 9cl AA/C Sawyer; 9bl AA/C Sawyer; 9br AA/C Sawyer; 10tr AA/J Holmes; 10cl AA/C Sawyer; 10cr AA/S McBride; 10bl AA/S McBride; 10bc AA/J Holmes; 10r AA/A Kouprianoff

LIVING ROME

11 AA/C Sawyer; 12/13bg AA/C Sawyer; 12tl AA/J Holmes; 12tc AA/D Mitidieri; 12tr AA/C Sawyer; 12c AA/C Sawyer; 12cb AA/J Holmes; 12b AA/S McBride; 13tl AA/S McBride; 13tc AA/J Holmes; 13tr AA/C Sawyer; 13cl AA/C Sawyer; 13cbl AA/S McBride; 13cbr AA/C Sawyer; 14/15bg AA/S McBride; 14tc AA/J Holmes; 14tr AA/A Kouprianoff; 14cl Rex Features Ltd; 14c AA/T Souter; 14b AA/S McBride; 15l AA/A Kouprianoff; 15tl AA/A Kouprianoff; 15tr AA/A Kouprianoff; 15c AA/D Mitidieri; 16/17bg AA/C Sawyer; 16tl AA/C Sawyer; 16tr AA/D Mitidieri; 16c AA/M Jourdan; 16cr AA/M Siebert; 16cb AA/J Holmes; 16b AA/A Kouprianoff; 17tl AA/J Holmes; 17tc AA/J Holmes; 17tr AA/A Kouprianoff; 17cl AA/J Holmes; 18/19bg AA/D Mitidieri; 18tl AA/J Holmes; 18c AA/J Holmes; 18r Rex Features Ltd; 18b AA/C Sawyer; 19tl AA/D Mitidieri; 19tc AA/C Sawyer; 19cl AA/D Mitidieri; 19c AA/C Sawyer; 19r AA/K Paterson; 19b Rex Features Ltd; 20/21bg AA/D Mitidieri; 20tl AA/S McBride; 20tc AA/D Mitidieri; 20r AA/J Holmes; 20b AA/J Holmes; 21tl AA/S McBride; 21tc AA/M Trelawney; 21tr AA/T Harris; 21c AA/A Kouprianoff; 21cr AA/J Holmes; 22/23bg Rex Features Ltd; 22tl Rex Features Ltd; 22tc Rex Features Ltd; 22cr Rex Features Ltd; 22r Rex Features Ltd; 22b Rex Features Ltd; 23tc Rex Features Ltd; 23tr Rex Features Ltd; 23cl Cinecittà Studios; 23cr Rex Features Ltd; 24bg AA/C Sawyer; 24tl AA/C Sawyer; 24tr AA/C Sawyer; 24cl AA/C Sawyer; 24c Rex Features Ltd; 24cr AA/C Sawyer; 24bcr AA/C Sawyer; 24b Rex Features Ltd

THE STORY OF ROME

25 AA/S McBride; 26/27bg AA; 26cl AA/P Wilson; 26cr AA/J Holmes; 26/27 AA; 27ct AA/S McBride; 27cl AA; 27cr AA/P Wilson; 27b Mary Evans Picture Library; 28/29bg AA/S McBride; 28ct Mary Evans Picture Library; 28c Hulton Archive/Getty Images; 28bl Mary Evans Picture Library; 28b Mary Evans Picture Library; 29c AA; 29b by courtesy of APT – Rome; 30/31bg AA/J Holmes; 30c AA; 30bl AA/C Sawyer; 30br Mary Evans Picture Library; 31l Mary Evans Picture Library; 31c AA; 31br AA/J Holmes; 32/33bg AA/S McBride; 32c AA; 32bl AA/C Sawyer; 32br AA/J Holmes; 33c AA/J Holmes; 33cr AA/C Sawyer; 33bl AA/S McBride; 33bc by courtesy of APT – Rome; 33br AA/P Wilson; 34/35bg AA/P Wilson; 34cr AA; 34bl Mary Evans Picture Library; 34bc AA/P Wilson; 34/35 AA/J Holmes; 35cl AA; 35cr AA/A Kouprianoff; 35b AA; 36/37bg AA/D Mitidieri; 36c AA; 36bl AA/S McBride; 36b AA/P Wilson; 36/37 AA; 37c AA/D Mitidieri; 37cr AA/J Holmes; 37b AA/D Mitidieri; 38/39bg AA/P Wilson; 38c Hulton Archive/Getty Images; 38cr AA; 38bl Mary Evans Picture Library; 38/39 Mary Evans Picture Library; 39cl Hulton Archive/Getty Images; 39bl AA/S McBride; 39bc AA/P Wilson; 40bg AA/J Holmes; 40c Hulton Archive/Getty Images; 40cr AA/A Kouprianoff; 40bl Hulton Archive/Getty Images; 40br Hulton Archive/Getty Images

ON THE MOVE

41 Digital Vision; 42t Digital Vision; 42c Digital Vision; 43t Digital Vision; 43c Digital Vision; 44t AA/S McBride; 44ct AA/S McBride; 44c AA/M Adelman; 44cr AA/S McBride; 45t AA/B Smith; 45c AA/S McBride; 45b AA/S McBride; 46t AA/B Smith; 46c AA/S McBride; 46bl AA/S McBride; 46bc AA/S McBride; 47t AA/B Smith; 47ct AA/S McBride; 47cb AA/S McBride; 47bl AA/M Jourdan; 47bc AA/S McBride; 48t AA/B Smith; 48c AA/S McBride; 49t AA/B Smith; 49c AA/S McBride; 50 AA/B Smith; 51t AA/C Sawyer; 51cr AA/J Holmes; 51cl AA/M Jourdan; 51b AA/J Holmes; 52t AA/P Wilson; 52c AA/J

Holmes; 52b AA/M Jourdan; 52/3 Digital Vision; 53t AA/C Sawyer; 53c AA/S McBride; 54t Digital Vision; 54b The picture used has been accorded by Regency San Marino srl www.accessibleitaly.com

THE SIGHTS

55 AA/S McBride; 60cl AA/S McBride; 60cr AA/S McBride; 61cl AA/J Holmes; 61cr AA/C Sawyer; 61b AA/A Kouprianoff; 62cl AA/A Kouprianoff; 62cr AA/C Sawyer; 63cl AA/J Holmes; 63cr AA/S McBride; 64c AA/J Holmes; 64b AA/C Sawyer; 65tl AA/D Mitidieri; 65tc AA/S McBride; 65tr Casa di Goethe; 66 main AA/S McBride; 66 inset by courtesy of APT – Rome; 67t by courtesy of APT – Rome; 67cl AA/D Mitidieri; 67c AA/P Wilson; 67cr AA/S McBride; 68c by courtesy of APT – Rome; 68b AA/C Sawyer; 69 AA/S McBride; 70 AA/T Souter; 71lcl AA/S McBride; 71cl by courtesy of APT – Rome; 71cr AA/D Mitidieri; 71rcr AA/S McBride; 72t AA/S McBride; 72c AA/J Holmes; 73 main by courtesy of APT – Rome; 73 inset AA/S McBride; 74 AA/S McBride; 75t AA/P Wilson; 75c AA/S McBride; 76c AA/C Sawyer; 76b AA/J Holmes; 76/77 by courtesy of APT – Rome; 78tl AA/C Sawyer; 78tc AA/C Sawyer; 78tr AA; 79tl AA/D Mitidieri; 79tr Allegory of Fame by Sebastiano Conca (1680-1764) Accademia di San Luca, Rome, Italy/Bridgeman Art Library; 80t AA/S McBride; 80c by courtesy of APT – Rome; 81 main AA/C Sawyer; 81 inset AA/S McBride; 82t AA/J Holmes; 82c by courtesy of APT – Rome; 82b AA/S McBride; 83t AA/J Holmes; 83c AA/T Souter; 83b AA/J Holmes; 84 by courtesy of APT – Rome; 85t AA/S McBride; 86cl AA/S McBride; 86cr AA/C Sawyer; 87 by courtesy of APT – Rome; 88 AA/A Kouprianoff; 89cl AA/S McBride; 89c AA/A Kouprianoff; 89cr by courtesy of APT – Rome; 89b AA/S McBride; 90tl AA/J Holmes; 90tc AA/S McBride; 91tl AA/A Kouprianoff; 91tc AA/A Kouprianoff; 91tr by courtesy of APT – Rome; 92 AA/D Mitidieri; 93t AA/K Gould; 93cl AA/D Mitidieri; 93c AA/P Wilson; 93cr AA/D Mitidieri; 94/95 AA/D Mitidieri; 94b AA/D Mitidieri; 95t AA/D Mitidieri; 95b Apollo and Daphne, 1622-25 (marble) by Giovanni Lorenzo Bernini (1598-1680) Galleria Borthese, Rome, Italy/Bridgeman Art Library (Lauros/Giraudon/Bridgeman Art Library); 96 The Prodigal Son (oil on canvas) by Guercino (Giovanni Grancesco Barbieri) (1591–1666) Galleria Borghese, Rome, Italy/Bridgeman Art Library; 97 The Ecstasy of Saint Catherine (oil on canvas) by Agostino Carracci (1557–1602) Galleria Borghese, Rome, Italy/Bridgeman Art Library; 98 AA/C Sawyer; 99t AA/C Sawyer; 99cl AA/S McBride; 99c AA/S McBride; 99cr AA/J Holmes; 99b AA/J Holmes; 100t AA/C Sawyer; 100b AA/C Sawyer; 101t AA/C Sawyer; 101c AA/C Sawyer; 101b AA/C Sawyer; 102 AA/C Sawyer; 103 AA/C Sawyer; 104 AA/J Holmes; 105t AA/C Sawyer; 105cl AA/S McBride; 105c AA/S McBride; 105cr AA/A Kouprianoff; 106 AA/S McBride; 108t AA/S McBride; 108c AA/S McBride; 109t AA/S McBride; 109b AA/J Holmes; 110tl AA/D Mitidieri; 110tc AA/C Sawyer; 110tr AA/A Kouprianoff; 111tl AA/J Holmes; 111tr AA/S McBride; 112t AA/S McBride; 112c AA/J Holmes; 113t Scala; 113c AA/S McBride; 113b A Gaul Committing Suicide, Pergamon School, 3rd century BC (marble) (b/w photo) Palazzo Altemps, Rome, Italy/Bridgeman Art Library (Bridgeman Art Library/Alinari); 114c AA/P Wilson; 114b AA/J Holmes; 115 AA/P Wilson; 116t Sleeping Hermaphrodite (marble) (b/w photo) Palazzo Massimon alle Terme, Rome, Italy/Bridgeman Art Library (Bridgeman Art Library/Alinari); 116c Seated women before a statue, detail from Room B of the Villa Farnesina (fresco) (b/w photo) Palazzo Massimo alle Terme, Rome, Italy/Bridgeman Art Library (Bridgeman Art Library/Alinari); 116b The 'Lancellotti' Discus Thrower (bronze) (b/w photo) Palazzo Massimo alle Terme, Rome, Italy/Bridgeman Art Library (Bridgeman Art Library/Alinari); 117t AA/S McBride; 117c Hippopotamus hunt with a view of the Nile, from Villa Maccarani (mosaic) (b/w photo) Palazzo Massimo alle Terme, Rome, Italy/Bridgeman Art Library (Bridgeman Art Library/Alinari); 118tl by courtesy of APT – Rome; 118tc AA/D Mitidieri; 118tr AA/J Holmes; 119tl AA/J Holmes; 119tc AA/A Kouprianoff; 119tr AA/D Mitidieri; 119b AA/S McBride; 120t AA/D Mitidieri; 120c AA/S McBride; 121 by courtesy of APT – Rome;

WHAT TO DO

OUT AND ABOUT

EATING

STAYING

PLANNING

Project editor
Kathy Gould

Interior design
David Austin, Glyn Barlow, Alan Gooch, Kate Harling, Bob Johnson,
Nick Otway, Carole Philp, Keith Russell

Picture research
Liz Allen, Chris Butler, Debbie Ireland, Charlotte Lippmann,
Vivien Little, Serena Mellish, Carol Walker

Cover design
Tigist Getachew

Internal repro work
Susan Crowhurst, Ian Little, Michael Moody

Production
Lyn Kirby, Caroline Nyman

Mapping
Maps produced by the Cartography Department of AA Publishing

Main contributors
Sally Roy (consultant), Giovanna Dunmall, Adele Evans, Tim Jepson,
Simona Marchetta, Lee Marshall, Michael Nation

Copy editors
Audrey Horne, Janet Tabinski

ISBN 1-4000-1384-4

Published in the United States by Fodor's Travel Publications and simultaneously
in Canada by Random House of Canada Limited, Toronto.
Published in the United Kingdom by AA Publishing.

Fodor's is a registered trademark of Random House, Inc., and Fodor's See It is a trademark of
Random House, Inc. Fodor's Travel Publications is a division of Fodor's LLC.

© **Automobile Association Developments Limited 2004**
10 9 8 7 6 5 4 3 2
Color separation by Keenes
Printed and bound by Leo, China

This book is available for special discounts for bulk purchases for sales promotions or premiums.
Special editions, including personalized covers, excerpts of existing books, and corporate imprints,
can be created in large quantities for special needs. For more information, write to Special
Markets/Premium Sales, 1745 Broadway, MD 6-2, New York, NY 10019 or e-mail
specialmarkets@randomhouse.com.

A02580
Mapping in this title produced from:
Map data © 1997–2003 Navigation Technologies BV. All rights reserved.
Mapping © GEOnext (Gruppo De Agostini) Novara

Relief map images supplied by Mountain High Maps ® Copyright © 1993 Digital Wisdom, Inc

Weather chart statistics supplied by Weatherbase © Copyright 2003 Canty and Associates, LLC

Important Note: Time inevitably brings changes, so always confirm prices, travel facts, and other
perishable information when it matters. Although Fodor's cannot accept responsibility for errors, you
can use this guide in the confidence that we have taken every care to ensure its accuracy.

Fodor's Key to the Guides

AMERICA'S **GUIDEBOOK LEADER** PUBLISHES GUIDES FOR **EVERY KIND OF TRAVELER**. CHECK OUT OUR MANY SERIES AND FIND YOUR **PERFECT MATCH**.

FODOR'S GOLD GUIDES
America's favorite travel-guide series offers the most detailed insider reviews of hotels, restaurants, and attractions in all price ranges, plus great background information, smart tips, and useful maps.

COMPASS AMERICAN GUIDES
Stunning guides from top local writers and photographers, with gorgeous photos, literary excerpts, and colorful anecdotes. A must-have for culture mavens, history buffs, and new residents.

FODOR'S CITYPACKS
Concise city coverage in a guide plus a foldout map. The right choice for urban travelers who want everything under one cover.

FODOR'S WHERE TO WEEKEND
A fresh take on weekending, this series identifies the best places to escape outside the city and details loads of rejuvenating activities as well as cool places to stay, great restaurants, and practical information.

FODOR'S AROUND THE CITY WITH KIDS
Up to 68 great ideas for family days, recommended by resident parents. Perfect for exploring in your own backyard or on the road.

FODOR'S TRAVEL HISTORIC AMERICA
For travelers who want to experience history firsthand, this series gives in-depth coverage of historic sights, plus nearby restaurants and hotels. Themes include the Thirteen Colonies, the Old West, and the Lewis and Clark Trail.

FODOR'S FLASHMAPS
Every resident's map guide, with 60 easy-to-follow maps of public transit, parks, museums, zip codes, and more.

FODOR'S LANGUAGES FOR TRAVELERS
Practice the local language before you hit the road. Available in phrase books, cassette sets, and CD sets.

THE COLLECTED TRAVELER
These collections of the best published essays and articles on various European destinations will give you a feel for the culture, cuisine, and way of life.

FODOR'S HOW TO GUIDES
Get tips from the pros on planning the perfect trip. Learn how to pack, fly hassle-free, plan a honeymoon or cruise, stay healthy on the road, and travel with your baby.

KAREN BROWN'S GUIDES
Engaging guides—many with easy-to-follow inn-to-inn itineraries—to the most charming inns and B&Bs in the U.S.A. and Europe.

BAEDEKER'S GUIDES
Comprehensive guides, trusted since 1829, packed with A–Z reviews and star ratings.

OTHER GREAT TITLES FROM FODOR'S
Baseball Vacations, The Complete Guide to the National Parks, Family Vacations, Golf Digest's Places to Play, Great American Drives of the East, Great American Drives of the West, Great American Vacations, Healthy Escapes, National Parks of the West, Skiing USA.

At bookstores everywhere.   www.fodors.com/books

Dear Traveler

From buying a plane ticket to booking a room and seeing
the sights, a trip goes much more smoothly when you have
a good travel guide. Dozens of writers, editors, designers,
and cartographers have worked hard to make the book
you hold in your hands a good one. Was it everything you
expected? Were our descriptions accurate? Were our
recommendations on target? And did you find our tips and
practical advice helpful? Your ideas and experiences
matter to us. If we have missed or misstated something,
we'd love to hear about it. Fill out our survey at
www.fodors.com/books/feedback/, or e-mail us at
seeit@fodors.com. Or you can snail mail to the See It
Editor at Fodor's, 1745 Broadway, New York, New York
10019. We'll look forward to hearing from you.

Karen Cure
Editorial Director